NICK DRAKE

Remembered
For A While

JOHN MURRAY

Remembered For A While . . .

A few years ago, my husband Louis de Wet gave me Lucasta Miller's book *The Brontë Myth*. In it, she says of Emily Brontë:

During the first half of the twentieth century, many of Emily's admirers had difficulty in allowing her to remain shadowy: they wanted to anchor her in a world of real-life relationships because it would somehow stop her slipping from their grasp. Perhaps what was needed, instead, was a form of biography which could acknowledge her elusive and ambivalent nature, and which was able to incorporate what Keats called 'negative capability', the ability to be 'in uncertainties, mysteries, doubts, without any irritable reaching after fact and reason'.

It occurred to me then that, one hundred years later, this could just as well have been written about Nick Drake.

People who have tried to analyse Nick, in an attempt to anchor him in their world, have nearly always exposed more about themselves than they have about their subject. For Nick has been like a mirror: lit from the front with a glaring light, he has thrown back a sharp-edged image, not of himself, but of the person attempting to illuminate him.

So this book will not try to expose Nick to the full beam of an analytical spotlight. Rather, it will be a series of sideways glances; an attempt to cast a few shards of light on the poet, the musician, the friend, the son, the brother, who was also more than all of these, and as indefinable as the morning mist.

Gabrielle Drake

I had much the same sort of upbringing as Nick Drake. My prep school regularly played matches against his; I spent a year in Aix-en-Provence a few years after he did; I went to the same university. As a teenager I bought *Five Leaves Left* and *Bryter Layter* as they appeared, and saw him as an impossibly romantic figure, partly because he seemed to have transcended my world in a way that triumphed over it and yet retained an Englishness that was entirely true to himself. There was not a trace of affectation about his work.

Much later, I returned to his music when the familiarity was altogether less comfortable. When the world seemed too remote, too difficult to negotiate, I recognised in him a spirit brave and brilliant enough to articulate in music what was an incoherent fog within me. For weeks at a time Nick Drake's music – sometimes just a sequence of a few notes – has sustained me. I am sure that I am not alone in this.

Anyone who has attempted to play and sing in public knows the agonies of doubt, exposure and humiliation that attend it. By all accounts Nick found it unendurable. No one can listen to his songs without recognising the painful shyness and trouble that they reveal. Yet for all his softness of tone, Nick, on record at least, sang clear, exposing himself in word and tone. Perhaps the cost of this was too high. These things can be a kind of torture; but then, if you are a musician, it is a torture *not* to do them, too. Torment from every quarter.

Yet he played guitar with the clearest, strongest sound I have ever heard. Much of this is technical. His right-hand technique was extraordinary. Listen to 'Road' and then try and play it. The music isn't actually that complicated – yet it's almost impossible to play as he did. And in a very different vein, listen to the delicacy and subtlety of the shifting, liminal 'Place To Be', and the incredible depth and richness of one man and one guitar, alone in the dark. It is delicate and haunting, but powerful, too; and that power endures.

The fetishisation of Nick Drake as a kind of depressives' pin-up has to be acknowledged. There is much mileage in celebrating the tragic, doomed figure, with a skin several times too thin, destroying themselves. But there is no glamour in the bleak, empty grief that is depression, no comfort in another's loneliness; and now, when I think of Nick's life, this man I never met, it is with real sadness. However, there is an absolute triumph in making from it a lasting art that overcomes the useless wasted time.

So I celebrate from afar the life of a gentle, troubled man, but above all celebrate as a kindred spirit the songs that rose from this lovely ground.

Monty Don
Gardener, writer and broadcaster

Dedicated to the memory of Robert Kirby:
musician and friend.

The Seed

Certificate ~~Return~~ of BAPTISMS, being an extract from the Register of Baptisms.

When Baptised.			Said to be Born.			Child's Christian Name.	Sex.	Parents' Name.		Abode of Parents.	Quality, trade or profession of father.	Person by whom the ceremony was performed.		
Year.	Month.	Day.	Year.	Month.	Day.			Christian.	Surname.			Name.	Designation.	Signature.
1948	NOVEMBER	28	1948	JUNE	19	NICHOLAS RODNEY	M.	RODNEY SHUTTLEWORTH MARY	DRAKE	11 MISSION ROAD	MERCHANT.	RIGHT REVEREND G. A. WEST	LORD BISHOP OF RANGOON.	George Rangoon
								GOD-PARENTS						
									MCDOWALL					
									MC DOWALL					
									SHELLEY					
									HUGHES					

I of the (name of Church) Holy Cross Church Rangoon. do hereby certify that the foregoing returns are true and faithful copies of all the entries being — in number relating to European and Armenian Christians and celebrated according to the rites of the (name of Church) Anglican in the register of kept at the Church ~~or station~~ of Holy Cross Rangoon as therein entered and made ~~between~~ on 28th day of November ~~and~~ ~~day of~~ in the year of Our Lord one thousand nine hundred and forty eight

Place. Witness my hand. G. L. Tidey Signature.

Date. Priest-in-charge Designation.
Holy Cross Church Rangoon

The C. & M. G. Ltd., Lahore,—500.

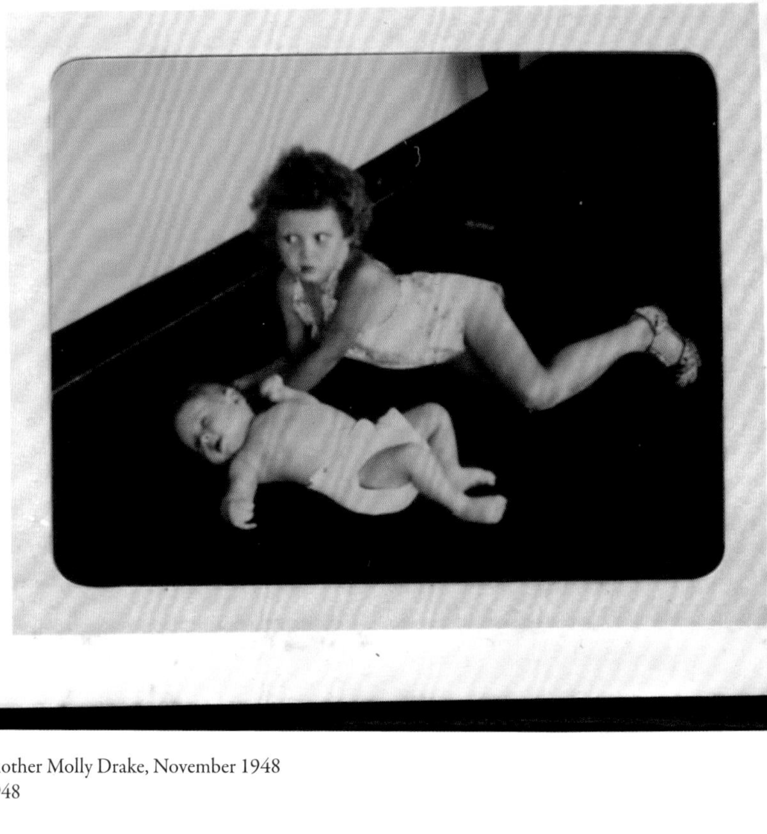

Above: Nick Drake's christening with his mother Molly Drake, November 1948
Below: Nick with sister Gabrielle Drake, 1948

Above: Nick at three months
Below: Nick with sister Gabrielle and nanny Rosie Paw Tun, 1950

Four-year-old Nick out front, Tanworth-in-Arden sports day, 1952; Far Leys behind

Primary Colour

My son is three, so his views
Are not over mellow;
I gave him a violet to smell
And he said it smelt yellow.

'Smells sweet, you mean,' I said:
The intractable fellow
Replied that it didn't smell sweet
It smelt yellow.

Poem by Molly Drake, photos by Rodney Drake

The Drake Family: Molly, Nick, Rodney, Gabrielle

Give Me A Place To Be

by Gabrielle Drake

Rodney Shuttleworth Drake was born in 1908, the only son, and youngest child, of Violet and Ernest Drake. His father, Ernest, was an eminent Harley Street physician, and was able to send his son to Marlborough College – the school he had himself attended.

The original intention was for Rodney to go to university after leaving school, study medicine, and follow in his father's footsteps. However, the family fortunes were badly affected when Ernest Drake suffered a heart attack and had to give up his lucrative London practice and retire to the country. Rodney had to leave Marlborough, and there was now no question of him going to university.

Thanks to the kind offices of 'a wealthy relation', Rodney secured an apprenticeship with the London and North Eastern Railway, and trained at their depots in Darlington and York, whilst studying for his engineering degree at night school.

If this change of plan dismayed Rodney, he certainly never showed it. Indeed, he might even have secretly welcomed it, for he seemed to be a born engineer, and always looked back on his time in the North-East with considerable affection.

However, his training accomplished, he decided that a future with the railways was not for him; so in 1930, ripe for adventure, he applied for, and got, a job as an Engineer Assistant with the Bombay Burmah Trading Corporation (BBTC) – an established British company in the Far East, with extensive interests in the teak industry.

Rodney was posted to Burma (now Myanmar). This must have been the first time he had been out of Europe – maybe even out of England, bearing in mind the restricted travel conditions of his time. But, from the moment he set foot on board the SS *Gloucestershire*, bound for Rangoon (Yangon), he seems to have been in his element. His first letter home to his parents is an enthusiastic, day-by-day chronicle of his first week at sea – by the end of which he had already been commandeered by the Captain to organise a gala day of games, had formed a committee to do this, and been, as he puts it,

'attacked by a crowd of energetic females who complained that there were not enough events for the women. I asked the leader of this deputation to become a member of the committee (a stroke of tactical genius on my part!) . . .[and] we got the games drawn up by midnight.'

All the elements that were key to his success in life are apparent in this little incident: leadership, tact, an ability to delegate, and a self-deprecating irony, all packaged in a charm that made it easy for these talents to be recognised by his superiors.

These included his boss at the BBTC in Rangoon. Rodney described their first meeting thus:

'I was introduced to one Macnamara – an enormous great genial fellow who, I have since learned, is an important man to keep on the right side of. It appears that he can be extraordinarily nice when he likes (and vice versa!) . . . we were soon involved in a long discussion on a series of calculations he had been making in connection with a steam plant – I found myself to be in complete disagreement with several of his solutions and informed him of the fact. However, we got on very well.'

Indeed they did, for Rodney advanced speedily in the company, and was soon given the responsibility of constructing a large new sawmill in Rangoon, which he then operated as Mill Manager. Many years later, it would be Macnamara who would offer him the managerial job that brought him back to England.

But for now, Rodney threw himself into his new life, declaring to his parents, 'I think I am going to like the job enormously, and the life as well.'

'The life', for the young men who had come out East to help run either the British Administration or British industrial enterprises, consisted of playing as hard as they worked: swimming, golf – played very early in the morning to escape the heat – tennis, squash, rowing, as well as expeditions into the jungle to shoot snipe, were all interspersed with a hard day's work at the office. And in the evenings there were dances, dinners in the Club – the great hub of social life – and amateur plays and concerts: for 'Out East' there was no choice but to provide your own entertainment. Rodney was a popular performer: he played the piano well enough to entertain his friends after dinner (sometimes with his own compositions: he once wrote an operetta based on life on board a ship bound for the East), and sang in a fine bass voice – a fact attested to by this review of the Boat Club Concert, lovingly kept by his mother:

Mr R.S. Drake's 'Droop Not Young Lover' brought the house down. Before he opened his mouth, there was applause, but this is due to Mr Drake's popularity. Not even the singer took the song seriously. I felt that Mr Drake himself was doing his best not to laugh. But in spite of this, he sang extremely well . . . The audience begged for more . . .

The year 1933 was to prove momentous for Rodney – not that he realised it at the time. He would have known the Deputy Commissioner, one Idwal Lloyd, and his formidable wife Georgie; and also known their eldest daughter, Gwladys, a noted beauty who had come out to Burma with her parents shortly before he had. In December of that year, the Lloyds returned from leave, bringing with them their second daughter, Molly, then aged eighteen.

Molly Lloyd was born in 1915 in Rangoon. Her father, Idwal, was a serving officer in the elite Indian Civil Service, and had been posted to Burma – then a province of India. She was christened Mary, but Molly seemed a much more appropriate name for the little girl with flaming red hair – and Molly she remained for the rest of her life.

In those days, the Far East was not considered to be a healthy environment for children; so, at the age of three, Molly had been taken back to England. There, she, and her two sisters – elder sister Gwladys, and younger sister Nancy – were brought up in the happy household of the Dunns. Aunt Helen and Uncle Willie, despite straitened circumstances, seem to have had a gift for creating happiness and giving their extended family of servicemen's children a haven in which to flourish. What could have been a time of disastrous unhappiness therefore turned out to be one of joyous development, where the bond between Molly and her younger sister Nancy was irrevocably forged. It would last their entire lives.

All three girls were eventually sent to boarding school. Molly always professed to having hated school, although she managed to scrape through her School Certificate. Having done so, she was, to her joy, allowed to leave school and return with her parents to Burma.

Her diary for the year 1933 shows great exuberance and *joie de vivre*; and her record of the sea journey out East curiously mirrors Rodney's description to his parents of his own voyage two years earlier. But, unlike Rodney, Molly was desperately shy. She felt herself to be gauche and awkward – and feared letting down her glamorous elder sister Gwladys, who had already cut a swathe through Rangoon society. However, with the casting aside of school uniform, ugly glasses, and straight hair (her first perm must have been a great joy to her), a butterfly emerged from the chrysalis, and, despite her fears, Molly seems to have had little difficulty finding her place in the carefree whirl of colonial life in those pre-war years in Burma.

Molly met Rodney Drake at one of the first parties she went to in Rangoon – unsurprisingly, since he was a sought-after guest at most social events. It was not love at first sight. But his easy wit and life-long ability to set people at their ease must have been a great comfort to the shy young Molly. However, it would be some time before either of them recognised that they had found a partner for life. They eventually married in 1937: it was to be a marriage that endured, vibrantly, for fifty-one years, until Rodney's death in 1988.

The early years of their marriage were set against increasing political unrest. Burma was granted separate colonial status in 1937, with much of the governing power devolving to the indigenous people. However, calls for total independence became ever louder, and strikes were frequent. Nevertheless, life for the colonials seems to have continued to be relatively carefree and easy. And despite the storm clouds that were gathering over Europe, when letters from 'Home' took several weeks to arrive, it was difficult to grasp the immediacy of any situation. If the 'Phoney War' in England was a time of unnatural calm, so much the more was it Out East.

The grim reality of the Second World War finally came to Burma in 1942 with the Japanese invasion. Hasty plans were made for the evacuation of the British women, and Molly and her sister Nancy – now married to Rodney's close friend in Burma, Chris McDowall – joined the great trek out of Burma into India. For the most part, this turned into a mad scramble, with evacuees suffering appalling hardship and loss of life. But Molly and Nancy had the good fortune to be part of a comparatively well-organised march. Nevertheless, it was gruelling: the terrain was difficult, and the threat constant, and underlying everything was a perpetual anguish as to the fate of their husbands, who were in the thick of the fighting in Burma.

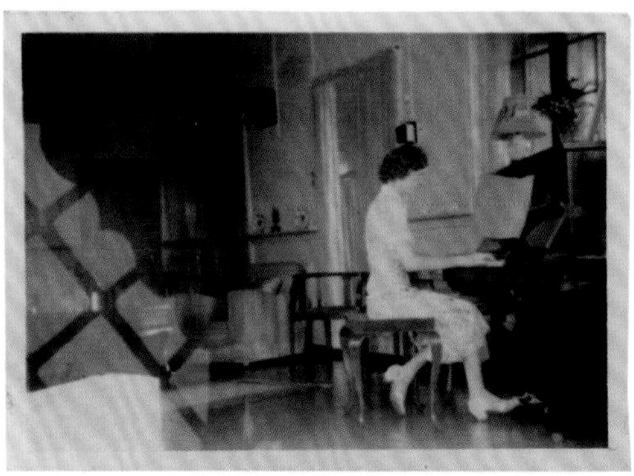

If Molly's exit from Burma was difficult, Rodney's was worse. He had already enlisted in the Burma Defence Force, but now, with the fall of Rangoon, he joined the Artisan Works company, where his engineering skills were used to lay charges for the demolition of bridges, which must, in itself, have been depressing for a construction engineer.

The Allied retreat from Burma was a desperate and disorganised affair and Rodney was in the thick of it. Starving, sick and wounded refugees clogged the primitive roads leading to India, and harassment by the Japanese, who had an intimate knowledge of the jungle terrain, was constant and effective. At Shwegin, Rodney had the unenviable job of Embarkation Officer. Here General Alexander's Burma Corps had to be ferried across the Chindwin River on ramshackle ferries, and under unceasing enemy attack. Eventually the Corps – depleted and with virtually no equipment – reached India, just as the monsoon broke. The demoralised men found their miseries added to when they were forced to camp in the open under torrential rain. Rodney, among many others, fell victim to dysentery. He was eventually granted sick leave, and was able to join Molly.

By now, Molly and Nancy had taken refuge with their aunt and uncle, Alan and Mary Lloyd, in Delhi, seat of the British Administration in India. Alan Lloyd, like his brother Idwal, was a member of the ICS, and part of the government – a government that seemed almost unaware of the war being fought on its borders. Life for the two sisters must now have taken on a surreal similarity to life in Burma before the war, not least since their Aunt Mary, though delightful and loving, was as formidable a member of the British Raj as ever their mother had been, and made it quite clear that the girls must not 'let the side down'. Stiff upper lips were the order of the day. The sisters took comfort from each other; and since both were musical it was perhaps inevitable, at a time when party pieces were expected, that they should form a duet, singing together, unaccompanied, in close harmony. So successful were they that they were asked to perform on All India Radio. Nancy, whose knowledge of music was more academic than her sister's, would arrange popular songs of the era for them to perform. For Molly, though, music was a private joy, as was her poetry. All her life, both provided a retreat and a place from which to draw inner strength. And though she was happy to play and sing her songs to friends and family, their composing was always an intensely private affair, and she would sit for hours alone at a piano, working out words and music. Her poetry, she would read to Nancy.

When Rodney eventually reached Delhi, riddled with dysentery, Molly's joy must have been laced with alarm. He arrived with only the ragged clothes he stood up in (he had already been refused entry into the British Club, because he was not wearing a dinner jacket!), and though six feet tall weighed no more than seven stone. His recovery was long and slow – particularly as dysentery developed into hepatitis.

By the time Rodney was declared fit, the Japanese

occupation of Burma had severed India's vitally needed supply of teak. So it was that Rodney found himself seconded out of the army, and commissioned by the Indian government to build a sawmill at the foot of the Himalaya mountains. This meant that he and Molly could live together again in the little hill station of Jhelum – provided he could find suitable accommodation. The mill duly arrived in packing cases from America and, once built, Rodney, ever ingenious, constructed a house for himself and Molly out of the redundant packing cases. 'Packing Case Villa' saw the birth of their first child, Gabrielle.

Rodney had given an undertaking to the BBTC that, as soon as the war ended, he would return to Burma. And immediately after the Japanese surrender in 1945, this is what he did, taking charge of the efforts to restore his firm's fortunes there. But much more than this, he had become deeply involved in the politics of country. He had grown to love Burma, and grieved at the devastation war had wrought upon a once wealthy country, rich in rice and oil and teak. Now ravaged by the scorched-earth policies of both the British and the Japanese, the country was in chaos. Rodney had spent many hours deliberating on a solution for Burma, and wrote a long paper detailing his ideas. The plan that he set out for independence was coherent, radical, and took into account all he had learned of the Burmese people. He always believed that independence for the country was both essential and inevitable. But he also believed that Britain had a moral responsibility to ensure that this happened gradually, and with the requisite amount of education and support from the British government. Although well received by the authorities – and this included Sir Stafford Cripps, at the time a member of the War Cabinet – it was, in the end, ignored. Nevertheless, when the post-war Administration was set up in Rangoon, Rodney was one of only four European members of the House of Representatives. All his tact and diplomatic skills were needed during this highly charged time of political instability.

(L-R) Rodney, Gabrielle and Nick Drake, Chris McDowall, Molly Drake and her sister Nancy McDowall, 1955

No doubt to Rodney's dismay, three brief years later, in January 1948, Burma was granted full independence. Much of the turmoil he had predicted would follow such a precipitate event, came to pass; and his tract 'Chaos in Burma' remains a fine analysis of the troubles that ensued.

However, the Drakes now also had personal matters on their minds. For five months later, in June, their second child – Nicholas Rodney – was born in Rangoon: possibly in the same hospital where Molly had herself been born. With the political situation becoming ever more volatile in the wake of independence, it must have been something of a relief when, in 1949, the BBTC offered Rodney promotion, sending him to their head offices in Bombay, where he became a director and joint chairman.

But not for long. In 1950, Rodney's erstwhile boss, that 'great genial fellow' Macnamara, wrote to him from England, offering him a job as managing director of a small Birmingham-based firm, the Wolseley Sheep Shearing Company. To leave India would be a wrench for the whole family – Rodney and Molly loved the life Out East. On the other hand, they knew they would soon be faced with the problem of their children's education, which would have to take place in England in a few years, and this would inevitably lead to the family being split up. Much as she had enjoyed her childhood with the Dunns, Molly didn't want the same fate for her children, and she and Rodney found the thought of separation from each other, if she accompanied the children back to England, intolerable. So with considerable sorrow, the Drakes packed up, lock, stock and barrel, and trundled back home, taking with them the children's Karen nanny, Rosie PawTun.

In fact, Nanny – as Rosie was always known (having been nanny in England to other retired colonial families) – knew more about 'Home' – an austere post-war England – than either Molly or Rodney did themselves. She it was who guided Molly through the complexities of post-war rationing, and helped her set up a household without servants, something Molly had never known before in her married life.

The family moved to the leafy county of Warwickshire: Shakespeare's county. Rodney bought his wife a house which, at the time, he could ill afford, but which Molly had fallen in love with. Far Leys was spacious and well-proportioned, and looked out over an expansive garden to the glorious Warwickshire countryside beyond. Molly made it both elegant and comfortable; and the sitting room, with its central feature of their grand piano, transported back from Bombay, became a hub of legendary social events – often music-based, for both Rodney and Molly were proficient piano players. In an age when television was still a rarity, this would not have been so uncommon. What was, perhaps, less usual, was the fact that many snippets of these parties were recorded: for Rodney, ever intrigued by new inventions, had brought home one day a large trunk-like contraption that turned out to be an early reel-to-reel tape-recording machine. Such a novelty was inevitably brought out at parties, and people delighted at the new phenomenon of being able to hear recordings of their own voices. More importantly, as it turned out, Rodney was able to persuade Molly to record her own songs. Understanding, as he always did, the private nature of her creative work, he would set up the machine and leave her to record her songs on her own. For the sitting room was also Molly's retreat, where, usually in the afternoons, she would sit at the piano, or at her desk, composing, or writing her poetry.

Meanwhile, Rodney rose rapidly in the Birmingham business world, gradually transforming the Wolseley Sheep Shearing Company into what would eventually become a global enterprise. Today, Wolseley plc is the world's largest trade distributor of plumbing and heating products; it was set on that track by Rodney, who developed the small agricultural firm he came to Birmingham to manage into a network of flourishing businesses. He was elected to the Council of the Birmingham Chamber of Commerce, and was president-elect, when history cruelly repeated itself. In 1964, like his father before him, he had a heart attack, and was forced to resign.

The Drakes sent both their children to the schools they had themselves attended. The fact that neither child followed a conventional career path after school worried them not one whit – they almost seemed to feel that their children were pursuing a destiny which was a natural follow-on from their own lives, in which music, drama and literature had featured so significantly in their leisure hours.

Both parents delighted in their son's songwriting ability, though they were not in the least surprised by it; and both were immensely proud of Nick's albums. And later, both faced the ordeal of their son's depressive illness – during the last years of which he spent the majority of his time at home – with baffled fortitude, with extraordinary patience, and with a never-ceasing desire to understand: Rodney with his keen analytic intelligence, Molly with her intuition. From her poetry, one realises that she must have understood much of what her son was going through – yet she was powerless to help him.

Nick's death on a bleak November morning in 1974 was the greatest tragedy of Molly's and Rodney's lives. No one can know the toll it took on them both. Outwardly they recovered, drawing strength, once again, from each other, as well as, over the following years, from any recognition given to their son's music – including the small stream of his fans that came to visit Far Leys from all over the world. Alas, neither of them lived to see the full extent of their son's burgeoning fame.

Rodney died in 1988. His obituary states:

Rodney Drake combined, to a most unusual degree, exceptional skill in all aspects of mechanical engineering with a high order of administrative ability and financial acumen. Intellectually gifted, his fertile brain was a constant source of innovative ideas, the acceptance of which he would seek to achieve by gentle persuasion rather than coercion. He was a thoughtful, sympathetic and wise counsellor to those with personal problems, but above all he was a man of sparkling humour, and laughter was never far away when he was in the room. Truly a man for all seasons, he earned the respect, affection and admiration of all with whom he came into contact.

Molly lived on until 1993. She earned no obituary – which was perhaps fitting for such an essentially reclusive person. What would she have made of the fact that strangers across the world are now listening to her own songs and reading her poetry? That both have achieved critical acclaim in America and in Britain? That she has been the subject of a radio programme and a live concert?

For someone who once scribbled her 'Epitaph' in pencil in her poetry book –

Here lies one who was felled at a touch
Who purposing many a many thing
Almost did so much and so much
And never quite did anything.

– might she not perhaps have said, to quote another line from one of her songs, 'It's the laugh of the year'?

Four Karen nannies in traditional dress, Naw Rosie Paw Tun seated with Naw Ma Naw far right

The Regency Buck

by Gabrielle Drake

I don't remember when I was told that I was to have a sibling. I only remember being terribly excited at the prospect of the arrival of my sister: for I was determined that the growing bump my mother carried in front of her contained a girl. I christened her Gaylibar (I don't know where I conjured that soubriquet from – maybe it was just an extension of my own name as I knew it, for everyone called me Gay, and never Gabrielle). I held long conversations with Gaylibar, my ear pressed against my mother's tummy, but heard not a word in reply. Nick started as he meant to go on.

And then, my brother arrived.

The initial disappointment gave way to delight in this bouncing baby with jet-black hair, which grew in a Regency-style quiff.

> Who's my Regency Buck?
> No one but Nicholas Rodney.

Those were the words of my mother's first song about her new-born son, christened Nicholas Rodney Drake by the Bishop of Rangoon.

Within a year, black hair had given way to a flaxen thatch. And always he remained what our Scottish grandmother would have called 'a bonnie boy': perfectly proportioned with smooth unblemished honey-coloured skin. I don't ever recall being jealous of him, despite envying his straight blond hair – as I struggled to get a brush through my tight tangled curls – and his neat figure, which contrasted with my gangling legs and perennial untidiness. Nor do I remember any feeling of resentment towards the newcomer – quite the contrary: it was good to have him there. No doubt this testifies not only to the baby's chortling charm, but also to my parents' loving tact and patience. With hindsight, I realise such patience would have been easier for them than for many a harassed parent back in post-war England, for in Burma the sun invariably shone, and servants were plentiful. These included our beloved nanny – a gentle soul called Dwe Mai, who, like many nannies chosen by the British community in Burma, was a Karen. The Karens were a hill race living mainly in South East Burma. Many had been converted to Christianity by British missionaries, and that fact, coupled with their renowned sweetness of nature and their loyalty, made the women a favoured choice for the Colonial community's childcare needs.

For the British in post-war Burma were in need of loyalty. The country – and in particular the capital, Rangoon – was in political turmoil, with the situation becoming increasingly tense after independence was granted. Which no doubt meant that my father was happy to accept his firm's offer of promotion to their office in Bombay.

The only way in which this upheaval impinged upon the emotional tranquillity of our lives – Nick's and mine – was the departure of our dear Dwe Mai, who felt that her health wouldn't allow her to leave Burma. In her place came another angelic, but quite different Karen, Naw Rosie Paw Tun. Never shall I forget the arrival of Naw Rosie, or Nanny: Nanny, who was to be a pivotal part of our lives; Nanny, so wise and calm and strong; Nanny, who became a third parent.

She arrived in a rickshaw, her belongings heaped

'Oh Cowboy Small
Oh Cowboy Small
All the other cowboys
Call Cowboy small'

The earliest known Nick Drake song, displaying an economy of words later to be perfected on *Pink Moon*.

up beside her. She was dressed in traditional costume of flowered longyi and white lawn aingyi, with a lotus flower pinned into the glossy black hair piled high on her head. Her round National Health-type glasses seemed to be a part of her strong pleasant face, wreathed in a smile that showed her strong white teeth. She fitted without any difficulty into the family structure – perhaps because she was used to doing so: we were by no means the first European family she had looked after. But we were the last: for she stayed with us for fifteen years before retiring to, as she put it, 'lay her bones' in her mother country. She accompanied us to India – a period that was, in fact, no more than eighteen months, although it stretches endlessly in memory, throwing up alternate images of city life in Bombay, and seaside weekends in our little mud-floored shack at Marvie – and then she came back with us to England, and life in Warwickshire.

With our return to England, the prelude to Nick's and my lives ended, and we started the process of becoming proper people. Nanny became the bridge between East and West, ensuring that the prelude was ever present: we all became mutually reliant – we children and, indeed, our parents – on Nanny, and she, I do believe, on us: dependency across cultures. It enriched us all.

A Memoir Of My Childhood Friend

by Andrew Hicks

It is strange that although Nick Drake was one of my closest childhood friends, I only came to learn of his musical fame relatively recently. I was born a little more than a year before Nick and I spent all of my childhood at our family home just outside the Warwickshire village of Tanworth-in-Arden, where Nick was brought up. It all seems an awfully long time ago, though the impressions of the people around me are still strong.

Becoming addicted to his music has been a strange experience for me in the last few years. At any time I can put on a CD and Nick will sing for me. I can recognise his voice, which stirs memories, and I have come to learn something of his adult life. Now free of commitments to a growing family, I have more time to renew contacts with old friends from the distant past, and I feel the loss keenly that Nick cannot be one of them. Instead I visited his grave on what would have been his fiftieth birthday.

All I want to do now is to share a few memories of the childhood of a gentle and happy person. So much has been written of the later stages of Nick's life, often creating a shadowy mystique of a strange and haunted individual. This bears no resemblance to the person I knew, to the real Nick. I do not want to dwell upon his tragedy as so many have done; I hope to celebrate what he really was and to shed a little light on the impression he left on one of the young companions of his early childhood.

I remember Far Leys, the Drakes' Tanworth home, from before the family moved in. It was the home of Jim Smith, a stockbroker with Albert E. Sharpe in Birmingham. His daughters, Judy and Rosemary, were the same age as my elder sister and me. They appear as attractive children gazing out of a number of sepia photographs taken in our garden. At one of my parties Rosemary bit my arm leaving livid teeth marks. I forget what I did to warrant this. My sister and I used to go to the Smiths at Far Leys for a little pre-school or playgroup run by a Miss Tonks. When the Smiths moved to a house in Edgbaston, I thought 'Drake', the name of the newcomers, a bit strange, like a family of ducks.

Rodney Drake worked for Wolseley Hughes, an engineering company, and not with Wolseley the car company, as stated by Patrick Humphries in Nick's biography. (Wolseley is now a major listed company with varied interests including a builders' merchants.)

The most accessible private schools for small children were in Henley-in-Arden, some five miles distant from Tanworth. Nick and Gabrielle were sent to Hurst House, a pre-prep school in Henley. I have the Holiday Circular for the end of the summer term (I think of 1953), the term when Nicholas Drake along with six others joined the school.

I was one year ahead of Nick. From the time the Drakes arrived in Tanworth, my parents and a number of other families shared a car pool with them for the trip to Henley. So for over ten years we were closely connected with the Drake family and were in and out of each other's cars and houses on a regular basis.

I remember my first day at Hurst House, proud of my independence in being taken not by my mother, but by one of the other mothers, possibly Molly Drake. As you leave Henley on the road to Stratford-upon-Avon, there is a steep private drive to the right, until recently Ardenhurst School. This was the amalgamation of Hurst

House, the pre-prep school, and Arden House, the prep school to which I later went, aged eight. Hurst House is the square 1830s house up the drive on the right, now in private occupation. My impression of going to school there is still etched in my memory . . . of each classroom, the swings at the side, the entrance hall, the stairs that I had to be carried up after breaking my leg at the Drakes' house. Hurst House had a pleasant, happy atmosphere with dedicated staff. Was it Miss Jones who took the charming photo of me, Antonia Adey and Rodney Hammonds peering into the bucket of frogspawn on the gravel in front of the school?

Nick would have started in Miss Jones's class in the room on the right at the bottom of the stairs. After lunch we sat or lay on blankets and had 'rest' and were read a story. Then in our second year we progressed upstairs to Miss Franey's form, and then to Mrs Ince and finally downstairs to Miss Smith, a fire-breathing Catholic. When I fell heavily on the hard slate floor, she interpreted this to me as a punishment from God for infringing the school rule of not running along the corridor.

Andrew Hicks with Joanna Lodder

The school was run by Dennis and Jill Bennett and was, I believe, owned by Jill's family, the Nelsons. Their older son Jeremy has had a distinguished career as producer of historical and other television documentaries. The younger post-war children, Mary and Oliver, were my contemporaries at the school. And there was Marcus, the dachshund who appears front centre in all the school group photographs. I have several of these photos showing about sixty attractive, smiling children of ambitious middle-class fee-paying parents, arrayed in front of the school's solid late Georgian facade. Gabrielle – Gay, as I knew her – Drake is in the photographs I have, but they must pre-date Nick's arrival. I can also see Gay in several photos of our birthday parties at home, but somehow Nick must have avoided the camera.

Hurst House was an easy-going school where we learned the basics of reading, writing and arithmetic. Like me, Nick had an older sister to see him into school, at least for the first term, and I am sure he settled in well. I remember that both the Drake children were good at swimming, a skill learned in the Far East. The Holiday Circular I still have shows Gay Drake as winning the One Length Swimming Race, and coming second in the obstacle race. It also requests children not to bring sweets to school in future. Morning school is to begin with prayers at 9.20 a.m. and end at 12.30 p.m., while afternoon school finishes at 3.40 p.m. All children are asked to arrive and be called for punctually. Those under seven are requested to bring a pair of dungarees for games wear. Rubber boots should be marked with marking ink. Such was life's pattern, so safe and so secure and middle class, a world away from the classless milieu of the media and popular music that Nick was later to face.

We travelled to and from Henley in our small black Standard Eight, Molly Drake's succession of Morris Minors, and the cars of a number of other parents. We knew every inch of the five-mile journey to Henley – the old windmill at Danzey, now in the Avoncroft Museum, and of course the mushroom tree. For Molly and Rodney, dull or sullen silence in the car was anathema. Partly to subdue fighting in the back, but also because performance should be a universal pleasure, stories were told and songs were sung as we travelled. After leaving Danzey we always sang 'Shall we see the mushroom tree?' to the tune of an old nursery rhyme. For the Drake family, successful performance, both music and drama, were a way of life and an essential value.

The Drakes' house was sometimes the collection point for the children. I have a strong recollection of Far Leys from the many times of waiting there to be picked up by my mother, and of wonderful children's parties there. In summer we played in the extensive garden behind the house. The lawns sloped down to the fields and to a marshy stream flowing out of a pond on the other side of the road where Nick and I would happily get ourselves covered in mud.

On one occasion we were playing inside in the upstairs corridor between Nick's bedroom and the playroom. Our game was to rush down the corridor together, to throw ourselves onto a mat and slide along on the polished wood floor. On this occasion I fell badly, with Nick on top of me. The pain in my left leg below the knee was excruciating. The family's Karen nanny came and carried me to the couch in the playroom. I was howling as she massaged my leg. My mother was called urgently and I was taken to Solihull hospital where an X-ray diagnosed a fractured tibia. My leg was plastered right up to the groin and I was on crutches for six weeks.

The accident was nobody's fault, but the Drakes were most concerned that it had happened while in their care. Molly and Nick visited me, still prostrate in my bedroom. They brought me some presents – activity games and a Noddy book – and signed my plaster. I distinctly remember Nick saying that I had been very brave; strange how a trauma preserves these little details.

Tanworth was a beautiful setting for a childhood, but it was not all soft-focus summer days. It is easy to characterise it as a dreamy Miss Marple backwater, but in fact it was a time when British industry was boldly facing the future and there was optimism about modernising for a prosperous future. But there was still some rationing in the early Fifties and much austerity remaining after the war. Rooms were cold, we relied on coal fires, and many of the luxuries of today were absent, though our families were among the better off. In the Drakes' playroom was a wind-up gramophone and downstairs in the drawing room a spool-to-spool tape recorder. This was the first time I had ever heard a voice being recorded. I now realise that the purpose of this expensive tape machine was to record their own music.

Andrew Hicks

The larger houses in Tanworth attracted many of the business owners and managers from Birmingham and its industrial hinterland. While it was in unspoiled countyside, it was close to the factories of the Midlands and had good communications.

The tiny Post Office was manned by a loquacious gossip, appropriately named Miss Chattaway, and her mother. The store was run by the Tibbles family, the butcher's by Mr Simmons. Jack Hood, the ex-champion boxer (not Jack London as Humphries calls him) was publican of The Bell, and Canon Dudley W. Lee and then Mr Willmott the vicars. There were still some old characters around from an earlier agricultural age, survivors from before the industrialisation of farming. I remember Mr Hussell, always clad in old tweed jacket and trousers, heavy boots and a cloth cap that he would doff to my parents. Was he farm labourer, gardener, carpenter? His grave, marked by a simple wooden cross that will soon decay, is just a few yards from Nick's headstone in the churchyard.

Far Leys stands in a lane just off the village centre. Opposite, a track led to the village cricket pitch. Next to this lived the Pattersons, Muriel and Pip, who built their house in the early Fifties. Pip worked for Dunlop, had a well-polished Triumph 2000 and plus fours. He smoked a pipe with herbal tobacco which he collected from the hedgerows and dried in his garage. Then in the next house was the Richards family, whose daughter rode with my sister and in whose pool we occasionally risked hypothermia. Next to the Drakes was a large late-Victorian house down a long drive where village fetes were sometimes hosted. There lived Mr Onions, a retired industrialist, and his wife, the sister of Mrs Williams, our much loved next-door neighbour at Old Forge Cottage. And opposite, in one of the houses built in the late Fifties or early Sixties, lived my friend from a later school, Nick Hallam, now a doctor. Tanworth was small enough that we knew many of the families living there.

This was the context of our childhood: mostly positive, except perhaps a little sleepy and isolated and lacking in companions and unstimulating in comparison to city life. On thinking about it, Nick was one of the very few accessible contemporaries of about my own age that my parents would have seen as an appropriate social fit. So I became used to my own companionship, went for long bike rides alone or took walks through the field with the dog. I suppose life was much the same for Nick.

We all went to the same children's parties. Nick was always immaculately turned out in neat shorts and cotton shirts, Clarks sandals and, horror of horrors, white ankle socks . . . I would sooner have died horribly in a pool of piranhas. He was a delightful friend at the party, never aggressive or pushy and always without malice. Nick would not knock down your castle when you turned your back, eat your sweets, hide your favourite toy, nor punch you in the face when you were down. Childhood is red in tooth and claw and we gained real insights into those around us. Nick was not the most boisterous among us but he was sociable, joined in all the fun and got messy like everyone. He was happy, healthy and normal. With adults his behaviour was impeccable, his goodbyes and thank yous perfectly rehearsed, always addressing Mr or Mrs Double-Barrell by name. Even unbroken, his voice had a hint of the low huskiness we hear in his singing. He was the handsome, delightful child that every parent would want their own to be.

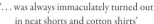

'. . . was always immaculately turned out in neat shorts and cotton shirts'

Similarly, the Drake family were charming and attractive; anyone would aspire to be like them. With great warmth they would welcome and show genuine interest in all their neighbours. They excelled as hosts and I remember their adult parties to which we were invited. At Christmas the church choir came and sang carols in their large hallway. As I stood awkardly on one leg speaking in monosyllables, the adults chatted volubly and fiddled with small eats. I can clearly remember Molly and Rodney, Molly beaming at her guests, Rodney and my father standing together ramrod straight gripping their glasses, discussing what they had in common – wartime experiences, Suez, fuel consumption, engineering, and Wolseleys; both their fathers had bought early examples of this car.

Gabrielle was generally there, strikingly lovely and with that special capacity of putting people at ease, passing round drinks, asking the right questions and dazzling everyone. She was a rising star of theatre and screen and we watched her career with pride and delight. We went to see her on stage whenever we could, my father a particular fan. He would always buy us tickets; I remember Malvern and Nottingham and going backstage to see her afterwards. She was a hard act for a younger sibling to follow and we did not even know of Nick's musical aspirations.

Were the Chatwins at those parties at Far Leys? After Hurst House, Nick did not go on to Arden House but was sent to board at another prep school. I remember a sense of disappointment and mild betrayal when I heard this as I would then not see him daily as I had before. Patrick Humphries' book documents his time at Marlborough where he boarded from the age of thirteen. Humphries mentions a number of famous old boys of the school, one of them the travel writer and novelist Bruce Chatwin. What he omitted to mention was that the Chatwins were a Tanworth family and were almost certainly part of the Drakes' social circle.

The parallels between Nick and Bruce Chatwin are close: both sons of upper middle-class families, strikingly good looking men who would never go unnoticed. They were of artistic temperament, brought up in Tanworth, going on to public school at Marlborough, both dying young and being lionised in death with biographies and growing critical acclaim and attention. Chatwin of course achieved success in his lifetime, becoming well-known as a writer and social animal.

Such early deaths are not uncommon. In our school car pool to Henley was another family with two sons. Again the father was a managing director, they were good looking and charming people, the older son brilliantly clever at school, the younger perhaps struggling socially and academically. Unable to compete with his older brother he took up artistic interests, studied art, suffered mental breakdowns and finally killed himself in his twenties. It happens everywhere . . . mental ill health is normal and Tanworth does not show a special cluster of such tragedies. All are an absolute waste, though Bruce and Nick's short lives were remarkably full and productive and are now widely remembered and valued.

After Hurst House Nick and I went to different boarding schools and so I rarely saw him, except at the occasional party in the holidays. The last time was at a party to which we invited him after I had left school. There was an old barn attached to our house which was perfect for noisy parties: ring round friends with the date . . . get in some kegs of beer . . . set up some music and wait for them all to arrive . . .

I am not sure which party it was; possibly the one on the evening of my sister's wedding, which took place at Tanworth church. The Drakes came to the wedding and to the reception; their familiar presence is in the wedding album and Gay and Nick were asked to the party afterwards in the barn. This would have been May 1968 when I was at university reading Law.

Whichever party it was, I retain a clear image of Nick

entering the barn and coming up to me and chatting. All was familiar but also much changed, with our experiences and interests diverging, me feeling a bit conventional and boring, Nick, all studied cool and glamour. He had by then adopted his standard image of long hair and dark jacket, possibly a polo neck and dark trousers that didn't taper. He was very tall, slightly stooped, with a pleasant warmth but evidently shy . . . He kept a distance, not quite engaged, just as everyone has described. I am so sorry I did not have time with him on his own. Like me, perhaps he functioned better on a one-to-one basis and not in a crowd of people yelling to be heard over the loud music.

During the evening one of the girls came up to me and said, 'Who's that gorgeous man?' She then asked me to introduce her to Nick but she was way out of his league. As people do at parties, he slipped away some time during the evening and I never saw him again.

My best Warwickshire friend at the time was Jane. She had been in Nick's year at Hurst House so knew him well. She was a competent guitarist and she and I loved nothing better than to sit around singing to the guitar – popular but pedestrian stuff. I am haunted by the possible memory that she said to me after the party that Nick had arrived with his guitar hoping to sing, looking for an audience. It was far too big and raucous a party, not the moment for this. But had it happened, had he played, we would have been transfixed by his talent; we must surely have met up again. Even then I knew nothing of his growing musical career.

Nick in the nursery of peril at Far Leys

After graduating from Southampton University, I spent two years with a law firm in Birmingham and became a solicitor in London. Inevitably I drifted away from the safety and security of the friends that I once knew in my childhood. Then I accepted a lectureship in law at a university in Nigeria to enable me to join my girlfriend who was working there. This was towards the end of 1973. My mother told me shortly before her death that Molly Drake had said at that time that Nick was at home in Tanworth and would I come over to see him. I have no memory of this, but then it is a long time ago. At that time Nick did not have much more than a year to live and I am not sure how a meeting between us would have gone. I was on the crest of a wave, having given up my career in private practice to follow my heart on an immensely exciting trip to Africa. He would have found my high mood difficult and I could not possibly have understood his predicament. At that time we so little understood or acknowleged depression, and at that age I had no insight or experience of it.

I remember where I was when I heard the news of Kennedy being shot, but I do not remember being told of Nick's death. It may even have been some years after he died. Letters to Nigeria took many weeks, if they got there at all, and phones were only for decoration. We were now expatriates with new lives, and were substantially out of touch with our old ones. We spent fifteen years abroad in West Africa and the Far East as a family, the greatest loss being separated from our roots and old friends.

Returning to UK in 1988 with two small children and two careers to establish here, life was hectic. I rediscovered Nick to my great surprise listed in a *Daily Telegraph* colour supplement table of the hundred best post-war albums. I was aghast. I had no idea of Nick's critical acclaim. I had been on another planet for years and had missed it all. I went out and bought *Way To Blue* but didn't have a CD player. So I took it round to the flat of some Malaysian Chinese friends in their mid-twenties and listened to Nick's voice for the first time with great pleasure and emotion. As the typeface of the sleeve notes was too small and I could not read it, Tieng read it out to me. It gave a moving account of Nick's life and achievements and of his death, a poignant description of Molly and Rodney's terrible loss. Tieng and Say were then amazed to see me, a middle-aged greying law lecturer almost twice their age, silently listening to a background of Nick's songs, in floods of tears.

Since then I have played Nick's CDs perhaps more than any other music I have ever listened to. In 1995, after a severe virus, I began to suffer from an unexplained chronic illness which left me in physical distress and with too much time on my hands. Nick became a daily feature of my life, a special pleasure never rationed, who released many emotions for me and helped me through a barren and difficult time. His music is haunting and sombre, but its beauty never fails to lift me. I do not always feel robust enough to face it, but when I do it is always to good effect. It seems strange that I knew so little of his music for so long but now am addicted.

It was during this time that my mother became ill and was dying of cancer. I came up to Cheltenham to see her. We talked together in the hospital about the Drake family and about Nick. I can date the time because it was June 1998, fifty years after Nick's birth. On the nineteenth, which would have been his fiftieth birthday, I went back to Tanworth for the first time for many years. As I walked among the graves looking for Nick's, I saw so many names that I had known in life. At last I found the headstone, so simple and dignified. 'And now we rise and we are everywhere.'

In the church I leafed through the visitors book. There were numerous entries from people who had come to Nick's graveside on that particular day, his birthday, to thank him for his music. I added my own with Don McLean's line about Van Gogh: 'This world was never meant for one as beautiful as you.'

Psychologists are fine until they pretend fully to understand the human psyche. And amateur psychologists who jump to conclusions are even worse. But it seems to me that the personal pressures on Nick could have broken a much stronger man. In families such as his, achievement is assumed and appears easy. How difficult it must have been for Nick to go from the strong support and discipline of such a home, through the institutionalisation of private schooling and Cambridge, and then to drop out into nothingness. No routine, no structure to his life, no supporting community, just time stretching out ahead, during which he had to produce creative and magical work. It had to be not only good but also good of the type that attracts a broad public and sells records. The alternative was commercial failure and rejection . . . hard for any artist who wants his work to be heard and appreciated. (Having just published a novel and awaiting a public response, I find the silence excruciating.) Leaving university for a music career was a huge and daring gamble for Nick.

Nick, Rodney and Gabrielle on holiday

Then there was the difficult transition to be made from Old Marlburian and Cambridge undergrad; for Nick to cease being so pukka and transform into a cool, classless artist with universal appeal. Did he curse where he came from? Did he swear in the night? And when unable to communicate with those around him and suffering an attack of diffidence, did he retreat into the distance? 'I'm a poor boy and drive a Rover.' These were real contradictions that would have challenged anyone. The Sixties and Seventies were fast moving; it was no time to feel a remnant of something that's past. When the ban on feeling free was lifted, when the prohibition on sweets in school and other more powerful pleasures no longer applied, Nick's new freedom from formality and routine in an unforgiving world must have been immensely difficult for him.

After discovering Nick's music, time now suddenly stretched ahead of me, too, because of my illness, and it gave me the opportunity to write this account of Nick. I have found it hard to lose the structure of my life, even though in middle age and no longer with anything to prove. For Nick setting out on life's adventure, commercial failure must have been devastating.

If I now want to conclude anything from my ramblings, it is this. Do not forget Nick. Enjoy and treasure his work. But do not play up the mystery of the shadowy tragic figure who nobody ever knew. This is all rubbish. I knew Nick and so did many others; he was sociable in a quiet way, a pleasure to know, and very real and substantial. And I also want to add that clinical depression, or whatever you may call it, is normal and is all around us. It hits the best people, including the cheerful ones, and is often not apparent.

I sense that if Nick had been born twenty or thirty years later things might have turned out differently for him. The Sixties was a tumultuous time, more of a revolution than it would seem in retrospect, requiring much of those wishing to reinvent themselves and become their own person. It is always hard to escape the expectations and conditioning of your upbringing,

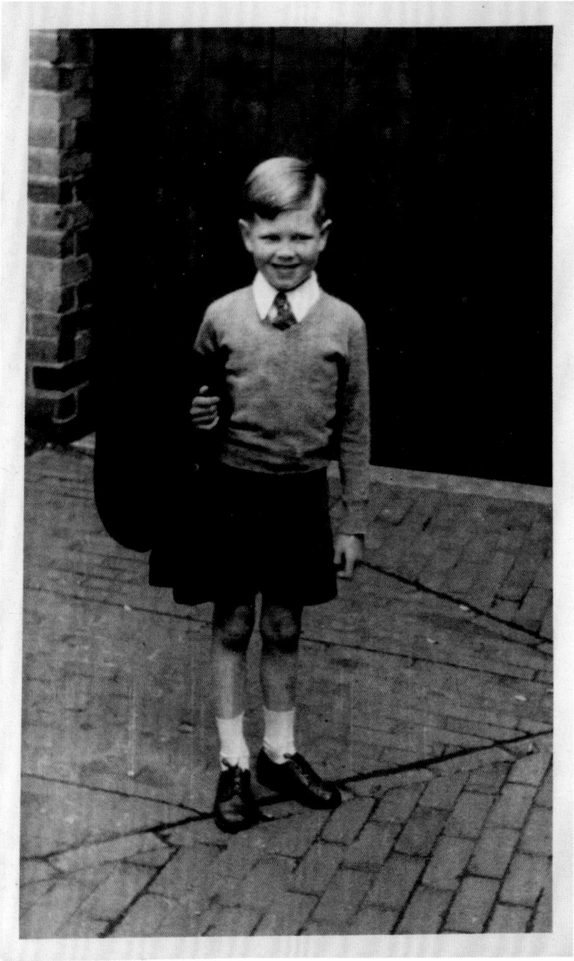

Nick all set for school

even though society is now much more mobile. There is perhaps a greater realism today; we know that the world does not owe us a living and that it is a hard world out there. We know we have to plan cautiously before making the big gamble.

The Sixties was a melting pot in which people like Nick took great and romantic risks. As a result we now have his music, but I feel his loss keenly. If only things had been different; if he could have had a whole long lifetime, if he could have stayed for more.

Nick had strong views on his record collection from an early age. Note glowing comments on his mother's songs

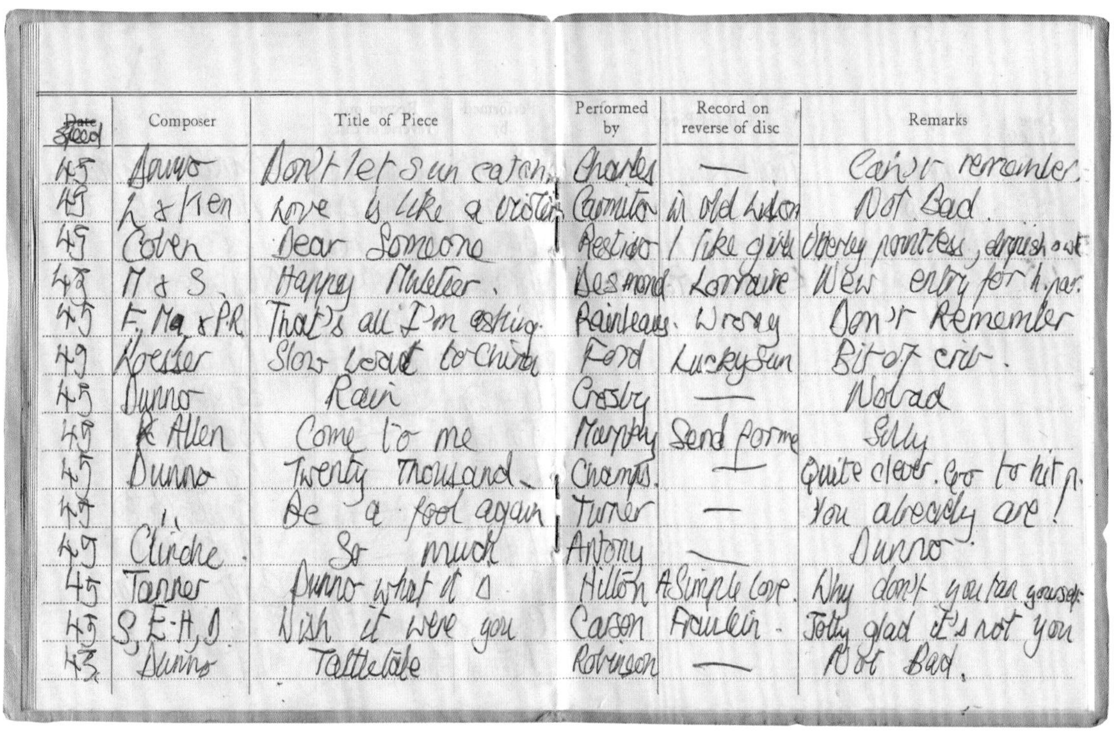

Date Played	Composer	Title of Piece	Performed by	Record on reverse of disc	Remarks
45	Dunno	Don't let sun catch..	Charles	—	Can't remember.
49	L & Ken	Love is like a cigarette	Carmita	In old Lisbon	Not Bad.
49	Cohen	Dear Someone	Restivo	I like girls	Utterly pointless, droppish out
49	M & S	Happy Muleteer.	Desmond	Lorraine	New entry for h. par.
45	F, Ma & P.R.	That's all I'm asking.	[illegible]	Wrong	Don't Remember
49	Koesser	Slow boat to China	Ford	Lucky Sun	Bit of crib.
45	Dunno	Rain	Crosby	—	No bad
49	R Allen	Come to me	Murphy	Send for me	Silly
45	Dunno	Twenty Thousand	Champs.	—	Quite clever. Go to hit p.
49	"	Be a fool again	Turner	—	You already are!
49	Cliche	So much	Antony	—	Dunno
45	Tanner	Dunno what it is	Hilton	A Simple Love	Why don't you ban yourself
45	S, E-H, D	Wish it were you	Carson	Fraulein	Jolly glad it's not you
45	Dunno	Tattletale	Robinson	—	Not Bad.

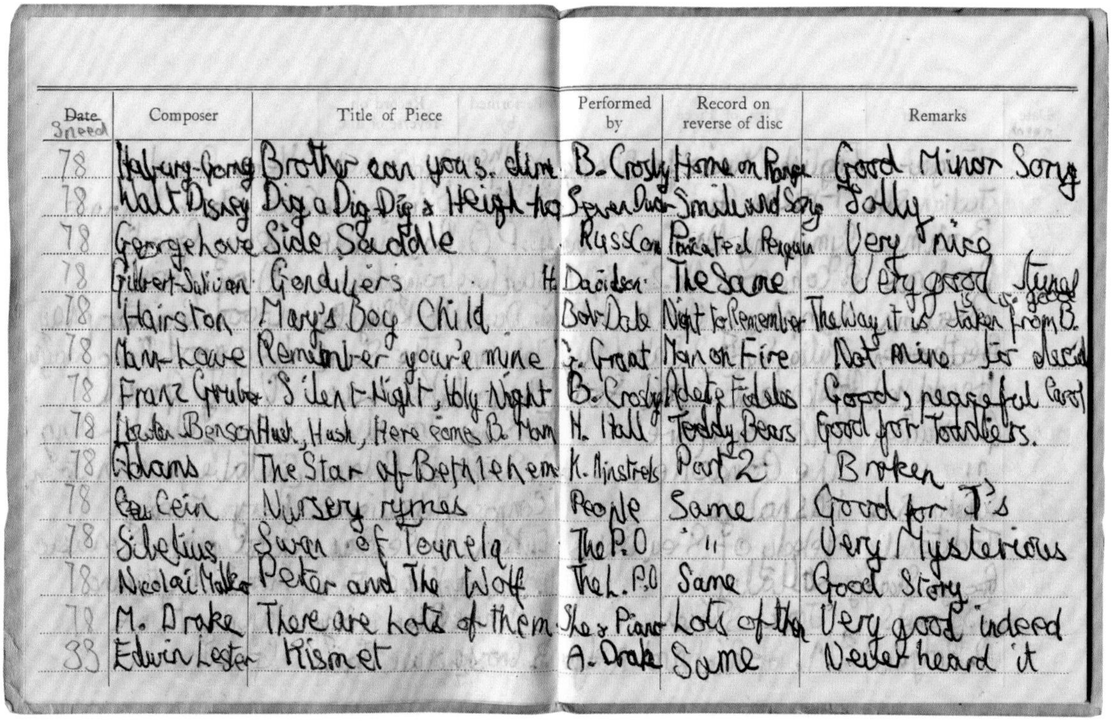

~~Date~~ Speed	Composer	Title of Piece	Performed by	Record on reverse of disc	Remarks
78	Harburg-Gorney	Brother can you s. dime	B. Crosby	Home on Range	Good Minor Song
78	Walt Disney	Dig a Dig Dig & Heigh ho	Seven Dwarfs	Smile and Sing	Jolly
78	George Love	Side Saddle	Russ Conway	Pixilated Penguin	Very nice
78	Gilbert-Sullivan	Gondoliers	H. Davidson	The Same	Very good singing
78	Hairston	Mary's Boy Child	Bob Dale	Night to Remember	The way it is taken from B.
78	Mann-Lowe	Remember you're mine	F. Grant	Man on Fire	Not mine to decide
78	Franz Gruber	Silent Night, Holy Night	B. Crosby	Adeste Fideles	Good, peaceful Carol
78	Lester Benson	Hush, Hush, Here comes B. Man	H. Hall	Teddy Bears	Good for Toddlers.
78	Adams	The Star of Bethlehem	K. Minstrels	Part 2	Broken
78	Gou Cein	Nursery rymes	People	Same	Good for J's
78	Sibelius	Swan of Tounela	The P.O	"	Very Mysterious
78	Nicolai Malko	Peter and The Wolf	The L.P.O	Same	Good Story
78	M. Drake	There are lots of them	She & Piano	Lots of them	Very good indeed
33	Edwin Lester	Kismet	A. Drake	Same	Never heard it

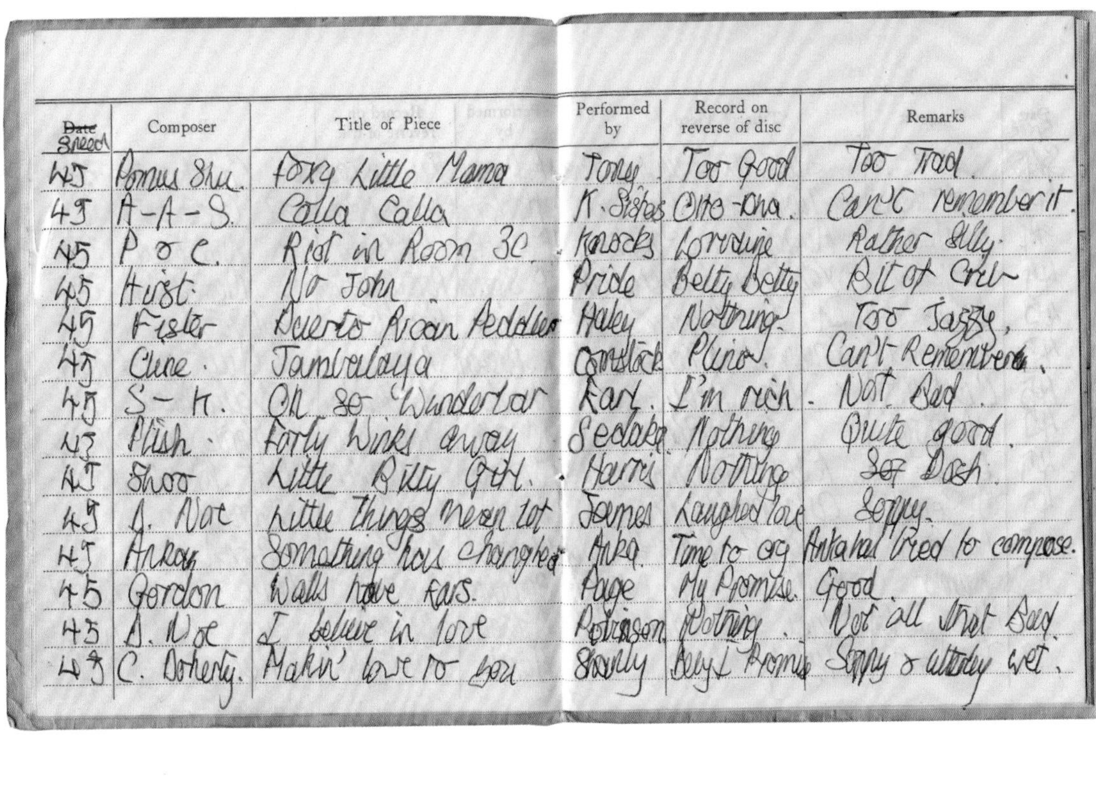

~~Date~~ Speed	Composer	Title of Piece	Performed by	Record on reverse of disc	Remarks
45	Pomus Shu.	Foxy Little Mama	Tony	Too Good	Too Trad.
45	A-A-S.	Calla Calla	K. Sisters	Cha-Cha.	Can't remember it.
45	P & C.	Riot in Room 3C	Knocks	Lorraine	Rather Silly.
45	Hurst.	No John	Pride	Betty Betty	Bit of Crib
45	Fisler	Puerto Rican Peddler	Haley	Nothing.	Too Jazzy.
45	Clune.	Jambalaya	Comstock	Pluria.	Can't Remember.
45	S-K.	Oh so Wunderbar	Karl.	I'm rich.	Not Bad.
45	Plush.	Forty Winks away	Sedaka	Nothing	Quite good.
45	Shoo	Little Bitty Girl.	Harris	Nothing	So Dash.
45	J. Noc	Little Things mean lot	James	Laughed Love	Soppy.
45	Anka	Something has changed	Anka	Time to cry	Anka had tried to compose.
45	Gordon	Walls have Ears.	Page	My Promise.	Good.
45	A. Noc	I believe in love	Robinson	Nothing.	Not all that Bad.
45	C. Doherty.	Makin' love to you	Shanty	Baby I Promise	Soppy & utterly wet.

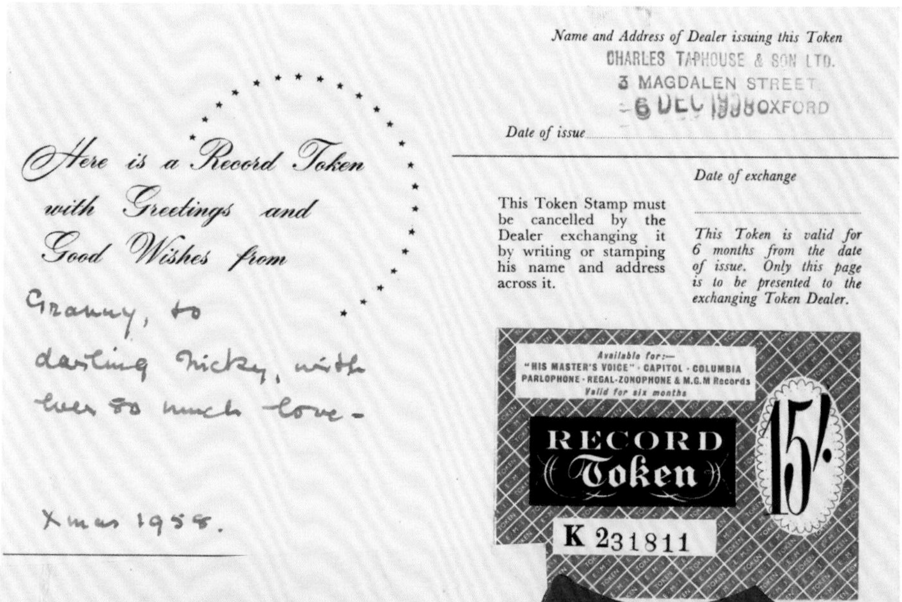
Here is a Record Token
with Greetings and
Good Wishes from
Granny, to
darling Nicky, with
ever so much love –
Xmas 1958.
Name and Address of Dealer issuing this Token
CHARLES TAPHOUSE & SON LTD.
3 MAGDALEN STREET
6 DEC
OXFORD
Date of issue
Date of exchange
This Token Stamp must be cancelled by the Dealer exchanging it by writing or stamping his name and address across it.
This Token is valid for 6 months from the date of issue. Only this page is to be presented to the exchanging Token Dealer.
Available for:—
"HIS MASTER'S VOICE" · CAPITOL · COLUMBIA
PARLOPHONE · REGAL-ZONOPHONE & M.G.M Records
Valid for six months
RECORD
Token
15/-
K 231811

— Butte Montmartre
Claude Marin
Artiste Français

NATIONAL STANDARD
JUNIOR GRADE 1
AAA

A record token from his grandmother, an Amateur Athletic Association blazer badge and a trip to Paris

The Flower

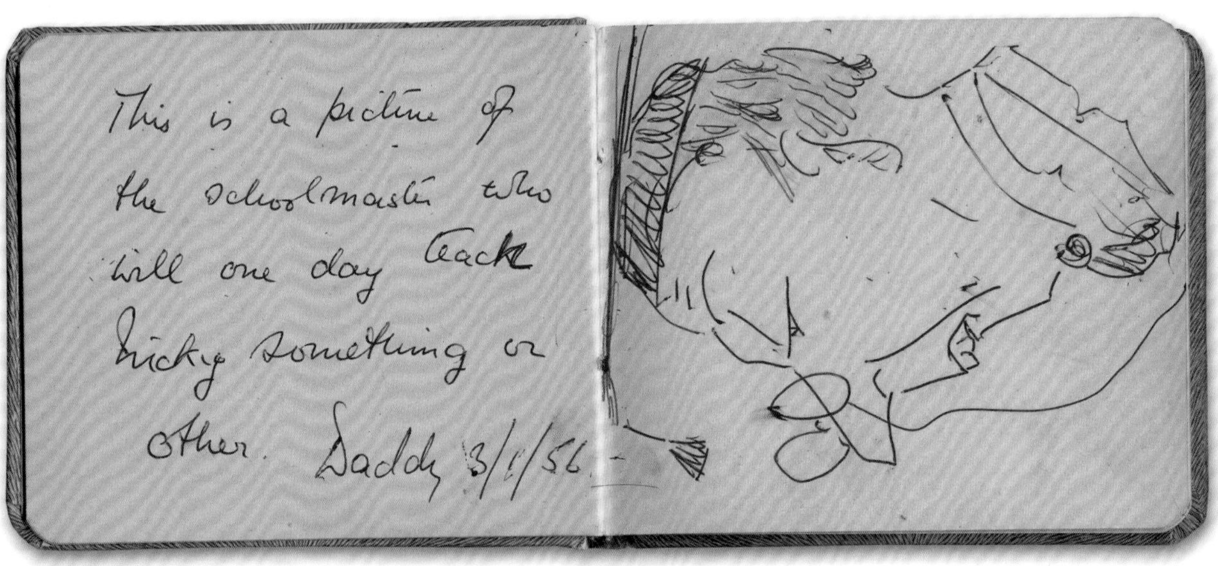
This is a picture of
the schoolmaster who
will one day teach
Nicky something or
other. Daddy 3/1/56

The Flower I

Family letters

Annotated by Gabrielle Drake

In common with many British boys from his background, Nick's education followed a traditional pattern. At eight years old, he was sent to boarding school – first a 'prep' (preparatory) school, Eagle House, and then, at the age of thirteen, to a 'public' school (public being in fact private: such are the vagaries of the British educational system). Marlborough College in Wiltshire was the school that both Nick's father Rodney and grandfather had attended. Nowadays, it is co-educational, but in Nick's time it was strictly boys only, and little had changed since his father was there.

One of the boarding-school rules was that children should write to their parents every week. Such a rule must inevitably have led to a fair degree of formal letters and stilted prose. And Nick's earliest letters from Eagle House (lovingly preserved by his mother) reflect this. But as he mastered the art of writing, his letters became increasingly expressive, and the correspondence between him and his parents is remarkable on two counts. First, for the liveliness of the exchanges, but also for the fact that so many letters, on both sides, are preserved. Nick, like his mother, was a hoarder.

Throughout his schooldays, Nick's letters were largely concerned with his two main interests: sport and music – with the emphasis gradually shifting from the former to the latter. Although in one of his earliest letters, written from his prep school at the age of eleven, he says:

'. . . Stapleton is being nice this term and we have good fun playing the piano. We have decided to go into the business when we grow up! (in music)!! . . .'

Rodney had been a keen sportsman in his youth, and both his parents were deeply interested in music of all kinds, so Nick could write to them freely about both. But he had also inherited something of his father's engineering ability, and was a willing and interested collaborator in the various mechanical experiments that Rodney conducted in the garden at Far Leys. These included a prototype Go-Kart, which occupied many hours for both father and son. This letter from his prep school covers all Nick's interests (including a nascent sartorial awareness):

EARLY SUMMER 1961
Eagle House, Sandhurst, Camberley
Dear Mum and Dad,

Thank you very much for your letters. Also for sending the cap and watch. The cap does fit this time apart from coming down towards my ears a bit.

We are having real summer weather here. It is absolutely baking. We have been playing a lot of cricket. Last Monday I scored 68 not out, but I'm afraid I only scored 1 yesterday . . .

Yes, Dad, I think it would be a very good idea to have pedals for the accelerator and break [*sic*], although perhaps rather more complicated. We might start off by having an ordinary little handle, and then gradually work up to the pedals.

Please could you tell Naw that, as she was asking what record I would like for my birthday I would like if possible 'The entry of the Gladiators' played by Nero and the Gladiators . . .

'Fraid there's no more news now. Please give my love to Nan and Naw.

Lots of love
Nick

Eagle House school

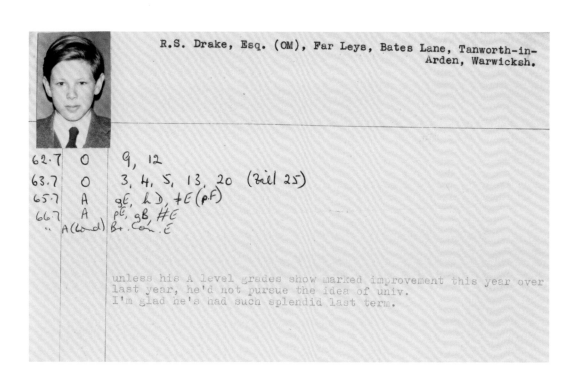

85 ~~69~~	DRAKE Nicholas R.odney	19.6.48.	62/1	P. Wootton, Eagle House, Sandhurst, Camberley	Cl ~~Barton~~ H.

62/1 62/2	Rem D	A sensible start. I.Q. 116 Generally satisfactory reports.	66/2	Captain
62/3	100d	Good term.		
63/1		House report makes good reading.		
63/2		Another good term		
63/3	His V	Jump from Lwer Sc. to Up.Sc. often coincides with the boy's emerging from "little boy" stage and can be disconcerting. That he should be at sea for one term is understandable, but mustn't make it two.		
64/2		For moment House rpt seems to me to be more important & I am glad to read it.		
64/3	HisUV	A term of real progress.		
65/2		Generally good rpts - though it looks as if his successes are going to come outside classroom more than in it.		
65/3	His.6	He gives me impression of being about a year younger than he actually is. It seems to me therefore just conceivable that coming year will see a notable increase in intellectual maturity. If that happened I thinkhe <u>could</u> make University.		? Camb.
66/2		He told me when he said goodbye he was thinking of going to crammers with view to univ. entrance. After reading rpts I'd like to express strong opinion that,		

Marlborough headmaster's record card, Rodney Drake coded 'OM' (Old Marlburian)

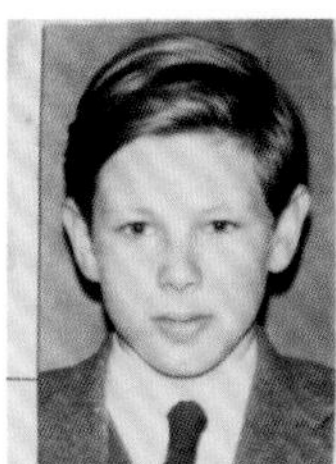

R.S. Drake, Esq. (OM), Far Leys, Bates Lane, Tanworth-in-Arden, Warwicksh.

62.7	O	9, 12
63.7	O	3, 4, 5, 13, 20 (Fail 25)
65.7	A	gE, hD, +E (p.F)
66.7	A	pE, gB, #E
"	A(Lond)	Br. Con. E

unless his A level grades show marked improvement this year over last year, he'd not pursue the idea of univ.
I'm glad he's had such splendid last term.

Nick's house wins the 1965 'House Shout' singing competition at Marlborough

In 1962, Nick moved to Marlborough College. To begin with, like all new boys, he was put into a junior house – presumably this was to lessen the impact of the change from a small 'prep' school to a major 'public' school. Nevertheless, in his first letter home from Marlborough, Nick confessed to being a little nonplussed:

SUNDAY, 21 JANUARY 1962
Barton Hill, Bath Road, Marlborough
Dear Mum and Dad,

. . . When you left, I found myself rather bewildered, and went up to the library and read. (It's a jolly good library with a lot of good books.) Then Mr Middleton called all of the new boys into the library to talk to them. He's very friendly and nice and the first thing he said was 'your parents pay a hell of a lot for you to come here, so for God's sake enjoy yourselves' which was, I thought, a very good piece of advice . . .

And one Nick took to heart. He started making his mark early, immediately getting into the main school choir (with his then treble voice), and soon after impressing the games master – thanks in part to his own enterprise. His second letter home shows a growing confidence:

28 JANUARY 1962
Barton Hill, Marlborough
. . . On Tuesday I had my first game of hockey. It was rather annoying as I found myself put on the left wing where I hardly got the ball. So at half time I beseeched the master to put me centre forward where I did much better . . . Towards the end of the game the master in charge of Junior Hockey came and watched. After the game he came up and asked me my name . . . On Friday . . . I turned up quite by accident on the wrong pitch . . . So I asked the master in charge of the game (the one who asked me my name) on what pitch I was supposed to be playing, and he remembered me and said he wanted to see me play, so . . . I went onto the right wing which I didn't find too bad . . .

On Wednesday I had my first piano lesson. I'm taken by a lady called Mrs Howe. She's not a bad old girl, and reminds me a bit of Granny. The only trouble is that she talks all the while I'm playing, and makes it rather difficult to concentrate. The pieces didn't go terribly well, but she was quite impressed . . .

Nick's desire to present a cool image started early:

6 MAY 1962
Barton Hill, Marlborough
. . . By the way, Mum, even people who weren't in the prep school 1st teams seem to have white trousers, so do you think you could send my cricket trousers. But please don't clean them, or people'll think I've sent home specially for new ones. I've been oiling my bat, and I now see what a beautiful bat it is. I can't remember what the price was, but it must've been d----mnd [*sic*] expensive. Thank you so very much, Dad.

And again:

5 JUNE 1962
Barton Hill, Marlborough
. . . P.S. Please could you send my swimming shorts as quick as poss. But please don't iron them.

By the following year, Nick was well into the swing of Marlborough life:

TUESDAY, 13 FEBRUARY 1963
Barton Hill, Marlborough
Dear Mum and Dad,

I really am most frightfully sorry for not writing till now, but on Sunday morning I was arranging a ping-

Molly, Nick and Gabrielle on holiday in Scotland

pong team to play Upcot, and on Sunday afternoon I was playing the competition, and in the evening I had rather a lot of prep to do. Still, that's not really a good enough excuse, considering you sent me so many nice letters. Thank you very much indeed for them. I'm glad you had a good time with the Lancasters. Thank you also for the news about Gay, which I very much enjoyed reading.

. . . I really am getting sick of this weather. We had yet another blizzard on Sunday, which added a couple of inches or more in three hours. I'm longing for a game of hockey. All we do at the moment is have physical jerks at the gym, which gets me down. Another thing which makes life pretty depressing is that we're not allowed to brew because of some burst pipe or something. So I now have piles of baked beans, ravioli, spaghetti bolognese etc. etc. just moulding [*sic*] in the locker (of course they're all in separate tins!)

I was rather annoyed about the ping-pong competition against Upcot, because it came on the day of the one concert I wanted to go to, which was Joseph Cooper (piano) who played all kinds of nice things like 'Sheep may safely graze!' By the way, Upcot beat us, but I managed to win my game.

Next week I am starting pieces for piano and clarinet, which will be fun. It'll also be fun for the holidays. In piano, I'm learning another boring piece.

I'm afraid there's no more news now. I've just had my fortnightly order. I came 5th in Physics and 5th in Chemistry. Please give my love to Nan and Naw.

Simply longing to see you on Sat.

Much love from Nick

In the autumn term of 1963, Nick started at his Senior House, C1, situated in the main body of Marlborough College. By now he was fifteen years old, and had already passed seven O-Level exams, and he and his parents had their sights set on a place for him at either Oxford or Cambridge University. Nick was fortunate to have as his new housemaster at C1 Dennis Silk, an exceptional teacher with whom Nick seemed to establish an immediate rapport, and who was to play a key role in Nick's school life, and university entrance. He is referred to variously in the letters as 'Silk', 'DWS', and 'Den'.

RODNEY TO NICK:
22 SEPTEMBER 1963
Dear Nickroach,

Just a line to add to Mummy's – I forgot to tell you that I did talk to Mr Silk about Oxford. He agreed that we should make the first move now that you have your 'O' levels and we decided that we would we would discuss it with him the first time we come down.

Hope you are settling down and have discovered where to go and what to do and when etc.! Always a bit difficult at first – however, you've been through that experience quite often now with Hurst House, Eagle House, and Barton Hill behind you and you must be getting progressively more expert at solving the problems involved.

I'm afraid having to say goodbye to old Nan has made the return to school a sad affair for you this term. I just can't think what we shall feel like on October 18th!

Best of luck, Nick. Longing to hear your news

Dad

October 18th was the date Nan – Naw Rosie Paw Tun – who had been with the family for fifteen years, was due to leave and set sail for Burma. Rodney's letter crossed in the post with Nick's first from C1.

22 SEPTEMBER 1963
C1 House, Marlborough
Dear Mum and Dad,

To start with, thank you very much indeed for such

Rodney and Nick on holiday in Scotland

a smashing holiday. I enjoyed every moment . . . I think Scotland was one of the best hols we've ever had . . .

. . . I'm beginning to find my feet in this place, but everything still seems a bit strange. Silk is a very nice chap and most helpful. There was a bit of a muddle over which form I was in. I looked on the board and saw the list of the History V on which I wasn't . . . I went and saw Silk about it, and apparently, when they saw I'd passed German, they fell flat on their faces with surprise and hurriedly and apologetically put me back on the Modern Languages side. This put me in a dilemma, wondering which side I should go on. Silk was very helpful and went through the various options and subjects of each side with me. I eventually decided to go into the History V. I do History (Alfred etc.) and English with Silk, European History with someone else, and Latin, French and German. So that's fine. Instead of what's called 'Study Periods', of which I have two or three a week, I have Latin extra tuition, with some other boys who haven't done Latin for a year.

Having eventually found out where the wardrobe is, I have unpacked my trunk. It's quite alright about the socks. I just walk in and help myself any time I want, and throw the dirty ones in a basket.

I don't really know anybody in house at the moment, and life's rather dull. I have been talking mainly to old junior house friends in other houses . . .

Please give all my love to Nan and Naw,

Much love Nick

MOLLY TO NICK:
10 OCTOBER 1963
Far Leys
My darling Nick,

Thank you so very much for your super & most amusing letter this week which was full of news . . . Took it over to Oxford on Tuesday to read to Gran who was most interested in it . . .

Well now what has been the news lately. Gay & I had a marathon at Stratford last Saturday – the Wars of the Roses – it was really terrific & we enjoyed it enormously. I think I enjoyed 'Henry VI' best – but that may have been because it was in the morning & I was most alert. I must confess by the time it came to 'Richard III' in the evening I was ready for a snooze and dropped off for a short space during Act 1!

Last night we had dinner with the Lancasters – it was to be what Norman called a Soirée Musical . . .

The music was lovely and we did enjoy it – though it was hard to get Norman to stop talking for long enough to listen to it! There were two other couples there – both doctors – one couple was called Jacques . . . & they have a son at Marlborough who is a month older than you but seems to be about two forms lower – the very nice (hugely tall) Dr Jacques kept saying to me 'Your boy must be brilliant – almost scholarship standard'. I wonder if you've come across their son.

Must stop darling as the post is about to go. Ghastly writing I'm afraid – masses of love from everyone – Nan's boat now sails Oct: 22nd – it would be very nice if you could send her a little note – all love Mum

13 OCTOBER 1963
C1 House, Marlborough
Dear Mum and Dad,

Thank you so very much indeed for your nice letter. So glad you enjoyed the marathon W[ars] of the R[oses]. The 'soiree musicale' sounds good fun. I know the Jacques boy very vaguely. He seems okay but is about –5 [i.e. minus five] inches tall, which seems strange since his father is so goliathan. By the way, you don't want to be taken in by these parents who say I must be clever. It just means that that they don't like to admit their son is below average intelligence.

A thing or two has been happening in the rugger world. Apparently I was to be promoted onto the second team, but the people in the third team persuaded the captain of games not to promote me. This suited me okay . . . On

Dennis Silk stands beside Nick's hockey team at Marlborough

Thursday night I went into Silk's study to get permission for something or other. He suddenly turned on me and said 'You, you lazy young lout,' (my heart froze) 'should be on the Colts team and end up with at least 2 years on the XV as a very fine three-quarter.' (My heart thawed) . . .
I went to the Mop fair again yesterday and spent another 10 bob. Mop fairs really are money-eating things, and I'm getting a bit hard-up financially (hint hint!). To explain about the whole holiday, it is, funnily enough, a whole holiday (that's helpful isn't it!) . . . It is a day when one can do anything one likes. A lot of people go up to London. I'm not sure whether I will or not. I think I'll probably just go to Swindon, cos it's cheaper, and they've got a selection of 3 cinemas anyhow.

I don't think I've told you anything about music this term. I've got the same old cow teaching me piano as I had before. She's hurriedly put me onto the most lifeless piece that ever survived, and stamped out any enthusiasm that I had. With the clarinet I'm struggling through that 'Valse des Fleurs' and slowly getting it. My teacher says that there's definitely something wrong with my clarinet and he's going to take it in again to have it mended. At the moment I use the mouthpiece of my own clarinet and the body of the school one.

No more news now. Please give my love to all.

Much love Nick

Financial hint taken!

20 October 1963

Dear Mum and Dad,

Thank you so very much indeed for your good letters. Thank you also so much for sending my watch, shirt and £3. I hope you got my postcard saying I'd love to meet up with you on whole holiday, at Victoria Bus station 10.30 a.m.

Very little has been happening this week. Last Tuesday was Field Day, and we had to do a most ridiculous exercise. We had to split up into groups of three and tramp all over the countryside for miles around, clocking in at various points to claim certain amounts of marks. If a group succeeded in getting 100 marks it was offered a prize. I'm sorry to say that we did not get 100 marks. We spent about an hour in thick fog, looking for a point which we later found out had never existed. It continued to drizzle throughout the day, the fog never lifted, and we arrived home extremely exhausted, and blistered to the core – not one of the most enjoyable days I have had.

Even after racking my brains until they ache, I'm afraid I still can't think of another item of news worth relating . . .

A run of three consecutive letters:

3 November 1963

CI House, Marlborough

Dear Mum and Dad,

Thank you so very much indeed for giving me such a super time last week-end. I really did enjoy it. The blow-out I had is still lasting me out, and probably will continue to do so for some time!

I did my lecture on the Claudian Invasion yesterday. It went quite well, and Silk was really quite complimentary about it . . .

Last night was 'Pop Nite', which is the usual session of music played by different school bands. It went very well, and everybody played pretty well, especially the four □ □ □ □'s [Squares]. At one stage there were 4 guitars, 4 saxes, three trombones, three trumpets, double bass, piano, and two people on drums, all playing at the same time, which was quite impressive. The Jerry Harmer Folk Trio was quite good, I thought. It consisted of Jeremy on guitar, with double bass and drums.

I'm afraid there's no more news now. Please give my love to Naw. The cake is simply delicious. Just about as good as Nan's.

'Brasser', a small orchestra consisting of brass and wind instruments. Nick seen clutching his saxophone in case it falls apart

MOLLY TO NICK:
6 NOVEMBER 1963
Far Leys
My darling Nick,

I am really feeling absolutely awful about you – I haven't written for so long darling and I am so sorry – I don't quite know how it is that I've been so busy. I suppose it's just the rush of housework to the head as a result of Nan's departure. And another reason why Dad and I are both feeling awful is that we suddenly realised we've never told you about 'Becket' – I do hope it isn't too late now to get tickets for same – we have booked at the C[astle]. & B[all]. for that w/e and of course we ought to have let you know days ago about it – d'you think you'd still be able to get some? If so get one for Gay too though it's not certain whether or not she'll be able to come that w/e. But get one in case. Thank you so very much for your lovely letter this week darling – we were terribly interested about the Claudian Invasion lecture and so very glad and delighted that Mr Silk was complimentary about it. Do try and keep a copy of it for us to see . . .

We had a lovely letter from Old Nan yesterday – written like a diary with a bit written each day. I'll try and remember to bring it for you to see. She sounds in good heart though she says she can't stop thinking 'Far Leys' – poor old darling – she sent you lots of love. The sea had been very calm all the way which was a good job . . .

Masses of love darling and longing to see you on the 16th – let me know if there's any change re: wanting a chocolate cake – so glad the last was edible.

All love again darling

10 NOVEMBER 1963
C1 House, Marlborough
Dear Mum and Dad,

Thank you so very much for your letters. It's alright about the tickets for 'Becket', as I got some on the off-chance before your letter arrived. I'm greatly looking forward to seeing you next week-end. I hear the Crockers are coming down that week-end too, so we can resume tradition after that slight break last time. I'm so glad to hear that Nan has had a good voyage so far, and that Naw is cheering up.

I went to a film put on by the Jazz Society yesterday afternoon. It was a filmed jazz session by Duke Ellington and his band. It was absolutely fabulous, I thought. I have heard that it's meant to have the finest saxophone section in the world, and they certainly proved it in this film. There was also some jazz played by some school groups, which seemed rather cheap up against Ellington . . .

Must stop now. Please give my love to Naw. If you were thinking of bringing a cake down next w-e, a fruit cake would be super. I'll show you my lecture when you come down, as I rather need it for some notes at the moment. Longing to see you.

Gradually, the music side of Nick's life assumed increasing importance. He set about becoming a performer rather than merely a member of the audience:

5 JULY 1964

. . . I told my music teacher about wanting to take up the sax, and he said it would be just about alright now, especially if I took up the alto. So I've had one lesson with him, which was great fun. He has now given me some pop music to transpose into the right key for the sax so that I can play it next week with him accompanying me on the piano. I look forward to that . . .

22 OCTOBER 1964

. . . I've recently been having a go on a sax which is much better than the one I took home last holidays, and I find that much of what I took to be my own lack of

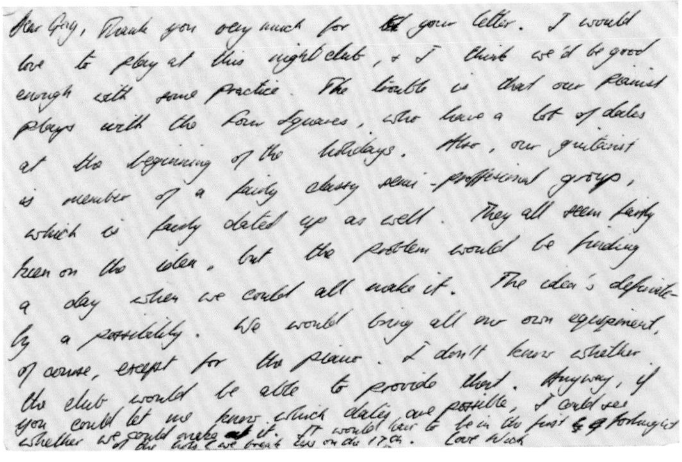
Dear Gay, Thank you very much for your letter. I would
love to play at this night club, & I think we'd be good
enough with some practice. The trouble is that our pianist
plays with the Four Squares, who have a lot of dates
at the beginning of the holidays. Also, our guitarist
is member of a fairly classy semi-proffessional group,
which is fairly dated up as well. They all seem fairly
keen on the idea, but the problem would be finding
a day when we could all make it. The idea's definitely a possibility. We would bring all our own equipment,
of course, except for the piano. I don't know whether
the club would be able to provide that. Anyway, if
you could let me know which dates are possible, I could see
whether we could make it. It would have to be in the first 2 fortnights
of the hols (we break up on the 17th). Love Nick

Nick responds to Gabrielle's suggestion of playing at Malvern

proficiency was in fact caused by the bad condition of the instrument. The time of the week I most look forward now is my clarinet lesson. As I think I told you, my teacher is a very capable musician and knows everything about music. He also plays just about every instrument, including the guitar. In my lessons I can talk to him about music in general as well as playing with him. He usually has a pretty varied assortment of music for me to play. I've asked him if he can get me something more modern in the way of pieces for piano and clarinet, so I don't know what he'll get. (In fact he'll probably forget to get anything at all!) He's taught me a bit about the guitar as well . . .

Monday, 10 April 1965

. . . Well, at this early stage of term there doesn't seem to be a great deal to tell you. I've had a go on the tenor sax, which I didn't really find difficult. It's now broken unfortunately. I'm now playing the alto in Brasser and have just been asked to play it in one piece for the orchestra, which is a bit of a laugh. I'm also trying to get up a jazz quartet to play at the Jazz Society. Jeremy has been writing off to all kinds of shipping companies. He got the first reply yesterday, and, believe it or not, it was refused!

18 May 1965

. . . I did a bit of running on Saturday in the match. It was a sort of 2nd team and I didn't do any of the sprints. I just did the 200-yds hurdles, and made rather a mess up of it, since I got my pace all wrong. I also ran in the relay, which we won. I have yet to get reasonably fit.

The term is proving to be a fairly dull one so far, with little out of the ordinary happening. Still, I suppose one has to expect that of school. Anyway, my time seems to be completely taken up one way or another. I'm playing in a jazz group at the moment which we've formed to play at the Jazz Society next week. It consists of a piano, sax, flute, trumpet, bass, and drums. We play rather more sophisticated stuff like 'Summertime' and 'Misty', and a few vocals like 'Sit right down and write myself a letter'. Just your sort of vintage, really!

There was the occasional diversion – such as the time Gabrielle decided to take a break from rehearsals at the Everyman Theatre in Liverpool, and come to Marlborough for the weekend with her friend – an exuberant actress called Sarah Buchanan – and take Nick and his friends out, landing them all in a fair degree of hot water. Curiously, brother and sister both wrote about this event to their parents (who were then enjoying a working holiday in India) on the same day:

GABRIELLE:
15 February 1965
Everyman Theatre, Liverpool

Well we've 'done' Marlborough! Thank God, wonders will never cease, the weekend was left free . . . Sarah rang up a pet place of hers called The Bell at Ramsbury which she thoroughly recommended . . . Very cleverly we guessed at booking a table for 5 – brilliant as Nick brought out 2 friends – Dace – as we are not allowed to call him! – & Andy Murison who is extremely nice – smaller than Nick & Dace, pleasant faced, & be-glassed – rather serious minded which seems paradoxical as he was the arch baddy on last term's drunken exploit! Nick was in excellent form – I've never seen him so gay & forthcoming. They all seemed thrilled at the prospect of going to the Bell, but tentatively stated that they thought it might be a bit expensive. Actually Sarah had said this too, so we were prepared. And my goodness it certainly was! But a really excellent place – Sarah very kindly paid for drinks & liqueurs which she kindly offered us, and we had a marvellous evening. I think all the boys thoroughly enjoyed themselves – no shyness or any nonsense of that

WILTSHIRE GAZETTE AND HERALD, THURSDAY, JUNE 23, 1966.

WILTS ATHLETIC CHAMPIONSHIPS

M. R. Drake, of Marlborough College, winner of the junior 100 yards at the Wiltshire championships on Saturday.

Junior men

100 yards: 1 M. Drake (Marlborough) 10.4sec., 2 K. Hall (Swindon), 3 J. Worthington (Marlborough).

220 yards: 1 M. Drake (Marlborough) 22.8secs., 2 J. Worthington (Marlborough), 3 K. Hall (Swindon).

440 yards: 1 N. Grist (Trowbridge) 51.7sec. (record), 2 D. Lyall (Calne), 3 C. Darby (Bradford-on-Avon).

880 yards: 1 N. Grist (Trowbridge) 2min. 1.9sec., 2 S. Barnes (Swindon).

One mile: 1 J. Bednarski (Swindon) 4min. 26sec. (record), 2 J. Glague (Marlborough), 3 P. Wright (Marlborough).

Long jump: 1 M. Phillips (Marlborough) 20ft. 6¾in., 2 P. Millard (Swindon), 3 A. Oruston (Marlborough).

Triple jump: 1 P. Millard (Swindon) 40ft. 5in., 2 A. Oruston (Marlborough).

Javelin: 1 G. Rudkin (Marlborough) 146ft. 10in., 2 S. Barnes (Swindon) 3 D. Arthur (Marlborough).

Discus: 1 C. Cox (Marlborough) 125ft. 5in., 2 M. Wood (Marlborough).

Shot: 1 M Wood (Marlborough) 40ft. 2¼in. 2 C. Cox (Marlborough).

Wiltshire Gazette and Herald, 23 June 1966

Other sport

ATHLETICS

WILTS A.A.A. CHAMPIONSHIPS (at Marlborough). Winners. Senior Men.—100 Yards: A Walker (Swindon), 10.2s. 220: A Walker, 23s. 440: G Grist (Trowbridge), 52.3s. 880: G Grist, 1m 56.5s. 1 Mile: D Bratt (R.A.F.), 4m 29.8s. 3 Miles: D Bratt, 14m 54s. 2 Miles Walk: W Pickett (Trowbridge), 15m 34s. High Jump: A Kilpatrick (London), 6ft 4in. Long Jump: R Tigwell (unattached), 19ft 9¾in. Triple Jump: R Ryan (Salisbury), 42ft 10½in. Javelin: H Bowron (R.A.F. Swindon), 178ft 7in.

Junior Men. 100 Yards: M Drake (Marlborough), 10.4s. 220: M Drake, 22.8s. 440: N Grist (Trowbridge), 51.7s. 880: N Grist, 2m 1.9s. 1 Mile: J Bednarski (Swindon), 4m 26s. Long Jump: M Phillips (Marlborough), 20ft 6¾in. Triple Jump: P Millard (Swindon), 40ft 5in.

Women. 100 Yards: B Gill (Swindon), 12.1s. 220: B Gill, 27.3s. 4 x 110 Yards Relay: Swindon, 54.2s. High Jump: B Gill, 5ft 2in. Long Jump: B Gill, 16ft 4¾in. 880: C Lovelock (Salisbury), 2m 28.1s.

kind – not that one could be with Sarah around! As I said Nick was very au fait & adult seeming – as indeed they all were. They all said that as Silk was not there it didn't matter what time they got back, & and we eventually dropped them off at 11.15! Apparently, quite contrary to what they said, house captains had been tearing their hair out & ringing up police to see if there had been an accident between Marlborough & Swindon, & were about to ring the Swindon bowling alley as a last resort when they eventually appeared. However the next day they assured us nothing terrible would happen & that there was <u>no</u> reason for us to go & 'chat-up' house captains or house tutor – probably afraid we'd muck the whole thing up to an even greater degree! . . .

NICK: 15 February 1965

. . . Gay & Sarah decided to come down this week-end in spite of my away match at Millfield. I'm certainly very glad they did. They picked me up around 7.30 (I couldn't take me out any earlier as a result of my away match). I took Dave Wright & Andy Murison out too, and we all went to the Bell at Ramsbury, which is a really elite little restaurant. We had a wonderful meal with lots of wine and rounded it off with coffee & liqueurs. I hate to think what it cost. Gay insisted on paying for it all (with Sarah paying for the drink). It really was terribly kind of them. Unfortunately we couldn't get a table till nine, and consequently we weren't back until 11.30, & to our great surprise we found they had been quite worried about us back at house. They're really quite cross about the whole thing, & I have to go and see Den tonight, stupid man. I don't suppose he'll do anything about it . . .

GABRIELLE:

. . . Nick brought out another member of his 'clique' to breakfast – Arthur Packer – funny looking boy – who Nick says is even vaguer than he is <u>if</u> that's possible – but <u>so</u> nice & very polite & appreciative. We'd decided, Sarah & I, that we'd go to St Peter's if only to see who could cadge the most looks! We met up with Dace & Andy & all went into church together – it was lovely to do a proper Marlborough weekend again. After church we took them all for a drink to one of 'their' pubs! Then Nick came out to lunch alone this time. Unfortunately he had a (dance band) practice in the afternoon, and as we had to leave at tea time . . . we thought we'd go to some of the dance band practice & then be on our way. Well, going to the practice was Sarah's idea, and we rather insisted on doing it. I'm afraid Nick was rather pulverised with embarrassment, but it was fun – Nick seemed to be doing very well. Didn't spare us a look I need hardly say! . . .

NICK:

. . . Anyway, I went out on Sunday as well with another friend & had a very good breakfast at the C&B. Then we all went (plus D.W. & A.M.) to St Peters & occupied the back row. It was quite a laugh. I stayed out for lunch by myself, Sarah & Gay still paying for everything. But then I had to go back to a dance band practice so they set off back to Liverpool. It was really good of them to come down & treat us all so generously . . .

No mention by Nick of the embarrassment of having the girls gatecrash his rehearsal! Too uncool, no doubt . . . But the evening had its repercussions: Nick's debauchery, instigated by his sister, led to the only recorded incident of a fall-out between him and Dennis Silk:

. . . Saw Den last night about being really late last Saturday. He really got quite uppish about it. I really had

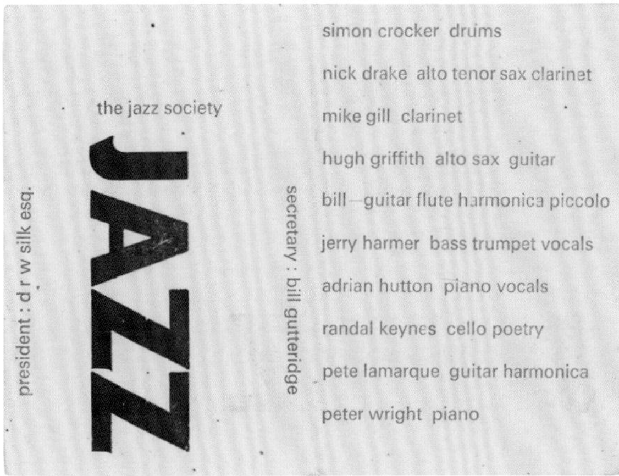

to put him in his place. He's now got us doing sweats before breakfast every morning as a punishment which is really nasty of him. I did one this morning, & practically fell asleep over me corn flakes! Still it's not the end of the world, & no doubt it'll do me a lot of good . . .

But good relations between pupil and housemaster were soon restored: history does not relate what the 'report' below was in relation to, but the mutual respect is apparent:

4 April 1965
C1 House, Marlborough
Dear Dad,

. . . I plucked up courage and went and saw Den about my report the other night. He seemed very pleased, and said he has realised since writing the report that it is pointless for a captain of classroom to hope for complete authority, since he is in charge of boys who are all his own age and level. He also said that he now realises that the classroom went much better than he in fact thought. So all is well there. He said he was very glad I'd come to see him about it, and that it was very 'brave and sensible' of me. So I obviously did the right thing . . .

By now, Nick's enthusiasm for sport was increasingly on the wane, although he had a natural athletic ability. Whereas music, in almost all forms, occupied him ever more.

24 October 1965
C1 House, Marlborough
Dear Mum and Dad,

. . . Well, as usual there are lots of exciting events to recall after yet another thrill-packed week at Marlborough Coll. I had to face two rugger matches last week, one on Thursday and one yesterday, which virtually put an end to me. We lost both of them, much to my disappointment. Had the most nerve-racking time yesterday, as we were playing army apprentices, who had an even less human approach to the game than most rugger players.

The musical side of life seems to be thriving at the moment. Jeremy's group is in full swing . . . and the other group I was talking about, which I really do enjoy playing in, featured last night at the Jazz Society. It went very well once we got started, but unfortunately that took some time, since all the amplifiers, plugs, and everything else conceivable took it in turns to go wrong or blow up or something, which was a little off-putting. However, it was a very informal meeting, so it didn't matter much.

The week before last I went up to London in a small party to see 'Carmen' at the Sadler's Wells Theatre. I found there were quite a few familiar tunes in it, and I thoroughly enjoyed it, except that I always think it's rather a pity that in operas the young hero has to be a most undesirable little fat man. Still, I suppose he's the only type who can sing in the right way. However, I thought Carmen herself, who was played by a girl called Joyce Blackham, was magnificent.

The work is plodding on, and is not particularly inspiring.

I'm afraid that's about all the excitement I can provide . . .

6 February 1966
C1 House, Marlborough College
Dear Mum and Dad,

Thank you very much for your letters with all your news.

Life here seems to be really rather tolerable at the moment. I'm almost enjoying my work at times, and that's something I don't think you'd have heard me say during

the last two years. In English I'm at present studying Milton's 'Paradise Lost', which is a bit heavy going, but at the same time I'm doing 'Othello', which certainly keeps me alive. We're going to see that same play done at the Malvern Festival Theatre of all places, so it'll be grand to be back. [Gabrielle had spent a season at the theatre the previous summer, and Nick had visited her several times.] British Constitution is also fairly interesting, since before I started I knew virtually nothing about it. Being at school does seem to have one or two advantages. I'm treated as an adult and there's quite a feeling of independence in a way. Unfortunately there are rather too many disadvantages as well. I wouldn't mind giving up games now, so as to have more time for things like art and music, but no doubt all the various authorities would have respective heart attacks if I suggested such a thing! Anyway, I suppose it's quite a good thing to get fit now and then, since seventeen seems rather an early age to relapse into complete physical chaos! Incidentally, I'm still on the second hockey team, which is rather a relief, since there's not such a frighteningly keen atmosphere about it as there always is on the first. We had a match against the town the other day, which we won (no thanks to me, of course, since I was in a state of continual exhaustion from start to finish).

I've abandoned that group which came to such grief in its one and only performance, and have now started another one . . . To begin with, I did the singing, but soon found that playing the piano and harmonica, and singing at the same time, was a bit too much, and anyway my voice isn't really up to it. So we've now imported someone and are trying to teach him to sing. The dance band is due to play before some film show, and I'm getting a selection of new numbers for it to play, which should improve its reputation.

Anyway, must stop now, as I have to write a critical appreciation of Dryden's 'Absalom & Achitophel'!

4 May 1966

Dear Dad,

This is really to send you many happy returns on this historic annual event! I'm sorry to be missing out on the birthday card stakes again, but as usual the Marlborough selection is laughably bad, and I thought you'd probably rather not have some gaudy card with 'To Father from his Son' or 'Now you are 57' or any other such delightful message! Anyway many happy returns all the same.

Things seem to be generally okay at this end . . . The study has turned out quite nice. It's really quite big and the carpet fits just about right. Incidentally it looks amazingly plush in its present surroundings, which perhaps doesn't say much for the present surroundings. Still, they're not bad, especially as far as space goes. There's room for two beds which makes things rather comfortable. It's quite satisfactory from my point of view, since the other two are always going off somewhere, so that I have the study to myself for quite a lot of the time.

I seem to be doing a lot of training at the moment, though nothing very strenuous as yet. I now find that I get less exhausted than various other people because I take half the number of steps that they do!

Please thank Mum for her letter with all the news. I was interested to hear about Gay's reviews. What a turn up for the books getting such a good one from Gareth Lloyd-Evans. I thought he got it bang-on in those few words, and his phrase 'reluctant viciousness' seems to sum up the mood of the part exactly. I do hope the first night of 'Simpleton' went well. Gay must have looked delicious!

Must stop now. Once again best wishes for a h[appy]. b[irthday]. Thank you very much for a really good holiday, and especially so for that marvellous financial bonus. It really was generous of you. Please thank Mum for the party and everything. See you on the 21st.

Love to Naw and Gay,

Much love Nick

The Simpleton of the Unexpected Isles: Linda Marlowe, Benjamin Whitrow and Gabrielle with the black wig that covered her ears

RODNEY TO NICK:
7 MAY 1966
Far Leys

Dear Nick,

Many thanks indeed for your birthday wishes letter – very clever of you to remember – though actually I rather encourage people to forget this annual event nowadays. But I'm sorry you didn't manage to find a 'Now you are 57' card, because this would have flattered me by one year! Awful thought, isn't it! Mum has given me an extremely smart dressing gown which will put me right on the map in the Cote d'Azur, after which it will be locked away from your covetous eyes!

Glad to hear the training is not proving too onerous ... I hope the new starting blocks will function effectively. You don't say anything about D.W.S. and your proposed extra coaching in Latin grammar, but perhaps that's too horrible to talk about.

News – we went to see Gay in the opening night of 'The Simpleton of the Unexpected Isles', which we much enjoyed. It's a very strange play (written by Shaw when he was well over 80) where the characters are really instruments used for the expression of various pet theories of his – but it is nevertheless very original and amusing. Gay has a fairly small part as one of the four children, produced by an experimental union of Western and Eastern parents, who charge about dressed in exotic oriental costumes. She was in the end allowed to have a full wig (long black hair), and didn't have to show her ears ...

And then Rodney, who had already suffered one heart attack two years previously, had another one:

RODNEY TO NICK:
30 MAY 1966
Far Leys

Dear Nick,

Well this is a fine state of affairs is it not – the old man crocked up again for no apparent reason that I can see. Doctor says doing too much but I don't quite see how I can do much less. However it's not so bad this time and I hope to start getting about again in about 4 weeks' time ...

At the moment the position is as follows – Bank Holiday – 6 p.m. – perfect day. Self sitting up here in Mum's bed, to which I have transferred, looking out from time to time through the open window, framed in wisteria blossom nearing its fullest, down the garden to the purple lilac (at the bottom of the lawn) which is a breathtaking spectacle this year. Yer Ma is planting some new roses judging from the sounds emanating from the beds and, again judging by ear, Gay, who has been stretched out on the terrace in her bikini like a fish on a cold slab for the whole afternoon, has been dragooned into doing some watering ... She went to a lunch party yesterday ... and on afterwards to a supper party ... So she arrived home well wined and dined though not, I think, altogether spiritually sated as I think, at these affairs, she finds fewer people operating on her wavelength than she does amongst those who accompany her to the night clubs of Birmingham after the theatre. Incidentally I think her Isabella [In Marlowe's *Edward II*] is attracting a certain amount of attention in informed circles – for instance Paul Scofield went up to see the show last week and was reported to have commented favourably on her. But of course I am not permitted to repeat this so please don't pin it on the notice board or anything like that. She may be going up to London next week for the interview she told you about but she seems less keen on the venture

now as apparently the film is to be made in England and not in Hollywood as we originally thought . . .

We were of course very interested to hear your news when you rang up and also rather more fully from Pam [Rodney's sister, then on holiday from her home in Canada] and Gay when they got back from Marlborough . . . Afraid it sounds as though Music is a bit of a casualty this term – but it's all in a good cause. No doubt you find Latin in particular a tiresome distraction from the proper pursuit of living. Whilst I don't subscribe to the old-fashioned belief that the effectiveness of a medicine is directly proportional to the nastiness of its taste, nevertheless I do think that it is essential when one is young to learn to discipline one's mind and body to do things they don't want to. One of the several important benefits derived from the process is an increase in the powers of concentration – (an important matter in the case of N.R.D.?) and you'll need that, whatever you go in for – just as the sun requires the assistance of a magnifying glass before it can start a fire. End of lecture.

Must stop now as you will never finish this. I was going to go on to say that there is usually a reward for doing a worthy but mundane thing – like the pleasant view at the top of a steep hill one has been made to struggle up much against one's better judgment, but I think this might be overdoing it a bit and might cause you to burst into tears – so I will refrain.

The big news is that Mr Daniels has started to sing in the Davenport advertisements. Mum disloyally claims that it is dubbed but I am attributing the rich baritone to the great man himself.

We are enjoying a return of 'Not Only But Also' once a week – an amusing sketch last week, the two tramps discussing sex. 'The Frost Report' on doctors also very funny.

Masses of love as per from your Ma, Gay and Naw and also your Dad

Mr Daniels was a local bigwig who had suddenly started to star in a beer commercial, much to Nick and Rodney's amusement.

June 1966
Marlborough College
Dear Mum and Dad,

Hope all goes smoothly at your end, and that you are already on the way to a speedy recovery, Dad. Glad to hear this is such a mild bout, and no doubt you'll be back in action fairly soon.

Please thank Gay for coming down last Sunday with Pam. It really was a good day. I was very impressed with our aunt, and I must say she is remarkably elegant for her age! It seemed ridiculous to be seeing a close relation for the first time in 10 years and for the last time for several more. Still, she says she'll be back once the dogs are disposed of!

Life here progresses in the normal hair-raising fashion. The really alarming thing is that I have an 'A' level in about a week's time. The British Constitution papers always happen a few weeks before all the others. It's a bit worrying really, but it'll be nice to get one exam out of the way . . .

I at last seem to be getting rid of my cold . . . I must say that, bore as it was, it had its advantages. Not having been able to taste anything for the last week, I've been putting back the college food in a most impressive style. It's really not bad at all when you can't taste it! My cold has also provided an admirable excuse whenever my athletics hasn't been up to scratch. My enthusiasm for running has been dying fast, especially when I did my trick of coming second but doing exactly the same time as the winner in both the 100 & 220 yards the other day. I've decided that running is perhaps more stupid than rugger, which is saying something! Still, I'm rather committed to it now, and anyway I don't mind doing it so much when I think that it's for the last time. I seem to be saying that about everything at the moment. The thought that in two months' time it'll be the end of Marlborough rather than just the end of term seems to make everything just tolerable.

Incidentally, there's been a slight development in the Fitzwilliam Affair. Mr Walters, the College Tutor, has written to Den to say that it's a bit doubtful for October '66 since he's fairly full up. He says that October '67 would be more of a possibility. I feel just a little doubtful about that, but am of course quite prepared to do it if it's the only way. If I was lucky, I might get in for '67 on my 'A' levels, but on the other hand they might want me to take university entrance, in which case Den suggests I go to a crammer for a term. I don't know how that idea seems to you. Anyway, it all needs consideration.

This letter seems to be rambling on without any hope of ever ending. Still, since I don't seem to have written for so long, I'll let it meander on a little longer. It's now Thursday if you please. I have received both your letters, and thank you very much for them. Very glad to hear of Dad's good progress. Also impressed by Paul Scofield's favourable attitude to Gay's acting, and especially shattered to hear that Mr Daniels has started to hold forth in song.

We had an athletics match today against Wellington. Needless to say we lost, but their sprinters were not very good, and I won the 100 and 200 yards. Then just to enhance the humour of the situation I have been awarded my colours!

I think this must be one of the most uninteresting letters ever written, and if you're still with me at this point I admire your powers of concentration. Anyway, I'll draw to a long awaited close now.

Please give my love to Naw and Gay, and wish G much luck from me in her interview, although of course that job's not worth getting now, since it's not even being filmed in Hollywood!

Much love

Nick

And so Nick left Marlborough: but without having secured a place at university. In the end, Dennis Silk's advice was followed. And after a summer holiday hitching through France with some of his Marlborough friends –

AUGUST 1966

La Ciotat, South of France

Dear Mum and Dad,

We eventually had to take the train down to Marseilles as hitching is quite impossible. We're now working our way east along the coast by bus. We spent one night at Cassis, then the next at a place called La Ciotat, and then the next night we were at Toulon, where I visited all the old sights. All hotels and youth hostels seem to be full up, so we're spending our nights in the most interesting of places, e.g. last night on the beach, the night before in a cave with some Germans, and the night before that on a town football ground! We haven't enough money to get home by train so we are planning to hitch up through Italy, Switzerland, Germany and Belgium. Weather is perfect and I'm having a very good time. Love Nick

– Nick came home, went to a crammer and had some private tuition. By all accounts, his tutor was not over-impressed by his academic abilities, and doubted – as did his headmaster at Marlborough – his chances of getting into Cambridge. Nevertheless, due undoubtedly in large part to help from Dennis Silk, who pulled several strings on Nick's behalf, he was offered a place at Fitzwilliam College.

However, as predicted, that place did not become free until the autumn of 1967, and this left nine months to be filled.

(L-R) Richard Mason, Nick Drake, Hugh Griffiths, Con Claque and Jeremy Mason, 5 April 1966 (Photo supplied by Jeremy Mason)

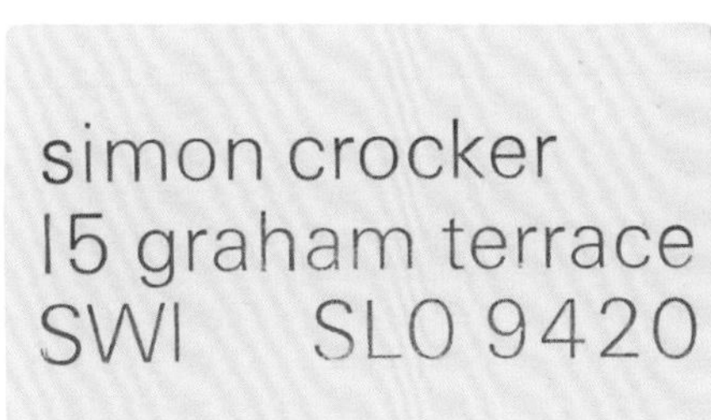

simon crocker
15 graham terrace
SWI SLO 9420

Nick's feet and guitar, France, 1966 (Photo and silhouette: Simon Crocker)
Simon Crocker's calling card found in Nick's wallet

Nick's 'Aix' guitar, an Estruch, made by a family-run luthier company based in Barcelona since 1888 (Photo: Paul Rider)

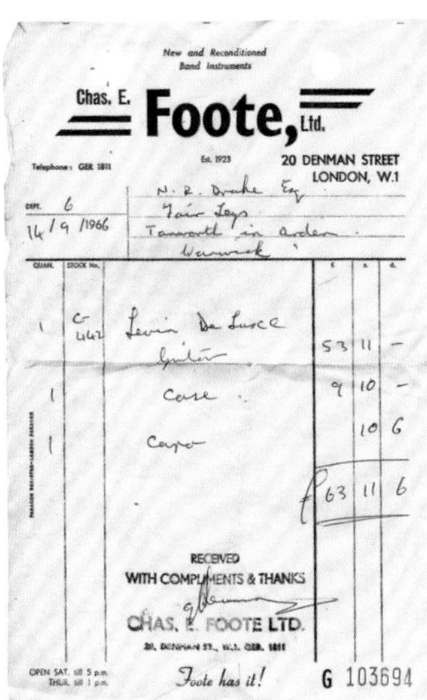

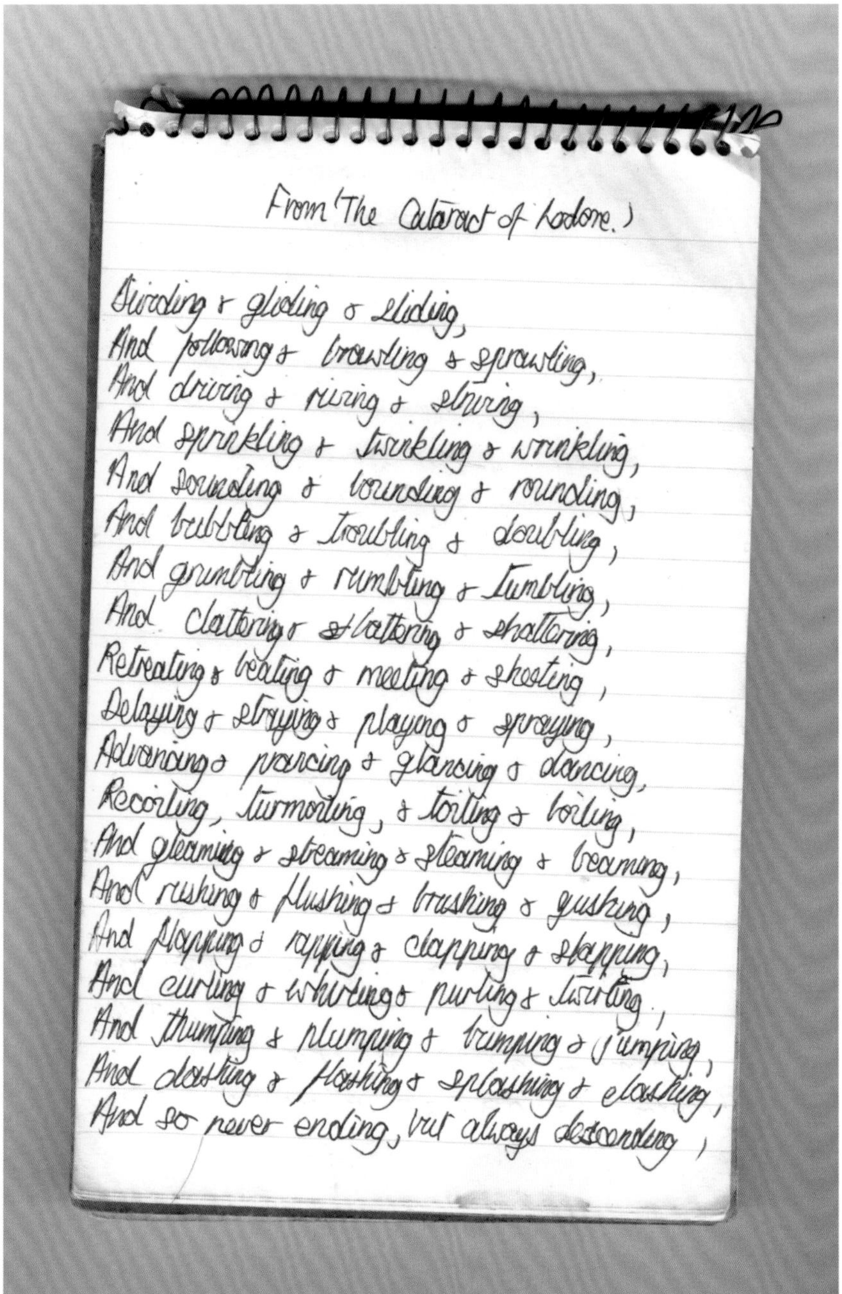

Marlborough: Nick writes out 'The Cataract of Lodore' by English poet Robert Southey (1774 –1843). Written in 1820, the poem describes the Lodore Falls in Cumbria. Using onomatopoeia, and when seen in print, the body of the poem takes on the shape of a waterfall

Nick in France playing the Swedish-built Levin guitar

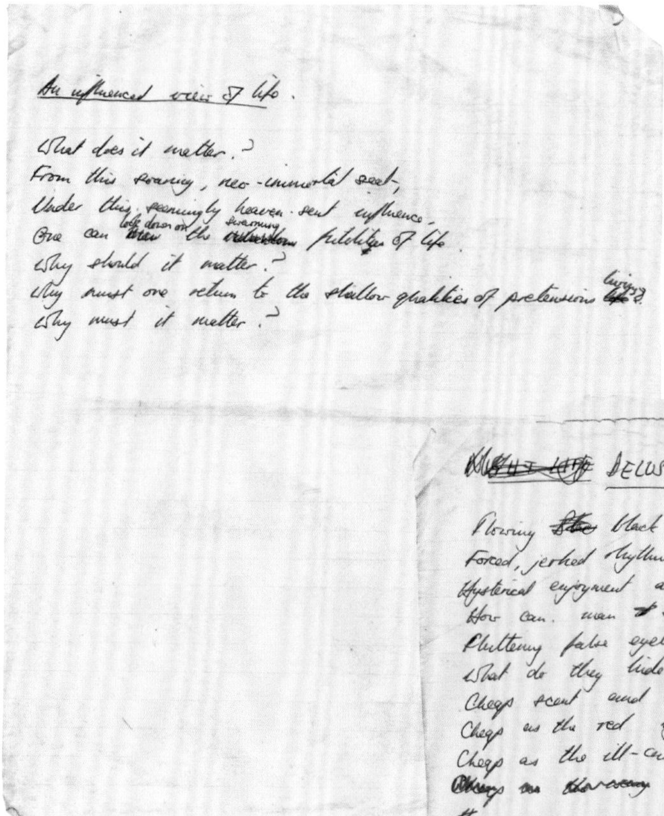

An influenced view of life.

What does it matter?
From this soaring, neo-immortal seat,
Under this seemingly heaven-sent influence,
One can look down on the swarming futilities of life.
Why should it matter?
Why must one return to the shallow qualities of pretensious living?
Why must it matter?

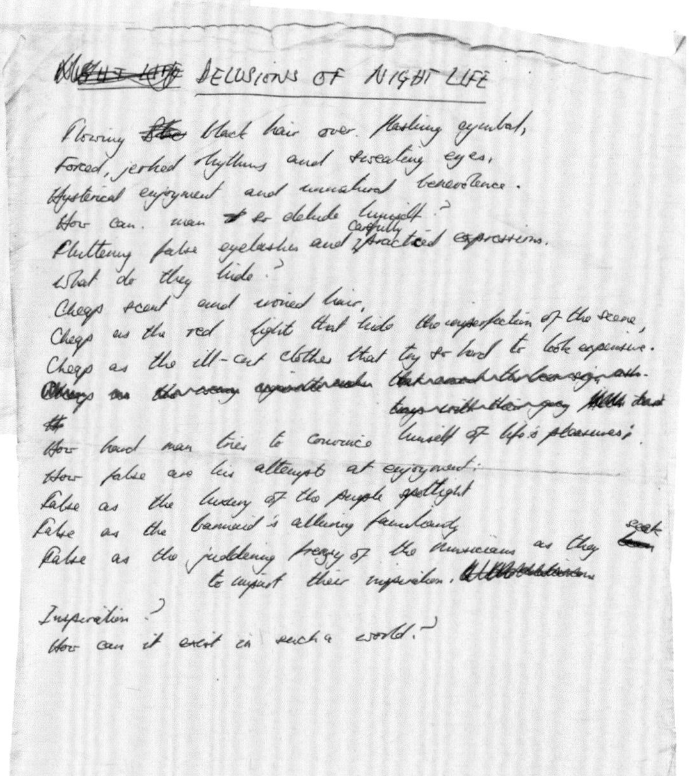

DELUSIONS OF NIGHT LIFE

Flowing black hair over flashing cymbal,
Forced, jerked rhythms and sweating eyes,
Hysterical enjoyment and unnatural benevolence.
How can man so delude himself?
Fluttering false eyelashes and carefully practiced expressions.
What do they hide?
Cheap scent and waved hair,
Cheap as the red light that hides the imperfection of the scene,
Cheap as the ill-cut clothes that try so hard to look expensive.

How hard man tries to convince himself of life's pleasures;
How false are his attempts at enjoyment:
False as the luxury of the purple spotlight
False as the barmaid's alluring familiarity
False as the jiddering frenzy of the musicians as they seek
to impart their inspiration.

Inspiration?
How can it exist in such a world?

Early poems by Nick Drake found in his Marlborough exercise books

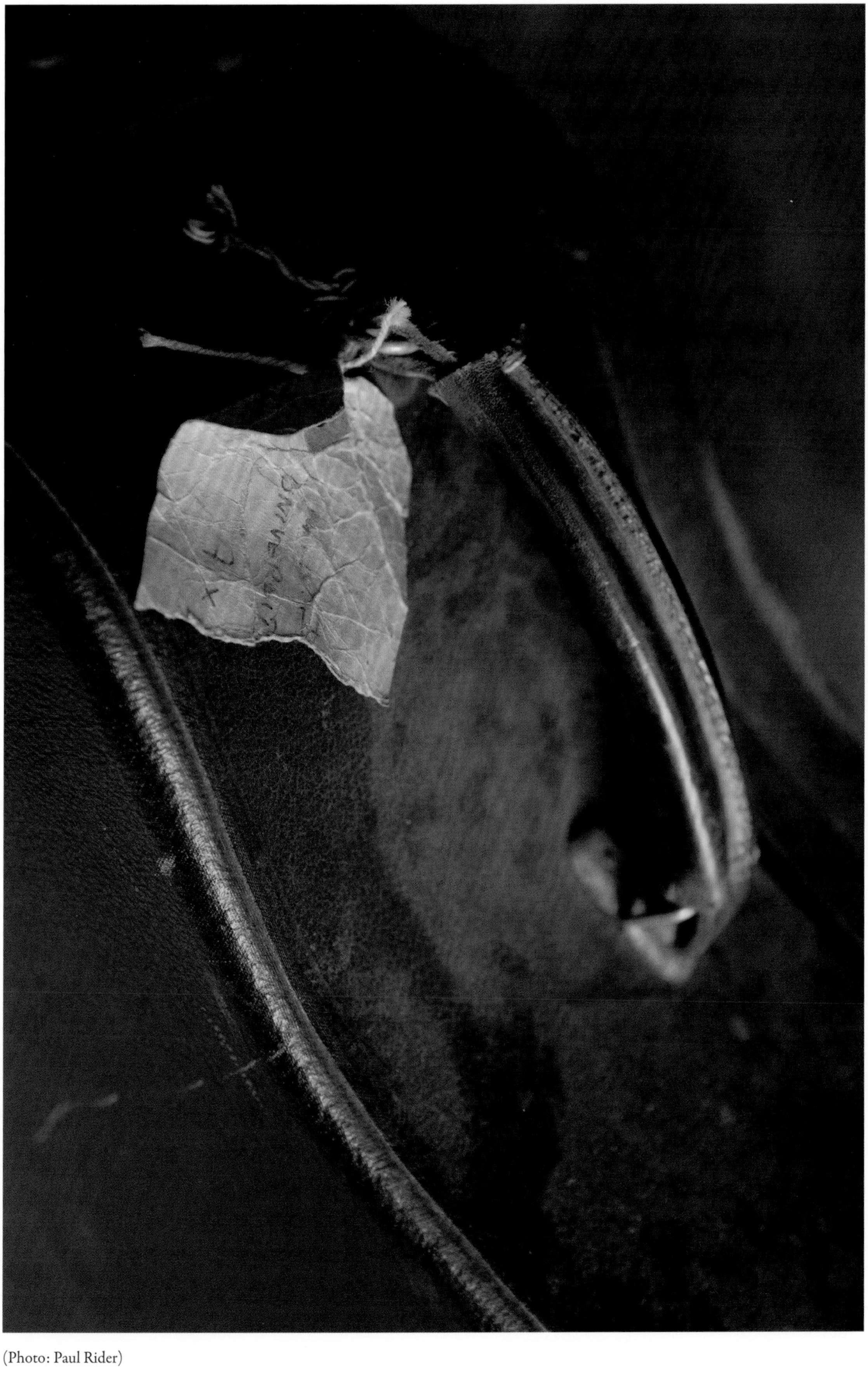

(Photo: Paul Rider)

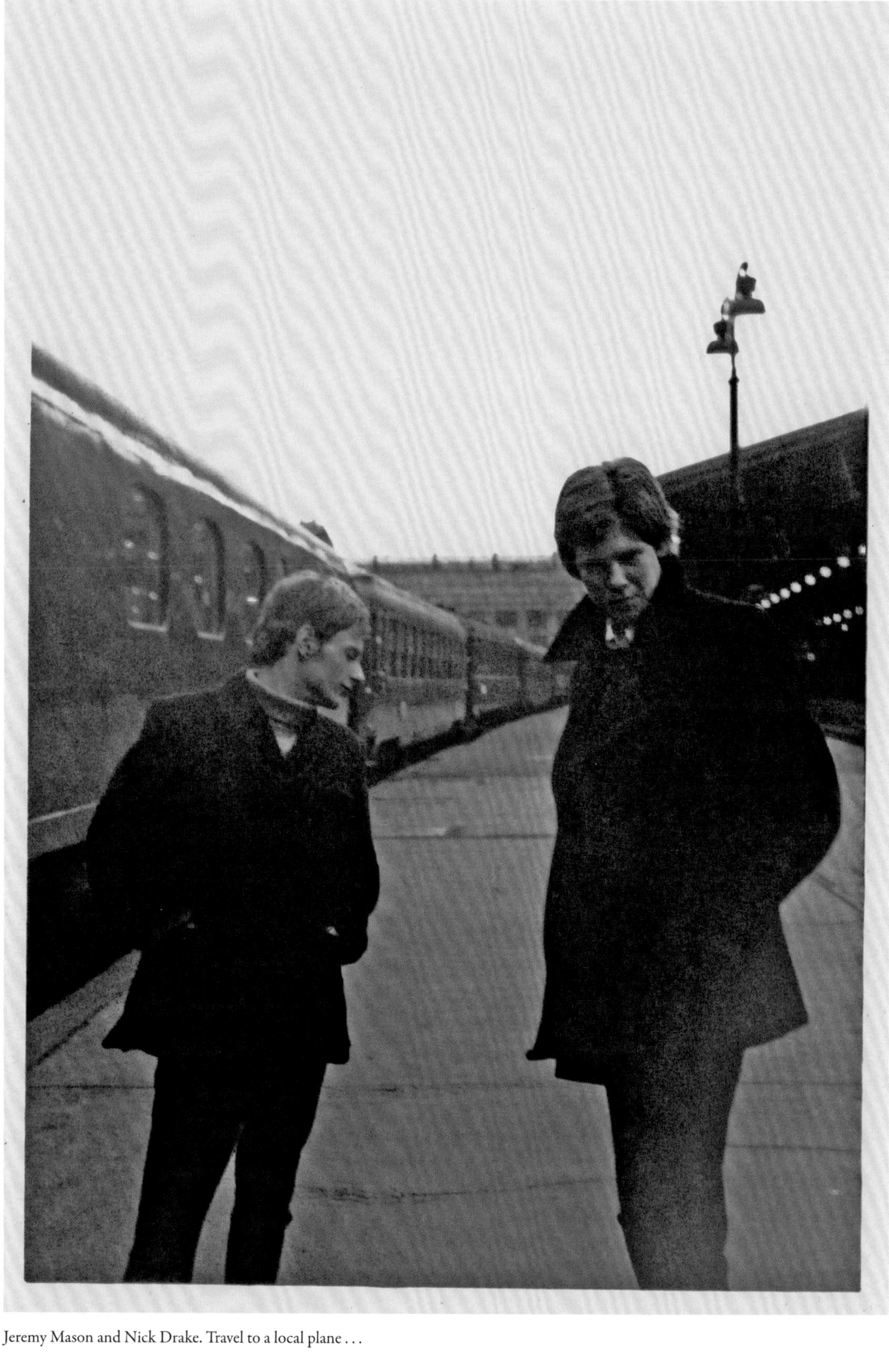

Jeremy Mason and Nick Drake. Travel to a local plane . . .

The Flower II

Family letters

Annotated by Gabrielle Drake

It was decided that Nick should join his two Marlborough friends, Jeremy Mason and Simon Crocker, on a three-month course for Foreign Language students at the University of Aix-en-Provence. It was a life-changing experience – or perhaps it would be more accurate to say that it was an experience that caused Nick to emerge from his childhood into his particular adulthood.

His letters from Aix, and later from Morocco, to some extent chart that experience:

Saturday, 20 February 1967
Batiment C2, Residence Sextius, Chemin du Petit Barthelemy, Aix-en-Provence
Dear Mum and Dad,

I'm happy to say that I'm now finally established in some extremely smart rooms on the outskirts of Aix. However, before I tell you more about them, perhaps I'd better fill you in with some earlier news.

After spending a successful evening in London which Gay has no doubt told you about, I was picked up at the crack of dawn by the Crockers and taken to the station. We eventually came across Jeremy, who was in the process of searching Victoria Station for his fiancé, who had come to see him off. That side of it was eventually settled, and we set off crammed into a carriage amongst our very varied selection of belongings. Everything went very smoothly, in particular the crossing, which saw the Channel at its very smoothest. We had a meal in the boat restaurant, which saw us though to Calais, where we disembarked and got straight onto the train for Paris. At Paris there was a certain amount of flustering while we tried to discover whether or not our train did in fact shunt round to the Gare de Lyon, from where the Marseilles train was to leave. We eventually decided to risk it, hoping that our gamble would not result in our swift return to Calais. However, it proved to be alright, and we arrived at the Gare de Lyon for a 3-hour wait before the Marseilles train left. By this time I was beginning to regret very sincerely the weight of my suitcase, and I still don't know how I managed to arrive in Aix with both arms still in their sockets. However, we eventually did arrive, having successfully found couchettes on the train, and went straight to the Institute to try and get lodgings. The woman in control there spoke not a word of English, which set our French speaking off with a bang. She gave us various possibilities, most of which fell through straight away. However, we ended up having rooms with this very charming family, and the possibility of getting a flat the next Tuesday morning. The set-up with the family was that the other two slept in a double bed in Madame's house, while I had a room in the neighbouring house, belonging to Grandmère. I had some fairly hair-raising experiences with the latter, who could speak no more English than the rest of the family. She seemed to be the French equivalent of Gran, only slightly more fire-breathing, and added to that was an ex-concert pianist and slightly round the bend. It was quite impossible for me to get in or out without being grabbed and submitted to a long volley of powerful French dialogue. I think she was getting rid of conversation that had been building up inside her for twenty years, and was delighted to find such a totally defenceless victim. Whenever she seemed to be running out of ammunition, she would repeat the

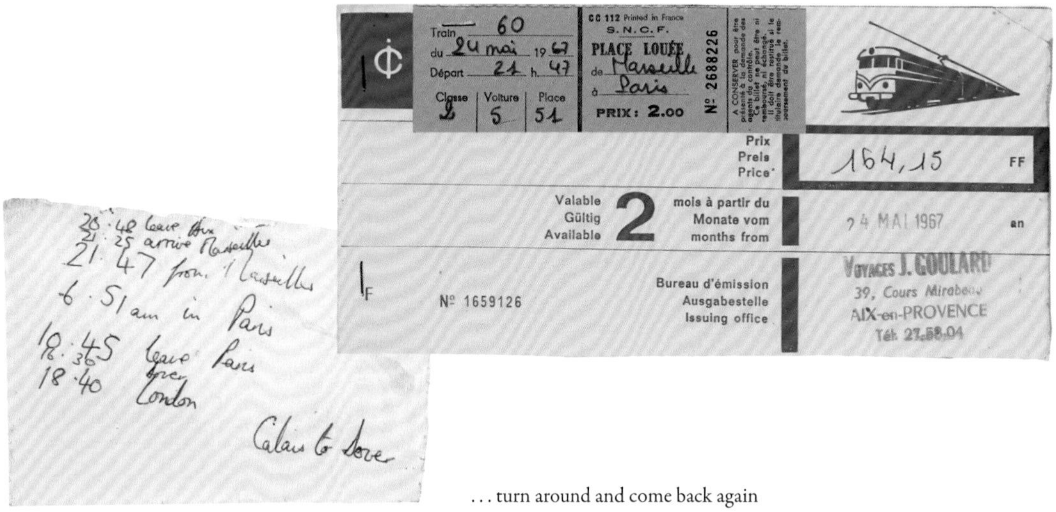

. . . turn around and come back again

last point again and again until a new topic occurred to her. However, I shouldn't run them down, since they were all extremely kind, as well as providing excellent opportunities for practising our French.

Monday proved to be our real trial of strength, since it was on that day that we had to make all our university arrangements. This involved going first to the Institute (the Etudiants Etrangers bit, which is devoted entirely to foreign students and has no connection with the big French university as far as work is concerned) and filling in the biggest pile of forms you've ever seen, all of which were naturally in French and extremely complex. We then had to go to a shop and obtain photographs of our passports before setting off for the 'Nouvelles Facultés', the huge collection of new and most impressive buildings which make up the French university itself. Here we had to slog from building to building, first paying for the course, then filling in more forms and getting our student cards, then moving on to get our restaurant cards, then getting restaurant tickets. After all that we had to return once more to the Institute to find out about courses. Also, at some stage during the day, I can't remember which, we paid a visit to the bank to make arrangements there, which was a comparatively easy process. So one way or another it turned out to be quite a day. In the evening we tried out the eating hall, which is another part of the Nouvelles Facultés. It really is most impressive, seating about 15,000, and the food is pretty good in quality, and totally unrestricted in quantity, which is quite pleasant.

Tuesday morning provided a most bitter blow. We had been told by the woman at the Institute to go along to this flat at nine o'clock on Tues. morning and see the lady in charge. Since all the other possibilities had fallen through, we had come to absolutely depend on this one prospect. So there we were at 9 o'c. in the morning, looking the very epitome of respectability, when the woman appeared and informed us in the most light-hearted fashion that the flat had been taken even before we had arrived in Aix. So after drowning our sorrows in several large cups of coffee, we set off round all the agencies of Aix. Most of them had nothing to offer, except for this one that sent us round to the 'Residence Sextius', a huge block of rooms, which have only just been completed. The rooms are extremely nice, with two beds, shower, basin, loo and cupboards etc. We have in fact taken two, one of which they have let us have for half-price, which was nice of them. Simon and I sleep in one of them, while the other serves as a bedroom for Jeremy as well as a sitting room for all of us, which works out quite well. The rent works out at about 200 francs a month each, which is pretty reasonable. The money situation seems to be fairly satisfactory at the moment, and I have made all the necessary arrangements with the bank.

As for the Institute itself, I have been to two lectures so far, but gained rather little from both of them, mainly because I didn't have the necessary books. However, I've now just about put that right, and plan to start properly next week. I intend going to lectures on French grammar and speaking, as well as some philosophy, which in this case deal with existentialism, and in particular with Albert Camus. There is also a course on Surrealist poetry,

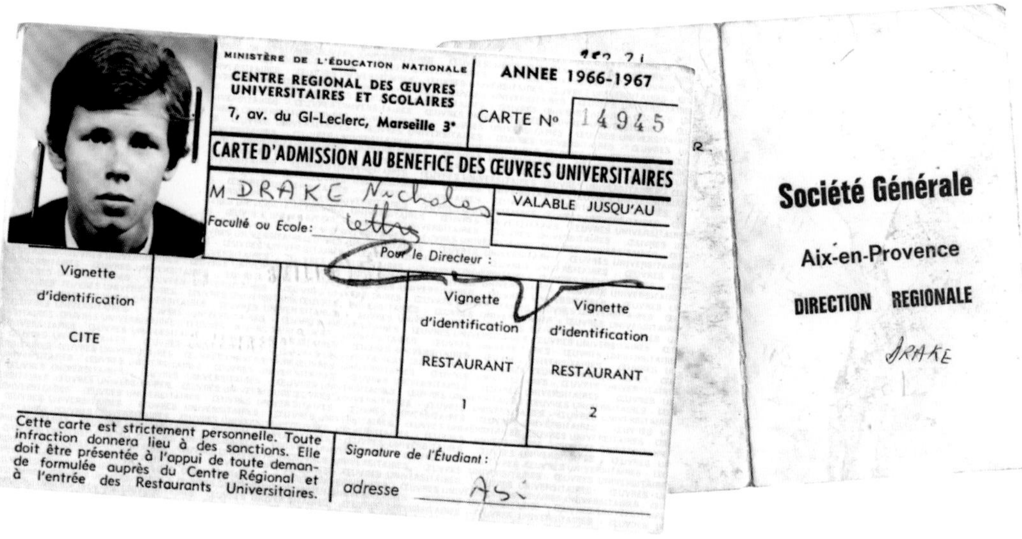

which I might try and cope with later on. I seem to have met a great many people down here already, although none of them are quite the ideal type, since they're either English or American. The majority of them seem to be rich young Londoners who have been sent out here for want of something better to do, have at no stage had any intention of learning French, and who are constantly bored stiff. All nice guys, but not the sort of type who help one improve one's French.

I think that just about brings you up to date, and it seems to have taken me rather a long time to do it, so I'll end off now. I hope all goes well at your end, and that Gay's telly programme is making good progress. Please send my love to her and Naw. Incidentally, I forgot to mention that a car does not seem at all necessary here really, since Aix is not really a very big town, and everything is fairly well within walking distance. Anyway, I should probably be absolutely terrified if I was driving one!

Will probably be writing again quite soon.

Much love Nick

RODNEY to NICK:
Saturday, 25 February 1967
Far Leys
Dear Nick,

We were very delighted, I need hardly say, to get your nice long letter and also your postcard sent off soon after your arrival. I rather feared that you would have had about enough of that suitcase by the time you reached Aix! I am a bit surprised that the handle didn't come off. You will probably have to get something lighter if you start touring around down there. We were much amused at your account of your sojourn with Grandmère and indeed it seemed a pity, from the point of view of your French, that you couldn't have stayed on there! – particularly as the old lady appears to have repeated everything several times for your benefit. What a job it seems to have been finding accommodation. Perhaps you really ought to have gone down a week before the *semestre* started; however, what you've got now sounds reasonable enough – I assume you are all talking French to each other?? . . .

All goes well here but we've had an awful lot of rain. Bab [Nick's car: all the Drakes gave names to their cars] is now safely locked up . . . having been serviced and made all ready for when it is next required. We had the usual difficulty over starting it and Holmes had to give me a push down the hill in time-honoured fashion. It did the trick and I raced on to the crossroads to turn round, only to find that I had run out of petrol! (you certainly cut it pretty fine). Holmes eventually turned up in the van and was vastly tickled by what he regarded as a very shrewd piece of budgeting on your part . . .

Friday, 3 May 1967
Batiment C2, Residence Sextius, Aix
Dear Mum and Dad,

Thank you so much for your letters, which arrived yesterday & the day before, and which I thoroughly enjoyed. I was very interested to here all your news, in particular the reports on Gay's progress. Her name certainly does seem to be getting somewhere, although I was horrified to hear that she has turned down a job involving a lot of money and little work – a criminal act in my opinion, of course!

Life here seems to have become very settled, and now that most of the cold weather has gone, leaving us with a sort of English summer-type climate, everything is really rather pleasant. Unfortunately the weather didn't change until after the weekend, which was a pity, since last Friday we decided to make our first visit to Jeremy's house near Nimes. It was not, on the whole, a particularly successful outing. We set off on Friday afternoon, myself and Jeremy hitching, and Simon on his newly acquired *mobilette*, which cost him 150 francs, and has since proved rather too temperamental to be considered a resounding success. At that stage the sun was burning ferociously, and we shrewdly left behind all forms of clothing which might have provided any warmth. No sooner had we arrived at Ledenon, the village where stands the house of Mason, than the weather underwent a miraculous change. The journey, which is no more than some 90 kiloms, had incidentally taken us 6 and a half hours, and was, as you can imagine, something of an ordeal. Anyway, the house is essentially a summerhouse, and a large part of the weekend was spent in tramping up hills in the pouring rain to find wood for the fire – altogether rather fun. However, the visit did have its merits, since the village folk are immensely friendly to the English, who provide for them a great curiosity, and we chatted gaily with all and sundry as they dropped in to pass the time of day. This was in a way almost as taxing as my attempts with the veritable Grandmère, since the French peasants, in particular those of Provence, never render the French language in its most comprehensible form. Still, we got by. The journey back to Aix also proved useful on that score, since I got lifts from one or two fairly chatty folks. One lift proved particularly beneficial, since it came from a guy with a white sports car who lives in Aix, and who took me back to his luxury apartment, plied me with cognac, and then returned me to my residence, leaving me with the offer to go back to his place any time and meet his friends – a most useful contact I feel. In fact that journey back was considerably more lucky than the unfortunate Jeremy, who *malheureusement* was picked up by two successive queers – a most harassing experience, you will agree, for a man engaged to be married. He informs us that his French has never come so hard and fast as it did in dealing with those two!

The prospects of improving my French do, on the whole, seem to be improving. I am getting to find the English group rather tedious, which is probably a good thing. Although individually they are mostly very nice, as a group they are thoroughly nauseous. I have made one or two contacts with French people, though not nearly as many as I'd like to. Apart from the sports-car man, I have met one or two female French students, which is of course rather pleasant. I have also met a fellow [who] would pass anywhere as English, but who speaks four languages like a native, and is enrolled at Aix as a French student, and he could be useful. I'm finding the lectures a bit tough, and think I shall probably stick to the actual French lessons for a while, and perhaps keep going on the philosophy lectures, which I find easier than the rest.

I'm thinking of going to Morocco for the Easter break, since I've been offered a lift down, and it's a place the idea of which rather appeals to me . . . My plans are by no means certain, since the fellow who offered to take me is one of the English students, who is at the moment in either Paris or Geneva, and no one is quite sure whether he's coming back. Anyway, I'm sure I shall find something entertaining to do.

I'm looking around for an opportunity to start playing my guitar in public. There have in fact been one or two chances already, but I've been rather lazy about it. I went to a jazz club in Aix the other night, and stood in for about half an hour with some other students. I mostly played piano, but also had a go on an alto. My saxophone playing proved regrettably to be somewhat rusty. There don't seem to be many concrete activities about which I can inform you, since life here seems to revolve largely around moving from café to café – very pleasant in its way.

Must stop now – love to all – Much love, Nick.

And indeed, he did decide to go to Morocco for the Easter break with a carful of friends. It proved to be a memorable trip, and would be recounted in future years by more than one of the participants – but all of them were talking about it in retrospect. Here is Nick's personal account, which is contemporary: the following three letters – quoted below verbatim (save for the patches where a mouse decided to snack on a part of a couple of the pages) make up 'The Morocco Letters'.

6 April 1967

Dear Mum and Dad,

Thank you very much for your letter, which I received on arrival back at Aix. I'm afraid I have a few apologies to make, firstly for not keeping in touch for some time. The main trouble was that we had the most terrible delay in getting back from Morocco, as a result of a certain mishap with the car, which I will come to later in the letter. I was planning to get back to Aix before writing to you again, since apparently letters sent from Morocco have only about a 50-50 chance of getting to their destination during the same year . . . I'm also very sorry about knocking off a few days before the beginning of the Easter break. The thing was that I really was very keen to go to Morocco, and the only chance I had was to go when I did. Also, I had nothing else lined up for Easter, and didn't really fancy being stranded in Aix. Although I don't mean this as any form of excuse, the students here do come and go much as they please, since the Institute shows very little interest in them on the whole. If it provides any consolation, I did in fact improve my French a lot more in Morocco than I have done in Aix, as far as speaking is concerned. However, I'll also mention that later, and I think I'd better start trying to give an account of the expedition.

The first events seem to be a very long time ago. I set off from Aix with three others in the morning, and before going further perhaps I'd better give a few details of the dramatis personae. Leading the expedition was one Mike Hill, heir to some five titles and endowed with private means of fairly notable proportions. He drives a Spitfire in England, but bought a Cortina GT just to come out to Europe. Quite a useful car on the whole. It was originally entered for the Monte Carlo rally, but the sponsors ran out of money, and Mike managed to buy it. However, he did not unfortunately have the patience to run it in properly, an oversight from which we were all to suffer later. Anyway, the other members of the safari were Bob, a really great guy, who at first gives the impression of being thick as boots, but who is in fact very intelligent, and is going up to Cambridge next Oct. to read science, and Julian . . . a sort of far-gone intellectual who has a classical scholarship to Oxford.

Anyway, we set off and drove through the day and night, or at least Mike did, stopping only for an hour's sleep, and arrived in Granada about lunchtime the next day. We decided to stay there the rest of the day and that night, and in fact spent the next morning there as well, since it proved to be such an intriguing place. Granada provided our first taste of Moorish civilisation, and I must say I was immensely impressed. The main features at Granada, as you may already know, are the Alhambra Palace and the Summer Palace, both fantastic in their different ways. I never knew the Moors were so advanced artistically. In the Alhambra every wall and ceiling is carved into the most devious and intricate patterns, some of which are imprinted with simple but very effective colouring. Also impressive are the open courtyards that one keeps coming across, containing long, fish-ridden pools surrounded by marble paving stones. The Summer Palace is full of luscious gardens, with Moorish pools and fountains, laden orange trees, and violent greenery. One can so clearly imagine the great fat Moorish rulers lounging around there, surrounded by their oozing, silken females.

Anyway, to continue, we eventually set off from Granada to Gibraltar. The road from Granada to Malaga is a particularly hair-raising mountain road, and since Mike rather fancies himself as a would-be rally driver, there was a certain amount of hanging on involved. I think we must have set up a few records. We arrived at Gibraltar that evening, and found that we were not allowed to take the car in, as a result of all the trouble that's going on. So we left the car at the Spanish border, and walked the hundred yards of no-man's land into Gib. It really gave me quite a shock, since I never had any idea that it was quite so English. What with the English policemen, street signs, voices etc., it really is extraordinary. We spent a very pleasant evening, eating in a fish-and-chip shop as English as they come, and then sitting in the Bull & Bush drinking pints of bitter. We in fact spent two nights in Gib, spending the next day going up the rock to take a look around. Very impressive view from up there.

There's a fabulous deep, deep cave halfway up the rock, with dim lighting and beautiful choir music drifting around – I just sat there for about an hour in a complete trance! We eventually got round to leaving Gib, and drove to Algeciras, where we caught a ferry across to Tangier. The weather was brilliant by now, and we had a delicious crossing, sunbathing on the first class deck (our tickets being 4th class!) It was rather nice to be sailing out of Europe for the first time in 15 years.

I've now just come back from telephoning you, and I think I'll follow your suggestion and send off the first instalment now, since this seems quite a good place to break off.

Don't miss next week's thrilling instalment, packed full of high Moroccan adventure!

Love to Gay and Naw,

Much love, Nick

April 1967

Dear Mum and Dad,

Thank you very much indeed for your letters, and for sending the contact lens. It does indeed 'open out' very nicely thank you. I'm sorry this second instalment is rather delayed, but I have just been away for a short weekend stay with an English girl called Jo, who has access to a flat in Cassis. However, before reporting on that, perhaps I had better move on and complete the account of the Moroccan expedition.

I think I left off last time at our arrival in Tangier. It was about two minutes before we were set upon by an Arab trying to make money out of us. This was something we were to encounter just about every two minutes for the rest of our time in the country. This first one, unusually enough, proved to be quite useful, since he showed us round the town. However, he tried to ask us for a ridiculously large tip, and we got rid of him hastily. Then we went and signed in at a hotel before going to look round the town. It seemed that by now word had spread around that we were new arrivals, since at every turn we had someone coming up to us with a new offer. The Arabs really are extraordinary people. Not content with attempts to flog us old currency etc., we even had little boys coming up and offering to sell us their brothers! Only one encounter proved to be of use to us, and that was the one I think I mentioned on my postcard, the little guy who claimed to work in the Regent Palace Hotel, Piccadilly. We were naturally very suspicious of him at first, although we were gradually reassured, firstly by a perfect cockney accent which he kept coming out with, and secondly by a little English bird whom he suddenly produced, and who was apparently his wife! His name was Muhammhed, and he offered to show us all around the Arab quarter. Tangier, like almost every other Moroccan town, is in two halves, one the French quarter and the other Arab, and since we had as yet only seen the French part, we were quite happy to go along with him.

Tangier has, in my opinion, the best *medina* (the term, as you probably know, referring to an Arab market-place and quarter in general) in the whole of Morocco, and since it also happened to be the first one I'd seen, I was fairly bowled over. It really is the most intriguing and fascinating place, what with the dark little streets, no bigger than English pavements, littered with ragged little children, tiny shops, and weird hooded figures in every direction. To provide the atmosphere there is the *inevitable* collection of different smells, and of course the music, which booms from all the cafés. As I think I mentioned, Moroccan music scored a major hit with me, although it's probably not every European's cup of tea. I find it to be the most mournful, but at the same time one of the most dignified forms of music that I've ever heard.

We got a good dose of it on our first night, when Muhammhed took us to a tumble-down old café called the 'Dancing Boy', an extraordinary place where all the Arabs sit around smoking their marihuana pipes, drinking mint tea, and listening to the band. Star of the show is a boy, dressed in white silk, who sings and occasionally hops up and does a dance! The fact that it is a little boy, and not a woman, may seem rather strange to you, as it did to us, but of course such activities are totally taboo for the Arab women. It seems in fact that most things are equally forbidden for them, and I think they must live a peaceful, but rather boring life.

I don't think there's much else of particular note to tell you of our stay in Tangier, except perhaps for the last night, when it was generally agreed that I should play the guitar in public. By then we had discovered that the Rolling Stones were in town, and hoping to make contact with them, we went down to their hotel, the celebrated El Mingah. Having seen them going in, looking quite extraordinary even by their own standards, we marched in and I made a request to play in the bar. After I had been turned down very politely, Bob, whose nerves seem to stop at nothing, proceeded to ring up the Stones' suite and ask if they might be wanting a little musical entertainment! This was unfortunately refused in a similar fashion, and it was decided that my fortune should be made elsewhere. So we made a quick tour of the night clubs, asking if I could play. Fortunately, one of those which accepted the offer was the Katoubia Palace, Tangier's most exclusive night spot, which is done up in the style of a Moorish palace. I couldn't help feeling a little out of place, but all the same I played for about quarter of an hour. The reception was extraordinarily good, and we all got stood rounds of drinks, which was rather pleasant.

Anyway, to continue the story, we decided the next day to move on down to Marrakesh, via the big road on the west coast. So we moved quickly and I received my first surprise as regards the Moroccan countryside. In the north, near Tangier, it is just as green as England, and the colours even seem to be deeper and more luscious. Just outside the town there is a whole stock of fabulous villas, belonging to various wealthy Americans and English. I think that is probably where I shall move to after making my proverbial million!

We passed fairly quickly through Rabat and Casablanca, spending about a couple of hours in each, taking a look at the one or two points of interest such as the king's palace at Rabat which in fact was not particularly impressive, and then pressed on to arrive at Marrakesh late that evening. We began to look for the French quarter, since we had by now decided that French quarters were a better bet as far as staying was concerned, owing to the fact that Arab hotels tend to be rather subject to bed bugs and the like. However, we proceeded to get ourselves hopelessly lost in the Arab quarter, which at night is a rather depressing experience. If one asks the way to an Arab, he will never admit that he doesn't know and will immediately direct you, regardless of the fact that it is totally the wrong direction. After completing about 50 perfect circles, we eventually discovered a European, who informed us that the French quarter was in fact some 2 miles away. We were then able to find it quite easily, had a meal and went to a hotel.

The next day we did a tour of Marrakesh's noted landmarks, various palaces, towers and tombs. They were quite good, but by no means up to Granada standards. Perhaps the most notable feature of Marrakesh is its market-place, a huge crowded gathering place where one finds musicians, magicians, soothsayers, acrobats, snake-charmers, dancers, and various other oddities which I am unable to find a name for.

Best of all was a set of African drummers and dancers, who produced about the most infectious rhythms I have ever been infected by. The snake-charmers were rather disappointing since the snakes were so sleepy they could hardly lift their heads, let alone be charmed! However the music was quite fun, since it came from 3 funny old men, who sat cross-legged in a line, swaying around and blowing with all their might, producing the strangest noises imaginable. While watching the African dancers, who should we see watching with us but our friends the Stones, and we decided on another attempt at contact at some stage. It so happened that late that evening we saw them eating in a small restaurant, and Bob, displaying once more his nerve, marched in and told them I wanted to play guitar for them. Surprisingly enough, they accepted this time, so I went in and did them a few numbers. We in fact got quite chatty with them, and it was quite interesting learning all the inside stories.

The next day we intended to move down south, touch on the north tip of the Sahara, and then return upwards again, stopping at a few places on the way. However, it was today that our major mishap was to occur, an occurrence which was to cast something of a slur on the rest of the trip. We started off, covering large distances in fairly short spaces of time, and eventually began to come into what one thinks of as 'African' countryside – bush land, gulches, etc. Then we were hurling along an open round when we suddenly came upon a sharp bend in the road. A lot of gravel had been blown across the road, and we skidded off the road, turned over, bounced on the roof of the car, and eventually ended up on all four wheels in the middle of the bush land! It was rather hair-raising really, but we all succeeded in climbing out quite unscathed, bar a few bruises. Though, I must say I have become even more endeared to safety belts as a result of it, since I was sitting in the front passenger seat, and the windscreen was smashed, and the roof completely caved in about 6 inches in front of my nose, so, had I not had the belt on, one can imagine the sort of mess there might have been.

30 April 1967

Dear Mum and Dad,

Nice to hear you on the telephone, and thank you for your telegram. I will certainly act according to instructions and keep you informed as to my whereabouts. As it is, I'd better press on now and try and complete the saga, which already seems to have taken longer to relate than it did to happen.

I think I left you sitting upside down in the car in the middle of the desert, and I hope you haven't been finding it too inconvenient. Anyway, a car pulled up quite soon, longer to relate than it did to happen.

I think I left you sitting upside down in the car in the middle of the desert, & I hope you haven't been finding it too inconvenient. Anyway, a car pulled up quite soon, & the driver offered to take one of us back to the nearest town, which was fortunately only about 60 miles back. So Bob got in & set off, while we started to try & get the car back onto the road. We found that the engine did in fact still work, & after bashing out one of the wings with a jack, we were able to drive it back onto the road. However, the steering

was very wobbl[y]
the headlights
decided to w
someone whom
town, which
delicious san
hours later
a taxi, & w
it at a ve
eventually sl
a few miles f
that the dri
stop for th
11 oclock, we decided to do likewise, & set off again at first light. We were received

and the driver offered to take one of us back to the nearest town, which was fortunately only about 60 miles back. So Bob got in and set off, while we started to try and get the car back on the road. We found that the engine did in fact still work, and after bashing out one of the wings with a jack, we were able to drive it back onto the road. However, the steering was very wobbly, and since it was getting dark and the headlights were not working too well, we decided to wait until Bob returned with someone whom we could follow back to the town, which incidentally rejoiced in the name of Ourzazate. About four hours later he eventually did get back with a taxi, and we began to wobble along behind it at a very subdued pace. The taxi eventually stopped at a very small village a few miles from Ourzazate, and it turned out that the driver lived there and wanted to stop for the night. Since it was by now 11 o'clock, we decided to do likewise, and set off again at first light. We were received with great hospitality, provided with an excellent meal at the village tavern, and after being taught how to play Moroccan cards (not a particularly complex game – a rather simplified version of Happy Families, and rather typical of the Arab mentality) we were eventually allowed to kip down on the floor of the local surgery.

We got up very early the next morning, and completed the trip to Ourzazate in a fantastic dawn drive, which really was exhilarating. Having got there, we took the car to a garage, so that the steering could be fixed, and the car could be made generally capable of getting to one of the big cities, where the major damage could be dealt with. The garage completed the job fairly quickly, and that afternoon we set off for a 300-mile journey with no windscreen, and the roof bashed right in on the passenger side. This was in fact one of the few occasions on which I drove, and I was very glad to, since it proved to be the most delightful journey. We had to go slightly eastwards before heading north towards Meknes, the place where we had decided to take the car, and this meant going across the northernmost part of the Sahara. The land is mostly fairly flat, but one keeps coming across the most extraordinary red rock and sand formations, clusters of palm trees, and, every now and then, patches of the brightest greens imaginable. In the distance, on every side, there is always a ring of multi-coloured mountains, which in some strange way one never manages to reach.

We also passed a fairly interesting selection of people, mostly Berber tribesmen. We did not in fact make it as far as Meknes that evening and stopped at a smallish town called Ksar-es-Souk for the night, and it was here that our next colourful incident was to take place.

We booked in at a hotel, and Bob went on down to the adjoining café and started to get into conversation with the proprietor's son, who was a sort of would-be with-it type. He mentioned the fact that I had played for the Stones, but unfortunately this was misheard and taken to mean that we were the Stones. Bob, determined not to miss such an opportunity, quickly informed the fellow that I was Mick Jagger, on a quiet, private holiday. Everyone had heard of Mick Jagger, but no one was quite sure what he looked like, so they all happily convinced themselves that there was a celebrity in their midst. I was surrounded by requests for autographs, and we were given free dinner, rooms in the hotel, breakfast, as well as an invitation to go swimming at a nearby oasis with the proprietor's son, and have a couscous lunch with him afterwards. However the whole thing had by now become thoroughly embarrassing, and we were feeling extremely guilty, so we decided to push off after breakfast. The car hardly had the ritzy touch about it, since we virtually had to climb in through the windscreen. But this did not seem to worry anyone much, and we departed amongst the cheers and waves of the assembled community!

We arrived at Meknes that afternoon, and left the car in the hands of one Moullay Ahmed, who assured us that it would be completely put to rights in as short a time as possible. We then spent a couple of days in Meknes, but quickly discovered that it had very little of interest to offer, and consequently decided to hitch out and see some of the surrounding parts.

First stop was Fes, which is meant to be rather well known as far as points of interest are concerned, but which I was not very impressed by. It has a vast *medina*, in which we got hopelessly lost, as well as rather nauseated by some rather unsavoury scenes such as cats getting kicked to death. It also happened to be the time of the Moroccan fiesta, the main feature of which seems to be chopping up every goat in sight, alive or dead! The best thing there was, in my opinion, the fascinating antique shops, with their ancient Berber weapons, and brass and silver works.

After Fes, we planned to hitch up north-east, get just over the Algerian border, and go up to the coast for some Mediterranean sea-bathing. However, the route proved to be somewhat deserted, and after taking about 2 days to travel 20 miles, we gave up the ghost and ploughed back once more to Meknes, deciding instead to go westward and hit the sea somewhere near Rabat. We found that progress was going quite satisfactorily with the car, set off, and completed the journey to the coast quite successfully, ending up at a small resort called Kenitra. This proved to be quite an interesting place, since it is an American naval training base. It has naturally been taken over in grand style, and is full of fantastic American cars. We spent a very cheap three days there, since we were stood a fair amount

of free food and drink, both by the Americans, and also by various rich Moroccans, who keep villas around there. For sleeping purposes, we took a room in a shack just by the beach, which was rather too full of cockroaches and bed-bugs to be entirely satisfactory, but which was at least a roof over our heads. After about thee days at Kenitra, we decided that the car must be nearly ready, and so we returned once more to Meknes, a place which we were by now pretty sick of. We found that the car was quite a long way from being ready, and that, in true Arab style, the initial enthusiasm shown at the garage had fairly quickly died off. So we once more applied the whip and told them that it must be ready in two days at the most.

These two days proved to be about the worst of the whole trip, since it was during them that we learnt the full extent of Arab stupidity and inefficiency. Since the cost of the repairs on the car were going to come to about £75, we had to try and get some money sent through from France. We struggled to do this with every bank and consulate in Meknes, but they all seemed to be in such chaos that it proved to be quite impossible to do any such thing. By some very lucky chance Mike was eventually able to cash a cheque, since he has a French chequebook. The car was not in fact ready in two days, and we ended up having to

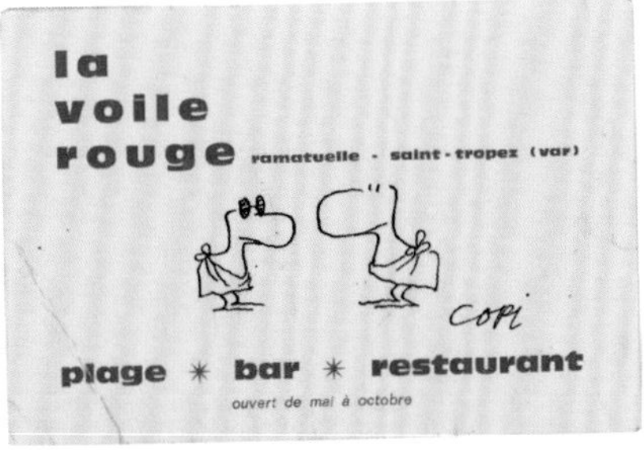

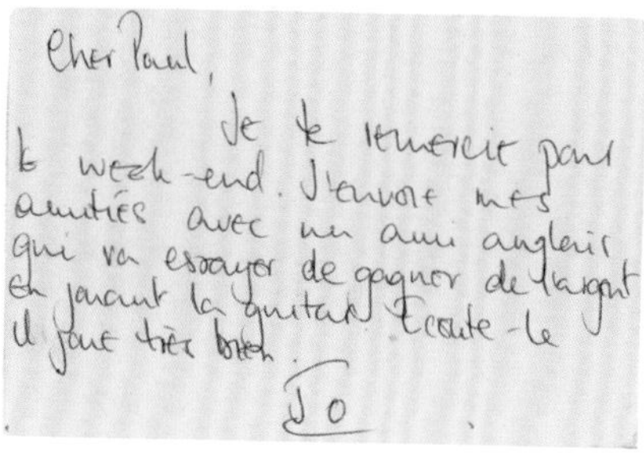
Cher Paul,
Je te remercie pour le week-end. J'envoie mes amitiés avec un ami anglais qui va essayer de gagner de l'argent en jouant la guitare. Ecoute-le il joue très bien.
Jo

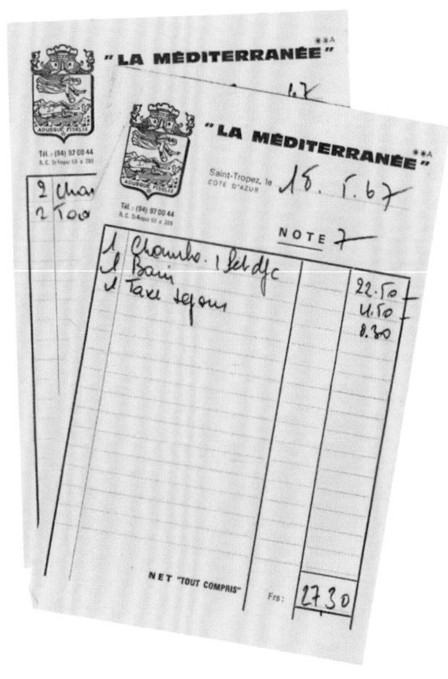
"LA MÉDITERRANÉE"
Saint-Tropez, le 18.5.67
NOTE 7
1 Chambre 1 lit dfc 22.50
1 Bain 4.50
1 Taxe séjour 0.30
NET "TOUT COMPRIS" Frs: 27.30

stand over them right through the night until 11 o'clock the next morning to make them finish the job.

So at last, after a delay of about ten days, we were eventually able to set off home. I don't think the journey back is worth relating, except to say that it was absolute hell, and every conceivable thing went wrong with the car in turn, ending with the engine boiling over five miles outside Aix!

I'm afraid you may be feeling fairly starved of news concerning my life in Aix, but there has in fact been very little worth telling you about, since very little of note has happened. I've made a lot of friends and learnt to speak quite a bit of French, and my life has been quite enjoyable in its own way, but I can't think of any particularly positive events that have taken place. I'm in fact quite glad that I'm moving on elsewhere. I've now moved out of my room in the Residence Sextius, and am kipping in the flat of a friend until I get sufficiently organised to go down to St Tropez. I will drop you a line as soon as I get there. Hope all goes well with you, Gay and Naw.

Much love Nick

That last paragraph is tantalisingly brief! Perhaps Nick just got sick of writing . . .

He did finally make it to St Tropez, as we know from two postcards, crammed to capacity, as Nick's postcards usually were, with tightly written script – almost as much of a challenge to read as his father's letters. The reward for deciphering them was to be transported into the immediacy of his experiences.

Although Nick's arrival in St Tropez was hardly auspicious, we know from Colin Betts, in his book *Frozenlight*, that he did, eventually, play in the nightclubs there, before moving on to Paris. The final glimpse we have of Nick through his own eyes, before he took his place at Cambridge in the autumn of 1967, comes in this postcard to his parents from Paris:

July 1967
Dear Mum & Dad,
Am still in Paris, & have found myself a job, playing in a night club.

Not particularly lucrative, but it passes the time. Have just got your letter with all the cards. Thank you for sending them. I've now moved out of the flat into a very nice hotel, which has all I need, the only drawback being that the manager is always beating up his wife, which tends to be rather disconcerting.

I'd been in the hotel only five minutes when I looked out the window to see the poor woman tearing into the street screaming for the police! The address incidentally is Hotel du Bon Marché, 22 Rue Saint-Placide, Paris 6.

Haven't been doing anything in particular, though have seen quite a few films.

My job has now taken temporary set-back, since the bar I play in has been shut down for a few days owing to fact that the barman is ill.

Don't think I'll be wanting insurance extended thank you. May even be home before end of July. Hope all goes well.

Love Nick

~~Drive my Cars~~

Drive my Car

✓ Ain't get you

✓ Mess around

Since I met you baby

✓ Kids are all right

✓ I don't mind

Legal matter

Louie Louie

✓ We can work it out

✓ Watch your step

✓ LSD

✓? Jump back

Look away

✓ Down the road apiece

✓ Roberta

✓ Bright Lights B.C.

✓ [illegible]

Good morning little schoolgirl

Sticks & Stones ✓

My Babe

Panhman F. ✓

Let me down easy

Please do some— ✓

Untie me ✓

Climbin' up a hill.

Watermelon man

Song Of Aix

by Robin Frederick

Adapted from a sleeve note to the Family Tree *compilation* (2007)

Aix-en-Provence in the south of France, 1967. What I remember is a sudden, explosive sensation of freedom. Flocks of foreign students wheeled from one end of town to the other, settling in the cafés and around the fountains, speaking a dozen different languages. The ancient, buff-coloured buildings echoed with the clatter of cheap motorbikes and the songs of street musicians. We were escapees. The well-bred Brits worked hard to ditch their boarding-school pallor. The German kids loosened up their stiff spines by studiedly slouching against the sun-drenched walls. The Americans tried to forget hometowns with names like Kalamazoo, where Middle America had been slowly squeezing them into button-down suits. We lived on our own or with room-mates or newly discovered lovers in rented flats in this place where the rules of childhood no longer applied. Most of us felt like we'd been holding our collective breath for eighteen or nineteen years. In Aix, we finally got to let it out. We breathed in deep lungfuls of excitement and began looking around at this brave new world. What would we do with it? What wouldn't we do with it?

Slowly, we began to blend in, picking up slang and small mannerisms. We studied each other, looking for new ways to be. Amid the carnival colours and exotic accents, being an American girl with a guitar didn't seem terribly interesting. I shed my California beach tan, sewed a couple of hippie dresses and bought a mod pantsuit and French mini on the Cours Mirabeau. I couldn't decide who I was; I wanted to be a lot of different people.

The music in the air was equally eclectic, from the Johnny Hallyday and Georges Brassens songs the French students played to the American blues and folk songs of the buskers. At a local club, I sang the usual blues and folk numbers mixed with my own original songs. One evening, after a set, Nick Drake introduced himself. Over the next couple of months he would turn up at my flat with his guitar, often late in the evening, to play music, share a glass of wine and a toke if there was any smoke around. Like most folksingers, we knew a lot of the same songs but I don't remember ever singing together. Nick often experimented with tempos and rhythmic feel in his songs, making them difficult to play along with. (Maybe that was part of the reason he did it.) I preferred playing my own songs and he seemed content to listen. He didn't strike me as being shy about playing. He knew he was good and, like a proud bird, he liked to display his feathers.

Unlike the rest of us, Nick never varied his costume; his hair grew a little longer but the jeans, white shirt and dark, fitted jacket never changed – he knew what he wanted the world to see. Amidst the chaos and the freedom, he seemed to remain still. Slowly, however, he was sculpting his music to suit his vision. When I listen to the recordings Nick made during that time – the tracks on this CD, many of them from Aix – I hear someone trying on a wardrobe of music. Listening to *Five Leaves Left* decades later, it sounds inevitable, doesn't it? The album is a perfect fit for Nick's restrained style and manner. But it wasn't inevitable then. What makes these early recordings so interesting is what they are not – they are not like the three albums he made for Island Records. They are explorations of musical pathways that led him, by inspiration and force of will, to a place where he finally found the songs that matched his image of himself.

Robin Frederick, Aix-en-Provence school yearbook, 1966

Nick Drake, folksinger

The things that attracted my generation to folk music may not seem so obvious or understandable now but, even years later, I can recall the powerful pull of folk songs. There was a purity there, an honesty and simplicity and sense of community that helped us define our unease. There was nothing overtly wrong with our lives; we ate well but never seemed to satisfy a deeper hunger.

Group singing played a big part in the feeling of connection that folk music gave us. Songs like 'Michael Row the Boat Ashore' were easy to learn and share. They didn't have that 'lowest level of the musical food chain' stigma that has been attached to them since. 'All My Trials', 'Kumbaya', and other sprituals of the American South had been passed down through generations, sung in churches and community groups, eventually becoming part of the Civil Rights movement that helped to change the political landscape of America in the early 1960s. The ease with which these songs could be learned ensured they would spread like wildfire as more and more teenagers picked up guitars in the mid-Sixties and needed a quick repertoire. As songwriters, we cut our teeth on them; sometimes, like Bob Dylan, adapting the melodies and writing our own lyrics. It's hard to imagine Nick Drake singing these folk standards, but that's because we are looking back through the veil of the sophisticated, solitary songs of his Island albums. In those days in Aix, he was just beginning to write songs and the folk influence was helping to shape his future direction.

Nick picked up his folk-song covers from a variety of sources. British singer-songwriter/guitarists like John Renbourn and Bert Jansch had moved through the folk canon on the way to finding a unique voice and style of their own. Renbourn's eponymous 1966 release included traditional folk songs like 'Winter is Gone' and 'John Henry' alongside the distinctive guitar style he was developing at the time. 'Strolling Down the Highway' is a catchy Bert Jansch song with a simple structure and folk-inspired lyric theme. It was frequently covered by street musicans. Nick had Jansch's 1965 self-titled album, studied it, and performed at least one other song from it during the time I knew him ('Courting Blues'). Jansch's great instrumental guitar tracks, 'Smokey River' and 'Casbah', are also on that album. I suspect these are some of the tracks Nick was getting his hands around during those long hours of practice in his room in Aix when friends like Jeremy Mason heard him constantly tuning and detuning his guitar. The evidence would turn up later in songs like 'Three Hours' and ''Cello Song'.

Bob Dylan's 'Tomorrow Is a Long Time' was endlessly covered by others. Nick played this song for me when I visited him and his friends in his room at the Residence Sextius one evening and I remember thinking, 'What is he doing to the rhythm of that song?!' He replaces Dylan's straight fingerpicking rhythm with a light, bluesy, triple feel that adds forward momentum and bounce to the song. On the recording, he fluffs the lyrics on the first couple of lines but doesn't miss a beat of the unusual guitar rhythm. It's always steady on.

Robin Frederick onstage in Aix-en-Provence, 1966
(Photo: Jean-Louis Pujol)

Jackson C. Frank's songs were everywhere in the air in the spring of 1967. 'Catch a boat to England, baby, maybe to Spain . . .' Bridget St John sang to me recently over the telephone, 'Oh, everyone knew that one!' Songs like 'Blues Run the Game' were quickly passed from one singer to the next. I don't even remember where I learned that one, maybe Nick. There's no question that Frank was influential in the development of Nick's music. What's interesting is how much of that influence can be traced to just one song: 'Milk and Honey'. The unusual melodic phrasing beginning on the third beat of the measure, the guitar picking patterns, the sense of embracing sorrow and accepting loss, even the lyric references to seasons – all of these can be found in Nick's later songs. In fact, he could have been using 'Milk and Honey' as a template when writing 'Day Is Done', these two songs are musically so similar. One thing Nick did not pick up from Jackson C. Frank and other folksingers of the time was the 'ramblin' guy' persona of songs like 'Here Come the Blues'. We all seemed to be 'leaving on a southbound train' except Nick. In his songs, he was more concerned that we were all leaving him.

The Palest Blues

When I heard Nick play blues guitar in Aix, it was obvious that he had already mastered the style. He knew dozens of blues riffs which he handily strung together over changing chords, all the while keeping the rock-steady beat that characterised his guitar work. The guitar style Nick favoured – blues licks on the treble strings played over a solid beat on the bass strings – is called Piedmont Blues. It blends Delta blues riffs with ragtime piano rhythms. Early blues recordings by Josh White are a good example of the sound.

Two of the songs Nick recorded on a home demo in 1967/68 are traditional songs which he might have heard on Dave Van Ronk's album, *Ballads, Blues & a Spiritual* (Folkways F-3818): 'My Baby's So Sweet,' and 'Black Mountain Blues'. In addition, he recorded a Van Ronk original, 'If You Leave Me Pretty Momma' from the same album. (As for 'Cocaine Blues,' there were so many versions of this song circulating in the mid-1960s that it's difficult to pinpoint a single source.) Jeremy Mason, Nick's room-mate in Aix, recalls Dave Van Ronk's music, alongside albums by John Renbourn and Bert Jansch, turning up at their flat.

Van Ronk's gritty guitar performances summon up the original spirit of these four songs, evoking their raw, earthy roots. Nick's arrangements, on the other hand, are intricate and sophisticated. Despite his mastery of the blues-guitar vocabulary, no one could mistake Nick Drake for an authentic purveyor of the blues! Rather, his fast, riff-filled guitar arrangements were perfect for entertaining friends and busking on the streets – the kind of thing that made tourists stop in their tracks and toss several francs. (One franc would buy you a lunch at the university cafeteria.) In these blues tracks you get an idea of what an engaging showman Nick was at that time.

Robin Frederick playing the autoharp Carter-family-style at an informal singalong in a classroom in Aix, 1966 (Photo: Jean-Louis Pujol)

I wrote 'Been Smoking Too Long' a couple of months before meeting Nick. He quickly picked up the song and began performing it in his characteristically fluid blues style. Almost immediately he changed my lyric from 'Got the marijuana blues' to 'Got no other life to choose'. He knew the original line because he had my handwritten lyrics and he didn't do this kind of rewrite on any of the other blues songs he covered. (When he changes the lyrics on other songs, it's usually a line that's difficult to understand on a recording.) Whether he felt this was a more effective blues lyric or a statement he personally wanted to make – or both – I don't know.

Nick Drake, songwriter

'Strange Meeting II' is musically very much in the folk-song style Nick adopted in Aix. The descending bass line and chord changes are reminiscent of 'Winter Is Gone'. The change from a minor to major feel also occurs in 'Winter Is Gone'. Like almost all of the songs Nick covered at the time, it consists of a string of verses with a repeated refrain, no bridge or stand-alone chorus. While it's clear that this early work derives from the songs Nick was playing in Aix, interestingly, it also prefigures the songs he would write a few years later for *Pink Moon*, songs with a simple folk form.

On the Aix tape, referring to 'Strange Meeting II', Nick says: 'This is my surrealist song. A sort of funny dream.' Nick sets the scene with a cinematic eye, sweeping in from distant horizon to the details of foam and pebbles at his feet. The characters are Magritte-like: a silent woman, a lost message, a brief, unaccountable meeting of strangers. I can't help but think of French surrealist films like Alain Resnais's *Last Year at Marienbad* (1961). There's a disconnection from time and a clear-edged quality to both. I think people underestimate this lyric when they interpret it simply as an adolescent love song.

There is, of course, a powerful, haunting poem by Wilfred Owen titled 'Strange Meeting'. Nick would certainly have been aware of it, having studied English Literature at Marlborough. Owen's poem also concerns a dream, but it is one of war and death. Other than the oneiric quality of both works, I don't find compelling parallels between the two. Since 'Strange Meeting' is an apt title for his song and Nick was aware of another work by this title, he may have distinguished his by simply adding a number.

The other original song Nick recorded on the Aix tape is 'They're Leaving Me Behind'. These two songs, 'They're Leaving Me Behind' and 'Strange Meeting II', are almost certainly among the first songs he wrote and yet they couldn't be more different. While 'Strange Meeting II' is derivative of the folk songs he had been covering, 'They're

Leaving Me Behind' doesn't sound like anything else. Here Nick is beginning to reach for his own unique sound. The guitar part with its fast 1-2-3, 1-2-3, 1-2 picking pattern suggests a light Afro-Cuban feel (which Nick would come back to later, playing a slowed-down version of it in 'Harvest Breed'). The long, sustained phrases of the vocal melody require a lot of breath control. It's rare for a singer-songwriter to create a melody that is so challenging. Why would you do that to yourself?! Nick obviously had an effect he was trying to create; it sounds like he was attempting to 'float' the melody, disconnect it from the chords and guitar accompaniment, as he would do so successfully in a track like ''Cello Song'. He knows what he wants but he doesn't know exactly how to make it happen . . . yet. In a remarkably short time, he would have it all figured out.

But soon 'the sun went down and the crowd went home . . .' and Aix became just a memory. It haunts the lyrics of 'Time Of No Reply' and hovers behind the songs on his first album, in the wistfulness of 'Saturday Sun', the bluesy rhythms of 'Man In A Shed', and the modal drone of 'Three Hours'. But there the similarities end. When I first happened across *Five Leaves Left* in the import bin at Tower Records, I was thrilled that Nick had made a record. I rushed home and played it. I was seduced by its beauty but also a little perplexed. On the cover of the record was my friend, still wearing the same jacket and jeans he wore in Aix, still sure of his image. But on the album was someone I hardly recognised. The voice seemed to float in some strange way, detached from the guitar rhythm. The playing was rock solid as always, but more complex and there were those amazing cluster chords. In less than twenty-four months, Nick had somehow rocketed light years ahead of the rest of us. He had found his musical persona. It was, to be sure, built on the blues and folk songs he played in Aix but, when all is said and done, he had remade it all in his own image.

The Aix Tape

The tracks recorded in Aix come from a session Nick did in April or May 1967 with a friend and fellow student who was living in a flat on the Rue Manuel. The friend, James, had with him one of the original Philips cassette recorders. He recalls:

'The flat, being conveniently situated not far from Les Deux Garçons, the Mistral nightclub, and that great pinball haunt, the Café Leydet, was a very popular place for social gatherings, ranging from a few drinks to the occasional all night poker session. I can't remember where I first met Nick but it was probably at one of these places and it wasn't long before he was giving impromptu performances in the flat. One knew immediately that he was a cut above your average teenager doing a Bob Dylan impression and I asked him if he would like to commit some of his songs to tape. He leapt at the idea and we arranged a time when no one else would be in the flat to try and keep background noise to a minimum. Because this session was prearranged and therefore not spontaneous it meant that he was a bit too sober for his own liking when playing! All the times I heard him play he was happy, comfortable and enjoyed the attention and respect that his obvious talent commanded.'

Estruch guitar (Photo: Gavin Bush)

Get Together

by Colin Betts

From his book *Frozenlight*, based on his contemporary diaries

It will be some time before you can regard your own country with any affection. In the early spring of 1967 there is only one thing on your mind: you need to get out of here. For eighteen years you've twisted and turned in a cold, hard cage and suddenly the door is open.

First stop is the passport office in Petty France, followed by a two-day wait that allows a glimpse of how London has changed, is still changing, into a scene that promises to be something special. But you've done your bit for a New England, put in the miles and paid the dues. You'll come back when it's warmer and a little less painful. Right now you're ready for a holiday in the sun.

As the white cliffs recede and the French coast takes shape, you feel like singing. Never mind the bluebirds astern in the wake (which anyway look suspiciously like seagulls), ahead lies abroad. There's a whole world out there, big and beautiful. And it doesn't know what it's missing.

Fit, strong, rested and well fed, you stay in Paris only long enough to busk up a stake, smoke a lot of expensive hash and sleep a few nights under bridges. It's all fresh and new, exotic and exciting, but that's not enough. For the first time there's a chance to connect with a lineage, to walk where Kerouac trod, blow joints where Ginsberg smoked, and that can only mean Tangier, Morocco.

Hitching down through France, Andorra and Spain is slow and tough, but if you keep thumbing and walking, smiling and thumbing, it can be done in four days. You can eat and sleep when you get there, where it's warm and friendly and beatniks are welcome, where a hotel room costs ten bob and the best zero-zero from Ketama is threepence a gramme; where a big bowl of couscous sets you back tuppence ha'penny, and the mint tea is virtually free. What a place!

And it's full of beatniks like you, plus a new breed of rebels and travellers who call themselves hippies, whose music is tuneful and relevant to a skinny white boy with a dope habit. Unlike the boring old blues. With nowhere better to go and nothing to run from, you can relax here, unpack all the senses and emotions from their boxes and throw the boxes away. Kill a little time, erase a few memories. Be whatever you want to be.

In Tangier Andy Pandy and Teddy could play around all day, while Bill and Ben wouldn't have to go back into their flowerpots, because the gardener never returns from having his dinner. You feel about five years old, and are far from being the only one.

As the new book records:

'There's only one place to be in the spring of 1967 and that's Morocco. The hippie generation is on the move and Tangier is a magnet for European and East Coast American kids who need to be somewhere different that also has dope. The old city alleyways buzz like a beehive with Arab traders, rich-kid students, ageing pederasts, beats on the Kerouac trail, long-term tokers, Dharma Bums, nervous smugglers, bemused straight tourists and unpublished writers. The hippies have taken over the Medina.'

Farther south in Marrakesh the Stones are holding court and having a song written about them, but all is not well. Mick and Keith are on bail for a bust and Brian's losing his girlfriend, Anita, to Keith. Still, the Moroccan government thinks the Stones are good for tourism, so they're on national TV every night, dubbed in Arabic.

Even farther South, Nick Drake and his pals are rolling a dark-blue Mark One Ford Cortina in the Atlas mountains and are lucky to crawl out of the wreckage alive. But their karma is good. They are four young, friendly English guys escaping their public schools at the best time in British history. Most earlier generations were fighting wars at eighteen, or administering colonies. These chaps have the best days of their lives ahead of them. No one has to worry about university, marriage or a career for several glorious months to come.

It's not enough to be at the right place at the right time, you need to be the right age too. And to be eighteen in 1967 is perfect. If you also realise that it can't last and will never come again, that's the spirit of '67 and you'll never forget it. But every moment must count: right here, right now. Trouble is, you need money to live and breathe, even at Moroccan prices. And right now you're broke in Tangier, the tourist season is starting and you need to get to Paris or somewhere fast. The busking season starts there in April. The American tourists love to hear some credible R&B, while the French are grateful for anything.

The only option is to hitchhike for three or four days through Spain again, then two more through France, and you've only got two pounds in francs left. So when you see a happy band of hippies in a battered car with GB plates you have to be interested. They board the ferry to Algeciras too and head for the sundeck. The tall skinny one has a guitar and you gravitate towards them. There must be two hundred hippies on the boat, having a high old time, trailing a cloud of smoke in their wake. Everyone knows the Spanish fascists bust smugglers for six years and a day, so they're getting rid of their stashes. While the Rock of Gibraltar glides by.

It's a brilliant, sparkling Mediterranean morning, cobalt blue and golden bright. The hippies are grooving away around little cassette players (the Americans) and guitars (mostly Brits). The latest vibe is Acid Rock from California, so the yanks are playing Big Brother, the Grateful Dead, Jefferson Airplane. Some English Beats are singing 'Cocaine' and Nick Drake's playing an arabesque instrumental in a tuning that leaves his long, hammerhead fingers free to improvise on the open chords, magic fingers that make you glad you didn't start playing first.

Nick's style has the clean, technical dexterity of the bearded folkie brigade, who can all play 'Anji' faultlessly. There are also bluegrass, clawhammer, jazz and classical elements, and a drone effect on the bass strings he can only have discovered in Morocco, where every radio blares out the music of Oum Khalsoum and other Egyptian divas all day long.

You found a vaguely Arabic tuning yourself, over a month in Tangier, and proudly unleash it. Should have known better. Nick promptly retunes two strings and it's twice as good. You sadly decline to sing a couple of songs for the moment and roll a joint instead, talk about music, trade credentials. He's a Gemini too; ten days younger. Gets every allusion and laughs at your cynical jokes.

Nick says he'll be busking in Aix-en-Provence and it sounds like a cool place; thousands of students from all over Europe and the USA pretending to study French. He asks where *you're* going and you say: 'France'. A moment later he offers you a lift all the way up through Spain, non-stop, about six hundred miles. You'll write a song about it.

Can relax now, enjoy the trip, that's the biggest problem solved, just have to negotiate Spanish customs. But the English Boys on Tour breeze right through, like you steamed past the Rock: full speed ahead and keep on trucking. Too many kids forget where they put their stash, or try to smuggle a lump of hash, and will spend the rest of the decade rotting in one of General Franco's jails.

You're crushed in the back of the Cortina, Julian and Richard to the right, buried under luggage and guitars. Nick and this other guy are up front and your job is to keep them awake while you're driving. You talk about the Stones first, not failing to mention your slight connection. But Nick met them down in Marrakech and actually played for them. The Stones were originally a beatnik group and although it's good to know the hippies like them too, it makes you feel old.

Nick wants to know your busking set list: 'Walkin' the Dog', 'House of the Rising Sun, 'Get Together', 'San Francisco Bay Blues', 'Not Fade Away'. He nods. There is mention of Leadbelly and Woody Guthrie, then a debate about Acid Rock versus pure acoustic folk. You maintain that the punters in 1967 want four or five chords and a chorus they can learn to play at home. Every skinny white boy's got a guitar these days, must have been a dozen of them on the boat. You're worried that in a year or so there'll be buskers everywhere and say so: 'You'll have to queue up to get a good pitch.'

'That's good,' says Nick. 'Music on every corner and lots of competition.'

You're not so sure. Apart from knowing only about ten

chords, you wouldn't want to try so hard. The songs you like the best are simple. Most people are like that about music. They can't sing a note or even bang a tambourine in time, but they know what they like. And what they like at the moment is the next step up from a twelve-bar blues: tuneful, folkie R&B with a hook-line, guitar solo and a chorus. The Mamas and Papas are having the same idea, the Byrds and Spoonful.

'So if you want to make a living out of rock and pop,' you conclude, 'get a group together with acoustic guitars, vocal harmonies, a pretty girl, and Bob's your uncle. You can sing, right?' Nick nods that he can, comes in with 'Goodnight Irene' in D, and you supply a higher harmony. Then you switch over a verse (he must have seen the Leadbelly song book) and you both forget the rest of the words at the same time. Then Nick says:

'Did you bring anything back?' And you say:

'Just a bit in my mouth, in case I had to swallow it. You?'

'Just a bit, but I'm driving, so we may as well smoke yours.'

His hunched shoulders quiver with mirth around the wheel. Every part of everyone is scrunched and cramped in the tiny Cortina, but that's OK when you're young and spreading your wings of freedom . . . is how it feels after a nice joint of zero-zero. And from where you're sitting Nick really does look like a watchful bony eagle in the Spanish sun, cruising at 50 mph, left hand on the wheel, right hand trailing smoke out of the open window. So the joint's burning too fast and if a bit drops off he might burn a hole in his jeans and crash the car.

'Don't let it go out,' you say.

Once you get over being jealous of Nick's guitar picking, he's quite a cool guy. By early 1967 the hippie revolution might not have evolved a comprehensive philosophy as such, but everyone you met in Morocco smiled all the time and was ready for anything. There are unspoken rules that really matter: you don't play games, go on ego-trips, rip people off or put them in danger. That's selfish. Otherwise you can pretty much do as you like, as long as no one gets hurt. Basically, if you can't do good, at least don't leave the planet worse than you found it. But above all never lose your cool. You've found some rules you can live by. Being a hippie is alright.

While Nick has a doze, you talk to Richard about his plans and hopes for the future. It seems they're all bound for university after the summer. Already the spring has been so good everyone is talking about the Movement by now. That'll be the American influence, and they're all over Europe with their Acid Rock music, five dollars a day and funny little joints with only one paper. They really believe we can stop the war and change the world for the better – that this will happen because it's right. The very idea is militant, liberating. Why settle for anything less? If everyone turns on and tunes in we'll all be fine, the earth can be protected and Mick and Keith won't have to go to jail. How could you not support a proposition like that? Say what you like about Americans, they think big.

There's a stop for a stretch and a breath of air. No food, just water in bottles and canteens, plenty of fags. Then the new banger groans as you all pile back in and knock up some more miles. Time doesn't matter: it was light, now it's dark. Bob Dylan's on the agenda, another Gemini – indeed Grand Master of the House of Gemini. Nick's caught every LP from the start. You don't mention you've had 'Fixin to Die' tattooed on your arm since Approved School, and sing 'Blowin' in the Wind' instead. It's a song borrowed permanently from his Bobness, on which you owe him busking royalties. Nick too, has obviously loved it since first setting eyes on Mary out of Peter, Paul and. You share every cultural reference since 1948, know all the Beatles and Dylan songs by heart, really dig Phil Spector. You do 'Be My Baby' way down low, with vibrato.

'Three chords and a chorus!' you gloat.

'No, four,' says Nick, and both giggle like schoolboys who've pulled a stroke. The other poor guys are asleep, passively smoking, while two Geminis try to keep each other awake. Nick says it's easy to score in Aix, prompting you to roll another one. He asks where *exactly* you are going.

'Paris.' It's almost a question though. You're also ready for anything.

'You could come to Aix. There's always a place to sleep at the Sextius.'

'Huh? Sex what?'

'Residence Sextius, it's a hall of residence without the supervision. And you can eat free at the university, everybody does. What do you think, Jules?'

But Jules has crashed out. So you say:

'Sounds great. "Follow your karma," this American Beat in Tangier used to say. Thanks a lot.'

Conversion is complete: from loner-tramp to flower-power evangelist. Just have to be nicer to everybody, try to love them. And it really does sound like the right place to busk for a while, with warm weather and thousands of wealthy students. Every student loves a singalong in English. If they also smoke you won't have to play crap tunes.

Could be the Pyrenees out there, judging by a rugged star-lit horizon. One of the headlights is wonky but the motor's running fine. Nick says it's 'rally-tuned', and then you're a little surprised to learn that he takes Donovan seriously. Here's a hippie who gets by on two and a half chords and a chorus. To prove a point you do 'Don't Think Twice' and just know Nick plays it inside out, 'Wildwood Flower' all that stuff. It's been the standard Beat repertoire for several years now. Hippies haven't sprung from nowhere, perfectly formed. They had to be Beats first; dig Miles, Coltrane and Mingus; Woody Guthrie, Robert Johnson. It's essential. But:

'Acid Rock is all you need,' you blurt out. Dope's getting low and you held it down too long: 'I bet you a joint in Aix that your favourite track this year is Jorma's guitar instrumental on the Jefferson Airplane LP. Pure Acid Rock.'

Got it in one, and you can tell he's thinking about it. You also know if you had ten per cent of his talent and Nick had ten per cent of your brass neck you would both be stars, the new Peter and Gordon, only better looking, with far better tunes.

'Why don't *you* get a group together, then?' says Nick.

'Because it would mean staying in one place, getting a pad, money for dope and food. And then organising people. Besides, I'd have to practise for years to be any good at the guitar or songwriting.'

Colin Betts, his dog and mum (Photo supplied by Colin Betts)

Nick agrees that this is so. 'You've thought about it though,' he says.

'Not really, and certainly not for a while. I'm trying to get to California, that's where it's at. I want to drop acid and peyote in Big Sur and Yosemite, see San Francisco before it's too late. How about you?'

'Oh, I suspect I'm doomed to Cambridge.'

'How do you mean, doomed?'

'We'll, it's all organised from the moment you're born, whether it's suitable for you or not.'

'So drop out! If you change your mind you can always go back.'

'If only it were that simple.'

'If we can't afford to put off our lives for a year or two we're really in trouble.'

'Yes well, we'll see,' says Nick.

'I just don't think there'll be a better time than this. And if *we* don't do something, nobody will. It's all up to us. It's scary.'

Now suddenly you're an expert on revolution already, but all you hope is that these kids will remember the spirit of '67, that even if they become lawyers or politicians they'll still give hippies lifts. And this Aix place sounds better than Paris, where you'd have to sleep rough and sing 'Catch the Bloody Wind' on the Boulevard Montparnasse. In Aix there'll be lots of stoned bright hippies who know the words of 'We Shall Overcome'. You might meet an heiress from Santa Barbara or Nob Hill, maybe do a bit of busking with Nick. Those pretty little rich girls will just love two good-looking, six-foot-three-inch guitar-pickers who can really hold a tune.

California Dreaming

On waking up in Aix-en-Provence, you lie low for a while, waiting for Jules to surface and show you around. The bright sun outside is inviting and you're keen to check out the scene, but need to establish your status with the Residence Sextius before regarding it as any kind of base-camp. It was still dark when the trashed Cortina pulled up outside and five grubby, wasted travellers stumbled into the newish building. You stuck close to Julian, the friendliest of the other four, and it's his floor you crashed on. Now he's invisible under a white quilt, but it's good to know he's there.

From experience you've learned that the camaraderie and promises of the reckless road can vanish when static reality re-imposes itself, but you don't think that's likely on this occasion. Still it's best to know where you stand before assuming any kind of squatter's rights, just in case these upper-class hippies turn out to be mere ravers who won't want to know you in the warm light of a *provençale* morning. So you skin up a weakish one and bring the book up to date:

'Aix, April? 1967. The spirit of Neal Cassady was with us yesterday. From Morocco to France the road unspooled like a film, or Kerouac's manuscript that day he unrolled it across a New York publisher's floor: here, the beat bible is ready now, the youth of the world can make of it what they will. And it was fine to be in Tangier only ten years after he was there with Ginsberg and Burroughs, on the streets of Africa; to smoke a hookah in The Dancing Boy nightclub, make love to strong American girls on the roof of the Hotel Tetouan, watch freighters from New York unload long-haired dreamers onto the beach-head of an anti-authoritarian invasion that will change this tired old world. Bogart's black and white *Casablanca* will never be the same here come the technicolor armies of the star-filled daytime sky to paint rainbows on your walls and . . .'

'Good morning, Colin.'

'Huh? Oh Jules, hiya man. Lovely day.'

Indeed it is. After a casual stroll from city wall to pavement café and art gallery to record shop, you enjoy a lentil stew at the university cafeteria and return to the Sextius for a siesta. Everyone's friendly and cool. The kids in the residence are a lively bunch of proto-toffs in the process of stretching their social parameters. The cultural revolution in Britain has elevated oiks of every stripe to iconic status, from scouser pop stars to cockney actors, models and snappers. The arts and entertainment industries could no longer function without them. All of a sudden it is fashionable to dress like a colour-blind tramp and drop your aitches. In French ideally.

Of course the English elite can tell you're a climber, if not admire you for it. What helps is roadworthiness, street-wisdom and a thorough knowledge of popular music from both sides of the Atlantic. In this regard your busking repertoire earns you larger audiences and more money than Nick's does. He'll have to learn to smile more often, and to stand up when he performs.

One morning he comes down for coffee, to borrow some skins (and hash) and you're working out 'Je Ne Regrette Rien', by Edith Piaf. It's got great vocal harmonies and so has 'Milord', which Nick can play, and 'Hymne D'Amour'. Piaf had a close-harmony male chorus, most prominently on 'Les Trois Cloches', which sold a million copies as Little Jimmy Brown's 'Three Bells', for heaven sake. You jammed for six hours in the end. Entirely in French.

You can hear him practising through the walls and ceilings every day and night of the week – marvellous stuff that makes your ears burn with envy and puts your own plunking progress to shame. And on the Mirabeau, outside La Rotonde or the other crowded café-bars, he's invariably surrounded by eyelash-fluttering beauties, whereas you attract the poorer hippie-types, French teenagers and singalong drunks. But he's very shy, tends to ignore the punters, looks down all the time, as though concentrating hard on the fretwork and finger-picking, which you know for a fact he doesn't need to do. On those occasions late at night when you smoke and jam together, he can play, talk and listen at the same time without missing a note or buzzing a fret.

You're both doing fine for francs and centimes though, these Aix kids have money to burn. In a couple of twenty-minute sets you can afford to eat in a brasserie, score five grammes of decent hash from Mahmoud the Rotonde waiter and buy new guitar strings which last about a week.

Robin Frederick would be a star in any folk-music heaven; in the candy-floss sky of Aix-en-Provence she's a supernova, shines on everyone in town. You meet her on the street, where else, and while you're emptying the new guitar case (which cost more than the guitar) into the old school satchel, she invites you back to the jazz-folk club where she has a residency. It's a smoky dive with gentle lighting, cool clientele and a message board with ads for shared-petrol rides, gigs on the coast and communications between passers-through:

'Swedish Erik to English Annabel – gone to Istanbul. See you whenever xxx' kind of thing.

Robin is a graduate of an LA scene that produced the Byrds, Spoonful, Mamas and Papas, who also knows Acid Rock inside out, although her own material is more eclectic. Nick's here too and you've never seen him quite so animated. Around the English-party circuit, he's a luminous butterfly, flitting from one clique to another without lingering anywhere particularly, but tonight he's wherever Robin is, looking vaguely sheepish.

During a break between live acts (and anyone can play) Pink Floyd are on the sound-system and you pass on the rumour that Syd's on the skids of a bad acid-trip lately.

'Too much acid'll scramble your brain,' says Robin.

You still haven't tried it, are happy with dope, but Nick looks away, so perhaps he has. You can read him pretty well by now and detect he's on *something*.

'You don't approve?' you ask her.

'Too much of anything'll screw you up.'

'Even hash?' you persist. Nick nods as if he's heard the answer before.

'Sure,' Robin replies. 'After a while it flattens everything out. If you're high all the time it isn't a high any more. Then you need something stronger.'

There is sound logic in this, but before turning on you were low all the time and will settle for not feeling like that any more, whatever the consequences.

'So that smoking song isn't satirical?' She sang her own bluesy number about having been stoned for too long and you obviously missed the point.

'Not really,' she replies, looking distant for a moment, and you guess there's rather more to it than that. At any rate the suspicion is it's a sensitive subject, so you change it:

'You two ever play together?'

Robin smiles enigmatically and you could swear Nick blushes, though it's quite dark in there. After Morocco he was lightly tanned but has faded since to a nocturnal pallor, albeit one that glows in the dark.

'Sometimes,' Robin smiles, 'we do cover versions, but those fancy tunings tie my fingers in knots.' Could fall in love with a lady like this, but she's out of your league and you know it. You're not so sure about Nick though and an hour or so later, when they leave together, are even less so. But she seemed wiser than either of you, maybe both of you combined, and in the book you describe her as:

'. . . an old soul who knows more than she lets on, with the grace and charm to make allowances for lesser mortals.'

You got her address though, and if you're ever in LA . . .

Despite its groovy scene in Aix, it's a small pond really, and you keep bumping into its sides. For one thing, although the busking is dead easy, you can't play more than a couple of times a day without running out of punters. The tourist season has yet to arrive and you can extract only *so* much cash from people who've heard you a dozen times before. And since you've got about ten good songs, the novelty is beginning to wear off. It helps to hook up with Julian's friend John Molloy from time to time. He's an ace clarinettist and you rehearse a few instrumentals together; 'Summertime', 'Yesterday', that sort of stuff, but it's hardly progressive and the same problem recurs: after a week you're back where you started. Imagine doing that every day for a living!

The busy social whirl is also getting boring. For a while it's fresh and exciting to hang out with all the right people, playing bridge in rented chateaux and dancing till dawn, stoned on hash and champagne; flirting with heiresses and debs and getting stoned with the more radical Americans, with their stereo systems, good grass and cocaine. At this stage hair-length is a fair guide to the contents of the mind underneath it. Longer than six inches is a sure sign of degeneracy, it means that guy's been a head for quite a while. But you're not likely to meet any revolutionary gurus, as such, in a place catering for rich kids on gap years.

Jules and John have an old school chum with a Deux Chevaux, permitting busking raids on Avignon, Arles and Marseilles, followed by excursions to the resorts on the Med. As the book records:

'France is two years behind England at least, which is good news for a street musician but otherwise dull. Meanwhile London is really happening by all the accounts arriving on the hippie grapevine. Everybody's dropping acid, Jimi Hendrix is the new Hank Marvin, Brian's cracking up and Syd's broken down. The backlash has set in too, so we must be doing something right, we children of illusion. Mick and Keith will be in court soon and might be sent down, and now Hoppy Hopkins from UFO has been busted. The pigs are raiding everyone, while in Aix you can smoke on the street. We've hardly started the revolution yet and already the jails, mental hospitals and cemeteries are filling up with victims. We will be seen and heard, though, before this is over, and one day everyone will know that we were right.'

You pause to roll another one, then:

'The music scene in France is pathetic. The big international bands visit Paris, but even here most people are still into Johnny Hallyday and Françoise Hardy, and Daevid Allen is considered avant-garde! It's even worse down here in the provinces. Happily, Terry Reid is in St Trop this weekend.'

Not surprisingly, Nick also turns up in St Trop to see Terry and his band. You spotted him playing the harbour cafés, but there is no conflict of interest because you and John arrived yesterday, made four hundred francs in an hour after lunch and secured a booking to appear at Le Stereo Club for another three hundred tonight. You're a pop star on the Côte d'Azur already, they're so desperate for some of that Swinging London rock and roll. You turned down an invitation to play at a party on a million-franc yacht. The owner *was* wearing make-up, so you crashed on the beach instead. It's quite a rush to find you can freewheel anywhere you like, earn a packet and make it up as you go along. And another buzz to catch up with good old Terry again. Last time you saw him was at a dead-or-alive gaff in Yorkshire where you were the only true bluesman for fifty miles.

You meet Nick at the door. He's pretending to be on the guest list. You noticed earlier he was busking with another guy (or rather some bloke was banging away on a tambourine) but now he's trailing around a Jewish-American girl called Emily Stone. She's got a car, a dinky blue Simca Mille, in which you promptly blow a joint, talk bollocks for a while. You are all very stoned and glowing after hours in the hot spring sun. In England it is raining and this would normally be bedtime.

Terry has a huge, soulful voice for such a little guy, and his band lay down some solid R&B but the French audience need to smoke more dope and you're the only ones who noticeably appreciate it. Afterwards, Terry and his drummer join you for a couple of joints.

'Hard work with this lot,' you console them.

'Money's good though,' Terry grins, 'and we can work every night. England's gone crazy. Must be a hundred bands chasing every fifty-quid gig.'

And there'll be a hundred buskers coveting every five-quid pitch, you're sure. How could it last? There'll be a hippie on every corner.

In the car park Emily said that music isn't everything, and neither will it change the world. No sooner have you become what you want to be, than suddenly it's not good enough; you have to save the planet too. You thought the world of music but:

'The system will institutionalise it, give a few hundred stars too much money so they can destroy themselves with sex and drugs and fast cars.'

That's a heresy in this company, of course, but would be true of you. All the way back through the complacent French night, the conviction grows that America is the place to be in the summer of 1967. Kids over there are taking over the streets, parks and campuses. The civil rights and anti-war movements are challenging the establishment head-on, literally fighting for the soul of their country, while the greatest enemies of people like the Beatles and Stones are the tax-man and the drug squads.

How can you ever enjoy a seven-shilling coffee again? Poncing through the ancient ruins of history, lurking in posh shop doorways singing 'Baby Let Me Follow You Down' isn't going to change anything. And besides, compared to Nick and Terry you're crap.

It's a lot to assimilate, and within minutes you also understand what a transformation will be necessary to actualise this theory of enlightenment. But three things are immediately clear: first, it's time to get out of Aix; second, you have to smoke less dope; and third, you need a stiff joint *tout de suite*. Before the new regime starts officially.

Up early next morning, determined to have a little less fun, start building the stake that will get you to America as soon as possible. How simple it would be to chase around Europe, just ahead of the pack, having a high time and just growing old. So you talk to people instead, especially Americans, fill up the book with addresses from Boston to Berkeley and lots of places in between. Like Emily, many of these students admire all things European and their invitations to 'look me up in St Louis' or Ann Arbor are warm and genuine.

It's also true that the Aix class of '67 will be leaving soon, back to their own universities and bright futures. Within a few weeks the various residences and rented villas will be vacated, cleaned up, prepared for a new intake of rich kids arriving for their 'French courses'. Once the summer vacations begin hardly anyone you know will be left. At that stage the busking will pick up again, fresh faces will dominate the places to be seen in. You could easily waste a whole year in Provence.

The weather, like the party season, is coming to a boil. Those foreigners who still care about such things have finished their exams, are making plans for their final weeks of freedom, while most of the French students have cleared off already. The message board at the club is crowded with ads for redundant books and cheap Citroëns. Lifts are further available to all points of the Tarot card. Kids are teaming up for further adventures together, so there are also lots of unwanted airline tickets around. If you had fifteen hundred francs you could fly one-way to the East Coast of America; for half as much again it could be Los Angeles or San Francisco.

Unfortunately the busking is terrible: students' allowances have run out, or now have to stretch longer than originally planned. So when, on the way to the Rotonde, you come across Nick perched on one of the fountain walls, it's with a nagging sense of gloom.

'Aix has had it,' you announce. 'I didn't make a hundred francs yesterday. You?'

He just nods and won't look at you, which is unusual. Yesterday he was full of beans at another Marlborough boy's leaving party and you rolled home together singing Beatles' songs. At one point your eye caught across this sea of bobbing heads: 'You Really Got Me'. You were the only two standing still. An eyebrow from Nick suggested a matter of mutual interest. In the shrubbery you blew a few chillums of Ketama Number One.

'What are you on, man?' you accuse. He scrabbles in his old suit-jacket pocket, unwraps a twist of silver paper and shows you three little blue pills.

'Blue Cheer,' he mumbles, 'from California.'

Wow! Owsley acid! It's a legendary brand of high quality and purity that comes in several colours: Orange Sunshine, Purple Haze, White Lightning. There are successful bands named after Owsley acid.

'Where can I get some? How much are they?'

For an answer he picks two out and passes them over with a lopsided grin. You're uncommonly grateful and say so, not least because you really need to put in a little research before heading to the West Coast, *insh'allah*. Ought to know what to expect.

'Emily split this morning,' he explains, 'didn't want to risk taking it through customs.' Which clarifies more than one point. Americans are so civilised. No English hippie would have any tabs of Owsley left over.

You pop one down with a handful of water from the fountain, fire up a cheap Spanish fag and wait for the earth to move. At last! Nick unpacks his guitar and so do you. Thus far you've been the big brother in matters of the road and street but now he's ahead, psychedelically as well as musically. You only hope he'll still be around if you end up on what you've heard and read described as a 'bad trip'. But expect to find that we are all one.

With charitable restraint Nick sticks to easy tunes: 'House of the Rising Sun', 'Got My Mojo Working', 'Don't Think Twice', 'SF Bay Blues', 'Cocaine', 'Baby Let Me Follow You Down' – by which time the Owsley kicks in and you find yourself (lose yourself?) spending the next hundred years messing around with 'Season of the Witch'.

You still can't stand Donovan, but his songs are so simple that any cack-handed divvo on acid can keep up, and a small crowd has gathered in the coruscating sunshine. The happy sound of tinkling water and coins plinking into guitar cases is also rather pleasant. Kids are getting comfortable, joints and an incense stick are ignited. An American girl called Beth-Anne is dancing with earnest abandon. People are clapping and tapping along.

The vocals have become somewhat impressionistic, because you never did know the words too well, and neither do a couple of German hippies who also join in. But it's a diamond afternoon and the spirit of '67 is strong today. You and Nick (and Robin of course) have provided a soundtrack to these beautiful people's golden days and nights, and now they're almost over it's a nostalgic occasion too. In fact it's quite embarrassing, so that the rhythm escapes along with the lyrics and you have to stop. Except there isn't a 'you' any more in any familiar context; rather what continues to exist is a more general, plural you that is both here and watching itself being here at the same time. Far out, man.

Then Nick stops playing too, plonks his guitar on top

of the money and gently fastens the case. You glance at him shyly with a question mark; another appears above his head; in fact wherever you look the shimmering air is dotted with symbols; vaguely oriental glyphs and syllables appear and disappear, morphing into one another, and vibrating, pulsing with a life and energy of their own, as though all matter and space is interchangeable, insubstantial, essential and non-essential, neither spatial nor material in any permanent or relative sense. Crikey. It all boils down to a *symbol.*

'How are you doing?' says Nick, who is sparkling currently.

'How shoe doing? How's who I mean,' the pair of you blowing rainbow bubbles that burst in the air, or maybe it's water; the fountain is sun-rays refracting through air-drops. Cartoon fish you are, roseate dolphins trailing balloons of honeysuckle bubble gum whose words explode with poof puff poff on the edge of hysteria and if you laugh you'll never stop, so maybe it's safe to cry. But people are staring now, you might lose it, and Nick says:

'You ready?'

'For anything,' you forgot to say. 'Huh?' Ready for What?

'Race you up to the place?' Nick's vowels are liquid roses.

Which one, up or down? But with the last atom of ego, all that's left of you, throw the dice, you say:

'Yeah, that's good, but you dropped a bit of something, look it's down there . . .' Pointing, and as his eyes fall out on the ground (more bubbles) you grab your guitar case, take off like Gemini wind, it isn't fair or foul or far. You were the 440-yard champion at Ardale, but he catches up and passes, past the Tabac selling MAIZ skins from Spain, past a gawping population, round the corner up the stairs, guitars bumping. You are Van-go-go-Gogh and it's so good to make some money out of music. All the plumbers make a living, but a muso's in a lottery, only so many survive. And it's good you listened to Emily's schtick before the acid hit too, or else these dreams of California would be chemically induced instead of real, man, and you might go back to Morocco, smuggle hash through Algeciras in desperation, end up back inside. Insecure isn't the word when you can't afford a train to the next town but want to be in California, six thousand miles away. Where the revolution is at. The revolution that needs you. Leave the music in Nick's magic hands. You're just not good enough.

'How many sugars?'

'That's a tricky one, is that the time?' Nick is dissolving. 'I've put two in.' He remembered.

'Thanks, Nick.' You can see right through his skin. Red and blue inside.

Now it's getting dark, the coffee's free and so is Miles – if still in pain – it makes you sad that Vincent died so poor and lonely. Was it Churchill said the hard part's getting off a tiger? You're coming down, but not with a bump, with a whisper, and Jules is here too, hi man, my good friends, I love you, always will. It's like sliding down a big old wooden fairground helter-skelter; hurdy-gurdy girls with candy-floss cheeks 'Jailhouse Rock'ing through busted speakers. Yeah man.

After a little while the spinning stops and that's sad too, but good to know the option exists to start again whenever. You're trying to work out whether it's better to have another arrow in the quiver or another string to the bow, then give up, turn to face the wall – it'll keep until tomorrow. You passed the acid test, that's the main thing. And nothing bad happened.

There's only one page left in the book and you waste it on a summary of the months it took to fill it and a list of places you've been. Might come in handy, when you're old and quite mad, to know exactly what happened. It's doubtful you'll ever forget but it's possible the memory bank will fill up and overload, or you might unlearn how to read, burn out the brain-cells completely, so just in case . . . and the last line says:

ACID + REALISE = RADICALISE

It will be decades before you notice the extra E.

All of a sudden everything speeds up again. The lift you arranged to Paris will depart a day earlier than planned and there's only time for quick goodbyes, vague promises to meet in London, and a last couple of joints with Julian, Nick and John. There was another leaving party last night, a Harvard bash that got a little out of hand, so the blinds are down to protect those nerve-endings that remain from the unforgiving sun. The place is also a mess, you've seen Soho skippers in better shape, but everyone except Nick will be gone within a week and it would take longer than that to repair the damage.

'So . . .' you conclude awkwardly, 'thanks for everything, chaps.'

These guys have been so kind it hurts, shown you a whole world. But how on earth did you spend six weeks in Aix and go busking together only once? In fact you feel guilty about lots of things: that you never really listened to Nick's own songs; contributed no harmonies or percussion; that on the road from Morocco you had the arrogance to insinuate that his style is dated and lecture him on how to make it more commercial by adding bells, whistles and girlie vocals; but most of all because you failed to see beyond his impeccable exterior to the lonely schoolboy inside. Soon he has to go back there, to that life. You've been so engrossed in managing the personal psycho-drama going on in your own mind you hardly noticed Nick's got his own problems.

It was easy to assume that these rich kids bound for Oxford and Cambridge would float through the rest of their lives on a golden cloud of privilege and success. While you hope and pray they'll remember 1967 and keep the spirit alive, the suspicion is their Acid Rock records will end up in the attics of Chelsea townhouses and country piles along with their cricket bats, existential novels and hookah pipes from the Medina in Tangier. But Nick sounds so bitter, as he regards the future, that even a meretricious hippie tramp like you has to feel for him:

'I'm *supposed* to stay here until August,' he complains, stabbing out the joint and lighting a fag, 'then three years at Cambridge reading dusty old books.'

A week ago you might have settled for that: May Balls, lovely rich girls; get a band together with prospects, sign up for Footlights – but now this deluded notion makes you squirm. Hoping to cheer him up, you blurt out:

'In Approved School they let you out after a year. Even Borstal's only eighteen months.'

You haven't admitted this before, wouldn't sunbathe with the others for fear the crude Ardale tattoos on your arms might worry people. But Owsley acid has amended both your self-image and aspirations. You are what you are now, and if not exactly proud of it, no longer see any reason to deny it either.

After only a few minutes of imagining yourself in Nick's scuffed holey moccasins, yet another illusion falls away. Until now you've envied as well as admired him. You would have traded all but that stubborn corner of the mind which pulled you through the worst times to look and play and speak like Nick, but not any more. Whereas you had fifteen years of obscurity and relative misery to slough off, people like Nick have generations of conditioning, expectation and investment to defy. That kind of pressure must be terrible. Precisely when The Movement is ready to rock.

But he'll be fine, surely. With such enormous talent and all the contacts he'll make, wherever Nick goes the record company scouts will scramble over each other to sign him up and make him a star. And that's what he wants more than anything. More than girls and nice clothes and a car, or even dope and acid. Why else would he practise all night and busk for fun – sometimes without bothering to lay out the guitar case? That's what broke your musical heart: how easy it was for Nick. Until you met and studied him, you had musical ambitions of your own. Not any more. You'll have to write the Great post-Beat novel instead. But that beeping noise outside must be the Yank with the Camper waiting to haul you off to Paris.

You know you'll see Jules and John again, so a brief cuddle will do. Skinny white English boys can get away with that by now without being suspected of homosexuality. But with Nick it turns into a swaying hug that ends in wet eyes. May all the Buddhas bless you, little brother, and may everybody get together and love one another right here, right now, or we'll *all* have wasted our time.

by Valentine PRINTERS & PUBLISHERS, DUNDEE & LONDON
Love from Ben and Alex and Sophia and Sarah and Rose and David
Nick Drake,
5 Cyril Mansions,
Prince of Wales Drive,
London
S.W.11.

A postcard from the Isle of Mull to Nick, staying with his sister in London

I know you all, and will awhile uphold
The unyok'd humour of your idleness . . .

Henry IV, Part 1

The Jeunesse Dorée

by Gabrielle Drake

'We were Nick's playmates.' This is how Ben Laycock described the group of young upper-class hippies into which Nick found himself drawn on his return from Aix-en-Provence in 1967. And, in the few brief months between that return from France and the start of his first term at Cambridge University, Nick formed friendships within it that seem to have brought him some of the most carefree and joyful times of his life.

Nick's entrée into this group came in Aix-en-Provence. To begin with, he seems to have been somewhat disparaging about his fellow countrymen in this foreign city:

'I seem to have met a great many people down here already, although none of them are quite the ideal type, since they're either English or American. The majority of them seem to be rich young Londoners who have been sent out here for want of something better to do, have at no stage had any intention of learning French, and who are constantly bored stiff. All nice guys, but not the sort of type who help one improve one's French.'

And again:

'The prospects of improving my French do, on the whole, seem to be improving. I am getting to find the English group rather tedious, which is probably a good thing. Although individually they are mostly very nice, as a group they are thoroughly nauseous.'

But probably sooner rather than later he sorted the wheat from the chaff. And maybe this was when he started to enter Aix's music scene:

'I'm looking around for an opportunity to start playing my guitar in public. There have in fact been one or two chances already, but I've been rather lazy about it. I went to a jazz club in Aix the other night, and stood in for about half an hour with some other students. I mostly played piano, but also had a go on an alto. My saxophone playing proved regrettably to be somewhat rusty.'

But it was his guitar that brought him his real opportunity to meet congenial company. We know, from his old school friends Simon Crocker and Jeremy Mason, with whom he shared lodgings in Aix, that Nick spent many hours – as he would do for the rest of his life – practising his guitar. And it must have been in Aix that his talent started to be honed into something exceptional. We know that he soon met up with Robin Frederick, the beautiful golden American girl who wrote 'Smokin' Too Long' (was she his Princess of the Sand?) and was herself a fine guitarist and musician; we know that he not only played in nightclubs but also busked in the streets of Aix; and we know that, gradually, he gathered round himself sympathetic souls whose enthusiasm for the contemporary music scene was matched by an appreciation of a stimulant so suited to the heady optimism of the day: marijuana. For, of course, it was here in Aix that Nick acquired his fabled taste for pot.

It is thanks to James, an Old Etonian who possessed one of the early Philips cassette recorders, as well as the foresight to ask Nick to put down on tape some of his

Nick Drake, Sophia and an obscured David Ward (Photo: Alex Henderson)

repertoire, that we have a record of Nick's emerging skill on the guitar, as well as the first examples of his own original songs. The playing already seems polished, though at one point Nick apologises for 'the poor quality of this performance, which is due to the fact that I am too damn sober'.

One evening, when he and the gathering were, presumably, not so 'damn sober', Nick met Ben Laycock – son of the distinguished ex-Governor of Malta (and World War Two hero) Major General Sir Robert Laycock.

Ben had just returned to England from India and, reunited with his girlfriend (now wife) Rosie, they decided to drive over to France and visit their friends Nick Lewin and Derek Fitzgerald in Aix-en-Provence. They arrived in Aix one evening and were taken by their friends to a gathering that included Nick Drake. As the night became more convivial, first their host started playing his guitar, followed by Ben himself. And finally the quiet young man in the corner was persuaded to play.

Ben's verdict? 'It was quite obvious from the outset that this chap was way outside our league: I had never heard anyone of my own generation play with such skill. It was quite astonishing.'

However, they were not to meet again for some months. Ben and Rosie took off the next morning, and Nick, before he returned to England, was to have his Moroccan adventure, and would play in the nightclubs of St Tropez and Paris. Writing to his grandmother from Paris in July of that year, Nick says he has a job playing his guitar in a nightclub, but that it was 'not altogether satisfactory' and that he would be returning to England 'quite soon'. Which he did, eventually pitching up in London – much to the delight, apparently, of his Old Etonian friends from Aix, who were keen to introduce him to their Chelsea set.

Ben Laycock in particular took Nick under his wing, and soon Nick was hanging out with the scions of some of the most prominent families in Britain: the Astors, the Ormsby-Gores and, perhaps most notably for Nick, David Ward (now Earl of Dudley), who was himself a guitar player of note, and a songwriter who had had his work picked up and recorded by the blues singer Alexis Korner. Here was someone who could exchange musical ideas with Nick on an equal footing.

Then there was Ben's great friend Alex Henderson, a budding young photographer – extrovert and easy-going – and his beautiful girlfriend Sophia, who seems to have wrapped herself around Nick's heart, though no one heard him say as much. Certainly this did not prevent him and Alex having a light-hearted friendship that lives on in the latter's memory:

Sophia and Ben Laycock on the King's Road, London   to: Alex Henderson)

'What people all seem to forget in the midst of all this stuff, is that Nick was just a really nice guy. We had a lot of laughs. He used to stay with me and Sophia in London . . . And he came with us to Scotland – my mother had a tiny cottage on the Island of Mull, overlooking the Western Isles. It was a stunning place. A whole group of us used to go there – David Ward and his girlfriend, Ben Laycock and Rose, myself and Sophia – and Nick. Because it was so small, Nick had to sleep in this tiny room called 'the Captain's bed' – all it contained was a fold-up bed, and Nick had to fold his enormously tall frame into it. But he always managed it . . . We used to play the guitar and sing . . . and smoke – and laugh a lot. Those were really good days . . . we were all having a lot of fun – Nick wasn't at all withdrawn – quiet, maybe, but not unusually so.'

Once again, Nick was the 'Oddefellowe' – the outsider who was made welcome.

'I was quite possessive of Nick,' recalls Ben Laycock, 'because I felt I had discovered him – this marvellous creature, so talented, but so reticent about it.' At the time Nick was staying temporarily with his sister Gabrielle in Battersea, where Ben would visit him. 'Once I went round to show him my new motorbike. He pronounced it "a fine machine", and accepted my invitation to go for a ride. But he was hopeless at riding pillion. I mean, hopeless! For a start he had these long long legs – and then he would always forget to lean in the right direction round a corner. He was too busy looking at something else – or looking at the sky . . . We laughed a great deal . . .'

On another occasion, he remembers Nick playing a clutch of songs that he didn't recognize. 'Where do they come from?' asked Ben, and Nick said they were his own – but nothing much, just strumming. 'No they're not,' said Ben – and declared that he would manage Nick and introduce him to a wider public. An impulsive offer – and who knows how Nick viewed it? But surely such faith would have helped to steady his ever-vacillating ego.

And faith in his talent was what this whole group of friends showed Nick. It was a faith worth having, for the group was by no means musically illiterate. On the contrary, the acoustic canons of the likes of Josh White, Woody Guthrie, Pete Seeger, Bert Jansch and Davey Graham were already staples of their musical diet – and they had been avidly following Bob Dylan from his first album onwards. Tough acts for the unpublished, untested Nick Drake to follow. Nevertheless, despite his reserve, Nick would frequently give them the first airings of newly fledged works.

Julian Lloyd recalls evenings at his flat in Fulham. 'I remember Nick singing, say, a Dylan song and then turning to one of his own compositions. His whole stance changed; leaning over his guitar, he would hold it tighter to himself, he would fold his head close to his instrument, his eyes no longer looking out into the room – he was now "apart".' At one such occasion, David Ward remembers Nick playing 'Things Behind The Sun' to them all, saying that he hadn't played it to anyone before, and that it was still unfinished. If this was so, then it was an act of great trust on Nick's part – a trust that was not misplaced.

David Ward and Sarah at Parson's Sally (Photo: Alex Henderson)

For Nick was just accepted – and cherished. Although most of the group were already in couples – Ben and Rosie, David and girlfriend (later wife) Sarah, Julian Lloyd and Victoria Ormsby-Gore, Alex and Sophia – no one regarded Nick as an intruder: no one felt he was in the way. Even at the concert on the Isle of Wight, when Nick was crammed into a caravan with David and Sarah, they simply felt, said David, that it was a privilege to have him there. For the girls adored him as much as the men did; and although sex was pulsating through the air everyone breathed in those heady days of the Sixties, with Nick it just didn't seem to be an issue: 'I had too much respect for him as a musician to indulge in blokes' talk,' says David Ward. 'Nick was just gorgeous,' Rosie Laycock remembers, 'and sort of ethereal, and so beautiful – sex was somehow irrelevant.'

So if Nick had any sexual demons, he didn't have to confront them with these friends. And Sophia? She seems to have become one of Nick's romantic, unattainable goddesses: another Princess of the Sands.

Nick's written references to this group are sparse – though he spoke of them frequently. During his first disappointing days at Cambridge, some of them came over from nearby Hatley Park, seat of the Astors, and were appalled at the bleak functionality of his lodgings. They scooped him up and took him back to join the weekend party. As Nick wrote to his parents: 'On Saturday Stella Astor and a couple of friends came over from Hatley and took me back for the night. Needless to say it was a very comfortable little stay indeed.'

And Nick continued to see these friends throughout his time at Cambridge, mostly during visits to London, but also on various jaunts – to Mull; to Wales with Julian Lloyd, one of the few photographers apart from Keith Morris who managed to capture Nick on camera extensively; and, perhaps most notably of all, to the legendary Isle of Wight Festival in 1969, where Bob Dylan inspired a crowd of over 150,000 and the air was pungent with hope and love.

The trip to the Isle of Wight was organised by Alex Henderson's mother: in an act of extraordinary generosity and empathy, she hired three caravans, and brought a brace of grouse down with her from her family's Scottish estate, which, while her young son and his friends listened to the concert, she somehow managed to roast. Thus, when they all returned from the concert, body as well as spirit could be nourished – nourished so that late into the night they could play and sing their own songs round the campfire. No doubt this was a scene that was repeated right across the site of the concert. And in the embers of those fires, a phoenix of faith in the future rose. Certainly Nick, for one, came home elated, and declared that now, finally, the world would change, and peace would prevail. It was one of the few political statements he ever made.

It was inevitable that disillusion should set in. As the Sixties turned into the Seventies, life took on a harder edge. The carefree group of friends grew up and, to some degree, grew away from Nick – and he from them, as he became more involved with the grim reality of trying

Ben Laycock on guitar
(Photo: Alex Henderson)

to be a professional musician. Their meetings became sporadic and then all but petered out.

Nevertheless, in the despair of his final years, in the depths of his depression, Nick would visit them individually, these now grown-up golden ones: all recount the same sad tale of Nick arriving unannounced on their doorsteps, of being unable to talk or sit, let alone explain his plight. Alex remembers him turning up looking 'shell-shocked – that's the best way of describing it'; Ben and Rosie, now coping with parenthood, spent an awkward evening with him in their home, unable to get a word out of him. Only when Rosie went to bed did Nick, on the point of leaving, confide to Ben that he was 'being pursued by a black dog'.

With David Ward, himself disillusioned with the West and on the point of returning to India to the ashram of his teacher, Nick was eventually able to give voice to some of his desolation. But still, it seems, he sought but did not find that elusive essence he was trying to recapture.

So what was it he was seeking to recapture? Why was this group of privileged young people important to him, as they so patently were? From the evidence that exists, it could be inferred that, as a group, they were all that Nick disdained. His references to the 'nauseous' group of 'rich young Londoners' who were 'constantly bored stiff' at Aix, and the fact that none of his significant friends from either Cambridge or the music world came from the upper echelons of British society, would seem to point to a young man shaking off the shackles of his youth and background. Yet it is quite obvious that the friends who comprised what Joe Boyd called 'The Jeunesse Dorée' gave sustenance and joy to Nick's life at a crucial time of creativity.

The term 'Jeunesse Dorée' – gilded youth – is often used disparagingly about the idle and wealthy young. Yet it is interesting to note that the term was first coined in France to describe a young bourgeoisie in rebellion against *La Terreur* – the French Revolution in all its horror.

Nick's young aristocratic friends were themselves in rebellion. None of them followed the traditions of their family or class. None were idle or, in fact, particularly rich. The cars they drove were old bangers, and while life might have been carefree, all had to earn their livings, even if somewhat haphazardly. But they had joined the

Alex Henderson
(Photo supplied by Alex)

throng of those who were disillusioned with values that had led to two cataclysmic wars within fifty years. It had taken a decade and a half for the world to lick its wounds and recuperate from the last one. But by the late Sixties an exhilarating revolution of love and peace was tangible: values were being tossed in the air, and you smoked a joint while waiting to see which way up they would land.

And at the heart of this benign insurrection? It was surely music. Music was the unifying factor – and the music makers were the revered magicians.

As for Nick, he was no revolutionary; no fiery advocate of any political stance. And it took sensitivity and gentleness to understand his very personal, yet detached message. Few did, in those early days. Few, in the precipitate rush of new ideas, slogans and the tearing down of ancient barriers, had time to appreciate one whose motto was rather, to quote Shakespeare, 'I'll be a candle-holder, and look on'.

But his friends, the young golden ones, had time: time and generosity and musical perspicacity – as well as a necessary light-heartedness. Their particular qualities – individually and as a group – and their unreserved appreciation of Nick, must have had a vital impact on his emerging gift. No matter that the time span of their camaraderie was short. In its intensity, it burned as brightly as magnesium, and left as indelible an imprint on the retina of experience. For them, he was not so much the 'Oddefellowe' as the Orpheus. For him, they were, at one point in his life, a collective Muse.

Bliss was it in that dawn to be alive,
But to be young was very heaven . . .

Wordsworth's words, written about the heady days of optimism that preceded the French Revolution, could have equally applied to the period of Flower Power during the late 1960s. That both were false dawns is perhaps less important than the nuggets of lasting worth that emerged from them. In the ashes of all the ensuing tragedies – including Nick's personal tragedy, tiny though it was by comparison – small slivers of silver can be picked out, which remain to comfort us. Maybe Nick Drake's songs can be counted among them. And, if so, then we should not forget the contribution made to them by the Jeunesse Dorée.

By all accounts Nick was a furiously competitive croquet player (Photo: Ben Laycock)

Nick sits beside a much updated ruin (Photo: Ben Laycock)

The beginnings of an informal photo session by Julian Lloyd in Harlech

RELEASED BY THE PRESS DEPARTMENT

ISLAND

Dear Mr. & Mrs. Drake

Many thanks for your letter about Nick's photographs. The pictures were taken by Julian Lloyd, about whom I know nothing. Some of the photographs were taken on the beach at Harlech in North Wales during the winter of 1967/8 while others were taken the following summer at Lloyd's parents' house in the country (exactly where I don't know).

The last known address for Julian Lloyd (it was found with the pictures) was The Globe (or it could be The Glebe), Leixlip, Co. Kildare, Ireland.

I hope this is of some use to you.

Yours sincerely

Rob Partridge

The reply from the late Rob Partridge (head of press at Island Records) to Rodney Drake when Rodney decided to search for the Harlech photos after Nick's death

Further Thoughts On Nick

by David, Earl of Dudley

Attempting to construe the personality traits of a late friend, or a family member, in fine detail – so as to portray and truthfully assess their innermost motivation – is exceptionally difficult.

The first pitfall that presents itself is the risk of conflating bona fide details of occasional meetings and aspects of character, with received assumptions based on fragments of recovered memory which might have been suggested by others within their own written or recorded assessments. These chimerical mistakes can filter down into the record of the individual and become part of the established version of the recollected image. All that one can possibly hope to extract, from even the most thorough piece of biographical research, on a person as highly reclusive in their thoughts as Nick Drake, will be an impressionistic pastiche, containing certain glittering pointers of factual experience to light the path forward.

Nick was formidably invested with a highly tuned ear, a prolific melodic creative imagination, a well-practised precision of instrumentation, a curiosity to explore original and potential facets of the chosen tool of his craft, and a pleasant, intrinsic, unprepossessing vocal delivery, with those understated, ethereal qualities that begged for undivided attention from the listener.

Artistically, he was something of a lone wolf. This was due to, and added to, his distinction as a performer. His music perfectly reflects his careful social contact – since it displays a piercing, discriminatory eye; but it is an eye with strong reservations about thrusting his cannily opinionated conclusions upon the listener. It wasn't in his nature to put himself about much.

Nick was a highly educated man in literary terms, and had an enlightened and excellent taste in harmony and counterpoint, for music-arrangement purposes. The background of music in his family, which he had enjoyed as a child, clearly had much to do with the laying down of strong foundations, which permitted his evolving creations to happen, fearlessly. It is very clear that his creative process was natural, unhesitating and uncomplicated.

Many of his lyrics are presented as a deliberately random selection – using the scansion or rhyme pattern of the opening lyrics as scaffolding. Once armed with a favourite line, or notion, he occasionally allows the development of the work to run freely towards clearly unmediated destinations. This breathes life into his unknowable, yet somehow familiar, and particular, disposition. Mysteries which evolve from an original, but recognisable, viewpoint become mysterious even to the artist himself – and yet, without really knowing why, we are no strangers to them. Similar if not identical evolutionary processes occur within the world of nature. Nick's work was dressed in multi-layered adornments emanating from the rural surroundings of his youth, and his unbiased, appreciative, early concern with all things bright and beautiful.

I first knew him at a period when his most telling musical influences were Bert Jansch and John Renbourn. The first original song I heard him play – in a private residence in the company of mutual friends – was 'Mayfair'. The admiration in us, as his audience, arose from Nick's execution of it, rather than any curiosity as to the possible sources of his inspiration. But the immaculate precision, and the dynamics of his performance, swiftly convinced us that a growing public recognition was inevitable.

At this point, almost forty years after his untimely death, it is good to remind ourselves that the only real, surefire, unarguable remaining evidence – the one and only key which we can use in our attempts to unlock the Nick Drake 'code' – is to be found almost exclusively within his musical legacy. There is no adult footage, made at performances or anywhere else; no recorded interview; no taped 'snippets' of choice 'live' phrases from any recital or live performance. Beyond his timeless songs, we are left with just a few albums' worth of still photographs and the inexorably fading memories of those who knew him.

This unusual set of conditions is another clue to the measure of the man. I feel that he wouldn't have wanted it any other way. Nick's avowed method of communication was via his music, as applied to the social context of his everyday existence, both in terms of those around him and to people he had never met. Like most performers, he maintained a subconscious intent to arm and project his personality via the course of his professional experience – to obviate any misunderstanding of his true nature. It provided him, in theory at least, with a means of self-protection. It saved him from having to justify himself; and allowed him to keep his quiet counsel, with pride intact. His portfolio of creations was his CV: his passport to universal belonging. Many professional entertainers have these traits, but in Nick's case they were accentuated. His background of disciplined good manners balanced out the extrovert contortions then expected of stage artists. His performances – both public and private – had so much more to reveal of him than he was willing to disclose without them. He was capable of transmitting his ideas, feelings and personal expressions on a higher plane than might be possible for the average individual. It was his privilege to become modestly averse to over-exhibiting them. Might the limited nature of Nick's enduring legacy therefore be facetiously interpreted as his gentle private joke at the expense of those he left behind?

The joke would broaden if viewed in the context of those ambiguities that arise from the variations in his personal enigma. His successors were provided with no more than a set of riddles to decipher – in their attempts to discern where, how and why his beacon was lit. That situation is laced with archetypal British irony. It allows for innumerable errors to surface, such as the assertion, so regularly repeated by the morbidly fascinated, that Nick intentionally prophesied his own early demise in the line from 'Fruit Tree': 'It can never flourish / 'til its stock is in the ground'. Should we further deduce, therefore, that when he wrote, in ''Cello Song', 'while the earth / Sinks to its grave', that he is, doubtless, predicting Armageddon? Or that the line he sang, in 'From The Morning', 'And now we rise from the ground', foresees his own future semi-messianic status: providing him, and others, with the ability to resurrect? Anyone suggesting and maintaining such notions must know absolutely nothing of the craft of songwriting.

Before long, reports began to arrive via mutual friends that Nick was beginning to lose faith in the validity of public performance. Discontinuing public performances, in those days, spelled curtains for an artistic career – unless, like The Beatles, your public recognition had become so great that you no longer had need of gigs.

Nick was totally unaware of the extent to which his reputation had spread internationally. I know for a fact that by the time of his death, he had already become the principal pop-music icon among the young residents of, for example, an out-of-the-way, spliff-and-surf town on North Island, New Zealand. Doubtless this was the case in numerous other such locations under the Anglo-Saxon umbrella.

A relative of mine who met Nick a number of times sent me this succinct verdict recently on her opinion concerning the symptoms of his withdrawn later state:

'N.D. was a victim to cannabis smoking at a young age which is now known to block neural pathways, [and] make[s] you [feel] paranoid & isolated . . .' This is doubtless an over-simplification of the facts, but it remains a useful appraisal.

My own experience of Nick's deterioration into silent paranoia was not a gradual one. There must have been a large gap, at some point, between our meetings – perhaps as much as two years. The difference in his behaviour between the two occasions was notable and pronounced. I had heard reports from mutual friends of the changes in him. But I was very surprised when I experienced it for myself. For he came to see me in my new house, and simply sat there, and all my attempts to engage him in conversation were met with monosyllabic replies and avoidance of eye-contact. From then on, whenever he came by, he would stay for half an hour or so, saying nothing, then rise uncomfortably and leave. He would absolutely not be drawn into discussing what was troubling him.

I always thought Nick was too intelligent and aware to indulge in the excessive use of any drug but marijuana. I can do no more than surmise that heavy and regular smoking of pot exacerbated the introverted, reserved complexites of his personality, and aggravated the condition of overwhelming anxiety he was suffering from, over the lack of progress in his career.

On the last day I spent in Nick's company, he became more conversational as the hours went by. Questions regarding his grievances and the causes of his malaise were answered briefly but frankly – and yet with smiling irony. He definitely spoke of two major concerns: firstly, at the feeling of to some extent having let down his family, by his career not achieving greater recognition and financial success. There was no launching into any great detail, but I think Nick was desperately keen to repay his parents for the gifts supplied to him through his education.

The nature of Nick's complaints against Joe Boyd, on the other hand, were not musical: they were exclusively about Boyd's – and Island Records' – promotional support.

Despite all these issues, I saw no reasons on that last occasion to believe that there were any major causes for concern. Nick was his own man, in my rose-tinted opinion, and would eventually triumph. Of course, I wasn't wrong in this. I was simply unaware of just how discouraged Nick was by the fact that progress seemed so unbearably slow. I knew – as we all did – that he had alternating groups of friends. We assumed that he was obtaining from other people the moral support he didn't get sufficiently from us alone. This included female companionship – which I suppose we imagined him as being simply too discreet to mention.

Was Nick actively pursuing some form of spiritual quest? By the time the Seventies began, I believe the answer to this question, as it applied to many of our generation, might have been 'yes'. The changes in attitude that took place in the previous decade, and the widening of horizons and increasing immediacy in the field of international communications, brought more diverse global references into the fields of spiritual philosophy and metaphysics. So we were bombarded by novel ideas that took root in the idealistic spirit of our youth.

Nick was far too intellectually secure to be bowled over by a one-off sudden sermon. I think he would have needed to apply himself to an in-depth study of any teaching before approaching a serious level of conviction about its merits or demerits. In my opinion, such a radical proposition hadn't as yet begun to figure largely in his agenda. His trip to my spiritual gathering in Cambridge occurred not because of the purpose of the meeting or its venue, but merely for the agreeable consequence of our mutual companionship. The seeds of Nick's own, personal form of musical Gospel had already spread far into the multitude, to assist and succour needy souls.

The tragedy was that he had been left so unaware of it.

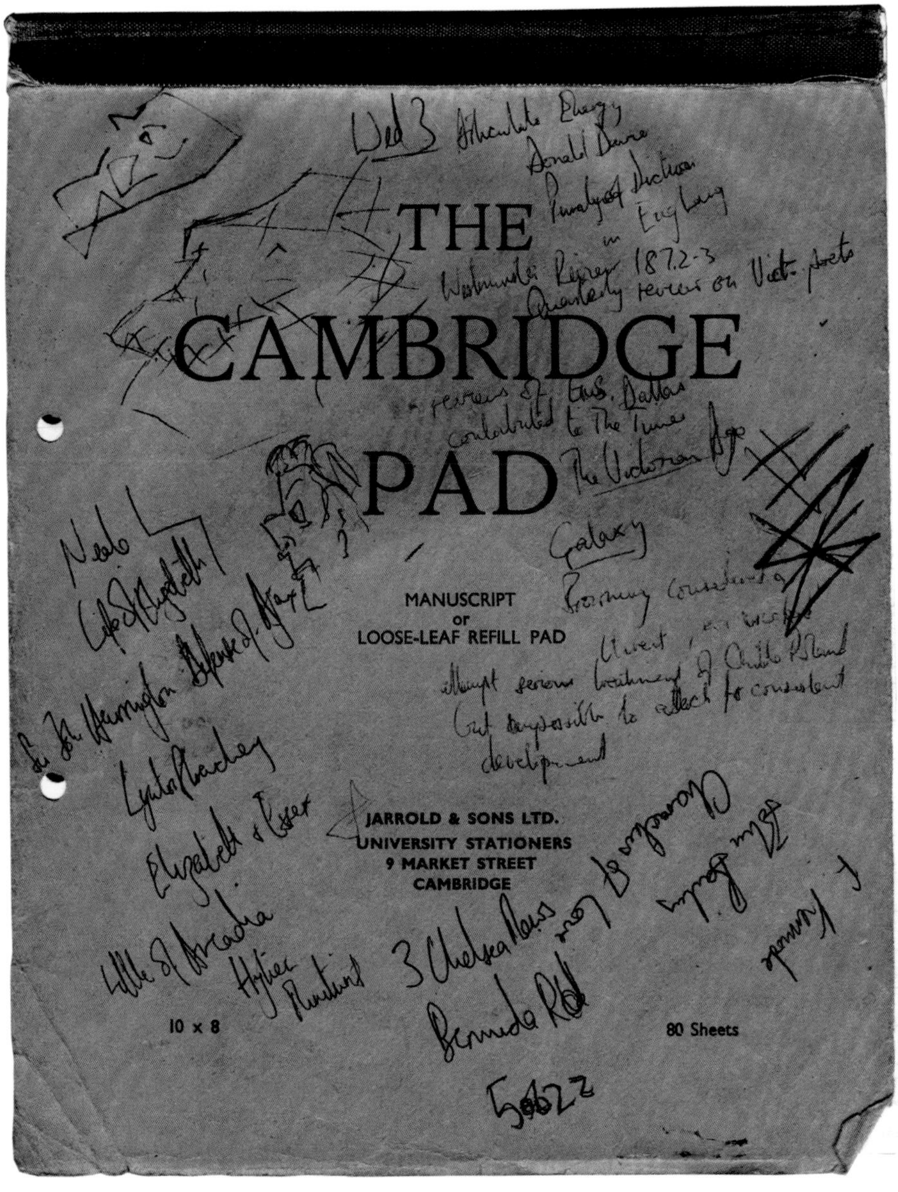
THE
CAMBRIDGE
PAD
MANUSCRIPT
or
LOOSE-LEAF REFILL PAD
JARROLD & SONS LTD.
UNIVERSITY STATIONERS
9 MARKET STREET
CAMBRIDGE
10 x 8
80 Sheets

The Flower III

Family letters

Annotated by Gabrielle Drake

RODNEY TO NICK:
10 OCTOBER 1967
Wolseley Engineering Ltd., Birmingham
Dear Nick,

Just a line to tell you that 'Dezzy' [Nick's friend, Desirée Burlison Rush] rang up last night to get your address in Cambridge (which I gave her). She said she had taken your tape round to Chris Blackwell (have I got the name right?) and that she was present when it was played and that they were 'delighted' with it. I imagine that she will be writing to tell you about this. So that all sounds very promising and I wonder what the next step will be? As you may imagine, Mum and I celebrated with an extra drink!

I'm afraid the news about your recorder is not so good. The amplifier and the loudspeaker have gone. You really did a job on it and I can't imagine how you can have been such an ass!

A new deck has been sent for and there is some hope that Philips may agree to do the job for half price as a special concession – but I fear it will be another week at least.

A miserable day here today – have you a raincoat of any sort??

Hope the general outlook is improving.

Congratulations on the tape, anyway!

love Dad

MONDAY, 17 OCTOBER 1967
Fitzwilliam College, Cambridge
Dear Mum and Dad,

Thank you very much for your letters. I hope all continues to go well with you. I really do feel stupid about the tape recorder, & thank you very much for getting it done cheaply. I'll send you a cheque as soon as you know the exact price.

There doesn't really seem to be much news from this end. Life has got better and will probably continue to do so, but I don't see that it's going to be the fantastic existence that people like to make out. From what I've seen of the social life so far, it's just great, if you happen to like talking about games and getting drunk with the chaps every night. However, I think, & hope, that my views on this particular aspect will change fairly soon. I have in fact met one or two quite nice people, mostly in Trinity. I discovered one of the people I went to Morocco with, who is at Trinity, and met various people through him. I've also met one or two people in St Catharine's, through Colin Tillie. As yet I've met virtually no one in Fitzwilliam, and from what I see around me I'm not sure that I terribly want to. Terrible attitude, of course, but I don't seem to be cut out to be one of God's gifts to the community life. The main trouble with Fitzwilliam is that it's so far out. It's easier now that I have a bike, but it's still rather a long way from the centre of things.

. . . The various intentions I had on coming up here don't seem to have come to much as yet! There is a Classical Guitar Society, but it is on rather an unsatisfactory system. As far as Karate is concerned, it doesn't happen here at all, but it seems they may be starting a club quite soon. Apart from that, I think I may join the Asian Music Society . . .

. . . My guitar is still out of action at the moment, since the shop has had to send up to the factory for a new part. This of course does not greatly help my state of mind. While it's been away I've been writing quite a few words, but am in the deeply frustrating position of not being able to set them to music!

My Chinese friend Calvin is up here for a couple of days, doing a bit of lecturing, and it is naturally a relief to find someone so interesting and unusual for a change . . .

12 November 1967
Fitzwilliam House, Cambridge
Dear Mum and Dad,

. . . It was very nice to get your letters. I'm glad you've finally seen 'Bonnie & Clyde'. A rather interesting theory of yours on it, Dad, and one that I must confess hadn't occurred to me. I would certainly enjoy being a psychologist, by the way, since it always interests me to try and understand other people. I only wish I could understand myself! . . .

. . . My views on Cambridge seem to undulate continually from good to bad, although I'm still not particularly knocked out by the people I meet. However, I think most people going up to university suffer from misconceptions about the types they will meet there. Thinking they are going to find a place brimming over with interesting and enlightened people, it doesn't take them long to discover that the average student is in fact extraordinarily dull. So one just has to be patient and hope that one will eventually discover some of the above average. There does at the moment seem to be a hope of better things to come.

I went to an extremely interesting meeting of the Asian Music Circle the other night. It consisted of a lecture given by an Indian dancer about the themes and rhythms involved in Indian dancing, as well as the philosophy behind it. There were also practical demonstrations given by him and his rather beautiful wife. It was all fascinating, but so complicated that the mind boggled, and it made one aware of how far ahead of us the Indians are in certain artistic fields.

My guitar is now back in action. I eventually went up to London for an afternoon and bought a new part, as well as a few decorations for my room. I managed to retrieve my Indian pictures from the flat, which are now hanging in state above my desk. I haven't yet played my guitar in public, since I haven't found a suitable place.

Must stop now, since this is my last bit of writing paper.

Love to Gay and Naw – hope the BBC is going well.
Much love Nick

These two letters from Nick – and possibly others – apparently prompted this response from his mother!

MOLLY to NICK:
29 November 1967
Far Leys
Darling Nick,

I was rather grief-stricken to hear your condemnation of all things pertaining to Fitzwilliam. It seems your disappointment and disillusion are complete – I can't help wondering if the disappointment is one-sided – your entry into Fitzwilliam was, we know, governed to a <u>small</u> extent by Den's good report of you – by his telling them that they were getting in you not only a fine athlete but also one who was a good mixer and popular with his colleagues. And what have they got? A toffee-nosed recluse? It could appear that way . . .

Life at Cambridge took a turn for the better for Nick the following term, when he started to meet more kindred souls – in particular, his friend and soon-to-be orchestrator, Robert Kirby, and also a fellow singer-songwriter, Paul Wheeler. Both these two were at Gonville and Caius College, and Nick started to spend more time in that ancient college than he did in his own. He was invited to be the 'Oddefellowe' – the one outsider – in a club of ancient origin – The Loungers – revived by one of the scholars of the college, Mike Schutzer Weissmann, which met regularly to do nothing much more than play albums from Mike's eclectic collection of music. Nick had by now moved to more congenial lodgings in the centre of Cambridge itself.

12 February 1968
Dear Mum and Dad,

It seems quite a while since I last got in touch with you, for which I'm very sorry, but life has been quite full recently. I was very glad to get your letters and to hear your news . . . I myself had rather a pleasant weekend. On Saturday Stella Astor and a couple of friends came over from Hatley and took me back for the night. Needless to say it was a very comfortable little stay indeed.

On Sunday, Calvin had asked me up to meet Françoise Hardy, who was filming an International Cabaret, which I duly did. She was going to have supper with us at Rupert's after the show, but unfortunately had to go to something with her agent instead, so I did little more than say hello. I've never really thought much of her before, but seen

Hatley House, 1967: Nick rides with the Astors

close to in the flesh, I must admit she's quite something. The show itself was quite an experience too. If, when watching the show, you've ever imagined the audience indulging in the high luxuries of a top nightclub, you can forget it! One is presented with what looks very much like champagne, but which as far as taste is concerned, might just as well be an advertisement for Squeezy! Look out for the programme, for we got in rather late and had to sit quite near the edge of the stage. You might recognise me by my hands, behind which I hid for most of the programme, for fear of being spotted by a passing camera.

Things are slowly going ahead with my music. My musical friend, a guy named Robert Kirby, is working quite hard on arrangements for some of my songs, and seems to be pretty competent. He's a rather splendid fellow, and looks rather like Haydn or Mozart or someone, being rather short and stocky, with long wavy hair and rimless spectacles. However, he's quite hip to my sort of music, being quite a proficient folksinger himself. He's done a rather beautiful string quartet arrangement for 'Day Is Done', and is now working on 'Time Of No Reply'. Naturally, it's a rather lengthy process, and I don't know whether he'll be able to get enough done by Feb 23rd, the date of the concert in which our music is scheduled to be performed. Incidentally, he's made it clear to me that I'm well out of studying music, since it's obviously an extremely difficult as well as rather tedious course.

It may surprise you to hear that during the last few weeks I've been extraordinarily happy with life, and I haven't a clue why! It seems that Cambridge can in fact do rather nice things to one if one lets it. And I'm not sure that I did let it before. I think I've thrown off one or two rather useless and restrictive complexes that I picked up before coming here. This seems to be becoming rather self-indulgent and boring, so I'll stop.

By the way, think of me next Saturday, the day of my initiation for transcendental meditation. I went to a talk on it last week, and it seems to be a thing that is impossible to explain. So the only way to discover what it's all about is to do it oneself. I don't know what happens at the initiation, but I have to take along some fruit, some flowers, and a clean white handkerchief, which is rather a nice idea.

The work isn't too bad at the moment. I'm doing sort of 17th, 18th century poets, people like Swift, Pope, Blake, etc., who have quite a lot to offer in their way. But they seem to be very difficult to write about.

Must stop now and go to bed. I do hope all goes well at home. Must try and make it back sometime for a weekend, though the next 2 seem rather busy.

Love to Naw,

Much love, Nick.

Then came the famous concert at the Roundhouse, and Nick's subsequent meeting with the already legendary Joe Boyd. Joe became interested in working with Nick on an album of Nick's songs, and Nick found himself increasingly irked by university life:

Nick at Hatley, home to the Astor family
(Photos: Victoria Waymouth)

The Monkey Island Hotel, Bray, a favourite retreat of the Drakes

23 JANUARY 1969
56 Carlyle Road, Cambridge
Dear Mum and Dad,

Here at last I'm fulfilling my promise to write you a letter – sorry it's such a long time since the last one! . . .

Cambridge has been quite pleasant this term, but here I am, becoming increasingly sure that I want to leave soon, in spite of the well-meaning advice that I receive from every direction.

I'm afraid that everything I say in this respect is likely to have a distinct air of ungratefulness about it, but I hope you realise that I am in fact very grateful for everything you've done, and I'm sure we'll achieve more if I tell you just how I feel. I won't say more than necessary, since I'm sure that our various conversations have made clear my general feelings. To use your word, Dad, my life at the moment is indeed a pretty 'passive' one, and I don't really see much likelihood of it being anything else until I leave Cambridge. To be 'active' here in anything other than purely academic pursuits seems to involve a form of irresponsibility and amateurism which is worse than useless to me at the moment. I am obviously getting onto the subject of my music here, and this may appear as a very arrogant statement, since as far as performing is concerned, I myself am certainly no more than amateur. However, with regard to my songwriting, I can only progress from the stage that I have reached so far by developing a purely professional approach. It is hard to do this with things as they are at the moment, and since the only professional people involved with a university are apparently the academics, it seems unlikely that my approach will find much sympathy or outlet at Cambridge. I know for a certainty that I must make this progression with my music in order to achieve any sense of fulfilment in my present life. You also said, Dad, and also quite rightly, that I seemed to be leading a rather escapist form of existence. This results from a sort of restlessness and dissatisfaction which I think anyone in my situation would encounter.

This all seems to be getting very intense and serious-minded, but I hope you can perhaps appreciate that the idea of having my music as a 'vacation hobby' for another year and a half is not a particularly happy one. It seems that Cambridge can really only delay me from doing what at the moment I most need to do. There are other aspects, but I have already produced quite enough boring monologue for one letter. It's just that, all things considered, I would really like to leave Cambridge quite soon . . .

. . . I'm getting Robert Kirby to do me a couple of arrangements for me . . .

Will probably be ringing you sometime, and will be interested to hear how you take my rather feeble attempt to explain rationally what is perhaps a rather irrational problem!

Much love,
Nick

To which Rodney replied:

RODNEY TO NICK:
LENT TERM [1969]
Dear Nick,

I have taken rather a long time to answer your letter which you posted last Monday because I wanted time to reflect upon it and to talk it over with Mum.

Obviously it is for me to try to give you the best advice I can and for it to be based upon the clearest understanding of your problem that I can manage. I *can* understand your impatience to get on with the career of a professional musician which you have decided upon and I can also understand that in the light of your overwhelming interest in this, other activities appear either irrelevant or frivolous or both. So what are we waiting for – why not leave at once? Obviously it is a step which we have to consider

carefully because it is an irrevocable one – there is no going back.

There are two aspects which we have to think about, I think – firstly – and obviously uppermost in your mind – are you more or less likely to succeed at your chosen career if you leave now? Secondly, what advantage unconnected with your career may you be throwing away if you leave now?

On the first aspect – it must be accepted, you will agree, that a man is more likely to succeed in any walk of life if he has developed his intellectual powers as fully as possible and also his ability to apply them. We are slow developers in our family and you I believe are no exception to this. I would go so far as to say that you will surprise yourself in the next two years by the changes and development that will occur in your personality, your understanding and your outlook. In addition to this, any career involving self-employment demands a high degree of self-discipline, and a will to overcome one's weaknesses, and making the effort required to tackle problems which do not come easily. I think you have a long way to go here. You believe that the problem of turning yourself from an amateur into a professional can be solved merely by transferring yourself from Cambridge to somewhere where you are surrounded by, and under the influence of, professionals in your chosen field. From what you say I take it that you must believe that it was the prospect of returning to Cambridge for 8-week periods during the year that prevented you, in the long summer vac, from getting into the swim, so to speak, and of starting to acquire the professionalism which you are rightly seeking.

But I doubt this very much and I would regard as far more likely reasons your reticence – which you must overcome – your difficulty in communicating – which you must overcome – your reluctance to plunge in and have a go, which you conceal from yourself by self-persuasion that more *solo* practising and *solo* listening are required before the move is made. Don't shrug these views off, rather reflect in them. (To thine own self be true, make that your motto all the time.)

If I am right in what I say, and the real trouble is that you have not yet overcome your weaknesses (and God knows we all have them), then you may well find that you have thrown over Cambridge simply to continue indefinitely on the outskirts of what you are looking for.

At Cambridge you have a chance to fight your weaknesses and overcome them (and fight like hell you MUST) to discipline yourself from inside, and take a more active interest in your fellows (another weakness of yours – I am being very blunt, aren't I) and generally to prepare and develop yourself to make a real success of what you want to do. And in the meantime your creative powers will be developing, not stagnating, do please believe me. It is not as though you have been shoved into an office or a factory where a routine existence and a preoccupation with materialistic problems might mould you into something different from what your true inclinations want to make of you . . .

On the second aspect – what advantages unconnected with your career may you be throwing away – there is not a great deal to say except that it is a rounded personality which is most likely to lead its owner on a happy and full road though life. To specialise too early and to have interest in only one activity makes Jack a very dull boy . . .

One and a half years may seem a long time to you. Allow me to assure you it is not – but it is a terribly important time in the *development* of you as a person into something that you are going to *start to* be at about the age of 23. To be able to spare a little time when one is young to . . . hear great argument not only adds enormously to one's intellectual strength but opens up to one vistas which perhaps otherwise might not have been considered.

The winning of a degree may seem to bear little significance to you, and the argument that it is a safety net, if you come a cropper with your music, will doubtless evoke the response that a safety net is just what you don't want. I would say to you however that the self-discipline which it involves apart from anything else at all is a priceless asset in whatever you do want to tackle during the rest of your life.

So there we are, Nick – there's my views. I urge you to resolve to see Cambridge through and make a success of it . . . I have heard so many people say that it wasn't until their last year of University that the penny dropped and they realised what it was all in aid of . . .

Maybe as a result of his father's letter, Nick did stay on at Cambridge for a further nine months. But in October 1969, he came to the conclusion that he had to leave University. This was perhaps more understandable, since in the interim (on 3 July that year) *Five Leaves Left* had been released. Nevertheless, it appears Nick went to see his tutor, Dr Kelly, to ask if he could have a year's sabbatical from Cambridge, rather than leaving forever. However, this dispensation was not granted, and Nick had to make an irrevocable decision. He communicated this to his parents by telephone, which led to one final attempt by Rodney to make him change his mind:

RODNEY TO NICK:
THURSDAY MORNING: OCTOBER 1969
Dear Nick,

Thanks for ringing last night. Of course we were both terribly disappointed to hear of the decision you have reached, but we have said all there is to say on our side and no doubt you have weighed up all the pros and cons very carefully.

I thought I had better have a word on the telephone with Kelly this morning as I thought he might think it rather strange that I had not said anything to him at all (he would be thinking me, perhaps, a callous father!) and also I thought I ought to thank him for listening so sympathetically and so on.

So I did that and he told me that he was very sorry indeed that you had decided to go, having got so far and being only within *nine months* of your BA degree, which in this day and age is such a tremendously useful piece of equipment to have behind you *wherever* you may be going.

Well, Nick, it does seem an *awful* pity and I still feel that you may live to regret it bitterly and it is my duty to say that to you. To us of course it seems a tragedy now – to you perhaps it will do so one day. I think it probably could.

Have one more think about it. You can still withdraw your notice when you see Kelly (he said so). In your own interests I feel I must make this final appeal to you.

Whatever happens, we are so hoping you will be able to come to see us soon and the sooner the better. (And whatever you've decided we shan't have a go at you.) . . .

Very much love from us both,
Dad

But Nick did leave Cambridge – and, true to their word, Rodney and Molly never reproached him for this decision – never said 'I told you so' when, in later years, Nick seemed to regret it, offering instead support, and, indeed, advice, when asked for it:

RODNEY TO NICK:
6 MAY 1969
Wolseley Engineering Ltd., Birmingham
Dear Nick

I am returning herewith the Agreement Form of which I have taken copies & I will let you know in due course if I succeed in getting any professional advice on the terms. You may rest assured that any advice I do get will be confidential between me & whoever I approach & there will be no danger of Warlock Music Ltd getting to hear about it. If I do get anything worthwhile in the way of professional comment I will pass it on to you to make use of or not as you like.

Of course in all these sorts of things a good deal depends on the man you are dealing with, and however carefully an agreement is drawn, it won't work unless the two participants trust each other, whilst, conversely, however badly an agreement is drawn it will still work if there is trust. One has to make up one's mind about people oneself & one gets better at it as one goes on. You remember the old Arab saying 'If a man deceives me once, shame on him – if a man deceives me twice, shame on me.' . . . When you sign you will of course keep a copy for yourself for reference.

It seems to tie you up rather for three years but then I suppose that if they are going to invest a lot in launching your music, they must have some guarantee of you going on with them for a decent period.

Anyway I think it's all a very fine effort on your part . . .

By the way I am crediting your account with Lloyds Bank with £10 for the car repairs as our agreement was that I pay insurance, registration & major repairs not due to bad driving!

Lots of love from us all,
Dad

The Drakes' home recording suite
(Photo: Gavin Bush)

RODNEY TO NICK:
28 MAY 1970
Wolseley Engineering Ltd., Birmingham
Dear Nick,

Very many thanks for your letter – do hope the *UHER* [tape recorder] will help.

We have been enjoying your record so much on the stereo – the first time we have ever heard it properly. You really must hurry up and do another one – it was such a delightful work of art and it's high time there was another like it! You've got it in you, all right.

I have had a number of sessions with the equipment and have now mastered the transfer from one tape to another plus the addition of another instrument or voice. One can go on doing that indefinitely apparently. But I'm still mystified about the tuner . . .

That little switch in the middle of the mixer has the joint purpose of enabling you to balance the recording level of the two tracks and also indicates if the battery is charged.

The rectangular push button between the two reels (on top of the recording heads) changes the recording from two-track to four-track, but I haven't quite grasped the significance of this yet. The trouble is, the instructions are not very well translated from the German I think.

All well this end – see you soon

Love from all, D

As always, Nick and his father communicated well and easily on technical matters.

MAY 1970
112 Haverstock Hill
Dear Dad,

Thought I'd just write you a note to thank you for the Uher. It's certainly a very fine thing to suddenly have in one's possession, and I really am grateful. I know it's going to come in very useful in various ways, be it for recording new things to hand in to the publishing woman, or entertaining British Rail passengers with rural sounds etc. etc. Thank you very much indeed.

I hope your studies on your machine are progressing, and that when I next see you your recording skills will be up to professional standards! Will let you know about Saturday, and in any case will be seeing you soon. Hope you and Mum have got rid of your colds as I have mine. Love to all, and thank you again so much for the recorder.

Nick

Now Nick started work on his second album, *Bryter Layter* – and life became grimmer for him. Friends talk about him starting, at this time, to withdraw and become more remote. At the same time, the recording process was not without its frustrations and difficulties, in addition to which there were complications with the design for the album cover – the first one was entirely rejected, causing a delay in the release of the album. Contrary to the published date of November 1970, *Bryter Layter*'s release was in fact postponed until well into the New Year. This must have been frustrating and anguishing for Nick – something he obviously managed to communicate, even if indirectly, to his parents:

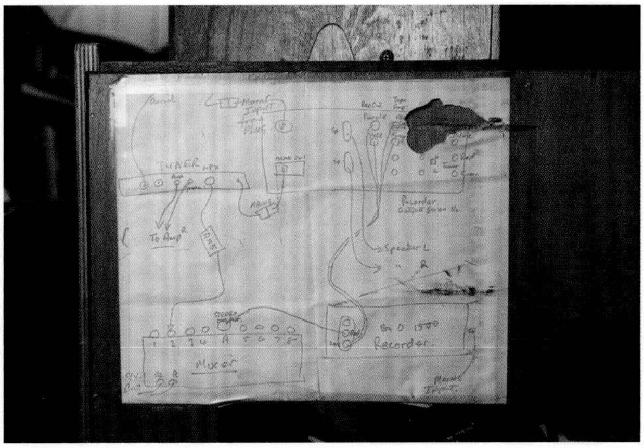

The Drakes' home recording suite, not to be confused with Sound Techniques'. Note diagram alteration by mice (Photo: Gavin Bush)

RODNEY to NICK:
6 October 1970
Far Leys
Dear Nick,

From our short talk on the phone on Monday evening I rather gathered that things are a bit sticky for you at the moment and this is just to say 'hope they'll soon be better' – for what it's worth. Try not to let things get you down. If your record is held up for some reason and you can't see how to get it going again or – still worse – if the whole thing comes to a sticky end – try to get a bit of a change to sort yourself out. Speculate for a while on the fact that most disastrous and exasperating situations always have their humorous side in retrospect, and therefore must contain the elements of humour even while they're happening. I have found this a helpful reflection in many dire and seemingly hopeless situations.

Come home for a bit and listen to my new records and cheer me up in my temporary depression over the impending end of my career as a (not so) hard boiled business man . . .

Cheer up, Nick, and don't lose belief in yourself – you're one of the few who've got something.

Very much love from all
Dad

And written by Rodney at the same time:

. . . Don't forget, by the way, that now I am retired I am free to meet you anytime during the week if you suddenly feel like popping up for a night, and per contra I am free to pop up to London any day if there is suddenly a chance of hearing a recording session (or even meeting your Joe Boyd!) . . .

Presumably Nick did not take up this invitation. Or did he? Here is evidence of a meeting in London with his father – though not, apparently, a very communicative one:

RODNEY to NICK:
11 December 1970
Far Leys
Dear Nick,

Nice seeing you for lunch yesterday and I also enjoyed our meeting at Haverstock Hill.

But it is rather strange for me to reflect as I sit writing this how very little indeed we know about your life and how it is developing.

This, I think, however, is how you want it – to some extent it is perhaps that you do not know yourself and anyway you want to keep your options open – and I presume your independence of action without commitment of any sort to anyone.

The outcome of it all anyway in so far as your Ma and Pa are concerned is that we do not know:

(a) if you are jogging along more or less on course
or
(b) if things are going well for you
or
(c) if things are going badly for you
or
(d) if you are extremely worried about the future
or
(e) if you are pleased about the future
or
(f) if you aren't bothered about the future anyway
or
(g) if your finances are down to the last bean
or
(h) if your finances are in particularly good shape
or
(i) if your plans for your musical career are
(1) O.K.
(2) Developing rapidly
(3) Lying in shattered ruins around your feet
or
(j) if you are satisfied with the life you are leading

or

(k) if you are dissatisfied with the life you are leading

or

(l) if you are home every evening and are

(1) miserably depressed and bored

(2) perfectly contented with your own company

or

(m) if you have a large circle of friends and go out every night,

and so on and so on and so on.

Well – the purpose of this letter is not to ask you to provide answers to all these things – indeed nor to any of them. My object is simply to remind you that whilst we are very much in ignorance of your way of life etc., at the same time we are hoping very much that if at any time you are considering a change of course, or are confronted with a problem that greatly worries you, or find yourself in an impasse that you can't see any way out of, you will not regard us as only a last resort for consultation and help.

I know that you want to make your way on your own but in doing so you may make use of any allies you may have, and families are surely a traditional source of succour.

As you said yourself – both your generation and mine have had enough disillusionments to bring them within range of each other.

All this does not mean that I don't think you are capable of looking after yourself (I am indeed going to 'pay you that compliment'!). But I just would like to feel that we are not so cut off from you that you wouldn't at least see what we had to say if you were in a worry about anything . . .

What Rodney did not realise was that Nick was starting the long slow path towards cutting himself off from everyone. Was getting rid of his car part of this process?

A gentle piece of irony from his father:

RODNEY TO NICK:
15 DECEMBER 1970
Far Leys
Dear Nick,

. . . In reflecting upon the problem of how I am going to keep myself occupied after my retirement, I am disturbed to think that you no longer have a car, because paying your parking fines has become quite a part-time occupation lately. The technique of ignoring any individual claim until reminders get to the stage of threatening court proceedings and then making sure that one has not already paid the fine has been interesting work and will leave quite a gap in my day's programme.

I deliberated for some time as to whether I should give them your name and address but in the end decided that, as the end was in sight, I would shoulder the burden myself as a contribution to your career, and I shall expect a free record of 'Bryter Layter' in return for payments of the collective 35 fines. But when you next have a car you will have to conform a bit more, or you will find most of your royalties will have to be devoted to your parking fines . . .

Bryter Layter was eventually released – to a largely indifferent and lukewarm press – though Nick's mother chanced upon one of the few reviews that was favourable:

MOLLY TO NICK:
19 MARCH 1971
Far Leys
Darling Nick,

I have been meaning to write this since the day the postal strike ended to tell you how very impressed and delighted I am with your record. I love it all and each different song grows on you the more you play it – and fresh subtleties come to light with each hearing. I particularly love 'Sunday', which is so haunting and I find it continually running through my brain – I am becoming very fond too of 'Northern Sky' – and as for 'Poor Boy' I think it is splendid and deserves to be a great hit – it has such terrific rhythm that even these ageing old bones can not stay still when it is played. I suppose you will say it's a case of 'If the management only thought the same as Mother', but in this instance it seems to me that the management does think the same as Mother – witness this review by Michael Cable that I enclose and which appeared in the *Daily Mail* this morning – Don't you think it's an excellent review – Dad and I were terribly thrilled.

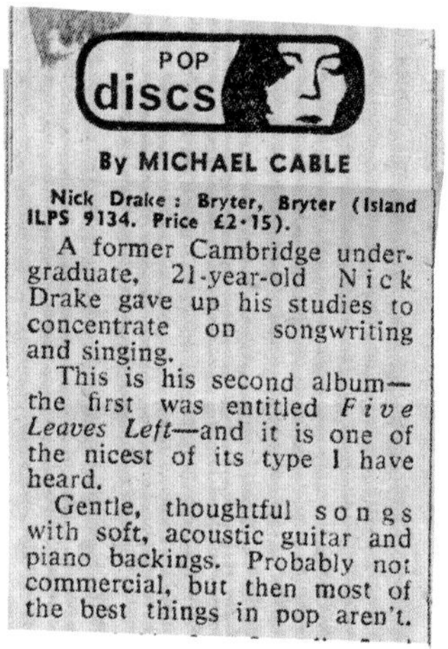

POP discs

By MICHAEL CABLE

Nick Drake: Bryter, Bryter (Island ILPS 9134. Price £2·15).

A former Cambridge undergraduate, 21-year-old Nick Drake gave up his studies to concentrate on songwriting and singing.

This is his second album—the first was entitled *Five Leaves Left*—and it is one of the nicest of its type I have heard.

Gentle, thoughtful songs with soft, acoustic guitar and piano backings. Probably not commercial, but then most of the best things in pop aren't.

I was most interested to hear that you had popped over to Paris for a change of scene – what a good idea.

Well, my darling – see you soon I hope and meantime all love and so many congratulations. Mum

And so the correspondence draws to a close, ending with Nick's withdrawal from London and retreat to his parents' home as the clouds of depression closed in upon him. Throughout, one of its most notable features was the courtesy and respect with which all participants treated each other. The simple philosophy behind this could perhaps be summed up in an undated letter from Molly to her son:

MOLLY TO NICK:
My darling Nick,

On the vexed question of the Davis invitation . . . will you write at once to Mrs Davis darling . . . because it is supposed to be good manners to answer as soon as possible if you are going to refuse an invitation – the idea being that the inviter can then rush some less desirable mortal into the lamentable gap. And when I say Good Manners I don't mean some stuffy old Victorian concept of Decorum. I mean that thing which I have always fervently believed oils the wheels of the entire world. I think one of the reasons the world is in such a pitiable state at the moment is that people – from the highest to the lowest, from the oldest to the youngest, have largely forgotten how to use good manners (and consideration, tolerance and gentleness – they're all the same thing) towards each other. To my mind, good manners are the only investment in the world that cost nothing but at the same time pay huge dividends. As a matter of fact I think this is something that you have discovered for yourself in your own life and do, to a very large extent act upon. And so my darling will you please answer the Davis invitation without delay! . . .

Let us leave the last word with Rodney. By 1971 he was beginning to become seriously worried about his son, but, true to his own belief 'that most disastrous and exasperating situations always have their humorous side', he wrote (almost undoubtedly without any hope of a reply):

RODNEY TO NICK:
SUNDAY, 10 JANUARY 1971
Far Leys
Dear Nick,

. . . Just finished lunch:–

The Sunday crossword had a down clue (7 letters): 'Having lost control, father sits on little Nicholas':

Answer: P
A
N
I
C
K
Y

The first part of the clue is very topical but it's a long time since the second has been applicable. The answer often applies anyway!

Lovely day today – hope you're out on the heath!

Lots of love from us all

Dad

(Photo: Victoria Waymouth)

The Oddefellowe With The Global Brain

or, A Friendship Nipped In The Bud

Gabrielle Drake reflects on a conversation with Peter Russell

'Nick Drake – I remember him as being very kind.' So said Peter Russell, physicist, philosopher and author, to his and Nick's mutual friend, Paul Wheeler.

Peter Russell's many books – including his best-seller *The Global Brain* – attest to a life spent in the study of the evolution of the human mind, the nature of consciousness, and the necessity for humanity to develop a new kind of spirituality to deal with the technological age in which we live. The fact that his ideas have gained such popularity point to a rare ability to communicate, and to translate complex scientific theories into a clear and cohesive philosophy where Western science and Eastern mysticism meet. In 1969, however, he was studying at Cambridge University, and it was here that he and Nick met – thanks to Nick's newfound colleague, Paul Wheeler.

Both Wheeler and Peter Russell were scholars at Gonville and Caius – one of the oldest colleges in Cambridge, and one to which Nick seems to have been keenly drawn. It provided two of his most significant friendships: Paul Wheeler himself – also a singer-songwriter – and Robert Kirby, who so famously went on to arrange many of Nick's songs.

Peter Russell was not one of Nick's intimates – though both were members of the Loungers Club: an ancient institution within Caius, revived at that time by a group of like-minded college members. Not that they were like-minded in the subjects they were reading, which ranged from Physics to English, to Classical Music, and even Chinese. The Club allowed for one outsider – 'the Oddefellowe' – and Nick was invited to be that outsider. Both the title, and the one rule of the club, to 'stand by ye gate once a day and observe what strange creatures God hath made', would seem to have suited Nick admirably.

Only one other tradition was observed by members of the Club: once a month, one of them would provide for the rest a gargantuan and exotic breakfast. Otherwise, their meetings seem to have consisted of the playing of varied and eclectic albums of music, and the unofficial smoking of much pot.

It must have been during the evening meetings of the Club that the seed of a friendship between Nick and Peter formed. The fact that it never fully germinated is perhaps not surprising, though possibly a personal misfortune for Nick. A road not taken.

On the surface, it might seem that the two men had little in common: Peter had come up to Cambridge on a scholarship two years earlier than Nick, to study theoretical physics. At Caius, he found himself 'exactly where I thought I wanted to be, studying with the best minds in the best of places'. Nick, on the other hand, had scraped into Cambridge to read English, and found himself in one of the modern colleges, Fitzwilliam, situated some way out of the centre of town. He was less than enthusiastic when he arrived:

'I don't see that it's going to be the fantastic existence that people like to make out . . . It seemed reasonably easy to put my brain back in action, which was lucky, and the work in fact seems to be about the most acceptable thing about the place so far . . .'

Luckily for Nick, fairly soon after this, he met Paul Wheeler, and a new side of Cambridge's social life opened up to him. He also managed to move from his cramped and uncongenial room in Fitzwilliam College to rooms nearer the centre of the city – rooms by the river, on the other side of a little bridge, which he crossed daily. It was here that Peter Russell remembers visiting him with Paul. Was it to vet him for Oddefellowe status? If so, he apparently found Nick congenial enough to approve.

By the time he met Nick, Russell must have been on the brink of a major leap in his personal evolution. He had already realised that the physical sciences he was studying could never provide the answers to questions that were increasingly occupying him, and which would, eventually, produce his key works concerning mind and consciousness. Despite the fact that he had arrived at university with a deep distrust of the dogma of conventional religion, so much of which was at odds with scientific facts, he increasingly felt that science did not hold all the spiritual answers.

For Nick, too, conventional religion was a problem.

In an undated fragment of a letter to his parents – a letter which may have been just a draft, for it was torn up in pieces (presumably by Nick) but saved by his mother in a cellophane bag tucked into the back of her writing case – Nick writes:

'I'm glad you realised that the reasons for my absence from the Christmas service amounted to more than mere lethargy. I have in fact given the matter quite a lot of thought . . . It is difficult to say exactly what I feel, since I am by no means clear in my own mind yet . . . As regards the communion service itself, I find myself understandably hampered by an inability to believe in the authenticity of Christ himself. The stories concerning Christ are, after all, the product of an age governed by superstition. Where factual knowledge is lacking, superstition automatically takes over, making it possible for any man of outstanding ability to be thought of as possessing supernatural powers, and to be looked on as nothing less than a god. One of the few things I feel convinced about is that none of the miracles took place, and that Christ did nothing that was the result of supernatural powers. However, I do feel sure that he was an exceptional leader and teacher, even if it was in a completely human context, and I was interested in the idea you suggested that joining with other people in order to hear the teachings of a great man is sufficient reason for going to a church service. However, I don't feel entirely convinced by this, since it doesn't seem quite right that one should worship, in the way that the Christian church requires one to worship, someone who is no more than a mere human being.

I am by no means entirely atheistic, since I do believe that there is some kind of 'divine inspiration', and this is coupled with a firm belief in predestination. However, I don't accept that this inspiration, or whatever one calls it, has ever existed in human form . . .'

This rejection of conventional religion is neither surprising nor unusual in a young man starting to think for himself. What is interesting is Nick's cogent, reasoned argument. He is arguing as his father, Rodney, a trained engineer with a fine analytical mind, might have argued. But it is also obvious that here is a young man groping towards an individual spirituality: a groping that resonates in his songs.

Undoubtedly, Nick inherited his mother's poetic and intuitive grasp of 'things behind the sun'. But he differed from her, in that part of his make-up included his father's equally profound but more scientific mind. Here, maybe, Nick and Peter Russell found some common ground.

Nick must have been intrigued by a student who had walked away from a degree in Theoretical Physics, and taken a six months' leave of absence from university to try and come to terms with his quest for the answer to some fundamental truths. Now, Peter Russell had returned to Cambridge, and was studying for a degree in Experimental Psychology, which allowed him to pursue his exploration of the inner world of consciousness. As part of this exploration, he had become interested in various forms of meditation – Transcendental Meditation in particular – which he started to practise regularly. It was only natural that a man who was an inherent teacher should involve his friends, and arrange sessions of Transcendental Meditation for interested people. Of whom, Nick, it appears, was one. In February 1968, he wrote home to his parents:

'It may surprise you to hear that during the last few weeks I've been extraordinarily happy with life, and I haven't a clue why! It seems that Cambridge can in fact do rather nice things to one if one lets it. And I'm not sure that I did let it before. I think I've thrown off one or two rather useless and restrictive complexes that I picked up before coming here . . .

By the way, think of me next Saturday, the day of my initiation for transcendental meditation. I went to a talk on it last week, and it seems to be a thing that is impossible to explain. So the only way to discover what it's all about is to do it oneself. I don't know what happens at the initiation, but I have to take along some fruit, some flowers, and a clean white handkerchief, which is rather a nice idea.'

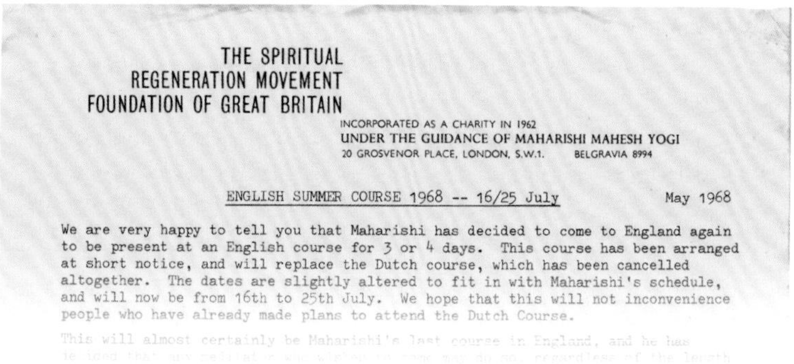
THE SPIRITUAL
REGENERATION MOVEMENT
FOUNDATION OF GREAT BRITAIN

INCORPORATED AS A CHARITY IN 1962
UNDER THE GUIDANCE OF MAHARISHI MAHESH YOGI
20 GROSVENOR PLACE, LONDON, S.W.1. BELGRAVIA 8994

ENGLISH SUMMER COURSE 1968 -- 16/25 July May 1968

We are very happy to tell you that Maharishi has decided to come to England again to be present at an English course for 3 or 4 days. This course has been arranged at short notice, and will replace the Dutch course, which has been cancelled altogether. The dates are slightly altered to fit in with Maharishi's schedule, and will now be from 16th to 25th July. We hope that this will not inconvenience people who have already made plans to attend the Dutch Course.

This will almost certainly be Maharishi's last course in England, and he has

We do not know who gave that initial talk – was it Peter Russell himself? Though there is no stated correlation, Nick's profession of happiness – the only one so positively expressed in a letter – is consistent with someone who perhaps feels enlightened for a brief moment.

Sadly, this euphoria did not last. We have no direct record of Nick's reaction to the initiation, but Brian Wells, who accompanied him, said that they both dismissed the session as 'a load of rubbish'. Can this have been the entirety of Nick's experience? Or was it that the commitment involved in a consistent practice of TM would have been of insufficient importance to him then, involved as he was in his music and song-writing? Easier to reach another dimension by smoking marijuana. And, perhaps, by listening to Asian music, which we know Nick found beguiling and beautiful, and which Peter Russell remembers them listening to together.

So Nick obviously did not underestimate Russell himself. How could he, anyway, have dismissed a friend who had introduced him to an extraordinary experience? As Paul Wheeler remembers:

'Pete used to listen to music on headphones in the car – and in those days, no one listened on headphones much, let alone in their cars. He suggested this to Nick, and Nick was amazed. He thought this was brilliant – that you could put on headphones and have an absolutely intimate experience whilst driving – as you know, Nick loved driving . . . you say this to someone today, and they say so what? But in 1969, it was unknown – a revolutionary idea.'

Nor can Nick have entirely dismissed the practice of meditation. Sometime later, when Nick had left Cambridge and was living in London, Peter Russell remembers visiting him, and the two of them meditating together in Nick's London flat. That was probably the last time they saw each other. Although Russell tried to visit Nick when the latter was living in Hampstead, Nick didn't answer the knock at his door.

Life is full of 'might have beens' and 'what ifs'.

What if Nick had answered that knock at his door? At the time Peter Russell made that final visit, Nick must have already begun his long, final, downward spiral. Russell, on the other hand, had recently returned from a year spent in India, at the ashram of his teacher, Maharishi Mahesh Yogi. It was a year that had resulted in his decision to become a teacher of Transcendental Meditation, but also to return to university in England to study further the effects of meditation on the human mind, paralleling his metaphysical studies with a degree in computer science and eventually forming his own philosophy, which would lead to his seminal book *The Global Brain*.

The Global Brain is an important work for anyone trying to understand the connection between what we have come from, and what we might become: with elegant simplicity, Russell traces an evolutionary path that began with the Big Bang, and continues through to our uncertain future, marrying contemporary physics with ancient mysticism to produce a vision of humanity as a vast, inter-functioning organism: in fact, a global brain. Published before either the Internet or the World Wide Web came into being, it could be said to have predicted both.

And it could be argued – certainly Paul Wheeler does – that it was the Internet that finally launched Nick to a wider public.

We know that Nick had a desire to communicate. He once said, in anguish, to his mother, 'If only I could feel that my music had ever helped a single person.' Yet we also know that he was incapable of getting his message across in the only way known at that time: that of tramping the folk-club circuit, gigging and gagging, and struggling for air-play; selling himself as a package at the centre of which was the music. Most artists – certainly those in the music world – are able to protect a creative inner core with an outer, brasher, carapace: one that serves the double function of keeping their spirit pure, whilst selling it to their listeners. Nick had no outer skin; no defences with which to parlay. But perhaps, also, sure and tenacious as he always was with regard to his work, he became increasingly aware that his fragile muse would shatter in a harsh surrounding. Certainly his few, less-than-successful, public appearances would have borne this out. Did he, somewhere in himself, know that there had to be, that there would be, another way?

Paul Wheeler again:

'We know that, in the long term, what was initially an inhibition, turned into an absolute godsend – which maybe he even foresaw: because by *not* going through the gigging process, by *not* getting the exposure, Nick Drake was not saddled, as artists like Fairport Convention were, with the baggage of the Sixties. He was not seen, by the younger generation of the 1990s – the first Internet generation – as being part of their parents' hippie culture. I mean he *wasn't* in everybody's mother's and father's album collection. He *hadn't* been done to death . . .

In the early days of the Internet, the experience of listening to stuff on it was very, very mysterious: almost like being in a séance. You'd go into your computer, and you'd know that people all around the world were tuning in and trying to find voices and music that hadn't been heard before. You were alone – and yet linked to thousands and thousands of others. Nick absolutely fitted into that situation. So when people say 'Oh, Nick gave up, he should have soldiered on', you could answer that, on the contrary, he was extremely astute to know that there had to be another way for him to get himself across, sooner or later. It just happened to be much later.'

Is this crediting Nick with too much prescience? Possibly. However, let us reconsider Nick's response to the experience Peter Russell introduced him to: that of listening to music on headphones in a car. The depth of his reaction would seem to indicate that this was more than merely an enjoyable sensation. Could it be, as Paul Wheeler said, that 'Nick realised there could be a technology which would enable you to have a direct contact with your audience. And your music would be in their ears. At the time the idea was radical. But I remember Nick thinking "It can be done: you can skip all the usual paraphernalia . . ." And you see he was proved right. That was exactly what happened.'

Nick's songs are not political, nor, for the most part, are they autobiographical. Instead, they seem to take him on an inner journey – a quest to find a purer place to be. That the quest doesn't always succeed is what makes the songs so poignant and, perhaps, timeless.

Although they are rarely ego-based, that is not to say the songs don't treat of 'I' and 'my'. In his book *The TM Technique*, Peter Russell draws the distinction between the ego-based self – the individual image we all have of ourselves – and the pure Self, the Universal Self that underlies all experience: the Self that is rarely perceived, and only known in a state of transcendental consciousness. This is how he describes it:

'In this state, there is no longer any experience of "I am". It is a field which lies beyond individual consciousness, and for precisely this reason, there is an absence of individuality . . . One begins to experience that, at the most fundamental level, we are all one and the same . . . in the words of the psychologist Carl Rogers, "the deeper we go into ourselves . . . the more we find the whole human species".'

This state of transcendental consciousness was undoubtedly familiar to Nick – as it is to a number of creative people – and it was at this level that Nick, so withdrawn and reserved on the surface, sought to communicate with his fellow human beings, with a desire – maybe naive and of his time (he was, after all, a child of the Sixties) – to make the world a better place.

Yet was that desire so naive?

In *The Global Brain* Peter Russell talks of humanity being in a state of severe crisis, and that we face an evolutionary test as to

'whether or not [we are] psychologically and spiritually fit to live on planet Earth, whether we can change at a very fundamental level the way we relate to others and the environment, whether we can work in harmony rather than conflict, whether we can balance centuries of material progress with an equal amount of inner growth, whether we can connect with that level of unity that we know theoretically (and, in those privileged, magical moments, know experientially) lies at our core . . . If we fail, we will probably be discarded [by Nature] as an evolutionary blind alley, an experiment that, for one reason or another did not quite work out.'

But the anguished question presents itself: how do we change? In a world apparently dominated by conflict and disunity, it is easy to feel despair. The clamour of war is always louder, but not necessarily more persistent or constant than the still small voice of love, if only we would know where to look for it.

For help, humanity has always turned to its artists, its music makers. Not for nothing did Robert Kirby, Nick's orchestrator, call his first group 'The Gentle Power of Song'.

And today, our advanced technology means that we

do not have to rely on the campfire singalong, the concert hall, or even a CD player for the dissemination of that power.

The growing number of people captivated by Nick's music appears to be increasingly diverse. Fans come from different countries, different age groups, and from all walks of life. But the most remarkable phenomenon is not so much their differences, spread as they are across the world but, rather, the unanimity of their reaction to the music: compassion, gratitude for comfort derived from the songs, and courage gained from them to face problems similar to Nick's. Overwhelmingly, it is one of connection and love.

To quote for one last time Nick's not-quite friend, Peter Russell: 'Humanity has to find the courage to express our deeper values and use our technology to create the world of our dreams. Perhaps then the global brain can awaken to its global heart.'

If this is so, then maybe the most important function any artist can have is to help humanity find its global heart.

To be numbered amongst those artists would surely be a legacy Nick would have deeply desired and endorsed.

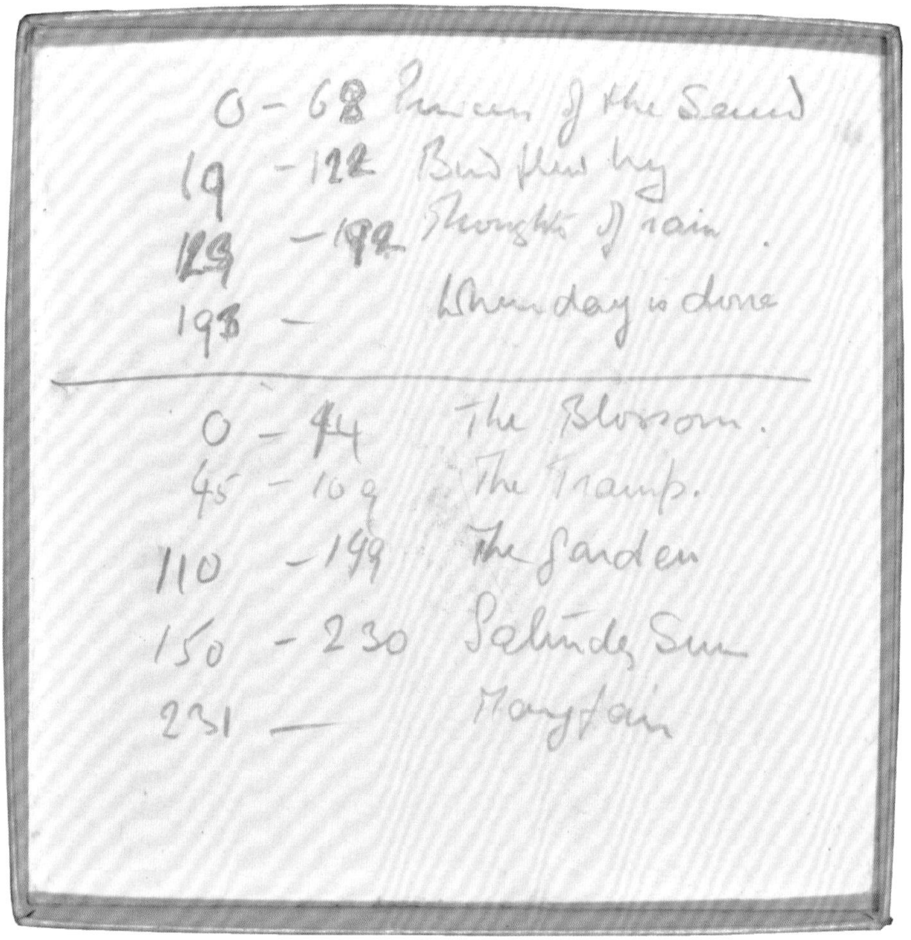

Rodney's track listing inside the lid of Nick's home recordings

Come To The Garden

by Pete Paphides

It was clear when he returned from his travels – first to Aix-en-Provence and then on to Marrakesh – that Aix had changed Nick Drake. His hair was longer, his air somehow both worldly and otherworldly. Unencumbered by the schedules of school and family, Nick had finally been free to experience at first hand a life that – up until that point – he had only experienced by proxy, through the writing of Sartre and Kerouac. A life brought almost within touching distance by some of the records that had accumulated turntable miles back in Marlborough and Tanworth-in-Arden. On the many tapes that Nick made in 1966, the songs to which he gravitated were those which eschewed attachments and obligations for the romance of a solitary, itinerant life: Bert Jansch's 'Strolling Down the Highway'; Jackson C. Frank's 'Blues Run the Game'; Bob Dylan's 'Don't Think Twice, It's All Right'. It isn't hard to see why these songs would have appealed to Nick Drake as he accelerated out of adolescence and – as so many great songwriters, from Dylan to Tom Waits, have done – hit upon songwriting as a means by which to mould a persona from the raw ingredients of his personality. Nick's extended stay in Aix, accompanied by Simon Crocker and Jeremy Mason, afforded him the space and distance to do just that. Interviewed by Patrick Humphries, Jeremy recalled that the three friends spent much of their time 'playing pinball at a café called Les Deux Garçons'. Occasionally, Nick would busk, with Jeremy tasked to collect the money from passers-by.

Prior to Aix, Nick's friends have no recollection of him writing songs, but on a trip from Aix to Mason's parents house 'somewhere near Avignon', Crocker remembered having to hold the microphone for Nick, whilst he set about recording some of his first compositions. The tape has since been lost, but Simon told Humphries that 'I'm pretty sure "Time Has Told Me" was one of them.' Later, though, Robin Frederick, the American student and guitarist who was 'nominally' studying in Aix, recalled that 'Nick never sang any of his own songs.' In fact, he had written at least one song at this point, although Robin may have been forgiven for not realising it was an original composition. On the famous 'Aix tape', which surfaced in 1998, Nick can be heard performing eight songs amid an atmosphere of general revelry. Among them is 'Princess Of The Sand' (later retitled 'Strange Meeting II') – by any criteria, an extraordinarily assured songwriting arrival. If Nick hadn't heard Davy Graham's 'Anji', he was certainly familiar with the version that Bert Jansch recorded on his 1965 debut album. Musically, 'Princess Of The Sand' sounds like perfect assimilation of Graham's game-changing instrumental and Jackson C. Frank's 'Milk and Honey' (a song Nick frequently played), albeit with words that tread a well-worn lyrical path: a mysterious encounter with a figure so beautiful that the whole episode may be nothing more than a figment of the narrator's imagination.

Using Aix as a base, Nick and three friends embarked on a month-long adventure that took them to Morocco. Their arrival coincided with that of the Rolling Stones, whose trip was captured for posterity by Cecil Beaton. Perhaps inevitably, Nick found himself in a local restaurant playing a short set for them. Writing to his family, he recalled that 'we in fact got quite chatty with them, and it was quite interesting learning all the inside

stories'. By the time he returned, the Marlborough friends who accompanied him in Aix noticed a change in Nick. In Humphries' book, Crocker elaborates on what he saw as a loss of 'light-heartedness' and a 'more drug-orientated' outlook: 'We had an old guitar he smashed up and set light to, and he hung it from the ceiling and looked at it, like, "Wow, man!"'

The fomentation of Nick Drake's artistic persona and his adult persona appeared to be one and the same – and although this lack of distinction may have caused him problems later on in life, it seems at this point to have had the effect that Nick wanted it to. On his return from Aix, Nick could legitimately call himself an artist. He had songs – and given the formal manner in which he appeared to present them to his family, he must have been very proud of them. 'He came back home,' Gabrielle recalled:

'He played for us . . . three songs that he'd composed for himself. And that was very thrilling, but it was somehow both thrilling and unexpected – and yet, at the same time, totally expected. It was somehow a natural progression, because it was something that we'd grown up with, with my mum composing all the time and my parents playing on the piano . . . It was somehow natural, but nevertheless exciting.'

Gabrielle's clearest recollection of her brother's performance was that of him playing 'Princess Of The Sand', his parents, Rodney and Molly Drake, recalling the other two songs as 'Bird Flew By' and 'Rain'.

Perhaps, then, these were the first three of Nick's fully-fledged compositions. If, as Simon Crocker seems to recall, Nick had written 'Time Has Told Me' as well, surely he would have deemed it strong enough to show off alongside the aforesaid three? Setting that issue aside for a moment, 'Bird Flew By' tells you far more about where Nick came from than where he was heading. The sound of Nick pondering the seasonal cycle, with its indifference to our carefully tended dreams, recalls nothing so much as the songs written by his mother, which radiated a similar air of reluctant pragmatism: 'Happiness' and 'Poor Mum'. The changing of the seasons also figures in 'Rain', and in another song from this time: 'Blossom'. At this early stage, the emotional vernacular of Nick's songs was strongly intertwined with the imagery of nature: 'This was our season / We said it couldn't end / But my love left with the rain.'

Over the ensuing period, Nick's repertoire expanded to take in at least three more songs. Some eighteen months before he came to Joe Boyd's attention, fledgling music conglomerate Hansa offered Nick a publishing deal. Shown on the contract are four songs, only one of which – 'Day Is Done' – would make it onto his debut album over a year later. Dated 31 August 1969, the document also makes reference to 'My Love Left With The Rain', 'Leaving Me Behind' and 'Life Flies Away'. Outside of this contract (which, in the end, Nick elected not to sign),

Gabrielle insists on a more complex chord structure for their recording of 'All My Trials' during Christmas at Far Leys. Lady Lloyd (grandmother) and Molly otherwise occupied

there is no trace of any song written by Nick which might answer to the name of 'Life Flies Away'. However, it may have been a title swiftly conferred upon a song which he subsequently renamed. 'Leaving Me Behind', on the other hand, is familiar, perhaps as a result of the sort of pensive descending chord progression which he would deploy more effectively on 1970's 'At The Chime Of A City Clock' and 1974's 'Tow The Line'.

All told, then, it's perhaps no wonder that Nick's fellow undergraduates remember him as a confident, charismatic individual who, in his own quiet way, seemed to draw people towards him. By the time he arrived in Cambridge, his adventures in France and north Africa had made a relatively seasoned traveller of him. And with a small armoury of original compositions to boot, he had effectively turned into the Nick Drake that discerning music fans would soon see gazing out of a Wimbledon attic window on the sleeve of *Five Leaves Left*. 'We were long-haired groovy people with greater vision than people cycling off to their lectures,' recalled fellow Cambridge student and musician Brian Wells. 'We both had bikes when we went up to Cambridge, but within a week they were stolen and we didn't give a damn. When he found his again, he didn't want it back because he preferred to walk. It was too studenty and Hooray Henryish – too uncool – to cycle around Cambridge.'

By every account of his contemporaries, Nick knew how good he was. The only thing at which he appeared to make any sort of effort was his playing. Wells recalled standing outside his room and hearing him 'doing the same riff over and over and over for half an hour, and when I banged on the door and went in, he still carried on.' At that point, everything at which Nick had succeeded had appeared to come easily to him. His sprinting prowess at school was impressive to everyone except, seemingly, himself. Any shortfall in academic application seemed to be made up for by other people's belief in Nick. Having initially failed to get a place at Cambridge, he finally passed the entrance exam, but, according to Gabrielle, it was a robust commendation from Nick's Marlborough housemaster, Dennis Silk, that secured his passage into Fitzwilliam College. By the end of 1966, failure was something that Nick had never seriously had to countenance. Why should that change when it came to music?

His hunger to get on with the business of being a famous musician is well evidenced by his first billing on a London stage. With barely enough songs to perform a set of original material, Nick secured himself a booking during the Christmas break of 1967 at the Camden Roundhouse – one of many performers on a five-day benefit show headlined by Country Joe and the Fish. By this time, he had written the song that would go on to open his debut album. According to Paul Wheeler, the title of 'Time Has Told Me' came to Nick whilst the pair were drinking in the Footlights bar. Rodney and Molly Drake suggested that it was written about a girl he met in Cambridge. Quoted in Gorm Henrik Rasmussen's book

Pink Moon, the Drakes (Rasmussen doesn't say which one) are quoted as saying that 'it was clear that he was head over heels in love with her'.

At the Roundhouse gig, Fairport Convention's Ashley Hutchings was sufficiently struck by Nick's 'demeanour and charisma' to introduce himself and suggest that he and Joe Boyd make contact. Working for himself under the aegis of the publishing–production–management imprint Witchseason, Joe had secured deals with Island for two of his acts: Fairport Convention and The Incredible String Band. As it happens, Nick was already on the radar of Island Records' owner Chris Blackwell, thanks to a mutual friend, Desirée Burlison Rush. It was Burlison Rush who played Nick's tape to Blackwell before reporting back to Molly and Rodney Drake that Blackwell had enjoyed it. In the event, however, it was Boyd who proved the vital catalyst in building a team around Nick that would, in time, bring out his songs' vast potential.

Alongside 'Time Has Told Me', the reel-to-reel tape recorded in Tanworth over the Christmas break and hand-delivered by Nick featured two more new songs: 'The Thoughts Of Mary Jane' and 'Magic'. The effect that these 'mysteriously original' songs had on Joe Boyd is a matter of record. Already suspicious of the post-Dylan milieu of earnest acoustic troubadours, Boyd immediately recognised something in these three Nick Drake songs that set him apart. Unlike Nick's very earliest songwriting attempts, the recordings that he proffered Joe Boyd revealed not the merest hint of blues guitar. Instead, they prompted Joe's right-hand man Todd Lloyd to surmise that, in Nick, they had found 'an English chansonnier'.

Up to that point, the idea of a practitioner of specifically English chansons had pretty much begun and ended with Jake Thackray – a Yorkshire-born singer-songwriter whose tendency to skip between social satire and sentimentality (often within the same song) made him similarly difficult to categorise. Written around this time, and described by Robert as 'a very cynical song about the rich people of Mayfair', Nick's 'Mayfair' was similar in tone and content to much of what could be found on Thackray's recently released debut album. Two years later, it would become the first of Nick's songs to be recorded by another singer – Millie Small of 'My Boy Lollipop' fame covered it for her album *Time Will Tell*. The 2004 album of Nick's (mostly) unreleased music, *Made To Love Magic*, includes a recording he made in Robert Kirby's room at Caius College, playing both 'Mayfair' and what, for many, would come to be known as his signature song: 'River Man'. Speaking shortly before the 2004 album's release, Robert contended that his friend's performance 'on my naff Spanish guitar' was better than those captured on the records. On 'River Man', in particular, he said, 'the playing is incredible': more so, arguably, for the fact that Nick had only recently completed work on it.

That Nick's songwriting was now in vertical ascent is demonstrated by Robert's account of the pair's first encounter, 'during the spring term, March or April, 1968'. Three of the four songs presented by Nick on that first meeting were brand new: 'Day Is Done', 'Way To Blue' and 'Time Of No Reply'. In addition to 'The Thoughts Of Mary Jane', these would form the basis of the set that Nick would perform at Cambridge, often on a weekly basis at college balls and dances. 'We would be the act between the rock groups,' recalled Robert in a Swedish radio interview, 'and we would do four songs with the orchestra. Then the orchestra would do one or two classical pieces, and then Nick would do four or five pieces on his own.'

Shortly after the 1969 May Ball (always, paradoxically, held in June), Nick emptied out his room at Fitzwilliam College, knowing that when he returned to start his second year, he would have already commenced work on his first album.

If Songs Were Lines In A Conversation . . .

An analysis of Nick's songs by Chris Healey

Nick Drake's songs have a rare ability to resist sounding dated or genre-bound. Although they developed from an initial love of playing blues and folk, when he began writing his own songs he seemed to go out of his way to avoid anything which might link him too closely to stock forms. You can certainly see how players like John Renbourn and Donovan, for example, or tunes like Jackson C. Frank's 'Milk and Honey', were an influence on his earliest work. But very quickly he began finding ways to generate new chords and harmonic progressions, often through alternate tunings, as if unsatisfied with the straightforward chord patterns he grew up learning.

Such influences did survive more noticeably in structural terms, though: like most blues and a lot of folk, his songs almost never have a chorus.

Of course, a lot of guitarists have used alternate tunings to create different flavours. But often we're still left with a sense of familiarity – our ear grows used to the kind of sounds that folk guitarists get out of the most common tunings, like DADGBE ('dropped D'), or DADGAD, for example. Nick seems to have wanted to make his guitar parts sound unlike anyone else, if he possibly could. The three albums released in his lifetime contain only five songs in standard tuning (and even then 'River Man' and 'Poor Boy' manage to find some really unusual chords in it), and only two songs in common folk detunings.

His two signature tunings of BEBEBE and CGCFCE allowed him to develop his own individual harmonic landscape, while his other tunings seem to be attempts to get the notes in each particular song to speak to each other in exactly the way he wanted, rather than just an exercise in coming up with something unusual. You can imagine him playing with a simple Asus9 to D pattern in standard tuning, thinking 'I wish I could get a top A note in here', and then capoing up the neck and tuning the G string down to F# . . . and ''Cello Song' taking shape. Or playing the chord shapes that became 'Place To Be' in his regular CGCFCE tuning and realising there was no good way to get the Em chord he wanted . . . so tuning the top C down to a G to enable him to do it . . . and finding that the open G added great new texture to all the other chords too.

The notes attached to each song here just concern aspects of them that seem original, or musically interesting, or particularly inspired. I've tried to steer clear of technical language as much as possible, though there are places where I've had to leave in some terms that non-musicians might not understand. Where possible I've explained them as they occur.

But trying to write about how a piece of music works is a tricky business. Quite apart from the fact that a song's harmonic effects may not cause the same reaction in every listener, no one wants to listen to a song or piece of music and have running through their head a constant commentary explaining what each chord change 'means'.

And songwriting is not always a conscious process. Part of writing songs is the ability to know when something 'just works' – when a chord sequence or a melody or a guitar arrangement that you're playing around with goes from being a possible idea into something which suddenly sounds like it has its own perfect inner logic, or seems to express some emotion, or sits so perfectly with the lyric that it feels like the two were created together. Sometimes you can see why it works; sometimes you half know (and half don't want to know); sometimes it's a complete mystery.

So this isn't an attempt to provide a logical reduction of Nick Drake's art, or a manual for 'How To Be Nick'. I hope the pieces are illuminating and interesting as far as they go. But art that resonates will always take you somewhere beyond explanation; playing unusual chords in random tunings will not make you another Nick Drake. Years after most of his contemporaries' work has faded or dated, his songs continue to move people profoundly, and they do so in ways that can't, ultimately, be broken down.

What follows are Nick's lyrics as sung and, where they exist, as written.

Bird Flew By

Bird flew by and wondered, wondered why
She was wise enough to stay up in the sky
From there she could wonder the reason
What's the point of the year or a season?

Your life flies away as the night turns to day
If you stop once to think, your hair will soon turn grey
But one would like to wonder the reason
What's the point of the year or a season?

The list of false starts and crumbled, broken hearts
Comes from a need to play so many parts
One would like to wonder the reason
What's the point of the year or a season?

The wind and the rain shook hands again
Untouched by the world they managed to stay sane
They were able to wonder the reason
What's the point of the year or a season?

Bird flew by and wondered, wondered why
She was wise enough to stay up in the sky
From there she could wonder for the reason
What's the point of the year or a season?

What's perhaps most striking about 'Blossom' and 'Bird Flew By' is how much like pop songs their chord sequences are. Although unremarkable compared to Nick's later work, they're still decent first outings for a teenager who'd not been playing long, showing a good ear for straightforward harmonic changes, and also a few wrinkles that hint at the originality to come – the unusual E7sus4 at the end of each verse line in 'Blossom', for example, with the E note rising to an F# and G# and clashing with the A note above, or the C#7 with a G# bass (e.g. under 'the cider and . . .'), resolving upwards to a D chord but downwards in the bass to an F# ('. . . the wine').

'Rain' has some similar chord moves to 'Blossom' and 'Bird Flew By', but seems to come as much from the folk-picking tradition as pop writing. It also shows how much ability Nick had even then – it's actually quite a tricky song to sing and play at the same time.

By the standards of his mature work, though, they can seem a bit primitive – both musically (the bridge of 'Blossom' in particular) and lyrically. You can see why he would later describe these early songs as 'childish and foolish'.

'Come Into The Garden' is more successful. Although it wears the musical influence of (folk blues standard) 'St James' Infirmary' pretty clearly, it nonetheless comes together quite convincingly in its own right, with an atmosphere of oppression (partly caused by the dark, fluttery echo effect on the vocal) and stillness, and a lyric that speaks of an inability to connect and seems almost prescient about the difficulties Nick himself would eventually face.

Equally prescient is the remarkable 'Leaving Me Behind'. Musically, this shows Nick trying to make something new from his influences. The guitar part derives from a standard blues riff (the same one whose harmonies lie behind the 'Nobody knows . . .' section from 'Poor Boy'), but is picked out here with a 3/3/2 rhythm in a low register. This brings a dark and unsettled undercurrent to the singer's frail resignation that he may not be able to join in with life as others live it, producing an almost spectral sense of dislocation that wouldn't be out of place on *Pink Moon*.

Nick might have been just beginning to find his own path musically, but both these songs sound every bit as much from the heart as anything he would go on to write later.

Leaving Me Behind
(also referred to as The Tramp)

The tramp moves on to the end of the street
I listen to the echo of his hobnail feet
For some there's a future to find
But I think they're leaving me behind

The world hurries on at its breakneck pace
People fly by in their lifelong race
For them there's a future to find
But I think they're leaving me behind

The chances they come, but the chances have been lost
Success can be gained but at too great a cost
For some there's a future to find
But I think they're leaving me behind

The wind sweeps up, and goes back to its tree
The rain flows by and moves on to the sea
For them there's a future to find
But I think they're leaving me behind

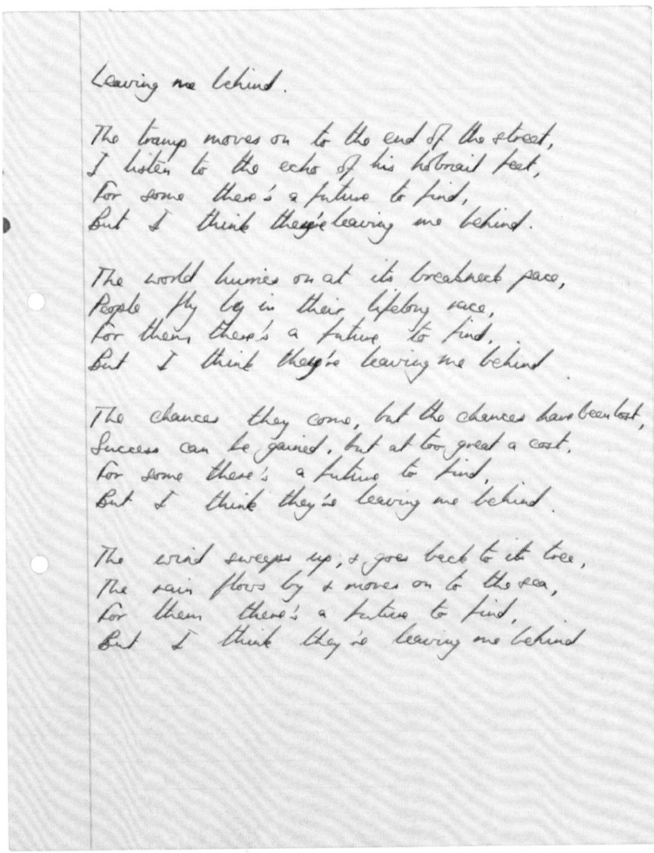
Leaving me behind.

The tramp moves on to the end of the street,
I listen to the echo of his hobnail feet,
For some there's a future to find,
But I think they're leaving me behind.

The world hurries on at its breakneck pace,
People fly by in their lifelong race,
For them there's a future to find,
But I think they're leaving me behind.

The chances they come, but the chances have been lost,
Success can be gained, but at too great a cost,
For some there's a future to find,
But I think they're leaving me behind.

The wind sweeps up, & goes back to its tree,
The rain flows by & moves on to the sea,
For them there's a future to find,
But I think they're leaving me behind

Rain

Thoughts of rain at sunset
Clouds of rainbow blue
Thoughts of sun on sand dunes
Where the seabirds flew
This was our season and we said it couldn't end
But my love left with the rain

Thoughts of leaves in autumn
Falling from the tree
Thoughts of horizon tree tops
Leading to the sea
This was our season, no lies and no pretend
But my love left with the rain

Thoughts of springtime rainfall
Touching flowers that bend
Thoughts of wind in willows
Days that never end
This was our season we said it couldn't end
But my love left with the rain

Rain's the way you move now
Sun the way you seem
Leaves the way you wonder
Flowers the way you dream
This was our season, but sorrow waited round the bend
For my love left with the rain

This was our season, we said it couldn't end
But my love left with the rain

Rain

Thoughts of rain at sunset,
Clouds of rainbow blue,
Thoughts of sun on sand-dunes,
Where the seabirds flew,
This was our season, & we said it couldn't end,
But my love left with the rain

Thoughts of leaves in autumn
Falling from the tree,
Thoughts of horizon tree tops
Leading to the sea,
This was our season, no lies and no pretend,
But my love left with the rain.

Thoughts of springtime rainfall
Touching flowers that bend,
Thoughts of wind in willows,
Days that never end
This was our season, but sorrow waited round the bend,
For my love left with the rain.

Rain's the way you move now,
Sun the way you seem,
Leaves the way you wonder,

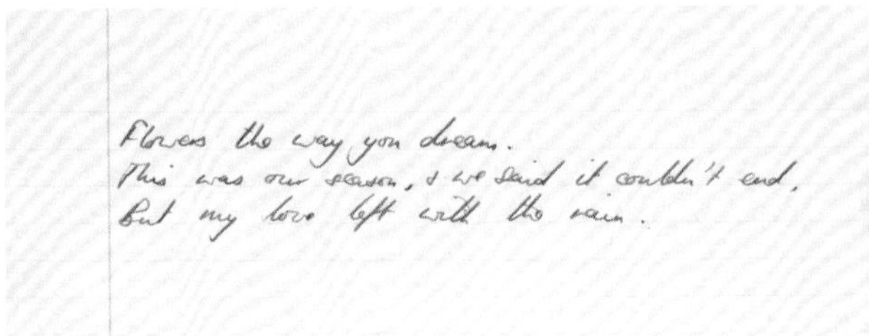
Flowers the way you dream.
This was our season, & we said it couldn't end,
But my love left with the rain.

Come To The Garden

In a bright red sky, in the heat of an evening
When only prisoners sleep
She said she couldn't come to the garden
See an old man weep

She said her dreams were too far to be thought of
Her scars too white to view
She said she couldn't come to the garden
See a blind man kneel

She sailed away to a blue horizon
In floating thoughts she'd sway
She said she couldn't come to the garden
See an old man pray

She wished them luck as they left on their journey
Maybe she'd join them soon?
But she lost her grip at the tip of life's finger
Went home and worshipped the moon

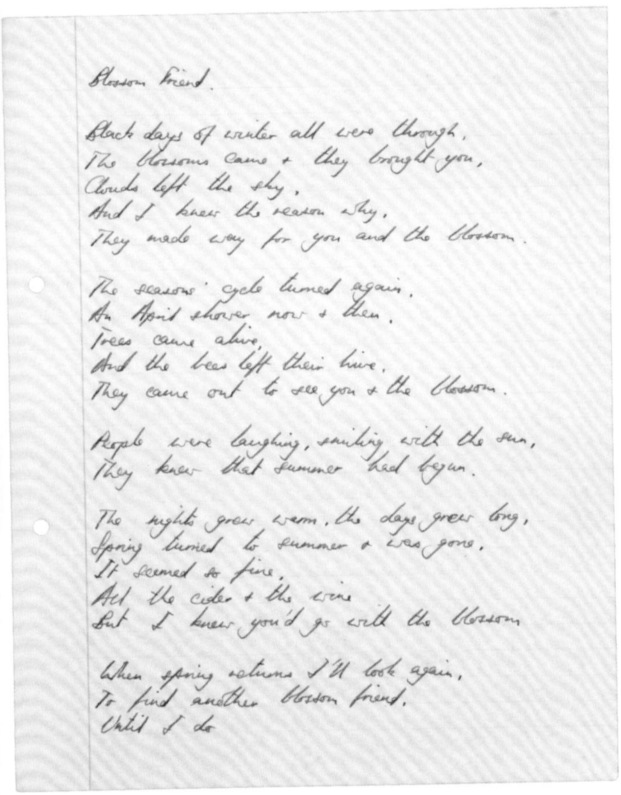
Blossom Friend.

Black days of winter all were through,
The blossoms came + they brought you,
Clouds left the sky,
And I knew the reason why,
They made way for you and the blossom.

The seasons' cycle turned again,
An April shower now + then,
Trees came alive,
And the bees left their hive,
They came out to see you + the blossom.

People were laughing, smiling with the sun,
They knew that summer had begun.

The nights grew warm, the days grew long,
Spring turned to summer + was gone,
It seemed so fine,
And the cider + the wine
But I knew you'd go with the blossom

When spring returns I'll look again,
To find another blossom friend,
Until I do

Blossom

(also referred to as Blossom Friend)

Black days of winter all were through
The blossoms came and they brought you
Clouds left the sky
I knew the reason why
They made way for you and the blossom
And the blossom
The season's cycle turned again
An April shower now and then
Trees came alive
Bees left their hive
They came out to see you and the blossom
And the blossom

People were laughing, smiling with the sun
They knew that summer had begun

*The days grew warm, the nights grew warm**
Spring turned to summer and was gone
It seemed so fine
And the cider and the wine
But I knew you'd go with the blossom
With the blossom

When spring returns I'll look again
To find another blossom friend
Until I do
Find something new
I'll just think of you and the blossom
And the blossom

I'll just think of you and the blossom

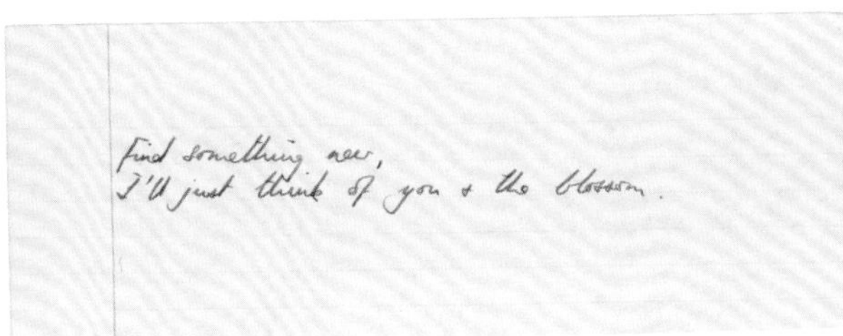
Find something new,
I'll just think of you + the blossom.

* Though Nick clearly wrote 'The nights grew warm, the days grew long', when it came to the home recording he mistakenly sung the line as written here

Clothes Of Sand

Who has dressed you in strange clothes of sand?
Who has taken you far from my land?
Who has said that my sayings were wrong?
And who will say that I stayed much too long?

> *Clothes of sand have covered your face*
> *Given you meaning but taken my place*
> *So make your way on down to the sea*
> *Something has taken you so far from me*

Does it now seem worth all the colour of skies?
To see the earth through painted eyes
To look through panes of shaded glass
See the stains of winter's grass

Can you now return to from where you came?
Try to burn your changing name
Or with silver spoons and coloured light
Will you worship moons in winter's night?

> *Clothes of sand have covered your face*
> *Given you meaning but taken my place*
> *So make your way on down to the sea*
> *Something has taken you so far from me*

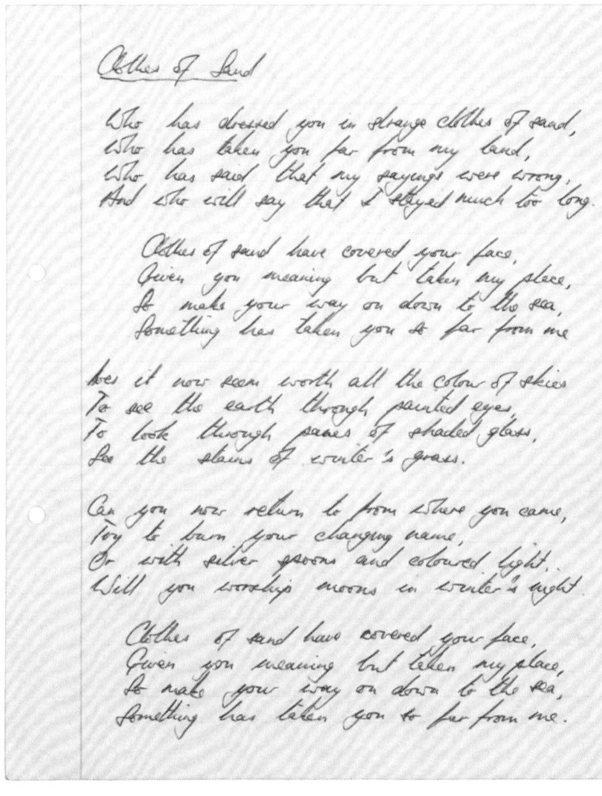

Clothes of Sand

Who has dressed you in strange clothes of sand,
Who has taken you far from my land,
Who has said that my sayings were wrong,
And who will say that I stayed much too long.

Clothes of sand have covered your face,
Given you meaning but taken my place,
So make your way on down to the sea,
Something has taken you so far from me

Does it now seem worth all the colour of skies
To see the earth through painted eyes,
To look through panes of shaded glass,
See the stains of winter's grass.

Can you now return to from where you came,
Try to burn your changing name,
Or with silver spoons and coloured light.
Will you worship moons in winter's night.

Clothes of sand have covered your face,
Given you meaning but taken my place,
So make your way on down to the sea,
Something has taken you so far from me.

Just one re-tuned string does a lot of work here. The extra A note given by tuning the B string down generates cluster effects in three of the four verse chords, producing the doubt of the add9s and the tension of the Eadd4 ('your changing name'). Nick's precisely constructed picking patterns as usual add their own pleasing logic and structure.

Most interestingly, though, the re-tuned string provides a base chord at the beginning and end of the verse with a nagging, doubled tonic note, but no firm major/minor status. Nick's melody provides the minor note, but crucially the music doesn't. The vocal is asking if things are actually not as good as they seem. But if you put a minor note in the chord, the song sounds sad from the off – it has already decided the issue for you and the singer's questions no longer work. (A similar effect happens in 'Time Of No Reply', where the minor in the B section being in the melody but not the chord matches the lyric's suggestion that things are potentially serious, not doomed already.)

Blue Season

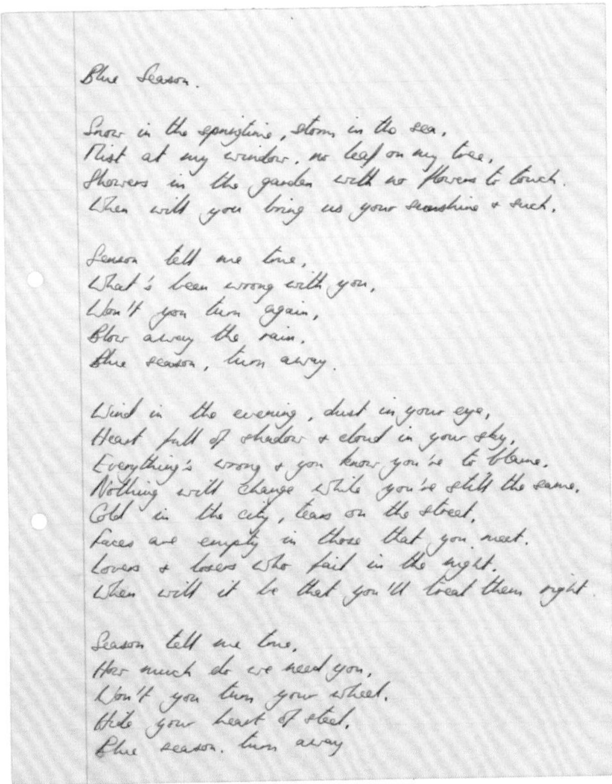
Blue Season.

Snow in the springtime, storm in the sea,
Mist at my window, no leaf on my tree,
Showers in the garden with no flowers to touch.
When will you bring us your sunshine + such.

Season tell me true,
What's been wrong with you,
Won't you turn again,
Blow away the rain,
Blue season, turn away.

Wind in the evening, dust in your eye,
Heart full of shadow + cloud in your sky,
Everything's wrong + you know you're to blame.
Nothing will change while you're still the same.
Cold in the city, tears on the street,
Faces are empty in those that you meet.
Lovers + losers who fail in the night.
When will it be that you'll treat them right.

Season tell me true,
How much do we need you,
Won't you turn your wheel.
Hide your heart of steel.
Blue season. turn away

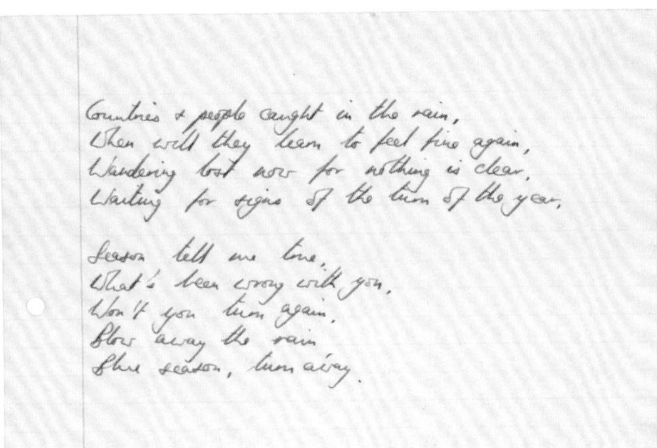
Countries + people caught in the rain,
When will they learn to feel fine again,
Wandering lost now for nothing is clear,
Waiting for signs of the turn of the year,

Season tell me true,
What's been wrong with you,
Won't you turn again.
Blow away the rain
Blue season, turn away.

Snow in the springtime, storm in the sea
Mist at my window, no leaf on my tree
Showers in the garden with no flowers to touch
When will you bring us your sunshine and such?

Season tell me true
What's been wrong with you?
Won't you turn again
Blow away the rain?
Blue season, turn away

Wind in the evening, dust in your eye,
Heart full of shadow and cloud in the sky
Everything's wrong and you know you're to blame
Nothing will change while you're still the same
Cold in the city, tears on the street
Faces are empty in those that you meet
Lovers and losers who fail in the night
When will it be that you'll treat them right?

Season tell me true
How much do we need you?
Won't you turn your wheel
Hide your heart of steel?
Blue season turn away

Countries and people caught in the rain
When will they learn to feel fine again?
Wandering lost now for nothing is clear
Waiting for signs of the turn of the year

Season tell me true
What's been wrong with you?
Won't you turn again
Blow away the rain?
Blue season, turn away

Joey In Mind

When Joey first came the light seemed to rise
Though it came in the night and left with her eyes
And I wish that her face would return once again
Just once to remind me of Saturday's gain

As I sit in her city in fog and in steam
Everything's blurred, for blurred is my dream
So I'll leave for my terrace and tea laced with rum
And wait for this day when Joey will come

And come all the dreamers that ever did try
To live on a memory or float on a sigh
Together we'll sit in this Sunday rain
And dream of Joey or Mary Jane

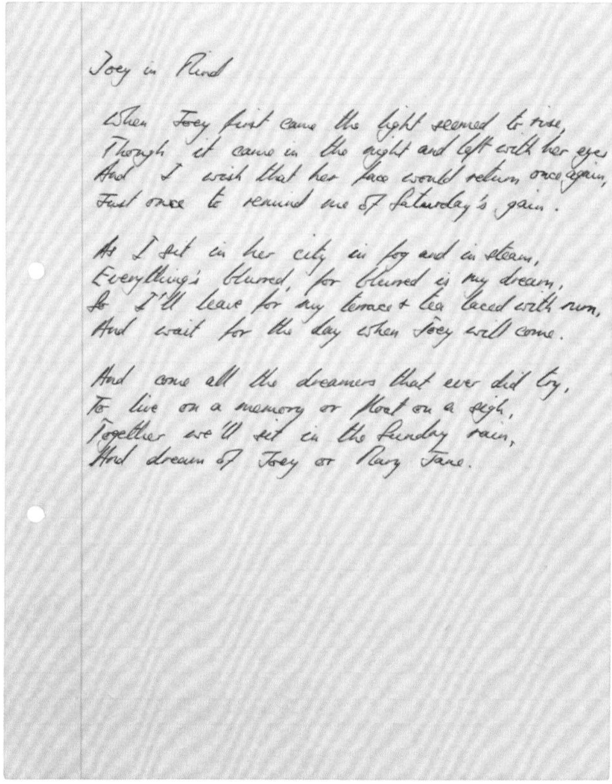
Joey in Mind

When Joey first came the light seemed to rise,
Though it came in the night and left with her eyes
And I wish that her face would return once again,
Just once to remind me of Saturday's gain.

As I sit in her city in fog and in steam,
Everything's blurred, for blurred is my dream,
So I'll leave for my terrace + tea laced with rum,
And wait for the day when Joey will come.

And come all the dreamers that ever did try,
To live on a memory or float on a sigh,
Together we'll sit in the Sunday rain,
And dream of Joey or Mary Jane.

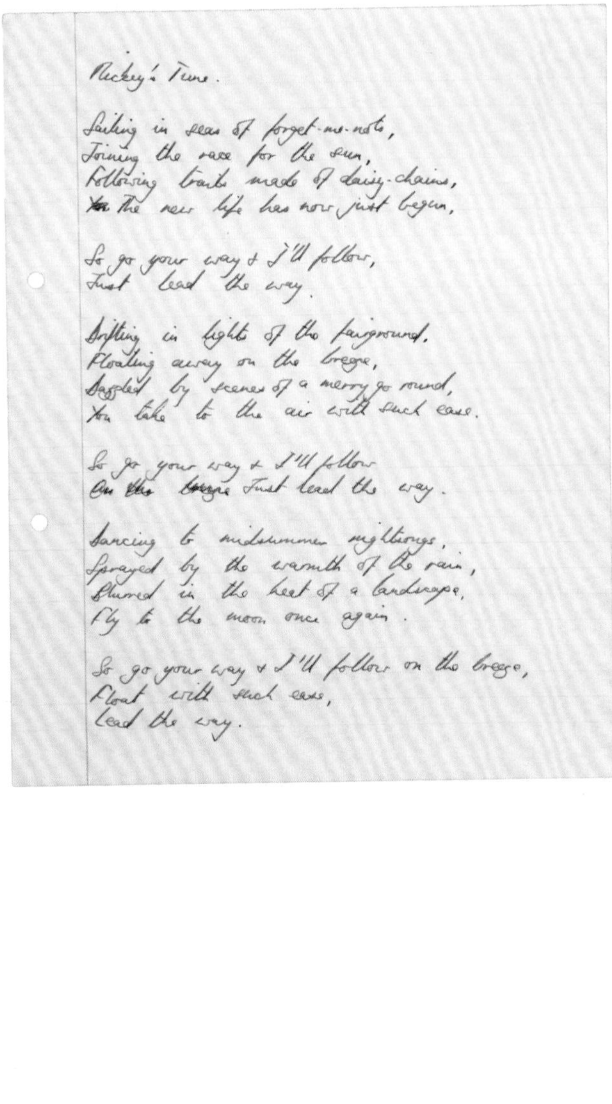
Mickey's Tune.

Sailing in seas of forget-me-nots,
Joining the race for the sun,
Following trails made of daisy-chains,
~~You~~ The new life has now just begun,

So go your way & I'll follow,
Just lead the way.

Drifting in lights of the fairground,
Floating away on the breeze,
Dazzled by scenes of a merry go round,
You take to the air with such ease.

So go your way & I'll follow
~~On the breeze~~ Just lead the way.

Dancing to midsummer nightsongs,
Sprayed by the warmth of the rain,
Blurred in the heat of a landscape,
Fly to the moon once again.

So go your way & I'll follow on the breeze,
Float with such ease,
Lead the way.

Mickey's Tune

Sailing in seas of forget-me-nots
Joining the race for the sun
Following trails made of daisy chains
The new life has now just begun

So go your way and I'll follow
Just lead the way

Drifting in lights of the fairground
Floating away on the breeze
Dazzled by scenes of a merry-go-round
You take to the air with such ease

So go your way and I'll follow
Just lead the way

Dancing to midsummer nightsongs
Sprayed by the warmth of the rain
Blurred in the heat of a landscape
Fly to the moon once again

So go your way and I'll follow on the breeze
Float with such ease,
Lead the way

Outside

Seems the time is near for finding a place outside
Seems the time is here for holding the window wide
So I'm going to try
To open up one eye
But if the world is too wide
I'll be home to hide
Keep it warm inside, if it's strange, outside.

Seems the time has flown, when we lived inside a cloud
Seems the time has gone, when nothing we said was out loud
Going to find a word
Make myself be heard
But if the world is too loud
I'll be home from the crowd
Keep it soft inside, if it's strange, outside.

Seems the time has come for banging our feet to the ground
Seems the time has come to see if the world is round
Sweep the smoke away
Reach the earth today
But if the world is all wrong
I won't be staying long
Keep it cool inside, if it's strange, outside.

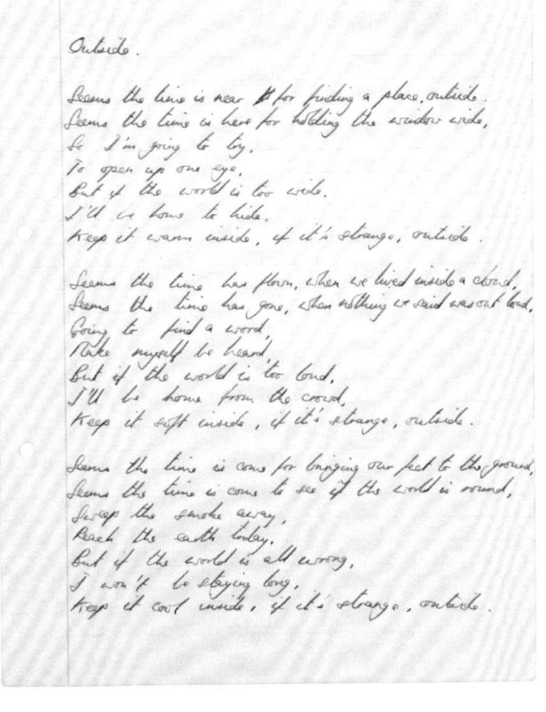
Outside.

Seems the time is near for finding a place, outside.
Seems the time is here for holding the window wide,
So I'm going to try,
To open up one eye,
But if the world is too wide,
I'll be home to hide,
Keep it warm inside, if it's strange, outside.

Seems the time has flown, when we lived inside a cloud,
Seems the time has gone, when nothing we said was out loud,
Going to find a word,
Make myself be heard,
But if the world is too loud,
I'll be home from the crowd,
Keep it soft inside, if it's strange, outside.

Seems the time is come for banging our feet to the ground,
Seems the time is come to see if the world is round,
Sweep the smoke away,
Reach the earth today,
But if the world is all wrong,
I won't be staying long,
Keep it cool inside, if it's strange, outside.

Just Another Girl

Love come today gone tomorrow
Picture of joy turned to sorrow
So I'm searching for another world
We thought it could last forever
But seems it must end now or never
Is it true then was she just another girl
We talked of a new world together
But now I just talk 'bout the weather
So I'm searching for another world
Face that once shone in the light
Now has faded in the night
Is it true then was she really just another girl
Once you would fly on a cloud
But now you just mingle with the crowd
So I'm searching for another world
So go your way I'll go mine
Life will continue just fine
So it's true then she was really just another girl
Another girl

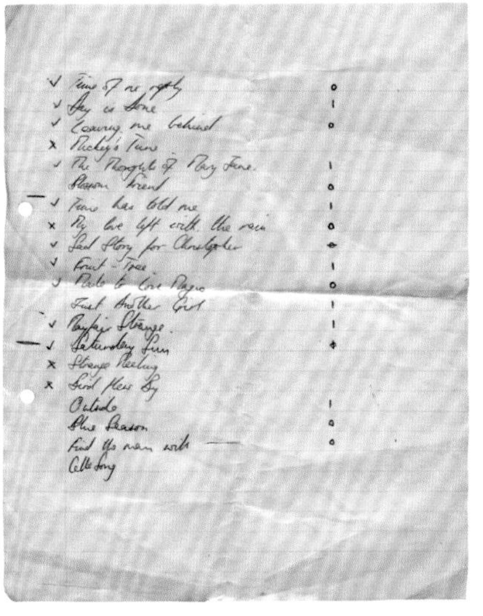
✓ Time of no reply
✓ Day is done
✓ Leaving me behind
× Mickey's Tune
✓ The Thoughts of Mary Jane
[illegible]
✓ Time has told me
× My love left with the rain
✓ [illegible] for Christopher
✓ Fruit Tree
✓ [illegible]
Just Another Girl
✓ [illegible] Strange
✓ Saturday Sun
× Strange Feeling
× [illegible]
Outside
Blue Season
[illegible]
Cello Song

Time Of No Reply

Summer was gone and the heat died down
And autumn reached for her golden crown
I looked behind as I heard a sigh
But this was the time of no reply

The sun went down and the crowd went home
I was left by the roadside all alone
I turned to speak as they went by
But this was the time of no reply

The time of no reply is calling me to stay
There's no hello and no goodbye, to leave there is no way

The trees on the hill had nothing to say
They would keep their dreams 'til another day
So they stood and thought and wondered why
For this was the time of no reply

Time goes by from year to year
And no one asks why I am standing here
But I have my answer as I look to the sky
This is the time of no reply

The time of no reply is calling me to stay
There's no hello and no goodbye, to leave there is no way

Summer was gone and the heat died down
And autumn reached for her golden crown
I looked behind as I heard a sigh
But this was the time of no reply

Time Piece

Still it's time that grows in my brain
Still it's time that calls me the end

Still I scream when time ticks
Still I cringe when time strokes

Still I groan for time's lapse
But still I'll try for time perhaps

Robert Kirby's original written score for 'Time Of No Reply'

This is the first appearance of BEBEBE tuning – one of Nick's favourites and, as far as I can discover, his own invention. It's a remarkably strong song to have been left off a debut album. (It was recorded during the sessions for *Five Leaves Left*.)

The way each line of the verse functions is interesting. The simple descending first line and its second-line repeat describe external circumstance; the third line gets its hopes up, coming up musically by an interval of a fourth, and usually refers to an attempt to engage with or explain the situation; but the last line always slaps them down, with its return to base and chromatic descent echoing the main intro theme and thereby telling us the song's main tale: that there is no escape anywhere from this isolation.

Still, I think the B sections ('Time of no reply, is calling me to stay . . .') are the key to this song's effect. The major note drops out of the home chord and the melody becomes minor as Nick coolly considers a potential future of complete isolation. Without these sections the song might seem too delicate, pastoral even, to have serious effect. With them we're in no doubt of the gravity of the situation.

Strange Meeting II

(also referred to as Princess Of The Sand)

Deep down in the depths of forgotten dreams
So far away. so long ago it seems
The memory comes of a distant beach
With the pale sand stretching far from reach
It was there I found my princess of the sand

As I traced the foam, with the pebbles beneath my feet
I looked behind, and I saw this one so sweet
She came to me and I saw in her eyes
The heavy toll of a thousand sighs
I called her my princess of the sand

She stared at me and my mind was in a maze
As we moved along in a summer sea-dream haze
She moved her mouth but it made no sound
The message she brought can never be found
But I called her my princess of the sand

One moment we walked with the night breeze in our face
Then I looked, she'd gone, of her presence there was no trace
Where she went or came from who can know
Or if she'll ever return to help me know
Who she is my princess of the sand

Someday when the summer nights come back
I'll go back to the sea, and I'll follow that sand swept track
I'll look around and I'll hope to find
That strange young dream ...
I'll call her my princess in the sand

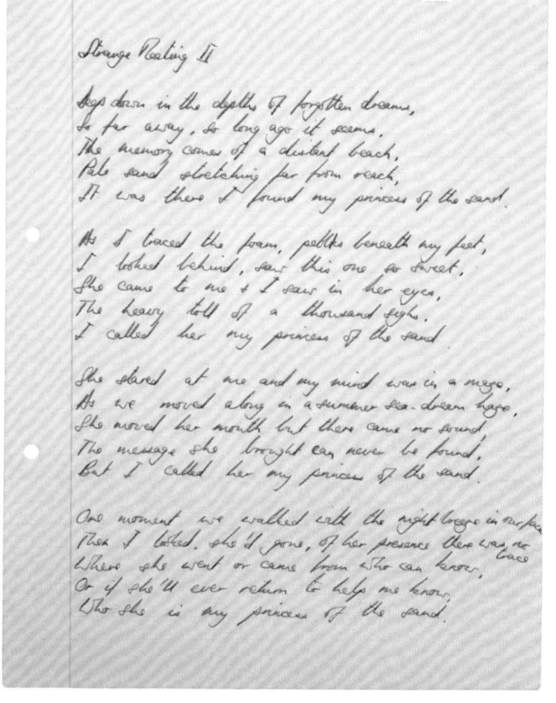

Strange Meeting II

Deep down in the depths of forgotten dreams,
So far away, so long ago it seems,
The memory comes of a distant beach,
Pale sand stretching far from reach,
It was there I found my princess of the sand.

As I traced the foam, pebbles beneath my feet,
I looked behind, saw this one so sweet,
She came to me + I saw in her eyes,
The heavy toll of a thousand sighs.
I called her my princess of the sand

She stared at me and my mind was in a maze,
As we moved along in a summer sea-dream haze,
She moved her mouth but there came no sound,
The message she brought can never be found,
But I called her my princess of the sand.

One moment we walked with the night breeze in our face
Then I looked, she'd gone, of her presence there was no trace
Where she went or came from who can know,
Or if she'll ever return to help me know,
Who she is my princess of the sand.

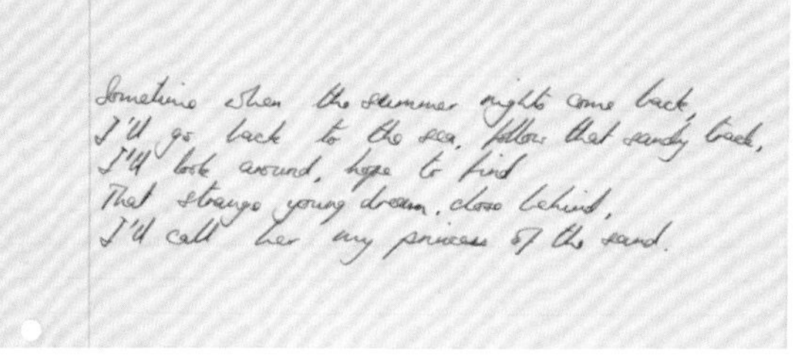

Sometime when the summer nights come back
I'll go back to the sea, follow that sandy track,
I'll look around, hope to find
That strange young dream, close behind,
I'll call her my princess of the sand.

Like 'Mayfair', you could view this early composition as a song where Nick was finding his feet (and indeed some of it re-uses sections of his own cover versions of John Renbourn and Jackson C. Frank material). Unlike 'Mayfair', though, you can see where this song led him. In taking the well-known formula of a four-chord descent from A minor, and trying to make something original of it, he's showing us a plan he would return to – with new ideas – in 'Day Is Done' and 'Fruit Tree'. (Compare Robin Frederick's 'Been Smoking Too Long', covered by Nick on the *Time Of No Reply* album, which feels much more like a straightforward blues take on the formula.)

Along with the slightly unusual downward progression (Am-D/F#-Dm/F-E), the tension of the C melody over the third chord in every line (much like the variation on an F chord at the same point in 'Things Behind The Sun') gives this song an emotional resonance, lifting it above its simple roots.

Mayfair

(also referred to as Mayfair Strange)

Mayfair strange in the morning light
Mayfair strange in a summer night
Mayfair strangest in the afternoon
Mayfair stretching far above
Full of fame but lacking love
Could it be we see the Mayfair moon?

Mayfair strange across the park
In the day or in the dark
There's no need to walk or even run
Mayfair faces clean and nice
But beauty here is cold as ice
Could it be we see the Mayfair sun?

Mayfair strange at every hour
Hidden frowns with mystic power
Starry heights and golden throne
Down below you're on your own

Mayfair strange for passers-by
Sights of wonder for the eye
Could it be that they'll pass by again?
Mayfair calling far and near
For even trees are wealthy here
Could it be we hear the Mayfair rain?

Mayfair strange in the morning light
Mayfair strange in a summer night
Mayfair strangest in the afternoon
Mayfair stretching far above
Full of fame but lacking love
Could it be we see the Mayfair moon?

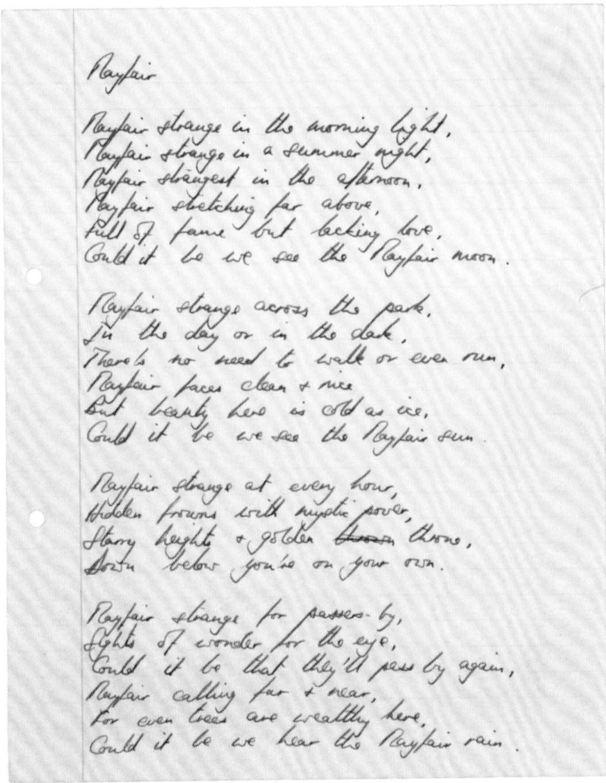

Mayfair

Mayfair strange in the morning light,
Mayfair strange in a summer night,
Mayfair strangest in the afternoon,
Mayfair stretching far above,
Full of fame but lacking love,
Could it be we see the Mayfair moon.

Mayfair strange across the park,
In the day or in the dark,
There's no need to walk or even run,
Mayfair faces clean + nice
But beauty here is cold as ice,
Could it be we see the Mayfair sun.

Mayfair strange at every hour,
Hidden frowns with mystic power,
Starry heights + golden ~~[illegible]~~ throne,
Down below you're on your own.

Mayfair strange for passers-by,
Sights of wonder for the eye,
Could it be that they'll pass by again,
Mayfair calling far + near,
For even trees are wealthy here,
Could it be we hear the Mayfair rain.

This is a very conventional three-chord pattern, with a little bit of walking bass under it. It feels like the sort of simple song, both musically and lyrically, a songwriter might write while learning his trade. It seems slightly ironic, given the heights Nick went on to, that this was the first song of his to be covered commercially.

Joey

Joey will come to see your flowers
Joey will come to while away your hours
But she will tell you you're not so good for her
She wouldn't be there if it could be that you were

Joey has loved, but never shown her tears
So she may laugh in the autumn of your years
And when you're with her you'll wonder if it's true
All that they said of a world without you

Where she may come from, where she may go
Who she may run from, no one will know
Why she was late may trouble you so
Still you wait for Joey to come

Joey will come when once more it looks like snow
Joey will come when it's really time to go
And you may smile when you find that you've been wrong
You thought you'd found her but she knew you all along

But Joey will come to say hello,
Joey

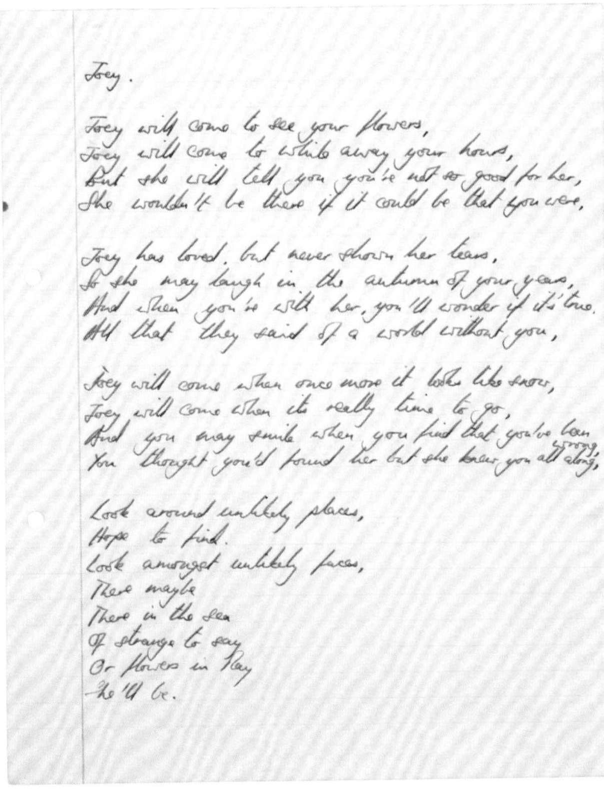
Joey.

Joey will come to see your flowers,
Joey will come to while away your hours,
But she will tell you you're not so good for her,
She wouldn't be there if it could be that you were,

Joey has loved, but never shown her tears,
So she may laugh in the autumn of your years,
And when you're with her, you'll wonder if it's true.
All that they said of a world without you,

Joey will come when once more it looks like snow,
Joey will come when its really time to go,
And you may smile when you find that you've been wrong,
You thought you'd found her but she knew you all along,

Look around unlikely places,
Hope to find.
Look amongst unlikely faces,
There maybe
There in the sea
Of strange to say
Or flowers in May
She'll be.

These chords are also pretty familiar (and in standard tuning), but there's more than enough melodic interest generated by the picking variations, the extra-high note lines, and the odd clever chord voicing (like the 0x6700 E7 under 'She wouldn't be there . . .') to make this feel like a true composition, not just a backing. My favourite bit comes in the last verse, where after the normal sequence begins under 'And you may smile when you find that you've been wrong', the Dm/G unexpectedly repeats for 'thought you'd found her' but is then trumped by the extra surprise of returning to Bm7/E7 for 'but she knew you all along': like the moment someone realizes they've been double-crossed.

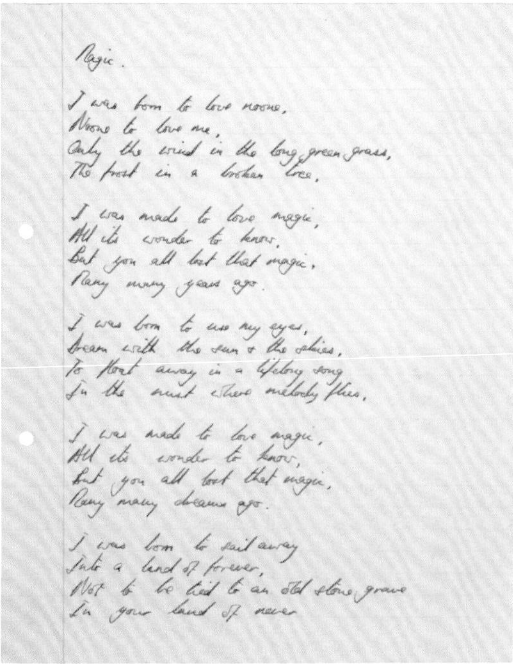
Magic.

I was born to love noone,
Noone to love me,
Only the wind in the long green grass,
The frost in a broken tree,

I was made to love magic,
All its wonder to know,
But you all lost that magic,
Many many years ago.

I was born to use my eyes,
Dream with the sun & the skies,
To float away in a lifelong song
In the mist where melody flies,

I was made to love magic,
All its wonder to know,
But you all lost that magic,
Many many dreams ago.

I was born to sail away
Into a land of forever,
Not to be tied to an old stone grave
In your land of never

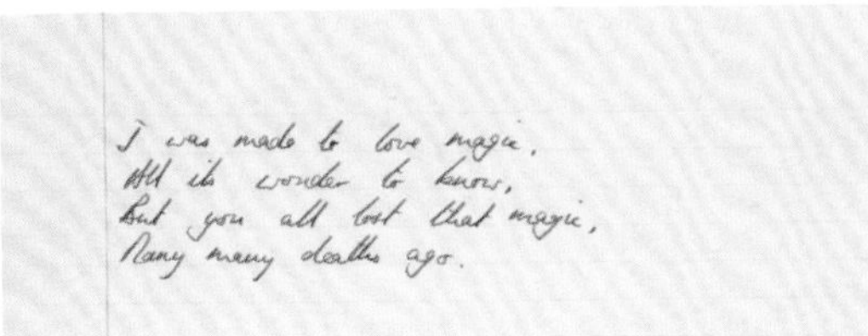
I was made to love magic,
All its wonder to know,
But you all lost that magic,
Many many deaths ago.

Robert Kirby's original written score for 'Magic'

Magic

I was born to love no one
No one to love me
Only the wind in the long green grass
The frost in a broken tree

I was made to love magic
All its wonder to know
But you all lost that magic
Many, many years ago

I was born to use my eyes
Dream with the sun and the skies
To float away in a lifelong song
In the mist where melody flies

I was made to love magic
All its wonder to know
But you all lost that magic
Many, many years ago

I was born to sail away
Into a land of forever
Not to be tied to an old stone grave
In your land of never

I was made to love magic
All its wonder to know
But you all lost that magic
Many, many years ago

The original (and unreleased) guitar version of this was, unusually for Nick, in DGDGBbD, a simple minor-chord tuning. Equally unusually – although several chords did have typical Nick harmonic quirks in them – there was not much in the picking pattern that was composed or constructed much beyond a typical folk fingerpicker's same-thing-on-every-chord right-hand routine. (It was a very early composition, though.) Maybe this is why Nick felt it would be worth trying as an orchestral piece?

It's perhaps easier to see why this track was left off *Five Leaves Left* than it is to understand why 'Time Of No Reply' was omitted. The lyrics do flirt with self-pity, while the switch from minor to major for 'I was made to love magic', and quickly back again for 'But you all lost that magic', is a bit heavy-handed. 'Way To Blue' pulls off something similar with rather more subtlety.

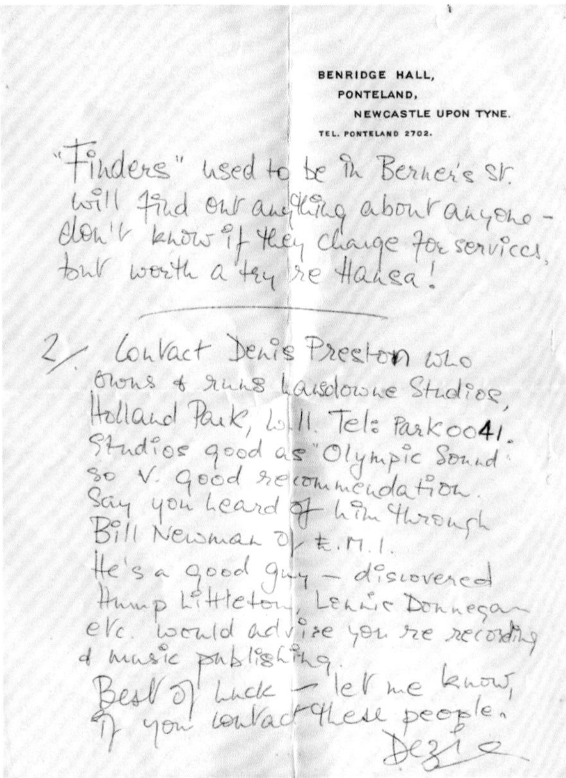

BENRIDGE HALL,
PONTELAND,
NEWCASTLE UPON TYNE.
TEL. PONTELAND 2702.

"Finders" used to be in Berner's St.
will find out anything about anyone –
don't know if they charge for services,
but worth a try re Hansa!

2/ Contact Denis Preston who
owns & runs Lansdowne Studios,
Holland Park, W.11. Tel: Park 0041.
Studios good as "Olympic Sound"
so v. good recommendation.
Say you heard of him through
Bill Newman of E.M.I.
He's a good guy – discovered
Hump Littleton, Lennie Donnegan
etc. would advise you re recording
& music publishing.
Best of luck – let me know,
if you contact these people.
Dezie

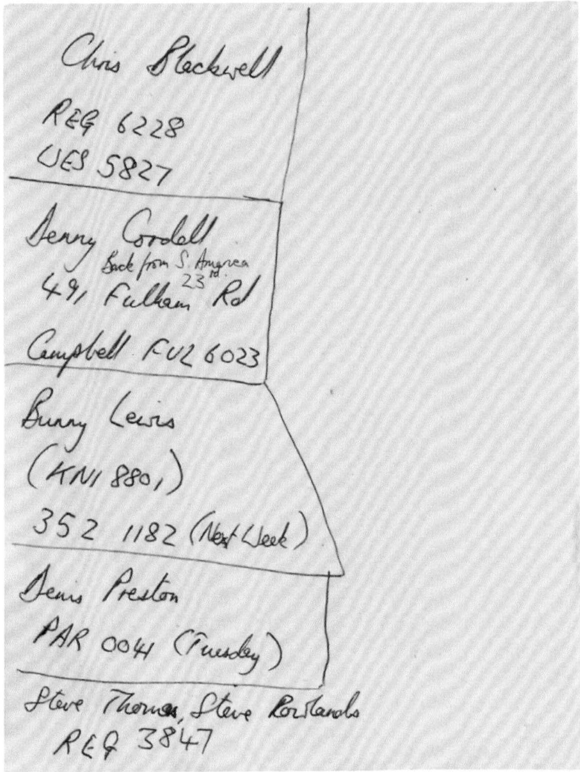

Chris Blackwell
REG 6228
UES 5827

Denny Cordell
Back from S. America 23rd.
49, Fulham Rd
Campbell FUL 6023

Bunny Lewis
(KNI 8801)
352 1182 (Next Week)

Denis Preston
PAR 0041 (Tuesday)

Steve Thomas, Steve Rowlands
REG 3847

Assisted and advised by his friend Dezie (Desirée Burlison Rush), Nick set about finding himself a recording or publishing contract. His list puts Island Records' Chris Blackwell at the top followed by Denny Cordell of Straight Ahead Productions. Songwriter and producer Steve Rowland, then working at Hansa Music Publishers, is at the bottom

Hansa offered the first deal, here annotated by Rodney Drake but never taken up. Note mis-spellings of songs and 'Life Flies Away', possibly a misheard 'Bird Flew By'. Rowland went on to produce the album *Coming From Reality* by Sixto Rodriguez, an obscure artist rediscovered almost Drake-like in 2012 due to the film *Searching For Sugar Man*, directed by Malik Bendjelloul

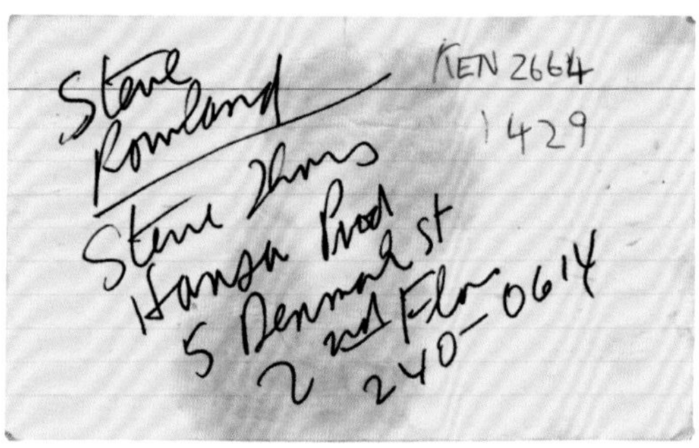

This Agreement is made the thirty first day of August one thousand nine hundred and sixty seven.

BETWEEN NICK DRAKE

of 62 Sloane Street, London, S.W.1.

and

of

(hereinafter referred to as "the Assignor(s)" of the one part and

HANSA PRODUCTION LTD. of 5 Denmark Street, W.C.2.
Reg: 142 Charing Cross Road, W.C.2.

in the County of London (hereinafter referred to as "the Publishers") of the other part WITNESSETH that in consideration of the payment by the Publishers to the Assignor(s) of the sum of 1/- (one shilling) (the receipt of which is hereby acknowledged) on account of the Royalties and Fees mentioned below the Assignor(s) hereby assigns to the Publishers ALL the Copyright as defined by the Copyright Act 1956, throughout the territory to which that Act may now or may at any time hereafter extend, together with all other rights of a like nature as are now conferred by the laws in force in all other territories throughout the world, including the renewal Copyright as conferred by the law of the United States of America, and such other rights as may hereafter be conferred or created by law or international arrangement or convention in any part of the world whether by new or additional rights not now comprised in Copyright or by way of extension of the period of then or now existing rights of and in the musical composition(s) entitled:—

"MY LOVE LEFT WITH THE RAIN"
"THE DAY IS DONE"
"LEAVING ME BEHIND"
"LIFE FLIES AWAY"

Copyright for ever

(hereinafter referred to as "the said work(s)")

TO HOLD the same unto the Publishers their successors and assignees absolutely AND the Assignor(s) hereby agrees on demand to execute and sign any other documents and to do all other acts and things which may hereafter be required of the Assignor(s) for vesting in the Publishers the premises expressed to be hereby assigned AND the Assignor(s) hereby warrants and declares that the said work(s) is a new and original unpublished work and does not infringe the Copyright in any other work and that he the Assignor(s) has good right and full power to assign to the Publishers free from all encumbrances the premises expressed to be hereby assigned and every one of them in the manner aforesaid.

In the event that the said work(s) is an instrumental composition then and in such event the Assignor(s) hereby irrevocably grants to the Publishers the sole and exclusive right and privilege to cause to have lyrics written for the said work(s) by a writer or writers designated by the Publishers which lyrics shall require only the approval of the Publishers whereupon the Assignor(s) shall be entitled only to one-half of the Royalties provided for in this Agreement in respect of the vocal edition only.

Can change anything

The Publishers shall have the right to make and publish adaptations and arrangements of the said work(s) and to make such additions and adaptations and alterations in and to the words and/or music of the said work(s) and such changes of title as they may desire, and to provide and translate the lyric thereof in any and all languages.

It is understood and agreed that the performing rights hereby assigned are subject to the rights of the Performing Right Society Limited or any affiliated Society of which the Assignor(s) is a member.

The music room at Far Leys

The Fruit

In Search Of A Master

by Gabrielle Drake

There are three key people who have been the channels through which Nick Drake's music has become known to a wider public. All three have been remarkable men in their own rights. All three were friends of Nick's, as well as collaborators. All three championed Nick's music long after his death; and to them, Nick owes much of his present renown.

They are (in order of Nick's meeting them) Robert Kirby, Joe Boyd, and John Wood.

Robert Kirby: Orchestrator

Robert Kirby was born in Bishop's Stortford in Hertfordshire, on 16 April 1948, in the kitchen of a house in Cherry Gardens, which was perhaps appropriate for a man who went on to develop a passion for food. Robert was a man of many passions. He had an enormous appetite for life.

His family was working-class, as he himself always said. His father was a skilled carpenter and cabinet maker; so skilled, in fact, that during the war he was co-opted into a satellite company for De Havilland, to make Mosquito planes, since these planes were constructed largely of wood. He was still an apprentice when he met and married Robert's mother – herself not long out of school. So, Robert grew up in a humble but happy household, with his older brother, Stuart, whose first comment on seeing his baby brother was: 'Hasn't he got beautiful pink ears?'

Robert's parents were determined to give their sons the education that they had never been able to have. So, from a very young age, both children had piano and singing lessons. In the early days, it was Stuart who was considered to have the fine voice, and who was always chosen to sing the solos in the church choir. Until, that is, the day he developed tonsillitis just before the Carol Service at which he was due to sing the boy soprano solo in 'Once in Royal David's City'. The choirmaster came round to the Kirby house to see whether there was any chance Stuart might recover in time to perform. And it was at this point that the seven-year-old Robert piped up that he knew the solo and could sing it. Which, to everyone's astonishment, he proceeded to do – and a musical career was launched.

Robert's voice became his gateway to music: he joined the church choir, became their solo singer, and formed friendships which were to last his whole life through – and this included his best friend Geoffrey James. For Robert's enthusiasm for life included a fierce and enduring loyalty to family and friends.

Both the Kirby boys were bright, and both were offered places at Bishop's Stortford College. Both flourished. The young Robert developed interests in music, sports (cross-country running and swimming in particular), drama, and literature, as well as a propensity for cheekiness and the odd prank, which was probably easy to forgive in a pupil who excelled in all subjects. Although the day he crashed his moped onto the local railway line – an incident from which he emerged unscathed, but which stopped the trains for a couple of days – must have taxed the patience of both his parents and teachers – and British Rail.

But singing remained Robert's overriding love: he joined the school choir, but then, as his interest in folk

THE GENTLE POWER OF SONG

TV TIMES WINTER '67

This group couldn't be better named—they really do have The Gentle Power of Song. Six past and present Cambridge choral scholars (below), they used to sing together in chapel. And the way they mix pop and serious music is delightful to hear. "It's not a gimmick," they say firmly. "We want to break down the barriers between different kinds of music. You could say our sound was a mixture of medieval and commercial." This month they follow up their first LP—of Christmas carols—with *Circus*, on the Polydor label. You'll love their original versions of songs like *God Only Knows*

32

THE OBSERVER REVIEW, 12 NOVEMBER 1967

JOHN HODDER

Six serious singers, making medieval commercial sound.

Robert Kirby (Photo and cuttings supplied by Henry and Constance Kirby)

music developed, he formed a folk group with his friend Geoffrey James. To begin with they toured the local pubs, then later went further afield, to Germany, where the group played Bob Dylan covers.

And it was singing that was to gain Robert a place at university: in 1966 he won a choral scholarship to Gonville and Caius, one of Cambridge University's most distinguished colleges.

By now he was studying music and orchestration, and seemed to be destined for a life as a music teacher. Robert found Cambridge challenging in a way school had never been. Nevertheless, he threw himself into life there with his customary zeal. Determined to take advantage of all the university had to offer, he decided to audition for the famous Cambridge dramatic society, the Footlights. Somewhat to his surprise, he failed to get in! But the audition was to be momentous, though he did not realise it at the time, for at that same audition was a tall, willowy, somewhat introverted student called Nick Drake. History does not relate whether the unsuccessful candidates (for Nick also failed to get into the Footlights) had any kind of actual exchange at this time. The first significant meeting between the two of them was to take place a while later, in Robert's rooms at Caius.

By now, Robert had joined a harmony group, formed from the chapel choristers of his college and called The Gentle Power of Song, as well as a pop group – Fab Cab – and he was gaining a reputation within the university as a music arranger. Nick had heard about this, and turned up with his guitar to ask Robert to add some arrangements to his own songs. The ebullient Kirby and the reticent Drake would appear to have been polar opposites. Musically, however, they were kindred souls. Robert, by his own admission, was deeply impressed when he heard Nick's songs; and Nick knew he had found the person he was looking for, as this extract, from a letter to his parents, shows:

'My musical friend, a guy named Robert Kirby, is working quite hard on arrangements for some of my songs, and seems to be pretty competent. He's a rather splendid fellow, and looks rather like Haydn or Mozart or someone, being rather short and stocky, with long wavy hair and rimless spectacles. However he's quite hip to my sort of music, being quite a proficient folk singer himself. He's done a rather beautiful string quartet arrangement for "Day Is Done", and is now working on "Time Of No Reply".'

Robert was not displeased with this description of himself when shown it many years later: for, as he used to say, 'Mozart is my favourite composer – although The Beatles run him a close second.'

Robert Kirby died in 2009.

John Wood: Sound Engineer

In 1964, John Wood, together with Geoff Frost, founded the remarkable and innovatory Sound Techniques Studio. It was here that Nick recorded all three of his albums.

Born on 4 November 1939, in Sevenoaks, Kent, John Wood was a scholarship boy who found exams easy, but disliked school intensely. Consequently, he never made it to the sixth form, and left without attempting to go to university. Instead, since he had excelled in Maths and Science at school, he became a research assistant at BICC Research Laboratories in London, whilst studying for a diploma in metallurgy. However, this became as tedious to him as school had been, and so after eighteen months he left, not knowing what he would do.

Then it occurred to him that he could find employment doing something he actually enjoyed.

In his boyhood, John had developed a love of classical music, and, like his father, had become a hi-fi enthusiast, building up a fine record collection, and thus inevitably training his ear from an early age. At this crossroads in his life, John made the momentous decision to combine his love of music with his scientific ability, and to try for a job in the expanding recording industry.

Decca Records was the home of classical music, and so the young John wrote to them, but hedged his bets by writing to EMI as well. Rather to his surprise, both offered him a job. He took Decca's offer, and flourished, quickly acquiring a considerable degree of expertise in stereo mastering.

It was this expertise which led to an offer of work at Levy's Sound Studio – a very different set-up from Decca's. Here, John was forced to confront the problems of recording popular music. It was a baptism of fire.

As John himself recollects:

'Levy's main products were Woolworths' cover records. My job was to make the cover version sound like the original. This was just a nightmare, Every three or four weeks the A&R man for Embassy (as the label was called) would decide what was going to be a hit and would then get someone to cover it. No one ever had a clue about any of the techniques that were employed on the original versions.

'They'd bring me the original, plus their cover version – which for a start probably only used half the amount of musicians – and they would ask, 'Could you just twiddle the knobs and make it sound like that?' So I suppose that was how I developed an interest in popular music.'

But it was here, at Levy's Sound Studio, that John Wood met Geoff Frost, then their chief technical engineer. Both

John Wood at Sound Techniques, 1974 (Photo: Willi Murray)

men obviously found the conditions under which they were working to be far from ideal, and, after a year, both thought: 'We can do better than this.'

So, with a loan of £10,000 from Geoff's mother, the two young men set about finding premises for their new recording studio.

'We found two upper floors of an old dairy in Chelsea,' remembers John. 'In those days, Chelsea wasn't fashionable: it was classed as a light-industrial zone, and recording studios were thought to be light industry. There was a builder's merchant round the corner and an art shop where you could get big dyeline drawings done for circuit diagrams. So, although it wasn't ideal, we settled on the dairy.'

This was 46a Old Church Street. The plaster cow's head which marked the doorway became a landmark for musicians and recording artists alike. But to make it work as a recording studio required a certain degree of ingenuity, as John himself recalls:

'We had to lift out the centre of the top floor, ending up with a long, almost shoe-box like shape, which was fifty feet by twenty feet, and about twelve feet high – it went right up to the roof so it was double the height.

'At one end we had the control room which looked down on two-thirds of the studio, and at the other end we had the workshop, with the office and an entrance downstairs, made out of what had originally been a garage entrance. Then there were the windows: it was unusual in those days to have windows in a studio. We had to triple-glaze them, and line the roof part of the ceiling with extra sound-deadening materials. It was all pretty fundamental. Nevertheless, we started off with four-track recording, which was state of the art in those days.

'We didn't have very much money and, being of a technical bent, Geoff Frost made all our own equipment.

Anyway, in those days, there wasn't much equipment you could buy. It was a very different industry from now, pretty much run by inspired amateurs.

'However, even before we'd finished making our own mixer, we'd already started making them for other people. To begin with, we were constructing mixers upstairs and recording downstairs. We used to have a red light in the workshop which went on whenever we were recording a take, and all the sawing and hammering would have to stop until it went out. We went on to develop the construction side of the business and Geoff ran that, while I ran the studio. By the time we were making Nick's records, the equipment-building side had moved out to Suffolk.

'In 1976 we came to the end of the lease on 46a Old Church Street, and we tried to buy the building, as it was up for sale. But our bankers at the time thought it would be a bad investment! I think we could have bought the building we were in, plus two shops at the front and a flat over the top for £180,000. I don't know what it would be worth today – 12 million pounds? More?

'I didn't feel like starting again, so we arranged a deal whereby Cliff Adams, who owned Olympic Studios, and was always interested in property investments, purchased the freehold of the entire site and continued to run the studio as a satellite of Olympic. I'm not sure how long they ran it for. I know I went on using it for mixing and recording sessions until the mid Eighties. Eventually the whole site was redeveloped. It's now a block of flats. Probably somebody's got a bathroom where Nick used to play his guitar.'

'Whenever I pass the old dairy and see the flats that have replaced the studio,' wrote Joe Boyd in *White Bicycles*, 'I feel a wrench. It's hard to find places like Sound Techniques today. There is a small anti-digital movement, but even studios with this approach rarely have a room that sounds anywhere near as good.'

Joe Boyd: Producer

Joe Boyd was born in Boston, Massachusetts on 5 August 1942. Like Robert Kirby, he developed a love of music from a very early age, and with it, a discerning ear. By the time he was eleven years old (and by now living in Princeton, New Jersey) he had discovered, and was avidly listening to, blues and jazz, at a time when neither was fashionable – certainly not in the respectable, white, American middle-class milieu in which he was growing up. But the young Joe Boyd knew, from an early age, that he would never be a musician himself. Rather, he decided, at the tender age of eighteen, he would be a record producer: he would be the facilitator, the necessary channel by which the musician's work would reach a wider audience.

Just before he started studying at Harvard, he managed to track down the once celebrated, but almost forgotten blues singer Lonnie Johnson, at that time working as a cook in a Philadelphia hotel. Joe organised a concert for him in a friend's living room, and thereby re-launched Johnson's career. And the young Joe Boyd, even before he went to college, was set firmly on his chosen path.

Joe's first job after leaving Harvard in 1964 was as tour manager for the American Folk Blues and Gospel Caravan: a line-up of legendary blues and gospel singers – Muddy Waters, Sister Rosetta Tharpe, and the Reverend Gary Davies amongst them – set to tour principally in the UK. To his surprise, Joe discovered at the first rehearsal in London that most of the performers did not know each other, and that the degree of resentment amongst them was high. Disaster loomed, and Joe's nascent management skills were put to a severe test. But he – and above all the tour – emerged triumphant, and the concerts have become the stuff of legends. At the end of a few short weeks, animosity had turned to friendship, and the performers vowed they would repeat the experience. Alas, this was never to be – but such was the enthusiasm

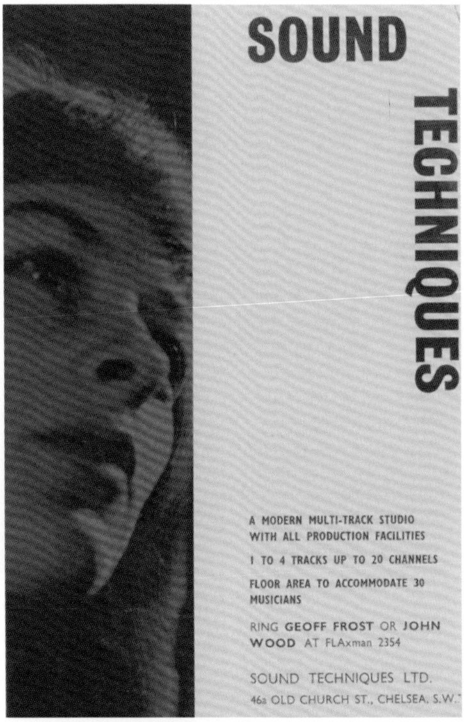
SOUND
TECHNIQUES
A MODERN MULTI-TRACK STUDIO
WITH ALL PRODUCTION FACILITIES
1 TO 4 TRACKS UP TO 20 CHANNELS
FLOOR AREA TO ACCOMMODATE 30
MUSICIANS
RING GEOFF FROST OR JOHN
WOOD AT FLAxman 2354
SOUND TECHNIQUES LTD.
46a OLD CHURCH ST., CHELSEA, S.W.

of the British audiences for these and other blues concerts that it changed the course of Joe Boyd's life: he decided to leave America, and to live and produce music in Britain.

This ambition was furthered when Jac Holzman gave Joe the job of opening up a London office for Elektra Records, with the opening brief of finding a blues band featuring British talent to appear on a compilation album Elektra were planning to release called *The Electric Blues Project* (an album later released in the US as *What's Shakin'*). Within a few months, Joe had met up with Paul Jones, lead singer with Manfred Mann, who suggested putting together an all-star band to mark the occasion. Between them they formed a group that included Eric Clapton (the group was called Eric Clapton and the Power House), Steve Winwood and Paul Jones himself.

But Powerhouse was never intended to be more than a short-lived studio project, and Joe continued his search for a British band to sign. However, *The Electric Blues Project* had produced two key connections for him: Eric Clapton became a friend, and, in getting clearance for Steve Winwood to play in his group, Joe made his first contact with Chris Blackwell of Island Records, who would figure prominently in his subsequent professional life.

It soon became obvious that Joe's quest for new talent was at odds with Jac Holzman's need for a straight marketing man, and, before two years were out, Joe had left Elektra Records. But not before his significant meeting with John Wood.

Elektra Records had started using John's recording studio, the emerging Sound Techniques, for two orchestral concept albums, and when the musicians needed paying, Joe, as label manager, was sent to 46a Old Church Street with a wad of cash. There he met John Wood, owner and chief engineer; the two men found an instant sympathy, both with each other, and with their ideas about the recording of music. It was a partnership that was to lead to seminal albums from The Incredible String Band, Fairport Convention, John and Beverley Martyn – and, of course, Nick Drake.

Before this, however, Joe Boyd, having lost his job at Elektra, had become an integral part of London's Underground movement, discovering The Pink Floyd, and founding his radical and subversive club, UFO. By the time he met Nick Drake, he had started his own production company, Witchseason, and had become a record producer of some renown – a youthful *éminence grise*: 'a role to which I had aspired ever since I had first understood the expression,' as Joe himself puts it in his enticing autobiography, *White Bicycles*, in which he describes all of the above, and much more, in full and fascinating detail.

THE A&R MEN

No 10.
JOE BOYD

"IT was in my early teens that I made up my mind that one day I was going to be a record producer," said Joe Boyd, a tall, thoughtful American. "I was involved in blues and folk when I was young, but my first steps toward this ambition came when I was at Harvard. I got to know a lot of the people when the folk thing started—at one time I was rooming with Tom Rush—and I started a small distribution agency for specialist blues and folk labels for the Boston area.'

"My first real connection with producing came when I took a term off from college and managed to get a job in a studio doing odd jobs and generally helping out. Although I wasn't doing anything important, I learnt a lot".

Joe has had an important association with Paul Rothchild, now Elektra's chief producer. They'd been friendly for some time working on Paul's small independent label when Rothchild was offered a job with Prestige, an up-and-coming blues and jazz label. Joe followed him as unofficial assistant and together they worked on records by, among others, Geoff Muldaur, Tom Rush and the Kweskin Jug Band.

Meanwhile, Joe had been to England. "I had been struck by groups like Manfred Mann and the Stones who were playing white electric blues, which was unheard of in America. Sam Charters took me down to a Chicago club to see a band, which he said was incredibly good and made up of black and white musicians. It turned out to be the Butterfield band, and Paul was asked to leave Prestige to produce them for Elektra. He did, and we got them in the studio with Mike Bloomfield brought in on guitar. They were the first of their kind in America.'

"The first session with me in control came later on. Elektra had a number of blues tracks by the Spoonful, Butterfield, Al Kooper and others, and they wanted to get launched in England with a British band. It was decided to get it all together in a follow-up amplified anthology to the acoustic *Blues Project* album. It was Paul Jones who offered to get a blues band, and he came up with Steve Anglo and the Powerhouse—in reality, Steve Winwood, Eric Clapton, Pete York, Jack Bruce and Paul himself on harmonica. As it happened, Jac Holzman, the Elektra boss, suddenly turned up in England to keep an eye on me on this session. But what a way to start".

MORE WORK

More work began to come Joe's way, recording English folk artists with Bill Leader for Transatlantic. Two notable singles to emerge were *Arnold Layne* by the Floyd and *Granny Takes A Trip* by the Purple Gang, both produced by Boyd. At around this time, Joe was running the epoch-making UFO club along with John Hopkins, taking charge completely when Hoppy was jailed, so he had a very full plate of business.

By this time he had recorded the Incredible String Band, for which he is best known. "I'd come across Robin Williamson and Clive Palmer in Edinburgh in '65 when I was managing the Blues and Gospel Caravan tour. They were playing a sort of Scottish bluegrass, and were obviously something very special. When I returned to England a year later, the first thing I did was to go up and find them. By this time Mike Heron had joined and the three of them were doing more of their own songs—but nobody had signed them up, luckily. It was agreed that I should manage them and produce their records, and we went into the studio as soon as we could.

"My philosophy as a producer is simply to set as good an atmosphere as possible for the artists to play their best and then put them in front of a microphone and record them as faithfully as I can. I don't want to impose my personality on the record, and I don't like using electronic trickery. Robin and Mike like to come in and record a song straight, listen to it, and then decide if they want to dub on any more instruments, although at first they were horrified at the thought of tracking. Now they've discovered the possibilities".

In addition to the Incredibles, Joe also records Fairport Convention, Nick Drake, the Chris MacGregor Group and Beverly —a fair selection of the best new folk and jazz artists, as yet not fully accepted. Joe Boyd is important now, but it looks as if he can only grow in stature along with these artists.

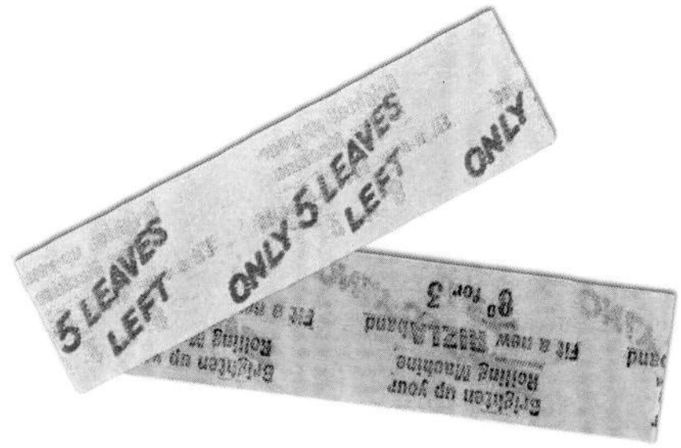

Five Leaves Left

by Pete Paphides

When Joe Boyd first told Nick that he envisaged string arrangements for his songs, Nick responded positively. He too had envisaged something similar. Listen to the recording of 'River Man' in Kirby's room or, much later, the demo of 'Hazey Jane I', and much of what you hear the strings playing in the recorded versions of the songs is traceable to those early versions. Travelling for the first time to John Wood's Sound Techniques Studio in Chelsea, Nick had yet to tell Joe Boyd about Robert Kirby – and, at this point, it probably wouldn't have made much difference if he had. If Joe had a strategy for Nick's first album it was one based on the phenomenal success of Leonard Cohen's debut, which had raced towards 100,000 sales since its release in December 1967. A world-class songwriter would require nothing less than a world-class arranger and, after a few enquiries, it was decided that Richard Hewson was the right man for the job. Having arranged the strings on James Taylor's debut album and Donovan's first two albums, Hewson seemed a safe pair of hands.

It's hard not to wonder what must have been going through Nick's head as, playing live alongside a string quartet and bass guitar, he heard Richard Hewson's arrangements for 'The Thoughts Of Mary Jane', 'Day Is Done' and 'Magic' for the first time. Hindsight has been dismissive of these versions, in particular 'Magic' (erroneously titled 'I Was Made To Love Magic' on 1987's *Time Of No Reply* compilation), but Hewson's arrangements are far from without merit. If anything, they suggest that he'd heard Nick described as an 'English chansonnier' and placed the songs in a setting that teased out those similarities. Hewson's versions were perfectly pretty – but they were created at something of a disadvantage: he had never seen or spoken to Nick. He had no idea who this unknown singer was trying to emulate; who he saw as his peers; whether his aspirations were mainstream or underground. On the early version of 'The Thoughts Of Mary Jane', any indication that Nick might be singing about marijuana (as per the vernacular of the day) is lost in Hewson's fragrant arrangement. But perhaps the measure of Robert Kirby's immediate bond with Nick's music can be apprehended by comparing his arrangement of 'Magic' with that of Hewson. Having lain in Kirby's potting shed until 2003, his score for the song dramatically came to life when Nick's vocal was finally reunited with it for the following year's *Made To Love Magic* anthology. It had only taken thirty-five years, but finally John Wood and Robert Kirby were able to fashion a version that did justice to Nick's vision for the song. The existence of Nick's voice on one separate stereo track on the multi-track master meant that, with a little studio trickery, his vocal performance could be isolated in readiness for Kirby's belatedly realised arrangement.

In the liner notes for *Made To Love Magic*, Robert Kirby described the moment the orchestra first played his original arrangement for 'Magic': 'When I stood at the rostrum and Nick's solo voice, onto which I was to lay the orchestra again after thirty-five years, came through the headphones, I closed my eyes and it was a highly emotional experience. I swear I could smell and feel Cambridge in the late Sixties again.' It was a moment that Wood himself described as 'jaw-dropping', adding that the musicians on the session were 'pretty overawed too'.

Indeed, the Kirby arrangement of 'Magic' is so strong, one wonders if it might have supplanted any of the songs that did make it on to *Five Leaves Left*. Eschewing attempts to imbue the song with any sort of pop sensibility, Kirby's string arrangement holds back from sweetening the deep-seated fatalism of the lyrical sentiment; indeed, on the achingly mournful bridge, he seems to echo it.

In the aftermath of the Hewson session, it's hardly surprising that Nick was unsure how to voice his dissatisfaction. This was his first time in a recording studio. The trouble and expense involved in arranging the session would have fazed many a more experienced musician. Sitting beside engineer John Wood at the console, Joe Boyd had already made up his mind. 'From the beginning you could just tell it was wrong,' he recalled.

'It was sweet, corny and cute . . . [but] you had to finish the session. People were gradually packing up, and John Wood and I and Nick sat there looking at each other, and [once Richard Hewson] was out the door, I turned to Nick and said, "Sorry about that, it didn't really work." And Nick was so relieved because you could tell he loathed it and was a little too shy . . . I mean, he didn't know what I was going to say, and he was worried about what would happen if I liked it. And we said, "Well, what are we going to do?" And Nick said, "Well, I have a friend at Cambridge . . ."'

At this point, Boyd was faced with two conflicting instincts. On one hand, his stated ambition to embellish Nick's songs with a 'world-class arranger' couldn't be further removed from the idea of using an untried undergraduate 'who had never done anything professional in his life'; on the other, Nick had barely proffered anything by way of verbal input, so the fact that he had said anything at all made it worth listening to. The pairing of Robert Kirby and Nick Drake – the working-class extrovert and the upper-middle-class introvert – was an unlikely one. But when it came to working in a recording studio, neither were lacking in confidence. One Friday in October 1968, still only twenty years old, the relatively untried Kirby accompanied Nick to his sister Gabrielle's Battersea flat, where the pair stayed before heading across the river to Sound Techniques the following morning.

Only the most dogged of rationalists would refuse to believe that some divine hand was at play when a mutual friend suggested to Nick that fellow undergraduate Robert might be able to supply Nick's songs with the arrangements he was after. Both were unconventional in their approach. Kirby's love of great pop was matched only by his disdain for the Cambridge music department's embrace of such modern conceptualists as Stockhausen and Boulez. 'Nuts and bolts in a dustbin have never been my forte,' he later explained. Recalling the first piece of music he submitted as a student there, he recalled that it 'had a line struck right through it and my lecturers wrote "Corn Flakes commercial" underneath. But I was delighted. I thought: "Is this really good enough to be in a Corn Flakes commercial?"' If Kirby was immediately struck by Nick's charisma, the feeling was no less mutual. Kirby had the sort of experience which Nick so readily craved. He had toured Europe with groups since the early Sixties and, as part of a Cambridge-based collective called The Gentle Power of Song, had already released a single – a wonderfully odd marriage of choral vocals and freakbeat guitar called 'Constant Penelope'. In the winter of 1967, The Gentle Power of Song had even appeared on the wildly popular chat show *du jour*, *Dee Time*.

Kirby's openness mirrored Nick's own eclectic approach. Friends at Cambridge remember albums by Van Morrison, The Fifth Dimension, Mose Allison, Randy Newman, John Coltrane, The Beach Boys, Jimmy Webb, Ravel and Vaughan Williams all competing for airtime on Nick's record player. Prior to that, of course, Nick had hurled himself headlong into the set texts of the folk-guitar revival, but these seemed to have tailed off slightly by the time he reached Cambridge. As Nathan Wiseman-Trowse wrote in his book *Dreaming England*, Nick's 'interpretations of a number of songs from two specific albums, *Dave Van Ronk Sings* and Jackson C. Frank's eponymous debut album from 1965, point to a budding guitarist who has been devouring momentary musical obsessions to learn his craft.'

That he had finessed that craft to a level of peerless virtuosity was apparent when he entered the studio. In a session that began at 10 a.m., Nick Drake – assisted by Robert Kirby, John Wood, Joe Boyd and the assembled players – achieved an extraordinary feat. In just three hours, almost half of his debut album had been recorded: 'Way To Blue', 'The Thoughts Of Mary Jane', 'Fruit Tree', and 'Day Is Done'. Joe Boyd remembers that 'the first track was "Way To Blue", and just hearing [the session musicians play their] individual parts was so tantalizing and interesting, and I was so impatient with John Wood because he wanted to listen at first to the violas and then the violins and then finally I heard it all together and I was, like, "This is fantastic!" It was so, so far beyond what we were expecting or hoping for.'

The first time Nick played 'Way To Blue' to Robert

Kirby would have been in the late winter of 1968, shortly after the pair met for the first time:

'I had a 1959 Series 3 Ferrograph (valve) mono tape-recorder . . . [on which] he recorded "Way To Blue", "Magic", and "Saturday Sun" . . . He was extremely patient as I boringly dissected each one – writing down exactly how any complex chords were voiced . . . I was interested in the songs of Debussy and Ravel; and so we would talk a bit about Impressionism. And in some of the arrangements, I tried to get a bit of an Impressionist feel. But, there again, say on "Way To Blue", I tried to handle it completely as a baroque song, like Handel or Bach, and that's why we dispensed with the guitar and just had the orchestra and Nick singing. It seemed to suit the mood of the song . . . It was almost like a Bach chorale; it was a religious song, I thought, a spiritual song.'

The passing decades have done nothing to dissipate the effect of 'Way To Blue'. Robin Frederick attributes much of the song's power to 'the resolving of the suspended fourth to the major third':

'If you sing the word "amen" as it is sung at the end of a hymn, you will hear exactly that. This song is filled with the "amen" phrase . . . This prayer-like quality is underscored in the lyric: its metaphysical questions – "Have you ever heard a way to find the sun?", "Can you understand a light among the trees?" – hang suspended in the air, quietly demanding an answer that does not come.'

Unlike Hewson, Robert Kirby's arrangements made no concessions to accepted notions of what the components of a pop song should be. As a 'mad Beatles freak since 1963', he noted the way that George Martin fashioned an uncompromisingly stark setting for 'Eleanor Rigby' (1966). And, indeed, having used Handel as a jumping-off point for 'Way To Blue', it was the Beatles song that emboldened him to do something similar on 'Day Is Done'. 'The cellos had the rhythm part,' he recalled, 'which was an unashamed homage to George Martin.' While Hewson's arrangement played against the lyric, the strings on Robert Kirby's version seem to impassively serve the words. Nick was finding more sophisticated expressions of the fatalism that characterised his very earliest lyrics. The book on Nick's bedside table at the time of his death was Camus's *The Myth of Sisyphus*: an atheist's argument against suicide. Frederick points out that, 'like Sisyphus [the mythical giant condemned to repeat his arduous task], the vocal melody is forced to return again and again to its starting point . . . The repetitive quality of the song, its continual return to the beginning, and its bleak lyrics all invoke the philosophy of Absurdism and the question which lies at its heart: How do you go on living when you know that life is meaningless?'

Early versions of the song were, if anything, even more repetitive. A home recording of 'Day Is Done' contains two extra verses – three if you include a mumbled fourth verse. On the two verses that precede the closing reiteration of the first verse, we hear Nick sing, 'When they have sung the song / Maybe you won't feel quite so strong / Your hopes won't last quite so long / When they have sung the song.' And then: 'When they have sung the [this?] song / Won't be / Not so sure [*indeterminate mumbling*] / When they have sung the [this?] song.' What is striking here is Nick's eagerness to keep singing the song, in spite of the fact that the lyrics have yet to be finessed. The unselfconscious expressiveness of his vocal also depicts a songwriter in the first flush of enthusiasm for a new composition. What we appear to be hearing is a lyric that is, in part, being improvised into life. By the time 'Day Is Done' made it to Sound Techniques, Nick sounded less emotionally invested in the lyric, a change which freighted an appropriate sense of weary indifference into Nick's words that perfectly complemented Kirby's arrangement.

To what degree was Nick philosophically invested in these sentiments? Was he essaying a view, or describing the world as it truly seemed to him? To what degree had he been seduced by the ideas he was reading and singing about? These are all questions that circle around key songs in his oeuvre – and none more than 'Fruit Tree', a rumination on posthumous fame, whose contents seems to bear out Nick's comment in a letter to his parents that he was enjoying studying 'people like Swift, Pope, Blake etc, who have quite a lot to offer in their way'.

It seems almost irresistibly easy to make a connection between lines such as 'Don't you worry / They'll stand and stare when you're gone' and the almost unacknowledged passing of their creator, six years later. But, of course, Nick was a student of English literature and, as Frederick points out, 'He would have known that poets like Keats and William Blake (a favourite of his) died without the recognition they deserved.' Similarly, a few months previously, when Nick visited Kirby's room and played 'Fruit Tree' into his tape recorder, his friend 'saw it as somewhat inspired by Shelley or Byron or Buddy Holly', and made a note of Nick's ideas for how the finished song should sound: 'He said that he possibly heard oboes on it, and strings, and that was about it.' Interviewed for the 2002 documentary *A Skin Too Few: The Days Of Nick Drake*, he elaborated further: '[the oboe and cor anglais] are really just playing one long tune and one takes off after another . . . Because I didn't want it to ever take over from the guitar playing.'

Kirby thought his 'simple' arrangement of 'The Thoughts Of Mary Jane' constituted 'a step forward' in the sense that 'we weren't trying to copy anyone'. Nevertheless, for Robin Frederick, this was the first of Nick's songs to suggest a perceptible bossa nova influence – João Gilberto refracted through Tim Buckley, perhaps. In Hewson's arrangement, it's a similarity brought closer to the surface by the languorous tapping of brush on snare. Two months later, Nick would attempt the song a third time, with Richard Thompson contributing electric guitar, but it was the October 1969 version that made the final cut, in the process ousting 'Time Of No Reply', which Nick deemed too similar. The failure of 'Time Of No Reply' to make it onto the first album came as a surprise to Brian Wells, 'because it was something he played quite a lot [at Cambridge]'. In fact, it would be another thirty-five years before Kirby would finally get to hear his arrangement for 'Time Of No Reply' in a studio, when it was finally recorded for the *Made To Love Magic* album.

More than any other single location in Britain, Sound Techniques was the hub of the British folk-rock boom. The albums released between 1968 and 1972 by Fairport Convention, Sandy Denny, John and Beverley Martyn, Fotheringay, and Nick Drake tend to be united in people's minds by the fact that Joe Boyd produced them – but John Wood with his then-unfashionable insistence that acoustic instruments needed to be recorded in a large, live-sounding room is no less crucial to the picture. As the late Scott Appel, a guitarist and fastidious early student of Nick's music, wrote: 'Wood had arrived at a system of using four mics, in the truest sense of ambience, placing one completely across the room.' Along with chief technical engineer Geoff Frost, it was Wood – a former Decca engineer who had grown up on classical music – who set about converting two floors of an old dairy into a recording studio. In the 1960s, no two studios were the same. Recording hardware, which is now mass-produced, was more often than not made from scratch. 'The industry was run by inspired amateurs,' recalls Wood. In time, he settled into the role of in-house engineer while Frost specialised in building mixers to order for anyone who wanted to buy one.

By the time Joe Boyd came knocking on the door of Sound Techniques, John Wood had developed an interest in pop, largely because of the demands placed upon him as the producer of cover records released on Woolworths' budget Embassy label. Wood saw his resourcefulness routinely stretched to breaking point as he was charged with the task of creating sonic facsimiles of popular hits using the sparest of means. So when Joe Boyd suggested he engineer Judy Collins's *In My Life* album, Wood had accrued a wealth of experience. Though he didn't realise it at the time, Collins's album was effectively a dry run for processes that would dramatically bear fruit on *Five Leaves Left*. Collins's arranger, Joshua Rifkin, was insistent that the musicians on her album would need to be classically trained players who had resisted the lure of pop sessions and adverts. The effect was palpable enough to distinguish Collins's album in a crowded subgenre. Furthermore, her version of Leonard Cohen's 'Suzanne' was pivotal in introducing the singer-songwriter to a mainstream audience.

Also featured on Collins's album was a song by a then-unknown writer called Randy Newman called 'I Think It's Going to Rain Today' – which, in itself, was enough to establish an early bond between Nick and the man who would go on to engineer all of his studio recordings. Newman's self-titled debut album had entered Nick's orbit before it had even secured a UK release and, without delay, proceeded to make a lasting impression. 'About the time of the very first recording sessions,' recalled Wood, 'I talked to [Nick] about his musical influences, and he came up with Randy Newman . . . I had an empathy with Nick because of that; I could see where he was coming from.' Patrick Humphries picks up on the 'striking similarities' between *Randy Newman* (1968) and Nick's own first album: 'most obviously the lush orchestrations which punctuate the songs – particularly the opening "Love story" and the spellbinding "I Think It's Going to Rain Today" . . . It was the orchestral accompaniment, massed and used as an instrument, that gave the record its real impact, and made such an effect on Nick.'

Having allowed Richard Hewson to choose the players on the aborted first session for Nick's album, John Wood and Joe Boyd reverted to the process that they had seen work so well for Judy Collins. From thereon in, recalled Wood, 'we never went to the regular sources: we booked people from the London Symphony Orchestra or the English Chamber Orchestra.' Indeed, Boyd's meticulous selection of players 'who could bounce off Nick, rather than just provide a kind of colour or something', was unrelenting. Even on the songs that required no orchestral accompaniment, every musician involved was unique in their field.

New York pianist Paul Harris was the very first musician to be pencilled in by Boyd on his first encounter with Nick's music – for the piano accompaniment to

'Time Has Told Me', which was the first song he heard on the demo tape. And the finished album version of the song is performed by a small but stellar ensemble, all of whom treat Nick's music with the utmost respect. Accompanying Paul Harris's piano, and moonlighting from Pentangle, was the pre-eminent double-bassist of his generation, Danny Thompson – to whose 'aggressive cockney affection' (as Joe Boyd called it) Nick took an instant shine. According to Boyd, Danny's namesake Richard Thompson, the session's guitarist, 'would listen to a song of Nick's, ask to hear it again, then again, frowning in concentration, then come up with a great part. He would stand in the door of the control room listening to a playback, concentrating quizzically. Richard likes to figure out every kind of music he hears, but Nick puzzled him – "Where did that *come* from?"' In a bid to find out the same thing, Paul Harris spent hours talking to Nick, feeling increasingly protective of him as he did so.

The presence of Harris on the 'Time Has Told Me' session dates the recording some way into 1969. This much we know because Harris had already begun work with John and Beverley Martyn that year in Woodstock on their *Stormbringer!* album, and it was on arriving in London to finish work on that album that Harris first met Nick. It must have been thrilling for Nick to hear one of his earliest songs brought into new focus by the casual synergy that his illustrious sidemen had summoned for it.

It's almost impossible to overestimate the influence of The Band's *Music from Big Pink* at this period, and either by design or osmosis, there's something of that record's rootsy languor in the execution of 'Time Has Told Me', especially in the contributions that Richard Thompson overdubbed after the main session. These undercurrents were further finessed when Elton John covered the song (along with 'Day Is Done', 'Way To Blue' and 'Saturday Sun') for a privately pressed album of Witchseason-published songs. But even here, there are compositional flourishes that confound all expectations. Robin Frederick draws attention to the song's bridge ('So I'll leave the ways of making me be . . . ') which, she says, 'quietly takes a giant step into the world of jazz. Here the key centre shifts abruptly and we hear chord substitutions typical of Coltrane-style Sixties bebop.' 'It's a deceptive song,' according to Richard Thompson, 'with three chords; but the bridge is bizarre, going into an unexpected, jazzy realm. What ended up on tape was a mixture of two or three takes. I got a session fee of £9 or £10. Our weekly wage with Fairport was £12 a week, and rent was £3, so it wasn't bad for a morning's work.'

Paul Harris's piano on 'Time Has Told Me' and 'Man In A Shed' suggests that both songs were recorded around the same time – 'probably the same day', as Joe Boyd remembers, although the subsequent realization that Harris was out of tune on 'Man In A Shed' meant that Boyd had to fly to New York to get him to do it again. Asked by John Wood what the song was about, Nick told him it was about his father, 'who was always fiddling around with things'. In terms of sound, however, Boyd feels that the song – originally titled 'Sad Story For Christopher' – 'is more influenced by Nick's mother, Molly. It had a light touch about it, like "Mayfair".' Relative to what surrounds it on *Five Leaves Left*, 'Man In A Shed' is perhaps the least loved track on the record. Biographer Patrick Humphries called it 'a facile rewrite of [The Beatles'] "Fixing a Hole".' Frederick traces the song's DNA back to to his days in Marlborough, where friends recalled him playing Mose Allison's 'Parchman Farm' at the piano. 'It's also possible,' she adds, 'that Allison's breathy, laid-back singing style influenced Nick's approach to his own vocals.' Again, the end result is an unexpectedly harmonious marriage of incongruents: the zestful fluidity of Harris's piano, alongside what sounds like a shy plea for companionship.

The one other song on Nick's first album to give similar vent to Nick's love of jazz and blues also doubled up as the record's working title: 'Saturday Sun'. Written early in 1968, 'Saturday Sun' suggests an anxiety that, in some ways, life has been too idyllic; that life will never again seem as easy as it did in the hot high summer of youth: 'Saturday sun brought people and faces / That didn't seem much in their day / But when I remember those people and places / They were really too good in their way . . . So Sunday sat in the Saturday sun / And wept for a day gone by.' Robin Frederick hears elements of Ray Charles's 'You Don't Know Me' – elements teased out further by Elton John's version – while Gorm Henrik Rasmussen compares Nick's piano work to Oscar Peterson's 'Hymn To Freedom'. Nick's readiness to co-opt elements of jazz instrumentation into his songs – in particular, vibraphone – may have also been abetted by his affection for Van Morrison's *Astral Weeks*, an album recorded in just two sessions with a collective of jazz musicians with whom Morrison was only minimally acquainted. Certainly, Boyd recalls that the vibes were Nick's idea – and, having played with both Duke Ellington and on *Sgt Pepper*, Tristan Fry was deemed perfect for what the song needed. 'I think it was going to be just vibes, piano and bass,' recalls John Wood. 'And then someone decided it would be a good idea to have drums. Whether it was Nick or Joe, I don't know. But Tristan had got a drum-kit with him! And at that time he wasn't known for playing drums at all. He just didn't do it, and so why on earth he'd got a kit in the car, I can't imagine!'

Over the course of the sessions, Nick Drake had effectively amassed a close-knit team of believers, none of whom countenanced the notion that his records might not sell. With Joe Boyd dividing his attentions between a growing roster of artists, and with Nick still at Cambridge, his visits to Sound Techniques were sporadic, but over time they yielded more songs than were needed for the final track listing. A relatively early session in November 1968 saw Nick return to two of his very earliest songs: 'Joey' and 'Clothes Of Sand'. Speaking to Gorm Henrik Rasmussen, Molly Drake said that 'Joey' dated back to her son's time in Aix, and addressed a particular girl called Jo with whom Molly felt he may have been in love. If 'Joey' was indeed inspired by her, it seems reasonable to suppose that another early (unrecorded) song, 'Joey In Mind' has . . . well, Jo in mind. Both 'Joey' and 'Clothes of Sand' are exceptionally strong examples of Nick's early ascent – and had lain forgotten until 1985, when Joe Boyd found himself in the Island archives going through Sandy Denny's master recordings for the *Who Knows Where The Time Goes?* anthology. It was here that Boyd also found all the original masters of what, at the time, were thought to be all of Nick's sessions.

Of course, this hasn't quite turned out to be true. One of the most thrilling finds on 2004's *Made To Love Magic* anthology was a newly surfaced version of 'Three Hours', which pre-dated the version that appeared on *Five Leaves Left*. Lining the two up side-by-side is fascinating for all sorts of reasons. Recorded at north London's Morgan studios and featuring sometime Traffic cohort Rebop Kwaku Baah on congas, alongside an unknown flautist, the earlier version has a more improvisational feel. Its unrelenting rhythmic momentum lures the listener into a reverie that is instantly punctured by the arrival of the flute with just under two minutes remaining. The ensuing forty-five years have done nothing to diminish the hair-raising intimacy of this small ensemble performance. But, as John Wood recalls, 'This was an instance of Nick doing something, not liking it and deciding he wanted to do it again.'

We can perhaps infer something of what Nick didn't like about this version of 'Three Hours' by listening to the one that made the cut. Out goes the flute and in comes Danny Thompson, with Rocki Dzidzornu – best known for his work on The Rolling Stones' 'Sympathy for the Devil' – stepping in to play congas. Though described by Boyd as 'the flavour-of-the-month percussionist in London at the time', Dzidzornu didn't seem to find much more favour with Nick than his predecessor. Fellow Cambridge student Brian Wells recalled Nick saying that 'it was a nightmare in the studio because of all the frustrations with the conga player'. Filling in the space vacated by the flute is a display of staggering virtuosity from Nick, made all the more incredible by Nick's counter-intuitive way of beginning almost every line at the end of the previous bar.

The song's compositional oddness is further accentuated by its content, and the drone played by Nick on the lower strings of his guitar. As Robin Frederick explains, 'The song is essentially modal, meaning it is not based on chords, as most contemporary Western music is, but on a scale or mode, in this case a minor scale (Dorian) which is frequently heard in Arabic, Turkish and Spanish folk music.' The exotic feel of the melody was enhanced further by a lyric that has been subject to more scrutiny than most of Nick's songs. 'Three Hours', remembered Boyd, was the time it sometimes took to drive from London to Cambridge. 'Three Hours' was also Jeremy Mason's phrase for 'anything that would take a tiresomely long time'. And, of course, there's a Jeremy referenced at the very beginning of the song. Understandably, Mason asked Nick if the song was about him. Nick's response is recounted in Humphries' book: 'He said yes. I said: "Well what does it mean?" He said: "Well, if you don't know, it doesn't matter . . . it's the way I perceived your situation at that time." And believe me I've listened to it a thousand times.' Equally, it's not inconceivable that Nick might have simply been telling Mason (one of two Jeremys he knew at Marlborough) what he thought his friend wanted to hear.

In truth, not even the existence of an extra unsung verse in the inside sleeve of *Five Leaves Left* can hang a coherent story upon 'Three Hours' beyond the discomfiting sense – provided in part by Nick's playing – of sand slipping through an upturned hour glass as its protagonists search in vain for some resolution that ultimately never comes. For Joe Boyd, 'Three Hours' offers a textbook example of Nick's 'incredibly rhythmic' playing:

'The spine [of any arrangement] was provided by Nick's guitar. His playing was so clear, so strong, his fingering, his whole approach was so unique. If you put that right in the middle, you could figure out things to put around it that would play off it and take their cue from that . . . [so] if you listen to the way Rocki and Danny play, they're picking up so much from Nick's thumb . . . and responding to it.'

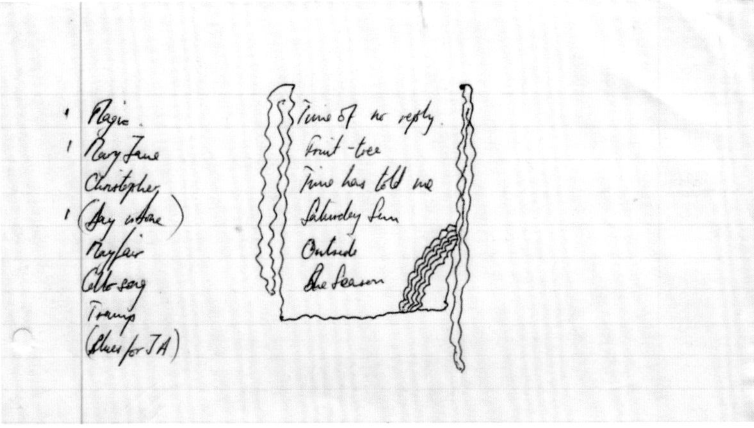

Nick's early running order

The presence of Dzidzorno and Thompson on ''Cello Song' (the apostrophe seems to be an acknowledgement of the instrument's full name: the violoncello) almost certainly dates it to the same session. Also present on the song is Clare Lowther, who had recently worked on records by Fairport Convention and earnest folk-guitar troubadour Marc Brierley. Robert Kirby recalls that he had 'come up with a cello line, but that was really Nick's line as well; he used to sing that. [Then] a lady cellist called Clare Lowther; she just came in and blew it, ad libbed it.' Turning to the inspiration for the track, the music critic Ian MacDonald surmises that ''Cello Song' might be one of a group of songs addressed to female muses during 1967 and 1968: 'some pure, heaven-redolent soul to "Lend a hand and lift me / To your place in the cloud".' Robin Frederick sees it as a preview of 'the kind of simple, bare-boned song to which Nick would return on *Pink Moon*:

'The feeling of floating, of being disconnected from solid ground, is central to Nick's music. You can hear it on song after song ("Hazey Jane I", "Free Ride", "Fly", "Which Will", "Pink Moon", "Place To Be" and others). He generally accomplishes it in two ways: (1) by shifting the emphasis around among different beats; and (2) through the use of melodic phrases that do not begin or end where we expect. Over and over, he finds ways to make the first beat of a bar – that rock-solid anchor of popular music – into an ambivalent question mark. "'Cello Song" is a great example. After setting up a steady drone in the intro, emphasising Beat 2 then shifting to Beat 1, he abruptly changes to a precise fingerpicking pattern that alternately emphasises Beats 1 and 3. When the cello line eventually enters on Beat 3, we feel ourselves losing touch with solid ground: where is Beat 1? Then, the vocal delivers us into a floating world: some of the lines begin on Beat 1, others Beat 3; phrases are five bars long instead of the usual four. By playing with the emphasised or "strong" beat, Nick cuts us loose from our anchor. We are drifting, no longer sure where we are.'

The one conundrum that required resolution during the sessions for Nick's first album came with the song that imprinted itself on the memory of every Cambridge student who saw him play it. The 5/4 time signature of 'River Man', and its astral sense of remove, made the prospect of offering any sort of arrangement for the song a job for only the most dauntless of musical minds. Robert Kirby held that – in terms of Nick's playing – the performance in his room which eventually appeared on *Made To Love Magic* supersedes that of *Five Leaves Left*. Certainly, it's easy to understand why, on hearing 'River Man', Kirby threw up his hand and declared the job beyond his capabilities. 'I thought it was for clever jazzy people,' he said in 2004. 'Now I realise that medieval church composers use it all the time.' In 2009, shortly before his death, Kirby told *Mojo*'s Mat Snow that 'Dave Brubeck's "Take Five" aside, ["River Man"] was the only time in my life I'd heard a piece of music consistently in 5/4. I could not for the life of me work out how to write a piece of music that didn't stagger along like a spider missing a leg, how you crossed over and ignored bar lines.' For all of Kirby's misgivings, it was an obstacle that – freed from the constraints of formal composition – at least two contemporaneous groups managed to overcome. In the summer of 1969, fellow Island act Jethro Tull scored their biggest hit with 'Living in the Past', while one year previously The Byrds' 'Tribal Gathering' also employed a 5/4 time signature.

Over four decades on, in that first recorded performance of 'River Man', it's possible to hear how much of the eventual arrangement Nick had stitched into the song, in particular the introduction of a discordant F# note in the C chord at 1:34. None of Nick's songs have been as extensively analysed as 'River Man'. Ian MacDonald suggested that the song was evidence of Nick's ability to relinquish earthly attachments, exist in the eternal present and achieve momentary glimpses of the state of enlightenment referred to in Zen as 'satori'. For MacDonald, the song's protagonist, Betty, represents the tension between the workaday demands of the empirical world and an altogether higher plane of existence. In the aforementioned *Mojo* article, Mat Snow raised a possible connection between the Betty in 'River Man' and her namesake in William Wordsworth's rural ballad 'The Idiot Boy': 'And Betty o'er and o'er has told / The boy who is her best delight, / Both what to follow, what to shun, / What to do, and what to leave undone, / How to turn left, and how to right.'

It is ironic that, perhaps more than any other of his early songs, Nick Drake's most otherworldly song should be most firmly rooted in an actual time and place. 'He moved into a room near by the river,' recalled Paul Wheeler. 'The house was outside the town centre as such, which meant that he had to cross one of the old bridges every day on his way to and from the university. He would often stop and watch the currents and the leaves floating by. I know that "River Man" is a portrait of the situation Nick found himself in, both geographically and emotionally.' Arriving at Cambridge a year after Nick, flautist and saxophonist Iain Cameron recalled an afternoon visit to Wheeler's room – 'this would be April or May 1969' – and seeing Nick play a selection of songs. 'I definitely remember "River Man", and just remember thinking what a dream of a song that was. How utterly stunning as a piece of music, partly because of the concentric guitar part in 5/4, the harmonies, very evocative, slightly mournful words. He also looked very impressive, like he looked on the records. A very beautiful person by any standards.'

Although Wheeler contends that if you 'get a guitarist to explain to you what's happening . . . he won't be able to', Robin Frederick nonetheless manages to convey some sense of the astonishing skill that the song's floating sense of reverie conceals:

'Almost all pop, rock and folk music is written in 4/4. We are accustomed to hearing music divided into four beats. By using groups of five, Nick creates the feeling that each bar is spilling over into the next, like overlapping waves . . . "River Man" showcases Nick's use of cluster chords. These are chords that have more than the usual three notes of a major or minor chord with the extra notes occurring very close to, or clustered around, the notes of the standard chord. These extra notes introduce a dissonant sound which, when combined with the basic triad, generates a new chord with added complexity, depth and warmth.'

On the face of it, Harry Robinson might not have seemed an obvious candidate to arrange Nick Drake's most iconic song. Ten years previously, as the leader of Lord Rockingham's XI, Robinson topped the charts with 'Hoots Mon' – a pacey sax number which featured no words save for a comedy Scottish voice declaring 'There's a moose loose about this hoose!' But when Nick said that he wanted the arrangement for 'River Man' to sound 'like Delius', it was to Robinson that John Wood's thoughts immediately turned. The two had worked together on a variety of commissions for the Children's Film Foundation. Wood had noted Robinson's talent for writing arrangements in the style of any composer. But it still remained to be seen whether Robinson could deliver what it was that Nick had envisaged for 'River Man'. In pursuit of an answer, Joe Boyd took Nick with him to meet Robinson. In his memoir *White Bicycles*, Boyd recalls the pair venturing out to Robinson's house, 'hidden in the middle of Barnes Common, just below the tree that was to kill Marc Bolan ten years later. Having heard a tape, Harry was already intrigued when we arrived. Nick played the song through, then strummed chords as the tape played, showing Harry the textures he wanted for the string parts. I had never heard him so articulate or demanding. Harry made notes and nodded.' John Wood adds: 'He clearly got across to Harry what he wanted in [his performance of] the guitar part – even to the point where on the demo, he says "fade".'

To his credit, Robert Kirby was never shy of paying tribute to Robinson for perfecting the job that had bamboozled him from the outset: 'Harry's string arrangement is barely in 5/4 – it goes along like a limpid river all the way, moving regularly and crossing all over the beats and the 5/4 with it.'

What Ian MacDonald quite rightly called 'one of the sky-high classics of post-war English popular music' was recorded live, with Nick singing alongside the orchestra, in less than three hours. The session seemed to leave a mark on everyone who played on it. 'Whenever I saw Harry in later years,' wrote Joe Boyd, 'he would talk about the day we recorded it, with Nick surrounded by the orchestra, playing and singing while Harry conducted – just like Nelson Riddle and Frank Sinatra.'

With a song as breathtaking as 'River Man' on a debut as accomplished as *Five Leaves Left*, it isn't hard to understand why no one within Nick's immediate

Nick Drake before and after his deft work with a biro

circle stopped to consider the notion that it might not sell. Nick's decision to inform his parents that he would not be returning to Cambridge for his final year must therefore have made a certain amount of sense.

Bookended by 'Time Has Told Me' and 'Saturday Sun' – songs that are both shaded in with the same world-weary sense of stasis – the album's track sequencing perhaps gave the impression of having had more thought expended on it than had really been the case. John Wood recalled the rather more prosaic process by which he and Joe Boyd had established the running order: namely, by writing down each song title on a piece of paper whose length was proportionate to that song's duration. Once the bits of paper were arranged in such a way as to represent two sides of a record, roughly equal in length, the job was done. The album tapes were then taken to Apple's mastering facility on Lisson Grove. Just a matter of weeks before the album's release was announced, however, Nick informed Joe of one final change. He had thought of a better album title than the originally proposed 'Saturday Sun'.

It's strange to think that the title of the record – a title inextricably bound with the Nick Drake myth – came at the very end of a process which had lasted over eighteen months. 'All smokers will recognise the meaning of the title,' began *Melody Maker*'s brief review of *Five Leaves Left*. The titular reference to the warning found towards the end of a pack of cigarette rolling papers was, according to Robert Kirby, an 'in-joke' for anyone who might have used Nick Drake's album as a surface on which to roll a joint.

Gabrielle Drake recalls that she and her brother were briefly sharing a flat when he returned home with the album. 'He was a man of few words, my brother – and he said [mumbling] "There you are," and he threw down on to the bed the complete record of *Five Leaves Left*. I was absolutely astonished. I couldn't believe this was my brother – my little brother – who had produced a full long-playing record, as it was then. It was amazing!'

Following the record's release in July 1969, the few reviews that took notice of *Five Leaves Left* were slightly more equivocal. There's little to the *Melody Maker* one beyond the aforesaid quote, while the one that ran in the 3 October issue of *New Musical Express* struggles to find anything positive to say:

I'm sorry I can't be more enthusiastic, because he obviously has a not inconsiderable amount of talent, but there is not nearly enough variety in this debut album to make it entertaining. His voice reminds me very much of Peter Sarstedt, but his songs lack Sarstedt's penetration and arresting quality. Exceptions are 'Mary Jane', a fragile little love song, and 'Saturday Sun', a reflective number on which the singer also plays a very attractive piano.

Quite how Nick must have felt, having delivered songs such as 'Way To Blue', 'River Man' and 'Fruit Tree', only to find himself being compared unfavourably to Peter Sarstedt, is a matter of conjecture. But he was by no means the only singer-songwriter operating at a cult level. Ralph McTell's debut album had achieved comparable sales, as had Bridget St John, with whom Nick would sometimes share the bill at Les Cousins from 1969. Between the completion of *Five Leaves Left* and the beginning of sessions for Nick's second album, Vashti Bunyan descended upon Sound Techniques to record *Just Another Diamond Day* – a chronicle of her two-year odyssey to Donovan's hippie commune in the Outer Hebrides. To her absolute devastation, sales of the record in the months and years immediately following its release were virtually non-existent.

Nick, at least, had options ahead of him. *Five Leaves Left* had been relatively inexpensive to make and both Island and Joe Boyd were committed to making another record with him. He had sung his songs both on Radio 1's underground stop-off *Top Gear* and on BBC2's new colour arts show *Late Night Line-Up*. A live set in September 1969, supporting Fairport Convention – the group's first show since the motorway collision that killed their drummer Martin Lamble – was greeted with hushed reverence. Scheduled for March 1970 was a further series of dates opening for Fotheringay. And perhaps most encouragingly of all, Nick's prodigious songwriting output showed no sign of relenting.

Time Has Told Me

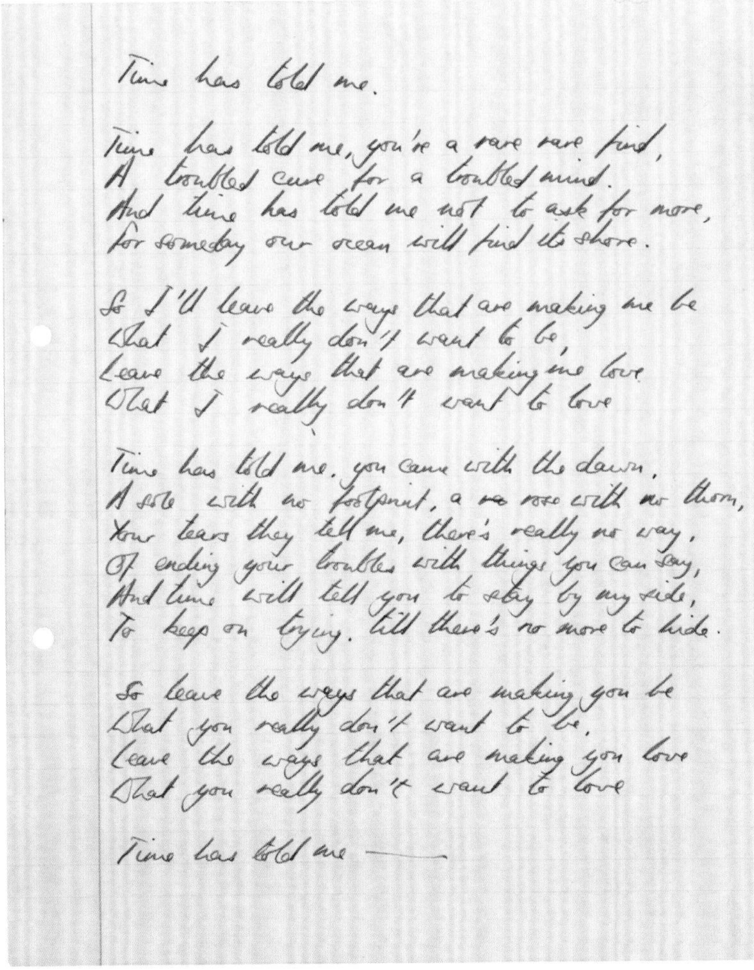

Time has told me.

Time has told me, you're a rare rare find,
A troubled cure for a troubled mind.
And time has told me not to ask for more,
for someday our ocean will find its shore.

So I'll leave the ways that are making me be
What I really don't want to be,
Leave the ways that are making me love
What I really don't want to love

Time has told me, you came with the dawn,
A sole with no footprint, a ro rose with no thorn,
Your tears they tell me, there's really no way,
Of ending your troubles with things you can say,
And time will tell you to stay by my side,
To keep on trying. till there's no more to hide.

So leave the ways that are making you be
What you really don't want to be,
Leave the ways that are making you love
What you really don't want to love

Time has told me ——

Time has told me, you're a rare, rare find
A troubled cure for a troubled mind
And time has told me not to ask for more
For someday our ocean will find its shore

So I'll leave the ways of making me be
What I really don't want to be
Leave the ways that are making me love
What I really don't want to love

Time has told me you came with the dawn
A sole with no footprint a rose with no thorn
Your tears they tell me there's really no way
Of ending your troubles with things you can say
And time will tell you to stay by my side
To keep on trying till there's no more to hide

So leave the ways that are making you be
What you really don't want to be
Leave the ways that are making you love
What you really don't want to love

Time has told me you're a rare, rare find
A troubled cure for a troubled mind

And time has told me not to ask for more
For someday our ocean will find its shore

Chris Healey: Unusually for Nick, this uses mainly simple chords, and is in standard tuning. But it manages to escape sounding like something we've heard before, thanks to the particular inversions and voicings (that is, the precise pattern of notes in the fingerings of each chord) that he uses.

The demo version he made for Island in 1968 illustrates this rather well: played with standard shapes and fewer chords, at a faster tempo and with a plain rhythm, the verses sound wholly unremarkable. The changes he made between then and the final recording completely transformed the song.

The music also supports the lyric in clever ways. The back-and-forth of the quick changes in the verse seems, like the words, to be weighing things up and coming to conclusions. The jazzier modulations of the 'So leave the ways . . .' section outline a tension – something is trying to drag the tune into a different key (Ab) but Nick wrestles it back towards C at the end of each line. The chords here are trying to make him be what he really doesn't want to be. But he won't let them.

River Man

Betty came by on her way
Said she had a word to say
About things today
And fallen leaves

Said she hadn't heard the news
Hadn't had the time to choose
A way to lose
But she believes

Gonna see the river man
Gonna tell him all I can
About the plan
For lilac time

If he tells me all he knows
About the way his river flows
And all night shows
In summertime

Betty said she prayed today
For the sky to blow away
Or maybe stay
She wasn't sure

For when she thought of summer rain
Calling for her mind again
She lost the pain
And stayed for more

Gonna to see the river man
Gonna tell him all I can
About the ban
On feeling free

If he tells me all he knows
About the way his river flows
I don't suppose
It's meant for me

Oh, how they come and go
Oh, how they come and go

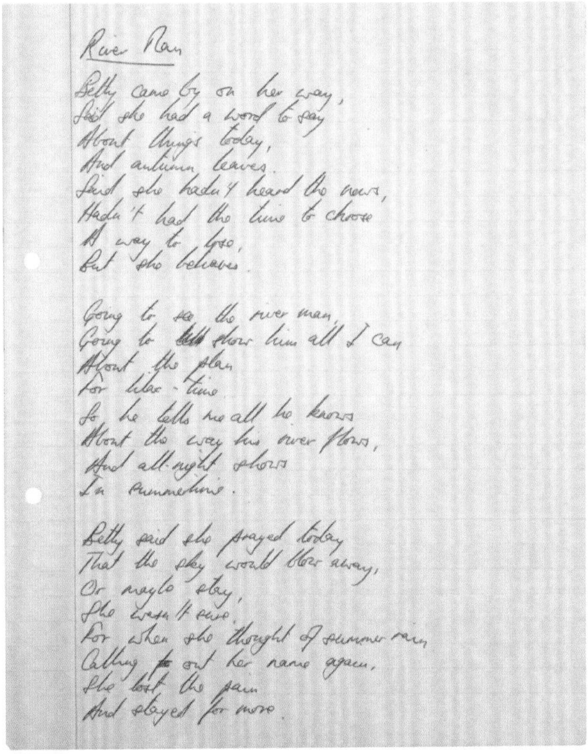
River Man

Betty came by on her way,
Said she had a word to say
About things today,
And autumn leaves.
Said she hadn't heard the news,
Hadn't had the time to choose
A way to lose,
But she believes.

Going to see the river man,
Going to ~~tell~~ show him all I can
About the plan
For lilac-time
So he tells me all he knows
About the way his river flows,
And all-night shows
In summertime.

Betty said she prayed today
That the sky would blow away,
Or maybe stay,
She wasn't sure.
For when she thought of summer rain
Calling ~~fo~~ out her name again,
She lost the pain
And stayed for more.

Initial pressings of the vinyl edition of the *Five Leaves Left* inner gatefold printed the second half of the lyrics as:

Betty fell behind awhile
Said she hadn't had time to smile
Or die in style
But still she tries

Said her time was growing short
Hadn't done the things she ought
Where teacher taught
And father flies

Going to see the river-man
Going to tell him all I can
About the ban
On feeling free

If he tells me all he knows
About the way his river flows
I don't suppose
It's meant for me

Betty said she prayed today
For the sky to blow away
Or maybe stay
She wasn't sure

For when she thought of summer rain
Calling for her mind again
She lost the pain
And stayed for more

Oh, how they come and go
Oh, how they come and go

Almost everything in 'River Man' is uncertain. The rhythm is a drifting, elusive five-time feel. The bass notes of the guitar pattern don't start on a solid root, while an added 9th undermines the confidence of the major chord intro. Then the verse begins with a switch to a minor tonality (still with the 9th) – this song is forever casting around, trying to find anything to hold on to. Each line has a moment of possible clarity when the second chord resolves to a simple major, but these feel like moments of wishful thinking, followed immediately by a return to uncertainty.

The end chord is very unusual: rather than invoke some extreme jazz scholarship on Nick's part, it seems more likely to me that his little finger just missed on one of the 00242x chords and happened upon 00204x instead. But if it *was* a mistake, you can see why he kept it in: the effect, of pain (the discord of the 5th and b12) and numbness (the 3rd – the note that gives you the traditional happy/sad major/minor marker – is absent), works brilliantly, as Nick drifts towards an unknown future.

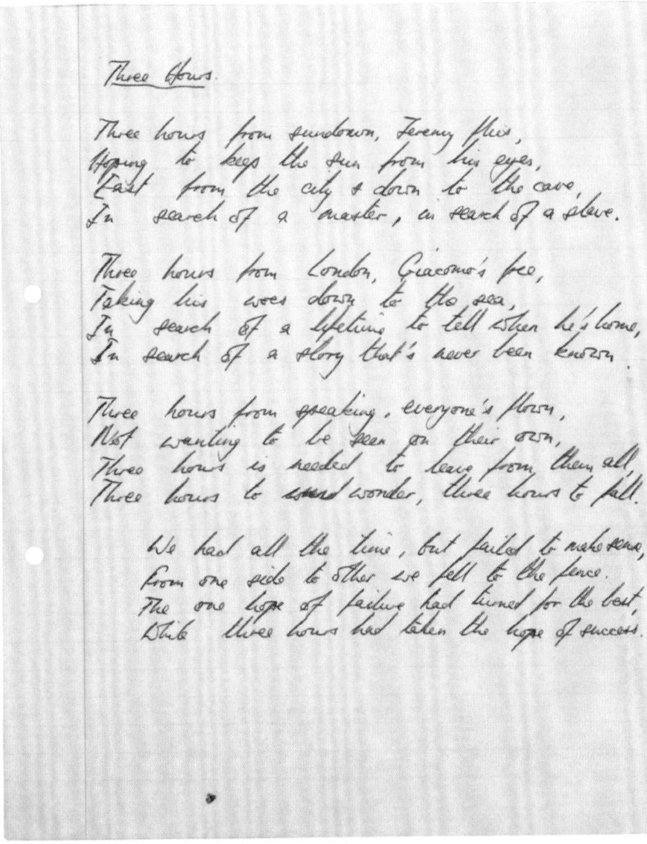
Three Hours.

Three hours from sundown, Jeremy flies,
Hoping to keep the sun from his eyes,
East from the city & down to the cave,
In search of a master, in search of a slave.

Three hours from London, Giacomo's free,
Taking his woes down to the sea,
In search of a lifetime to tell when he's home,
In search of a story that's never been known.

Three hours from speaking, everyone's flown,
Not wanting to be seen on their own,
Three hours is needed to leave from them all,
Three hours to wonder, three hours to fall.

We had all the time, but failed to make sense,
From one side to other we fell to the fence.
The one hope of failure had turned for the best,
While three hours had taken the hope of success.

Three Hours

Three hours from sundown
Jeremy flies
Hoping to keep
The sun from his eyes
East from the city
And down to the cave
In search of a master
In search of a slave

Three hours from London
Giacomo's free
Taking his woes
Down to the sea
In search of a lifetime
To tell when he's home
In search of a story
That's never been known

Three hours from speaking
Everyone's flown
Not wanting to be
Seen on their own
Three hours is needed
To leave from them all
Three hours to wonder
Three hours to fall

Three hours from sundown
Jeremy flies
Hoping to keep
The sun from his eyes
East from the city
And down to the cave
In search of a master
In search of a slave

Initial pressings of the vinyl edition of the *Five Leaves Left* inner gatefold carried the following as a 'last verse':

We had all the time
But failed to make sense
From one side to the other
We fell to the fence
The one hope of failure
Had turned for the best
While three hours had taken
The hope of success

Here the song was titled 'Sundown', not 'Three Hours', suggesting that the sleeve designer was given an early version of the song to work from and not the subsequently recorded version

'Three Hours' has a largely modal feel – by which I mean here a melodic scale over a drone, without harmonic progressions to give you a 'home chord' – although the verses do feature some harmonic movement. The tuning (BBDGBE, with the bottom two strings an octave apart) is very uncommon, and seems likely to be another Nick invention.

Like 'Time Has Told Me', the guitar part was obviously in the process of being refined even as recordings began – the fingerpicking in the version recorded two months before the one on *Five Leaves Left* is both simpler and more vague. The album version brings in some fast arpeggios in the instrumental section, which are some of the trickiest parts in Nick's repertoire, and remind us that he could do the complex stuff with the best of them – he just rarely included any of it in his own work.

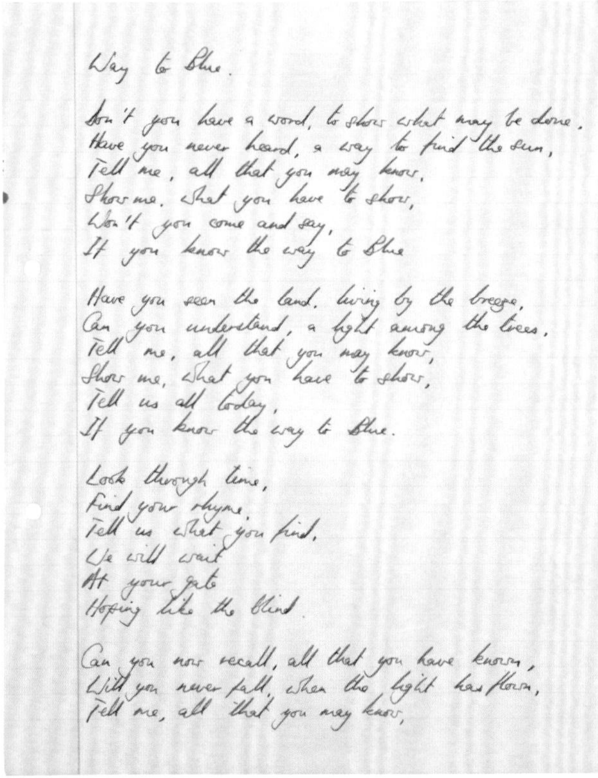
Way to Blue.

Don't you have a word, to show what may be done.
Have you never heard, a way to find the sun,
Tell me, all that you may know,
Show me, what you have to show,
Won't you come and say,
If you know the way to Blue

Have you seen the land, living by the breeze,
Can you understand, a light among the trees,
Tell me, all that you may know,
Show me, what you have to show,
Tell us all today,
If you know the way to Blue.

Look through time,
Find your rhyme,
Tell us what you find,
We will wait
At your gate
Hoping like the blind.

Can you now recall, all that you have known,
Will you never fall, when the light has flown,
Tell me, all that you may know,

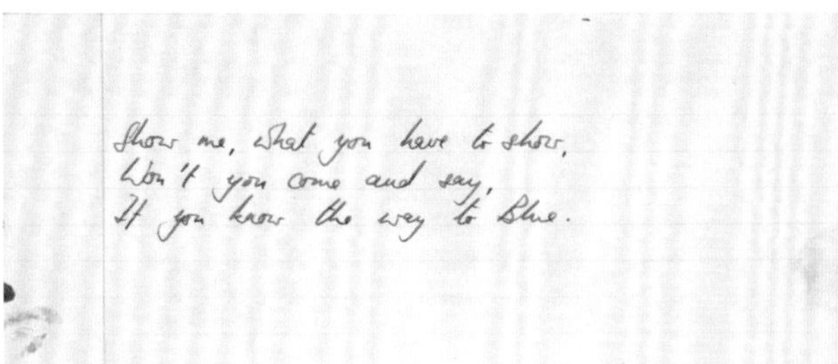
Show me, what you have to show,
Won't you come and say,
If you know the way to Blue.

Way To Blue

Don't you have a word to show what may be done?
Have you never heard a way to find the sun?
Tell me all that you may know
Show me what you have to show
Won't you come and say
If you know the way to blue

Have you seen the land living by the breeze?
Can you understand a light among the trees?
Tell me all that you may know
Show me what you have to show
Tell us all today
If you know the way to blue

Look through time and find your rhyme
Tell us what you find
We will wait
At your gate
Hoping like the blind

Can you now recall all that you have known?
Will you never fall
When the light has flown?
Tell me all that you may know
Show me what you have to show
Won't you come and say
If you know the way to blue

Perhaps the most noticeable aspect of this song is its constant switching from major to minor tonality. Rather than being an attempt to highlight different moods in the lyrics, here this feels like a constant searching – something that's even more obvious in the home piano recording. (As to the 'Blue' he's searching for, my guess, given Nick's familiarity with French symbolist poetry, is Mallarmé's 'Azure' – the impossible ideal of poetic insight. 'Look through time and find your rhyme,' Nick implores: 'Tell us what you find.')

Another thing that leaps out of the home demo is that most of the vocal lines start on the first beat of each line. In the final recorded version the vocals begin at some point after the first beat, which makes the vocal feel more diffident and much more natural – songs with first-beat vocals seem to wear their construction on their sleeve. Late-starting vocals became a fundamental part of Nick's style, and is a big reason they seem to connect so directly with listeners.

Day Is Done

When the day is done
Down to earth then sinks the sun
Along with everything that was loſt and won
When the day is done

When the day is done
Hope so much your race will be all run
Then you find you jumped the gun
Have to go back where you begun
When the day is done

When the night is cold
Some get by but some get old
Juſt to show life's not made of gold
When the night is cold

When the bird has flown
Got no one to call your own
Got no place to call your home
When the bird has flown

When the game's been fought
Newspaper blown across the court
Loſt much sooner than you would have thought
Now the game's been fought

When the party's through
Seems so very sad for you
Didn't do the things you meant to do
Now there's no time to ſtart anew
Now the party's through

When the day is done
Down to earth then sinks the sun
Along with everything that was loſt and won
When the day is done

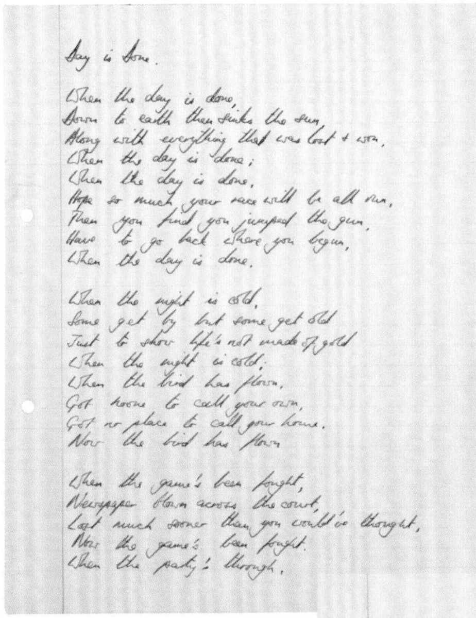
Day is Done.

When the day is done,
Down to earth then sinks the sun
Along with everything that was lost + won,
When the day is done;
When the day is done,
Hope so much your race will be all run,
Then you find you jumped the gun,
Have to go back where you begun,
When the day is done.

When the night is cold,
Some get by but some get old
Just to show life's not made of gold
When the night is cold,
When the bird has flown,
Got none to call your own,
Got no place to call your home.
Now the bird has flown

When the game's been fought,
Newspaper blown across the court,
Lost much sooner than you would've thought,
Now the game's been fought.
When the party's through,

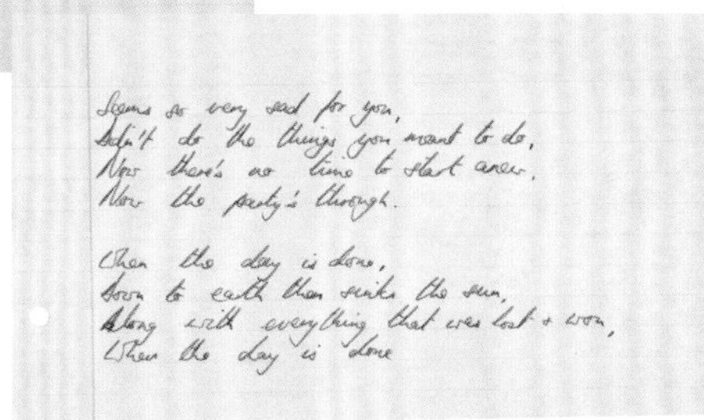
Seems so very sad for you,
Didn't do the things you meant to do,
Now there's no time to start anew,
Now the party's through.

When the day is done,
Down to earth then sinks the sun,
Along with everything that was lost + won,
When the day is done

In an earlier recording of the song, after identical first two verses, the lyrics were different:

When the night is cold
Some get by but some grow old
Just to show life's not made of gold
When the night is cold

When the night is cold
Weren't you ever told
It's the time when fear is bought and sold
When the night is cold

When the game's been fought
Newspaper blown across the court
You lost much sooner than you never would have thought
Now the game's been fought

When the party's through
Seems so sad for you
Didn't do the things you meant to do
Now there's no time to start anew
Now the party's through

When they've sung the song
Maybe you won't feel quite so strong
Your hopes don't last quite so long
When they've sung the song

When they've sung the song
Won't be so sure what's right, what's wrong
Not so sure where you belong
When they've sung the song

When the day is done
Down to earth then sinks the sun
Along with things that were lost and won
Along with everything that was lost and won
When the day is done

When the day is done
Hope so much your race will be all run
Then you find you jumped the gun
Have to go back where you begun
When the day is done

This is a deceptively difficult song to play. Despite being in ſtandard tuning, and being Nick's take on a fairly common guitar chord sequence (developing from Am over a bassline that descends in semitones), the unusual chord voicings and fiddly top line over a syncopated bass make it quite a trial. It troubled even Nick himself; on the home demo featured on the *Family Tree* album, he can be heard laughing at his own miſtakes and whispering, 'It's terrifying.'

The fact that he ſtuck to the part he wanted rather than simplify it is (like the precision of 'Hazey Jane I') quite telling: his guitar parts are compositions, not juſt backgrounds to sing over.

’Cello Song

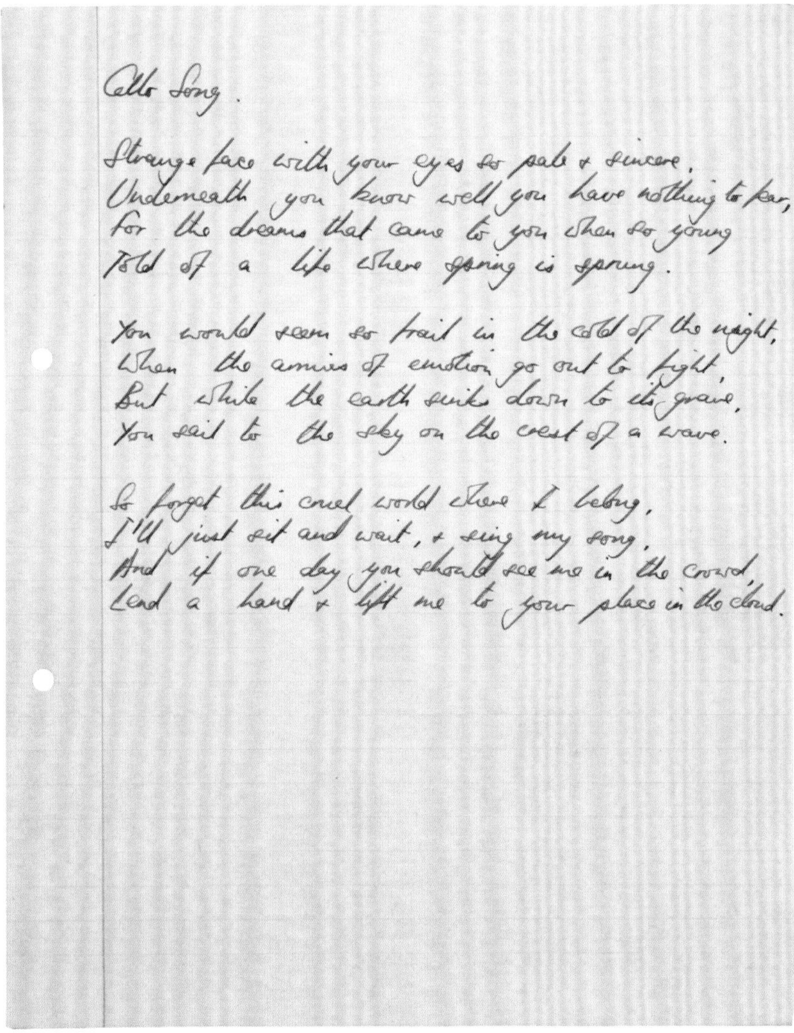

Cello Song.

Strange face with your eyes so pale + sincere,
Underneath you know well you have nothing to fear,
For the dreams that came to you when so young
Told of a life where spring is sprung.

You would seem so frail in the cold of the night,
When the armies of emotion go out to fight,
But while the earth sinks down to its grave,
You sail to the sky on the crest of a wave.

So forget this cruel world where I belong,
I'll just sit and wait, + sing my song,
And if one day you should see me in the crowd,
Lend a hand + lift me to your place in the cloud.

Strange face
With your eyes
So pale and sincere
Underneath you know well
You have nothing to fear
For the dreams that came
To you when so young
Told of a life
Where spring is sprung

You would seem so frail
In the cold of the night
When the armies of emotion
Go out to fight
But while the earth
Sinks to its grave
You sail to the sky
On the crest of a wave

So forget this cruel world
Where I belong
I’ll just sit and wait
And sing my song
And if one day you should see me
In the crowd
Lend a hand and lift me
To your place in the cloud

One sleight-of-hand this song pulls is to sound quite straightforward rhythmically, while constructing verses from three five-bar lines and a six-bar line. As always with Nick, it sounds completely natural, and indeed barely registers as anything unusual.

‘’Cello Song’ features some quick if fairly standard fingerpicking patterns over a constant alternating bass, but with lots of cute variations – a great song for inexperienced pickers to have a go at. The precision and regularity of his playing is remarkable.

The Thoughts Of Mary Jane

Who can know
The thoughts of Mary Jane?
Why she flies
Or goes out in the rain
Where she's been
And who she's seen
In her journey to the stars

Who can know
The reason for her smile?
What are her dreams
When they've journeyed for a while
The way she sings
And her brightly coloured rings
Make her the princess of the sky

Who can know
What happens in her mind?
Did she come
From a strange world
And leave her mind behind?
Her long lost sighs
And her brightly coloured eyes
Tell her story to the wind

Who can know
The thoughts of Mary Jane?
Why she flies
Or goes out in the rain
Where she's been
And who she's seen
In her journey to the stars

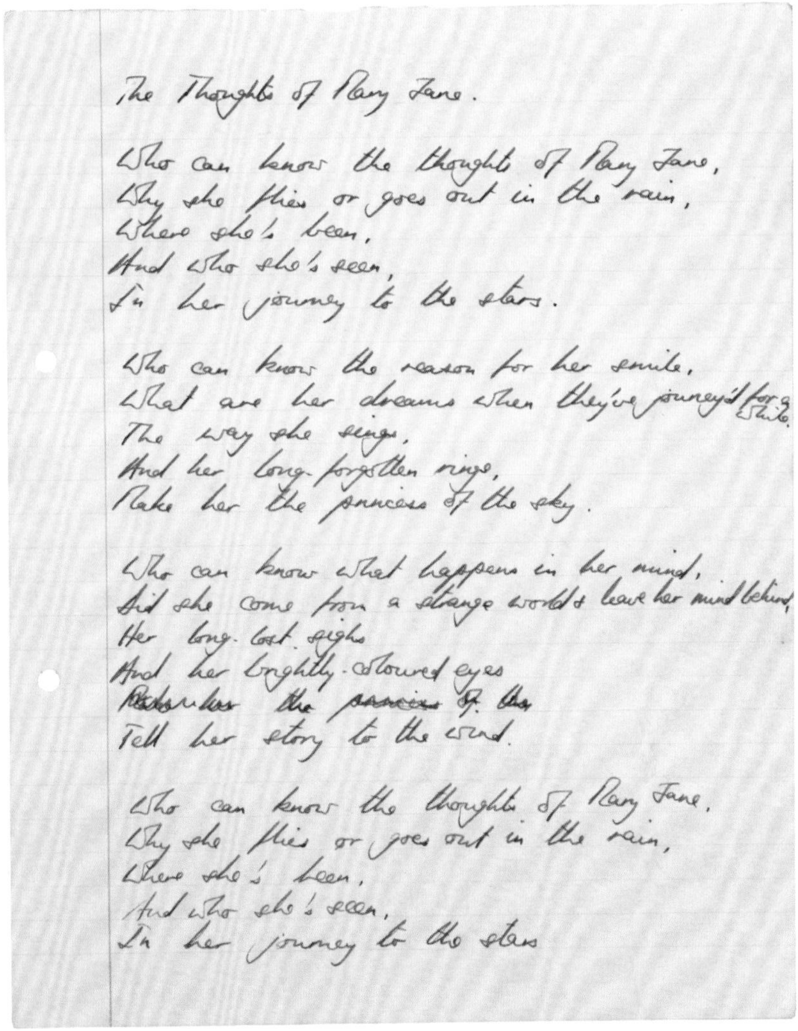

The Thoughts of Mary Jane.

Who can know the thoughts of Mary Jane,
Why she flies or goes out in the rain,
Where she's been,
And who she's seen,
In her journey to the stars.

Who can know the reason for her smile,
What are her dreams when they've journey'd for a while.
The way she sings,
And her long forgotten rings,
Make her the princess of the sky.

Who can know what happens in her mind,
Did she come from a strange world & leave her mind behind,
Her long lost sighs
And her brightly coloured eyes
~~Remember the princess of the~~
Tell her story to the wind.

Who can know the thoughts of Mary Jane,
Why she flies or goes out in the rain,
Where she's been,
And who she's seen,
In her journey to the stars

As with 'Cello Song', the G string is dropped to F#. Capoed up the neck, it's like a normally tuned guitar with no bottom string and an extra high string. The unusual voicings this one tweak creates transform a really simple basic chord structure (I, II, V) into something wonderfully open and pretty. The tuning doesn't dominate though: the song sounds different enough from 'Cello Song' for them to be sequenced next to each other without any obvious resemblance.

Man In A Shed

(formerly titled
Sad Story For Christopher)

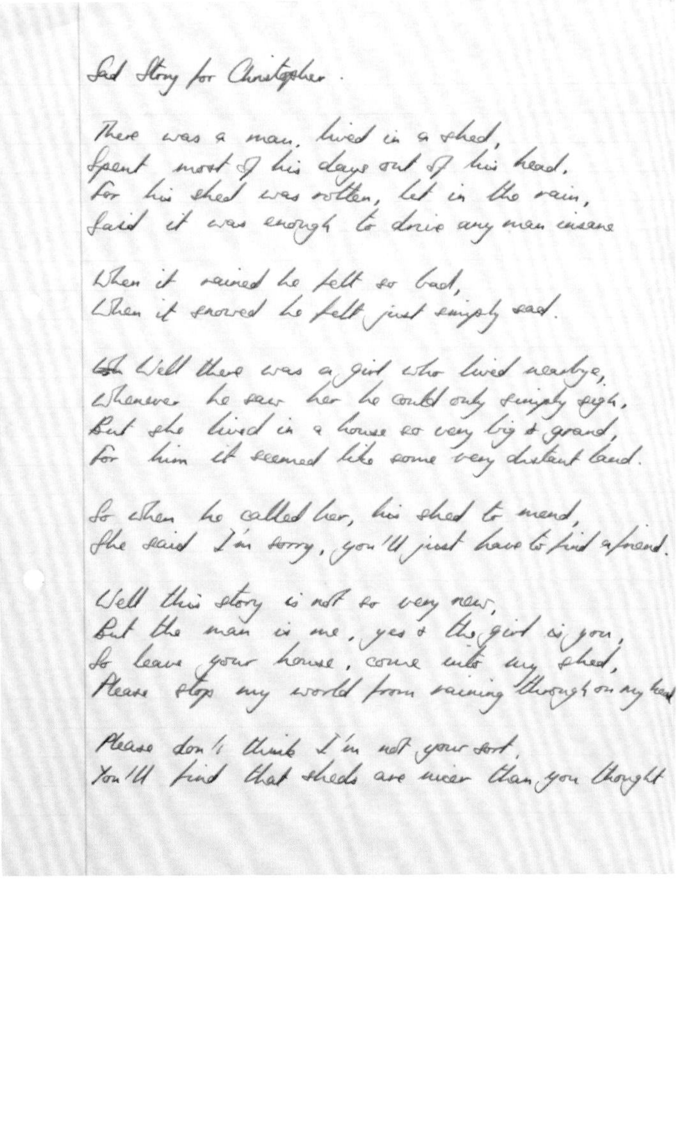
Sad Story for Christopher.

There was a man, lived in a shed,
Spent most of his days out of his head.
For his shed was rotten, let in the rain,
Said it was enough to drive any man insane

When it rained he felt so bad,
When it snowed he felt just simply sad.

Well there was a girl who lived nearbye,
Whenever he saw her he could only simply sigh,
But she lived in a house so very big & grand,
For him it seemed like some very distant land.

So when he called her, his shed to mend,
She said I'm sorry, you'll just have to find a friend.

Well this story is not so very new,
But the man is me, yes & the girl is you,
So leave your house, come into my shed,
Please stop my world from raining through on my head

Please don't think I'm not your sort,
You'll find that sheds are nicer than you thought

Well there was a man
Lived in a shed
Spent most of his days out of his head
For his shed was rotten, let in the rain
Said it was enough to drive any man insane
When it rained
He felt so bad
When it snowed he felt just simply sad

Well there was a girl
Who lived nearby
Whenever he saw her he could only simply sigh
But she lived in a house so very big and grand
For him it seemed like some very distant land
So when he called her
His shed to mend
She said I'm sorry you'll just have to find a friend

Well this story
Is not so very new
But the man is me, yes, and the girl is you
So leave your house come into my shed
Please stop my world from raining through my head
Please don't think
I'm not your sort
You'll find that sheds are nicer than you thought

As in many of Nick's songs, the combination of the tuning (BEBEBE) and the tricky right-hand picking patterns let some very simple left-hand fingerings create unusual and complex harmonic oppositions.

The note he bends up (after the lyric 'He felt so bad', for example) is interesting, as it's the only note with an obvious bend in all his recorded songs. As mentioned in the introduction, blues guitar was a major influence but in his own songs he seems to have gone out of his way to avoid anything that sounded like a typical blues lick. This bent note – and one very bluesy line ending you can hear underneath the piano solo – might be the closest he gets.

Fruit Tree

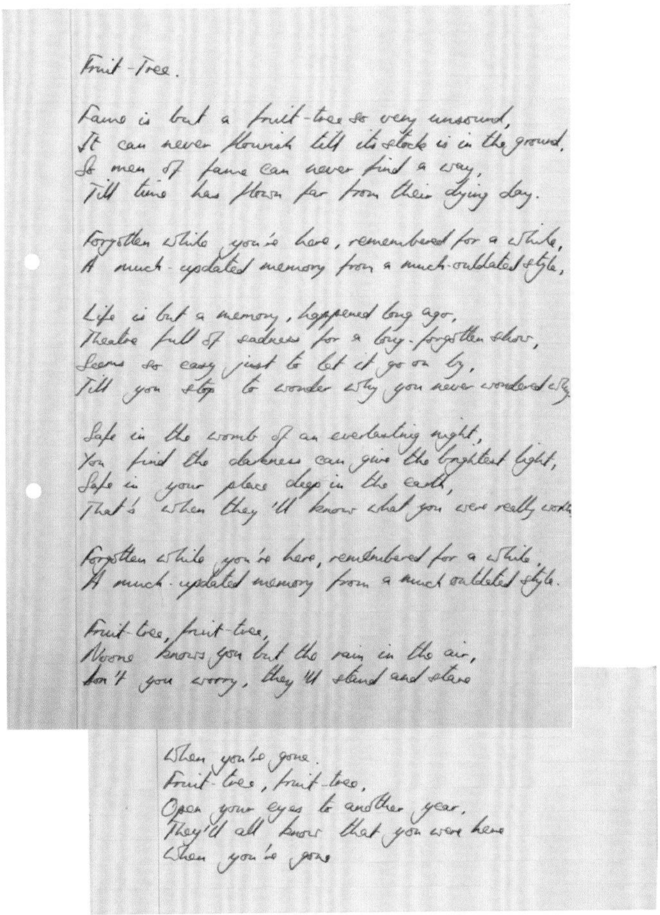

Fruit-Tree.

Fame is but a fruit-tree so very unsound,
It can never flourish till its stock is in the ground.
So men of fame can never find a way,
Till time has flown far from their dying day.

Forgotten while you're here, remembered for a while,
A much-updated memory from a much-outdated style,

Life is but a memory, happened long ago,
Theatre full of sadness for a long-forgotten show,
Seems so easy just to let it go on by,
Till you stop to wonder why you never wondered why

Safe in the womb of an everlasting night,
You find the darkness can give the brightest light,
Safe in your place deep in the earth,
That's when they'll know what you were really worth

Forgotten while you're here, remembered for a while,
A much-updated memory from a much outdated style.

Fruit tree, fruit tree,
Noone knows you but the rain in the air,
Don't you worry, they'll stand and stare
When you're gone.
Fruit tree, fruit tree,
Open your eyes to another year,
They'll all know that you were here
When you're gone

Fame is but a fruit tree
So very unsound
It can never flourish
Till its stock is in the ground
So men of fame
Can never find a way
Till time has flown
Far from their dying day

Forgotten while you're here
Remembered for a while
A much updated ruin
From a much outdated style

Life is but a memory
Happened long ago
Theatre full of sadness
For a long forgotten show
Seems so easy
Just to let it go on by
Till you stop and wonder
Why you never wondered why

Safe in the womb
Of an everlasting night
You find the darkness can
Give the brightest light
Safe in your place deep in the earth
That's when they'll know what you were really worth

Forgotten while you're here
Remembered for a while
A much updated ruin
From a much outdated style

Fame is but a fruit tree
So very unsound
It can never flourish
Till its stock is in the ground

So men of fame
Can never find a way
Till time has flown
Far from their dying day

Fruit tree, fruit tree
No-one knows you but the rain and the air
Don't you worry
They'll stand and stare when you're gone

Fruit tree, fruit tree
Open your eyes to another year
They'll all know
That you were here when you're gone

Here Nick uses the double-B tuning to different effect than on 'Three Hours': rather than a drone, he makes new variations on the semitone descent we saw in 'Day Is Done'. (Try singing a lower version of that over the first line of the verse here and you'll see the similarity.) As in 'Day Is Done', the feeling generated is cyclic, fatalistic.

The end section, where he seems to turn his attention to his own fate, is beautifully done. Although still based on the same descending root notes, the chords are now extended and reharmonised, as if the music suddenly finds its own late flowering, consoling Nick that his own material will survive him.

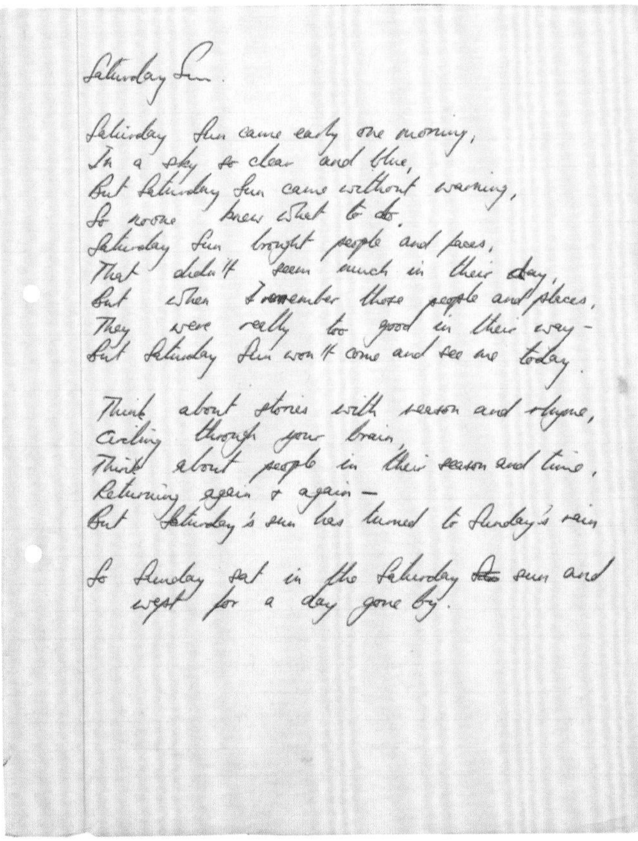

Saturday Sun.

Saturday Sun came early one morning,
In a sky so clear and blue,
But Saturday Sun came without warning,
So noone knew what to do.
Saturday Sun brought people and faces,
That didn't seem much in their day,
But when I remember those people and places,
They were really too good in their way -
But Saturday Sun won't come and see me today.

Think about stories with reason and rhyme,
Circling through your brain,
Think about people in their season and time,
Returning again & again -
But Saturday's sun has turned to Sunday's rain

So Sunday sat in the Saturday ~~the~~ sun and
wept for a day gone by.

Saturday Sun

Saturday sun came early one morning
In a sky so clear and blue
Saturday sun came without warning
So no-one knew what to do

Saturday sun brought people and faces
That didn't seem much in their day
But when I remember those people and places
They were really too good in their way

In their way
In their way
Saturday sun won't come and see me today

Think about stories with reason and rhyme
Circling through your brain
And think about people in their season and time
Returning again and again

And again
And again
But Saturday's sun has turned to Sunday's rain
So Sunday sat in the Saturday sun
And wept for a day gone by

Initial pressings of the vinyl edition of the *Five Leaves Left* inside sleeve carried incorrect lyrics

This gentle tune is quite unlike most of Nick's work. It's a chord sequence more typical of a simple cabaret or jazz ballad (his mother Molly's influence perhaps?). For example, it's the only time apart from a brief passing moment in 'Poor Boy' that he uses diminished chords ('In a sky . . .'). And he does it as an altered II in a II-V – an unusually stock 'songwriterly' move, by his standards.

One thing the song highlights which is really worth listening for is his vocal phrasing. The delicacy of precisely where he places the words is a huge part of how he makes his singing feel natural and effortless – it's only when you try to play and sing his songs exactly the way he did them that you realize the complexity of what he was doing. He really was an incredible singer, and this song one of his finest performances ('Time Has Told Me' is another great example). Try singing this dead on the beat and you lose entirely that sense of unforced, easy communication.

Tristan Fry's vibraphone work also adds greatly to the effect of the song, seeming to suggest bittersweet memories while tastefully adding a little more harmonic interest.

PARK WALK GARAGE

Nick seen here climbing into his own car. By the time he was recording *Five Leaves Left*, his friend Julian Lloyd had offered to take professional photos of Nick, which became his first ever session. Locations ranged from Stokenchurch Street in London to the Lloyd family's house in Selborne, Hampshire, where the famous blanket shots were taken. Julian Lloyd still owns the blanket, which forms the endpapers to this book

(Photo: Alex Henderson)

Keith Morris by Nick Drake

Keith Morris

by Gabrielle Drake

What happy confluence of the stars led to the unlikely pairing of a small, wiry, fiery photographer, who always described himself as a Londoner, with a tall, elegant, reserved young singer-songwriter from the English counties? On the surface, they seemed to have little in common. Yet it was apparent from the first photo shoot they did together that there was a rapport between them.

By the time Keith Morris met Nick Drake, he had already started to make a name for himself as a photographer of rock musicians. He had served an apprenticeship with the famous Sixties photographer David Bailey, and cut his photographic teeth on underground magazines such as *Oz*. Joe Boyd had used him to photograph Fairport Convention, Richard Thompson, and The Incredible String Band, and now felt that the time was right for Keith to photograph his first album cover. So the introduction took place, and Keith and Nick went off to talk over coffee. According to Keith, 'We were both naive and enthusiastic. It was a time of great optimism.' Probably each recognised fairly quickly that here was a fellow observer of life, the one making his comments in pictures, and the other in music. But above all, perhaps, each saw in the other, despite their very different natures, a steely integrity.

The best portrait photography is a co-operative venture, the subject subconsciously allowing the photographer access not only to his present mood, but also to his inner state. The photographer's art is as much about creating the trust that makes this possible as it is about camera technique. Nick, the guarded one, who could only bear to reveal himself in his songs, nevertheless let down his guard for Keith Morris's camera. And it is interesting to chart the singer's psychological progression through the three photo sessions that Keith did for the three Nick Drake albums.

Five Leaves Left

The photo shoot took place in four different locations in London: a derelict house in Wimbledon, on Wimbledon Common, outside a factory in Battersea (Keith, with an idea of the shots he wanted, had ascertained beforehand at what time the workers would be leaving work), and finally in Keith's photographic studio in Chelsea.

The photos show a very young Nick – shy, self-effacing, quizzical and amused, not entirely sure of himself, but nevertheless with a hint of that determination that could lead him to be quietly but unyieldingly obstinate about things that mattered to him.

The only shots that look slightly posed are the ones of him sitting in the grass on Wimbledon Common. Otherwise, the Nick you get is the Nick you would have met if you'd been in a room with him at that time: still a boy – a student – a dreamer of dreams as yet unshattered.

And the date the photos were taken? It turns out that the news-stand poster proclaiming 'Budget Day' was out of date: close inspection of the newspaper one of the bystanders was reading reveals the date to be one day later: 16 April 1969. Nick was twenty years old.

EVENING NEWS
BUDGET
SPEECH
EVENING
STANDARD

island
STEREO ILPS 9105
NICK DRAKE vocal & acoustic guitar
Side One
1. TIME HAS TOLD ME 3:56
Paul Harris piano
Richard Thompson electric guitar
Danny Thompson bass
2. RIVER MAN
Arranged by Harry Robinson
3. THREE HOURS
Danny Thompson bass
Rocki Dzidzornu congas
4. DAY IS DONE
Arranged by Robert Kirby
5. WAY TO BLUE 3:05
Arranged by Robert Kirby
Side Two
1. 'CELLO SONG
Clare Lowther 'cello
Danny Thompson bass
Rocki Dzidzornu congas
2. THE THOUGHTS OF MARY JANE 3:12
Arranged by Robert Kirby
3. MAN IN A SHED 3:49
Paul Harris piano
Danny Thompson bass
4. FRUIT TREE 4:42
Arranged by Robert Kirby
5. SATURDAY SUN
Nick Drake piano
Danny Thompson bass
Tristam Fry drums & vibraphone
All Songs By Nick Drake
© 1969 Warlock Music Ltd.
Photographs KEITH MORRIS
Design DIOGENIC ATTEMPTS LTD.
Engineering JOHN WOOD Sound Techniques
Produced by JOE BOYD
Witchseason Productions Ltd.
Printed & Made by ERNEST J. DAY & Co. Ltd.
island
ISLAND RECORDS LTD, BASING STREET LONDON W.11.

Joe Boyd: Not a lot of thought went into the sleeve for *Five Leaves Left*. I had a guy called Danny Halperin who was working in my office, who was a designer (and he ended up being the layout man for the *Telegraph Weekend Magazine*). His firm was Diogenic Attempts, I think Nigel Waymouth also did work for them on commission. Danny used to have an office at Track Records, he was an old friend of Track's owners, Chris Stamp and Kit Lambert. He got involved in my poster business and we rented him space in the back of our office in Charlotte Street and he did freelance work for other people. But part of the deal was he did our covers.

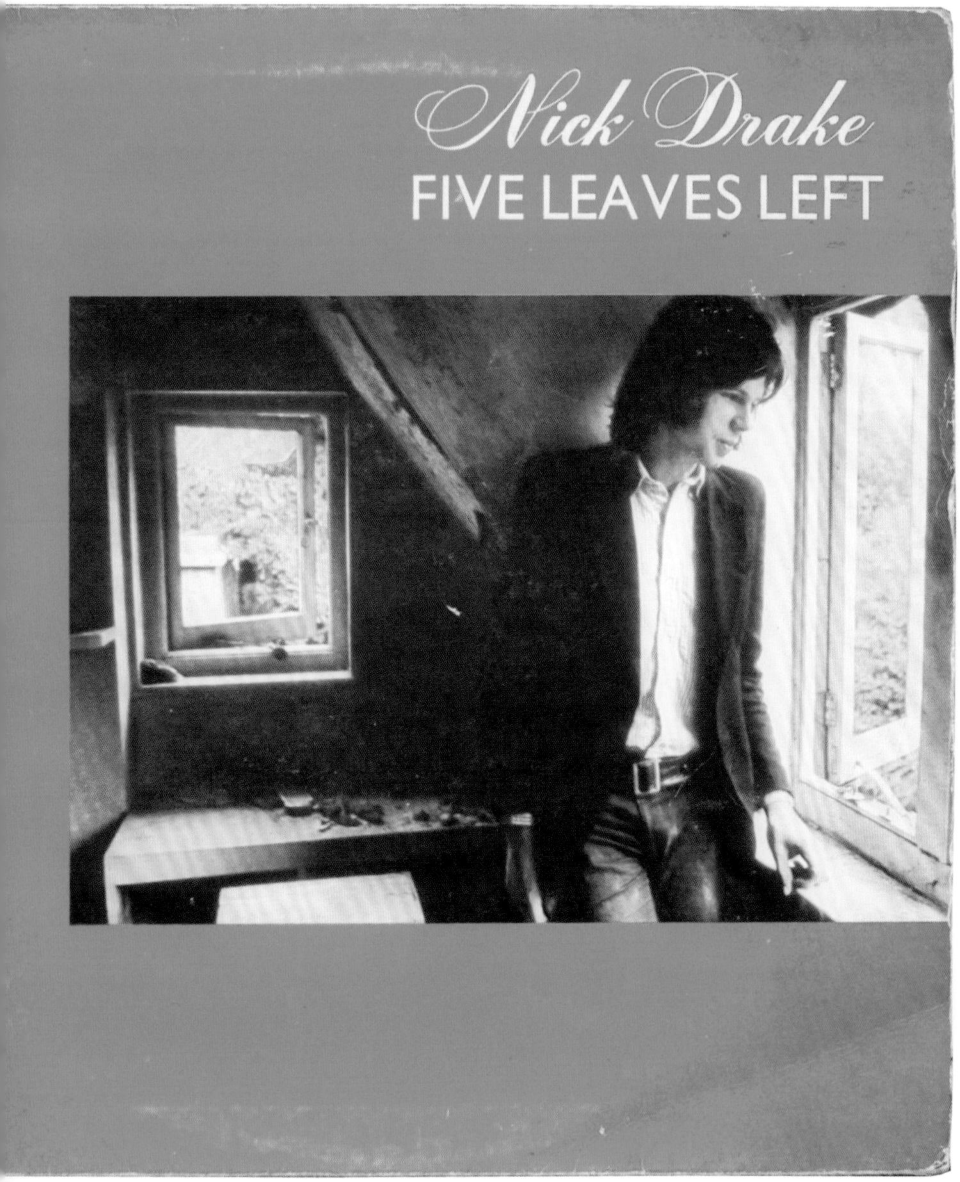

I can't remember how it came about but I remember we all liked Keith Morris's photo contact sheet. We all loved that thing of Nick standing still with people running past. That was very evocative. I think there was discussion at one point about that being the cover. It was, in America, on a compilation. At that time the mythologising of Nick as a solitary loner character had not yet really kicked in. Everybody knew he was shy but still it did seem to represent something.

I don't know why the photograph on the cover of *Five Leaves Left* is so small but that's what Danny's design was and we were in a hurry and it looked OK.

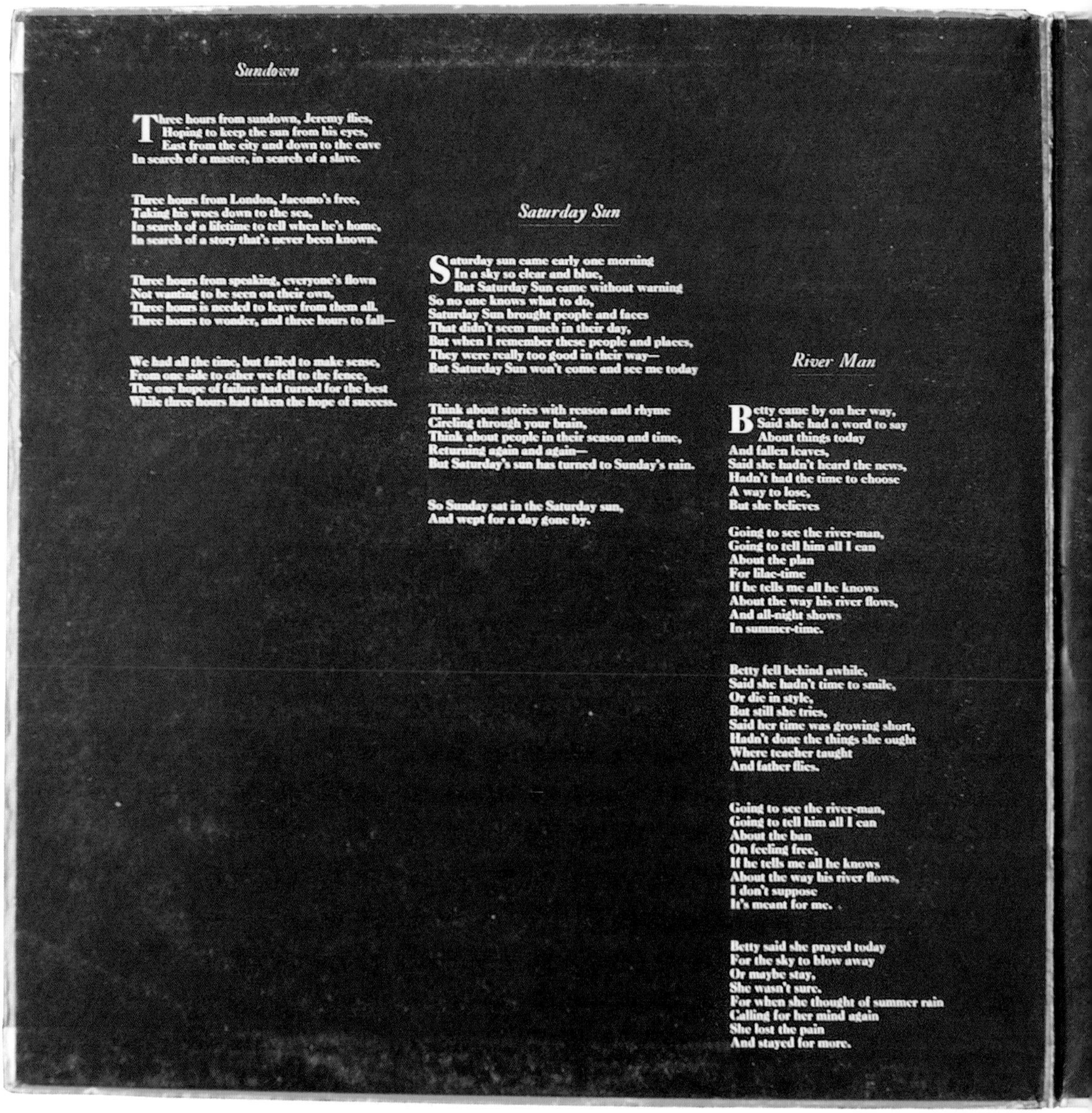

Sundown

Three hours from sundown, Jeremy flies,
Hoping to keep the sun from his eyes,
East from the city and down to the cave
In search of a master, in search of a slave.

Three hours from London, Jacomo's free,
Taking his woes down to the sea,
In search of a lifetime to tell when he's home,
In search of a story that's never been known.

Three hours from speaking, everyone's flown
Not wanting to be seen on their own,
Three hours is needed to leave from them all.
Three hours to wonder, and three hours to fall—

We had all the time, but failed to make sense,
From one side to other we fell to the fence,
The one hope of failure had turned for the best
While three hours had taken the hope of success.

Saturday Sun

Saturday sun came early one morning
In a sky so clear and blue,
But Saturday Sun came without warning
So no one knows what to do,
Saturday Sun brought people and faces
That didn't seem much in their day,
But when I remember these people and places,
They were really too good in their way—
But Saturday Sun won't come and see me today

Think about stories with reason and rhyme
Circling through your brain,
Think about people in their season and time,
Returning again and again—
But Saturday's sun has turned to Sunday's rain.

So Sunday sat in the Saturday sun,
And wept for a day gone by.

River Man

Betty came by on her way,
Said she had a word to say
About things today
And fallen leaves,
Said she hadn't heard the news,
Hadn't had the time to choose
A way to lose,
But she believes

Going to see the river-man,
Going to tell him all I can
About the plan
For lilac-time
If he tells me all he knows
About the way his river flows,
And all-night shows
In summer-time.

Betty fell behind awhile,
Said she hadn't time to smile,
Or die in style,
But still she tries,
Said her time was growing short,
Hadn't done the things she ought
Where teacher taught
And father flies.

Going to see the river-man,
Going to tell him all I can
About the ban
On feeling free,
If he tells me all he knows
About the way his river flows,
I don't suppose
It's meant for me.

Betty said she prayed today
For the sky to blow away
Or maybe stay,
She wasn't sure.
For when she thought of summer rain
Calling for her mind again
She lost the pain
And stayed for more.

Cassette shows early running order. Album running order was changed at the last minute

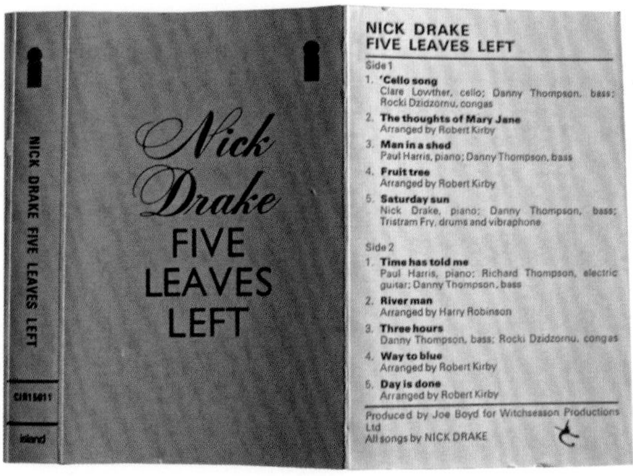

NICK DRAKE FIVE LEAVES LEFT
CIR15011
island
Nick Drake
FIVE LEAVES LEFT
NICK DRAKE
FIVE LEAVES LEFT
Side 1
1. 'Cello song
Clare Lowther, cello; Danny Thompson, bass; Rocki Dzidzornu, congas
2. The thoughts of Mary Jane
Arranged by Robert Kirby
3. Man in a shed
Paul Harris, piano; Danny Thompson, bass
4. Fruit tree
Arranged by Robert Kirby
5. Saturday sun
Nick Drake, piano; Danny Thompson, bass; Tristram Fry, drums and vibraphone
Side 2
1. Time has told me
Paul Harris, piano; Richard Thompson, electric guitar; Danny Thompson, bass
2. River man
Arranged by Harry Robinson
3. Three hours
Danny Thompson, bass; Rocki Dzidzornu, congas
4. Way to blue
Arranged by Robert Kirby
5. Day is done
Arranged by Robert Kirby
Produced by Joe Boyd for Witchseason Productions Ltd
All songs by NICK DRAKE

CIR 15011
(04)
FIVE LEAVES LEFT
TIME HAS TOLD ME, RIVER MAN, THREE HOURS, WAY TO BLUE, DAY IS DONE.
NICK DRAKE
ISLAND
2
Island Music Ltd.
℗ 1969
All rights of the record producer and of the owner of the work reproduced reserved. Copying, public performances and broadcasting of this recording prohibited.
For full copyright details see inlay card.

From the Drake family scrapbook.

Our second album from Fairport Convention. It may even be better than the first.

A discussion on Fairport Convention and their first Island album, reprinted from Zig Zag No. 1, April 1969.

"When you go and see the Fairport Convention, you can't go wrong—they always impress. Their singing and playing falls between categorical stools, but lands on a wide, luxurious musical carpet. They're like a growing city, phagocytically swallowing the peripheral satellite towns—they are always adding to their already rich anthology by absorbing adjacent styles, but allowing them to retain their own identity, a sense of locality if you like.

They just stand there, visually comparatively unappetising—no frenetic leaping or cavorting—but they seem to be haloed by an air of precise infallibility. Sandy Denny waits reticently, her hands clasped coyly as the introduction is played, but when she starts to sing, her personality and vocal succulence ooze over the song like melted chocolate, running through the articulated textures of Richard Thompson's guitar work, and subtly insinuating their way into the listener's mind.

The ecstatic plaudits I expected to see when their album came out never appeared. Inexplicable. To my mind the record towers like an aardvark in an ant colony compared with all 1969's other releases (except possibly the Family's which I haven't really had time to engulf myself in yet).

Any other English group attempting such variety on one album would find themselves stumbling through a musical minefield. But the Fairport, an eclectic group (their stage act ranges from traditional English folksongs to Muddy Waters and way beyond), but one which manages to do more than just invoke memories or comparison, come through on this their second album with almost unparalleled magnificence.

Joe Boyd, who turns up treasures like a beachcomber finds shells, discovered this cabal at the beginning of commercial underground activity in England, nuturing them through the days of the Electric Garden etc, and in the meticulous production of this record has yielded his masterpiece.

Ex folk club singer Sandy, who wrote the title track of Judy Collins' new LP, joined a few months ago and brought much of her background with her. It wouldn't be accurate or fair to say that she is the group's main strength, but her beautiful voice is certainly the outstanding feature of this album. She wrote 'Fotheringay', with an engrossing historical setting (I never imagined that a song about Mary Queen of Scots could get me going), and sings it exquisitely against an attractive lacework of acoustic guitars and harmonised humming which simply seeps warmth and folk nostalgia into the listener. (And those autoharp wisps—perfect!). She does an equally fine job on the two traditional tracks, 'Nottamun Town', which features an open tuned Indian influenced solo over Simon Nicol's sawed violin, and 'She Moves Through The Fair', a song exemplifying her ability and knowledge.

But the pilot of their conglomerate genius is lead guitarist Richard Thompson, who steers the group with a film director's vision. His songwriting accomplishment has leapt to match his instrumental excellence, which spans from butterfly delicacy on 'Fotheringay' to the crunchy rotundity on his own 'Meet On The Ledge', a superbly structured piece about dormant muses and flagging creativity. Here, as on most other tracks, Sandy's voice is complimented by Ian Matthews (who has since left the group) and they are both joined in the chorus by Simon, whose raucous edge gives the song its intensity. This track with its harmony, piano links and bass lyricism best sums up the polished achievement of the Fairport.

Thompson also wrote 'No Mans Land', an exuberant accordian dominated romp, which, despite the despondent lyric, conjures up visions of leathertrousered dancing Germans spilling beer (nice clapping in here too), and 'Tale In Hard Time'—vaguely Byrdian, but with a pumping harpsichord. Very nice.

'Book Song', straining the seams of familiarity, is a very pleasant cut. Delicate, dreamy and beautiful, with the congruous inclusion of Clare Lowther's tender cello. It also pinpoints Tyger Hutchins' bass technique. I have never heard such imaginative, inventive and lyrical bass playing anywhere—I found myself literally gurgling with delight on each track as I listened through the phones to the way he slid the riding embellishments and bubbling patterns into the music.

American listeners may be forgiven for misinterpreting the lyrics of the rumbustious 'Mr Lacey', written by Hutchins, as thinly disguised pornography—the sleeve reference to Prof Bruce Lacey will mean little to anyone outside Britain. He is a legendary underground figure, an inventor of radio controlled hominoids and strange gadgetry (some of which whirrs like power drills over the solo), and has appeared in all manner of happenings, including that theatrical extravaganza "An Evening of British Rubbish". In the song he is romanticised, not as the odd eccentric crackpot that many consider him to be, but as a leading pioneer in the field of mechanical invention whose greatness will one day be universally recognized. All this is conveyed in a cascading blues form.

The Fairport Convention work on an elastically wide canvas, but don't cover it by throwing buckets of paint. Everything is steeped in imagination from the vocals to the tasteful appropriate drumming of Martin Lamble, who sometimes has the bass drum motif blanching and other times is so gentle that only an almost imperceptable cymbal is heard. They don't put a foot wrong—lavishing care on each song (with particular attention to introductions and closes) so that each is a superbly arranged and polished entity, and yet an integral part of a most satisfying whole."

The new Fairport Convention, 'Unhalfbricking' available July 3.

The first Nick Drake album, 'Five Leaves Left', available July 3.

The first Dr. Strangely Strange, 'Kip of the Serenes', available July 3.

Like Fairport Convention, both Nick Drake and Dr. Strangely Strange co-produced their albums with Joe Boyd.

Nick Drake wrote all the songs on this first L.P. The unusual string arrangements were played on the session by Danny Thompson, Paul Harris and Richard Thompson.

Dr. Strangely Strange are greatly admired by the Incredible String Band, who have done so much to help them.

island

ISLAND RECORDS LTD. BASING STREET LONDON W11. TEL 229 1229

International Times, 4–17 July 1969

The Polydor axe falls and MBW asks...

HAS THE SAMPLER PROMO ALBUM OUTLIVED ITS USEFULNESS?

The latest CBS sampler for its progressive catalogue has already sold more than 70,000.

THE days of the sampler album are over. So said Polydor chief John Fruin, announcing the company's far-reaching price revisions.

And the result of his decision that samplers have outlived their usefulness will be the deletion, within the next few months, of all the Polydor 14s 6d sampler series — albums like "This Is James Last" and "This Is Kai Warner" which, as any dealer will confirm, have led to a significant increase in turnover of full-price product by these artists.

Fruin's pronouncement has been received with amazement in the trade. "It's absolutely crazy," was the first reaction from one record company marketing chief. And, indeed, too many companies have 100,000-plus-selling samplers working nicely for them to be likely to agree with him.

David Betteridge, sales director of Island, which has had great success with its "You Can All Join In" and "Nice Enough To Eat" samplers, is firmly convinced of their usefulness. "If you use them in the right way and don't flood your market with too many at one time they can be of enormous assistance in introducing little known names, like Nick Drake, to the public.

"It is important, of course, to put some strong-selling names on a sampler, but that isn't the object of the exercise. It is really just another exposure medium: giving the public and the retailer a good idea of range of your product."

Island's next sampler, "Bumper," features Clouds, John and Beverley Martyn, Dick Morrisey's band If and Cat Stevens alongside the label's big names like Jethro Tull and Blodwyn Pig. Said Betteridge: "If you can sell 500 copies of an album because of a sampler, you're doing well."

The new sampler will be retailing at a recommended 19s 11d, a 4s 5d increase, though it will now have 14 titles. "It's going up because we need to make a little more money," he said. "Royalty-wise, it's very tough going, especially as a lot of the product now is not just rehashed but fairly new material."

A and M's managing director Larry Yaskiel is another strong advocate of samplers, "but it depends on the purpose behind their release," he added.

"The word sampler is being used by different companies in different ways," he went on, "we use it to mean: sample our wares at this price, and if you like it, buy them at full price."

Since going independent last summer, the label has had three samplers. The Alpert "America" album has been phenomenally successful, selling over 150,000 to date. It has been followed by an "Introducing Sergio Mendes" album — it was released with a limited sales period, and will be withdrawn within the next month — which has sold more than 50,000.

"Our use of samplers is in keeping with our general policy of trying to reactivate our back catalogue," said Yaskiel.

With its 23-title "Fill Your Head With Rock" double album doing very big business, it is hardly surprising that CBS has no plans to scrap samplers.

In fact, there are two more already scheduled — one, at 19s 11d, for Straight, and a second Blue Horizon sampler.

"Samplers don't work in every area — we've found them to be most successful in the contemporary area," said David Howells, album co-ordinator for CBS.

The first progressive sampler, "Rock Machine Turns You On," sold 135,000 copies, the succeeding "Rock Machine, I Love You" sold only a few thousand short of that figure, and the new "Fill Your Head With Rock" two-record set has already topped 70,000.

Howells stressed the need to do more than simply put a sampler out. "If you don't back it up with a lot of promotional material it can easily become just a budget LP and be a fantastic seller, but not help you to sell your catalogue," he said.

The inclusion of an eight-page booklet in the double-album has proved extremely costly but, says Howells, has meant getting to the customer in his own home "where he can absorb what he is interested in."

Outside the progressive market, CBS's biggest success has been the Ray Conniff "His Orchestra, His Chorus, His Singers, His Sound" album, which has passed the 120,000 mark.

Said Howells: "We had a catalogue of 20 Conniff albums, but we needed something to give it a boost. This has been a very big success."

When CBS began its progressive samplers, the biggest names were Dylan and Simon and Garfunkel. Gradually, through samplers, the public have been made aware of groups like Spirit, Flock, Santana and It's A Beautiful Day. "We feel all our American progressive acts have benefitted from the samplers," said Howells.

JOHN FRUIN

Like A and M, CBS has a limited life period of six months to a year on its samplers. The current double album will be deleted before the end of the year. "That way you come out when you're on top," Howells explained.

He feels all samplers should be approached as loss leaders. "Obviously you make a fair profit if you sell them in quantity but we're more interested in how many full-price albums of the product featured on them we sell."

EMI's Barry Green, deputy marketing manager responsible for middle market product, feels the sampler is anything but dead. "Far from abandoning ours, I intend doing even more in 1971, and at least two pop material samplers will be coming from us before the end of the year," he said.

The company has had a trio of huge-selling Studio 2 samplers — "Breakthrough," "Impact" and "Ultimate Stereo Presentation," released at annual intervals. "Together they have introduced more than half a million people to Studio 2 material," said Green. "Breakthrough" sold more than 250,000 as a sampler, and is now, incredibly, going great guns for MfP as a straight budget album.

Green feels that the reason for EMI's success with the samplers is the choice of a good listening programme. Every track is considered carefully, and may even be re-mixed, before its eventual inclusion or otherwise.

The latest sampler, "USP," is the first to have 16 tracks and has been broadened to take in the Studio 2 "A Night At The Theatre" series and classical albums. "A good track we feel may not appeal to many of the public, such as a classical piece, we put at the end of each side, so the buyer can take it off before the end," he explained.

He is convinced the samplers have been of enormous benefit to the Studio 2 range generally. "Phase Four was on the market 18 months before Studio 2 was even thought of," he said. "Now Studio 2 is by far the best seller in its field."

Green sees other tangible benefits of issuing samplers. "You make money, you keep your factory working, it helps your cover commitment, and it's a definite contribution to overheads," he said.

Of Polydor's scrapping of samplers, he ventured: "I think they were putting out too many of them and not giving enough thought to it. It takes me a year to work properly at getting a sampler selected."

Certainly, its rivals think Polydor is going to lose business by getting out of samplers. After issuing so many, why now drop them?

Polydor's sales manager Eddy Webster told me: "We are not going to use the term sampler any more. It has in many ways outlived its usefulness. We virtually broke the ground on the sampler and we have worked it hard for four or five years. We have used it and used it and used it.

"In the past, we have done very well with it, but we don't get the same volume of sale out of it any more. And the volume of product in that price area is now very prolific — we are anxious to get into a new price category."

DAVID BETTERIDGE

The chosen price is 19s 10d (99p). "We'll be going into a sort of super budget line — a line of its own not specifically intended as a leader for full-price product, thought we may reintroduce some of the deleted samplers to it in a slightly different form," he said. "The marketing of this line will also have a decimalisation theme."

One can see the logic in establishing an attractive new price of 99p, but there seems to be no obvious reason for scrapping the sampler, at whatever price.

Polydor's greatest problem may be its seemingly indiscrimiate flood of samplers in the past. Perhaps it has over-worked them. And then, of course, there are the so-called "samplers" that are nothing more than a collection of old tracks. A recent Plastic Penny "sampler" from Page One was a case in point. These have served only to debase the term sampler and confuse the public.

But one would think there was still plenty of scope for the sparing use of a genuine sampler put out purely to increase interest in unestablished or new names with full-price product in the catalogue.

PETER ROBINSON

indeed.

* * *

In Britain there continue to appear new and promising young recruits to the singers of our time. Nick Drake, who made a brief but impressive appearance at a recent London concert, has an excellent LP of his own songs ("Five leaves left"—Island ILPS-9105) in which his own slightly hypnotic guitar is backed by Richard Thompson, Danny Thompson (bass) and Paul Harris (piano). His voice is slow, reflective and warm, and although the verse structure tends to melodic monotony, there is no mistaking the quality and the promise of "River man," "The Thoughts of Mary Jane," "Man in a Shed" and other items on this disc. (On Side One, incidentally, "Day is done" and "Way to blue" are in the reverse order to that given on the label and the sleeve).

Another newcomer, "Beau"

Music Business Weekly, 18 April 1970

Inset believed to be an early clipping from a Birmingham newspaper

FIVE LEAVES LEFT NICK DRAKE Island ILPS 9105

I don't think I've been so impressed with an album by an unknown singer/songwriter since I got the Duncan Browne album on Immediate, eighteen months ago, (why don't Immediate send us review copies? WHY DON'T IMMEDIATE SEND US REVIEW COPIES?), as I've been by the Nick Drake thing.

Unfortunately Drake's voice is going to be repeatedly compared to that of Donovan. But Don would be nowhere without his songs and Nick will get nowhere without his. They are beautiful, gentle breezes of cadent perfection which carry along reflective poems like dancing, golden leaves. Listen to the opening track on side two, 'Cello Song', for an excellent example of Drake's penchant for casting simple lyrics against a musical background of equal simplicity but of different beat and aural texture. This track's a little like some of the Pentangle's stuff actually and, ho and behold, Danny Thompson's on bass for much of the album! The arrangements, mostly by Robert Kirby, although some are handled by Harry Robinson and Nick himself, are excellent and match the mood of Nick's songs to a tee. The choice of backing instruments echos this too and the whole thing is put into a frame by Joe Boyd's tasteful production.

Nick Drake's songs are not of quite the same construction as folk tunes, they have a subtlety and originality that make this album a series of contemporary folk ARRANGEMENTS of just bloody, brilliant songs. The words of three of them are printed on the sleeve, for potential buyers to judge the man's worth. Also on the cover is a nice picture of a besuited grey running along to some unimportant appointment, or to catch his bus to the insurance office where he works, perhaps. Leaning on the wall watching him rush by, is the slightly puzzled Nick Drake. It's a nice touch and shows exactly where his music's at.

ISLAND: Island Records have a large July release. Out now are three Joe Boyd produced albums by the Fairport Convention, Nick Drake, and Dr. Strangley Strange. Coming on 25 July is the new Jethro Tull album, 'Stand Up' with a pop up cover, the first Clouds album, 'Scrapbook', and 'Ahead Rings Out' by Mick Abrams' Blodwyn Pig.
Matthew Wetmore

The first Nick Drake album, 'Five Leaves Left', available July 3.

The first Dr. Strangely Strange, 'Kip of the Serenes', available July 3.

Like Fairport Convention, both Nick Drake and Dr. Strangely Strange co-produced their albums with Joe Boyd.

Nick Drake wrote all the songs on this first L.P. The unusual string arrangements were played on the session by Danny Thompson, Paul Harris and Richard Thompson.

Dr. Strangely Strange are greatly admired by the Incredible String Band, who have done so much to help them.

island

Our second album from Fairport Convention. It may even be better than the first.

A discussion on Fairport Convention and their first Island album, reprinted from Zig Zag No. 1, April 1969.

'The ecstatic plaudits I expected to see when their album came out never appeared. Inexplicable. To my mind the record towers like an aardvark in an ant colony compared with all 1969's other releases (except possibly the Family's which I haven't really had time to engulf myself in yet).

Any other English group attempting such variety on one album would find themselves stumbling through a musical minefield. But the Fairport, an eclectic group (their stage act ranges from traditional English folksongs to Muddy Waters and way beyond), but one which manages to do more than just invoke memories or comparison, come through on this their second album with almost unparalleled magnificence.

Joe Boyd, who turns up treasures like a beachcomber finds shells, discovered this cabal at the beginning of commercial underground activity in England, nurturing them through the days of the Electric Garden etc, and in the meticulous production of this record has yielded his masterpiece'.

The first Nick Drake album, 'Five Leaves Left', available July 3.

The new Fairport Convention, 'Unhalfbricking', available July 3.

The first Dr. Strangely Strang 'Kip of the Serenes', availabl July 3.

Like Fairport Convention, both Nick Drake and Dr. Strangely Strange co-produced their albums with Joe Boyd.

Nick Drake wrote all the songs on this first L.P. The unusual string arrangements were played on the session by Danny Thompson, Paul Harris and Richard Thompson.

Dr. Strangely Strange are greatly admired by the Incredible ng Band, who have done so much to help them.

ISLAN

Record Releases

LOVE: The new Love album 'Four Sail' is due out in the States late July. Featuring all new members except for Arthur Lee, 'Four Sail' is a departure from their previous albums.

DOORS: 'The Soft Parade' album was released on 11 July in the States and will be released here mid-August. Tracks included their latest US single 'Tell All the People'.

TEN YEARS AFTER: Ten Years After have a new album called 'Ssssh . . .' which they produced themselves following their split with Mike Vernon. All but one of the tracks was written by Alvin Lee.

CROSBY, STILL AND NASH: The long awaited album by this trio is doing great business in the States and will be released by Atlantic here by early August.

BLIND FAITH: Their first album will be released on Polydor early August. The seven tracks include three Stevie Winwood songs and one sixteen minute opener by Ginger Baker.

JACK BRUCE: Jack Bruce's solo album, 'Songs for a Tailor', is expected at the same time. The album is dedicated to Genie the Tailor who died in the Fairp Convention crash last May, and featur many top name musicians.

GARY BURTON: RCA Records is comi up to date with the release last week 'A Genuine Tong Funeral'. This leav 'Duster' unreleased which might ha proved a better seller than his previo album, 'Tennessee Firebird'.

JEFF BECK: New album 'Beck-ola' w Nicky Hopkins and Rod Stewart due so on Columbia. Includes Beck's version 'Jailhouse Rock'.

WARNER REPRISE: Warner Reprise, nc an independent company in England, a planning to release a mass of albums he in September. Joni Mitchell's 'Clouds', t Grateful Dead's 'Aoxomoxoa', and both t Neil Young albums are included. V Morrison's 'Astral Weeks' will be releas 'any time now'.

ISLAND: Island Records have a large Ju release. Out now are three Joe Boyd pi duced albums by the Fairport Conventic Nick Drake, and Dr. Strangley Strang Coming on 25 July is the new Jethro T album, 'Stand Up' with a pop up cover, t first Clouds album, 'Scrapbook', a 'Ahead Rings Out' by Mick Abrams' Blo wyn Pig.
Matthew Wetmo

38

Above left: *International Times*, 18–31 July 1969 Above right: *Time Out*, 3 June–20 July 1969 Centre left: *Time Out*, 19 July 1969
Below left: *International Times*, 4–17 July 1969 Below right: *Time Out*, 19 July 1969

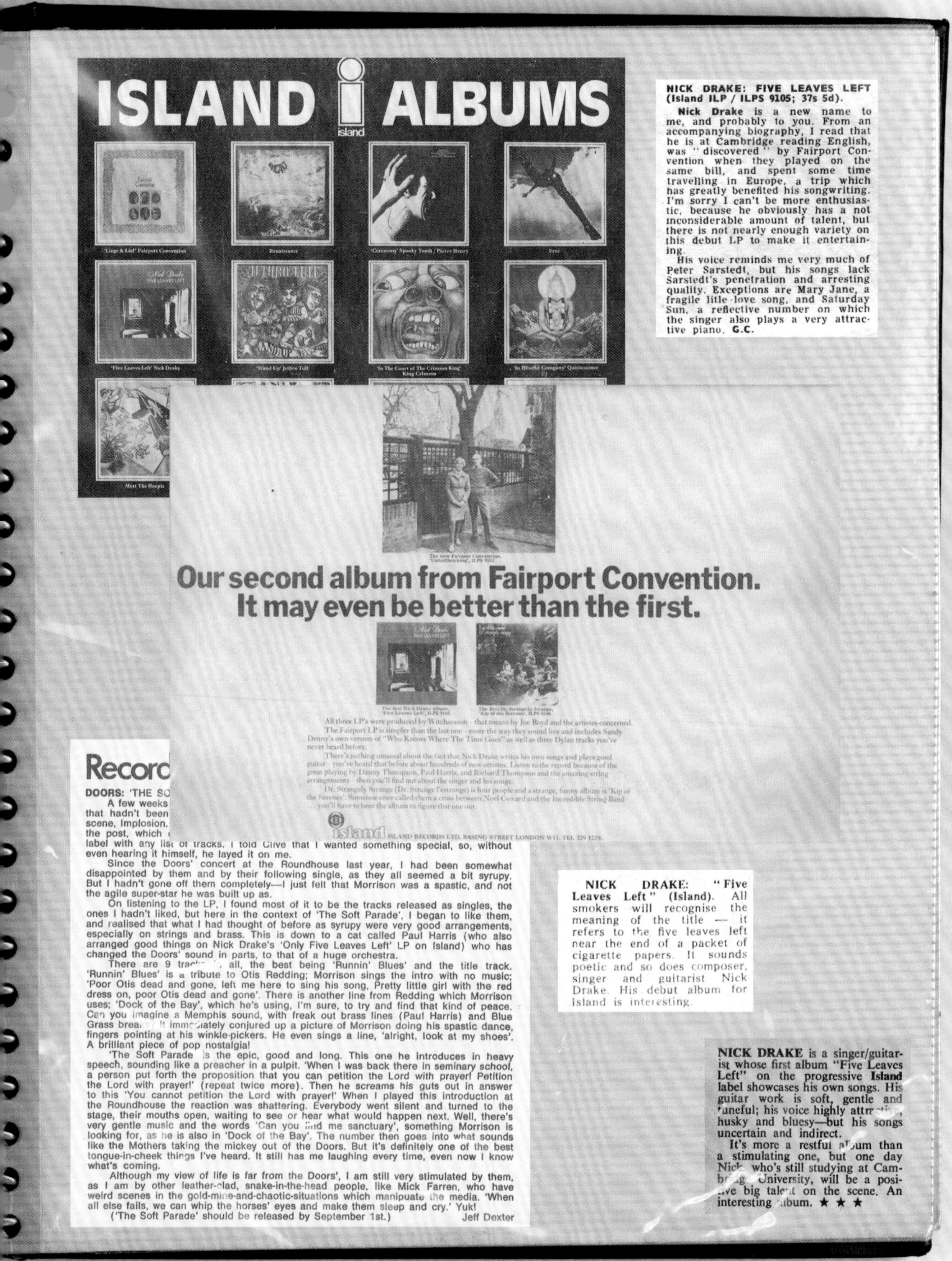

ISLAND
island
ALBUMS
'Liege & Lief' Fairport Convention
Renaissance
'Ceremony' Spooky Tooth / Pierre Henry
Free
'Five Leaves Left' Nick Drake
'Stand Up' Jethro Tull
'In The Court of The Crimson King' King Crimson
'In Blissful Company' Quintessence
Mott The Hoople

NICK DRAKE: FIVE LEAVES LEFT (Island ILP / ILPS 9105; 37s 5d).

Nick Drake is a new name to me, and probably to you. From an accompanying biography, I read that he is at Cambridge reading English, was " discovered " by Fairport Convention when they played on the same bill, and spent some time travelling in Europe, a trip which has greatly benefited his songwriting. I'm sorry I can't be more enthusiastic, because he obviously has a not inconsiderable amount of talent, but there is not nearly enough variety on this debut LP to make it entertaining.

His voice reminds me very much of Peter Sarstedt, but his songs lack Sarstedt's penetration and arresting quality. Exceptions are Mary Jane, a fragile litle love song, and Saturday Sun, a reflective number on which the singer also plays a very attractive piano. **G.C.**

The new Fairport Convention, 'Unhalfbricking', ILPS 9102

Our second album from Fairport Convention.
It may even be better than the first.

The first Nick Drake album, 'Five Leaves Left', ILPS 9105

The first Dr. Strangely Strange, 'Kip of the Serenes', ILPS 9106

All three LP's were produced by Witchseason – that means by Joe Boyd and the artistes concerned.

The Fairport LP is simpler than the last one – more the way they sound live and includes Sandy Denny's own version of "Who Knows Where The Time Goes" as well as three Dylan tracks you've never heard before.

There's nothing unusual about the fact that Nick Drake writes his own songs and plays good guitar – you've heard that before about hundreds of new artistes. Listen to the record because of the great playing by Danny Thompson, Paul Harris, and Richard Thompson and the amazing string arrangements – then you'll find out about the singer and his songs.

Dr. Strangely Strange (Dr. Strange l'estrange) is four people and a strange, funny album is 'Kip of the Serenes'. Someone once called them a cross between Noel Coward and the Incredible String Band . . . you'll have to hear the album to figure that one out.

island ISLAND RECORDS LTD. BASING STREET LONDON W11. TEL. 229 1229.

Recorc

DOORS: 'THE SO

A few weeks that hadn't been scene, Implosion. the post, which label with any list of tracks. I told Clive that I wanted something special, so, without even hearing it himself, he layed it on me.

Since the Doors' concert at the Roundhouse last year, I had been somewhat disappointed by them and by their following single, as they all seemed a bit syrupy. But I hadn't gone off them completely—I just felt that Morrison was a spastic, and not the agile super-star he was built up as.

On listening to the LP, I found most of it to be the tracks released as singles, the ones I hadn't liked, but here in the context of 'The Soft Parade', I began to like them, and realised that what I had thought of before as syrupy were very good arrangements, especially on strings and brass. This is down to a cat called Paul Harris (who also arranged good things on Nick Drake's 'Only Five Leaves Left' LP on Island) who has changed the Doors' sound in parts, to that of a huge orchestra.

There are 9 tracks in all, the best being 'Runnin' Blues' and the title track. 'Runnin' Blues' is a tribute to Otis Redding; Morrison sings the intro with no music; 'Poor Otis dead and gone, left me here to sing his song, Pretty little girl with the red dress on, poor Otis dead and gone'. There is another line from Redding which Morrison uses; 'Dock of the Bay', which he's using, I'm sure, to try and find that kind of peace. Can you imagine a Memphis sound, with freak out brass lines (Paul Harris) and Blue Grass breaks? It immediately conjured up a picture of Morrison doing his spastic dance, fingers pointing at his winkle-pickers. He even sings a line, 'alright, look at my shoes'. A brilliant piece of pop nostalgia!

'The Soft Parade' is the epic, good and long. This one he introduces in heavy speech, sounding like a preacher in a pulpit. 'When I was back there in seminary school, a person put forth the proposition that you can petition the Lord with prayer! Petition the Lord with prayer!' (repeat twice more). Then he screams his guts out in answer to this 'You cannot petition the Lord with prayer!' When I played this introduction at the Roundhouse the reaction was shattering. Everybody went silent and turned to the stage, their mouths open, waiting to see or hear what would happen next. Well, there's very gentle music and the words 'Can you find me sanctuary', something Morrison is looking for, as he is also in 'Dock of the Bay'. The number then goes into what sounds like the Mothers taking the mickey out of the Doors. But it's definitely one of the best tongue-in-cheek things I've heard. It still has me laughing every time, even now I know what's coming.

Although my view of life is far from the Doors', I am still very stimulated by them, as I am by other leather-clad, snake-in-the-head people, like Mick Farren, who have weird scenes in the gold-mine-and-chaotic-situations which manipulate the media. 'When all else fails, we can whip the horses' eyes and make them sleep and cry.' Yuk!

('The Soft Parade' should be released by September 1st.) Jeff Dexter

NICK DRAKE: " Five Leaves Left " (Island). All smokers will recognise the meaning of the title — it refers to the five leaves left near the end of a packet of cigarette papers. It sounds poetic and so does composer, singer and guitarist Nick Drake. His debut album for Island is interesting.

NICK DRAKE is a singer/guitarist whose first album "Five Leaves Left" on the progressive **Island** label showcases his own songs. His guitar work is soft, gentle and tuneful; his voice highly attractive, husky and bluesy—but his songs uncertain and indirect.

It's more a restful album than a stimulating one, but one day Nick, who's still studying at Cambridge University, will be a positive big talent on the scene. An interesting album. ★ ★ ★

Above left: *Melody Maker*, 20 June 1969 Above right: *NME*, 4 October 1969 Centre: *Melody Maker*, 5 July 1969
Centre right: *Melody Maker*, 26 July 1969 Below left: *Time Out*, 2–15 August 1969 Below right: *Disc & Music Echo*, 23 August 1969

The first Nick Drake album, 'Five Leaves Left', available July 3.

The new Fairport Convention, 'Unhalfbricking', available July 3.

The first Dr. Strangely Strange, 'Kip of the Serenes', available July 3.

Like Fairport Convention, both Nick Drake and Dr. Strangely Strange co-produced their albums with Joe Boyd.

Nick Drake wrote all the songs on this first L.P. The unusual string arrangements were played on the session by Danny Thompson, Paul Harris and Richard Thompson.

Dr. Strangely Strange are greatly admired by the Incredible String Band, who have done so much to help them.

ISLAND RECORDS LTD. BASING STREET LONDON W11. TEL 229 1229

NICK DRAKE: "Five Leaves Left" (ILPS 9105). A very attractive set from this young man — extremely poetic in concept and neatly scored throughout. Added instrumental support is given by Paul Harris piano, 'Pentangler' Danny Thompson bass, and Fairport's Richard Thompson on guitar. Not an album to set the charts alight but, nevertheless, very pleasant.

Brenda Ralfini to run Warlock Music

BRENDA Ralfini has been appointed general manager of Joe Boyd's new publishing company Warlock Music, after 10 years at Feldmans. Prior to that she worked for five years at Joe Henderson's publishing company, which she helped form in 1955.

At Feldmans, she was largely responsible for overseas licensing for the whole catalogue, as well as the Albert Grossman companies, which includes material by Bob Dylan, the Band, Janis Joplin and Paul Butterfield Blues Band.

One of her first jobs at Warlock, which publishes music by Richard Thompson of Fairport Convention, John and Beverley Martyn, Sandy Denny, and Robin Williamson and Mike Heron of the Incredible String Band, among others, will be to set up overseas publishing deals.

Boyd has also appointed Susannah Watson-Taylor as personal manager to John and Beverley Martyn and Nick Drake, and she will assist him with the Incredible String Band.

Above: *ZigZag*, 3 July 1969 Below left: *Top Pops*, 9 August 1969 Below right: *Music Business Weekly*, 7 March 1970

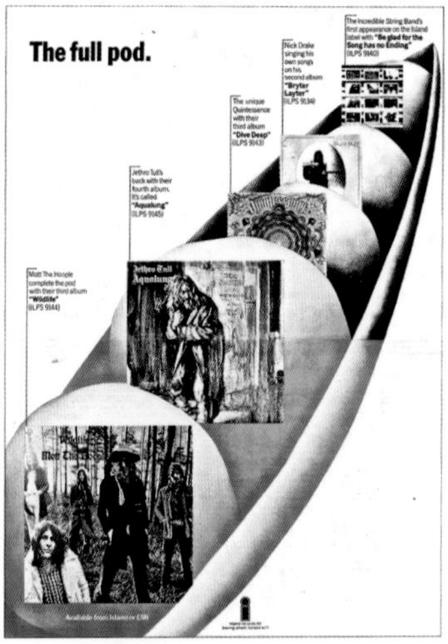

Island Records beat Apple to the iPod:
back cover of *Record Mirror*, 20 March 1971

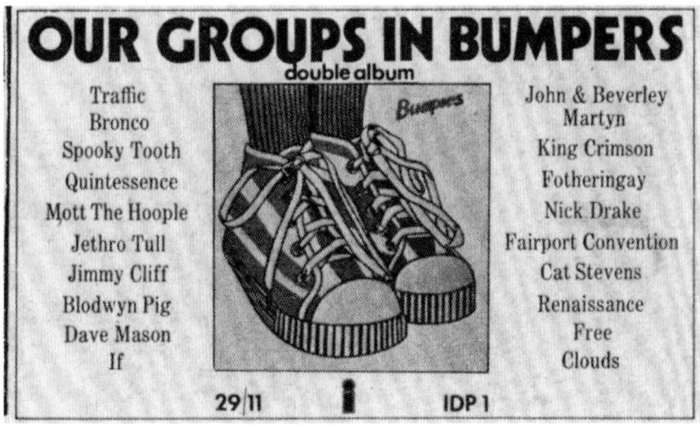

Along with CBS and Harvest, Island saw the benefit of releasing a selection of tracks by their key acts on budget-priced sampler albums, often running to double-album length. These included *Nice Enough To Eat* (14s/6d) which included 'Time Has Told Me'; *El Pea* ('One of These Things First') and *Bumpers* which included 'Hazey Jane' (not credited with either a I or a II, but including a long-lost colour photo of Nick pinned to a tree inside the sleeve).

Island also produced fully illustrated (and now highly sought-after) catalogues called 'The Island Book Of Records' in which Nick's albums were portrayed along with their track listings. Both of these marketing methods proved to be powerful ways of getting people to listen to Nick Drake, often by association with their bigger artists: Jethro Tull. King Crimson, Cat Stevens and Traffic, etc.

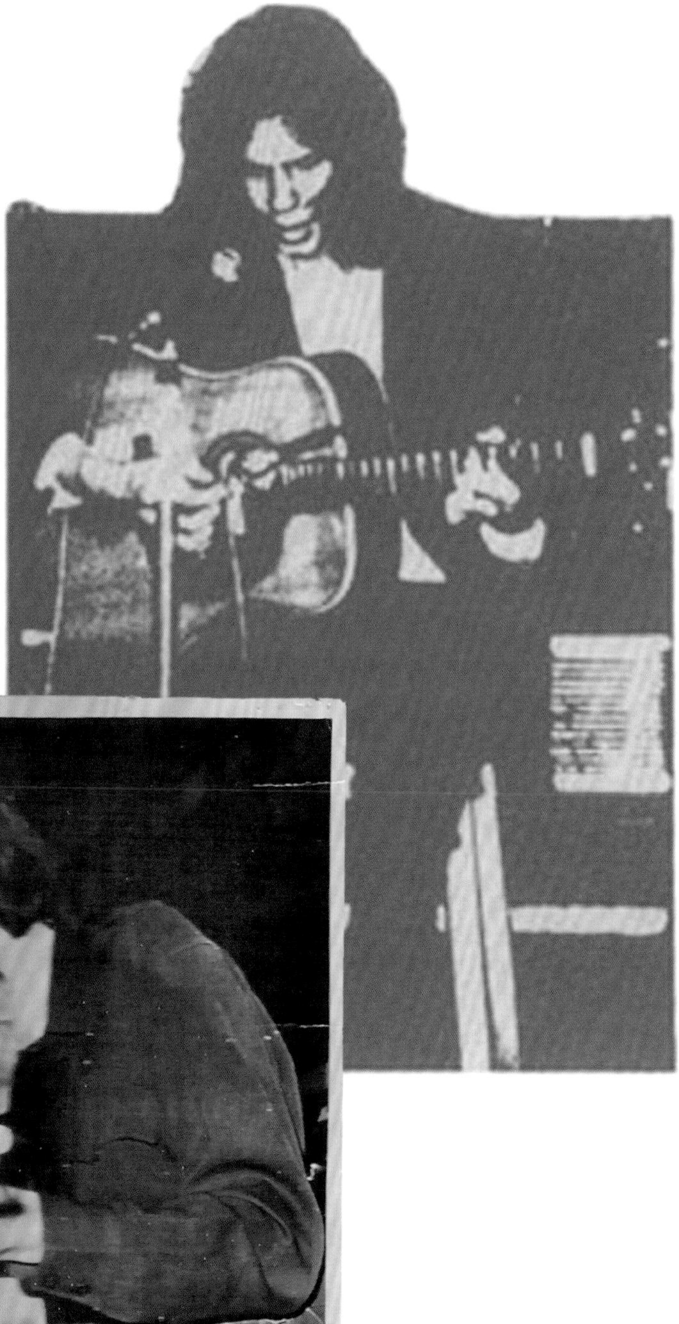

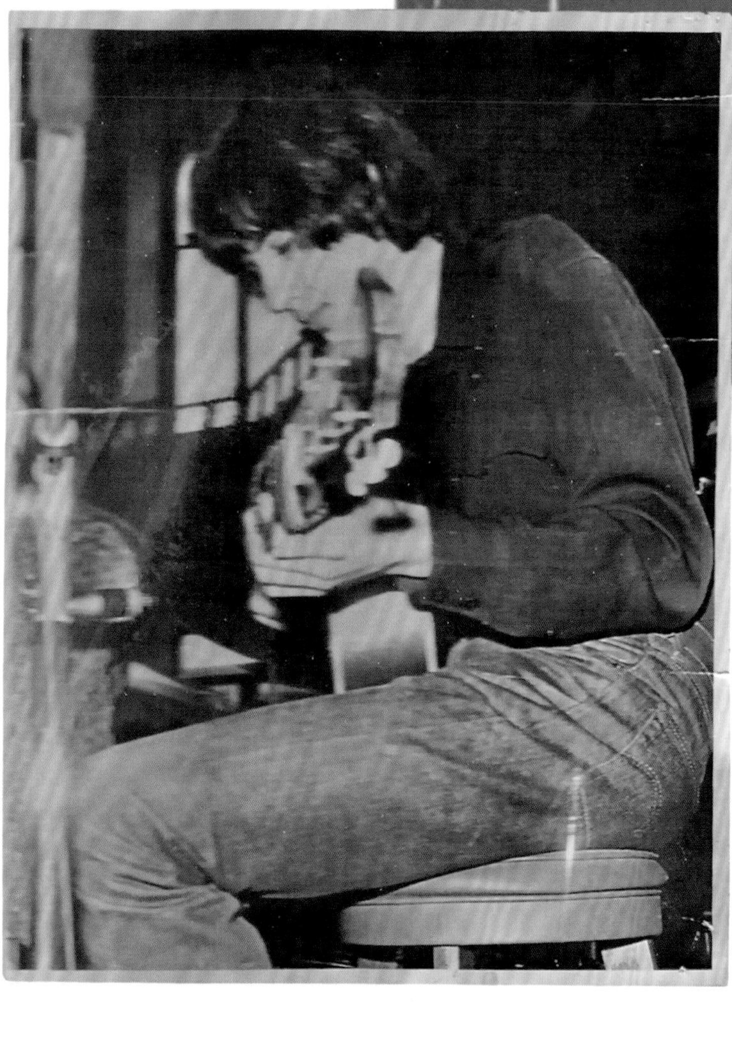

(Photos supplied by Paul Wheeler)

Never Sing For My Supper

Paul Wheeler in conversation with Gabrielle Drake

Paul Wheeler arrived in Cambridge in the autumn of 1968 – exactly one year after Nick. He had won a scholarship to Gonville and Caius College, the same college as Robert Kirby, who was by now working on arrangements for Nick's songs. Nick would undoubtedly have been keen to meet this new student who had already established himself as a singer-songwriter and musician, having previously worked with John Martyn on the latter's second album *The Tumbler* (1968). John Martyn was a rising young star in the Island Records stable, and Paul had played guitar on *The Tumbler*, and co-written one of the tracks ('Fly on Home'), as well as the album's sleeve notes. Paul and Nick found they had much in common, not only in music, but in other areas as well. And it was Paul who introduced Nick to John Martyn.

Nick and Paul continued to see each other, playing and singing together and sharing a friendship that lasted throughout, and beyond, their university days. They would meet in London, and then – when Paul's then wife, Diana, got a job as an assistant to John Lennon and Yoko Ono, and she and Paul moved to the Lennon estate near Ascot – Nick would visit them there, too.

Paul and Nick remained friends for the rest of Nick's life.

PAUL WHEELER: When I first heard Nick's songs, I thought 'Oh right, he's been driven more by the sounds and the rhythms of the words than by what they mean'. I don't think enough consideration has been given to the fact that writing a song is different from writing a poem. When you're writing a song, you're particularly concerned with the phonetics of a phrase. Meaning is very often secondary and is driven more by – OK, by the rhymes, but also by the *sound* of the word. You will know, as an actress, that when you're speaking lines from Shakespeare, what's happening in your mouth when you go from 'oh' to 'ah' to 'a' – is part of the expression. I'm certain Nick would choose certain phrases for the expression conveyed in the sibilances and in the vowel sounds rather than the actual meaning of the words. There's almost a sense of it being slightly un-cool to have too much meaning . . .

GABRIELLE DRAKE: When you think of lines like 'Sunday sat in the Saturday sun . . .'

PW: I think he was playing around with the phrase. And sure, you can turn it into a whole analysis of 'What does "Sunday" symbolise?' or whatever. But it's quite possible that it was simply the right sound! There has been much analysing of his songs . . . but analysis can get in the way. Analysts stop listening to the music. Most people who listen to Nick Drake are not analysing the philosophy behind the words. What they know is that it sounds right.

GD: Perhaps it's rather like an artist using the principle of the Golden Section in a picture? The spectator isn't aware that it has been used – only that the picture is visually satisfying.

PW: Yes. And to carry the analogy further, an artist could say: 'I intend to do my own thing, and if the Golden Section is the convention, then I'm never going to use it on principle.' Well, that's fine – that's a personal decision. But even the artistic rebel can't get away from the fact that the principle of the Golden Section *works*. And I think Nick, too, went beyond the breaking of the rules, and then came back to them. There's a certain . . . wryness – not cynicism, because that wasn't Nick – but certainly a wryness in using very simple lines – 'a rose with no thorn', 'you came with the dawn', almost as if Nick was saying, 'I know these lines and rhymes are stock-in-trade romantic symbols, but they actually do work.'

That, I think, is the first impression Nick's songs made on me. And it wasn't particularly the direction I was heading in at the time – or where anyone else we mutually knew was heading. But I could see what he was doing. At that stage his objective didn't seem to be to break the rules. The songs certainly didn't seem to be particularly political, or even adventurous, in terms of thinking, at that stage.

GD: You could say that they weren't trying to be anything more than an integral expression of his inner self.

PW: Yes. All I'm saying is that I think it can be a distraction to build up a whole academic and philosophical structure around his works. It's like looking at the paintwork rather than the painting, which is to miss the whole point. And I don't see much being said about the more sensual effect of his work.

Quite often, in the process of writing a song, you discover you're not just writing one song, but two or even three. It's a common experience for a singer-songwriter. And I'm pretty sure it would have been for Nick too. You find yourself with a phrase that doesn't fit – and you realise 'Oh, this is *two* songs.' So you put the phrase to one side, and you finish song number one. Then you come back to the phrase, or the thought, and put it into another song – and in doing that, you can find that it's actually *three* songs! Also, to be pragmatic about it, if you've just written a song of absolute despair, you'll write a positive song to balance the set. It might sound cynical, but that's the way it happens.

GD: It doesn't sound cynical to me: I think this is the way the creative process works. At its best, I think the creative process is a blend of the practical, the emotional and the spiritual.

PW: Yes! I'm sure that's right. There is the practical element – but on the other hand, it's not just a job. It's more than just being a job. I've certainly had times – I still have them – when I have something in my head, and I must write it down – I have no choice: I can't sleep, I can't eat, until I've written it down. It's not that I've got a deadline – I don't make my money from writing music anyway – but there's no question, it absolutely *has* to be written down – stop everything! Shut up! Get out of here! It's absolutely vital as to whether you make that note a G or a C. And when you're out of it, you think 'What was all that about?' But what can I say? It happens. You feel you'll die if you don't get the song down. Or worse, there's a danger you might die *without* finishing it.

GD: And you think Nick experienced that?

PW: I'm *sure* Nick must have experienced that.

GD: Do you think that part of his depression was because those moments weren't happening any more?

PW: Absolutely. Particularly as, in my experience, if you try to force them, they just don't come. I know some people say 'Oh you're just lazy – it's 1 per cent inspiration and 99 per cent perspiration.' But I'm not one of those. And I don't think Nick was. I can imagine him sitting there, playing around with stuff – because often the way you get into a new song is by playing through your old songs, or somebody else's songs – almost like a mantra. And out of that grows a new song, and you realise 'Oh, we're off.' But I can imagine – certainly in 1973, at the time of those last songs – I can see him playing old things – anything – planning to leap, and thinking, 'This just won't take off – it won't grow.' And that must have been profoundly depressing for him.

GD: Yes, and you are rather borne out by the fact that we've got a list, handwritten by Nick, of the titles of his last four songs, plus 'Tow the Line', which he obviously intended as one side of a new album, and then the list for side two is made up of titles of songs that have never been found . . .

PW: And there's nothing? No practice tape?

GD: No.

PW: People often speculate about Nick's lyrics: wondering where they came from. I'm often asked, 'What did Nick read?' Well, he was studying English Literature at university – what do you *think* he was reading? Shakespeare and Blake and things, of course! And then they say, 'Yes yes, but what was he *really* reading?' Well, that *was* what he was really reading! If you want to get through exams – OK, you have other books on your shelves, but the Blake and the Shakespeare are what you spend all your hours and homework on. Of course Nick's lyrics came out as classically romantic – but that's hardly surprising.

Again, you have to consider his songs within the context of his time . . . Because Nick was 'discovered' some thirty years after his death, and via a method (the Internet) which, during his time, was only vaguely dreamed of by a few people like Pete Russell, there's a tendency to think of him as a maverick – out of his time – unique. He *is* unique – but not because his work was so very different from what was going on around him. I mean, if you'd read a Shakespeare play without knowing anything at all about Elizabethan life or literature, you'd think 'Wow! What *is* this?' But if you had read or seen it *in* Elizabethan times, you'd know and understand the context, and you'd think, 'Oh yes, I saw something like this last week.' The same applies to Nick, I think . . .

GD: Trying to analyse what makes a work genius is pretty well impossible. It certainly doesn't depend on innovation: if you take Shakespeare again, his stories aren't original – he just tells them better than anyone else.

PW: And there's that quote: 'Good artists borrow, great artists steal' . . . Certainly with Nick, there are lines in his songs which anyone who knew him would have realised where they came from. For example, take one of his more upbeat songs, 'One Of These Things First' – which is a lovely song – it's one of the few times when that wry humour of his shows. Well, I remember one night in Cambridge, when we were all round at Mike's place . . . Mike Schutzer Weissmann. We were all part of this Loungers' Club: Nick, myself, Robert Kirby, Mike, and Pete Russell. And Mike had this amazing and eclectic collection of records. He would play Bach by the Leonhardt consort followed by Jaki Byard; William Byrd juxtaposed with Motown. Mike was our mentor. And one night, he put on this song by Smokey Robinson called something like 'The Way You Do the Things You Do', and they're brilliant lyrics: 'The way you knock me off my feet, you could have been a broom . . . the way you smell so sweet you could have been some perfume . . .' And I absolutely remember sitting in Mike's room and all of us laughing, and thinking, 'Wow, what an extraordinary way of using words!' And when I heard 'One Of These Things First' I could hear this . . . echo. There's also the way Nick sings it, in a slightly lighter way – a little bounce that you don't hear that much in his recorded work.

GD: I know exactly what you mean.

PW: There's something cheeky about it. I mean, he could be wry and cheeky. There's a little smile that very often runs through his work – it isn't all grim, of course it isn't – especially not *Bryter Later*.

GD: He had a delightful sense of humour.

PW: Absolutely. There are so many of his lyrics that are *not* to do with doom and gloom. Of course, there are times when I remember him being down – but there are more times when I remember him laughing and being very pleasant company – certainly in the first two years that I knew him. When you saw him, it wasn't, kind of, 'Oh dear, here comes Nick, poor guy.' Rather it was 'Great, here's Nick!'

Something that amused me recently – I was in the company of two young musicians – twenty-five years old or so – there was this young woman singer, who was German from Berlin – she was an extraordinary cabaret artist in the best German tradition, and she did this act which I thought was absolutely brilliant – sort of sardonic – and she had a guitarist – it was just her and the guitarist, and he was French. And I went up to them at the end, and said how I'd really enjoyed them – and, as is so often the case, the conversation came round to Nick, and the guitarist said, 'You know, I don't think I've ever actually heard his music – I've heard of him, but . . . what would you recommend that I listen to?' So I said, 'Well, for me, *Bryter Later*, because I just find it incredibly uplifting – and don't get too worried over all this stuff you hear about him being a miserable git.' And this German girl turned to me, and she said through gritted teeth, 'You don't listen to Nick Drake to cheer you up! You listen to Nick Drake when you're feeling like shit!' (GD *laughs.*) And it amused me – I'm glad it amuses you – because it sort of sums it up.

GD: It does! People don't want Nick to have been amusing and funny, or anything other than depressed and down.

PW: And in a way they're right . . .

GD: But at the same time, it makes him so much more of a complete character to have both sides. I remember so well, Nick had the most infectious laugh.

PW: Yes, absolutely, I remember that.

GD: He and his father shared such a sense of humour too: I remember, just after Daddy died, Mummy and I managed to find a sequence of letters from my father to Nick, and then Nick's replies to him. And we sat there, Mummy and I, with the tears rolling down our cheeks, we were laughing so much: we laughed and laughed and laughed. And we recounted this to someone – a close friend of my mother's, in fact – about having found this correspondence, and even she said, 'Ah, how sad that must have been for you!' But it absolutely wasn't. It was upliftingly funny. Not in a rollicking way – Nick didn't do rollicking humour. Nor did my dad.

PW: No, Nick's humour was very subtle. But he wasn't one for . . . I don't think Nick would ever laugh at other people's expense. He would maybe laugh at people's mannerisms, but that's superficial, it's not really getting at the person. It wasn't a vicious kind of humour.

GD: More wry, as you said before. It comes out in songs like 'Man In A Shed' and, for me, 'Mayfair'. But of course, one can't get away from the fact that the clouds did close in – there's not much to laugh about on *Pink Moon*.

PW: The good news is that *Pink Moon* got written at all. Because when you've gone beyond the depths, you can't write anything at all.

GD: There speaks the voice of experience, it seems to me.

PW: The salient difference between Nick and me was that although Nick tended towards depression, I was a manic depressive, as we called 'bipolar' at that time. So I certainly had depressed times, but I also had manic times. And I wouldn't say that Nick did. I mean, he had very blissful times, but not, kind of, excitable times. I think it amused Nick when I was manic. He enjoyed the ride when it happened.

On the other hand, when it came to my personal down periods, then we would be nearer to each other, and I suppose that, in both of our music and song writing, it was often our down periods that produced the music, rather than the high periods.

GD: It wasn't with Nick, as far as I can intuit. It seems to me that one of the contributing factors to the down periods was the fact that he felt he was no longer able to write songs.

PW: Well . . . it's tricky. I mean, actually *in* the down periods you might not write the songs, but you write them *about* being down. *Pink Moon* is about emerging out of the depression and looking back down into the abyss. I still find it very difficult to listen to *Pink Moon* – especially things like 'Parasite'. It's just too near the bone. Still today, years and years later, it's like looking down into the void.

But there was something I wanted to mention especially about *Pink Moon*: I have this very strong recollection of Nick in the Market Square in Cambridge. John Lennon had just released a song called 'Cold Turkey', and I'd heard it because Diana, my ex-wife, was working for him, and we'd probably heard it before anyone else. I remember meeting Nick, and he was looking particularly shaken and I said, 'Are you all right?' And he said, 'Have you heard John Lennon's "Cold Turkey"?'

And until that moment, I never would have thought of Nick reacting to a song like that – to something that was so stark. It was almost as though he had been punched in the face. And I remember thinking, 'This is a whole aspect of Nick I've not been taking on board.' I had thought he'd be able to float above that kind of naked emotion and despair. And I thought he did too. I mean, it wasn't the kind of thing he normally went out to listen to. So that stuck in my mind. Maybe it was a call to him, too. The dreamy days had gone. We were into an era of agony and pain. And certainly that's how it came out in *Pink Moon*.

BOULEVARD
FLY

Nick Drake had dropped out of a Cambridge literature scholarship to pursue his music at the time this album was recorded. Not unlike Van Morrison's **Astral Weeks,** its texturally comparable contemporary ('69), **Five Leaves Left** is a brilliant experiment in mood convocation. It is not so much questions and answers as it is a meditative talent for expressing observations. Life speaks for itself through Nick Drake. His concern was not with life yesterday or tomorrow, but with life for the moment—epiphany was the mysticism to which Drake's peculiar sensibility addressed itself. Zen-like epigrams on the nature of life and love's insides. He was as good a "jazz" singer as any white man—probably better. His crystalline melodies, so fragile, and his awesome arrangements (on this album, there is only his acoustic guitar, a jazz bass and congas) are labyrinths of emotional intrigue—listening to Drake is like reading Borges. Haunting melodies, frighteningly memorable. John Cale acknowledged this. His **Paris 1919** album, the epitome of the Neo-Romantic Ethos, was thoroughly inspired by his hearing the work of Nick Drake. And his voice—that jazz-inflected delicacy, that ethereal shadow voice: the transmutation of Astrud Gilberto's breathiness and Kevin Ayers' charm. Nick Drake was the John Coltrane of folk singers. French pop singer François Hardy was so enamored of Nick's verse that she summoned him to Paris to write for her. Nick wrote her an entire album which never surfaced. Drake was inspired and always inspired others. To John Martyn, fellow British jazz/folksinger, Drake was simply "the Guv'nor." But, for Drake, it was a meld of the two that constituted his art: his music and his words meshing as metaphors for each other, the creation of atmosphere. **Five Leaves Left** (which refers to the end of a pack of rolling papers) is desensitizing psychic seduction in which Drake's masterful musicianship eases the listener into his spine-tingling world of thinking boy's sensuousness. "Riverman" is hypnotism—an aura cast of oblique mystery. Drake's delicacy, his "sensitivity," was a ruse. He utilized subtlety as a masque to subdue the dangerous wanderings out of bounds of a hyperconscious mind. At his most deceptively feverish, as on "Three Hours" which introduced us for the first time to Drake's recurring image of autumn as symbol for the fall from grace, he was visionary.

Drake eventually became a recluse. He'd gotten a place in Hastings near friends, John & Bev Martyn's farm. It is said that Drake had rarely met with anyone from the record company. By the time of his third album, **Pink Moon,** he would simply send Island completed tapes of the new album and await payment via an anonymous post office box in Hastings. After cutting the most solipsistic **Pink Moon,** by which time his imagery had grown stark, hallucinatory and frequently terrifying, much like Van Gogh after the onset of glaucoma, Drake entered a psychiatric rest home. Upon exit, he vowed never to sing again, moved to Coventry and got a job as a computer programmer. Two years later, Drake was somehow inspired enough to pick up his guitar and begin to write again. The best material in his life according to his producer, Joe Boyd. He had laid down almost enough for a new album, and then perplexingly, Nick Drake died in his sleep on October 25, 1974 at his parents' home near Stratford-Upon-Avon; he was 26. It was from an overdose of an anti-depressant. The coroner's verdict was suicide, but this has been contested: there was no martyred death note, no grand curtain; accidental death had been know to occur with such drugs and after only one pill beyond the prescribed dosage. No, the conclusion amongst those close to him is that it was a hellish accident, a terrible tragedy. The greatest pity is that too few were ever given access to his wisdom.

—Bruce Malamut, January 1976

Side One

1. TIME HAS TOLD ME 3:56
   Paul Harris piano
   Richard Thompson electric
   Danny Thompson bass
2. RIVER MAN 4:28
   Arranged by Harry Robinsc
3. THREE HOURS 6:01
   Danny Thompson bass
   Rocki Dzidzornu congas
4. DAY IS DONE 2:22
   Arranged by Robert Kirby
5. WAY TO BLUE 3:05
   Arranged by Robert Kirby

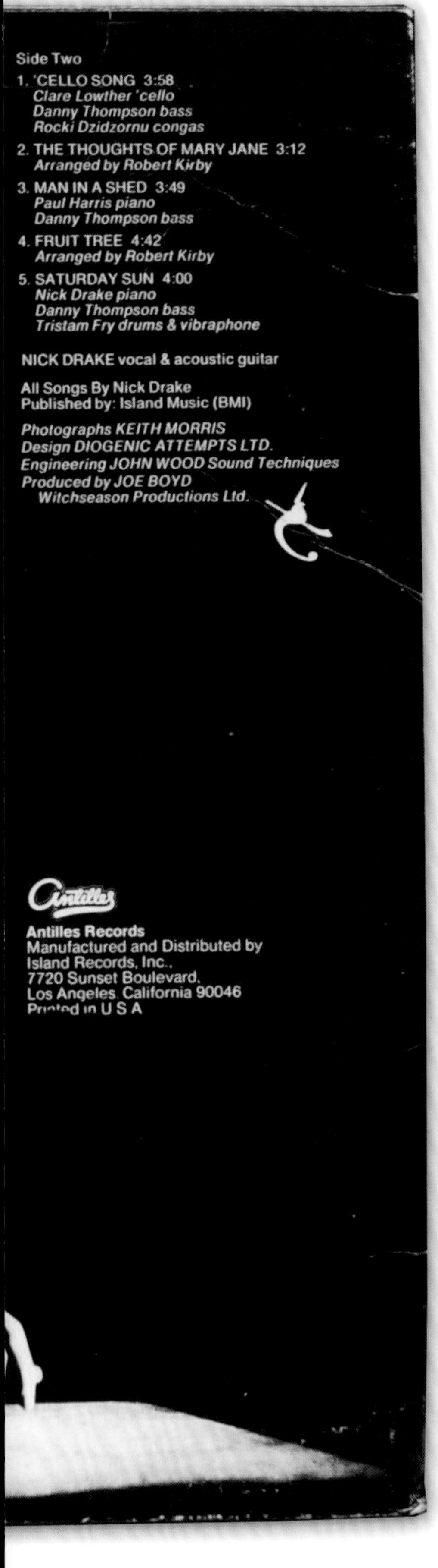

Side Two
1. 'CELLO SONG 3:58
Clare Lowther 'cello
Danny Thompson bass
Rocki Dzidzornu congas
2. THE THOUGHTS OF MARY JANE 3:12
Arranged by Robert Kirby
3. MAN IN A SHED 3:49
Paul Harris piano
Danny Thompson bass
4. FRUIT TREE 4:42
Arranged by Robert Kirby
5. SATURDAY SUN 4:00
Nick Drake piano
Danny Thompson bass
Tristam Fry drums & vibraphone
NICK DRAKE vocal & acoustic guitar
All Songs By Nick Drake
Published by: Island Music (BMI)
Photographs KEITH MORRIS
Design DIOGENIC ATTEMPTS LTD.
Engineering JOHN WOOD Sound Techniques
Produced by JOE BOYD
Witchseason Productions Ltd.
Antilles
Antilles Records
Manufactured and Distributed by
Island Records, Inc.,
7720 Sunset Boulevard,
Los Angeles. California 90046
in U S A

The first official US release of an original Nick Drake album was *Five Leaves Left*, in 1976 on the Island Records off-shoot label, Antilles. Sleeve notes were by Bruce Malamut

Photo taken for the front cover of *Bryter Layter*, by Nigel Waymouth

Bryter Layter

by Pete Paphides

Between leaving Cambridge and moving into his own flat in leafy Belsize Park, Nick briefly lived in Notting Hill Gate, with a girl whose name no one seems to remember, and her pet monkey. Robert Kirby, a frequent visitor to the Notting Hill flat, recalled Nick asking him what he'd like to listen to: 'Put on the monkey,' he'd say: '[The monkey] didn't need any goading, because as soon as the turntable would start spinning, the animal would jump on top of it. Then we would sit and watch the monkey go round and round.'

With no revolving primates to distract him, most of the songs proffered by Nick for inclusion on *Bryter Layter* were written in his spartan ground-floor flat. Beverley Martyn feels that public school and university had left Nick 'feeling institutionalised' and that these first months in London represented the 'beginning of his independence'. If this was indeed Nick's first experience of real independence, he nevertheless still had a support network that many in his position would have envied. Richard and Linda Thompson's flat in Haverstock Hill was a stone's throw away, while John and Beverley Martyn – both very protective towards Nick – were just up the hill in Hampstead. In the first weeks of 1970, the Bishop's Stortford branch of the Sound Techniques/Witchseason family welcomed Nick as he set about rehearsing his latest batch of songs. In the village of Little Hadham, Fairport Convention had taken residence in a disused pub called The Angel. Sandy Denny and Ashley Hutchings having recently left the band, the rest of Fairport – Dave Pegg, Dave Mattacks and Richard Thompson – spent three or four days with Nick.

Pegg recalled:

'You could never tell if he liked stuff or not, but we got an awful lot done in that time. He was just running through arrangements for *Bryter Layter*. He had all the songs and fairly positive ideas about how he wanted them done. His songs were fairly guitar-based, and he was a great guitarist. That was enough, really. On a lot of those things they were so complete with what he did, and it was early days, we were only learning rhythm-section things.'

Nick's satisfaction with these early sessions can be gauged by the presence of Pegg on nine of the ten songs on *Bryter Layter* and of Mattacks on four of them. (Thompson also tackles lead guitar on 'Hazey Jane II' – the only guitar part on the record not undertaken by Nick.) Augmented by a crisp, dewy string arrangement from Kirby, 'Introduction' is just Nick with the Fairport rhythm section – Mattacks deploying the sparest of punctuation by means of padded sticks on the tom-toms. It's also one of the first tracks that Nick had written for the album. Robert Kirby remembered that the pair had been working on it before the end of their final term at Cambridge:

'Nick talked a great deal about concept albums, which were out at the time, and wanting to use instrumental overtures and links between tracks. ["Introduction"] was an overture. It was always an overture. He wrote the guitar part, I recorded it on the trusty Ferrograph, I worked out some parts, played them to him on the piano, he'd say, "No, I don't like that . . . Yes, I do like those . . ."'

John Wood said he had tried to 'get out of Nick why he'd done the instrumentals' but hadn't got 'very far'. It might be that the idea of instrumentals interspersing songs with vocals was also seeded in the early concerts that Nick performed at Cambridge: shows that had seen Nick perform two or three original numbers, interspersed with classical pieces from a string quartet. Whatever Nick's vision was for the overall shape of *Bryter Layter*, it has long been established that it was one Joe Boyd did not wholeheartedly share. 'I was never happy about the three instrumentals,' he admitted. Boyd had heard Nick sing 'Things Behind The Sun' at the Fairport concert a few months earlier and suggested that *Bryter Layter* could certainly use a song of that quality, perhaps in place of an instrumental.

Nick ceded some ground – there are three instrumentals on the record instead of the intended four – but for the main part, this was the producer and engineer's first encounter with the 'obstinate integrity' that his sister Gabrielle has identified as one of her brother's defining character traits. It's also in the context of this 'obstinate integrity' that subsequent criticisms of the record are perhaps best examined. The creeping intimation among some fans and critics that Nick's vision was somehow compromised by a handful of relatively poppy arrangements is at odds with the recollections of some of those who worked on the record. 'Joe Boyd hardly said a word,' recalled drummer Mike Kowalski. 'Nick was very much in control. He did all the communicating. He was very demonstrative. He'd demonstrate just what he wanted in the studio, improvise, and let you groove with it.'

The mutual accommodation between structure and serendipity which seems to characterise so much of *Bryter Layter* is especially prevalent on the album's longest song, 'Poor Boy'. Having worked on an album by Chris McGregor in the morning, Boyd asked the South African jazz pianist to stick around for the 'Poor Boy' session, scheduled to take place in the afternoon. 'As I was hearing those jazz chords and the way the song was taking shape,' recalls Boyd, I just kept "hearing" Chris on the piano . . . Nick brought out his chord chart and they just ran through the chords first, a verse or two, then were recorded on the piano. What you hear on the album is the first and only take . . . the only solo Chris played.' It was a solo that left a clear imprint on the memory of Robert Kirby. Speaking to Patrick Humphries, he remembered 'being down there to watch Chris McGregor put down his stuff for "Poor Boy", Pat Arnold and Doris Troy wailing away, and Nick sitting there at the back, seeming quite happy.'

Nick's original demo of the song described by Joe Boyd as the album's 'symbol' signposts much of what the recorded version subsequently foregrounded, in particular the Greek chorus that gently sends up the song's protagonist: 'Oh poor boy / So sorry for himself / Oh poor boy / So worried for his health.' In the recorded version, of course, that role is assigned to Doris Troy and P.P. Arnold, both renowned solo artists and ubiquitous session singers – their inclusion another reference back to Joe Boyd's Leonard Cohen preoccupation: 'I had always been obsessed with those slightly mocking girls' voices on "So Long, Marianne" . . . and as soon as I heard Nick play, I said, "That's where I'm going to use those voices."'

And when 'Poor Boy' reached home to Far Leys, it would prompt another unlikely chorus. Unbeknownst to Nick, the song inspired his mother to write a riposte of sorts. 'Poor Mum' was a fleeting meditation on the hopes and ambitions that remained unfulfilled while the song's protagonist got on with the business of raising her children as best as she could. (If Molly Drake's response has a subtext, it's surely that angst isn't the sole domain of the young – should they be inclined to dwell on them, older generations have no shortage of accumulated compromises and regrets upon which to hang their anxieties.)

For Robin Frederick, the 'urban gospel' flavour of the backing vocals on 'Poor Boy' is superseded by a stronger influence: the bossa nova sound popularised in this country by Stan Getz and Astrud Gilberto's *Getz/Gilberto* album:

'A comparison with Nick's guitar track on 'Poor Boy' with João Gilberto's bossa nova guitar on 'Corcovado' ('Quiet Nights Of Quiet Stars') reveals a substantial similarity. Composed by Antônio Carlos Jobim and interpreted by

Gilberto on guitar and vocals, tracks like 'Corcovado', 'Desafinado' and 'The Girl from Ipanema' made use of complex chords, close voicings and progressions that circle around a cluster of common tones, all of which are present in 'Poor Boy'. Bossa nova is also characterised by a melody line or vocal with a smooth, detached quality, the result of starting melodic phrases around Beat 2 or Beat 3. You can hear exactly that kind of phrasing in 'Poor Boy' and, in fact, most of Nick's songs.'

Sequenced midway through side one, occupying the same position as 'Poor Boy' on side two, 'At The Chime Of A City Clock' sits on *Bryter Layter* as its distorted mirror image: the double bounce of a thumb on the bass string at the beginning of each bar; the presence once again of jazz players Mike Kowalski and Ray Warleigh; a minor-to-major shift on the chorus; and a lyric which returns to a common theme: its protagonist's inability to cling on to anything useful in the ceaseless tidal flow of city life: 'A city star won't shine too far / On account of the way you are.' Patrick Humphries describes the song as 'a big-city frieze, a fragmentary London portrait of the Soho streets Nick walked when he hitched down from the Marlborough to the Flamingo and the Marquee'. There are some inspired choices of musician on the album, and Warleigh's saxophone solo on 'At The Chime Of A City Clock' is a case in point, releasing a luminous vapour trail into the magic-hour half-light of Robert Kirby's string arrangement. 'Ray pops up on many of my records,' recalls Boyd, 'He's a really, really good player. He never cut a huge swathe through the British jazz scene, but for me, he just plays wonderful solos. It's sort of perfect what he did on "At The Chime Of A City Clock".' The same could be said of Kirby's work here. In 2002, Kirby explained how he sought to accentuate the 'lonely and bleak' aspect of the song by eschewing chords in favour of a reflective counter-melody on the strings.

Mike Kowalski's tendency to 'drive things a bit harder than Dave Mattacks' is, according to Boyd, key to the feel of the songs on which he played. Another case in point is 'One Of These Things First', which also benefits from an intuitive display on the bass from sometime touring Beach Boy Ed Carter (his only contribution to the album). The four-note phrase he plays twice, as Nick sings 'I could have been / One of these things first' nudges the whole thing into the realm of perfection.

As with so much of *Bryter Layter*, the gently efferverscent arrangement of 'One Of These Things First' almost serves to throw us off the scent of a lyric that sees its creator at something of an existential impasse. In the words of Robin Frederick, 'You hardly notice the song is about regret and lost chances.' Indeed, it's worth keeping in mind that outside of the harmonious studio sessions, Robert Kirby now darkly perceived Nick to be 'in crisis'. With every relocation, he seemed to be jettisoning more possessions. There was little more in his Haverstock Hill flat than a mattress dragged from the bed to the warmth of the gas fire. That 'One Of These Things' is sung in the past conditional tense suggests, at least subconsciously, that fatalism had set into Nick's worldview. On paper, the words read like a self-commiserating epilogue to 'Day Is Done', or a question that – from the depths of depression – he would appear to answer on *Pink Moon* with 'Parasite'.

But on *Bryter Layter* – what Paul Wheeler called Nick's 'city album' – questions easily outnumber answers, and no more so than on 'Hazey Jane I' and 'Hazey Jane II'. The prescience so often attributed to 'Fruit Tree' is perhaps even truer of 'Hazey Jane II': 'And what will happen in the morning when the world it gets so crowded that you can't look out the window in the morning?' asks Nick. By the time he reiterates the question a minute later, Kirby's bustling, kinetic arrangement has shaded in the remaining details of the never-ending London rush-hour portended by Nick's lyric. For this, the first song on the album to be recorded, Nick freighted in the Fairport rhythm section that had accompanied him in Little Hadham, but moving forward, Nick explained to Wood that he wanted the drums to feel 'more broken' on some songs, which led to Mike Kowalski supplanting Mattacks on tracks where his style was deemed to suit the songs better. Talking about the use of horns on the song, Kirby recalled him and Nick 'listening to various Stax things, but it came out very English. In the same way that George Martin's stunning brass arrangements for [The Beatles'] "Got To Get You Into My Life" could only be English. There was absolutely no attempt by me to make it sound like an American rock brass section. It sounds more like an English brass band.' Kirby's sentiments are echoed by Joe Boyd: '"Hazey Jane II" was a revelation because Robert came up with a fantastic horn part, which didn't sound like anything else at the time. It had nothing to do with R&B horns or jazz horns.'

The defiant Englishness of 'Hazey Jane II' – positing as it does a sort of red-brick response to Tijuana – must have sounded confusing to contemporary music fans in an era that saw rock bands almost exclusively using horns to import a little rootsy R&B authenticity into their sound. For Robin Frederick, the only thing that doesn't work on the song is what she sees as Nick's attempt to 'emulate the psychedelic lyrics of contemporary rock music', describing such lines as 'Take a little while to grow your brothers hair' as 'awkward and self-conscious'. She nevertheless notes that he 'ends this song with one of his most evocative and revealing lines':

'Nick, English scholar that he was, wrote an *envoy* at the close of 'Hazey Jane II'. Defined as a short verse of praise or explanation at the end of a poem, an envoy is a device that is not often used in pop songs. Because the end of a song is what stays with the listener, this is where the commercial songwriter puts what he wants you to remember.'

If this is true of 'Hazey Jane II', it would seem that what Nick wanted us to remember was: 'If songs were lines in a conversation / The situation would be fine.' If not exactly a cry for help, this parting shot seems to bear out the contrast between the Nick that his friends would encounter outside of the studio and the more assertive focused character communicating his ideas to the team of kindred spirits that surrounded him in Sound Techniques: Joe Boyd, John Wood and Robert Kirby.

'Hazey Jane I' was one of the earliest songs written for *Bryter Layter*. As with the first recordings of 'River Man', the most striking thing about the song in its home demo form is just how much of the string arrangement is rooted in elements of Nick's playing. The high, chiming notes picked out just ahead of each line in the verse form the basis of Kirby's work on the song – a perfect example of what Connor McKnight, writing for *ZigZag* in 1974, referred to as the arranger's 'literally fantastic empathy with Nick'. In fact, the interweaving of Nick's songs with Kirby's arrangements on *Bryter Layter* was down to more than mere empathy. They worked in close proximity together. Only once the basic tracks were recorded would Kirby look at what each song required in terms of an arrangement. As John Wood puts it, 'The tracks were scored up with Nick looking over Robert's shoulder. That was very different to the arrangements for *Five Leaves Left*, which were mostly put together with a view to the songs being performed live in Cambridge.'

Perhaps more than any other song on *Bryter Layter*, 'Hazey Jane I' shows how far Nick had progressed, both as a tunesmith and lyricist, since the compositional baby steps of 'Princess Of The Sand' three years previously. For Robin Frederick, 'the intricate guitar arrangement on this song is among Nick's best work. There are memorable guitar phrases at the top of the song and in the fills between verses. He also displays his ability to keep a rock-solid rhythm going, even when playing a complicated, fingerpicked arrangement like this one.' As with its namesake, it's a song which seems to resonate more with each ensuing decade. Writing for *Mojo* in 1999, Ian MacDonald asked, 'Can it be that the materialist worldview, in which there is no intrinsic meaning, is murdering our souls?' MacDonald seemed to think so, and posited the exponentially expanding popularity of his Cambridge contemporary as evidence. In 'Hazey Jane I' a series of similar questions seem to allude to a similar spiritual void: 'Do you like what you're doing? / Would you do it some more? / Or will you stop once and wonder / What you're doing it for?' Only with the mention of Jane does the song hint at resolution, and even her presence in the story is oddly chimeric: 'Sure that you would do the same for me one day / So try to be true / Even if it's only in your hazey way.'

In marked contrast to earlier home recordings, Nick's attempt to sing 'Hazey Jane I' during one of his final live performances at Les Cousins in 1970 was still imprinted in the meory of another performer decades later, though for all the wrong reasons. Having got to know him through mutual friends John and Beverley Martyn,

Brian Cullman opened for Nick that night. 'His shyness and awkwardness were almost transcendent . . . There was a new song he sang that night that he kept starting and stopping, never completing; he finally just sang the opening lines over and over again: "Do you curse where you come from? / Do you swear in the night?" It was chilling and morbidly fascinating.'

According to John Wood, the (barely audible) sound of Nick playing Hammond organ on the album version of 'Hazey Jane I' suggests that the recording took place relatively late into the *Bryter Layter* sessions. Wood suggests 'it was something he picked up from John Cale', who had arrived at Sound Techniques to help Joe Boyd finish work on Nico's *Desertshore* album and play on the sessions for Mike Heron's *Smiling Men with Bad Reputations*. Time and time again, Nick seemed to revel in the company of larger-than-life characters whose air of certitude would briefly send his own social anxieties into abeyance. John Martyn was one such character, as was Danny Thompson. Bob Squire – underworld-affiliated bespoke supplier of second-hand vehicles for touring Witchseason acts – was another. Writing about Squire's late-night liar-dice sessions, Boyd recalled: 'I never saw Nick more relaxed than in Bob's kitchen and few things seemed to give him more pleasure than winning a round of liar dice.' The impact that Cale had on Nick was immediate. In his memoir, Boyd recalls that:

'Cale put his feet up on the mixing desk, waved his arm imperially at John Wood, and said, "Let's hear what else you guys are working on." We played him a few things, and eventually got to Nick. Cale was amazing. "Who the fuck *is* this guy? I have to meet him, where is he? I mean, where is he *right now*?" I rang Nick and told him that John Cale would be over in half an hour. Nick said, "Oh, uh, OK." I wrote out Nick's address, John grabbed it, and ran down the stairs.

'The next morning I had a call from Cale. "We're going to need a pickup for the viola, an amp, a Fender bass and a bass amp, a celeste and a Hammond B-3 organ. This afternoon." I had scheduled a mix on another project that day but Cale had decided it was time to record "Northern Sky" and "Fly". They arrived together, John with a wild look in his eyes and Nick trailing behind. Despite his domineering manner, Cale was very solicitous towards Nick, who seemed to be guardedly enjoying himself: his only choice was to be relaxed and be carried along.'

Cale, for his part, remembered Nick as 'a very quiet guy': 'It was difficult to figure what was going on in his mind.'

Much later, possibly as a means to avoid having to go over familiar ground, Cale seemed to shut down further enquiries concerning his professional involvement with Nick. 'When that record was made,' he told the *Guardian*, 'Nick was not in the studio. I was the hired hand to come in and overdub and put some colour on the tracks. I finished the tracks, went on my merry way and met Nick much later.' This version of events seems to contradict not only the recollections of Joe Boyd, but Cale's own 2007 account of Nick's animated response when the older musician introduced him to his Martin D-12 12-string guitar: 'He'd never seen one before. He just picked up that guitar and it was just like this orchestral sound coming out. He went nuts, entranced. And all those chords were ringing. It was watching somebody get lost in an instrument. I didn't know about all the other problems, he was just very shy and very withdrawn. And I was trying to work out what the choruses were, but there weren't any.'

Within twenty-four hours of being played what had been recorded of *Bryter Layter*, Cale had masterminded the completion of two more songs. If Kirby felt any resentment at being supplanted by Cale, there's no evidence to suggest as much. Quite the reverse, in fact. His natural equanimity seemed to extend to the events in the studio that day, when he turned up to assist John Wood. Along with 'Hazey Jane I', 'Fly' dated back to the home recordings captured by Brian Wells a year previously in Tanworth-in-Arden. Indeed, the baroque accompaniment provided by Cale (viola and harpsichord) places it closer to *Five Leaves Left* than anything that surrounds it on *Bryter Layter*. Whether by coincidence or homage, the high, ornate harpsichord flourishes are strongly reminiscent of Larry Fallon's work on Van Morrison's 'Cyprus Avenue' – and the line 'come ride in my street-car by the bay' is all too easy to imagine tumbling from the mouth of the bead-wearing, free-spirited Morrison of the late Sixties. 'We were certainly listening to *Astral Weeks* heavily at that time,' confirmed Kirby.

For Robin Frederick, 'a sense of compromise and resignation' is unavoidable in 'Fly':

'From the world of poetry, popular music has borrowed the term "prosody" extending its meaning to refer to the way in which music underscores and intensifies the emotional content of language. "Fly" is a beautiful example of musical prosody. The verses all have essentially the same melody but they are sung in two different octaves, each with its own emotional character. Nick sings the first and third verses near the top of his vocal range. The words are pleading and vulnerable, the thin, high vocal conveys a sense of childlike helplessness and need. The second and fourth verses are sung an octave lower and in these the content is quite different. This low voice belongs to an adult who talks about "recompense" and "if"s, sounding more like an accountant than a lover . . . [If you] try switching the lyrics – sing the high verse lyric in the lower octave and the low verse lyric up an octave – you can feel the difference; the song is not as emotionally effective. Nick knew just what he was doing.'

'Those two tracks, "Fly" and "Northern Sky" sound full,' comments Joe Boyd. 'They sound top productions, but what's on them? On "Fly", there's viola, harpsichord, [Dave Pegg on] bass, Nick's guitar, that's all. On "Northern Sky", it's celeste, piano and organ, bass, drums and Nick's guitar. So the tracks are very self-contained, but they sound immense.'

Perhaps the one moment of transcendent joy in Nick's canon, 'Northern Sky' came to him during a stay at John and Beverley Martyn's new house in Hastings. By the time the couple had released their second album, *The Road To Ruin*, Beverley was pregnant with her second child. Despite the stresses of domestic life, both seemed protective of Nick. 'It was nice to try and make him laugh,' recalled Beverley, 'because he had such a good sense of humour':

'Sometimes he'd mutter something under his breath and you'd want to hear it, because, really, you wanted to hear anything he had to say. I was a bit mumsy with him, I'd say, "Have you eaten?" and he would say no. He would eat whatever you were eating. After I made mince pies for the first time, I remember him saying that they were "scrumptious". He wrote "Northern Sky" around us. We had a tree in the garden across the pavement – hence the line "Or felt sweet breezes in the top of a tree". The top of the tree came to the window where Nick was, and you could see the full moon on the sea at night.'

Paul Wheeler, a close friend of both John Martyn and Nick, echoes Beverley Martyn's recollection. 'It's all to do with the view from John Martyn's house in Hastings,' he says. 'There's the line "I never held emotion in the palm of my hand" – which is all to do with a remark that Nick made to me. He was holding a raspberry in the palm of his hand when he was stoned, and someone commented that it was actually a bunch of grapes. Nick laughed that this was unquestionably "true".'

For Robin Frederick, 'Northern Sky' is 'nothing more or less than a demonstration of the power of simplicity and repetition in the hands of a master songwriter, [consisting] of little more than two chords and two melodic phrases with a turnaround at the end.' 'Northern Sky' is also the nearest Nick ever got to writing a classic love song. Robert Kirby confessed to wondering what sort of person could have divined such feelings of unalloyed ecstasy in Nick. 'Is the "you" a girl on the scene or a generic Keatsian/Wordsworthian concept? It's hard to imagine a girl who wouldn't fall for him if he fell for them. At Cambridge, all our girlfriends fancied him like mad. It was infuriating!'

On a song whose protagonist fleetingly allows himself to float free of his existential moorings, the relatively speedy execution compounds a sense that we are privy to the crazy magic invoked by Nick in the opening line of 'Northern Sky'. Running through the centre of the song is an inspired musical conversation between Nick and John Cale on piano, each one a co-ordinate in a process of mutual discovery that can so often lose its sparkle with every subsequent attempt to get it right. Unusually for a Nick Drake song, there lurks a sense on 'Northern Sky' that everything might be all right: the dizzying ascent into the middle section which the protagonist dares to ask for a return on his pledge of devotion, and finally, with the reiteration of the opening first verse, something almost unprecedented for him: a positive sense of resolution.

Bookending side two of *Bryter Layter* are two of the album's three instrumentals. If nothing else, the title track and the closing-credits reverie of 'Sunday' bear testament to Nick's dogged faith in his original vision for the record. For Robin Frederick, the preponderance of instrumentals was quite simply a sign of the times:

'There was a lot of experimentation with the album format in the late 1960s. Both solo artists and bands recorded instrumental preludes, interludes, bridges between songs, interpolations, introductions with dialogue and sound effects – you name it, somebody did it. From Steve Miller's five minute "Song For Our Ancestors" [a favourite of Nick's] to the one-minute "Prelude" on *Chicago II*, to Brian Wilson's orchestral forays on *Pet Sounds*, instrumental tracks added a new dimension to the traditional album: they suggested there was more to it than just a haphazard string of songs.'

For all that, Frederick's view – that 'Nick was not playing to his strengths' – is one shared even by many of Nick's staunchest fans.

In the absence of a vocal, performances from two different flautists take centre stage on 'Bryter Layter' and 'Sunday'. Lyn Dobson (Georgie Fame, Manfred Mann, Soft Machine) steps forward to play on the former, while the latter sees Ray Warleigh switch from the alto sax he plays elsewhere on the album. Suffused with a marginally more melancholy, contemplative air, 'Sunday' is arguably the more successful track. Robert Kirby said that the song was a tribute of sorts to their time together in Cambridge: 'This is a driving song: you're meant to listen to it while you're driving. I can remember when Nick and I had this great thing where we used to drive around on Sunday.' In particular, Kirby drew attention to 'one section towards the end of the instrumental, a low string chord which is meant to be when you drive on a motorway on a nice day with the window open, and a lorry passes you.' In 1974, Kraftwerk would record their own driving anthem 'Autobahn', using a Heath-Robinsonesque agglomeration of synths, drum machines and Moog to simulate the sound of passing vehicles on a German motorway. Both artists had set out to evoke the sensation of driving through their native country through music. With 'Sunday', Nick Drake had beaten Kraftwerk to it by four years.

On the back cover-art of *Bryter Layter*, we see Nick gazing on at a speeding car under the Westway streetlights. It's an apt visual shorthand for what you hear when you place the record on the turntable. This is London seen through the eyes of a protagonist who has yet to find his groove in the bustle of the big city. 'Northern Sky' notwithstanding, resolution evades every song on *Bryter Layter*. It sounds like an album nervously anticipating its own reception. Together with Robert Kirby's string and brass arrangements, the title of the record (bastardised from the BBC shipping forecast) bears out a sense that, on balance, it was all probably going to work out fine. It was a view seemingly shared by everyone who worked with Nick on the record. 'I loved it. It was just great fun to record,' says Wood. 'You very seldom make a record and don't say, "It's a shame we didn't do this or that," [but] *Bryter Layter* to me is that record – I can't find anything I would have wanted to change . . . It was so obvious to me and Joe [Boyd] that this was special.'

Feeling that they had an album which could finally break Nick to a wider audience, Joe Boyd and John Wood took special care over the process of mixing it. Wood:

'First of all, we mixed *Bryter Layter* at Sound Techniques. Then we took the tapes to America and mixed it again at Vanguard. I didn't like either. Then we came back and I changed the speakers at Sound Techniques, and we mixed it again, and that's the one we used. Nick wasn't involved in the Vanguard ones because he wasn't in New York. He certainly came to the other mixes and made comments but I don't ever recall him being particularly vigorous in his opinions about what we did. Possibly he liked what we did – so he didn't have to be vigorous, I don't remember. I can certainly remember mixes we did with artists who *were* vigorous in their opinions, and he wasn't one of them.'

Quoted in Patrick Humphries' biography, Robert Kirby summed up the *Bryter Layter* sessions as 'happy times. Nick was quite high on it. The first [album] had got his name known. I think he felt this was going to be the one.' Also in Humphries' book, Paul Wheeler recalled having dinner with Nick just after the release of the album. 'He said he assumed that it would be much more successful than it was. And I do remember being surprised, because I didn't think he was in it for that.' Given their shared subcultural sensibilities, it's perhaps not surprising that Nick may have given Wheeler the impression that commercial success wasn't high on his list of priorities.

Three months after the release of the record, only another attempt from Island around this time to re-promote the record yielded any reviews. An equivocal *Melody Maker* review blithely dismissed it as 'late night coffee 'n' chat music'. Reviewing for *Record Mirror*, Lon Goddard was much more positive. 'Definitely one of the prettiest (and that counts!) and most impressive albums I've heard . . . Happy, sad, very moving.' Writing for *Sounds*, Jerry Gilbert placed much of the credit for the album at the feet of the musicians that surrounded Nick, going as far as to name them all.

It was Gilbert also who would have the distinction of being the only music journalist to interview Nick. At the time of the encounter, no reviews of *Bryter Layter* had appeared in the music press, and with this in mind the downcast tone of the interview is unsurprising. (Gilbert: 'You could have cut the atmosphere with a knife.') Nick's few utterances hinted that having seen *Bryter Layter* fail to shake the world off its axis, there was little sense in continuing the experiment by following it with a similar sort of album. 'For the next one, I had the idea of just doing something with John Wood,' he told Gilbert. In the intervening years – prompted in part by the fact that sales of *Bryter Layter* have lagged behind the records either side of it – Boyd himself has come to wonder whether he, John Wood and Robert Kirby 'were all so enamoured of Nick's music that [on *Bryter Layter*] we moved happily into the vacuum created by his diffidence.'

Possibly so; but then, as the Richard Hewson episode and Nick's refusal to complete 'Things Behind The Sun' had shown, Nick was perfectly capable of digging his heels in when he wanted to. It makes no more sense to blame someone for a triumphant outcome than it does to credit someone for a failure. Nick's contemporary Vashti Bunyan saw her Joe Boyd-produced album *Just Another Diamond Day* emerge in the same year as *Bryter Layter* to less than 1,000 sales. For decades, she had all but disowned the record, sometimes citing her dissatisfaction with Boyd's production and some of Robert Kirby's arrangements. Decades later, when the reissue of the album brought her universal acclaim, Bunyan returned to it anew and heard it in the same way that a new generation of fans were hearing it. There is no reason to believe that Nick's feelings about *Bryter Layter* were anything like those that Vashti initially envisaged for her record. Nevertheless, the underlying point remains the same. For almost any artist, creation and reaction are inextricably linked. Had *Bryter Layter* been an immediate hit, Nick may have thought twice before jettisoning all ornamentation for his next album.

Hazey Jane II

And what will happen in the morning
when the world it gets so crowded
that you can't look out the window in the morning?

And what will happen in the evening
in the forest with the weasel with the teeth that bite so sharp
when you're not looking in the evening?

And all the friends that you once knew
are left behind they kept you safe and so secure
amongst the books and all the records of your lifetime?

What will happen
In the morning
When the world it gets
so crowded that you can't
look out the window in the morning?

Hey, take a little while to grow your brother's hair
And now, take a little while to make your sister fair
And now that the family is part of a chain
Take off your eyeshade start over again

And now take a little while to find your way in here
And now take a little while to make your story clear
And now that you're lifting
Your feet from the ground
Weigh up your anchor
And never look round

Let's sing a song
For Hazey Jane
She's back again in my mind
If songs were lines in a conversation
The situation would be fine

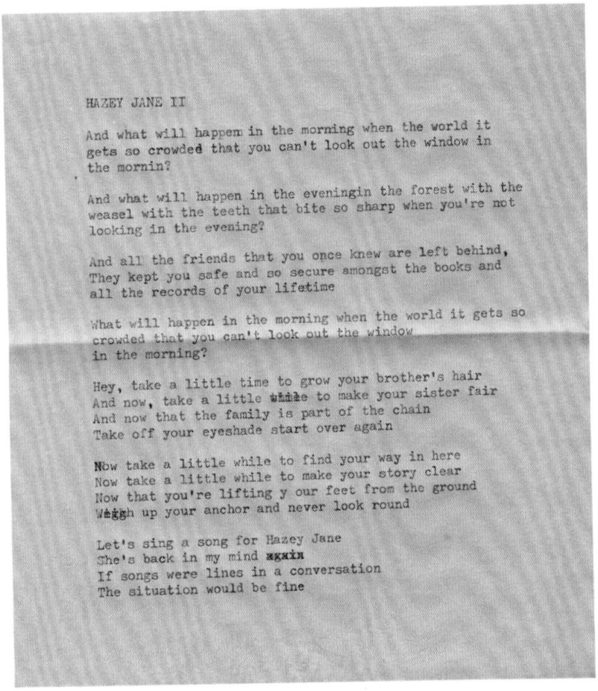

HAZEY JANE II

And what will happen in the morning when the world it
gets so crowded that you can't look out the window in
the mornin?

And what will happen in the eveningin the forest with the
weasel with the teeth that bite so sharp when you're not
looking in the evening?

And all the friends that you once knew are left behind,
They kept you safe and so secure amongst the books and
all the records of your lifetime

What will happen in the morning when the world it gets so
crowded that you can't look out the window
in the morning?

Hey, take a little time to grow your brother's hair
And now, take a little while to make your sister fair
And now that the family is part of the chain
Take off your eyeshade start over again

Now take a little while to find your way in here
Now take a little while to make your story clear
Now that you're lifting y our feet from the ground
Weigh up your anchor and never look round

Let's sing a song for Hazey Jane
She's back in my mind ~~again~~
If songs were lines in a conversation
The situation would be fine

Chris Healey:
'Introduction'
As with 'Man In A Shed', and indeed several of his songs, a complicated-sounding piece turns out, once you know the right tuning, to be simple fretting combined with some clever picking. Here flourishes of subtly shifting harmony turn out to be almost entirely playable with one finger of the left hand.

'Hazey Jane II'
Four of Nick's songs have strummed chords – 'Northern Sky', 'Pink Moon', 'Place To Be' and this one. But even shorn of any arrangement, none sound like typical singer-songwriter material. All are in tunings a long way from standard, so we are not hearing a string of chord voicings our ear is already used to. And here, the long wait for the vocal at the start of each line, and the playful way the tumbling streams of words extend the lines, mark it as something different right from the start.

We're also kept off-balance by the song's changes of key, with sections in F suddenly transforming themselves into C like a piece of close-up magic. And the structure is really unusual. The intro and verse are followed by what feel more like two bridges than anything resembling a chorus; there's no second verse; the end is a completely new section that seems to comment on what's gone before both musically and lyrically, finally concluding that even the song itself can't really help him. Somehow, Nick's easy phrasing and amused tone combine with the gentle arrangement to make all this oddness sound completely natural.

At The Chime Of A City Clock

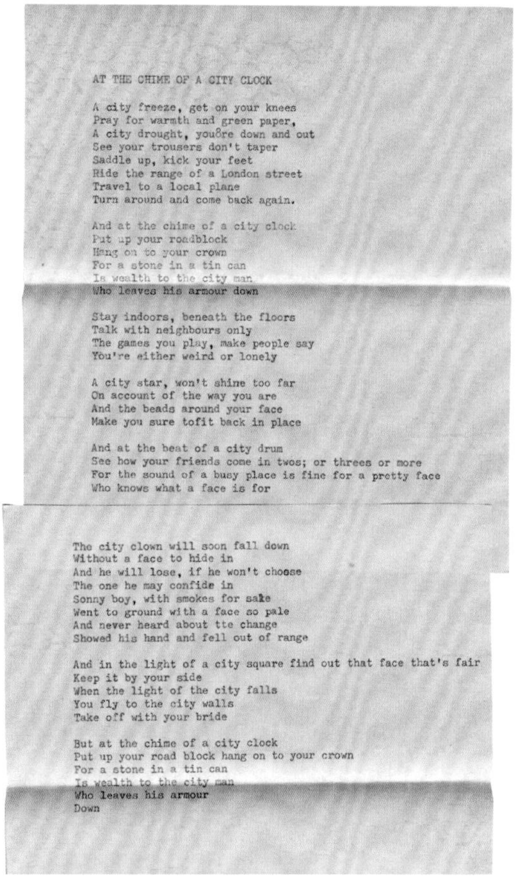

AT THE CHIME OF A CITY CLOCK

A city freeze, get on your knees
Pray for warmth and green paper,
A city drought, you8re down and out
See your trousers don't taper
Saddle up, kick your feet
Ride the range of a London street
Travel to a local plane
Turn around and come back again.

And at the chime of a city clock
Put up your roadblock
Hang on to your crown
For a stone in a tin can
Is wealth to the city man
Who leaves his armour down

Stay indoors, beneath the floors
Talk with neighbours only
The games you play, make people say
You're either weird or lonely

A city star, won't shine too far
On account of the way you are
And the beads around your face
Make you sure tofit back in place

And at the beat of a city drum
See how your friends come in twos; or threes or more
For the sound of a busy place is fine for a pretty face
Who knows what a face is for

The city clown will soon fall down
Without a face to hide in
And he will lose, if he won't choose
The one he may confide in
Sonny boy, with smokes for sake
Went to ground with a face so pale
And never heard about tte change
Showed his hand and fell out of range

And in the light of a city square find out that face that's fair
Keep it by your side
When the light of the city falls
You fly to the city walls
Take off with your bride

But at the chime of a city clock
Put up your road block hang on to your crown
For a stone in a tin can
Is wealth to the city man
Who leaves his armour
Down

A city freeze get on your knees
Pray for warmth and green paper
A city drought you're down and out
See your trousers don't taper
Saddle up, kick your feet
Ride the range of a London street
Travel to a local plane
Turn around and come back again

And at the chime of a city clock
Put up your road block
Hang on to your crown
For a stone in a tin can
Is wealth to the city man
Who leaves his armour down

Stay indoors beneath the floors
Talk with neighbours only
The games you play make people say
You're either weird or lonely
A city star won't shine too far
On account of the way you are
And the beads around your face
Make you sure to fit back in place

And at the beat of a city drum
See how your friends come in twos,
Or threes or more
For the sound of a busy place
Is fine for a pretty face
Who knows what a face is for

The city clown will soon fall down
Without a face to hide in
And he will lose if he won't choose
The one he may confide in
Sonny boy with smokes for sale
Went to ground with a face so pale
And never heard about the change
Showed his hand and fell out of ran

In the light of a city square
Find out that face that's fair
Keep it by your side
When the light of the city falls
You fly to the city walls
Take off with your bride

But at the chime of a city clock
Put up your road block
Hang on to your crown
For a stone in a tin can
Is wealth to the city man
Who leaves his armour
Down

Here both verse and chorus are descending lines typical of Nick, the verses over minor chords as he reflects on his own isolation in the city, while the choruses introduce a sudden shift to a major as he looks at the life of the wealthy and protected city dweller. The 'Saddle up' section goes to new places harmonically as the lyrics hint at someone's attempt to escape, but ends with a flip back to the original key, as they 'Turn around and come back again' (in a similar vein to the 'What I really don't want to be' sequence in 'Time Has Told Me'). The fast-repeated bass notes in the guitar part are unusual, but Nick liked the effect enough to use it in 'One Of These Things First' and 'Things Behind The Sun' too. Here it sounds like he might be using both sides of his thumbnail to do it.

One Of These Things First

I could have been a sailor
Could have been a cook
A real live lover
Could have been a book
I could have been a signpost
Could have been a clock
As simple as a kettle
Steady as a rock

I could be
Here and now
I would be, I should be
But how?

I could have been
One of these things first
I could have been
One of these things first

I could have been your pillar
Could have been your door
I could have stayed beside you
Could have stayed for more
I could have been your statue
Could have been your friend
A whole long lifetime
Could have been the end

I could be
Yours so true
I would be
I should be
Through and through

I could have been
One of these things first
I could have been
One of these things first

I could have been a whistle
Could have been a flute
A real live giver
Could have been a boot
I could have been a signpost
Could have been a clock
As simple as a kettle
Steady as a rock

I could be
Even here
I would be, I should be
So near
I could have been
One of these things first
I could have been

One of these things first

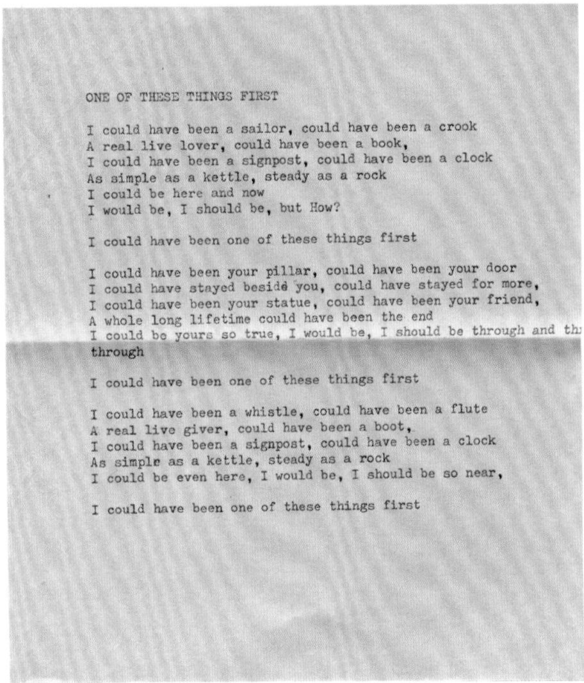

ONE OF THESE THINGS FIRST

I could have been a sailor, could have been a crook
A real live lover, could have been a book,
I could have been a signpost, could have been a clock
As simple as a kettle, steady as a rock
I could be here and now
I would be, I should be, but How?

I could have been one of these things first

I could have been your pillar, could have been your door
I could have stayed besidè you, could have stayed for more,
I could have been your statue, could have been your friend,
A whole long lifetime could have been the end
I could be yours so true, I would be, I should be through and th
through

I could have been one of these things first

I could have been a whistle, could have been a flute
A real live giver, could have been a boot,
I could have been a signpost, could have been a clock
As simplr as a kettle, steady as a rock
I could be even here, I would be, I should be so near,

I could have been one of these things first

One of the few conventional alternate tunings (a major chord) on the albums. Rarely straying from the bottom four strings, the doubled bass notes and busy picking combine with Paul Harris's equally busy piano to lend it a restless feel, suggesting the countless other possibilities (or incarnations perhaps) that the lyrics hint at.

Nick doesn't often let us see what he's capable of on guitar, but in the instrumental section towards the end he treats us to a few right-hand fireworks on the top strings. As always, though, everything's in the service of the song; the tricky stuff fits so well into the existing part that you still feel like you're listening to a balanced arrangement, not to a guitarist showing off.

Hazey Jane I

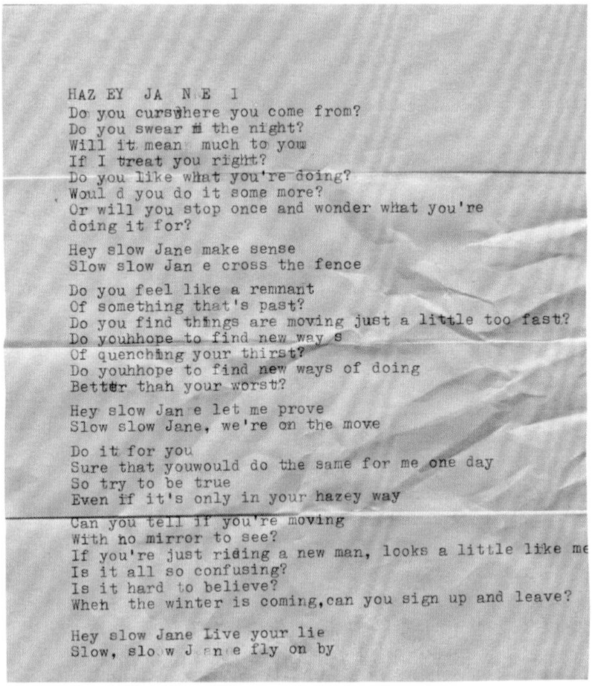

HAZ EY JA N E I
Do you curswhere you come from?
Do you swear m the night?
Will it mean much to you
If I treat you right?
Do you like what you're doing?
Woul d you do it some more?
Or will you stop once and wonder what you're
doing it for?

Hey slow Jane make sense
Slow slow Jan e cross the fence

Do you feel like a remnant
Of something that's past?
Do you find things are moving just a little too fast?
Do youhhope to find new way s
Of quenching your thirst?
Do youhhope to find new ways of doing
Better than your worst?

Hey slow Jan e let me prove
Slow slow Jane, we're on the move

Do it for you
Sure that youwould do the same for me one day
So try to be true
Even if it's only in your hazey way
Can you tell if you're moving
With no mirror to see?
If you're just riding a new man, looks a little like me
Is it all so confusing?
Is it hard to believe?
When the winter is coming,can you sign up and leave?

Hey slow Jane Live your lie
Slow, slo w J an e fly on by

Do you curse where you come from?
Do you swear in the night?
Will it mean much to you
If I treat you right?
Do you like what you're doing?
Would you do it some more?
Or will you stop once and wonder
What you're doing it for?
Hey slow Jane, make sense
Slow, slow Jane, cross the fence

Do you feel like a remnant
Of something that's past?
Do you find things are moving
Just a little too fast?
Do you hope to find new ways
Of quenching your thirst?
Do you hope to find new ways of doing
Better than your worst?
Hey slow Jane, let me prove
Slow, slow Jane, we're on the move

I do it for you
Sure that you would do the same for me one day
So try to be true
Even if it's only in your hazey way

Can you tell if you're moving
With no mirror to see?
If you are just riding a new man
Looks a little like me?
Is it all so confusing?
Is it hard to believe?
When the winter is coming can you
Sign up and leave?
Hey slow Jane, clear your eye
Slow, slow Jane, fly on by

The guitar intro to 'Hazey Jane I' is unusually long and loosely structured for Nick, and the picking patterns in the verses seem a bit less orderly than normal. You could be forgiven for thinking that he was just riffing around. But go back to an earlier demo version of this and every note is already there, exactly as they're played on *Bryter Layter*. Paul Wheeler has remarked that when Nick finally settled on a fingerpicking part, he generally played it exactly the same way every time. They are 'composed' – each note has a precise role.

Although the two 'Hazey Jane' songs on *Bryter Layter* have very different arrangements, they're very close musically. For example, the verses in both are made up of 222000 and 000200 chords in CGCFCE, and when the horn intro of 'Hazey Jane II' returns in the middle of that song, the chord sequence is identical to the 'So try to be true' section here – you can sing that over the top of it. They might well have developed from the same kernel.

Fly

Please give me a second grace
Please give me a second face
I've fallen far down the first time around
Now I just sit on the ground in your way

> *Now if it's time for recompense for what's done*
> *Come, come sit down on the fence in the sun*
> *And the clouds will roll by*
> *And we'll never deny*
> *It's really too hard*
> *For to fly*

Please tell me your second name
Please play me your second game
I've fallen so far for the people you are
I just need your star for a day

> *So come, come ride in my street-car by the bay*
> *For now I must know how fine you are in your way*
> *And the sea she will sigh*
> *But she won't need to cry*
> *For it's really too hard*
> *For to fly*

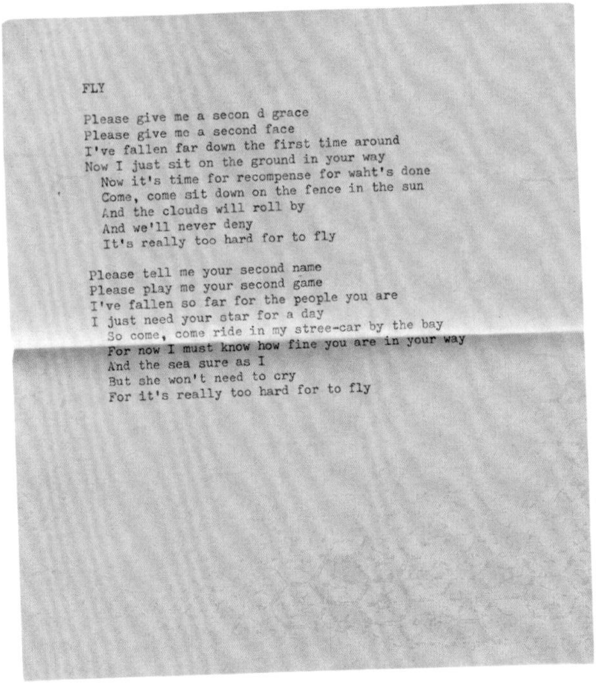

FLY

Please give me a secon d grace
Please give me a second face
I've fallen far down the first time around
Now I just sit on the ground in your way
Now it's time for recompense for waht's done
Come, come sit down on the fence in the sun
And the clouds will roll by
And we'll never deny
It's really too hard for to fly

Please tell me your second name
Please play me your second game
I've fallen so far for the people you are
I just need your star for a day
So come, come ride in my stree-car by the bay
For now I must know how fine you are in your way
And the sea sure as I
But she won't need to cry
For it's really too hard for to fly

'Bryter Layter'
Critics have argued that parts of this and 'Sunday' sound a bit like TV theme tunes, which is perhaps mainly down to the flute contributions. But while the guitar part might not be one of Nick's most memorable, it still works pretty well on its own, with enough unexpected constructions in the double dropped D tuning (such as the dissonant A/Bb's in the descending chords in the last section) to sustain interest.

'Fly'
If you had to pick one guitar part that best illustrated Nick's style, it might be this. (Although you might have to listen to the version on the *Time Of No Reply* album, as the guitar part is mixed rather low on *Bryter Layter*.) A descending pattern; his favourite BEBEBE tuning; an intricate sound which turns out to be simple in the left hand; and some neat regular work with the right. Newcomers to playing his songs are amazed to find they can coax such a gorgeous sound from under their fingers.

The falling pattern is actually a little unusual. Unlike 'Day Is Done', where the bass note in the guitar part descends, or 'Poor Boy', where the harmony descends over a constant bass note, here there is no bass note at all until the very end of the pattern. The guitar line begins high and rootless, before circling down. After it's ended, Nick sings about having 'fallen far down', and declares 'Now I just sit on the ground': the guitar has made the same journey.

Poor Boy

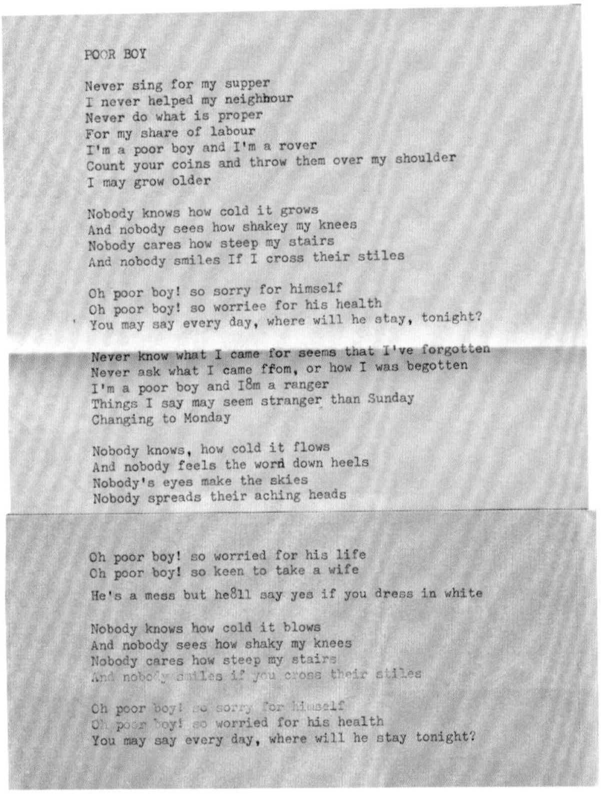

POOR BOY

Never sing for my supper
I never helped my neighbhour
Never do what is proper
For my share of labour
I'm a poor boy and I'm a rover
Count your coins and throw them over my shoulder
I may grow older

Nobody knows how cold it grows
And nobody sees how shakey my knees
Nobody cares how steep my stairs
And nobody smiles If I cross their stiles

Oh poor boy! so sorry for himself
Oh poor boy! so worriee for his health
You may say every day, where will he stay, tonight?

Never know what I came for seems that I've forgotten
Never ask what I came ffom, or how I was begotten
I'm a poor boy and I8m a ranger
Things I say may seem stranger than Sunday
Changing to Monday

Nobody knows, how cold it flows
And nobody feels the worn down heels
Nobody's eyes make the skies
Nobody spreads their aching heads

Oh poor boy! so worried for his life
Oh poor boy! so keen to take a wife

He's a mess but he8ll say yes if you dress in white

Nobody knows how cold it blows
And nobody sees how shaky my knees
Nobody cares how steep my stairs
And nobody smiles if you cross their stiles

Oh poor boy! so sorry for himself
Oh poor boy! so worried for his health
You may say every day, where will he stay tonight?

Never sing for my supper
I never helped my neighbour
Never do what is proper
For my fair share of labour

I'm a poor boy
And I'm a rover
Count your coins and
Throw them over my shoulder
I may grow older

Nobody knows
How cold it grows
And nobody sees
How shaky my knees
Nobody cares
How steep my stairs
And nobody smiles
If I cross their stiles

Oh poor boy
So sorry for himself
Oh poor boy
So worried for his health

You may say every day
Where will he stay tonight?

Never know what I came for
Seems that I've forgotten
Never ask what I came from
Or how I was begotten

I'm a poor boy
And I'm a ranger
Things I say
May seem stranger than Sunday
Changing to Monday

Nobody knows
How cold it flows
And nobody feels
The worn down heels
Nobody's eyes
Make the skies
Nobody spreads
Their aching heads

Oh poor boy
So worried for his life
Oh poor boy
So keen to take a wife

He's a mess but he'll say yes
If you just dress in white

Nobody knows
How cold it blows
And nobody sees
How shaky my knees
Nobody cares
How steep my stairs
And nobody smiles
If you cross their stiles

Oh poor boy
So sorry for himself
Oh poor boy
So worried for his health

You may say every day
Where will he stay tonight?

Oh poor boy
So worried for his life
Oh poor boy
So keen to take a wife

Oh poor boy
So sorry for himself
Oh poor boy
So worried for his health

Oh poor boy
So worried for his life

There are some complex sounding jazzy chords here, but the left-hand shapes turn out to be strangely familiar. The unusual 'for my supper' chord is just the simple minor 7 shape of 'Never sing' at the beginning, but with the barre finger a fret further back. Whether this came out of experiment or accident we can't say, but it could easily happen when you have large hands and you're playing high up the neck. However, Nick then extends the idea by moving the barre finger even further back for the 'I'm a poor boy' section, creating some odd 13th chords for himself and aching knuckles for the rest of us.

The 'Nobody knows' section is yet another descending pattern (it's actually a standard blues guitar lick re-imagined as a slower harmonic development). It doesn't do anything as crude as plunge you down into the depths, but seems to leave you back where you began, like walking down an Escher staircase.

Northern Sky

I never felt magic crazy as this
I never saw moons knew the meaning of the sea
I never held emotion in the palm of my hand
Or felt sweet breezes in the top of a tree
But now you're here brighten my northern sky

I've been a long time that I'm waiting
Been a long time that I'm blown
I've been a long time that I've wandered
Through the people I have known
Oh, if you would and you could
Straighten my new mind's eye

Would you love me for my money?
Would you love me for my head?
Would you love me through the winter?
Would you love me 'til I'm dead?
Oh, if you would and you could
Come blow your horn on high

I never felt magic crazy as this
I never saw moons knew the meaning of the sea
I never held emotion in the palm of my hand
Or felt sweet breezes in the top of a tree
But now you're here brighten my northern sky

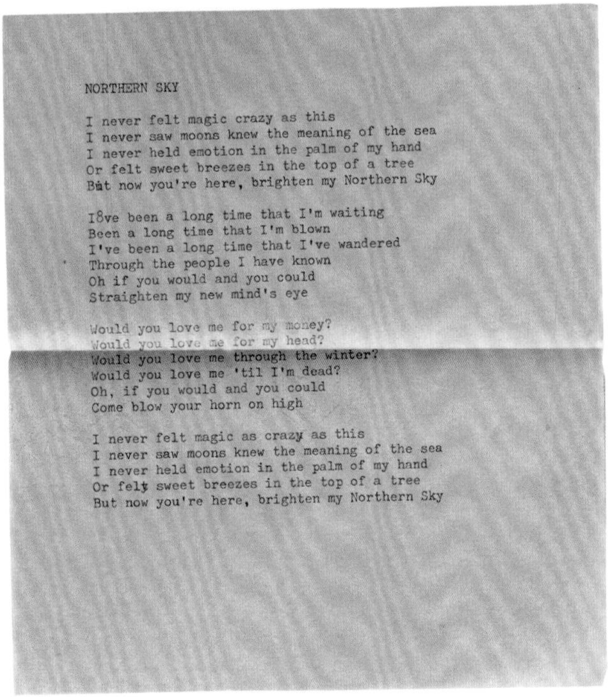
NORTHERN SKY

I never felt magic crazy as this
I never saw moons knew the meaning of the sea
I never held emotion in the palm of my hand
Or felt sweet breezes in the top of a tree
But now you're here, brighten my Northern Sky

I8ve been a long time that I'm waiting
Been a long time that I'm blown
I've been a long time that I've wandered
Through the people I have known
Oh if you would and you could
Straighten my new mind's eye

Would you love me for my money?
Would you love me for my head?
Would you love me through the winter?
Would you love me 'til I'm dead?
Oh, if you would and you could
Come blow your horn on high

I never felt magic as crazy as this
I never saw moons knew the meaning of the sea
I never held emotion in the palm of my hand
Or felt sweet breezes in the top of a tree
But now you're here, brighten my Northern Sky

'Northern Sky'

The pair of chords at the beginning of 'Northern Sky' make for an instantly recognisable opening statement, perhaps because the voicings he gets from BEBEBE are so distinctive and subtle. The first chord is a simple major 'home chord', but the note that tells you it's a major rather than minor (the *mi* in 'do-re-mi', or the 'happy' note, as it were) is unusually isolated and unsupported right at the top of the chord, leaving a fragile feel to this happiness. The second (minor) chord is all questions, with typical clusters of 7th/9th doubt. Five seconds into the song, two chords have expertly set the tone.

How they then resolve into the pure, straightforward, root-and-fifth-only of 'But now you're here', all previous complications and doubts swept aside, is even better – for me, one of Nick's finest moments. And as beautiful and atmospheric as John Cale's organ part is, it seems a shame to me that it rather buries all this compositional genius.

'Sunday'

'Work In Progress 7' from the home recordings is a piano piece full of arpeggios that is clearly the first version of what became 'Sunday'. It's interesting that when Nick transferred it onto guitar he chose to put it in BEBEBE: it would have been much easier to transfer a known chord sequence from piano into standard tuning on guitar. He must have been either extremely comfortable in BEBEBE or willing to experiment.

Robert Kirby's score for 'Sunday'

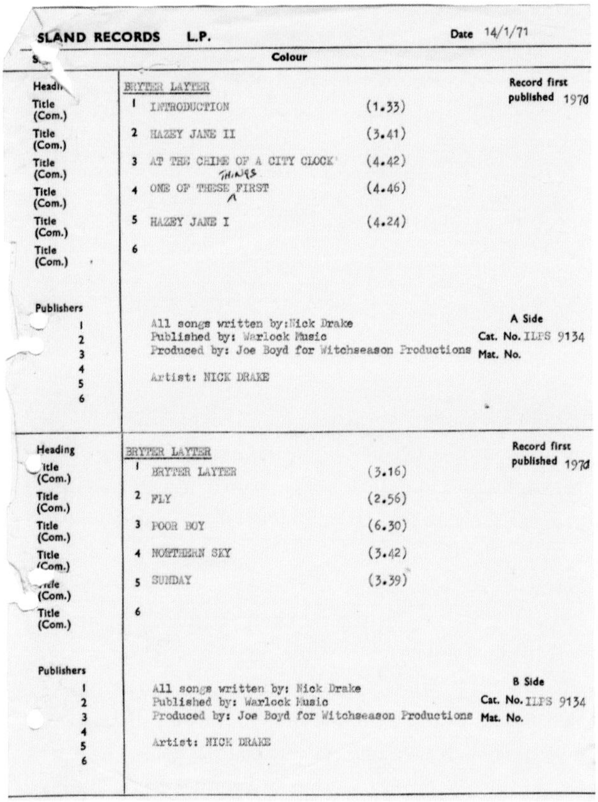

SLAND RECORDS L.P. — Date 14/1/71

Colour

BRYTER LAYTER — Record first published 1970

Title (Com.)	1	INTRODUCTION	(1.33)
Title (Com.)	2	HAZEY JANE II	(3.41)
Title (Com.)	3	AT THE CHIME OF A CITY CLOCK	(4.42)
Title (Com.)	4	ONE OF THESE THINGS FIRST	(4.46)
Title (Com.)	5	HAZEY JANE I	(4.24)
Title (Com.)	6		

Publishers 1 2 3 4 5 6

All songs written by: Nick Drake
Published by: Warlock Music
Produced by: Joe Boyd for Witchseason Productions

Artist: NICK DRAKE

A Side
Cat. No. ILPS 9134
Mat. No.

Heading

BRYTER LAYTER — Record first published 1970

Title (Com.)	1	BRYTER LAYTER	(3.16)
Title (Com.)	2	FLY	(2.56)
Title (Com.)	3	POOR BOY	(6.30)
Title (Com.)	4	NORTHERN SKY	(3.42)
Title (Com.)	5	SUNDAY	(3.39)
Title (Com.)	6		

Publishers 1 2 3 4 5 6

All songs written by: Nick Drake
Published by: Warlock Music
Produced by: Joe Boyd for Witchseason Productions

Artist: NICK DRAKE

B Side
Cat. No. ILPS 9134
Mat. No.

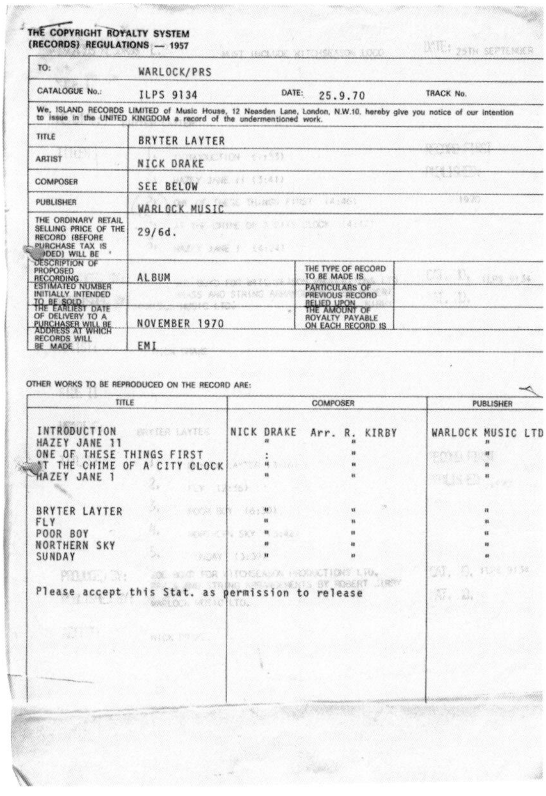

THE COPYRIGHT ROYALTY SYSTEM
(RECORDS) REGULATIONS — 1957

TO: WARLOCK/PRS

CATALOGUE No.: ILPS 9134 DATE: 25.9.70 TRACK No.

We, ISLAND RECORDS LIMITED of Music House, 12 Neasden Lane, London, N.W.10. hereby give you notice of our intention to issue in the UNITED KINGDOM a record of the undermentioned work.

TITLE	BRYTER LAYTER		
ARTIST	NICK DRAKE		
COMPOSER	SEE BELOW		
PUBLISHER	WARLOCK MUSIC		
THE ORDINARY RETAIL SELLING PRICE OF THE RECORD (BEFORE PURCHASE TAX IS ADDED) WILL BE	29/6d.		
DESCRIPTION OF PROPOSED RECORDING	ALBUM	THE TYPE OF RECORD TO BE MADE IS	
ESTIMATED NUMBER INITIALLY INTENDED TO BE SOLD		PARTICULARS OF PREVIOUS RECORD RELIED UPON	
THE EARLIEST DATE OF DELIVERY TO A PURCHASER WILL BE	NOVEMBER 1970	THE AMOUNT OF ROYALTY PAYABLE ON EACH RECORD IS	
ADDRESS AT WHICH RECORDS WILL BE MADE	EMI		

OTHER WORKS TO BE REPRODUCED ON THE RECORD ARE:

TITLE	COMPOSER	PUBLISHER
INTRODUCTION	NICK DRAKE Arr. R. KIRBY	WARLOCK MUSIC LTD
HAZEY JANE 11	" "	"
ONE OF THESE THINGS FIRST	: "	"
AT THE CHIME OF A CITY CLOCK	" "	"
HAZEY JANE 1	" "	"
BRYTER LAYTER	" "	"
FLY	" "	"
POOR BOY	" "	"
NORTHERN SKY	" "	"
SUNDAY	" "	"

Please accept this Stat. as permission to release

Original Island Records label copy with altered running order that appeared on Dutch pressings of the album by mistake, and original November release date

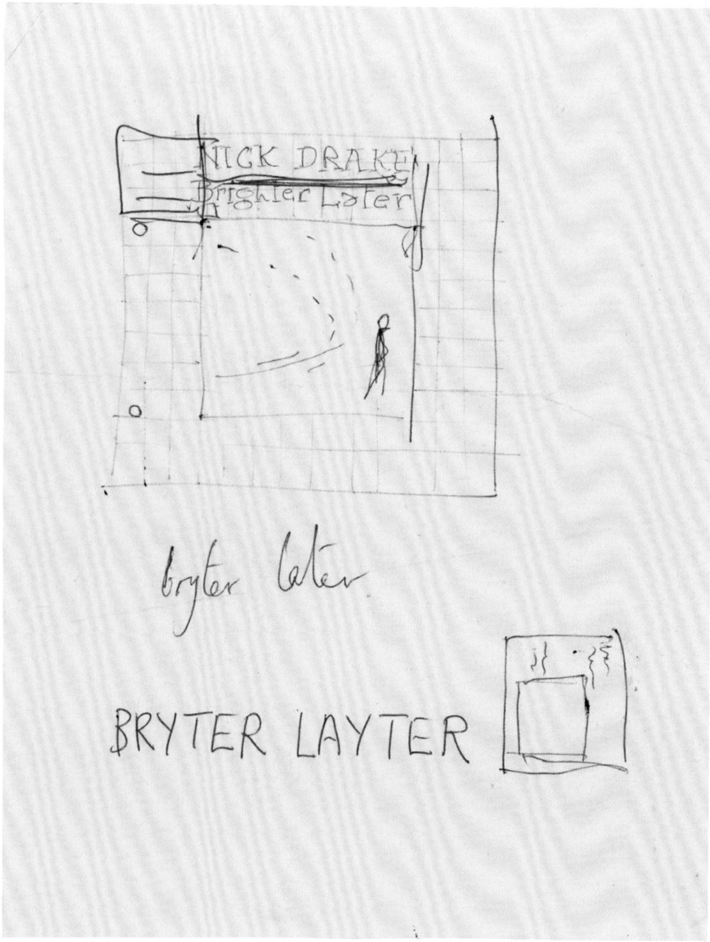

Nick's original sketch for the album front using the Keith Morris shot of him standing beside the Westway motorway flyover, London, and Nick's spelling of the album title

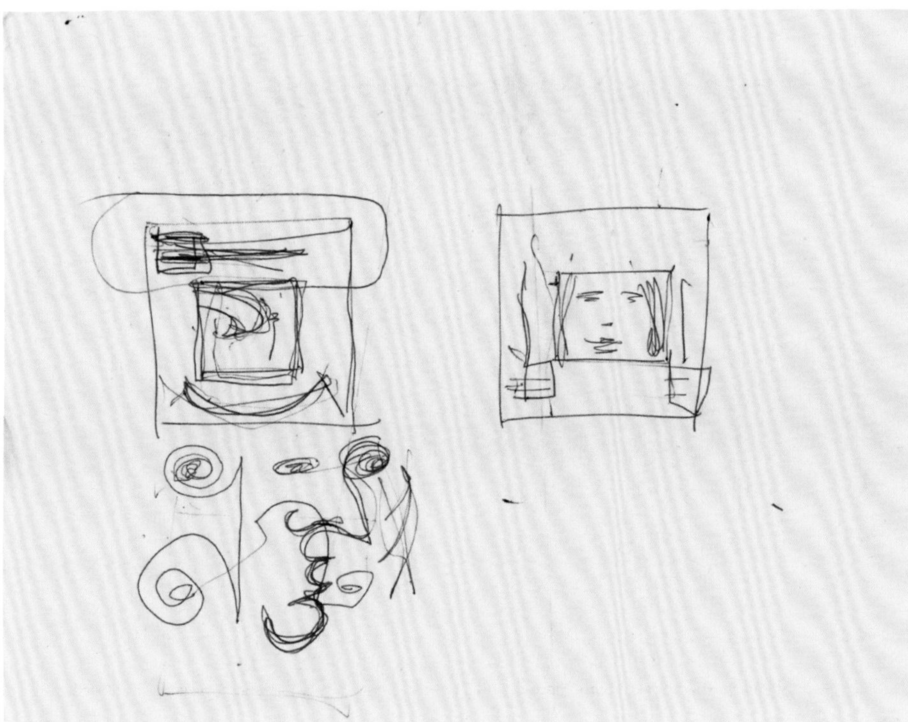

A second sketch using the Tony Evans colour photo on the front that was eventually used for the advance promotional copies

bryter layter
nick drake

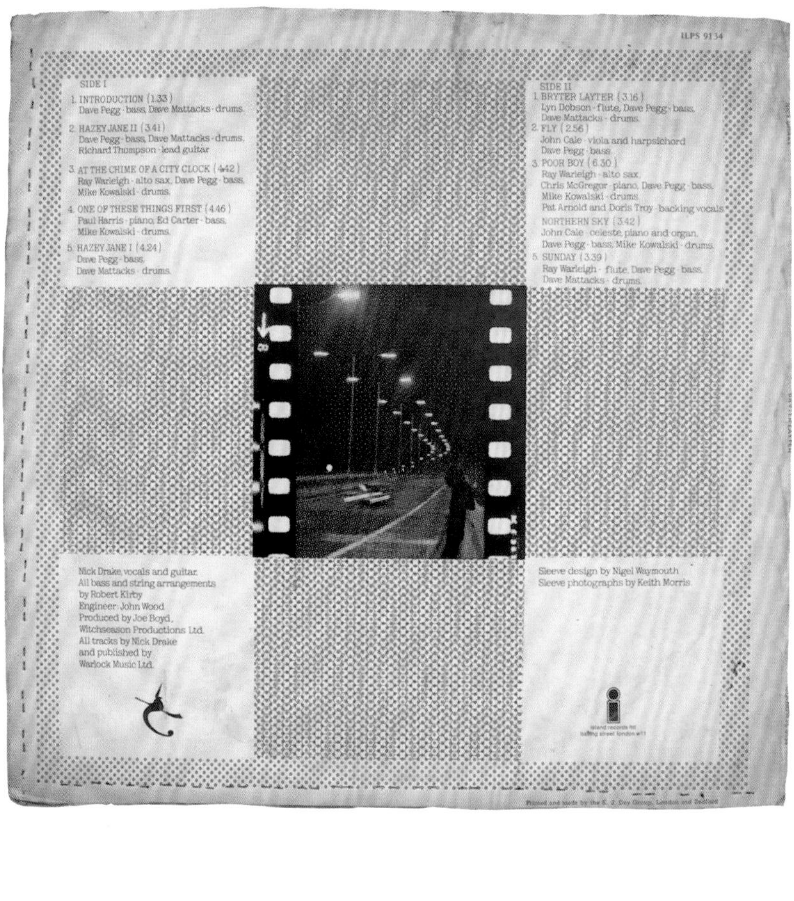
ILPS 9134
SIDE I
1. INTRODUCTION (1.33)
Dave Pegg - bass, Dave Mattacks - drums.
2. HAZEY JANE II (3.41)
Dave Pegg - bass, Dave Mattacks - drums.
Richard Thompson - lead guitar
3. AT THE CHIME OF A CITY CLOCK (4.42)
Ray Warleigh - alto sax, Dave Pegg - bass.
Mike Kowalski - drums.
4. ONE OF THESE THINGS FIRST (4.46)
Paul Harris - piano, Ed Carter - bass.
Mike Kowalski - drums.
5. HAZEY JANE I (4.24)
Dave Pegg - bass.
Dave Mattacks - drums.
SIDE II
1. BRYTER LAYTER (3.16)
Lyn Dobson - flute, Dave Pegg - bass.
Dave Mattacks - drums.
2. FLY (2.56)
John Cale - viola and harpsichord
Dave Pegg - bass.
3. POOR BOY (6.30)
Ray Warleigh - alto sax.
Chris McGregor - piano, Dave Pegg - bass.
Mike Kowalski - drums.
Pat Arnold and Doris Troy - backing vocals
NORTHERN SKY (3.42)
John Cale - celeste, piano and organ.
Dave Pegg - bass, Mike Kowalski - drums.
5. SUNDAY (3.39)
Ray Warleigh - flute, Dave Pegg - bass.
Dave Mattacks - drums.
Nick Drake, vocals and guitar.
All bass and string arrangements
by Robert Kirby
Engineer: John Wood
Produced by Joe Boyd,
Witchseason Productions Ltd.
All tracks by Nick Drake
and published by
Warlock Music Ltd.
Sleeve design by Nigel Waymouth
Sleeve photographs by Keith Morris

The sleeve to *Bryter Layter* had a difficult birth. By some accounts Witchseason were not happy with the Keith Morris photo session that took place in the summer of 1970. So, for the front cover, it was decided to use a colour photo of Nick smiling, taken from an impromptu session with Tony Evans. Nick put forward two sleeve design suggestions, one using this Tony Evans shot, the other using the picture at the foot of the Westway; a colour shot by Keith Morris taken on the evening of his 1970 session. It was at this point that Nick spelled out the title using two letter 'Y's, perhaps as a friendly jibe at his friend and fellow singer-songwriter John Martyn (not his real name). Photos for this colour session by Keith Morris are now lost.

Printed proofs were made of the sleeve proposal and the vinyl was titled 'Poor Boy', perhaps the album's working title. Advance promotional copies of the album were distributed to the trade in the autumn of 1970 but, for whatever reason, the sleeve was deemed unsuitable. A new design was sought and the release date delayed until early March 1971.

Nigel Waymouth was a colleague of Joe Boyd. He had formed the boutique 'Granny Takes a Trip' with Sheila Cohen and John Pearse in 1966 and was part of the design and musical outfit 'Hapshash and The Coloured Coat', alongside Michael English. An accomplished photographer, Nigel took the front cover photo of Nick and designed the new sleeve that was eventually used on the album.

Contrary to popular belief, the guitar on the cover was not one of Nick's. It is an early 1960s Guild M20, formerly the property of Eric Clapton who left it at his flat in The Pheasantry, Kings Road, as Nigel Waymouth moved in. It was given to Nigel who sold it in 1973 to Nick Laird-Clowes (later of The Dream Academy) for £100. The chair was reputed to have once belonged to Charles Dickens and the shoes were Nigel's own. The rest of the photo session is now lost.

The album advertising campaign still used a Tony Evans shot of Nick holding up a Yamaha guitar (later used on the front of the *Nick Drake – A Treasury* compilation) with the symbol of a sun added into the sound hole of the guitar for good measure.

Original copies of the sleeve have a machine-finished canvas texture and editions were printed in Australia (on the Festival label), in New Zealand (on Island), in Holland (on Island) and later in the USA.

nick drake bryter layter
ILPS 9134
SIDE I
INTRODUCTION (1.33)
Dave Pegg-bass, Dave Mattacks-drums.
HAZEY JANE II (3.41)
Dave Pegg-bass, Dave Mattacks-drums,
Richard Thompson-lead guitar
AT THE CHIME OF A CITY CLOCK (4.42)
Ray Warleigh-alto sax, Dave Pegg-bass,
Mike Kowalski-drums.
ONE OF THESE THINGS FIRST (4.46)
Paul Harris-piano, Ed Carter-bass,
Mike Kowalski-drums.
HAZEY JANE I (4.24)
Dave Pegg-bass,
Dave Mattacks-drums.
Nick Drake, vocals and guitar.
All bass and string arrangements
by Robert Kirby
Engineer: John Wood
Produced by Joe Boyd,
Witchseason Productions Ltd.
All tracks by Nick Drake
and published by
Warlock Music Ltd.
Sleeve design and front cover
photograph by Nigel Waymouth
Back cover photograph
by Keith Morris.
island records ltd basing street london w11
SIDE II
BRYTER LAYTER (3.16)
Lyn Dobson-flute, Dave Pegg-bass,
Dave Mattacks-drums.
FLY (2.56)
John Cale-viola and harpsichord.
Dave Pegg-bass.
POOR BOY (6.30)
Ray Warleigh-alto sax,
Chris McGregor-piano, Dave Pegg-bass,
Mike Kowalski-drums.
Pat Arnold and Doris Troy-backing vocals
NORTHERN SKY (3.42)
John Cale-celeste, piano and organ,
Dave Pegg-bass, Mike Kowalski-drums.
SUNDAY (3.39)
Ray Warleigh-flute, Dave Pegg-bass,
Dave Mattacks-drums.

NICK DRAKE
Bryter Layter
NICK DRAKE
Bryter Layter
Introduction : Hazey Jane 11
At The Chime Of A City Clock
One Of These Things First
Hazey Jane 1 : Bryter Layter
(Part 1) : Bryter Layter
(Conclusion) : Fly : Poor Boy
8
TRACK
STEREO

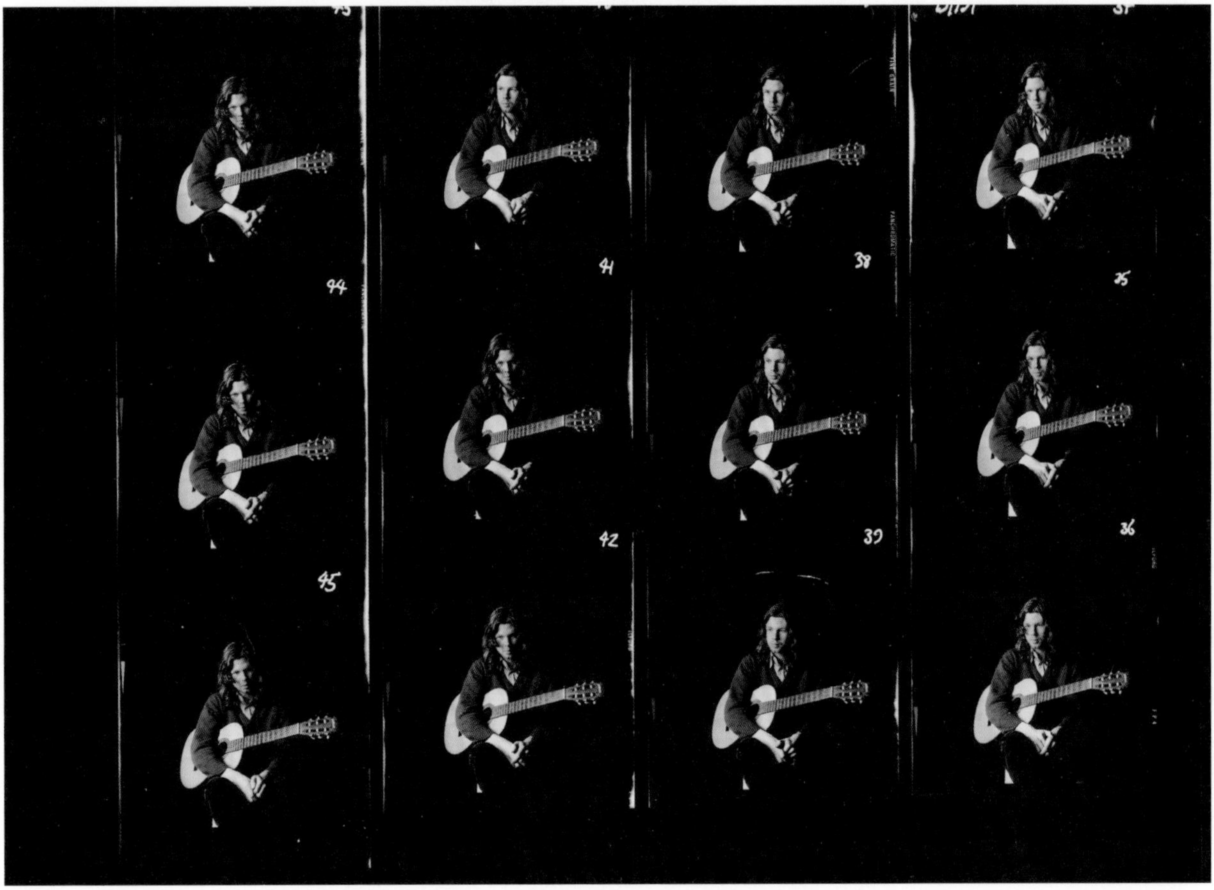

Nick poses for an impromptu photo session by Tony Evans, who was taking photos of John Martyn at the time and asked if he could shoot a few rolls of Nick (Photo supplied by the estate of Tony Evans)

Nick Drake

by Brian Cullman

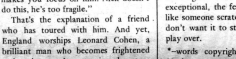

In John Martyn's house in Hampstead, Nick Drake sits over in a corner playing my guitar and smoking a very badly rolled joint. Sometimes he smiles, almost from behind his face, for he is incredibly shy ("He's known us for over a year," Beverly Martyn says, "and only now will he say things like, 'how are you?' ").

Nick has a very beautiful album out on Island Records over here, a record that will probably never reach the States . . . no one seems to have bought it. Joe Boyd, who produced the album, is the man who brought the Incredible String Band, Fairport Convention, and John & Beverly Martyn into studios; he has enough faith in Nick to begin recording his second album despite the commercial failure of his initial offering. But if the second one fails to catch on, things will be bad. Things aren't so good now.

Everyone has their own opinion about why no one is buying Nick's album. Those who like him say that it's because he's too good for public taste. Others aren't as kind. Selling records in England is hard because of the terrible radio situation, and so continual performances, perpetual gigs, are necessary to sell your album.

"Nick has no stage presence . . . he just gets up and sings, and he seems very self conscious, very shy. Someone like Ralph McTell has incredible presence . . . he draws your attention, makes you focus on him. Nick doesn't do this, he's too fragile."

That's the explanation of a friend who has toured with him. And yet, England worships Leonard Cohen, a brilliant man who becomes frightened and embarrassed every time he steps upon a stage. Somehow they accept that. I suppose it is simply a matter of a man not being able to be a prophet in his own home town; too often we see the present with out eyes firmly rooted in the past.

This is all leading up to the fact that Nick Drake is a gentle, happy surprise, a smile from a passing stranger. His album, FIVE LEAVES LEFT, is worth hunting around import stores for. He is a writer and singer of soft, rhythmic songs that are neither self-conscious nor self-pitying: a rarity. They are sung in a voice that some people compare to Donovan's, although it has none of Mr. Leitch's preciousness and is fuller. It wraps each song in fur.

His songs are of love, of friendships, of indecision, and of faith . . . faith in himself and faith in the ways of the world.

Time has told me you're a rare find
A trouble cure for a troubled mind.
And time has told me not to ask for more
*For someday our ocean will find its shore.**

He loves people and treats them in his songs the same way Truffaut handles all of the characters in his movies: with incredible tendernesss.

Betty said she prayed today
For the sky to blow away
Or maybe stay,
She wasn't sure.
For when she thought of summer rain
Calling for her mind again
She lost the pain
*And stayed for more.**

Backing him on the album are Fiarport's Richard Thompson, Pentangle's Danny Thompson, and everybody's Paul Harris. The arrangements and strings are exceptional, the feeling of the album is like someone scratching your back; you don't want it to stop, and so you let it play over.

*–words copyright 1969 by Warlock Music

Crawdaddy Magazine, Vol. 4, No. 14, September 1970, USA

Which Will

by Brian Cullman

Just past Tandy Crafts, a dark, unlovely store on the corner of 13th and 6th Avenue, there was a door that led to the shop's basement and storage area. Down there, tucked between the boiler room and the janitor's closet, you could find the editorial offices of *Crawdaddy!*

I was there because *Rolling Stone* was in California, because *Hit Parader* was no longer interesting, and because *Down Beat* was incomprehensible. *Crawdaddy!* was the only other music magazine I'd heard of, and it had the advantage of being in New York. It also had the advantage of not having a listed phone number, so I couldn't be turned away unseen. In my pocket I had two stories I'd written for my school paper. One was a review of John Fahey's *Days Have Gone By*, the other was an appreciation of The Paul Butterfield Blues Band. Neither was more than a few hundred words, and I'd probably spent more time tracking down the address of *Crawdaddy!* than I had in writing them. But there I was. It was the middle of April 1970, and all was right with the world.

The office looked like the sort of place where the right kind of people would plan a bank heist. Not necessarily a successful one. Everything was in shadow. In one corner there was a gum machine with no gum left in it. Cardboard boxes and file cabinets and what looked like thirteen or fourteen pieces of abandoned luggage lined the back wall. Two guys with long brown hair, one with a moustache, one without, sat across from each other at a desk. The one with the moustache swept whatever'd been on the desk into an open drawer, then shut it. The other one took a long drag off his cigarette and stared at me with a mixture of hope and panic in his eyes.

I couldn't find a chair, so I perched on the edge of a brown suitcase and pulled out folded copies of my stories. They passed them back and forth to each other. The one with the moustache turned out to be the editor, and he smiled once or twice, nodded in my direction and said, 'Butterfield,' as if it were a punchline or a benediction. 'Butterfield.'

I explained why I was there. I was going to London for a summer job, interning at a film company. Maybe I could do some stories for them while I was there. Some interviews. Or reviews.

'Right.' The editor nodded. 'Except . . . there's Miles.'

'Miles,' his friend agreed, and stubbed out his cigarette.

Barry Miles was their London editor. He was friends with The Beatles. He'd started the Indica Bookstore with Paul McCartney. John Lennon had met Yoko Ono at an opening in his gallery. He knew everyone.

The editor shrugged and leaned back in his chair. 'Leave us a number, someplace we can find you. Something turns up . . . we'll be in touch.'

The film company wasn't a film company any more. They no longer made films. An accountant had gone through their books and determined that none of their productions had made money in a long, long time. What kept them afloat was all the equipment they'd accumulated over the years, much of it from the 1940s: the cameras and tripods and dollies, the microphones, edit bays, widgets and mechanical whatnots that went into day-to-day filmmaking. Overnight, a company known for award-winning documentaries, news reports and music shows for the BBC had morphed into a rental office, grudgingly leasing their beautiful vintage gear to film-makers that hadn't gone bust yet.

The mood in the office was not sunny. The change had only gone into effect a few weeks before.

'It took the wind out of our sails,' the managing director told me when I first turned up. 'The cream out of our coffee. The spring out of our step. Can you imagine . . . ?' he asked me. He was wearing tweed. I nodded. 'No,' he snapped. 'No. You cannot.'

I was put into the hands of Mrs Pyne, a trim woman with tortoiseshell glasses and a style best described as crisp. She decided that I wouldn't be much use lifting of loading gear, nor was my knowledge of London sufficient to have me handle deliveries.

My job was to take all the various scraps of paper, all the inventory sheets, memos, cancelled cheques and invoice forms, and enter the information into an oversized ledger.

'In this column you'll list the pieces of equipment that were rented, the date of the rental and the price agreed upon. You'll do that in red ink. *Red.* Here,' she said, pointing to the opposite page, 'you'll enter the pieces of equipment returned, their condition on return, date of return and monies received. You'll do that in green ink. *Green*. Are we clear? The pens are in the middle drawer. They are not to be taken home. They are office property.'

This was not what I'd had in mind. It was probably not what they'd had in mind either. No wind, no sails, no cream, no coffee. I tried to hum while I made sense of all the bits of paper, but no songs were available.

It must have been two, three days later when the phone rang. Mrs Pyne held her hand over the mouthpiece and looked over to the managing director.

'Is his name Brian?' she pouted. He nodded. She handed me the phone and made a hurry-up motion with her hands.

'Hey,' a voice from somewhere far away drawled. 'How's it going?' It was the editor of *Crawdaddy!* He asked about clubs I'd never heard of, bars I'd never been to, bands I was only dimly aware of, parties I'd never been invited to. I mumbled affably. I was hoping that the sounds of despair and regret couldn't be heard transatlantically, that it could be put down to static on the line. The heat pipes coughed, and the tea lady down the corridor was rattling cups.

'So listen . . . Barry Miles is leaving England. He's moving to Woodstock to write a biography of Allen Ginsberg. We were wondering if you'd want to take over as our London editor. Is there anything you need?'

Looking in the rearview mirror, I should've said: 'An office! A phone! Money! A motorbike! Credit cards! Clothes! Pretty girls in tights!'

What I said was: 'A press pass. I need a press pass.'

No one in London had ever heard of *Crawdaddy!* No one. It didn't matter. All doors were open, everyone was home, and the world was aflame and alive with possibility.

I was backstage; I was on the side of the stage; I was onstage singing backup. People I didn't know bought me drinks, gave me their phone numbers. I looked up, and I was at the Baghdad House, a restaurant in north London with a private room downstairs where you could smoke hashish and drink rosewater honey. Frank Zappa was there. Peter Sellers was there. Sandy Denny saw me and dragged me off to a recording session, doing backup vocals for Stefan Grossman. The backing vocalists were Sandy, Linda Peters (soon to be Linda Thompson), Trevor Lucas, Heather Wood from The Young Tradition and myself. I was pleased to note that Heather Wood had a tendency to sing flat, same as I did, and we were both conveniently placed behind Trevor Lucas, who was exceedingly loud and reliably in tune.

'You're not flat,' he told me reassuringly. 'You and Heather just like to approach the notes from the south side.'

It was the summer of 1970. All was right with the world.

Hampstead Heath was my favourite place in London, and if I walked far enough along Primrose Hill Road I'd eventually get to John and Beverley Martyn's house, my home away from home. They took me in, the way they took in stray cats or drifters en route to Morocco or Spain.

The fact that I had some sort of magazine affiliation, however vague the affiliation, however distant the magazine, was, if anything, a strike against me. John loved talking, loved having an audience, but he hated answering questions and was deeply suspicious of the music press. The fact that I was an American who knew and liked his music, who had actually paid cash money for his *Stormbringer!* album back in America, and who had heard songs of his played on the radio in New York was a matter of amazement and pride. If he had a bad gig, if he broke a string, if the baby cried, if the weed or the whisky didn't take him where he needed to go, there was always that: somewhere in America someone was listening to his songs, someone liked his music. Over there. Somewhere.

'So,' he would say, leaning back, holding an *oud*, 'if we could wait till it was a really clear night, the stars out, not a cloud, man, not a cloud, and we could go up and down the radio dial, we could listen to the future as well as the past, hear a whole album I haven't even made yet, playing out there in the night. What do you think?'

'Save you the trouble of making it,' I ventured.

'Fuck off, Yank.'

A favourite pastime was making sense of Martyn's record collection, trying to organise it or relate it to a world I knew. Hamza El Din sat right next to Pharoah Sanders, Lord Buckley leaned up against Manitas de Plata, Baden Powell and Sandy Bull, and there was Archie Shepp, Bukka White, Geoff Muldaur, Anne Briggs; a record of bagpipe music; Koerner, Ray & Glover; *The Real Bahamas* and *A Love Supreme*. The records he loved, he played over and over again, until every note and every nuance was absorbed into the Turkish rugs on the floor, until the sounds were part of his life and his house.

Over time, I'd send him albums I thought he'd like, only to find them unapologetically unopened and unheard when I'd come by. Townes Van Zandt? 'It's the same song, over and over. And I know that song. I already wrote that song.' Tim Buckley? 'Too many octaves, man. Too many octaves.'

It was the second or third time I'd been to his house. It was late afternoon, there was a soft light coming through the curtains, and we'd been listening to the same album of classical guitar – Julian Bream? – for over an hour, when something by the window stirred and started to rise. I hadn't noticed anyone there, and it gave me a fright.

'Nick.' John nodded. 'This is Brian. Brian, Nick. Everyone present accounted for?'

The figure came into focus. It rose, and stretched, and where before it had looked like a small child that had folded itself into a ball, now I could see it was someone fairly tall with the physique of a tennis player, all arms and legs and elbows. A curtain of dark and uncombed hair hung around his face, hiding everything but his eyes. It looked like he was stoned. It looked like he was asleep. It looked like he was the most wide-awake person in the history of the world. All of the above. Each time I replay the scene in my mind, it's different. And each time it's true. He was wearing a frayed white shirt, and jeans and boots, and a black corduroy jacket that seemed a size too large. I don't usually pay much attention to clothes, but my first thought was . . . where can I get a black corduroy jacket?

How long had he been there? What was he doing? Meditating? Dreaming? Drifting? Watching?

Over the next few months, I'd have the same experience over and over again, and I never got used to it. I'd be in a room or a restaurant and wouldn't have a clue that Nick was there until he got up to leave. But, once gone, you'd notice the absence. It filled the air, like a chord that won't die out, that hangs there, loud, even in fading, especially in fading, that hangs there until the next note is played.

'You heard his record?' John asked, after he'd wandered off. 'No? Oh, man, how could you miss it? It's the best. It's alive!'

John handed me a well-worn copy of *Five Leaves Left*. I looked at the cover. When he left, a moment ago, he'd been wearing the same clothes he had on in the cover photo. And it looked like he might not have taken them off since then.

When I returned the record a few days later, I couldn't stop talking about how great it was, how it was something new and strong and pure. That voice! So smooth, so delicate, yet so hard to shake. Once you heard it, you couldn't get it out of your head. Those strings! The way they wove through the melodies like a Greek chorus, reminding you of the depths below, the darkness and the night just around the corner; maybe you can't see it now, but you will, you will! How he'd taken bits of John's guitar style and brought in some of the Brazilian shadings of João Gilberto, the soft, floating chord changes of Jimmy Webb, the sweep of *Astral Weeks*. How he'd invented a genuine British blues form, standing right there on the corner of Ralph Vaughan Williams and Brownie McGhee!

I went on and on. John might have winced a little, but I didn't notice. His wife Beverley did, and she took me aside.

'It's great that you love Nick's album. You know we love Nick's album. You know we love Nick. But maybe you shouldn't talk about it quite so much. To John, I mean.'

Point taken.

Martyn could be competitive and fractious, especially if he'd been drinking, and if I'd been raving about Bert Jansch or Richard Thompson, I'd have been bounced out on my ear. But when it came to Nick, different rules applied. John was fiercely protective of him, provided safe haven and no questions asked. Nick could leave his shadow behind; John would roll it up, put it in the hall closet, and it would be there safe when he returned.

I tried to tell Nick how much I liked his album. It was later that week, we were in the kitchen at John and Beverley's, drinking tea, and there was silence everywhere. I mentioned a few songs – ''Cello Song' and 'River Man' and 'Saturday Sun' – and he nodded and stared at the table. After a few minutes, he started fumbling through his coat pockets. There was a smell of mint and tobacco, maybe cloves, and he was pulling out scraps of paper, guitar picks, rolling papers and such. He looked up.

'Do you like chocolate?' he asked. He held an unopened bar of Cadbury's Dairy Milk Chocolate.

I had come to London with a Gibson Hummingbird guitar. It was beautiful and shiny and too good for me. In New York, it was like driving a Volvo: solid, reliable, safe. In London, it was like showing up in a Porsche.

I brought it to John's house to show it off, though John was only mildly curious. I played a few chords, and Andy the Greek, who ran Les Cousins, a club in the West End, began bombarding me with questions: Wasn't that the guitar on the cover of *Nashville Skyline*? What does it cost? Do you have a pickup for it? What strings do you use?

While I was answering, best I could, Nick materialised and asked if he could have a look. He picked up the guitar, carried it out into the hallway, and then shut the door tight. Through the closed door, I could just about hear bits of half-familiar melodies, the strings being coaxed into music.

'Do you ever play clubs?' Andy the Greek asked me while I was trying to hear the muffled sounds. I admitted that I'd played Bunjies a couple of times. Not very happily.

'They're a tough crowd there. You should try Les Cousins.'

'Sure. But who would I audition for?'

'Me.' He shrugged. 'And you already have. You can play there next Friday. Right before the ghost in the hallway.'

My performance at Les Cousins was forgettable. Nick's was memorable mostly for its awkwardness. Sitting on a small wooden chair, the kind favoured in most third-grade classrooms, he seemed to shrink, to recede further and further away from the microphone, as if we were all looking through the wrong end of a telescope. He hunched over a small mahogany guitar, a parlour guitar, and began fingerpicking with the ease and elegance and grace of the playing on his album, though he pulled the guitar tightly into himself, hugging it as he played, and the sound was distant and muffled and indistinct, as if he'd found a way to get up and walk out into the hallway and close the door on us while he sat there on the stage.

He began singing 'The Thoughts Of Mary Jane,' and you could hear the sound of the buttons on his jacket hitting the guitar, the sound of the chair creaking, and midway through, just as it seemed like he was getting warmed up and settling into the performance, he changed directions, changed songs. No one could tell if he'd forgotten the chords or lost the words or simply grown bored and decided to move on. He settled into a rolling guitar figure, beautiful and stuttered and strangely uplifting, and he began singing the opening lines to a new song; new to me at least:

> Do you curse where you come from?
> Do you swear in the night?

And then he would look away, even further away, and begin the pattern once again and continue the same words until they sprawled into a chant, slurred and strange and hypnotic:

> Do you curse where you come from?
> Do you swear in the night?

Nick inspects Fairport's *Full House* album in the Witchseason offices, Charlotte Street, London, 1970. Marian Bain takes notes (Photo: Joe Boyd)

The words seemed a challenge, a prayer and a whispered threat all at once, a quiet British voodoo sung to an unseen moon and an all-too-present dark:

> Do you curse where you come from?
> Do you swear in the night?

You couldn't watch. But you couldn't look away. And then it was over. I don't remember if there was any applause, but I know that there were no celebratory drinks, there was no after-party; the audience simply drifted off into their own version of the night.

We were driving to a late dinner. It was foggy and rainy and dark. I was there with John and Beverley and their friend Paul Wheeler, who was driving. He was with a woman in a dress that was much too pretty. Out the window we could see Nick driving somewhere in a battered white Chevy. We waved and honked, but I don't think he saw us. Maybe he didn't want to see us.

'He's like a phantom,' I said.

'The Flying Dutchman,' Paul Wheeler agreed.

'Jesus!' John snapped. 'Why does everyone think he's so gloomy? What, do you think he's off to wander through some abandoned graveyard and just look at tombstones and think about eternity? That's not who he is! That's not what he's doing!'

But that, in fact, was exactly what he was doing.

23 January 2012

Nick in his Haverstock Hill home (Photo: Keith Morris)

Keith Morris and *Bryter Layter*

These photos were taken in the summer of 1970, just over a year after the *Five Leaves Left* session. Nick's first album had been released – if not to resounding acclaim, at least to respectful and interested affirmation. And proof that Nick had the confidence of his record company Island was manifested in the commissioning of a further album – an album, moreover, that everyone was convinced would take Nick to the heights of recognition. In the summer of 1970, all must have seemed very right in Nick's world.

Keith's photos for this album would seem to reflect this. Nick appears more mature, more sure of himself – leaner of face, and lighter of heart. The shoot took place over three locations – still in London, but this time the landscapes were more urban. This was to be Nick's city album.

They started the day at Nick's flat in Hampstead, north London. Nick seems quite amused to be tangled up in his neighbour's washing line, and entirely relaxed playing his guitar in the garden. Then they moved southwards to Regent's Park. History doesn't relate what the huge tome was that Nick was perusing – was it a prop, or his actual reading material at the time? Finally they made their way to the industrial landscape of New Cross, with Nick sharply etched against a blurred background of Thames-side factories. Nick's reserved elegance seems easy and natural.

Not until well after this photo session did the problems with *Bryter Layter* begin to surface, which led to the postponement of its release from November 1970 to March 1971.

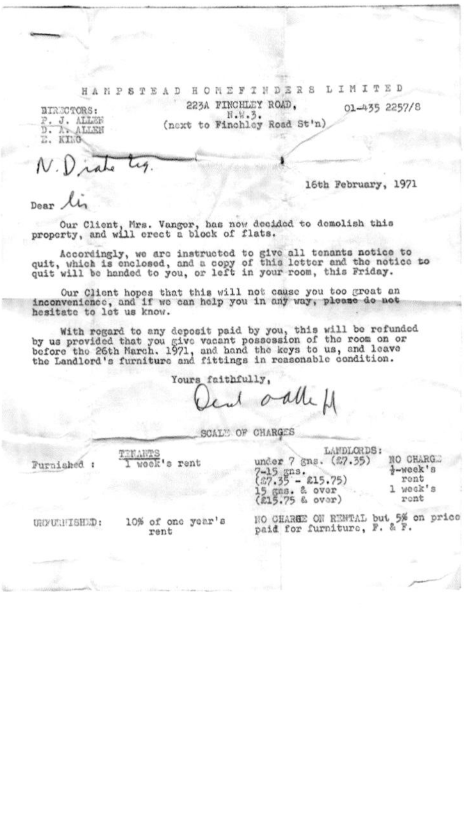

HAMPSTEAD HOMEFINDERS LIMITED

DIRECTORS:
P. J. ALLEN
D. A. ALLEN
E. KING

223A FINCHLEY ROAD,
N.W.3.
(next to Finchley Road St'n)

01-435 2257/8

N. Drake Esq.

16th February, 1971

Dear Sir

Our Client, Mrs. Vanger, has now decided to demolish this property, and will erect a block of flats.

Accordingly, we are instructed to give all tenants notice to quit, which is enclosed, and a copy of this letter and the notice to quit will be handed to you, or left in your room, this Friday.

Our Client hopes that this will not cause you too great an inconvenience, and if we can help you in any way, please do not hesitate to let us know.

With regard to any deposit paid by you, this will be refunded by us provided that you give vacant possession of the room on or before the 26th March. 1971, and hand the keys to us, and leave the Landlord's furniture and fittings in reasonable condition.

Yours faithfully,

SCALE OF CHARGES

	TENANTS	LANDLORDS:	
Furnished :	1 week's rent	under 7 gns. (£7.35)	NO CHARGE
		7-15 gns. (£7.35 - £15.75)	½-week's rent
		15 gns. & over (£15.75 & over)	1 week's rent
UNFURNISHED:	10% of one year's rent	NO CHARGE ON RENTAL but 5% on price paid for furniture, F. & F.	

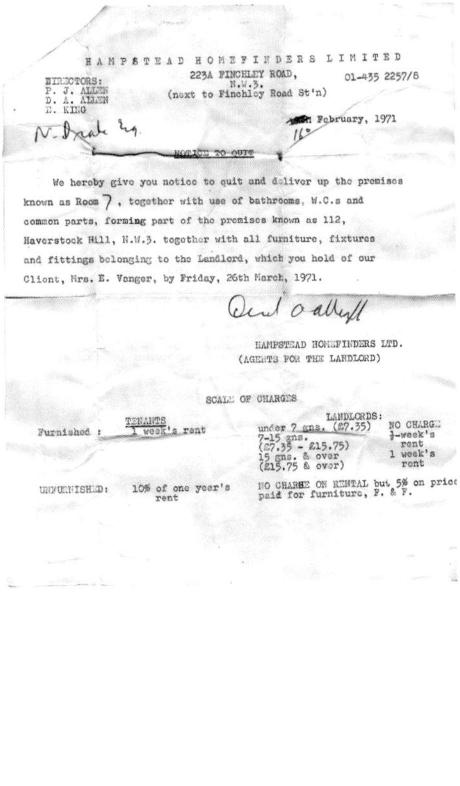

HAMPSTEAD HOMEFINDERS LIMITED

DIRECTORS:
P. J. ALLEN
D. A. ALLEN
E. KING

223A FINCHLEY ROAD,
N.W.3.
(next to Finchley Road St'n)

01-435 2257/8

16th February, 1971

N. Drake Esq.

NOTICE TO QUIT

We hereby give you notice to quit and deliver up the premises known as Room 7, together with use of bathrooms, W.C.s and common parts, forming part of the premises known as 112, Haverstock Hill, N.W.3. together with all furniture, fixtures and fittings belonging to the Landlord, which you hold of our Client, Mrs. E. Vanger, by Friday, 26th March, 1971.

HAMPSTEAD HOMEFINDERS LTD.
(AGENTS FOR THE LANDLORD)

SCALE OF CHARGES

	TENANTS	LANDLORDS:	
Furnished :	1 week's rent	under 7 gns. (£7.35)	NO CHARGE
		7-15 gns. (£7.35 - £15.75)	½-week's rent
		15 gns. & over (£15.75 & over)	1 week's rent
UNFURNISHED:	10% of one year's rent	NO CHARGE ON RENTAL but 5% on price paid for furniture, F. & F.	

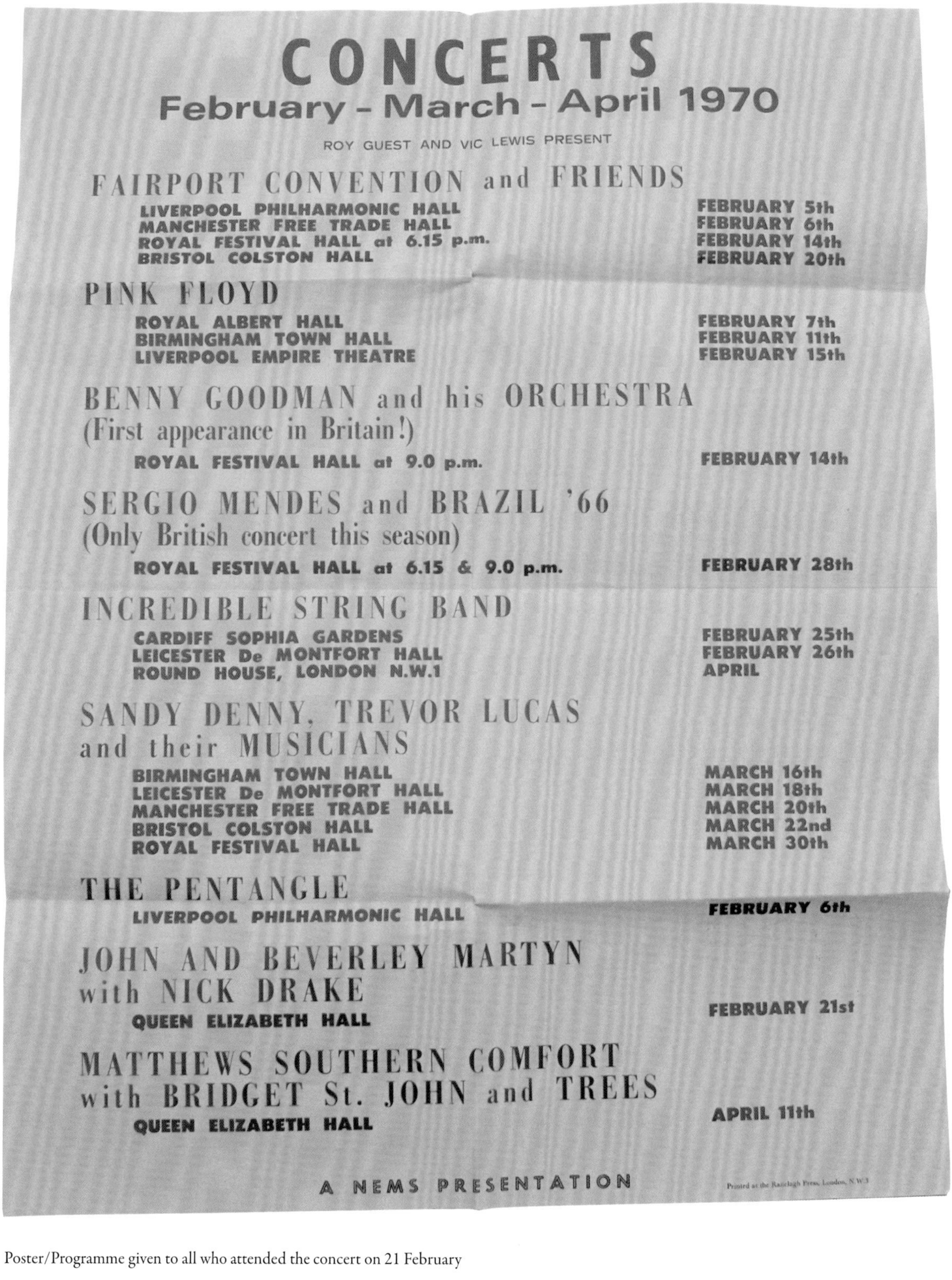

CONCERTS

February - March - April 1970

ROY GUEST AND VIC LEWIS PRESENT

FAIRPORT CONVENTION and FRIENDS

LIVERPOOL PHILHARMONIC HALL	FEBRUARY 5th
MANCHESTER FREE TRADE HALL	FEBRUARY 6th
ROYAL FESTIVAL HALL at 6.15 p.m.	FEBRUARY 14th
BRISTOL COLSTON HALL	FEBRUARY 20th

PINK FLOYD

ROYAL ALBERT HALL	FEBRUARY 7th
BIRMINGHAM TOWN HALL	FEBRUARY 11th
LIVERPOOL EMPIRE THEATRE	FEBRUARY 15th

BENNY GOODMAN and his ORCHESTRA
(First appearance in Britain!)

ROYAL FESTIVAL HALL at 9.0 p.m.	FEBRUARY 14th

SERGIO MENDES and BRAZIL '66
(Only British concert this season)

ROYAL FESTIVAL HALL at 6.15 & 9.0 p.m.	FEBRUARY 28th

INCREDIBLE STRING BAND

CARDIFF SOPHIA GARDENS	FEBRUARY 25th
LEICESTER De MONTFORT HALL	FEBRUARY 26th
ROUND HOUSE, LONDON N.W.1	APRIL

SANDY DENNY, TREVOR LUCAS
and their MUSICIANS

BIRMINGHAM TOWN HALL	MARCH 16th
LEICESTER De MONTFORT HALL	MARCH 18th
MANCHESTER FREE TRADE HALL	MARCH 20th
BRISTOL COLSTON HALL	MARCH 22nd
ROYAL FESTIVAL HALL	MARCH 30th

THE PENTANGLE

LIVERPOOL PHILHARMONIC HALL	FEBRUARY 6th

JOHN AND BEVERLEY MARTYN
with NICK DRAKE

QUEEN ELIZABETH HALL	FEBRUARY 21st

MATTHEWS SOUTHERN COMFORT
with BRIDGET St. JOHN and TREES

QUEEN ELIZABETH HALL	APRIL 11th

A NEMS PRESENTATION

Printed at the Ranelagh Press, London, N.W.3

Poster/Programme given to all who attended the concert on 21 February

Please Beware Of Them That Stare

by Cally

In the late 1960s the solo artists and bands that were signed to Island Records were encouraged to promote their record releases in accordance with its stated philosophy (one shared by other small independent labels such as Charisma): namely, that artists should sell their music without 'selling out'. Chris Blackwell, founder of the Island label, refused to employ a marketing department, because he had an aversion to the advertising of music – which he called 'numb selling'.

At the same time, a poster hung in his office which read: 'If you do not promote, a funny thing happens – nothing.'

There was, he believed, a fundamental difference between *advertising* – telling people what to buy – and *promotion* – making sure the public heard the music and then chose for itself.

At that time there were in reality only two methods by which an album could be promoted. The first involved 'broadcast exposure'. This included radio play – originally on the pirate radio stations, such as Radio Caroline, and, later, on the BBC's new Radio 1 by DJs such as John Peel, Pete Drummond, Mike Raven, Mike Harding and Bob Harris. Radio play would be greatly increased by a 'hit single', and Island acts, such as Free, Traffic, and Jethro Tull, had several. But they would often leave the 'hit single' off their albums for fear of appearing to be 'too commercial'.

'Broadcast exposure' could also include the playing of an album at live concerts: respected DJs such as Jeff Dexter (a fan of Nick's) and Andy Dunkley would command attention for the records they chose to play between the support and headlining groups. A favoured artist might be invited to perform live on BBC TV's *The Old Grey Whistle Test* – a programme often viewed by Nick at home with his father. And occasionally an artist or band would get lucky and their song would be chosen as the theme for a TV programme. When Brian Walden's *Weekend World* used 'Nantucket Sleighride' over their credits, Island band Mountain's profile was greatly enhanced.

The only other significant method of promotion involved live performances by the artists themselves. And this usually meant touring the country in less than salubrious conditions.

However, since Nick had first come to Joe Boyd's – and thus Island's – attention via his performance at London's Roundhouse theatre, it was a reasonable assumption that he would be able to handle the live-performance method of promoting his album. Yet in his years at Island Records he performed live barely twenty times – a tiny amount when compared to his friend and label-mate John Martyn. It is perhaps interesting to speculate why.

The accepted view is that Nick was daunted by audiences and too introverted and shy to relish performing live. But it is worth remembering that Nick had experienced no difficulty busking in the streets of Aix-en-Provence back in 1967, as is well documented in Colin Betts's book *Frozenlight*. Nor had he been averse to singing for his supper in the nightclubs of Morocco, St Tropez and Paris.

We know, too, that, though shy in manner, Nick played at the Cambridge May Balls while at university there, nor does his friend Robert Kirby, who first provided arrangements to Nick's music, record Nick being in any way intimidated by an audience that can hardly have been very attentive.

Above all, John Wood (Nick's sound engineer and friend), states categorically that Nick was always supremely confident performing in front of a live orchestra in the recording studio – surely the most daunting audience of all.

So, what might have changed between the time before the recording of *Five Leaves Left*, and the period after its release, when Joe Boyd – faithful to the Island ethic – tried to send Nick on a tour to promote his latest album?

Nick probably never had a very high opinion of his own voice. Even allowing for his characteristically ironic self-deprecation, this extract from a letter written to his parents while he was still at school at Marlborough College is revealing:

'My musical activities seem to be in full swing already. There was a film show on Saturday, and nobody seemed to be prepared to provide music before it, so I was asked to organise something. So I formed a small group, and after one practice, we went on and attempted to play. The result, as you may imagine, was pretty good chaos. For want of someone better, I had to sing myself, and I need hardly tell the trouble that was likely to cause. In one number I completely forgot the words of the last verse, and we ground to an embarrassing halt in the middle of the song! Fortunately Simon Crocker was in the group, so we were able to laugh a lot of it off, but it was somewhat embarrassing all the same. However, the most amazing thing was that quite a large number of people congratulated us afterwards, and said that they had thoroughly enjoyed it. The fact that 90% of all Marlburians are musical ignorami is certainly very helpful at times.'

Ever the perfectionist, Nick would surely have been aware that his voice was not a large one. It was at its least adequate whenever he tried to force it, as a recording of one of his performances at a Cambridge concert – where he had to sing over Robert Kirby's arrangements without the aid of foldback monitoring – reveals.

But when Nick went into the studio at Sound Techniques, John Wood would have mic'd Nick's voice as a separate instrument – and for the first time, Nick would have heard vocal qualities which, though hardly perfect in the accepted sense of the word, would enable him to get across his diffident but definite message. For although Nick's guitar playing was important to him – the hours he spent practising attest to that – it was never more than the necessary structure to support his songs. Nick was to be found – *is* to be found – in his songs: 'If songs were lines in a conversation, the situation would be fine . . .'

This profound gear-change in his perception of his own capabilities would only have been borne in on him gradually. To begin with, when Joe proposed the tour, Nick must have thought he would be on familiar territory, after his experience of playing in the bars and clubs of France, Morocco and Cambridge.

But as the inadequacies of the audio equipment at the venues he was touring became apparent, Nick must have become ever more frustrated and demoralised. For in those days, the audio equipment in the clubs and university campuses Nick was scheduled to tour would have been, at best, rudimentary. There would have been just two microphones: one for the voice, one for the (louder) guitar, all going through a four-channel mixer, amplification and puny 'WEM' or 'Laney' PA columns. Balance and finesse would have been noticeably absent. Nick, after hearing the possibilities that had been revealed to him in the recording studio, would surely have felt like a man banging his head against the walls of a soundproofed room.

Added to this was a further disadvantage. Nick's charisma depended on people being intrigued and coming into his world: he would not – could not – woo them on their terms. And he had no showman's patter. This was nothing new: if we look again at his letter from Marlborough College, we will see that a difficult situation was retrieved because 'Simon Crocker was in the group so we were able to laugh a lot of it off'. Not Nick.

There is one final point worth considering, and it is made by the writer and sound-recordist Martin Wilkinson, who also knew Nick:

'Despite its glamorous image, the reality of the "rock'n'roll" lifestyle was in fact corrupt and seedy . . . Cheap hotels, decaying dance halls, bad hours, sexual abandon, transport, girls, food, overindulgence in drugs and alchohol – all dangerous to health, mental balance and self-esteem.

'Given Nick's character and previous experience and the high quality of his music, it must have been a nasty shock for him to find out that this was the reality he was supposed to work within. Perhaps tougher people with less to say could survive it, and many did; but for someone like Nick it must have seemed a living nightmare at times.'

So, with hindsight, it is obvious that the 'live performance' method of promotion was not for Nick – but that was hardly apparent at the time. And the other method – that of 'broadcast exposure' – was simply unavailable to an artist with no apparent hit-single material, and practically no profile in the pulsating world of pop music, teeming as it was with vociferous candidates demanding their place on the airwaves.

But if Nick's one abortive tour had a positive outcome, it was perhaps its contribution to his dawning realisation that there had to be a different way for him to get his message across. Although another album was to come – *Bryter Layter*, which still depended on (very beautiful) orchestral arrangements – finally, though plagued by increasing mental depression, Nick, with his third album *Pink Moon* had the confidence to say: 'This is to be just me – my voice and my guitar.' The album, though stark, is a direct and intimate communication with the listener. And perhaps the greatest endorsement of the fact that he was right is the discovery many have subsequently made of Nick Drake's music in the intimacy of their homes, through that great invention which was hardly more than an inchoate thought in a scientist's mind at the time: the Internet.

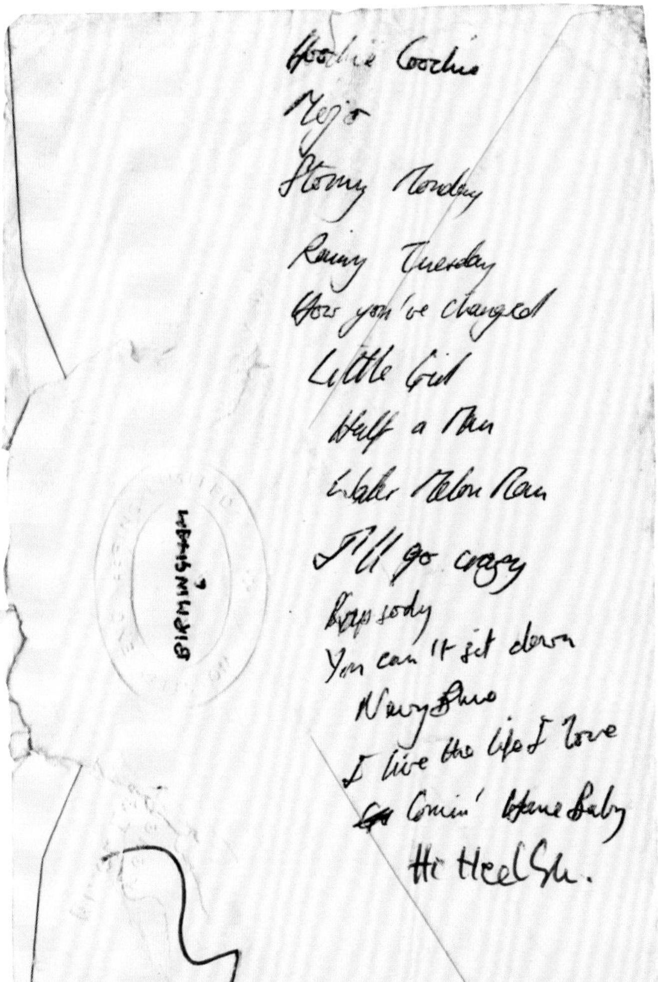
Hoochie Coochie
Mojo
Stormy Monday
Rainy Tuesday
How you've changed
Little Girl
Half a Man
Walker Below Rain
I'll go crazy
Rhapsody
You can't sit down
Navy Blue
I live the life I love
Comin' Home Baby
Hi Heel Sn.
BIRMINGHAM

A Chronology Of Nick Drake's Live Performances

1968	(unknown date)	Cambridge University: Bateman Room Concert
1968	(unknown date)	21st-Birthday Party for Brian Wells's wife (with full Octet)
1968	February	London. Roundhouse Peace Festival, on a bill headlined by Country Joe and The Fish
1968	May	Private party, Tanworth-in-Arden
1969	(undated)	Pitt Club, Cambridge, with orchestra
1969	10 June	Cambridge University: Gonville and Caius May Ball
1969	24 September	London Royal Festival Hall, supporting Fairport Convention, and John and Beverley Martyn
1969	4 October	The Goodwill To All Pub, Middlesex (supported by FolkOmnibus)
1969	15 November	Les Cousins Folk Club, London
1969	(unknown date)	Hull, Haworth Club, witnessed by songwriter and performer Michael Chapman
1969	(unknown date)	Coventry Apprentices Christmas Ball
1969	(unknown dates)	Birmingham, Smethwick; guest performer, Keen and Nettlefolds Works Social Club
1970	(unknown dates)	Three bookings at Les Cousins Club, London, one with John Martyn and Mike Cooper, one with Third Ear Band, and one with John James.
1970	24 January	The Adrian Mann Theatre, Ewell College Campus, Surrey; Ewell Technical College, Reigate, Surrey. Opening for headliners Atomic Rooster, plus Genesis
1970	6 February	Free Trade Hall, Manchester, supporting Fairport Convention
1970	14 February	Leeds University: Student Union Concert, supporting Genesis
1970	21 February	Queen Elizabeth Hall, London, supporting John and Beverley Martyn
1970	16 March	Birmingham Town Hall, supporting Fotheringay
1970	18 March	De Montfort Hall, Leicester, supporting Fotheringay
1970	20 March	Free Trade Hall, Manchester, supporting Fotheringay
1970	22 March	Colston Hall, Bristol, supporting Fotheringay
1970	30 March	Royal Festival Hall, London, supporting Fotheringay
1970	8 May	Regent's Park, London: Bedford College All-Nighter, featuring Graham Bond, East of Eden, May Blitz, Climax Chicago Blues Band, Raw Spirit, Black August, Group X, Jo-Ann Kelly, Spencer Davis, and John Martyn
1970	(unknown date)	Thought to have appeared at a Yorkshire Festival supporting Free as the headliners
1970	25 June	The Adrian Mann Theatre, Ewell College Campus, Surrey; Ewell Technical College, Reigate, supporting Ralph McTell
1970	14–16 August	Krumlin Festival, Yorkshire. This may be the venue where a tall man, not unlike Nick Drake, walked past a camera and was captured on film for all to see on YouTube many years later.
1973	April	Nick offered a ¼-hour slot at the London Palladium Charity Show

Nick was rumoured to have played – or not played – at the Dagenham Roundhouse (Essex) for the Village Blues Club in 1970, but 'didn't show so Krakatoa played instead'. He was also thought to have played at an all-nighter at the London Lyceum at some point between 1969 and 1971.

Live performance dossier compiled with grateful thanks to Richard Morton Jack, Steve Kelly, Steve Webb, and Bruce Lyall of Recycled Records in San Francisco

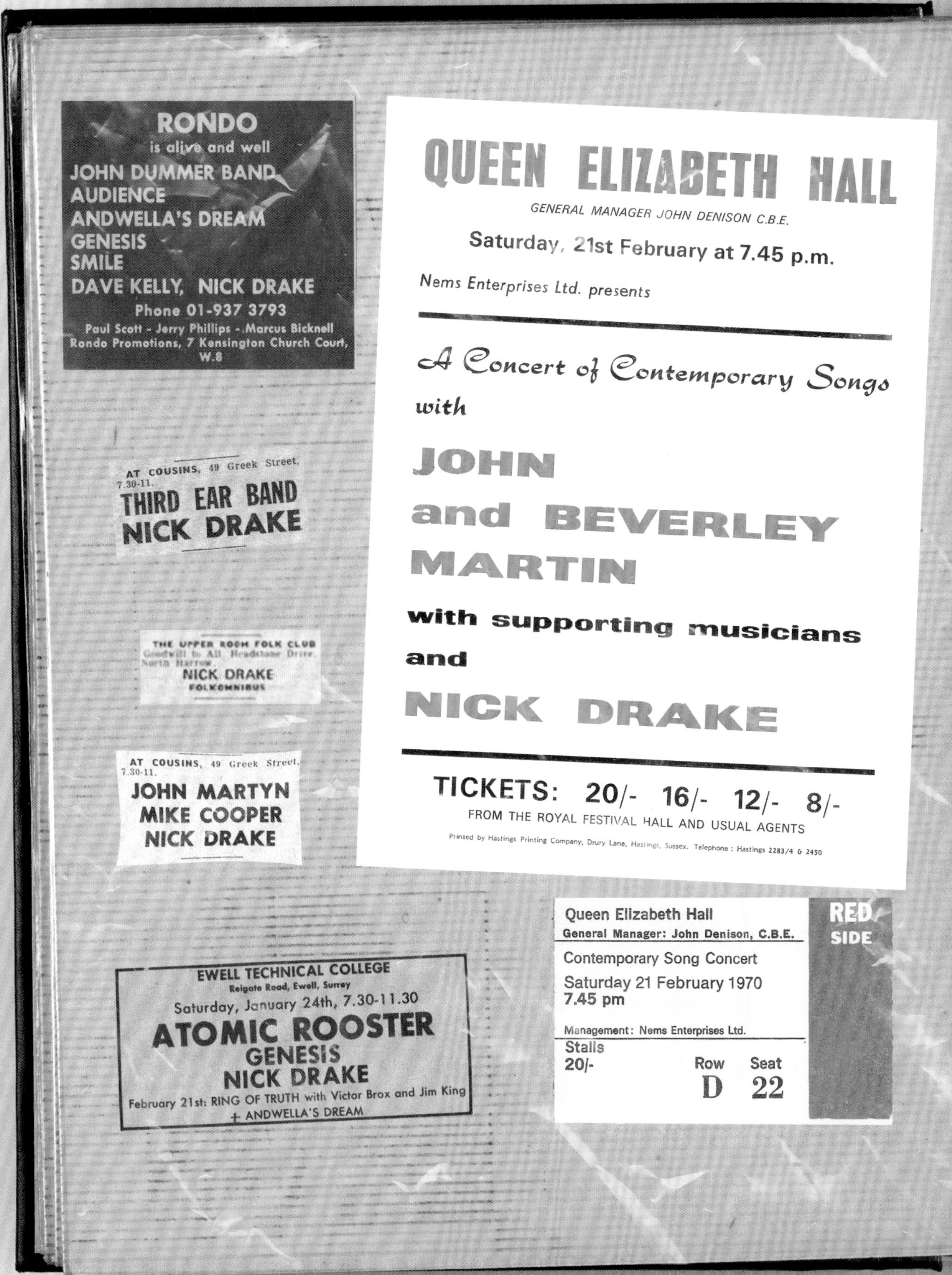

RONDO
is alive and well
JOHN DUMMER BAND
AUDIENCE
ANDWELLA'S DREAM
GENESIS
SMILE
DAVE KELLY, NICK DRAKE
Phone 01-937 3793
Paul Scott - Jerry Phillips - Marcus Bicknell
Rondo Promotions, 7 Kensington Church Court, W.8
AT COUSINS, 49 Greek Street, 7.30-11.
THIRD EAR BAND
NICK DRAKE
THE UPPER ROOM FOLK CLUB
Goodwill to All, Headstone Drive, North Harrow.
NICK DRAKE
FOLKOMNIBUS
AT COUSINS, 49 Greek Street, 7.30-11.
JOHN MARTYN
MIKE COOPER
NICK DRAKE
EWELL TECHNICAL COLLEGE
Reigate Road, Ewell, Surrey
Saturday, January 24th, 7.30-11.30
ATOMIC ROOSTER
GENESIS
NICK DRAKE
February 21st: RING OF TRUTH with Victor Brox and Jim King
+ ANDWELLA'S DREAM
QUEEN ELIZABETH HALL
GENERAL MANAGER JOHN DENISON C.B.E.
Saturday, 21st February at 7.45 p.m.
Nems Enterprises Ltd. presents
A Concert of Contemporary Songs
with
JOHN
and BEVERLEY
MARTIN
with supporting musicians
and
NICK DRAKE
TICKETS: 20/- 16/- 12/- 8/-
FROM THE ROYAL FESTIVAL HALL AND USUAL AGENTS
Printed by Hastings Printing Company, Drury Lane, Hastings, Sussex. Telephone : Hastings 2283/4 & 2450
Queen Elizabeth Hall
General Manager: John Denison, C.B.E.
Contemporary Song Concert
Saturday 21 February 1970
7.45 pm
Management: Nems Enterprises Ltd.
Stalls
20/-
Row
D
Seat
22
RED
SIDE

Above left: *Melody Maker*, 20 December 1970
Below left and above it: *Melody Maker*, 24 January 1970 and 17 January 1970

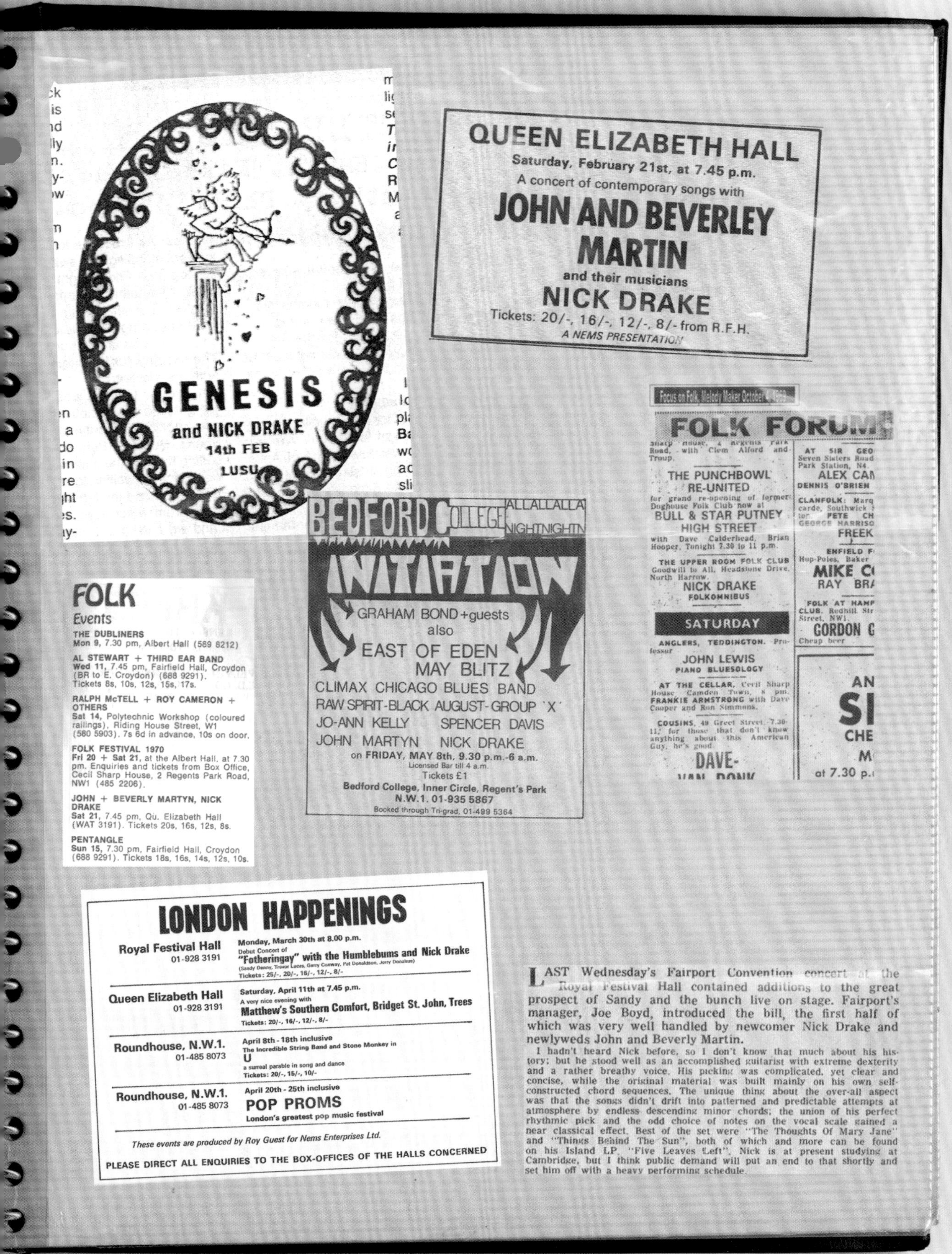

QUEEN ELIZABETH HALL
Saturday, February 21st, at 7.45 p.m.
A concert of contemporary songs with
JOHN AND BEVERLEY MARTIN
and their musicians
NICK DRAKE
Tickets: 20/-, 16/-, 12/-, 8/- from R.F.H.
A NEMS PRESENTATION

Focus on Folk, Melody Maker October [illegible]

FOLK FORUM

Road, with Clem Alford and Troup.

THE PUNCHBOWL RE-UNITED for grand re-opening of former Doghouse Folk Club now at BULL & STAR PUTNEY HIGH STREET with Dave Calderhead, Brian Hooper. Tonight 7.30 to 11 p.m.

THE UPPER ROOM FOLK CLUB Goodwill to All, Headstone Drive, North Harrow. NICK DRAKE FOLKOMNIBUS

SATURDAY

ANGLERS, TEDDINGTON. Professor JOHN LEWIS PIANO BLUESOLOGY

AT THE CELLAR, Cecil Sharp House, Camden Town, 8 pm. FRANKIE ARMSTRONG with Dave Cooper and Ron Simmons.

COUSINS, 49 Greek Street, 7.30-11, for those that don't know anything about this American Guy, he's good. DAVE-

Seven Sisters Road Park Station, N4.
DENNIS O'BRIEN
Hop-Poles, Baker
Street, NW1.
Cheap beer

FOLK
Events

THE DUBLINERS
Mon 9, 7.30 pm, Albert Hall (589 8212)

AL STEWART + THIRD EAR BAND
Wed 11, 7.45 pm, Fairfield Hall, Croydon (BR to E. Croydon) (688 9291). Tickets 8s, 10s, 12s, 15s, 17s.

RALPH McTELL + ROY CAMERON + OTHERS
Sat 14, Polytechnic Workshop (coloured railings), Riding House Street, W1 (580 5903). 7s 6d in advance, 10s on door.

FOLK FESTIVAL 1970
Fri 20 + Sat 21, at the Albert Hall, at 7.30 pm. Enquiries and tickets from Box Office, Cecil Sharp House, 2 Regents Park Road, NW1 (485 2206).

JOHN + BEVERLY MARTYN, NICK DRAKE
Sat 21, 7.45 pm, Qu. Elizabeth Hall (WAT 3191). Tickets 20s, 16s, 12s, 8s.

PENTANGLE
Sun 15, 7.30 pm, Fairfield Hall, Croydon (688 9291). Tickets 18s, 16s, 14s, 12s, 10s.

BEDFORD COLLEGE
ALLALLALLA NIGHTNIGHTN
INITIATION
GRAHAM BOND + guests
also
EAST OF EDEN
MAY BLITZ
CLIMAX CHICAGO BLUES BAND
RAW SPIRIT - BLACK AUGUST - GROUP 'X'
JO-ANN KELLY SPENCER DAVIS
JOHN MARTYN NICK DRAKE
on FRIDAY, MAY 8th, 9.30 p.m.-6 a.m.
Licensed Bar till 4 a.m.
Tickets £1
Bedford College, Inner Circle, Regent's Park
N.W.1. 01-935 5867
Booked through Tri-grad, 01-499 5364

LONDON HAPPENINGS

Royal Festival Hall 01-928 3191	Monday, March 30th at 8.00 p.m. Debut Concert of "Fotheringay" with the Humblebums and Nick Drake (Sandy Denny, Trevor Lucas, Gerry Conway, Pat Donaldson, Jerry Donahue) Tickets: 25/-, 20/-, 16/-, 12/-, 8/-
Queen Elizabeth Hall 01-928 3191	Saturday, April 11th at 7.45 p.m. A very nice evening with Matthew's Southern Comfort, Bridget St. John, Trees Tickets: 20/-, 16/-, 12/-, 8/-
Roundhouse, N.W.1. 01-485 8073	April 8th - 18th inclusive The Incredible String Band and Stone Monkey in U a surreal parable in song and dance Tickets: 20/-, 15/-, 10/-
Roundhouse, N.W.1. 01-485 8073	April 20th - 25th inclusive POP PROMS London's greatest pop music festival

These events are produced by Roy Guest for Nems Enterprises Ltd.

PLEASE DIRECT ALL ENQUIRIES TO THE BOX-OFFICES OF THE HALLS CONCERNED

LAST Wednesday's Fairport Convention concert at the Royal Festival Hall contained additions to the great prospect of Sandy and the bunch live on stage. Fairport's manager, Joe Boyd, introduced the bill, the first half of which was very well handled by newcomer Nick Drake and newlyweds John and Beverly Martin.

I hadn't heard Nick before, so I don't know that much about his history; but he stood well as an accomplished guitarist with extreme dexterity and a rather breathy voice. His picking was complicated, yet clear and concise, while the original material was built mainly on his own self-constructed chord sequences. The unique thing about the over-all aspect was that the songs didn't drift into patterned and predictable attempts at atmosphere by endless descending minor chords; the union of his perfect rhythmic pick and the odd choice of notes on the vocal scale gained a near classical effect. Best of the set were "The Thoughts Of Mary Jane" and "Things Behind The Sun", both of which and more can be found on his Island LP "Five Leaves Left". Nick is at present studying at Cambridge, but I think public demand will put an end to that shortly and set him off with a heavy performing schedule.

Centre: *Melody Maker*, 9 May 1970
Below left: *Time Out*, 21 March–4 April 1970

NICK DRAKE

HUMBLEBUMS

The Humblebums and Nick Drake opened and neither did much for me. The latter hunches over acoustic guitar and sings his own songs in a pleasant voice that seems to slide out of the corner of his mouth. The songs themselves are good but the fact that they were all in the same low key tended to send me to sleep.

Inset right: Live review by Nick Logan, *NME*, 4 April 1970

Roy Guest *presents*

FOTHERINGAY

THE HUMBLEBUMS

NICK DRAKE

Birmingham Town Hall	March 16th	1970
Leicester de Montfort Hall	March 18th	
Manchester Free Trade Hall	March 20th	
Bristol Colston Hall	March 22nd	
Royal Festival Hall (general manager: John Denison CBE)	March 30th	

No smoking in the auditorium

The taking of photographs in the auditorium is not permitted

In accordance with the requirements of the Greater London Council Persons shall not be permitted to stand or sit in any of the gangways inter seating, or to sit in any of the other gangways.

First Aid facilities are provided by the British Red Cross Society.

A Nems Presentation

MUSIC NOW LIVE!

THE INFLUENCE of contemporary folk music on the current scene verges on the phenomenal yet many of its finest exponents seem to be in a quandry as to how to project and progress their talents.

At London's Queen Elizabeth Hall last Saturday (21), John and Bevereley Martin shone through four acoustic backed numbers yet appeared totally run of the mill when joined by their electric guitar, bass and drums trio. Certainly the band came on with some tight, crisp sounds but so much of the duo's most worthwhile material demands a simple mood setting rather than raunchy heaviness.

John himself is an excellent musician, plugged in or not, but he seemed far happier with acoustic guitar across his knee singing songs like "Road To Ruin" and "Jelly Roll." Before launching into his famed "Black Roses" instrumental, during which he moves his capo up and down the guitar neck, he announced his intention of dropping the number from his act. Pity.

Earlier in the evening, Nick Drake, with one album out on Island and another to follow soon, exercised his throaty voice around a bunch of rather samey songs. "The Thoughts Of Mary Jane" and "Hey Slow Jane" came across well but Nick should endeavour to vary the tempo and setting of his songs rather more. Likewise, whilst his intricate guitar picking is superb, it would be something of a joy to hear him let rip with a simple free strum.

John and Beverley and Nick would, I believe, find wider, more appreciative response from audiences if they were to examine their presentation closely and retread their undeniable talents. (D.F.)

THE NEW SEEKERS have made it for themselves and what threatened to be shadows of the ghosts of you know who, turned out to be an evening of overwhelming enthusiasm and talent.

Naturally "Georgie Girl" and "I'll Never Find Another You" featured in the first medley, then the group swung easily into 'non-seekers' numbers such as "Island of Dreams" (Springfields) "Monday, Monday" (Mamas & Papas) and "Up and Away" (Jim Webb) with considerable verve.

A few comedy items followed and although enjoyable I felt they should not have 'knocked' Sandie Shaw so badly — However, this was the only discordant note.

The rest of the concert was almost 'whole family' entertainment including songs from 'Oliver' and such, and even items from Scotland, all of which proved that their whole range is so good that there must be a great future ahead of them especially in television spectaculars. Certainly they deserved all the audience's enthusiasm at the end of this memorable evening.

Below right: *Top Pops & Music Now*, 28 February 1970

WEREWOLF MANAGEMENT & AGENCY

now representing all WITCHSEASON artists

THE INCREDIBLE STRING BAND
FAIRPORT CONVENTION*
FOTHERINGAY
(Sandy Denny, Trevor Lucas, Pat Donaldson
Gerry Conway, Jerry Donahue)
JOHN & BEVERLEY MARTYN
NICK DRAKE
CHRIS McGREGOR'S GROUP AND BIG BAND
DUDU PUKWANA AND THE SPEAR

All enquiries to Huw Price, (01)-636 9436, (01)-580 5874

WITCHSEASON WARLOCK WEREWOLF
83 Charlotte Street, London, W.1

(*Shared with Nems Ltd. at this time)

BEDFORD COLLEGE UNION SOCIETY
presents
DEBUT SUPER SESSION
with
GRAHAM BOND
RIC GRECH
plus Guests
and also
EAST OF EDEN
MAY BLITZ
CLIMAX CHICAGO BLUES BAND
RAW SPIRIT • BLACK AUGUST • GROUP 'X'
and
JO-ANN KELLY • SPENCER DAVIS
JOHN MARTYN • NICK DRAKE
on
FRIDAY, MAY 8th, 9.30 p.m.-6 a.m.
Tickets £1
Bedford College, Inner Circle, Regent's Park, N.W.1. 01-935 5867

SATURDAY

ACTUAL PEANUTS. Kings Arms, 213 Bishopsgate.
NICK HARRISON
and guests.

ANGLERS TEDDINGTON:
JO ANN KELLY

AT COUSINS, 49 Greek Street, 7.30-11.
THIRD EAR BAND
NICK DRAKE

AT THE CELLAR. Cecil Sharp House, Camden Town, 8 pm. JOHNNY COLLINS, DAVE COOPER AND JENNY BEECHING.

FO'C'STLE, "Castle" Fairfield West, Kingston.
SANDY'S NIGHT

SATURDAY

"ANGLERS," TEDDINGTON
NIKKI
HORIZON

AT THE CELLAR, Cecil Sharp House, Camden Town 8.0 pm. COME ALL YE, DAVE COOPER AND JENNY BEECHING.

AT COUSINS, 49 Greek Street, 7.30-11.
JOHN JAMES
NICK DRAKE
and bassist friend

EWELL TECHNICAL COLLEGE
Folk Club Concert in the Adrian Mann Theatre
Thursday, 25th June, at 7.30
RALPH McTELL
NICK DRAKE
10/- S.U., 12/- Guests In advance from Social Secretary
Booked through Rondo Promotions, 01-493 0512/0559

Say John Martyn . . . LOUDER!

JOHN MARTYN's family are very proud of him. And to show that they are, they travel great distances to see him when he does big concerts like the Queen Elizabeth Hall in London.

"It makes me nervous. I was terrified when I did the Sandy Denny concert at the QE hall, because the wife's family, right down to Uncle George, came down from Coventry to watch. It's very unnerving."

John's wife, Beverly, has given up working with him in the clubs because she is too busy being a full-time mum to their two children. She still works on his albums and may well return to music when her children are a little older. She appeared on John's latest album "Bless The Weather" and there are plans for her to do a solo album when she gets the time.

"Beverly is anxious to work again. Being a good singer is a heavy thing, but being a mother is heavy, too. The two together don't always work. I feel the same about this album as I did about the last one, "Stormbringer" except this one is a litle purer.

"Also, I didn't have the hassles with this one. With 'Stormbringer' I had to travel to the States to get the musicians I wanted—like Harvey Brooks and John Simon—primarily for a rhythm section. The track 'Just Now' is the best thing I've done I think."

However, John had planned on doing something different with this album had he had a bigger budget to work with. But as "Stormbringer" didn't break sales records, the budget was kept to two thousand pounds.

"I might have done an electric album. That doesn't mean I don't dig "Bless The Weather," I do, but I may do the next album with electric instruments. I've been using them since the last album and it provides more scope. There isn't much adaptation, I just have to sing louder. With acoustic music, you can only do a few things a few ways but with a wider tonal quality, there are more possibilities."

Although he isn't really a typical singles artist, a single has just been brought out of his song "May You Never." John isn't ecstatic about it and thinks that it will probably just do nothing.

Although John did a few of the songs from the album at the QE hall, he generally tries not to emphasise his album in the way that many artists take the opportunity of plugging a record.

"Sometimes I consciously avoid pushing the album. The people in the audiences are sharp and they can suss anyone that's up there just to make a quick one. Everybody should have a good time at concerts.

"The music industry in general is looking for a shot in the arm, a new era, a new Beatles, but they are trying to manufacture one.

"It doesn't work trying to do that. As to the BBC's programmes on Radio 1—I don't hate them, but I resent them. I think, for instance, that they should devote a whole show to ethnic folk music because it's important. It's not the only music for me by any means, but I started out doing folk."

At the moment, John is half thinking about finding a bass player and a drummer, but wants to make sure he gets exactly the kind of musicians he needs.

"It's a matter of finding the right people. You have to consider what you like playing and also you have to keep a certain looseness so that ideas can be worked out. There are a few

JOHN MARTYN . . . good time concerts

artists I really admire, although I wouldn't say I wanted to play like them. I respect John McLaughlin and Nick Drake, because they are good guitarists. I'd like to be able to play as well, but not the same.

John has been taking a lot of work lately, but mainly around the South of England, within travelling distance of his home in Hastings. However, there is a chance that he will be doing some work in the States in the New Year and before then he will be going to Belgium and Holland for 10 days.

ROSALIND RUSSELL

Below: *Disc & Music Echo*, 11 December 1970

GIGS!!
FOTHERINGAY

ROYAL FESTIVAL HALL, Monday, March 30th.

FOTHERINGAY, AS EXPECTED, as expected had the largest PA system I,ve seen assembled on a British Stage for many a month and it also turned out to match its immense size with immense efficiency. Taking advantage of the tonal purity offered by the custom built system were the two supporting acts, the Humblebums and Nick Drake. Gerry Rafferty and William Connolly, who together with a three piece backing group make up the Humblebums, presented a humourous and varied selection of their original material which for me, bore little resemblence to that on their Transatlantic album but was nonetheless entertaining. Connolly was shouldered with the responsibility of providing the group's stage act, which he only just managed with his almost unintelligible Scottish humour and appropriate gesticulations – a sort of restrained tartan Jethro Tull.

There was a short burst of applause for Nick Drake's first number, 'Time Has Told Me', which must prove something about the sales figures for his first album, 'Five Leaves Left'. But Drake's music turned out to be stronger than his personality for his act lacked presence or vitality and the beautiful arrangements that mad the album so memorable. It seemed he felt a little uncertain as to whether or not he wanted to make public performances, there being little or no communication with the audience who nevertheless gave his basically excellent music a basically well deserved reception.

Feeling very sad, owing to some very bad-luck that I am having at the moment, I went along this evening to the **Royal Festival Hall** to attend the **Fairport Convention**, in the up-lifting company of **B. P. Fallon**, Press Officer for **Island Records**, I had a beautiful evening.

Have you listened to **"Five Leaves Left," Nick Drake's** new album? I reviewed it some weeks ago. Well Nick was one of the Fairport's 'friends', on the bill. He was very popular with the audience —as he deserves to be!

Other 'friends' of the Fairport were, **John Martyn** and his wife, **Beverley.** They have an album coming out in November on Island.

MAY 25, 1968, **BILLBOARD**

Above left: *International Times*, 9 April 1970   Right: *Billboard*, USA, 25 May 1968
Below left: 'Simon Stable's Stable Diet' column, *Top Pops & Music Now*, 4 October 1979

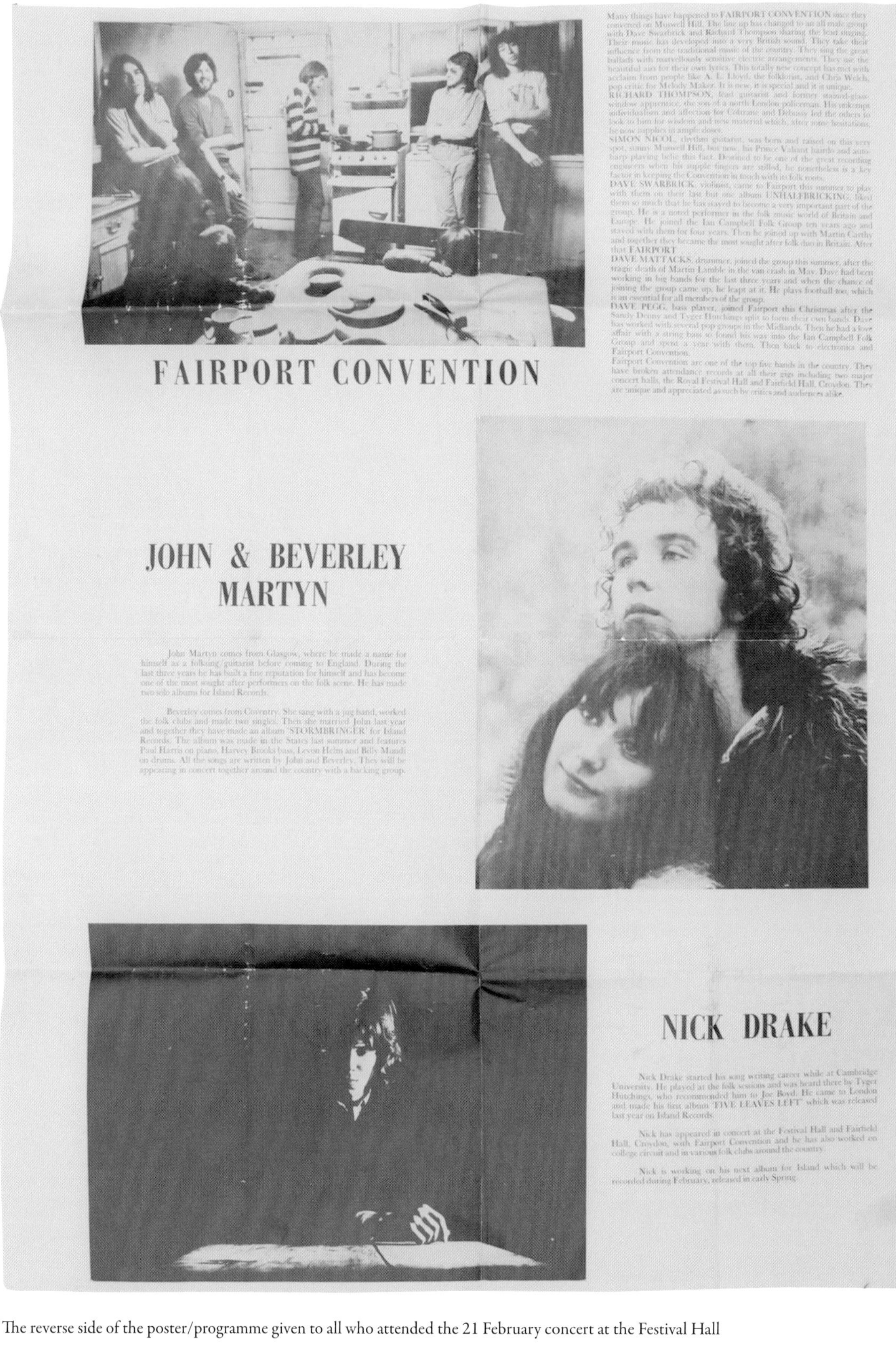

Many things have happened to **FAIRPORT CONVENTION** since they convened on Muswell Hill. The line up has changed to an all male group with Dave Swarbrick and Richard Thompson sharing the lead singing. Their music has developed into a very British sound. They take their influence from the traditional music of the country. They sing the great ballads with marvellously sensitive electric arrangements. They use the beautiful airs for their own lyrics. This totally new concept has met with acclaim from people like A. L. Lloyd, the folklorist, and Chris Welch, pop critic for Melody Maker. It is new, it is special and it is unique.

RICHARD THOMPSON, lead guitarist and former stained-glass-window apprentice, the son of a north London policeman. His unkempt individualism and affection for Coltrane and Debussy led the others to look to him for wisdom and new material which, after some hesitations, he now supplies in ample doses.

SIMON NICOL, rhythm guitarist, was born and raised on this very spot, sunny Muswell Hill, but now, his Prince Valiant hairdo and auto-harp playing belie this fact. Destined to be one of the great recording engineers when his supple fingers are stilled, he nonetheless is a key factor in keeping the Convention in touch with its folk roots.

DAVE SWARBRICK, violinist, came to Fairport this summer to play with them on their last but one album **UNHALFBRICKING**, liked them so much that he has stayed to become a very important part of the group. He is a noted performer in the folk music world of Britain and Europe. He joined the Ian Campbell Folk Group ten years ago and stayed with them for four years. Then he joined up with Martin Carthy and together they became the most sought after folk duo in Britain. After that **FAIRPORT** .

DAVE MATTACKS, drummer, joined the group this summer, after the tragic death of Martin Lamble in the van crash in May. Dave had been working in big bands for the last three years and when the chance of joining the group came up, he leapt at it. He plays football too, which is an essential for all members of the group.

DAVE PEGG, bass player, joined Fairport this Christmas after the Sandy Denny and Tyger Hutchings split to form their own bands. Dave has worked with several pop groups in the Midlands. Then he had a love affair with a string bass so found his way into the Ian Campbell Folk Group and spent a year with them. Then back to electronics and Fairport Convention.

Fairport Convention are one of the top five bands in the country. They have broken attendance records at all their gigs including two major concert halls, the Royal Festival Hall and Fairfield Hall, Croydon. They are unique and appreciated as such by critics and audiences alike.

FAIRPORT CONVENTION

JOHN & BEVERLEY MARTYN

John Martyn comes from Glasgow, where he made a name for himself as a folksing/guitarist before coming to England. During the last three years he has built a fine reputation for himself and has become one of the most sought after performers on the folk scene. He has made two solo albums for Island Records.

Beverley comes from Coventry. She sang with a jug band, worked the folk clubs and made two singles. Then she married John last year and together they have made an album 'STORMBRINGER' for Island Records. The album was made in the States last summer and features Paul Harris on piano, Harvey Brooks bass, Levon Helm and Billy Mundi on drums. All the songs are written by John and Beverley. They will be appearing in concert together around the country with a backing group.

NICK DRAKE

Nick Drake started his song writing career while at Cambridge University. He played at the folk sessions and was heard there by Tyger Hutchings, who recommended him to Joe Boyd. He came to London and made his first album 'FIVE LEAVES LEFT' which was released last year on Island Records.

Nick has appeared in concert at the Festival Hall and Fairfield Hall, Croydon, with Fairport Convention and he has also worked on college circuit and in various folk clubs around the country.

Nick is working on his next album for Island which will be recorded during February, released in early Spring.

The reverse side of the poster/programme given to all who attended the 21 February concert at the Festival Hall

Island set for album push

AFTER several months of apparent inactivity, Island has prepared a five-album release for March, to be followed in April and May with nine further albums, one of them a sampler of the new product.

Title and contents of the sampler have yet to be decided. The March releases is comprised of albums from Nick Drake titled 'Bryter Layter'; 'Dive Deep', the third by Quintessence; the first album by the Incredible String Band since moving to Island for Europe, title 'Be Glad, For The Song Has No End'; 'Wildlife' by Mott the Hoople and 'Aqualung' by Jethro Tull.

April and May will see albums by Incredible String Band's Mike Heron working solo, a new act called Tira Na Nog, Mick Abrahams who was formerly with Blodwyn Pig, Sandy Denny recording as a solo artist following breakup of her group Fotheringay, Fairport Convention, Emerson Lake and Palmer, Cat Stevens and Jimmy Cliff, making his album bow on Island since shifting from the Trojan reggae label.

Album." After the tour the group go to America.

The British tour begins at Liverpool Stadium on March 4 followed by Llandaff College, Cardiff (5 Apple, Brighton (6), Jazz Club (7), Birm Town Hall Bournemouth Gardens (10), D Top Rank Ballroo St. George's Hall B (14), Guildford C (15), Nottingham Hall (16), S University (19), Centre (20), Du Kinema (21) and City Hall (22).

On six dates, Birmingham, Bo Blackburn, Guil Nottingham the be joined by singer with Johnathan Swif

Heep in

URIAH Heep's America has forward an commence on five week iti

393, Fishpounds Rd.
Bristol. BS5 6RJ.
Oct. 22nd.

Dear Nick,

You're probably what on earth I'm writing to you for, only just recently I bought a copy of your 'Bryter Layter' LP, whilst buying the "Moody Blues' latest LP, and I bought it out of sheer curiosity.

Although this LP is by far one of the best I've got, forgive me please for being so rude in asking, but who are you? All I know is that you've been around sometime. (!!). If you can find the time to reply and tell me ~~how~~ who you are I would be grateful. Look after yourself, the man with big shoes,

with love,

Helen

...nd Beverley Martyn

...America to make an LP of their ...ongs. They returned with

"STORMBRINGER!"

The Players: JOHN MARTYN guitar & vocals, BEVERLEY MARTYN vocals, PAUL HARRIS piano, organ, arrangements, HARVEY BROOKS bass, LEVON HELM, BILLY MUNDI drums.

ILPS 9113.

JOHN & BEVERLEY MARTYN and NICK DRAKE in concert
21 February Queen Elizabeth Hall.

Above: *Record Mirror*, 20 February 1971
Centre: From Nick's wallet
Below: *Time Out*, 21 February 1970

Page 36—MELODY MAKER, March 6, 1971
YAMAHA
Nick Drake
Bryter Layter
Nick Drake is a folk singer who writes and sings all his own songs. He was discovered a little while back by the Fairport Convention. Bryter Layter, his second album, has been a long time in the making. It's been worth the wait.
Bryter Layter: Out now ILPS 9134

NME, 6 March 1971

DAILY TELEGRAPH
OCTOBER 13TH 1969

In Britain there continue to appear new and promising young recruits to the singers of our time. Nick Drake, who made a brief but impressive appearance at a recent London concert, has an excellent LP of his own songs ("Five leaves left"—Island ILPS-9105) in which his own slightly hypnotic guitar is backed by Richard Thompson, Danny Thompson (bass) and Paul Harris (piano). His voice is slow, reflective and warm, and although the verse structure tends to melodic monotony, there is no mistaking the quality and the promise of "River man," "The Thoughts of Mary Jane," "Man in a Shed" and other items on this disc. (On Side One, incidentally, "Day is done" and "Way to blue" are in the reverse order to that given on the label and the sleeve).

THE TIMES APRIL 1st 1970

Group of promise

Festival Hall

Fotheringay

Basically, Fotheringay, who made their debut at the Royal Festival Hall on Easter Monday, consists of some of the most talented members of three other groups — Sandy Denny from Fairport Convention, Trevor Lucas and Gerry Conway from Eclection, and Pat Donaldson and Jerry Donahue from Poet and the One-Man Band. At the moment they rather sound like it.

There is plenty of talent around in the group, no doubt of it. When they have, as the saying goes, got it together, Fotheringay will really dazzle all the time, as they did during Sandy Denny's slow recitative of "The Banks of the Nile", a traditional ballad from the time of Nelson, and in their encore, the country-styled classic tear-jerker, "Silver Threads and Golden Needles".

Guitarist Donahue showed his instrumental virtuosity in "The Claw" and more interestingly in his apt interpolations throughout the other songs. Conway hereby joins the ranks of the few rock drummers with sufficient sensitivity to accompany folk items and not smash them to pieces.

But generally, there is not yet a clear identity coming through the massive, specially built loudspeakers, successfully designed to balance the voices and electric sound of the group. It will come, certainly, for this was only their fifth public appearance.

It is one of the pitfalls of present-day pop that groups no longer have to slog their way round the lesser-known clubs, climbing their way laboriously into the front rank. A new group like Fotheringay can command a reasonable attendance at a top concert hall purely on the basis of word-of-mouth report and individual past careers. So it is not surprising that they show promise rather than fulfilment.

The same could be said of the two supporting items on the programme, the Humblebums, now well backed with an electric trio, and Nick Drake a contemporary song writer of talent but little stage presence.

The Humblebums have made the difficult transition from folk club duo to concert hall presentation with some success, though again their material seems to fall into separate pigeon holes. Gerry Rafferty's songs have the sweet tenderness of Paul McCartney in his "Yesterday" mood, while Billy Connolly, senior member of the group, has lustier material rooted still in the folk clubs that produced him

It seems somewhat unfair on Drake to pitch him straight into concerts without the grassroots training he'd get humping his guitar round the country from club to club. This is the third time I have heard him in concert, and each time more of his music has got through to me but still he remains a performer more for the intimate club, or the recording studio, I feel.

Still, if he were playing the club circuit, it is unlikely that he would have the chance of working with a bass player as good as Chris Lawrence, who really contributed a great deal to the instrumental passages in the songs.

Karl Dallas

NICK DRAKE
Island

Nick Drake — who is, despite his name, a singer/songwriter and not a prototypical 1942-vintage private detective radio hero — has made a first album that sounds vaguely like Donovan re-thinking "Astral Weeks", but lest you misunderstand me, it works wonderfully and adds up to one of those elusive but tenacious lps that simply won't stay off the turntable for very long.

There's a hint of the rogue about Nick Drake (betrayed not only by the photos of him that adorn the album jacket and by the songs he writes but also by the way he sings), a suggestion — and not much more than that — that he is the innocent, tousle-haired boy on the outside only and that inside, from whence his music springs, there lurks a wise heart, a well-educated soul. There's the slightest inclination that he's setting forth, in other words, a far more important kind of music than his soft voice and the mellow, jazz-flavored backgrounds that accompany it would at first lead one to believe. Beneath the voice, and sometimes hidden by it, are the words, and beneath the words (which are not all that good in most cases, by the way, at least not in the sense that they can be quoted out of context to illustrate, in this review, some pertinent point or other), there is a spirit, a feeling, a sense of wise mystery, of shrewd delineation of time and place and character, which is not specifically lyrical.

Drake's own guitar is big and full and confident; the other musicians are incredibly right: Chris McGregor (whose Brotherhood of Breath is probably the best big band in England) plays smartly ringing piano on "Poor Boy"; altoist Ray Warleigh soars through that song and through "At the Chime of a City Clock"; Clare Lowther's claret cello enrichens "'Cello Song" (what else?); Pat Arnold and Doris Troy swallow their infamous vibrations long enough to add a flowing, haunting chorus to "Poor Boy"; the effulgent John Cale plays celeste, piano, and organ on "Northern Sky" and viola and harpsichord on "Fly"; Paul Harris' piano brightens the buoyant, Buckley-like "One of These Things First"; Fairport Conventioneer Dave Pegg (who shares bass duties with Ed Carter and Danny Thompson) plays broad, linear patterns reminiscent of Richard Davis' work on "Astral Weeks" or on an album called "Tax Free" by the group of the same name, which also featured John Cale to good advantage and which otherwise resembles "Nick Drake" in its fluidity, its overall tenor.

What all this fine accompaniment adds up to, together with Drake's warm, elegant capacities as an abstract imagist, an innocent illusionist, is an album of great depth, great variety, (and yet) great unity, and great importance as an extension of a tradition of music-making that has not been articulated so consistently beautifully since that wondrous Van Morrison album of three years ago.

And if it sounds to you as though I'm having a little trouble, grasping and groping for the right words to express the way "Nick Drake" strikes me, I can only say Right On, Mr. Reader. A lot of what effects me so much is precisely what escapes me; self-conscious obscurity isn't worth a damn, but sly opacity, which this record is well misted with, is worth a great deal.

By Colman Andrews

Right: *Phonograph Record Magazine*, USA, December 1971

REVIEWS

land's answer to Simon and Garfunkel: they share the same, gentle lyrics, the same use of string arrangements, and they also came up from the world of smoky folk clubs to play their music to a wider audience.

Their album *Seasons* (Vertigo) is the best showcase of their talents to date; listen to it only once, and you will feel indefinably relaxed and peaceful. One half (the best half) of the record is taken up by the 'Seasons' suite, which is a pretty, almost medieval, series of songs about the different times of the year, written by group leader Chris Simpson.

The trio's vocal harmonies and guitar work is sometimes alarmingly similar to S and G, and perhaps they could do

Nick Drake – 'relaxing'

Amen Corner were always one of Britain's brightest pop groups, thanks mainly to a combination of booting tunes and **Andy Fairweather-Low's** distinctively pained voice. Fairweather-Low became

ance myself rather than at second hand.

Anoth… month… **Elton** … notes … depen… a hun… York's … a 'live … *17-11-* … It real… with J… the tr… previc… The I… and 'I… they a… fresh … full accompaniment to Elton's light-fingered piano technique from drummer Nigel Olsson and bassist Dee Murray.

I have always been rather disappointed with **Rod Stewart**

Best of the bunch this month, however, is the new album from **Nick Drake,** *Bryter Layter* (Island). Drake's first album, *Five Leaves Left*, was, commercially speaking, a failure, but it served to make us aware of Drake's talent, a talent which has blossomed spectacularly with Bryter Layter. It's a collection of songs and tunes of Drake's own composition, gentle, relaxing and beautiful. Regrettably it will probably pass unnoticed by the general public. **MB**

ISLAND: Island Records have a large July release. Out now are three Joe Boyd produced albums by the Fairport Convention, Nick Drake, and Dr. Strangley Strange. Coming on 25 July is the new Jethro Tull album, 'Stand Up' with a pop up cover, the first Clouds album, 'Scrapbook', and 'Ahead Rings Out' by Mick Abrams' Blodwyn Pig. *Matthew Wetmore*

OCTOPUS

A programme on Granada TV about new developments, be they in music and the arts, scientific research or literally anything that's happening today. Octopus goes out at 6.05 every Wednesday and is presented by Andrew Fisher, who used to co-edit OZ magazine amongst many other things. The programme has been running since January and Granada say that it might be extended

Considering that the show is relatively new and that its length is only 25 minutes some really nice people have been on— Bruce Beresford (of the British Film Institute), Harvey Matusow (large musician and computer-abolitionist), Buckminster Fuller, Nick Drake, Angelo Quatrocchi and groups like Love, Taste, and Quintessence to name a few. All this plus synthesisers, mobiles, inflatables and a galaxy of other wonders. Ron Geesin appears on 15 April while on the 22nd that excellent rock group Mighty Baby. Future plans include John and Yoko, Caroline Coon, Bridget St John and a feature on communes in Britain.

All the credit for these goodies must go to the Octopus team of Andrew Fisher and Sue Woodford, who have demonstrated that TV can be used as a communicator of ideas and energy and not just as a means of selling detergents. He is also fortunate in having aware producers and directors around him. With the exception of World In Action (which has a lot of money to spend) Octopus is certainly the best programme on Granada. The day might come when we see Granada do a midnight show as John Peel did so effectively on radio.

As a way of helping to promote the North West, on 29 April, Andrew will be presenting several local groups on Octopus. He hasn't heard them all and so if you play in/manage a group and would like to be considered for this programme, then write (don't telephone) giving full details to **Andrew Fisher, Octopus, Granada TV, Manchester 3.**

Above left: *Club International*, 1971

Centre left: *Time Out*, 19 July–3 August 1969

Below right: 'A Guide to the North-West', No. 2, *Time Out*, 11–25 April 1970

18 Rue Galilee (off Rue Victor Hugo)

LES COUSINS

POP discs

By MICHAEL CABLE

Faces: Long Player (Warner Bros. WS 3011. Price £2·15).

Rod Stewart and co. produced one of the most outstanding albums of 1970 in *Gasoline Alley* and the only trouble with that was that it made the task of following it up extremely difficult.

Almost inevitably *Long Player* is rather disappointing by comparison. It is far from being positively bad — apart from the bottleneck rendering of *Jerusalem*, which is a waste of good plastic.

It is just a bit of an anti-climax.

Richmond and *Sweet Lady Mary*, for instance, are both very good tracks but they just do not match up to their nearest equivalents on *Gasoline Alley*, *Jo's Lament* and *Lady Day*.

Nick Drake: Bryter, Bryter (Island ILPS 9134. Price £2·15).

A former Cambridge undergraduate, 21-year-old Nick Drake gave up his studies to concentrate on songwriting and singing.

This is his second album—the first was entitled *Five Leaves Left*—and it is one of the nicest of its type I have heard.

Gentle, thoughtful songs with soft, acoustic guitar and piano backings. Probably not commercial, but then most of the best things in pop aren't.

WEEK NIGHT SESSIONS
From 7.30 p.m.

FRIDAY **and** *SATURDAY*
ALL NIGHT SESSIONS
from
12.0 p.m. - 6.0 a.m.
12.0 p.m. - 7.0 a.m.

"LES COUSINS"
LONDON'S FOLK 'N' BLUES CENTER
49 GREEK STREET, LONDON W.1
GERrard 5413

MEMBERSHIP CARD

No. 4043

Available till 10/12/1967

Name

Age

Nationality

Members Signature

Directors Signature [signature]

Members May Introduce Two Guests.
THIS CARD IS NOT TRANSFERABLE

Nick's Les Cousins membership card
Left: *Daily Mail* review as mentioned in letter by Molly Drake

NICK DRAKE was discovered by Fairport Convention some time ago and **"Bryter Layter" (Island ILPS 9134, £2.15)** is his second album. He sings his own very personal songs in a strange, deep vaseline voice, probably more suited to crooning, accompanied at times by a really funky backing. There's an amazing array of faces featured—Dave Pegg, Richard Thompson, Dave Mattacks, Lyn Dobson playing flute on the title track, Chris McGregor and John Cale on lovely things like viola, harpsichord and celeste. An extraordinarily good hefty folk album.

Quality—good. Value for money—good.

NICK DRAKE: "BRYTER LAYTER" (ISLAND ILPS 9134).

I GET the feeling that only a Joe Boyd-Paul Harris alliance could have produced such a superb album as this. And once again a great slice of the credit must go to Robert Kirby, whose splendid arrangements are as noticeable on this album as they were on Nick Drake's last album. On their own merits, the songs of Nick Drake are not particularly strong, but Nick has always been a consistent if introverted performer, and placed in the cauldron that Joe Boyd has prepared for him, then things start to effervesce. Also joining guitarist Nick Drake on various tracks are Dave Pegg, Richard Thompson, Ray Warleigh, Mike Kowalski, Paul Harris, Ed Carter, Lyn Dobson, John Cale, Chris McGregor, Pat Arnold and Doris Troy; it seems nothing has been spared to make this album a success, and Joe Boyd and Nick Drake have certainly succeeded in their intentions. There has been a long gap between Nick's first and second albums, and anyone who has seen Nick performing at Witchseason concerts in the interim will recognise tracks like "Hazey Jane". And this, like all his songs, does take time to work through to the listener, with help from the beautiful backing which every track receives. — J.G.

NICK DRAKE: "Bryter Layter" (Island ILPS 9134). This is a particularly difficult album to come to any firm conclusion on. For one thing the reaction it produced depends very much on the mood of the listener. It's late night coffee'n chat music. The ten tracks are all very similar — quiet, gentle and relaxing. Nick Drake sends his voice skimming smoothly over the backing. The range of musicians used is apt to catch one unawares. Among the talents employed are Dave Pegg (bass) and Dave Mattacks (drums) both of Fairport Convention, Richard Thompson (ld gtr) ex-Fairport, John Cale (celeste, piano and organ) ex-Velvet Underground, Ray Warleigh (alto sax), Chris McGregor (piano) and Pat Arnold and Doris Troy (backing vocals). **A. M.**

October 17, 1970

E

tracked instead of using session men."

HOT TUNA

PETER KAUKONEN, brother of Airplane and Hot Tuna guitarist Jorma Kaukonen, is starting a rock band of his own to be based in San Francisco. He's looking for a drummer so if you're interested and thnk you're good enough write to Peter care of P.O. Box 1160, San Francisco, California.

FAIRPORTS

FAIRPORTS HAD to cut short their American tour when Dave Swarbrick had a recurrence of his ear trouble. He flew back for an operation in a London Clinic.

AIRPLANE

JEFFERSON AIRPLANE has celebrated its fifth birthday as a rock group — at least its fifth birthday in this life. Since their debut the group has had three gold albums — "Surrealistic Pillow," "Crown of Creation" and "Volunteers." And to celebrate, Grace Slick and Paul Kanter will have a baby in December. A cosmic baby, no doubt.

SON HOUSE sings on new Nick Drake double album . . . Red Bus and Dawn Records are promoting a concert tour for their groups Demon Fuzz, Heron, Titues Groan and Comus. Admission at all venues will be one penny!

NICK DRAKE: Bryter Layter (Island ILPS 9134). A beautiful guitarist – clean and with perfect timing – accompanied by soft, beautiful arrangements by Robert Kirby. Nick isn't the world's top singer, but he's written fantastic numbers that suit strings marvellously. Definitely one of the prettiest (and that counts!) and most impressive albums I've heard. Remember what Mason Williams did with 'Classical Gas'? A similar concept here, but Nick does it better – it's refined. Happy, sad, very moving. L.G.

Above left: *Disc & Music Echo*, 13 March 1971 Centre: *Sounds*, 13 March 1971 Above right: *Melody Maker*, 13 March 1971
Below left: *Sounds*, 17 October 1970 Below right: *Record Mirror*, 20 March 1971

El Pea
Traffic
Mott the Hoople
Fairport Convention
Mike Heron
Nick Drake
IDLP 1

Page 36—MELODY MAKER, March 6, 1971
Nick Drake
Bryter Layter
Nick Drake is a folk singer who writes and sings all his own songs. He was discovered a little while back by the Fairport Convention. Bryter Layter, his second album, has been a long time in the making. It's been worth the wait.
Bryter Layter: Out now
ILPS 9134

Good Shit Continued

couldn't have done it better. Mister Businessman bashing it out with the Youth of Today. Yukkh.

This parlour game of Freaks and Fascists is too bad to be true. But then seeing is believing. You see it on film, just as you read it in The Times, so it must be so.

Don't waste your money. Send it to the Monarchist League.

David Bowman

Nick Drake
Bryter Layter
Island ILPS9134

It seems that everything Joe Boyd touches turns to aesthetic if not material gold, not least his superlative production on both Nick Drake albums which sound as good on fab-gear, picnic, tin-lid throwaway record players as they do in the wonder of high fidelity.

It is now over eighteen months since Nick's last finely understated and predictably overlooked recording. A justifiable delay I would say, because when one makes use of arrangements as balanced and harmonious as those, it presents a considerable challenge to develop them further without allowing them to take over completely. To support them, colour them and give them life on this occasion are a fairly opulent gathering of talents, including Dave Pegg who contributes crisp, solid bass lines for all but one track, Ray Warleigh whose sweet tone enhances every bar he penetrates, and John Cale playing viola and various keyboards. Also present on various occasions is the ghost of that other sadly neglected Joe Boyd production, John and Beverley Martyn's 'Road to Ruin', in which both Paul Harris and Mike Kowalski - who also play here - were involved.

But ultimately it is not their album, nor arranger Robert Kirby's, nor Boyd's, but Nick Drake's alone. His simple, reflective words and smoky delivery glide gracefully over busy backgrounds to carve out songs which are difficult to describe.

Al Clark

ove left: *Melody Maker*, 24 April 1971 Right: *Melody Maker*, 6 March 1971 Centre left: *Melody Maker* (cutting), 1 May 1971 Below left: *Friends*, Issue 28, 23 May 1971

March 13, 1971

Something else for Nick?

NICK DRAKE is a shy, introverted folk singer, who is not usually known to speak unless it is absolutely necessary. But Nick is not the kind of folk singer who will drift into your friendly neighbourhood folk club; in fact, if you've seen him perform, the chances are that it was on the bill of a sell-out Festival Hall concert.

Last week I spoke to Nick, and eventually discovered that it has been precisely these kind of gigs that had hung him up — the reason why he has shied away from public performances almost without exception.

"I think the problem was with the material, which I wrote for records rather than performing. There were only two or three concerts that felt right, and there was something wrong with all the others. I did play Cousins and one or two folk clubs in the north, but the gigs just sort of petered out," Nick explained.

Nick pointed out that he was not happy with the way the gigs were working out and he couldn't get into them properly. Why, then, was he performing at such esteemed venues as the Festival Hall?

"I was under some obligation to do them, but it wasn't the end of the world when I stopped. If I was enjoying the gigs it would have made much more sense."

Don't, however, gain the impression that Nick is not a superb artist. Placed in the right context, his songs produce quite a stunning effect over a period of time. He has worked on two albums with Witchseason producer Joe Boyd, the latter having been released only last week. Entitled "Bryter Layter", it features some of the musicians who have contributed to the success of the John and Beverley Martyn albums, notably Paul Harris; and Robert Kirby's arrangements are just as important as Nick Drake's songs.

Says Nick: "I had something in mind when I wrote the songs, knowing that they weren't just for me. The album took a long time to do, in fact, we started doing it almost a year ago. But I'm not altogether clear about this album — I haven't got to terms with the whole presentation.

What's the next step for Nick? "I think there'll be another album and I have some material for it, but I'll be looking around now to see if this album leads anywhere naturally. For the next one I had the idea of just doing something with John Wood, the engineer at Sound Techniques."

Would there be any gigs to promote the album? "I don't think that would help — unless they were done in the right way. I'm just not very sure at the moment, it's hard to tell what will turn up. If I could find making music a fairly natural connection with something else, then I might move on to something else." — JERRY GILBERT

Nick Drake's debut album on Island records is probably the finest album of the year, and yet it's almost impossible to get without specially ordering it. In actuality, it's a composite album of tracks from his two British lp's, **Five Leaves Left** and **Bryter Layter**, and omits some of his best material. No matter, it's a good introduction to a brilliant songwriter. If Donovan had progressed from his **Mellow Yellow** album instead of slipping into children's candy dreams, this is the kind of album he might have produced . . . if he'd been lucky. This is a sad album, sad like old photographs, about a balance about to be shaken, about grace to be lost. "I've fallen so far from the people you are/now I just need your star for a day." The accompanying musicians are superb: John Cale, Danny Thompson, and Paul Harris, to name a few. The tone of the album is best expressed in a line by Kenneth Patchen: "It is the hour when the day begins to die in our arms, and we have not done much that is beautiful."

Above: *Sounds* (Nick's only printed interview)
Below: 'Neglected Albums of the Month', *Tumbril Magazine*, Brown University, USA, 22 January 1972

Island signs US distribution deal with Capitol

by PETER ROBINSON

ISLAND RECORDS has signed a three and a half year US distribution agreement with Capitol. The deal, which begins on January 1, was concluded by Island managing director Chris Blackwell with Capitol president Sal Iannucci during an American visit from which he returned last week.

A spokesman for Island said that no advances were involved in the deal. Capitol will pay all overheads, including promotion costs. First product to carry the Island logo is likely to be albums by Bronco, Amazing Blondel, and Nick Drake.

As contracts expire, other Island acts already committed in the US are expected to be transferred to the new label. Blackwell told MBW that Traffic would certainly be switching from UA when their American contract runs out next year.

Blackwell, who disclosed a month ago that he would not be accepting the $6 million Kinney National bid for outright takeover of Island, told MBW that he had from the outset been more interested in a distribution-only deal for the US rather than sale of the label.

Don England, Capitol marketing vice-president, commented this week: "We're very excited about the deal, and we are looking forward to a tremendous push behind the entire Island catalogue."

Precise details of the first release would be drawn up within a month.

England said that the marketing of Island would be handled by newly appointed vice-president, independent labels, Charles Nuccio, who is now responsible for the overall direction of sales, promotion and merchandising of Capitol's independent distributed lines. As well as Island, these include Apple, Harvest and a wealth of American labels, among them Invictus and Blue Thumb.

Only a small number of Island's major artists, notably Free and Cat Stevens, are management acts which can be placed direct by the label in America. The bulk of its other artists come via E&G Management (Emerson, Lake and Palmer, King Crimson, Lew Futterman (If) and Joe Boyd's Witchseason Productions (Fairport Convention, Fotheringay, John and Beverley Martyn, Nick Drake).

Boyd told MBW that the first three of these acts were already signed to American deals — the groups with A&M and the Martyn duo with Warner Bros. Though his overseas licensing was negotiated through Island, this did not mean that he would be signing new acts automatically to US Island.

But he has already agreed to place Nick Drake with the new label, and an album, "Bryghter Layter," set for British release in November, will be issued in America in the New Year.

Harrison and Jagger singles

EMI is rush-issuing the first George Harrison solo single. The double A-side titles are "Isn't It A Pity" and "My Sweet Lord" (R 5875), both taken from his forthcoming Apple solo album. Production is by Harrison and Phil Spector.

Decca is issuing a Mick Jagger solo single "Memo From Turner" (F 13067), sung by him in Performance and included on the Warner Bros. soundtrack album. It is a Jagger-Richard song.

ISLAND
Mott and Hoople (ILPS 9119)
King Crimson (ILPS 9127)
Fotheringay (ILPS 9125)
If "If" (ILPS 9129)
Spooky Tooth (ILPS 9117)
Free "Mr. Big" (ILPS 9120)
Quintessence (ILPS 9128)
Fairport Convention (ILPS 9130)
Nick Drake (ILPS 9131)

POP

NICK DRAKE—
Capitol SMAS 9307

From the opening tune, "Cello Song," Nick Drake has established his past, present and future, as he blends with the finest taste, the elements of jazz, classical and pop music with a mellow voice which whispers its message and soothes the ears of the listener. "Poor Boy" is a jazz based arrangement leaning heavily on piano and saxophone improvisations and a soul chorus; "Three Hours," is rhythmic and foreboding in parts.

Far more introspective, both professionally and musically, was Nick Drake, Cambridge dropout and guitarist of elusive, soft dimensions. Drake made two Island albums, "Five Leaves Left" and "Bryter Layter," with many of those same strong Witchseason folk featured on Martyn's works, and these were strong men indeed: Danny Thompson, Terry Cox, John Cale, and the list can go on for a few more lines.

Those two albums have been compressed for American consumption into "Nick Drake," and that release reflects the mellow quality of Drake's style by its surprising sense of coherence. No loose ends created by the compilation, but, instead, the smoky, hypnotic cadences of Drake's lonely urban folk sensibility.

Nick Drake
Island SMAS-9307

British singer-songwriter Nick Drake's American debut album is a beautiful and decadent record. A triumph of eclecticism, it successfully brings together varied elements characteristic of the evolution of urban folk rock music during the past five years. An incredibly slick sound that is highly dependent on production values (credit Joe Boyd) to achieve its effects, its dreamlike quality calls up the very best of the spirit of early Sixties' jazz-pop ballad. It combines this with the contemporary introspection of British folk rock to evoke a hypnotic spell of opiated languor.

The intention of casting a spell—perhaps the broadest and most powerful artistic impulse underlying Van Morrison's *Astral Weeks* (which *Nick Drake* resembles at moments, though this is not at all a "concept" album)—is here fully realized. Like *Astral Weeks*, and to a lesser extent Cat Stevens' *Mona Bone Jakon*, *Nick Drake* is an addictive record—perhaps even more than its predecessors, since Drake's voice is so softly, seductively sensual. Add to this Drake's own densely textured guitar, plus, of all unpromising elements, shades of Stan Getz and Ramsey Lewis, plus two of the most melancholy string arrangements ever written—and you get a head cocktail in which the "astral" of Van Morrison and the "transcendental" of Donovan are still present, yet seen as passively erotic distortions in a pool of sweet liqueur after a couple of downs and a few tokes.

Could this sort of thing be the Muzak of 1984? It would seem a fair guess. So what keeps *Nick Drake* from being the Muzak of today? The variety of its musical thought, the intensity of its aesthetic stance, and the superior musicianship of all concerned. Ray Warleigh's alto sax riffs are thrilling—tinged with the anarchic urban wail; likewise Chris McGregor's piano and John Cale's always distinctive contributions (celeste, piano and organ on "Northern Sky," and viola and harpsichord on "Fly").

Drake's songs vary considerably in style from the delightfully simple skipping-down-the-London-street "One of These Things First" to the Astrud Gilberto cafe-romantic ballad, "At the Chime of a City Clock." Drake's tunes, though more or less derivative, are melodically strong and harmonically kinetic. Their high degree of harmonic sophistication is enhanced by the brilliant arrangements, the most ambitious of which, by Harry Robinson, is lavished on "River Man," a mystical reverie with affinities to "Lazy Afternoon."

"Cello Song" is a tour-de-force of Indian-influenced erotic meditation, wherein guitar and cello (Clare Lowther) are interwoven with Drake's husky voice (itself taking a second cello part) to create the most sensuous of textures. On "Poor Boy," an outright gasp of self-pity, the soulful backup voices of Pat Arnold and Doris Troy repeatedly interrupt Drake's lament with the comment, "Oh poor boy/so sorry for yourself." This mockery of self-mockery is wonderfully ironic, but it also enhances the obsessively insomniac quality of the complaint itself—all six and-one-half gorgeous minutes of it.

Drake's greatest weakness—one he shares with all too many of today's male lyric troubadours, especially those from England—is the lack of verbal force in his song lyrics, which by and large could be characterized as *nouveau art nouveau*. In the case of Drake, this is less serious a liability than it is for artists who are more up front vocally. The beauty of Drake's voice is its own justification. May it become familiar to us all.

—Stephen Holden

ROLLING STONE/APRIL 27, 1972

Above left: *Music Business Weekly*, 31 October 1971   Above right: *Music Business Weekly*, 25 April 1970
Centre left: *Billboard*, USA, 7 August 1971   Centre right: *Billboard*, USA, 31 July 1971
Below left: *Billboard*, USA, 22 July 1972

Nick's first bona fide, non-imported USA release (July 1971), a combination of his first two albums on one record

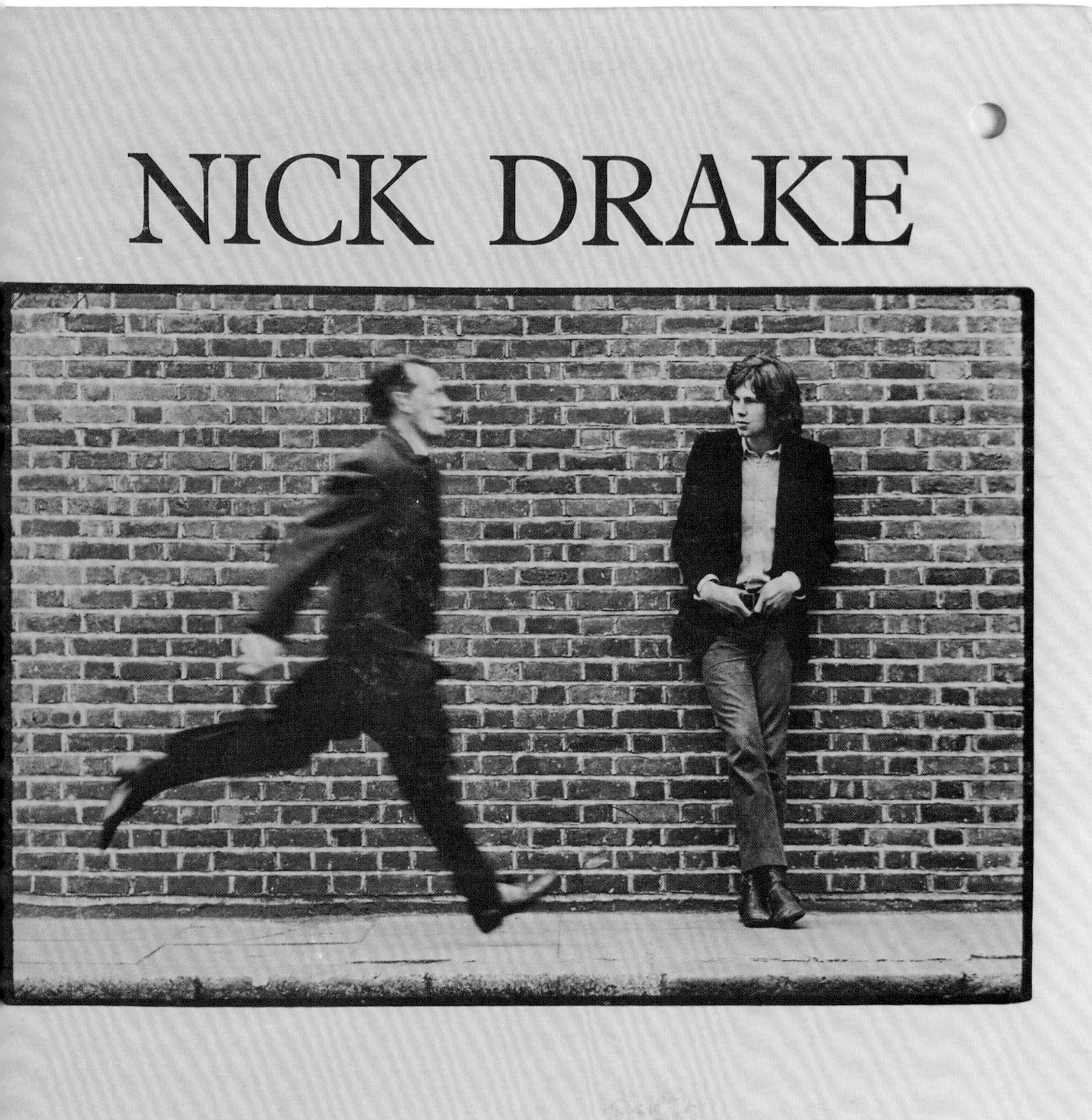
NICK DRAKE

The inside of the sleeve featuring a rare long-lost colour shot of Nick by Keith Morris.
The publishing credit was set as UFO Music Ltd, not Warlock as was normal

side one
'CELLO SONG (3:58)
clare lowther 'cello danny thompson bass rocky dzidzornu congas
POOR BOY (6:30) *
ray warleigh alto sax chris mcgregor piano dave pegg bass
mike kowalski drums pat arnold & doris troy backing vocals
AT THE CHIME OF A CITY CLOCK (4:42) *
ray warleigh alto sax dave pegg bass mike kowalski drums
NORTHERN SKY (3:42)
john cale celeste, piano & organ dave pegg bass mike kowalski drums
side two
RIVER MAN (4:28)
arranged by harry robinson
THREE HOURS (6:01)
danny thompson bass rocki dzidzornu congas
ONE OF THESE THINGS FIRST (4:46)
paul harris piano ed carter bass mike kowalski drums
FLY (2:56)
john cale viola & harpsichord dave pegg bass
* brass & string arrangements by Robert Kirby
vocals & guitar Nick Drake
all songs by Nick Drake
& published by UFO Music, Inc.
engineer John Wood
photographs by Keith Morris
produced by Joe Boyd
Witchseason Productions Ltd.
Recorded In England

ZCI 9184
PINK MOON
PINK MOON, PLACE TO BE, ROAD, WHICH WILL,
HORN, RIDE,
NICK DRAKE
island tapes
℗ 1972
NICK DRAKE
PINK MOON
Nick Drake
Pink Moon
island tapes

REVELATION, 7 *The end of the world*

said unto them, that they should rest yet for a little season, until their fellowservants also and their brethren, that should be killed as they *were*, should be fulfilled.

12 And I beheld when he had opened the sixth seal, and, lo, there was a great earthquake; and the sun became black as sackcloth of hair, and the moon became as blood;

13 And the stars of heaven fell unto the earth, even as a fig tree casteth her untimely figs, when she is shaken of a mighty wind.

14 And the heaven departed as a scroll when it is rolled together; and every mountain and island were moved out of their places.

15 And the kings of the earth, and the great men, and the rich men, and the chief captains, and the mighty men, and every bondman, and every free man, hid themselves in the dens and in the rocks of the mountains;

16 And said to the mountains and rocks, Fall on us, and hide us from the face of him that sitteth on the throne, and from the wrath of the Lamb:

17 For the great day of his wrath is come; and who shall be able to stand?

245 CHAPTER 7

AND after these things I saw four angels standing on the four corners of the earth, holding the four winds of the earth, that the wind should not blow on the earth, nor on the sea, nor on any tree.

2 And I saw another angel ascending from the east, having the seal of the living God: and he cried with a loud voice to the four angels, to whom it was given to hurt the earth and the sea,

3 Saying, Hurt not the earth, neither the sea, nor the trees, till we have sealed the servants of our God in their foreheads.

4 And I heard the number of them which were sealed: *and there were* sealed an hundred *and* forty *and* fou

580

Pink Moon

by Pete Paphides

Eighteen months after telling Jerry Gilbert that his next album would be recorded solo with John Wood producing, Nick called Wood and told him he was ready to do just that. Having not seen the *Sounds* interview in which Nick had declared his intentions, Wood's reaction was one of surprise. By this time, however, Joe Boyd had fled the scene. After a close succession of disappointments (a dispute with Fairport Convention over the track listing of their *Full House* album, Sandy Denny stalling on a solo album to join Fotheringay, and The Incredible String Band's conversion to Scientology), Boyd sold Witchseason and took up a new post in Los Angeles with the music division at Warner Brothers films. With Boyd gone, Wood living in Suffolk, and John and Beverley Martyn relocated in Hastings, Nick's world had narrowed. Robert Kirby was better placed than most to witness the deterioration in his friend throughout 1970 and 1971. In that time, any last flicker of the confidence he showed as a live performer in Cambridge had evaporated. Eyewitness accounts of his final shows suggest that they were as much an ordeal for those watching as they were for Nick. 'He wasn't like Keith Jarrett,' remembered Joe Boyd. 'He wouldn't stop and say "Shut up, I'm not going to play until you be quiet".' At Ewell Technical College in Surrey, that much was clearly apparent. Headlining act Ralph McTell watched as Nick abandoned his set halfway through 'Fruit Tree'. Beyond this, it is not known if he played live in front of an audience again.

Robert Kirby's concern for his friend and his eagerness to procure him work is striking. He enlisted Nick to play guitar on an album by singer-songwriter Mick Audsley and also on an educational album produced as a teaching aid by Longman. The latter, entitled *Interplay*, saw Nick play on three songs: 'I Wish I Was a Single Girl Again', sung by Vivian Fowler, featured the only bass guitar part ever to be recorded by Nick; while 'Full Fathom Five' and 'With My Swag All on My Shoulder' saw Nick playing guitar with Kirby tackling the vocal. Nick had also been invited to write songs for an album by his most glamorous fan, French pop icon Françoise Hardy – but by the time Hardy appeared at Sound Techniques with an agglomeration of folk-rock musicians *du jour*, Nick hadn't managed to come up with any songs for the resulting album (*Et Si Je M'en Vais Avant Toi*). He nonetheless turned up to at least one session around this time. Fotheringay guitarist Jerry Donahue recalled that Nick sat in the control room looking uncomfortable every time he was asked a question – while in her autobiography Hardy recalled that 'he would sit in one corner of the studio and would stay there for hours, without saying a word, as if it was enough for him to know that I liked his songs'.

By the time Nick was ready to start work on *Pink Moon*, he had reluctantly been prescribed antidepressants and also spent some time in Chris Blackwell's Spanish villa, at the personal request of the concerned Island Records boss. 'It felt like there was a kind of urgency about it,' recalled Wood – which may explain why Wood elected to record Nick's new songs at night when Sound Techniques was free, rather than wait for it to become available in the daytime. 'No frills' was Nick's directive – and Wood responded accordingly. Save for the title track's minimal, pretty piano solo, played on John Wood's Steinway, there are no overdubs on *Pink Moon*.

With just two extra room mics set up 'for ambience', the entire album – all twenty-eight minutes of it – was recorded over two nights in October 1971.

'There are two very different ways of interpreting the image of a pink moon,' suggests Robin Frederick.

'In folklore, the full moon in April is called the Pink Moon (other names are the Spring Moon, Grass Moon or Planter's Moon). This is the time of year when the snow melts and the first flowers of spring appear, a time of hope and regeneration. But there is another pink moon, the 'blood moon', which appears during a total lunar eclipse when the moon turns a deep pink colour. This has traditionally been seen as an evil omen, a portent of disaster. In the Bible's Book of Revelations, when the moon turns to blood, it is a sign that the sixth of the seven seals has been opened and God's wrath has come. Nick gave the lyrics of [the] song a biblical tone . . . Suggesting that he viewed the pink moon as a curse, a prophecy of dark days to come . . . [although later in the album] we'll get a very different sense of the future, one that is more in line with the pastoral promise of regeneration, the pink moon of folklore.'

Of Nick's three completed albums, no opening song has set the tone of what follows as wholly as *Pink Moon*'s title track does. Pregnant with symbolism and suggestive of some unspecified imminent reckoning, 'Pink Moon' bears a considerable weight – and like the beginning of any song cycle, that's what it has to do. In that sense, 'Pink Moon' bears comparison to the eponymous openers of *Astral Weeks* and *Sgt Pepper's Lonely Hearts Club Band*. And yet, none of that 'work' is consciously brought to the listener's attention: not Nick's decision to navigate the melody ('Pink, pink, pink, pink, pink, / Pink Moon') to a place below his vocal comfort zone; or the decision to accompany that descent with a comforting Em9 – thus bestowing upon the song what Rasmussen describes as 'a resigned calm . . . such as is found in someone who has settled his account and is ready to face the consequences of an important choice.' The first-time listener would be as likely to notice any of these decisions as they might notice the groundwork that had gone into creating the establishing shot of a favourite film. In other words, you don't have to notice something to feel its effect.

It seems that much of *Pink Moon* came together amid the relative isolation of Nick's Haverstock Hill flat – although the earliest written music on the record predates *Bryter Layter*. Featured alongside 'Hazey Jane I', 'Poor Boy' and 'Fly' on the 1969 'work tape' were 'Place To Be' and 'Parasite'. Between those performances and versions captured for *Pink Moon*, over two years had elapsed, yet they remain fundamentally unchanged. On 'Place To Be', the first half of each verse is immersed in the consolation of fonder memories ('And I was green, greener than the hill / Where flowers grew and sun shone still'), while the second half mourns the passing of more innocent times ('Now I'm darker than the deepest sea / Just hand me down, give me a place to be'). Somehow, the song itself is anything but bleak. The reference to 'Day Is Done' ('I thought I'd see when day was done') in the third verse is revealing. Whereas 'Day Is Done' is fated not to transcend its own fatalism, 'Place To Be' propels the listener to the transient succour of a nostalgic fever dream. Robin Frederick explains that 'Nick constructs the song so that we actually experience what he is talking about':

'The intro consists of a basic three-chord progression divided into even, two-bar phrases. It begins on the tonic chord, a kind of 'home base', and then moves through two more chords before returning home again. At this point, we're on very familiar ground. But then, in the middle of the progression, in the middle of a two-bar phrase, in a place where it shouldn't be, Nick starts the vocal. It has a disorienting effect; we're not sure where we are. He keeps us suspended in that place for three long bars before returning to the home chord and a welcome sense of familiarity and release. Then he does it again – twice in each verse – showing us each time how good it feels to return home.'

Referring to Nick's career, Robert Kirby remembered that there was 'a great deal of embarrassment among his peer group that what we thought was going to happen didn't'. For someone who had never seriously had to countenance the prospect, it might be that failure was little short of a living nightmare. It's unclear whether Nick was beginning to feel that way when he wrote "Parasite", but the resonances were seemingly inescapable by the time he recorded it. 'Some of *Pink Moon* was quite chilling,' recalled John Wood. 'It certainly was on the first day when we did "Parasite" . . . there was just something about it, you suddenly thought this was going to be very different.' Nick's London life is the backdrop of *Bryter Layter* and it's also unavoidable in 'Parasite' ('Sailing downstairs to the Northern Line / Watching the shine of the shoes'). If 'One Of These Things First' asks 'What am I?', 'Parasite' is the most dreaded of verdicts – played out over a descending chord sequence which strongly evokes The Beatles' 'Dear Prudence' (the White Album had been released just a few months before Nick wrote 'Parasite').

Poignantly, the final song that Nick ever played for Robert Kirby was one that had initially taken shape in Kirby's Cambridge room. In the spring of 1971, Nick moved to a bedsit in Muswell Hill, a stone's throw away from Kirby's flat. Speaking to Gorm Henrik Rasmussen, Kirby recalled that his friend 'would come by a couple of times a week, sit in a corner and stare into space':

'He didn't eat. He looked dishevelled. His clothes were dirty, his hair shaggy, his nails black with grime. His new room was horrible . . . [It] looked like a tomb. One day he took out his guitar and played me a song. I listened, not knowing that that would be the last thing he would ever play for me. The funny thing is that a few years prior I had recorded that exact song as Nick was jamming it. I still have that tape: a half-hour where he is jamming his way towards "Things Behind The Sun".'

Joe Boyd also had occasion to remember 'Things Behind The Sun'. This was the song that he had lobbied Nick to include on *Bryter Layter* when he heard him soundchecking with it at the Fairport Convention Royal Festival Hall show – and in some ways, it feels more suited to that album or even *Five Leaves Left*. That might be partly attributable to a host of influences that, by 1971, Nick had remoulded into something uniquely his. Robin Frederick talks about 'the unusual fingerpicking patterns, syncopations, drones and cluster chords' which unite early Bert Jansch songs with Nick Drake songs like 'Three Hours', 'Fruit Tree', 'Hazey Jane I' and 'Things Behind The Sun'. The rambling metre and riddle-like imagery of the lyric harks back to another of Nick's formative influences. Pick any segment from the lyric at random: perhaps 'Look around you find the ground / Is not so far from where you are, / But don't be too wise'; or ''Bout the farmers and the fun / And the things behind the sun / And the people round your head / Who say everything's been said.' It's as easy to imagine Bob Dylan singing those words as Nick Drake.

Bookending 'Things Behind The Sun' are two tracks which sit in direct opposition to that song's florid familiarity. 'It might be that Nick Drake does not exist at all,' *Melody Maker*'s Mark Plummer would conclude in his review of *Pink Moon* a few months later, and the same might almost be said of the 84 seconds that comprise 'Horn'. Coming at the end of side one, it's an intermission of sorts, but unlike its equivalent on *Bryter Layter*, one would be pressed to discern any sort of sonic landscape here. Ian MacDonald suggested that the predominant influence on 'Horn' might have been Indian veena music, while others have posited a North African influence. Whatever its inspirations, 'Horn' is defined almost entirely by what it has jettisoned. A low tolling bass note chimes in unison with a high, helpless echo of something which stops just short of a melody. In fact, what you can hear, in embryo form, might be 'Black Eyed Dog'. Just over two years later, it was an intro remarkably similar to 'Horn' that would usher in Nick's tormented allegorical address to his own depression.

Having been almost entirely absent from his original songs until this point, elements of the blues songs that Nick had covered in Aix-en-Provence could be heard filtering into his third album. No huge leap of imagination is needed to hear Robert Johnson or John Lee Hooker locking into the hypnotic four-note guitar phrase of 'Know', or indeed its sole stark self-negating verse: 'Know that I love you / Know I don't care / Know that I see you / Know I'm not there.' Perhaps the most startling detail about the song, however, is neither its lyric or melody, but the manner in which it is delivered: the increasing strength with which Nick picks at the strings of his guitar as if trying to make himself feel something, anything.

Also pared down to a single verse is 'Road', another second-person address which depicts two contrasting outlooks: 'You can say the sun is shining if you really want to / I can see the moon and it seems so clear'. In her song 'I Remember', Nick's mother also alludes to a disparity of outlook between the protagonist and the person she is addressing. But in that song, hers is the character straining towards the light, looking back in mild exasperation at her companion's inability to do the same: 'I remember firelight / And you remember smoke.' The protagonist in 'Road', however, seems to have exhausted his options. What little energy he has left is focused on mere survival: 'You can take the road that takes you to the stars now / I can take a road that'll see me through.' The characters that populated Nick's previous albums now seem like ancient history. The imagery too is stripped back to the barest fundamentals. Frederick notes that on 'Road' 'the fingerpicked guitar part consists of three chords with some variations':

'The melody line – both vocal and played on guitar – is strictly modal. The guitar plays the melody line on the low strings in parallel with the vocal while the upper strings provide an intricate rhythmic and harmonic accompaniment. This guitar style can be heard in traditional Appalachian folk music, played on both guitar and banjo by musicians like Roscoe Holcomb. It creates the impression that there are two instruments playing, ensuring that the track sounds full.'

Despite not having been deployed on any of Nick's previous albums, it's a technique that also surfaces on *Pink Moon*'s next track. Frederick compares 'Which Will' to 'a traditional folk ballad' – and, indeed, the universality of its sentiment and the softness of Drake's exhortations allow it to travel easily from one singer to another. On her 1992 album *Sweet Old World*, Lucinda Williams replaces Nick's intricate picking with contemplative strumming and, in doing so, accentuates the sense of quiet resignation made explicit with the song's penultimate question: 'Which will you take now? / If you won't take me.' Along with 'Hazey Jane I', the DNA of 'Which Will' is strongly detectable in the tone and lyrical conceit of 'Who Do You Love' from the 1998 debut album released by sometime Slowdive lynchpin Neil Halstead with his group Mojave 3.

That songs from *Pink Moon* have spawned so many cover versions (the title track alone has been recorded by artists as disparate as Robyn Hitchcock, Meshell Ndegeocello, Sebadoh and Beck – the latter having also tackled 'Which Will' and 'Parasite') in comparison to its predecessors may initially seem surprising. More likely, its very sparseness may be the reason more artists have felt emboldened to place their stamp on its songs. Interviewed by Amanda Petrusich for her 2007 book about *Pink Moon*, Kirby confessed that 'recently I have found myself starting to suspect that [*Pink Moon*] is just a demo of a series of unfinished masterpieces, absolutely perfect in this raw state, but unfinished.' If there's something in what Kirby has to say here, it follows that on *Five Leaves Left* and *Bryter Layter*, there is less room left for the interpretation of others.

Within twelve months of *Pink Moon*'s release, however, other musicians saw manifold possibilities in its sparsely furnished songs. Irish prog-folk group Tír na nÓg kicked off their 1973 album with a magnificently propulsive version of 'Free Ride' which seemed to owe as much to Roxy Music's marauding art-pop as it did to anything that Nick might have envisaged for it. In doing so, they further bore out Kirby's contention that 'each of the songs on [*Pink Moon*] contains a wealth of material that earlier [Nick] would have spent time developing'. By contrast, Nick's version of the song is static. The scenes depicted here – 'All of the pictures that you keep on the wall / All of the people that will come to the ball' – are sketched out as if witnessed under cover of night from a nearby parked car. The song's protagonist is describing someone who moves in rarefied social circles. 'Free Ride' was one of several lyrics that Nick asked his close friend Sophia Ryde to type for him at this time. Together with the notion that the song's title may be a play on her name, this has been enough to spark speculation that 'Free Ride' may be an address to her. In the event, it doesn't matter. If anything, the lyrical ambiguities of the song play to its strengths. It's a scene of privilege and entitlement, depicted by a protagonist suspicious of the former and long bereft of the latter.

The melody itself alternates exquisitely between the pensive observations of the first half of the verses and the beseeching hook: 'But hear me calling, won't you give me / A free ride.' For Robin Frederick, it's 'the droning bass, played in octaves with emphasis on the upbeats' – emphasis on the downbeats being the far more common practice – that distinguishes the song, and conspires to leave the listener feeling 'less than comfortable'.

As a voracious reader, it's unlikely that, along with other set texts of the counterculture (Kerouac, Sartre, Ginsberg, Camus), Nick wouldn't have come across Herman Hesse's *Steppenwolf* – and indeed, even the most cursory glance at 'Free Ride' makes it less likely still. The protagonist of Hesse's book (Harry Haller or Steppenwolf) is a loner on the margins of society who recognises a character seemingly identical to himself in a book he has been given to read. The book within Hesse's book is a treatise on the tension between higher and lower pleasures: man's spiritual state versus his lower, 'animal' state. It is, in fact, impossible to read *Steppenwolf* without alighting on themes echoed in and beyond several of Nick's songs. By softening his mistrust of the 'bourgeois', Harry's would-be saviour Hermine opens up a new world to him – one strikingly similar to that addressed in 'Free Ride'. And as with 'Free Ride', you can see the same ambivalence being played out in Harry's interior world. Elsewhere, in Hermine's compassionate reluctance to indulge Harry's self-pity, we see unmistakable shades of 'Poor Boy'. The description of Harry pacing the city streets in a bid to put off having to return home after insulting his friend's bust of Goethe calls to mind both 'Parasite' and 'At The Chime Of A City Clock'. It's impossible also not to think of 'Fruit Tree' in the author's description of Harry as one of the 'suicides' – people who carry an inner 'knowledge' that one day they will take their own life – and the concomitant contention that Harry is blessed with the potential for great deeds that will ultimately confer immortality upon him. We can only speculate how Nick might have contrasted his own continuing story (a story that appeared to lack a Hermine-like agent of change) against Hesse's narrative.

Beyond 'Free Ride', two songs remain on *Pink Moon* and both are characterised by a kind of acceptance, a sense that all available roles have been assigned and all that now remains is for the narrative to be played out: be it a play, a ritual sacrifice or a public execution. 'In all of the songs written for this album,' says Frederick, 'it seems he is simplifying, eliminating all non-essential elements, as if giving away his possessions.' In this regard, 'Harvest Breed' is no exception. Early drafts of the lyric featured several lines – all intimating some sort of imminent reckoning – that Nick eventually elected not to include. What remains, then, is a marriage of two incongruent parts. Frederick notes that

'the guitar plays a partial clavé rhythm – a pattern of beats that is the basis of Afro-Cuban dances like rumba – while the richly textured chords and limited, chromatic movement of the melody are reminiscent of bossa nova. Against this sensuous musical backdrop, the lyrics build to the haunting image of the "harvest breed" a term referring to birds that are raised to be hunted and killed. A less likely combination is hard to imagine. The effect is of a chilling embrace, a welcoming of death that sets the spirit free.'

For Robert Kirby, 'Harvest Breed' numbered among Nick's 'most optimistic songs . . . It's very depressing: "Falling fast and falling free / you look to find a friend / Falling fast and falling free / this could just be the end," and then he says, "And you're ready now / For the harvest breed . . ." Which could possibly be about death, but you're ready now for it. It means one is ready for one's environment; one knows what is coming.' Kirby's view was echoed by Ian MacDonald in his 1999 *Mojo* essay on Nick:

'The grim view [of the record] is unfair, the crowning misconception created by viewing Nick Drake as a troubadour of tragic sadness. He certainly went through his dark night of the soul . . . Nevertheless, he was a soul of light, a Romantic idealist – and this uncanny, magical record, far from bleak and ghoulish, is in truth, a stark, springy beautiful meditation on redemption through spiritual trial. *Pink Moon* isn't about death, but about resurrection.'

MacDonald's words are borne out by the album's final song. If 'Harvest Breed' represents the end of the fight, then 'From The Morning' inhabits the ensuing peace. Its significance in Nick Drake's canon has been underscored by the excerpt inscribed on the back of his headstone in Tanworth-in-Arden: 'And now we rise / And we are everywhere.' A sense of harking back to simpler times is compounded by a return to a folk-picking style that Nick had abandoned with some of his earliest compositions. Lyrically, too, 'From The Morning' resounds with what Frederick calls 'a visionary intensity and clarity; the focus is so tight and images so primitive and archetypal that it sounds almost incantatory . . . In the song, both dawn and nightfall – birth and death – are beautiful and personified as female. Life itself is merely a game. Ultimately "I" and "you" become "we", merged into one in a bodiless resurrection.'

No one was more startled by the brevity of *Pink Moon*'s execution than the man entrusted with the job of engineering and producing it. 'Afterwards,' recalled John Wood, 'when we sat in the control room and I listened to the tapes, I asked Nick how much of the material he thought we should keep. "All of it," Nick replied. I was surprised; we had never worked like that before. I realised that he had no more songs. It would be a short album – and an unusually intense one. "How would you like to have the songs arranged?" I asked. "I don't want them arranged," Nick said. "I want them to stand naked."'

The events immediately following the release of *Pink Moon* have long since fed into the myth of Nick Drake, in particular the manner in which Nick was said to have delivered the completed album. With Joe Boyd now in America, the story goes that the managerless singer delivered the master tapes at the reception of Island Records without exchanging any words with the receptionist – with the receptionist only realising several days later that what she had was the new Nick Drake album. However, the account offered by David Sandison – Nick's press officer at Island – was somewhat different. Speaking to Patrick Humphries, Sandison recalled:

'I saw him in reception after I came back from lunch . . . I saw a figure in the corner on the bench, and I suddenly realised it was Nick. He had this big master tape box under his arm, and I said, "Have you had a cup of tea? . . . Do you want to come upstairs?" So he went upstairs to my office . . . and he just sat in my office area for about half an hour, then said: "I'd better be going . . ." He went down the stairs with the tapes under his arm, and about half an hour later, the girl who worked behind the front desk called up and said: "Nick's left the tapes behind," so I went down and it was the big sixteen-track master tape box, and it said "Nick Drake: Pink Moon". So they called John Wood and said, "What's this?" and he said it was the new album. So we ran off a safety copy and said, "Let's hear it."'

If John Wood had intuited a certain urgency in Nick's declaration that he was ready to record *Pink Moon*, hindsight has shown just how wise he was to get Nick into the studio at the first opportunity. Shortly after the album's release on 26 February 1972, Nick's condition appeared to go into freefall. After some persuasion, he voluntarily commenced a five-week stay at the Louisa Raynes ward of the psychiatric hospital in nearby Warwick. Brian Wells, who visited him at the hospital, giving him a book about Bob Dylan, recalled that, prior to his admission there, Nick had 'been unforthcoming for quite some time . . . and when I got there, it was more of the same really.' On 9 June, the day after he was finally discharged, Rodney Drake drove Nick to London, where Françoise Hardy was once again at Sound Techniques, applying the finishing touches to her album *If You Listen*. However, having made it all the way to Chelsea, Nick could only summon the wherewithal to make the briefest appearance in the studio, before fleeing back to the sanctuary of the car. Despite Rodney's attempts to persuade him to re-enter, Nick couldn't bring himself to go in there again.

It's unclear to what degree Nick was aware of the few reviews which greeted *Pink Moon* at this time. Writing for *Sounds*, the previously supportive Jerry Gilbert was now beginning to show signs of impatience with an artist who he felt needed to stop 'acting mysteriously and [start getting] something properly organised for himself.' Most damningly of all, he added that 'the songs are not sufficiently strong to stand up without any embroidery at all'. Reviewing for *Melody Maker* several weeks later, Mark Plummer confessed that he was listening to the album on John Martyn's recommendation. 'The more you listen to Drake . . . the more compelling his music becomes – but all the time it hides from you.' *Pink Moon*'s most enthusiastic critical reception, however, would come from French writer, Hervé Muller. Writing in the May issue of *Best* magazine, Muller hymned 'the profound charm' of this 'extraordinary' album, 'all in nuances where humour and emotions are confusingly entwined . . . The spell is completed by the magic of his voice and music, but another asset of Nick's is being a wonderful poet who, by comparison, makes so many "wordy" singers seem ridiculous.'

As Nick attempted to manage his deteriorating condition, Island continued to show a level of belief in him which, by modern music industry standards, was unbelievable. The preceding year, Chris Blackwell had loaned Nick the use of his apartment on the Spanish coast. Now, in the wake of *Pink Moon*'s release, Island devoted the album's promotional budget on full-page adverts in the *New Musical Express*, *Melody Maker* and *Sounds*, which took the form of an open letter from David Sandison. In it, he recounted the unorthodox manner in which Nick had delivered the masters of *Pink Moon*: 'He came in, smiling that weird smile of his and handed over his new album. He'd just gone into the studios and recorded it without telling a soul except the engineer. And we haven't seen him since.' Sandison goes on to affirm Island's faith in Nick in a manner that surely hasn't been seen in any advert for a new album before or since: 'His first two albums haven't sold a shit. But, if we carry on releasing them, maybe one day, someone authoritative will stop, listen properly and agree with us. Then maybe a lot more people will get to hear Nick Drake's incredible songs and guitar playing. And maybe they'll buy a lot of his albums, and fulfil our faith in Nick's promise.'

Hindsight has conferred an irony upon Sandison's heartfelt address that couldn't possibly have been predicted in the wake of *Pink Moon*'s release. It did indeed take an advertisement to break Nick's third album to a wider audience, but it wouldn't be one for a Nick Drake record. In 1999, American advertising agency Arnold Worldwide were charged with the job of producing a 60-second television commercial for Volkswagen's new Cabrio convertible. The resulting film, entitled *Milky Way*, depicted four friends driving through the night with the top down beneath the light of a full moon. It transpires that they're on the way to a house party. They pull up outside the house, take one look at the scene taking place before them – frat boys staggering around the drive; one of them climbing into another car – take one look at each other, and drive back into the moonlit wilderness. The commercial wasn't just shown on television. Full page newspaper adverts directed readers to Volkswagen's website where the ad was waiting for them. As Nathan Wiseman-Trowse notes in *Dreaming England*, 'Soundscan data for 1999/2000 shows a marked increase in American sales of Drake's music. *Pink Moon*, which had sold 5,666 units in 1999, jumped, following the advert, to 74,696 sales, while the *Way To Blue* compilation almost increased its sales six-fold to 67,916 units over the same period.' A decade later, *Pink Moon* – by this time already Nick's highest-selling album – edged further ahead of its predecessors as a result of an AT&T campaign which used 'From The Morning'.

The use of well-loved songs in advertising campaigns can attract strong emotions. Only a tiny fraction of requests for the use of Nick's songs in adverts have been authorised, but the fact that there is a demand at all once again echoes Ian MacDonald's contention that Nick's music serves a purpose in the modern world that didn't always seem apparent to those who encountered it in his lifetime. Joe Boyd has said that *Pink Moon*'s commercial outperformance of its predecessors amounts to Nick having 'the last laugh'. For Boyd at the time, *Pink Moon* was 'emblematic of failure, of the blocks that would never permit Nick to succeed'. As the only other person privy to the *Pink Moon* sessions, John Wood was clearly affected by the experience. It would be years before he could even bring himself to play the record. 'After *Pink Moon*,' he recalled, 'Nick would just have this habit of arriving. I lived in Suffolk. He turned up on my doorstep more than once. He would ring about half an hour before arriving. He would stay and sit down and be part of the family. He wasn't bound by social obligations. I had two daughters who would sort of goad him into conversation.'

John Wood's recollection of Nick simply arriving at his house with barely any fanfare was consistent with the few other existing recollections people had of him in 1973. Beverley Martyn recalled Nick making an impromptu trip to the Hastings house she shared with John, only to stop short of being able to knock on the couple's front door: 'A neighbour saw him on the beach and duly reported this back to me . . . [Once he came in, he would] play the same album over and over again – or look out the window with a cup of tea in his hands for four hours.'

Pink Moon

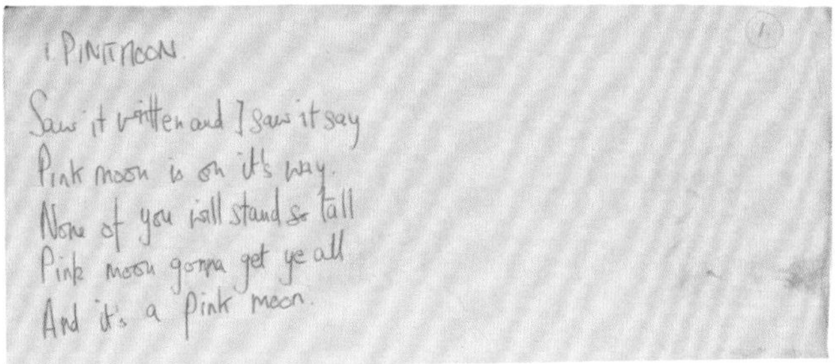
1. PINK MOON
Saw it written and I saw it say
Pink moon is on it's way.
None of you will stand so tall
Pink moon gonna get ye all
And it's a pink moon.

Saw it written and I saw it say
Pink moon is on its way
And none of you stand so tall
Pink moon gonna get ye all
And it's a pink moon
Yes a pink moon

Pink, pink, pink, pink,
Pink Moon

Pink, pink, pink, pink,
Pink Moon

I saw it written and I saw it say
Pink moon is on its way
And none of you stand so tall
Pink moon gonna get ye all
And it's a pink moon
Yes, a pink moon

Chris Healey: One of the ways this song manages to be so affecting is down to the way Nick uses his thumbnail and thumb to vary the texture of the strumming, generating everything from light accents to dug-in emphasis, and giving the whole song an intensely human feel. Try playing this song with a plectrum and you notice immediately how much flatter it sounds in comparison. The main riff is a triumph of minimal style, the back of his thumbnail accenting upstrokes, pulling out three descending notes in between the beats. An interesting comparison is with the opening to 'Hazey Jane I', which uses the same tuning and notes but to completely different effect.

Place To Be

When I was young, younger than before
I never saw the truth hanging from the door
And now I'm older see it face to face
And now I'm older gotta get up, clean the place

And I was green, greener than the hill
Where flowers grew and sun shone still
Now I'm darker than the deepest sea
Just hand me down, give me a place to be

And I was strong, strong in the sun
I thought I'd see when day was done
Now I'm weaker than the palest blue
Oh, so weak in this need for you

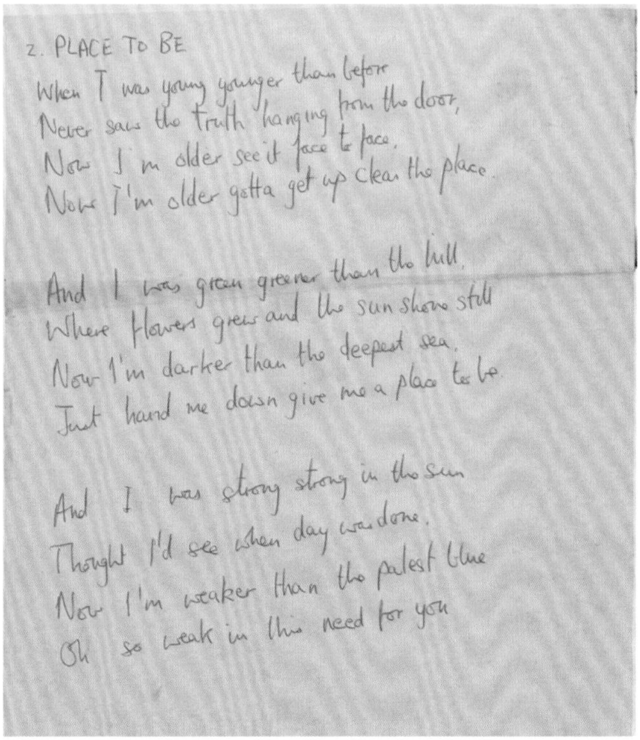
2. PLACE TO BE
When I was young younger than before
Never saw the truth hanging from the door,
Now I'm older see it face to face.
Now I'm older gotta get up clean the place.

And I was green greener than the hill
Where flowers grew and the sun shone still
Now I'm darker than the deepest sea.
Just hand me down give me a place to be.

And I was strong strong in the sun
Thought I'd see when day was done.
Now I'm weaker than the palest blue
Oh so weak in this need for you

There's a famous early demo of this that features an ornate and brilliant fingerpicked version of the guitar part. The song is a hard-won acceptance of the compromises and failings of an adult life, but in that demo version the vocal sounds almost like an afterthought, barely registering next to the crystalline guitar patterns. In the *Pink Moon* version, the guitar part is just gently strummed, allowing the vocal space to get across its understated but devastating self-analysis. Most guitarists would be unable to resist showing off their technique and would have stuck with the original part, but the song's much more affecting without it.

Road

3. ROAD
You can say the sun is shining if you really want to
I can see the moon and it seems so clear
You can take a road that takes you to the stars now
I can take a road that'll see me through

You can say the sun is shining if you really want to
I can see the moon and it seems so clear
You can take a road that takes you to the stars now
I can take a road that'll see me through

You can take a road that takes you to the stars now
I can take a road that'll see me through,
I can take a road that'll see me through,
I can take a road that'll see me through

Folk pickers normally use their thumb to provide regular rhythmic bass parts based around downbeats. This guitar part is unusual in that Nick uses his thumb on the bass strings to pick out the main tune. Doing this requires a lot of skill in both tonal control and syncopation. People have generalised from this song about Nick's thumb style being very unorthodox, but there aren't really many other examples (though 'Which Will' does do something similar).

The instrumental parts after the verses sound simple but are also really tricky to master. So not a great choice for your first Nick Drake song to try on guitar . . .

Which Will

Which will you go for?
Which will you love?
Which will you choose from?
From the stars above

Which will you answer?
Which will you call?
Which will you take for
For your one and all?

Tell me now
Which will you love the best?
Which do you dance for?
Which makes you shine?
Which will you choose now?
If you won't choose mine

Which will you hope for?
Which can it be?
Which will you take now?
If you won't take me

And tell me now
Which will you love the best?

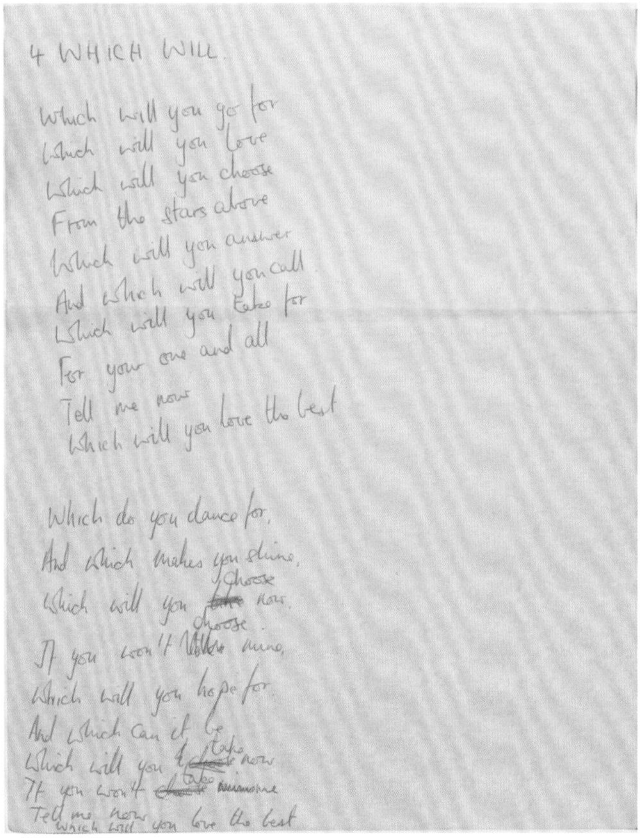
4 WHICH WILL
Which will you go for
Which will you love
Which will you choose
From the stars above
Which will you answer
And which will you call
Which will you take for
For your one and all
Tell me now
Which will you love the best
Which do you dance for,
And which makes you shine,
Which will you choose now.
If you won't choose mine,
Which will you hope for
And which can it be
Which will you take now
If you won't take someone
Tell me now
Which will you love the best

More bass string emphasis as Nick uses his thumb to pick out the riff which holds the whole song together. Not quite as tricksy-sounding or syncopated as its predecessor, it's still not straightforward to play.

Although in CGCFCE, the underlying chord sequence is very simple. But one nice touch is how Nick extends his range in CGCFCE by doing something new with his familiar and distinctive 222000 fingering (think of the sound of 'Pink, pink, pink, pink' in 'Pink Moon' or 'Hey slow Jane' in 'Hazey Jane I', for example). Here it occurs at the verse end ('For your . . .'), and he takes it up the neck to find 777070 ('. . . one and all'), and then 55505(0) ('I don't know, which will you love? . . .'). Both new chords are simple moves on the guitar, but subtle and satisfying variations on the standard V and IV chords, and great examples of what you can discover in alternate tunings.

'Horn'

A piece as minimal as this could feel completely redundant in the wrong hands. But Nick plays it with real artistry. The free timing, the varied dynamics, the vibrato; the way the bass note always happens fractionally before its top-note partner, before finally being brought together for the end of the tune as if in a longed-for integration; all these help a superficially slight piece to feel like it's speaking to you.

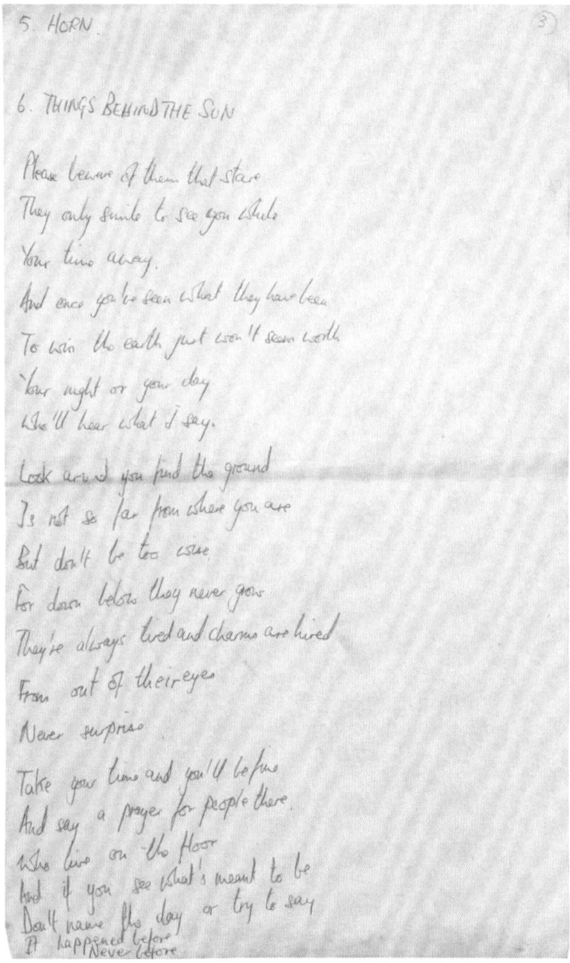
5. HORN (3)

6. THINGS BEHIND THE SUN

Please beware of them that stare
They only smile to see you while
Your time away.
And once you've seen what they have been
To win the earth just won't seem worth
Your night or your day
Who'll hear what I say.
Look around you find the ground
Is not so far from where you are
But don't be too wise
For down below they never grow
They're always tired and charms are hired
From out of their eyes
Never surprise
Take your time and you'll be fine
And say a prayer for people there
Who live on the floor
And if you see what's meant to be
Don't name the day or try to say
It happened before
Never before

Things Behind The Sun

Please beware of them that ﬆare
They'll only smile to see you while
Your time away
And once you've seen
What they have been
To win the earth
Juﬆ won't seem worth
Your night or your day
Who'll hear what I say?

Look around you find the ground
Is not so far from where you are,
But don't be too wise
For down below they never grow
They're always tired and charms are hired
From out of their eyes
Never surprise

Take your time and you'll be fine
And say a prayer for people there
Who live on the floor
And if you see what's meant to be
Don't name the day or try to say
It happened before

Don't be shy you learn to fly
And see the sun, day is done
If only you see
Juﬆ what you are beneath a ﬆar
That came to ﬆay one rainy day
In autumn for free
Yes, be what you'll be

Please beware
of them that ﬆare
They'll only smile
to see you while
Your time away
And once you've seen
what they have been
To win the earth
juﬆ won't seem worth
Your night or your day
Who'll hear what I say

Open up the broken cup
Let goodly sin and sunshine in
Yes that's day
And open wide the hymns you hide
You find renown
while people frown
At things that you say
But say what you'll say

'Bout the farmers
and the fun
And the things
behind the sun
And the people
round your head
Who say everything's been said
And the movement in your brain
Sends you out into the rain

Compositionally, this shares something with 'At The Chime Of A City Clock' – the cautionary minor-feel verses and subsequent major-key sections (here expressing hope); also the slightly ambivalent major ending. (It was actually written before the *Bryter Layter* album.) However, it's in standard tuning, so the more unusual voicings are not available. That said, it's amazing how much impact one simple bit of fingering has: the third chord in each verse line (under 'Your time away' in the first verse, for example) frets only two strings of the expected F chord, giving an unusual F/G hybrid which allows the picking hand to tell a complicated story with a few little moves, and gives the song a harmonic depth that takes it out of the range of simple folk tunes. This one chord is really the heart of the song, its own conflict the clue that there might be painful experience behind these simple-sounding injunctions.

Know

1. SIDE TWO.
2. KNOW
Knows that I love you.
Knows I don't care.
Know that I see you
Knows I'm not there

Know that I love you
Know I don't care
Know that I see you
Know I'm not there

What's interesting in 'Know' is what the guitar *doesn't* do – no chord, no harmonic progression, no ornament or even variation. There's nothing in the music to create any suggestions or lead the ear away from Nick's hypnotic focus, just one insistent four-note pattern to give a tonal base and a rhythm for the voice to work against. The result is that we are thrown into Nick's interior world and forced to engage with every emotional nuance in his vocal.

Parasite

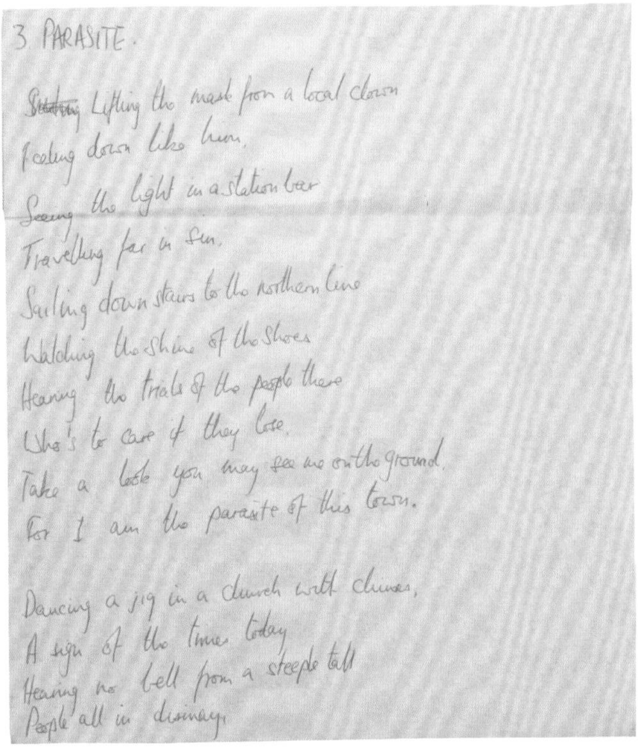
3 PARASITE.

~~Sailing~~ Lifting the mask from a local clown
Feeling down like him.
Seeing the light in a station bar
Travelling far in sin.
Sailing down stairs to the northern line
Watching the shine of the shoes
Hearing the trials of the people there
Who's to care if they lose.
Take a look you may see me on the ground.
For I am the parasite of this town.

Dancing a jig in a church with chimes,
A sign of the times today
Hearing no bell from a steeple tall
People all in dismay.

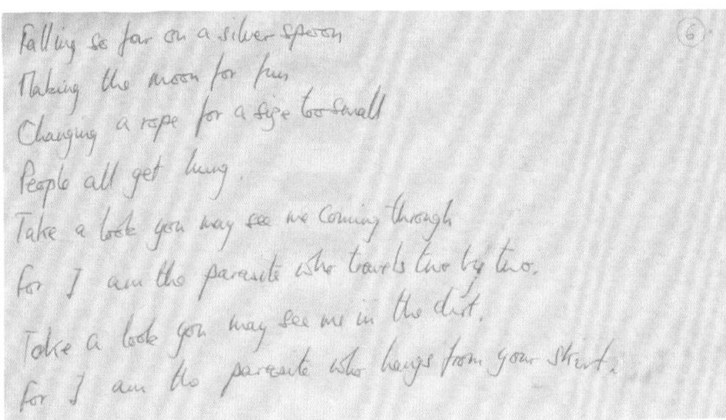
Falling so far on a silver spoon (6)
Making the moon for fun
Changing a rope for a size too small
People all get hung.
Take a look you may see me coming through
For I am the parasite who travels two by two.
Take a look you may see me in the dirt.
For I am the parasite who hangs from your skirt.

Lifting the mask from a local clown
Feeling down like him
Seeing the light in a station bar
Travelling far in sin
Sailing downstairs to the Northern Line
Watching the shine of the shoes
Hearing the trials of the people there
Who's to care if they lose

Take a look you may see me on the ground
For I am the parasite of this town

Dancing a jig in a church with chimes
A sign of the times today
Hearing no bell from the steeple tall
People all in dismay
Falling so far on a silver spoon
Making the moon for fun
Changing a rope for a size too small
People all get hung

Take a look you may see me coming through
For I am the parasite who travels two by two

When lifting the mask from a local clown
And feeling down like him
And I'm seeing the light in a station bar
Travelling far in sin
And I'm sailing downstairs to the Northern Line
Watching the shine of the shoes
And hearing the trials of the people there
Who's to care if they lose

Take a look you may see me on the ground
For I am the parasite of this town

And take a look you may see me in the dirt
For I am the parasite who hangs from your skirt

This is not just thematically and tonally the sibling of 'At The Chime Of A City Clock' – you can just imagine Ray Warleigh's sax chilling the air around it – but it's very close harmonically too.

Rarely can a song in a major key have sounded as sad as this. The first note of the riff is the flattened 7th, undermining any confidence or optimism that might have come from the tonic (or 'home' note) that follows. The riff then describes another descending pattern, with the bass part barely even giving you the root note to secure yourself on. The song also never goes to any other chord that a happy major base might typically aim for, straying only once, and then only a semitone up ('Take a look you may see me . . .'). These musical effects – compromised, ungrounded, circumscribed – back up the lyric of an alienated city life

Free Ride

I know you
I care too
I see through
All of the pictures that you keep on the wall
All of the people that will come to the ball
But hear me calling, won't you give me
A free ride
Hear me calling, won't you give me
A free ride

I know too
What you do
When you're through
Counting the cattle as they go by the door
Keeping a carpet that's so thick on the floor
But hear me calling, won't you give me
A free ride
Hear me calling, won't you give me
A free ride

I know you
I care too
I see through
All of the pictures that you keep on the wall
All of the people that will come to the ball
But hear me calling, won't you give me
A free ride
Hear me calling, won't you give me
A free ride

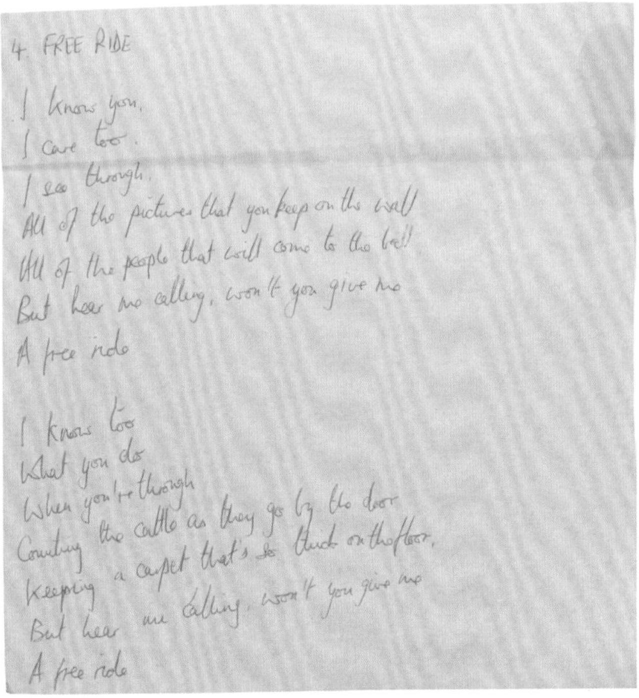
4. FREE RIDE
I know you.
I care too.
I see through.
All of the pictures that you keep on the wall
All of the people that will come to the ball
But hear me calling, won't you give me
A free ride

I know too
What you do
When you're through
Counting the cattle as they go by the door
Keeping a carpet that's so thick on the floor,
But hear me calling, won't you give me
A free ride

'Free Ride' seems to have the same sense of personal weakness and compromise as 'Place To Be', but also has darker, slightly accusatory overtones. Part of the latter effect comes from the bottom string being tuned all the way down to a low A; but it seems most to come out in the lines such as '*All* of the *pic*tures that you *keep* on the wall', where the left hand hits the chords for the italicised words with a sharp, fast slide from the fret below. This is a standard way for guitarists to add a bit of emphasis or just interest to a guitar part, and so typically would be exactly the sort of 'technique' thing Nick tends to avoid. But here it has a real, obvious purpose – it's like he's jabbing someone with his finger.

Harvest Breed

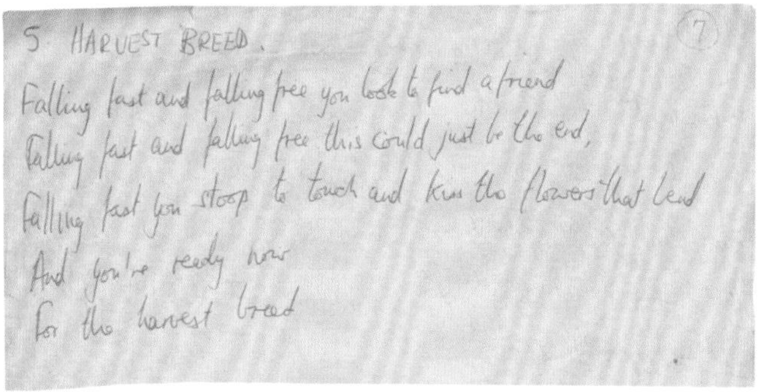
5 HARVEST BREED. (7)
Falling fast and falling free you look to find a friend
Falling fast and falling free this could just be the end,
Falling fast you stoop to touch and kiss the flowers that bend
And you're ready now
For the harvest breed

Falling fast and falling free you look to find a friend
Falling fast and falling free this could just be the end
Falling fast you stoop to touch and kiss the flowers that bend
And you're ready now
For the harvest breed

This song is in the same tuning as 'From The Morning' and uses similar shapes (based around 02400x in BEBEBE), but it does very different things with them.

Here the first chord (fingered 01300x) is a great example of something simple to play but harmonically unusual and cleverly used. Having two notes a fret down from the 'home' chord of 02400x could sound like a jazzy, chromatic move to start, but doesn't. Instead of the chord existing purely so that we can hear the tension resolve when it moves back up a fret (as, for example, the feeling coming back out of the second chord in the verses of 'Poor Boy'), the chord's own internal tensions themselves define the song. Explored by an insistent, unsettling picking pattern, they produce an immediate feeling of deep unease. This feeling is so strong that it persists through the whole number, as Nick considers what it might be to fall so far down that you embrace your own end.

From The Morning

A day once dawned and it was beautiful
A day once dawned from the ground
Then the night she fell
And the air was beautiful
The night she fell all around

So look see the days
The endless coloured ways
And go play the game that you learnt
From the morning

And now we rise
And we are everywhere
And now we rise from the ground
And see she flies
And she is everywhere
See she flies all around

So look see the sights
The endless summer nights
And go play the game that you learnt
From the morning

6. FROM THE MORNING
A day once dawned, and it was beautiful.
A day once dawned from the ground,
Then the night she fell,
And the air was beautiful,
Then night she fell all around.

So look see the days
The endless coloured ways,
And go play the game that you learnt f
From the morning

And now we rise
And we are everywhere,
And now we rise from the ground
And see she flies
And she is everywhere,
See she flies all around,

So look see the sights
The endless summer nights
And go play the game that you learnt
From the morning

Unlike its predecessor, 'Harvest Breed', the tone generated here from similar chords is not one of foreboding, but of a curious, resigned acceptance. Despite his struggle to find a way to live, he seems to be wishing for other people to be able to go out and enjoy life – an extraordinary gift with which to leave the stage.

Musically, it's remarkable how much he gets out of so little. Simple alternating bass from the thumb, two two-finger chords, his favourite 222000 for the fourth line 'chord-to-come-back-from' . . . and that's about it. Even the chord changes are, underneath it all, a basic three-chord pattern.

But softly picked in a low register, the three-note theme opening seems to reassure even as it hints at something darker. And the unusual inversion of the F chord, with no F in the bass strings, adds a qualified air: this is no straightforward emotion. Try this song with normal C and F chords on guitar – or even just add an F bass – and it feels completely different, somehow simplistic and lumbering where it was knowing and poised. Such small details can totally change a song, and part of Nick's art was making sure every detail worked.

A day once dawned,
And it was beautiful
A day once dawned from the ground.
Then the night she fell.
And the air was beautiful
The night she fell all around

So look see the sights
Of the endless summer nights
And go play the game
That you learnt from the morning

I have a giant love
That grows like a mountain bear,
Who scrapes the bark from the
edge of the trees
And hugs my past to death.

Keith Morris and *Pink Moon*

Photographer and subject met again in the latter months of 1971. In one short year, Nick had transformed into a man on the brink of oblivion. Only in part can this be attributed to the failure of *Bryter Layter* to make an impact on either the press or the public. Keith's shock at the change in his friend is revealed in his photos for Nick's final album.

This time there was only one location – Hampstead Heath, in north London, close to where Nick was staying before he finally retreated to Warwickshire. The shoot took barely an hour. Keith recalled later that they hardly spoke. But communication clearly took place at a deeper level. Keith seems to have had a profound understanding of a friend who could write:

(Photo: Christophe, 2004)

Know that I love you
Know I don't care
Know that I see you
Know I'm not there

Rarely has desolation been so bleakly distilled.
Rarely have photographs revealed that desolation with such spartan clarity.

Keith never forgot his friend and he never stopped taking photographs, but he heard his own stronger 'voice from the sea' and pursued his passion for marine diving at which he became a noted expert. He continued to give freely of his time to talk to Nick's fans who would contact him, by phone, by mail, or in person.
He did so until the day he drowned in a tragic diving accident in 2005.

AMERICAN ALBUM

ROLLING STONE/APRIL 27, 1972

Nick Drake
Island SMAS-9307

British singer-songwriter Nick Drake's American debut album is a beautiful and decadent record. A triumph of eclecticism, it successfully brings together varied elements characteristic of the evolution of urban folk rock music during the past five years. An incredibly slick sound that is highly dependent on production values (credit Joe Boyd) to achieve its effects, its dreamlike quality calls up the very best of the spirit of early Sixties' jazz-pop ballad. It combines this with the contemporary introspection of British folk rock to evoke a hypnotic spell of opiated languor.

The intention of casting a spell—perhaps the broadest and most powerful artistic impulse underlying Van Morrison's *Astral Weeks* (which *Nick Drake* resembles at moments, though this is not at all a "concept" album)—is here fully realized. Like *Astral Weeks*, and to a lesser extent Cat Stevens' *Mona Bone Jakon*, *Nick Drake* is an addictive record—perhaps even more than its predecessors, since Drake's voice is so softly, seductively sensual. Add to this Drake's own densely textured guitar, plus, of all unpromising elements, shades of Stan Getz and Ramsey Lewis, plus two of the most melancholy string arrangements ever written—and you get a head cocktail in which the "astral" of Van Morrison and the "transcendental" of Donovan are still present, yet seen as passively erotic distortions in a pool of sweet liqueur after a couple of downs and a few tokes.

Could this sort of thing be the Muzak of 1984? It would seem a fair guess. So what keeps *Nick Drake* from being the Muzak of today? The variety of its musical thought; the intensity of its aesthetic stance; and the superior musicianship of all concerned. Ray Warleigh's alto sax riffs are thrilling—tinged with the anarchic urban wail; likewise Chris McGregor's piano and John Cale's always distinctive contributions (celeste, piano and organ on "Northern Sky," and viola and harpsichord on "Fly").

Drake's songs vary considerably in style from the delightfully simple skipping-down-the-London-street "One of These Things First" to the Astrud Gilberto cafe-romantic ballad, "At the Chime of a City Clock." Drake's tunes, though more or less derivative, are melodically strong and harmonically kinetic. Their high degree of harmonic sophistication is enhanced by the brilliant arrangements, the most ambitious of which, by Harry Robinson, is lavished on "River Man," a mystical reverie with affinities to "Lazy Afternoon."

"Cello Song" is a tour-de-force of Indian-influenced erotic meditation, wherein guitar and cello (Clare Lowther) are interwoven with Drake's husky voice (itself taking a second cello part) to create the most sensuous of textures. On "Poor Boy," an outright gasp of self-pity, the soulful backup voices of Pat Arnold and Doris Troy repeatedly interrupt Drake's lament with the comment, "Oh poor boy/so sorry for yourself." This mockery of self-mockery is wonderfully ironic, but it also enhances the obsessively insomniac quality of the complaint itself—all six and-one-half gorgeous minutes of it.

Drake's greatest weakness—one he shares with all too many of today's male lyric troubadours, especially those from England—is the lack of verbal force in his song lyrics, which by and large could be characterized as *nouveau art nouveau*. In the case of Drake, this is less serious a liability than it is for artists who are more up front vocally. The beauty of Drake's voice is its own justification. May it become familiar to us all.

—STEPHEN HOLDEN

RECORD MIRROR, March 4, 1972

RODRIGUEZ
Coming From Reality (A&M AMLS 68073). He looks like A&M's answer to Jose Feliciano, but it's not so — he sounds like Donovan and plays like nobody else. Heavily orchestrated, Rod plays guitar out front of it all and the idea is slightly vague. I think he has a good voice and great musical ability, but this isn't right — it's over done and the arrangements plough through his lyrics like a buildozer in a flower garden. One fantastic track is 'Cause'. Better use of everything on this. L.G.

JAKE JONES
Jake Jones (MCA MUPS 432). Unusual approach involving less instrumentation, but more careful consideration for rhythm and vocals by a new group. Heavy use of acoustic guitars and tambourine, with piano, drums and organ to dress it up. Vocals are powerful and the entire effect is pleasing if just a bit under-done. Weird harmony and subdued instruments on Donovan's 'Catch The Wind'. Things could happen here. L.G.

TOAD
Toad (RCA Victor SF 8241). German group as heavy as imaginable and full of unobvious, uncommercial, maybe even unwanted chord progressions. Well produced and effective as a marathon mood effort, but by no means in the top of its class. They seem proficient at each part of this seven-track album, but nothing stands out as new, original or inspired — just passable. Ability has to be channeled properly. L.G.

FISHBAUGH FISHBAUGH AND ZORN
FFZ (CBS 64783). Hot new three-part harmony rock group from CBS and it looks like a lasting proposition. The Fishbaughs write it all and the approach may remind you of early Byrds, but updated and re-enforced with their own originality. Vocals are exceptionally accurate and clever. The accent is on acoustic picking in front of electric rock — just right for the vocal concept. Obviously three pros who know what they're doing — even the quiet solos are beautifully sung. Recommended. L.G.

NELSON EDDY/JAN PEERCE
World's Favourite Love Songs (Sunset SLS 50261). Eddy, star of Hollywood musicals; Peerce, Met Opera Company star. The songs are show stoppers from musicals like 'Kismet', 'Carousel' and 'West Side Story'.

JOHNSTONS
Now a duo, the Johnstons' light, traditional approach to original songs, makes them vocally unique. Backing them vocally are old pros like Tim Hart and Royston Wood, so the feel of this album is genuine English heritage, though the songs are new. In other words, it's an instant classic. Best on the melodic record is 'Continental Trailways Bus' with good acoustic guitar (reminiscent of Joni Mitchell's 'Carrie') and excellent ascending harmony lines. L.G.

NICK DRAKE
Pink Moon (Island ILPS 9184). Strange and mysterious voice from a mysterious and often scarce individual. Nick is a fine, timely guitarist — like Donovan always was, but more complex. His vocals are tuneful and full of a closeness you can't describe. The whole album has a delicacy about it that suggests a very fragile, but beautiful talent has been captured. Very interesting picking and chord structures perfectly defined, for Nick and his guitar are (wisely) the only elements present. Good stuff. L.G.

CLAIRE HAMILL
One House Left Standing (Island ILPS 9182). Very pretty, very dainty and sometimes full of insight and attractive expression. There are quite a number of young girl singer/song-writer/guitarists around who have made it and more who are trying, so it will be a tough job — but Claire has at least as much as any of them. Her style needs more character and songs a little more unification (dare I say pattern?), but overall, this is pleasing. It means that she's a natural and improvement will come easy. L.G.

HOOKY
Collected Tales Of Hooky No. 1 (RCA Victor SF 8247). Harmonies on this are grossly out of tune for the most part and many of the solo bits are even worse. The songs are weak already and appear to be played with a minor degree of capability, thus rendering this an unfortunate release all round. Production is flat and arrangements poor. I don't know whether the group or their connections are at fault, or whether everybody is. All I know is what my ear says and it says 'Ouch!' L.G.

LOS MACHUCAMBOS
Musica Latina (Decca Phase 4 PFS 4238). Latin material like 'El Condor Pasa', 'Frenesi', 'Ti-Pi-Tin' — excitingly recorded, even though of obvious speciality appeal. Fine instrumental work.

RECORD REVIEWS

Zenith Magazine (Oxford U.)

APRIL '72

PINK MOON by NICK DRAKE

Nick Drake's whispering vocals breathe their way through an aura of lyrical enchantment and tasteful guitar simplicity, creating the feeling of quiet contentment with life. The words are seemingly of nothing in particular, but they flow as gently and as freshly as morning dew.
Of the man himself I know very little, having only heard his first two albums and been greatly impressed, but not much seems to have been written about him. Anyway this is a remarkably fine album which comes in a really nice sleeve complete with words to all the songs. What more could you ask for?

EXPRESS & ECHO
EXETER 67-230
DAILY CIRCULATION 39,099

-6 APR 1972

E MAY BE R

Records by Jonathan Culverhouse

Sandpipers (A & M). The Sandpipers have an easy, relaxed way of singing things and on this album they do nice versions of "Never My Love", "How Can You Mend a Broken Heart" and "It's Too Late", plus seven others

**** Pink Moon—Nick Drake (Island). 'Bryter Later" was an album which received a good deal of attention when it came out last year and this, Nick Drake's second, looks like renewing the interest. He still sounds and sings a bit like Cat Stevens—maybe that is what I like.

Cheltenham Chronicle 15/4/72

RECORDS

ALBUM SPOT

NICK DRAKE—Pink Moon (Island): He is something of a mystery figure, which the record company have played on. At the same time, he is something of a cult figure among young, discerning album collectors. Drake falls into the singer-songwriter category, so popular at the moment. His songs are not the easiest to understand and he accompanies himself on guitar and piano. May be part of the fun of the album is unravelling what makes Nick tick. For no clear reasons the album does stand out, although Drake is very much solo.

GLOUCESTER CITIZEN

LATEST ALBUMS

NICK DRAKE — Pink Moon (Island): He is something of a mystery, cult figure among young, discerning album collectors. Drake falls into the singer-songwriter category — his songs are not the easiest to understand and he accompanies himself on guitar and piano. May be part of the fun of the album is unravelling what makes Nick tick. For no clear reasons the album does stand out.

Lincoln Echo
LINCOLN 67-365
Daily Circulation 37,000

11 APR 1972

THIS W

Albums

■ Nick Drake—Pink Moon (Island): He is something of a mystery figure, which the record company have played on. At the same time he is something of a cult figure among young discerning album collectors. Drake falls into the singer-songwriter category, so popular at the moment. His songs are not the easiest to understand and he accompanies himself on guitar and piano. Maybe part of the fun of the album is unravelling what makes Nick tick. For no clear reasons the album does stand out, although Drake is very much solo.

YARMOUTH MERCURY

14 APR 1972

Intimate

INTROVERT of the week: Nick Drake, with his Island album "Jink Moon" in its colourful Dali-esque surrealistic sleeve.

A tea cup, a shoe and a clown mask float in a greeny sky around a great cheesy moon. And the songs are the same: full of images that don't relate. Hinting at things, but never saying anything directly, clearly, out loud.

A song starts:

"Know that I love you,
Know that I don't care,
Know that I see you,
Know I'm not there."

End of song. So there's young Nick Drake trying to find himself in the alien landscape of his own mind. And being careful not to let us know very much about him.

But then the production and Drake's singing style are quite the opposite. They are intimate.

He has a high, breathy voice that sounds exactly like one of his female contemporaries, Bridget St. John (she has a low breathy voice).

He sings and hums to his own repetitive guitar or piano, and the result is softly hypnotic. But still the message is an all-too-familiar confusion, as if Drake is defying you to make your own sense of it.

In my case, his m lulled me and made me indolent to try.

Nick Drake . . . remote and in the shadows.

to resort to facile melodrama or gratuitous crowd-pleasing.

The album is an accurate indication of the strength and range of their music at the moment with the emphasis, if anywhere, on singer and guitarist Mick Rogers who measures his contribution beautifully. Manfred himself plays an assortment of keyboards, including a synthesizer which he operates in accordance with the material in hand. That's to say, its function is not particularly complex but it's not glib either, curling its way around 'California Coastline' like an epileptic jew's harp or weaving in and out of the layers of 'Tribute' like a weary electronic pogo stick.

The departure point in most cases is a good song. Steaming cauldrons of rhythm like 'Captain Bobby Stout' and Dr John's 'Jump Sturdy' are turned overundersidewaysdown and propelled with choral support. And Dylan's 'Please Mrs Henry' and Randy Newman's 'Living Without You' are driven along in a manner which, against all the odds, works. Manfred's own approach couldn't help but be affected by long exposure to these two heroes, with the result that 'Part Time Man', for instance, is the song of a different-ethnic-group Randy Newman and will strike a chord in anyone who's hung around outside a factory on a cold night hoping for a gig.

If there's no programming, no bogus structuring, melody and solidity can't fail. Manfred Mann's Earth Band have found themselves a happy relationship between excitement and expertise, in which the individual styles are compatible with the collective effort. They've made a record that's hot but abundant in detail and they're the most enjoyable band I've seen for a while. Gosh.

Al Clark

Nick Drake: 'Pink Moon'

(Island ILPS 9184)

It's a measure of Nick Drake's remoteness that, in these days of former folk singers getting it on with electric combos and using the whole range of effects available to them in the studio, he should choose to make his third album with only a guitar, piano and engineer for company.

The arrangements were an important feature of the first two records, especially the second. On that they reached a point of balance and harmony which, extended any further, might've resulted in their taking over completely. So it's understandable, now that Joe Boyd is no longer around, that Nick should want to approach his music in as bare and as personalised a manner as possible.

He writes striking and evocative songs and always has done, but most of the magic is in the delivery: a smoky, palpitating voice, reminiscent of the jazzier Donovan, gliding wistful words over the chord changes and creating moments of perfect stillness. Those who have tried their hand at his material haven't even scratched the surface yet.

'Pink Moon' features eleven new fragments of his head, including four of haiku length and a short instrumental. Several of the more substantial songs are very lovely: 'Things Behind The Sun', 'Parasite' and, especially 'From The Morning'. One, 'Which Will', sounds a bit like a John Martyn song but isn't.

Sadly, and despite Island's efforts to rectify the situation, Nick Drake is likely to remain in the shadows, the private troubadour of those who have been fortunate enough to catch an earful of his exquisite 3am introversions.

Al Clark

The Sutherland Brothers (Island)

What does it take to persuade you to lay out a couple of quid on a first album by an unknown band? A helluva lot, but this record is worth the risk. It would be a valid, but jaded, reaction to point out all the flashes of obvious influence which crop up as the record plays (particularly that of the Byrds), and to say that the band could get really interesting if they stay together and develop.

But somehow these callow youths have absorbed a lot of what's happened musically over the last fifteen years, added some lyrics which cause you to slap the nearest bit of soft flesh much more often than they make you snort with ancient derision, and produced the freshest bit of chunky-chunk in many a month. After you've taken the chance, bought the album and listened relaxed and attentive for half-a-dozen times, you'll find that at least half of the tracks will be fighting for precedence in that awkward corner of the head that constantly replays addictive melodies. In short (and this is a very short review) this is just about the first album to consider right now if you fancy taking a chance instead of settling for one of the obvious heavies.

John Collis

Time Out, 17 March 1972

CLOSE TO YOUR HEART

Paul and I were in the middle of laying out **LIQUORICE** with periodic assistance from Irena. I got up and fumbled for the post, Irena's still sleeping(!). There were two very nice letters , Jim Capaldi's single and an article on Nick Drake's "Pink Moon" for our "Close To Your Heart" series. We were really pleased, a first contribution to "Close To Your Heart" and it's about Nick Drake too. "Pink Moon" is a lovely LP, time to play its' haunting tunes again. Nick Drake hung on the clouds, the sun smiled occasionally, and one day time's river flowed swiftly out of view. There aren't that many real people making real music. Nick Drake was(is) one of them. It's a pleaure to have Nick Drake:Close To Your Heart.

It's not often that you hear two songs by an artist whom you've never heard before and are so impressed by them as to want to rush out and by all the singer's LPs as quickly as possible, but it happened to me in October last year when a white label Island sampler that I picked up for ten bob in a second-hand store yielded two songs so beautiful tat I dug out an old Island catalogue to work out that the tracks were "Things Behind the Sun" and "Pink Moon" from the LP of the same name by a guy who I'd previously only heard of fleetingly called Nick Drake.

A couple of weeks later I went round practically every record store in the centre of London to find just one with a Nick Drake LP in stock, the stunningly beautiful "Bryter Lyter". I tried every possible source to get information about Nick and eventually a friend sent me a photostat of Connor McKnight 's excellent article in ZigZag 42 Shortly afterwards a beautiful obituary in "Sounds" by Jerry Gilbert came as a bombshell-- Nick had died from an accidental overdose of tranquilisers at 6a.m on October 26. Words can't describe how the tragedy upset me and this isn't the place for the full story (it can be found in ZZs 42 & 49) but let it suffice to say that my copy of "Pink Moon" arrived two days later and it is the only record that has ever made me cry.

In the Autumn of 1971 Nick returned from a year in which he had been totally absent from the 'music scene' to record this LP. Gone were the beautiful elaborate arrangements of his first two LPs. Nick is the only person playing on the LP-- just him singing with his accoustic guitar (and piano on the title track). The only other person present at the sessions was his good friend (and brilliant engineer) John Wood. Everything that Nick recorded is on those sessions is on the LP.

The first track is "Pink Moon" and has just five lines. "Saw it written and I saw it say/ Pink Moon is on its way/ None of you will stand so tall/ Pink Moon gonna get ye all/ And its a Pink Moon.", sung twice against the guitar with a beautiful piano link Then there is "Place To Be" a sad (as are all the songs on the LP- by all accounts Nick was in a very depressed stage of his life from 1970 until a short while before he died) song about life, love, loneliness and searching....... ..for a place to be. "Road" is dominated by very strong guitar, a four line song the last two lines of which are repeated, once again, the search for a way to survive:

"You can take the road that takes you to the stars now,
I can take a road that'll see me through".

"Which Will" is a loving song to the girl who has rejected him ("Which way will you take now"/if you won't take me?") It is followed by "Horn", a brief instrumental that leads into "Things Behind the Sun", which, for what it's worth, probably means more to me than any other song I know. More so than any other song on the album it is a piece of advice, the lessons that Nick has learnt realised in the song:

"Please beware of them that stare/ they only smile to see you while your time away.... ....You'll find renown where people frown/ At things that you say/ But say what you'll say"

It is the longest track, the beautiful introduction breaks into the night like an anthem.. it's obviously very hard for me to express the wonders of this album.

Side two opens with "Know", a short scaring song, "Know that I love you/ Know that I don't care/ Know that I see you/ Know that I'm not there". "Parasite" is another moving song in which Nick tries to put himself down but ends up impressing me of his humility. "Free Ride" can be compared to "Know" in that it has a strong rhythm and is an expression of paranoia that sets the two songs aside from the togethrness of the rest of the album. "Harvest Breed" is a short song about, I think, reaching the depths of introspection/depression-- but the ending is optimistic (again, to me) "And you're ready now for the Harvest breed" The final song is, fittingly "From the Morning". (And at this point, a big round of applause to my favourite label, Island, both for supporting Nick by putting out his albums when no-one was interested in him, and for so carefully structuring the running order of this LP that it fits together perfectly.) Perhaps I've talked too much about each song on this album but let me say that, for a man who is so obviously close to suicide, it is a warm and optimistic close.

So there you are the LP only lasts about 29 minutes but that doesn't matter to me- each song is a gem and the record is so intense and moving that time ceases to exist for me when it is playing, it seems to be over in no time at all. The songs on the LP are like epigrams which, taken as a whole, display all that the artist has learnt in his life-- songs which transcend life and death, the songs of a wise and humble man.

Perhaps this article has seemed to be a little melodramatic to you; if so I don't apologise because that's what it means to me and that's what the series is about. The effect that "Pink Moon" has on me is consistent-- I can play it three times in a row without once losing it. Someone once called the LP "an album of 3a.m. introspection" which is close but too simplistic-- like Leonard Cohen's first three LPs it fills you with an air of seriousness, but the beauty of Nick's voice, guitar and songs give much more, the lyrics are so important and the emotion is so intense.

In closing, I know that most of us can't afford to fork out three quid on one guy's taste but if you ever get the chance to hear Nick Drake, please try.

The LP of Nick's that I haven't previously mentioned is his first "Five Leaves Left" and is excellent. The lyrics that I have quoted ought to be credited to Warlock Music, with thanks.

DAVE BELBIN.

LIQUORICE Magazine (Nottingham) 1974/5

NICK DRAKE: "PINK MOON" (ISLAND ILPS 9184).

ISLAND APPEARED to have forgotten about Nick Drake until he ambled into the offices one day and presented them with this album. No-one knew he'd recorded it except the engineer and it's a long way removed from the mighty sessions that Joe Boyd used to arrange for him. Nick Drake remains the great silent enigma of our time — the press handout says that no-one at Island even knows where he's living, and certainly he appears to have little interest in working in public again. The album consists entirely of Nick's guitar, voice and piano and features all the usual characteristics without ever matching up to "Bryter Layter". One has to accept that Nick's songs necessarily require further augmentation, for whilst his own accompaniments are good the songs are not sufficiently strong to stand up without any embroidery at all. "Things Behind The Sun" makes it, so does "Parasite" — but maybe it's time Mr. Drake stopped acting so mysteriously and started getting something properly organised for himself. — J.G.

New on Island

Nick Drake—Pink Moon
Island (SMAS-9318)

Nick Drake rarely performs live, but there is no doubt that he does communicate through his music and lyrics. Nick's first album (called "Nick Drake") came out last July and started a definite Nick Drake cult. Stephen Holden in Rolling Stone just recently reviewed the first album and said, "the beauty of Drake's voice is its own justification. May it become familiar to us all."

Platter Chatter

By Jim Conley

Nick Drake's Style Sincere

Every so often a record company, like a movie producer, floods a reviewer with so much advance publicity on some new talent that he can't help but be anxious to see if the artist can live up to his buildup.

This buildup can be a dangerous thing, like hopping you up so you expect too much.

Frankly, I didn't believe NICK DRAKE was going to be "another Cat Stevens" or would have "the kind of album Donovan might have produced. . .if he'd been lucky."

But the record is here now and everybody was almost right — except Nick Drake is not another Cat Stevens. There's a similarity of style but it's soon easy to forget.

So who is Nick Drake and what does he do? First of all, he's young, English, has a throaty, shaggy voice which is nevertheless captivating, plays acoustic guitar which could make a good LP by itself and he has just made his first American album "Pink Moon" (Island Records).

And how good is he? So good that you should listen for yourself before any more buildups spoil the spontaneous combustion of his music with your ears.

He lifts some unpolished, simple lyrics into a private world which you are made to share through his convincing sincerity. Where Cat Stevens seems to make a bit of fun of his situation, Nick Drake voices the sorrowful incompleteness of a man's who is struggling helplessly to be tender . . . like a drifter whose squinty, quick gaze is the facade of a scared-to-smile, too-often-hurt sensitivity.

Indeed, Drake — says his own recording sugar daddy — is somewhat of a loner, a mystery man who avoids interviews. That's fine for his image, too. Maybe his next album jacket will give more than a negative as a substitute for a perceptive photo of his face. And what will it take to bring the shy Nick Drake out of the shadows? Well, I'll bet coaxing with a gold album wouldn't hurt.

But whether or not he's as reclusive as his people say, I think he's where 1972's music is going, maybe where 1973's will be. At least I hope so, because it's a beautiful direction.

there's "Black Angel," a really unique song (it has been pointed out to me). It has marimbas, some harp punctuation and distinctively calypso-rock percussion. But they could have spared me the brass on the side's final cut, "Loving Cup."

We get more of Jagger's mean vocals and harp blasts on side 3, particularly on one cut whose title is enough to get it X-ed off the airwaves as well as the news pages. He shows once again the invaluable nature of the harmonica as a purveyor of whining excitation — I've always had a sneaking suspicion its high notes loosen the wax in your ears.

Side 4, to me, contains the best cut of the whole set, "Stop Breaking Down," a near perfect blues, rock combination — a hot, late night t u m b l i n' rhythm . . . a really snaky crying guitar and banging back-up piano.

It's the side which leaves you with a good taste in your mouth.

GOREN BRIDGE Q

by Charles H. Goren

Both vulnerable. East deals.

NORTH
♠ K J 9
♡ K Q 4 3 2
◇ A 9
♣ 9 4 2

WEST
♠ 8
♡ J 8 5
◇ K 10 8 5 3
♣ K Q J 6

EAST
♠ 7 4 3 2
♡ 10 7 6
◇ J 6 4
♣ A 8 7

SOUTH
♠ A Q 10 6 5
♡ A 9
◇ Q 7 2
♣ 10 5 3

The bidding:

East	South	West	North
Pass	1 ♠	Pass	2 ♡
Pass	2 ♠	Pass	4 ♠
Pass	Pass	Pass	

Opening lead: King of ♣

Although nine top tricks are available at no trump, it is natural for North and South to glide into a four spade contract. But for a gap in declarer's technique, the partnership would have scored a handsome profit on the deal.

West opened the king of clubs and continued to cash out the

Above left: *Sounds*, 25 March 1972 Below left: advert in *Rolling Stone*, 22 June 1972

NICK DRAKE: 'PINK MOON'
Pink moon; Place to be; Road; Which will; Horn; Things behind the sun; Know; Parasite; Free ride; Harvest breed; From the morning
Island ILPS-9184 (£2·30)

Sometimes I don't believe there is a Nick Drake—and, very often, Island have their doubts. It's a strange affair all round. Nick turns up at his recording company about once a year with a completed album in his hand, then disappears to goodness-knows-where, leaving Island to pay any forthcoming royalties into his bank account. Actually, the LPs hardly sell, thanks partly to Nick's reluctance to play promotional concerts and one is left with the feeling that his only ambition is to play the lead in the Howard Hughes story should anyone ever decide to make it as a musical. In the meantime, he employs his deliciously smokey voice in making these intimate, late-night sounds that I find myself playing time and time again. **[A: 1]**

NICK DRAKE / Pink Moon / Island 9318 We always have a hard time with this kind of young chap with acoustic guitar and his own poetry disguised as lyrics, probably for the same reason we have trouble with Joni Mitchell. As Stephen Holden says right on the hype sheet, "It [the album, Nick's third] combines this [dreamlike quality] with the contemporary introspection of British folk rock to evoke a hypnotic spell of opiated languor." Nick is from the land that loaned us Donovan, Van Morrison and Cat Stevens, and will no doubt become a popular favorite among popular circles.

NICK DRAKE. Pink Moon. Island ILPS 9184. £2.30.

NICK DRAKE IS an odd fish. He knows it, everybody knows it. He will not perform live because the prospect is too traumatic, Island can never find him 90 per cent of the time, and then out of the blue he walks into their offices with the tapes for his new album. Sung in a breathy, diffident, feathery voice, his songs are infinitely soothing and infinitely similar. So what. At certain times in one's life anything more emphatic is murderous. This album, just rippling acoustic guitar and that lullaby voice, is even more unassuming than the others, without the occasional string backing which lent a certain soporific lushness to the previous two. It is like intruding upon a private dream world in which even a murmur is indiscreet. Yet Nick Drake is not hiding anything. It is all there if you listen. He is simply saying 'These are my songs'. If you want them you can have them'. No cajoling, no hustling, not the slightest inducement of any kind by way of boppy arrangements or flashy lyrics. And people do take up the offer, not many but enough for it not to be a waste of time. Nick Drake will never strike it big. It is not in his nature or in the nature of his music. And that is another good thing too. Try and listen to it, above the roar of the city.

Above left: *HiFi News & Record Review*, May 1972 Above right: *Fusion*, No. 79, October 1972 Below left: Island Records' promotional poster for the quarter's releases: *Pink Moon* in the company of a Free offshoot, The Sutherland Brothers, Jethro Tull's latest epic and the *Pink Moon* sales-figure companion Claire Hamill Below right: *Records & Recording*, April 1972 sure, they could find themselves making more natural and important musical statements, than in the past, while consolidating their position as one of the most popular modern rock bands. — **C.W.**

NICK DRAKE: "Pink Moon" (Island). John Martyn told me about Nick Drake in ecstatic terms and so it seemed the natural thing to do, bag the album when it came in for review that is. It is hard to say whether John was right or not. His music is so personal and shyly presented both lyrically and in his confined guitar and piano playing that it neither does or doesn't come over. Drake is a fairly mysterious person, no-one appears to know where he lives, what he does — apart from writing songs — and there is not even a chance to see him on stage to get closer to his insides. In places he is a cult figure, and among the new younger sixth form and college audience there are pockets that go overboard to catch the latest glimmer of news that moves along the verbal news meanderings. The more you listen to Drake though, the more compelling his music becomes — but all the time it hides from you. On "Thing Behind The Sun," he sings to me, embarrassed and shy. Perhaps one should play his albums with the sound off and just look at the cover and make the music in your head reciting his words from inside the cover to your own rhythmic heart rhymes. Nick Drake does not exist at all. Four lines of "Know" — "Know that I love you, Know that I don't care, Know that I see you, Know I'm not there." It could be that Nick Drake does not exist at all. **MP.**

WAIT FOR IT!

island records ltd
basing street london w11

Full-page advert in *Record Collector (Including Record Bargains)*, February 1972
Above right: Mark Plummer, *Melody Maker*, 1 April 1972

Fusion, No. 77, August 1972

For the sleeve of Nick's last studio album, the Island in-house art director commissioned the illustrator Michael Trevithick to paint a cover illustration idea for the album based on a series of lyrics proposed for songs for the new album. Previously Michael had been to see Ann Sullivan at Island with his portfolio; he was already an established illustrator and had designed an image for a US edition of Island's Spooky Tooth debut album. Furnished with *Bryter Layter* and a few sheets of new lyrics, Michael extracted key lines from the songs and composed a sketch for the surreal image above (later painted in acrylic on board).

He took this into Island to show Nick who appeared to approve, though not resoundingly so, according to both Ann and Michael. 'He just shuffled in the background and nodded,' said Ann. Michael begged for two weeks to complete the final piece and his negotiated fee was £90 – triple what he was used to getting. The choice of gatefold or single sleeve was arbitrary.

Graphic Design company CCS took the painting into the finished artwork stage. It is assumed that the people at Island Records were not happy with Trevithick's original front cover typography (shown here), and mechanical type replaced this for the printed version under Trevithick's guidance.

Ann Sullivan had attended the the Keith Morris shoot on Hampstead Heath, but stayed in the background leaving Nick and Keith to it, sensing that her presence might be an intrusion. Her dog managed to get into some of the shots and Ann used one of these to advertise the album in the original *Record Collector* magazine. Left to her own devices, she added the headline 'WAIT FOR IT!'. This was later replaced by the letter from David Sandison when the advert appeared as a full page in *Melody Maker*.

Ann Sullivan left Island Records in 1972 to become the art director at Transatlantic Records, winning awards for her work. Michael Trevithick remains a successful freelance illustrator based in Kilburn, London.

'PINK MOON' - NICK DRAKE'S LATEST ALBUM: THE FIRST WE HEARD OF IT WAS WHEN IT WAS FINISHED.

The first time I ever heard Nick Drake was when I joined Island and picked out his first Album "Five Leaves Left" from the shelf and decided to listen to it because the cover looked good.

From the opening notes of "Time Has Told Me", to the last chord of "Saturday Sun", I was held by the totally personal feel of the music, the words, and by that strange feeling you get when you accidentally intrude on someone else's phone conversation.

The first time I ever saw Nick Drake was at the Queen Elizabeth Hall. He came on with his guitar, sat on a stool, looked at the floor and sang a series of muffled songs punctuated by mumbled thanks for the scattering of bewildered applause from the audience who didn't know who the hell he was, nor cared too much. At the end of his last song, his guitar still holding the final notes of the song, he got up and walked off; his shoulders hunched as if to protect him from actually having to meet people.

The first time I ever met Nick Drake was the week his 2nd Album "Bryter Layter" was released. He arrived an hour late, wasn't very interested in a cup of coffee or tea or anything to eat. During the next half hour he said maybe two words. Eventually I ran out of voice, paid the bill and walked him back to Witchseason.

The last time I saw Nick was a week or so ago. He came in, smiling that weird smile of his and handed over his new album. He'd just gone into the studios and recorded it without telling a soul except the engineer. And we haven't seen him since.

The point of this story is this: why, (when there are people prepared to do almost anything for a recording contract or a Queen Elizabeth Hall date) are we releasing this new Nick Drake Album, and (if he wants to make one) - the next?

Because, quite simply we believe that Nick Drake is a great talent. His first two albums haven't sold a shit. But, if we carry on releasing them, then maybe one day someone authoratative will stop, listen properly and agree with us. Then maybe a lot more people will get to hear Nick Drake's incredible songs and guitar playing. And maybe they'll buy a lot of his Albums, and fulfill our faith in Nick's promise.

Then. Then we'll have done our job.

David Sandison

Dave Sandison - December 1971
(Island's Press Officer)

NICK DRAKE
PINK MOON
ILPS 9184

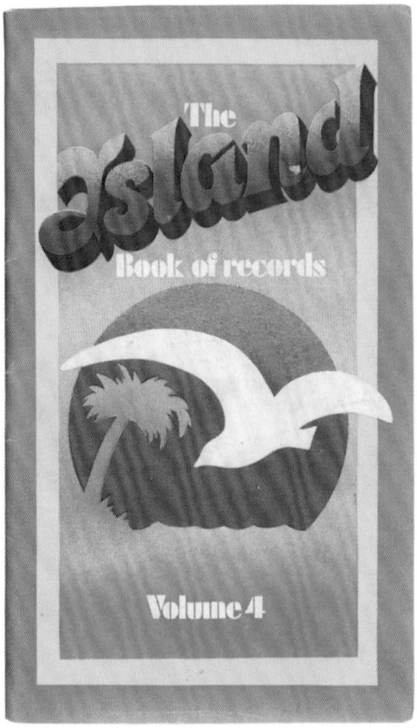

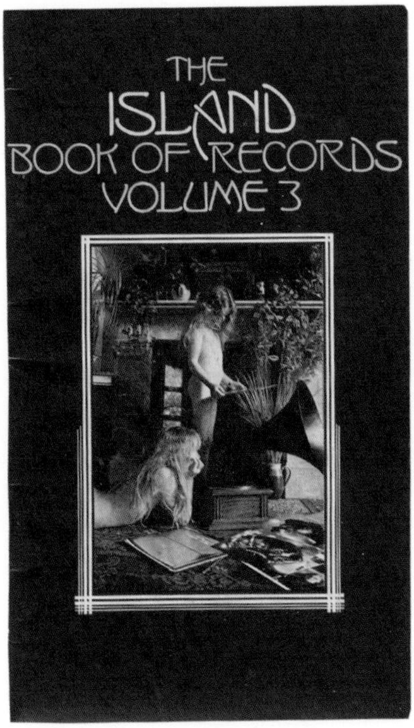

Three volumes of the iconic *Island Book Of Records* catalogues given away in record shops and now highly sought after, where many fans uncovered Nick Drake as well as through the Island budget sampler LPs

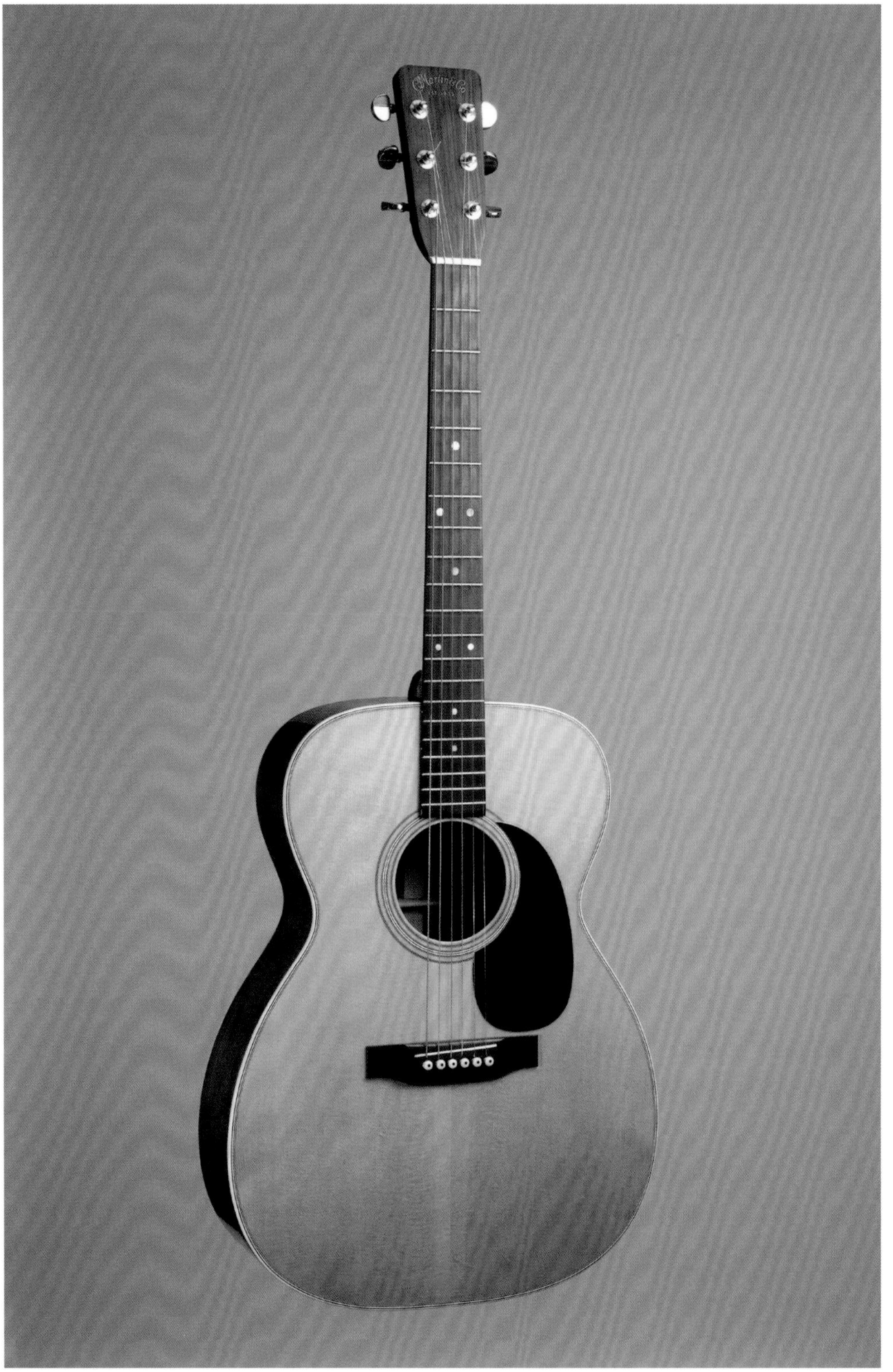

Nick's Martin guitar, model: 000-28, serial number: 313942 (1972)

Come Blow Your Horn On High

Paul Wheeler in conversation with Gabrielle Drake

PAUL WHEELER: This last guitar of Nick's – a Martin – is a smaller-bodied guitar than the one I remember him playing at Cambridge. I find that the particular quality of Martin guitars is their clarity: indeed, they tend to be almost too well balanced for someone like me. I play a Gibson J50, which has more of a drive on the bass. Whereas the Martins I've played were very evenly spaced, almost like a harpsichord.

I was not at all surprised that Nick played a Martin, because his playing didn't depend so much on a kick from the bass, but rather on precision and clarity. And when he needed the deeper notes, he simply tuned the bass down. Many guitarists tune bass E down to bass D, but he would frequently tune it down to C – and I thought this was his way of making the Martin into something deeper, while at the same time retaining its precision and delicacy.

It is interesting, anyway, that he chose to buy a guitar towards the end of his life, because it certainly implies that he was intending to develop in a new direction, not that he'd come to an end.

But what is also worthy of note is that he chose to go for a smaller-bodied guitar than before, which suggests to me that he was thinking in terms of playing with a higher timbre of sound: of getting away from the bass. You could start talking almost in philosophical terms about sounds of guitars, in that there's a certain kind of confidence if you're recognising the boom of the bass: you're acknowledging something that's resonant and emotionally centred underneath what you're doing. Whereas the exactitude of Nick's Martin suggests a certain distancing of yourself from the sound: it suggests a discipline, and an objectivity that comes with the clarity. And then too, there is the different way in which you have to hold the instrument. The Martin demands a much more upright posture than, say, my Gibson, which you have to pull into your body. (*He picks up and plays Nick's guitar.*) I would play this guitar, but it's not one I'd choose myself. But I can see exactly why Nick liked it . . . this Martin is particularly good at top notes . . . Guitars want to do different things. If I pick up a guitar, I'll play around a bit to find out what it wants to do – where it sounds best. You let the guitar tell you. And this guitar . . . tells me it wants to play Nick's songs! But at the same time, it's not a guitar on which I could imagine him playing something like 'Hazey Jane', because that does have a lower pitch.

GABRIELLE DRAKE: But if you think about his last four songs . . .

PW: Well, exactly, that fits, doesn't it? They're more plaintive – more a kind of wail; and he was singing in that high falsetto voice.

GD: Do you think that suggests that, had he lived, Nick would have turned to oriental or even early medieval music?

PW: I'm sure that is what he was exploring with, for instance, the last four songs. 'Black Eyed Dog' is a good example. The crossover between Indian music and, particularly, North African music on the one hand, and medieval European music on the other is no coincidence. It's like Morris dancing – the word comes from 'Moorish', apparently. The lute derives from the *oud*. And this was very much part of our generation's education, via people like Davy Graham, who specifically studied Moroccan music. And of course Morocco itself is a sort of storefront for Africa. People like Danny Thompson would then take his interest in African music further – with *Songhai*, for example. So Morocco is a kind of distillation of Arabic-African music, and that came back to Britain through Davy Graham, John Renbourn, the Incredible String Band, and then . . . then Nick . . . Yes, I think that was certainly the way he was going. It would make sense of his getting a smaller-bodied guitar.

Nick is known for using numerous different tunings, which again was something that people were experimenting with at the time – Joni Mitchell uses umpteen tunings, for example. But the tuning for many of the last songs, including 'Pink Moon', seem to me to go back to the root of something quite specific which, in guitar terms, is the tuning DADGAD. I first became aware of this tuning when it was used by Davy Graham. He set the whole ball rolling with regard to combining blues and jazz and Arabic music; and his working compromise between the Moroccan music he heard in Morocco, and the acoustic guitar that he played, was this tuning. Nowadays, it's become almost as common as the 'classic' tuning (EADGBE). There's a post-Nick Drake generation of guitarists who specifically and only use DADGAD – there's even a record label called Dadgad! If I play a bit of 'Pink Moon' . . . There, you see? Everything I played there is around the DADGAD tuning – and it suggests, not just moving towards this Arabic influence, but also absolutely returning to what would be considered the roots of that movement of acoustic guitars which began around 1968 with Davy Graham. I'm not saying that Nick stuck with this basic DADGAD tuning. I agree with the painstaking analyses that Chris Healey has done to identify the exact tunings Nick used, and that Nick tweaked and changed tunings restlessly. But for me, there is a musical relationship to that basic configuration. So in my opinion, it wasn't just that Nick stripped out all the strings and knobs from the arrangements of his songs, or that he reduced the size of his guitar – but rather that everything went back to a sort of disciplined minimalism, and to a much more direct relationship between Arabic and Western music.

GD: A liaison between East and West?

PW: Yes. But it's also the whole business of coming back to certain roots; and identifying the yearning, and the – almost muezzin – call of that music. At the same time, there's the physical way it feels to play this sort of music, which is quite different from the feeling when you're playing something like 'River Man', where there are subtle little shifts of movement of the body – tensions, and then the releasing of tensions. But this is a much more rigid way of playing – you have to bar a lot of chords . . .

GD: So, as you said, your posture has to be much more upright and rigid, and you have to slightly distance yourself from the instrument . . .

PW: Yes. And the whole thing is more ascetic.

GD: Are you saying that, with the album *Pink Moon*, Nick was not, as some people have suggested, simply rejecting what he might have seen as the 'commercialism' of *Bryter Layter* (which he had certainly fully endorsed at the time it was recorded), but rather that it was something much more positive: he was embracing a different discipline – rejecting the experimental to follow a recognised structure within which his work found a different freedom?

PW: In the early days, the way Nick played the guitar was different from the way you'd play jazz guitar, or classical music, where there are recognised procedures – recognised scales, recognised ways in which you should sit and hold the guitar, and so on. As ever in the Sixties, there was a spirit of rebellion about – a feeling of 'No one's going to tell me how to play the guitar' – so guitarists like Bert Jansch, Davy Graham, and John Renbourn didn't obey the rules. Nick was very much influenced by that spirit. And that went hand-in-hand with the experimental tunings. But with the album *Pink Moon*, he seems to be realigning himself with a path that is more, well, humble in a way.

GD: Do you think that he is bowing to a new discipline in a spirit of submission – which is perhaps captured in the last of his songs to be discovered, 'Tow The Line'?

PW: Well, that's an interesting way of putting it. It's more recognizable as a path that other contemporary guitarists trod; maybe *Bryter Layter* set out as being an 'indoors', comfortable album, whereas *Pink Moon* is back out in the cold, back out on the road . . .

PW: (*playing chords and bars from 'Time Has Told Me' and 'River Man'*) But there is something that hasn't been said about the way Nick played the guitar. It's tricky to put it into words – but I certainly think that, for me, the way that I use my hand, especially the left hand, is almost like a sign language – but a sign language to myself. If you're playing a certain kind of chord – this chord that Nick used, for example – there's a stretch, which gives you a certain specific feeling in your hand. Moving your fingers from one chord to another is almost an expression of what's going on in your mind. If you're playing a chord that is difficult to play, if it makes you strain, then your hand wants to get back to an easier position – apart from anything else, because it hurts your fingers. And this strain is included in the music: the strain comes out in the words, in the music, in the whole gesture. So to move from here (*minor chord*) to there (*major chord*) is the hand resolving itself. It's interesting, the way Nick fluctuates from the C major to the C minor. But there's a physical feeling in your hand when you do that, as well as in the shoulder: there's a strain – and then you relax. So if, as a guitarist, you experience the physical sensation of playing the song, you know, as you move your hand, what the song is reflecting, you know the inner life of the song – the words, the mood, the message that the song is trying to get across.

So for example this chord is very positive – very comfortable: a symmetrical feeling. And it sounds comfortable. That's part of the whole – what can I say? – the whole thing that Nick is famous for. And that has to do with the physical sensation: it may only be in the hands – but that's English minimalism for you! You express yourself in your hands, and not necessarily anywhere else. If Nick had been a Keith Richards or someone, he'd have stood up and agonised with his whole body as he played. But of course that's the very last thing Nick would do! But everything *is* there, in the movement of the hand, and I find that interesting.

And then there's the right hand: people quite often try to analyse Nick's right-hand movements, saying that they're strange because they don't stick to the conventions. But if you listen to the Tanworth demos, Nick did use very established claw-hammer techniques – techniques where you use a thumb and two fingers. But then he would add another note. So, essentially, he'd take recognised patterns, but he'd have constant cross rhythms, with extra fingers coming in. And if you put the two together – right and left hands – what you do affects the entire body movement. You can almost give yourself pain – well, certainly strain – and you can then resolve that strain: so that if something is troubling you, it will be reflected, and resolved, in the way your fingers move. Or if something's not quite right, you put in an extra finger – an extra note. So there's a kind of conversation that goes on with your fingers. And Nick, in my opinion, knew all about that. He was interested – not that I think he analysed it himself. But it's something I often think about.

GD: 'If songs were lines in a conversation . . .' My parents would sometimes hear Nick in what we called the Music Room, playing the same sequence of chords on his guitar over and over and over again. It usually preceded him taking some action – like driving off somewhere in his car . . .

PW: It's what I would do – I'd sit for hours and hours, and I would also drive off in the car until it ran out of petrol, as a matter of fact, so I can specifically identify with that . . . If you found something like this (*plays short passage from 'River Man'*), you'd play it over and over. I can imagine Nick sitting in his room literally for hours, repeating that series of chords. It is something that many guitarists do, as far as I can gather – it's a comforting thing to do – repeating something again and again. You could say it's almost like a mantra . . . It's not just the sound, it's not just the music, it's also the physical thing of how your hands are moving.

When I met Nick, the first song he played me – I think it was the first song – was 'Time Has Told Me'. And I remember thinking, 'How is he feeling?' Not deep in his soul, but in his hand: 'How is he feeling that in his hand?' And so I'd say, 'Show me – can I take the guitar? Do you mean this . . .' (*plays chord*), and he'd say,'Yes, yes, that's what I'm doing'; and I'd think 'Yeah, I *thought* he was' – because I could feel how he was holding the neck of the guitar.

What I love about the guitar is what it suggests and implies. For me, Nick's music was about the suggestions in the guitar. But that may just be one guitarist talking about another. I fully understand that not everyone feels like that, and that unless you put an arrangement on it, people won't hear it. I do believe that everyone involved with arranging and performing on Nick's albums thought they were doing it for the best. It was right for the time. However, I think the fact that Nick chose to record *Pink Moon* and the last four songs with just voice and guitar is hugely significant. For me, I far and away prefer to hear just Nick's voice and guitar. Because that's how I hear it, and that's how I love it.

Hampstead Heath (Photo: Keith Morris)

Voices ✓

Black-eyed dog ✓

Rider on the wheel ✓

Hanging on a star ✓

Tow the line. ✓

Saw you on a starship

Old fairytale

Even now

On this day

Long way to town

The Fourth Album

by Pete Paphides

Throughout 1973, Nick's only presence on a record was a proxy one. He was the subject of the song 'Solid Air' on John Martyn's eponymous album. Martyn's song achingly encapsulates the rising concern that those nearest to Nick had been feeling for the preceding years. Although, Martyn himself may not have been aware of it, 'Solid Air' was the second song about Nick to appear on one of his albums. Years later, Robin Frederick would reveal that her song 'Sandy Grey' – which Martyn covered on his 1967 debut *London Conversation* – had been written in Aix-en-Provence about Nick.

However, in the journal kept by Rodney Drake in an attempt to monitor the undulations of his son's condition, Rodney noted that on 22 February 1973 – not February or March 1974, as previous accounts have stated – Nick entered the studio with John Wood. It seems that at this time, Nick was struggling to write lyrics, confiding in those close to him that he felt he could only compose in the studio. 'Nick rang me up and said he wanted to record again,' recalls Wood, who feels that this may have been part of a greater deliberation concerning 'what he wanted to do with his life'. In the preceding months, Nick had shown some interest in working with computers – although when Rodney Drake arranged through a friend that he start work as a computer programmer, his son didn't make it to the end of the first day. Also mooted was the idea of joining the army.

'Previously, there would always be an album in stock, as it were' says John Wood, '[but] with these songs, one never had the feeling that there was a whole album waiting to reveal itself . . . He may have just wanted to get into the studio to amuse himself, for companionship or whatever. He certainly didn't have a lot of direction or focus on it.' Wood was also surprised that, for the first time, Nick did not feel up to the job of singing and play guitar at the same time:

'We went in and we did three songs – just tracks, because Nick hadn't got complete lyrics, which was very unusual for him. There were two versions of "Black Eyed Dog", one with heavy [guitar] strings and the other with light [guitar] strings – that's what the word "strings" denotes on the tape box. Then we did "Rider On The Wheel" and we did "Hanging On A Star" – again, both without lyrics – although what surprises me, having seen the tape box label, is that he must have had a bit more lyrically than he let on, because all the titles [for the three songs] are written on there.'

Having failed to persuade John Wood that he had enough material for a new album, the two agreed to put future sessions on hold for the time being.

Between the termination of these sessions and Joe Boyd's subsequent return to London, Nick's inability to come to terms with his lack of success intensified. On arriving from Los Angeles late in October 1973, Boyd rented a flat in London and it was here, a few months later, that a dishevelled and angry Nick confronted the man who had offered him his first and only record deal. With touring long since off the menu of options, there was little that Boyd could suggest beyond Nick making another record. Whether he was absolutely ready to do so at this stage is a moot point. 'Joe got on to Nick and sort of dragged him into the studio,' recalls Wood – but writing in *White Bicycles*, Boyd explained: 'I had no idea what would emerge, but it was the only therapy at my disposal.'

Among Nick's wider circle of friends, none seemed to have any greater idea of how best to help him escape what, by now, was a profound depression. One of the few people outside of his family who saw him in 1973 was Nick's old Marlborough friend and travelling companion Simon Crocker. 'In either April or May,' he recalled, 'I got this phone call out of the blue':

'And it was Nick. He sounded very incoherent. But he said, "I'd like to meet." So I said: "Great! Fantastic!" But he sounded shaky. Anyway, he came round to meet me in Chelsea . . . I'm amazed he even found his way there. He turned up, and he was completely incoherent. It was the most awful thing, because I wanted to take him and look after him. He sat there, completely shaking . . . He couldn't put a sentence together.'

It's perhaps worth dwelling momentarily on this image because – in between the abortive 1973 sessions and Nick's final recordings in July 1974, this was when Nick finally found words to accompany one of the instrumentals recorded with John Wood. And the resulting song seem to correspond completely with what Simon Crocker saw in Chelsea.

The depiction of depression as a black dog dates back to Cerberus – the many-headed dog of Greek mythology whose job was to guard the gates of Hades. As a scholar of blues guitar, it's likely that Nick would have been equally familiar with Robert Johnson's 'Hellhound on my Trail', either in its original form or through the version that Peter Green's Fleetwood Mac recorded on their eponymous 1968 album. In Johnson's song, only a single reference is made to the song's eponymous creature. The protagonist is fated to keep moving in a futile effort to shake off his tormentor. As with Johnson and his song, 'Black Eyed Dog' was one of the very last vocals committed to tape by Nick. If anything, 'Black Eyed Dog' is an even more disturbing piece of music than the blues song which may have helped inform its imagery. The protagonist of 'Black Eyed Dog' isn't going anywhere. Unlike Johnson's character, all escape routes have been exhausted: 'Black-eyed dog he called at my door / Black-eyed dog he called for more / Black-eyed dog he knew my name.' 'Black Eyed Dog' sounds like an SOS note sent from a building that its author is afraid he may never leave.

Indeed, prior to this point, it has been important – although not always easy – to observe a distinction between the protagonists of Nick's songs and the person who wrote them. While all three of Nick's completed albums were informed by the events of his life, as late as *Pink Moon* it is clear that Nick was honouring a conceit beyond merely writing about what was happening to him. On *Pink Moon*, 'Harvest Breed' and 'From The Morning' depict death as a necessary part of nature's continual renewal. Years previously on 'Fruit Tree', death was depicted as a process that keeps the pretensions of great artists in check, and ultimately realises them. Almost uniquely among Nick's canon, 'Black Eyed Dog' sits outside of the circle. Beyond the metaphor that it uses, there is no detectable conceit or 'story' here and perhaps most of all, that's what makes 'Black Eyed Dog' such uncomfortable listening. Joe Boyd:

'Nick was obviously a more sensitive, literate character than Pete Townshend penning the words, "I hope I die before I get old." Some people do get trapped in a persona and find it difficult to survive as a result. What I mean to say is that, even if Nick had imagined at the age of nineteen [as he appears to do on "Fruit Tree"] that he would only be remembered when he was gone, that's a very easy thing for a nineteen-year-old to think. Because you're not actually thinking about what it will actually mean to confront mortality before you're thirty. But when I met him in 1974, I think he saw what it meant.

And he was very upset by that, and angry. He saw that it was a dead end. And no fun.'

Nick's old university friend Paul Wheeler remembered feeling 'shock and respect' when he heard 'Black Eyed Dog'. Indeed, the sound of his friend venting his anguish put him in mind of John Lennon on 'Cold Turkey' – a song Wheeler had been surprised to hear Nick enthusing about when it had appeared in 1969: 'It's a really tough song. And I was quite surprised to hear Nick saying that it was a really interesting thing to do, because I didn't associate Nick with that kind of pain.' Two years later, it would turn out that Wheeler's then-wife Diana would find herself in the employ of Lennon and Yoko Ono. As one of Lennon's personal assistants based at the sometime Beatle's Tittenhurst estate, Diana, along with Paul Wheeler, frequently paid host to Nick. Speaking to Patrick Humphries, Nick's friend recalled that 'John and Yoko had gone [to America, never to return] and Nick seemed to fit in with the "ghost house" image of Tittenhurst.' In the summer of 1972, Wheeler recalled playing Lennon's unflinchingly cathartic *Plastic Ono Band* album to his friend for the first time and seeing him look 'visibly shocked'. Perhaps this would embolden him into similar lyrical candour in 'Black Eyed Dog' and some of his other final songs.

Whatever *did* inspire Nick Drake in 1974, it is now clear that as he entered the studio to record his final songs, the muses were far from finished with him. That 'Hanging On A Star' already had a title when Nick recorded it suggests, as per John Wood's earlier assertion, that he had an idea of what its lyrical content might be. Almost as startling as 'Black Eyed Dog' in its candour, 'Hanging On A Star' appears to be comprised of all the things Nick was waiting to say to Joe on his return from America: 'Why leave me hanging on a star / When you deem me so high?' If the words read accusingly, the rolling melody picked out by Nick's right hand edges the song away from anger and towards uncomprehending abandonment. 'I don't know how to describe the way he was [when he was recording the songs],' recalled Wood in 2002, 'but it was very agonising trying to see him do those recordings.'

Having lain in limbo since Nick laid down its guitar part in February 1973, 'Rider On The Wheel' also finally had a lyric assigned to it. Recalling the eloquent fatalism of 'Harvest Breed', the song – justifiably described by Humphries as 'one of the most beguiling of his short career' – sees its protagonist reconciled to the idea that he isn't (and perhaps never has been) the captain of his own destiny. Musically, it remains perhaps the prettiest of Nick's final songs. More Appalachian in style than anything else he committed to tape, the clockwork prettiness and precision of its circular melody strongly call to mind Lena Hughes, whose sole privately pressed album exerted a huge influence on one of Nick's teenage guitar heroes John Renbourn.

Five years had elapsed since Nick had first committed 'Voice From The Mountain' (or 'Voices', as it was often referred to in his notes) to tape. Now, in 1974, it seems that he was ready to record it. Described by Ian MacDonald as 'a heart-rending prayer for relief', the truth is that, rather like 'Parasite' and 'Fruit Tree', this was a song written in more hopeful times that would nonetheless acquire tragic resonances with the knowledge of what lay in wait for its author: 'Tell me my friend, my friend / Tell me with love / Where will it end, it end / This voice from above?' sings Nick, choosing to sing in a register that sits at the outermost perimeter of his comfort zone.

For twenty-nine years, it had been thought that these were the final songs that Nick had recorded before leaving Tanworth-in-Arden to spend a (by all accounts restorative) summer on a friend's houseboat in Paris. In the long interim period, the status of those final songs had been the subject of considerable debate. In a letter sent to the *NME* after Nick's death, Richard Williams, Nick's A&R man at Island, claimed that 'Nick himself expressed dissatisfaction with the four songs he recorded late last year, [and] consequently John Wood has destroyed the 16-track master tapes with our full approval.' However,

Wood has no memory of receiving such an instruction, although in 1979, when Boyd decided to append those four songs onto *Pink Moon* for the first issue of the *Fruit Tree* box set, Wood may have momentarily wished that he had adhered to words of Williams's letter. Wood's response to the release of Nick's final songs was to send Boyd 'a very strong letter about it . . . that, quite honestly, I don't think Nick would have ever wanted them released.' For his part, Boyd explained:

'I have generally been the bane of completists by insisting that out-takes and demos should not be released unless they are of high quality . . . As long as I was in a position to do so, I took the view that only tracks of high musical standard should be released, and I plead guilty to feeling that the four tracks . . . were – despite being chillingly stark and frightening – superb performances of very high quality. I don't think anyone has ever questioned that.'

In the years after of 1986's stand-alone disc *Time Of No Reply*, Boyd set out his position clearly: the Island vaults contained nothing else that was of a sufficiently releasable standard. However, outside of the vaults – in Robert Kirby's potting shed, to be precise – a handful of new discoveries set off a chain of events that would ultimately result in a new collection of non-album Nick Drake songs. As well as the versions of 'Mayfair' and 'River Man' recorded in his Cambridge room, Kirby found his original arrangements for 'Magic' and 'Time Of No Reply' – songs that, in the studio, had never made it beyond Richard Hewson's arrangements for them. With an earlier, significantly different version of 'Three Hours' having also come to light, this afforded a timely opportunity to effectively update *Time Of No Reply*. The versions of Nick's final songs which concluded *Time Of No Reply* had been monitor mixes – seven-inch mono 'listening' tapes of the songs in the raw, which had to be mixed for record. Reasoning that 'since they have been released anyway, they might as well go out in the best possible shape', Wood set about re-mixing them (and, in the case of 'Hanging On A Star', replacing the existing vocal with a stronger take). However, he has maintained the view that, had he survived long enough '[Nick] would have done them again.'

Commencing work on those final songs, Wood pressed play and began to make notes before getting to work in earnest. After the final song ran its course, he let the tape run on and, incredibly, a fifth song revealed itself. En route to a rehearsal that day, Gabrielle Drake happened to pop into the studio. 'I walked down the passageway and John said, "We've got another song!" He had forgotten. They had a fifth song, but he had forgotten all about it.'

'I can't say that I did [remember "Tow The Line"],' elaborated Wood, 'but I definitely did it. It was the last thing we ever did.' Having worked out the guitar part years previously on one of his many 'work' tapes, the version of 'Tow The Line' which Nick brought to his final session with Wood is, in the words of his sister, 'a song of some resignation': 'Today is the day that we rise or we fall / This night is the night that we win or lose all . . . If you call we will follow / If you show us we can tow the line.' Wood feels that 'if "Hanging On A Star" is about Joe Boyd, then "Tow The Line" probably is as well.'

Kirby, on the other hand, had his own view. Speaking in 2004, he offered up this interpretation: 'The "you" in "Tow The Line" is the muse, and "we" is all the different Nicks. So in that song you have both [the Nick of] "Black Eyed Dog" and [the Nick of] "Man In A Shed".' Kirby felt that there were certain musical 'safe places' to which Nick would gravitate when he wanted to 'be in control'. And one of those safe places was the sort of descending chord pattern shown here, which yielded 'Leaving Me Behind', 'Poor Boy' and 'At The Chime Of A City Clock'. Indeed, there's little beyond the difference of a mere semitone to separate the Nick's playing on the former to his part for 'Tow The Line'. For Kirby, 'Tow The Line' was a direct address to the muse which seemed to be deserting him in the latter part of his life: a final admission that 'he is prepared to play the game. He'll go on the road. He'll be commercial.'

The discovery of 'Tow The Line' solved one mystery while initiating another. In 2001, shortly after taking on the management of Nick Drake's estate, Cally Callomon set about putting the family archive into some sort of order and found a sheet of paper in Nick's handwriting which cast new light on his possible plans for the songs that he had recently recorded. Listed with ticks beside them, possibly to denote the fact that they had been recorded, were the five final songs: 'Voices' [sic]; 'Black Eyed Dog'; 'Rider On The Wheel'; 'Hanging On A Star'; and 'Tow The Line'. Then, separated as if to denote a different group – seemingly the second side of a record – are five more titles: 'Saw You On A Starship'; 'Old Fairytale'; 'Even Now'; 'On This Day'; and 'Long Way To Town'.

Along with these, Callomon discovered lyrics corresponding to the hitherto unknown titles, as well as two more that didn't make the track listing. Closer examination of their content is revealing. If nothing else, they go some way to tempering the view that Nick's final two years were marked by a steady deceleration in output. Without any surviving music, these lyrics offer only flickering glimpses of the emotional terrain that might have been marked out by a fourth Nick Drake album, but glimpses nonetheless. The bluesy tone in which the bleak sentiments of 'On This Day' are communicated suggests a possible companion piece to 'Black Eyed Dog': 'A train just don't run / Good time just won't come / On this day, on this day.' Similarly, 'Long Way To Town', the final track on this hypothetical album, reads like a postcard from a place far beyond all hope, almost apologetic in tone: 'Well I don't wish to deceive you more / And I don't wish to call you down / And I don't wish to deny my name / But it's a long long way to town / A long long way to town, to town / A long long way to town.'

Other lyrics take the form of a direct plea for company. Like a tantalising excerpt from an abruptly interrupted dream, 'Saw You On A Starship' sees its protagonist attempting to catch the attention of his subject as they whizz through space. Perhaps unsurprisingly, astronautical imagery was becoming increasingly prevalent in pop, and Nick's lyric here may have unconsciously taken some inspiration from recent hits by David Bowie ('Starman') and Elton John ('Rocket Man'). Albeit pared down to the bone, similar sentiments inform 'Sing A Song' – one of two lyrics whose titles Nick chose not to add to the above track listing. However, the second of those titles, 'Paid Brain', couldn't be more different in tone: 'Well they's paying him in gold / And they's paying him in smiles / And they's payin for his brain / And they's payin for his wiles.'

What would these songs have sounded like? It's a heartbreakingly unanswerable question – amplified in this case by the way the words sit on the page, their metre and vernacular offering leads that can never be verified. Looking at 'Old Fairytale' – especially the way each verse is gnomically rounded off with the pay-off, 'It's an old fairytale' – the mind races to a place that ultimately doesn't exist – like trying to locate a long-forgotten melody with only the faintest memory of how it made you feel at the time to guide you. Perhaps the most fascinating of these 'lost' lyrics is 'Even Now'. In the final months of his life, Nick showed signs of finding a focus and direction that had eluded him in the previous two years. His stay in Paris between the July session and the beginning of November appeared to arrest his decline. 'I can tell you that I'm changing too,' he says on 'Even Now', ushering in a sense of hope and resolution unheard in any of Nick's songs since 'Northern Sky'. 'And if you're losing what you started with / Don't you grieve for what you're parted with, broken-hearted with / You can bring it through / Maybe make it new / Even now, even now.' As his typewriter keys punched out the words, he must have surely believed the reassurances appearing in front of him. And, of course, if he had stayed a while longer, he would have seen that belief vindicated beyond his wildest imaginings.

Voices

Voice from the mountain
And a voice from the sea
Voice in my neighbourhood
And a voice calling me
Tell me my friend, my friend
Tell me with love
Where can it end, it end
This voice from above

A sound on the ocean wave
And a sound in the tree
A sound in a country lane say
Can you be free?
Tell me you crowd, you crowd
Tell me again
Tell me out loud, out loud, well
This sound is rain

A tune from the hillside
And a tune full of light
A flute in the morning
And a chime in the night
I know the game, the game
I know the score
I know my name, my name
But this tune is more

Voice from the mountain
And a voice from the sea
Voice in my neighbourhood
And a voice calling me
Tell me my friend, my friend
Tell me with love
Where can it end, it end
This voice from above

Tune from the hillside
And a tune full of light
Flute in the morning
And a chime in the night

I know the game the game
I know the score
I know my name my name
But this tune is more.

Voice from the mountain, voice from the sea
Voice in my neighbourhood & a voice calling me.
Tell me my friend my friend
Tell me with love
Where can it end it end
This voice from above

Voice from the ~~wood~~ mountain, voice from the sea,
Voice in my neighbourhood & a voice calling me
Tell me my friend my friend,
Tell me with love
Where can it end it end
This voice from above

Sound on the ocean wave
And a sound in the tree
Sound in a country lane say
Can you be free
~~Tell~~ Show me you crowd you crowd
~~Tell~~ Show me again
Tell me out loud out loud well
This sound is rain

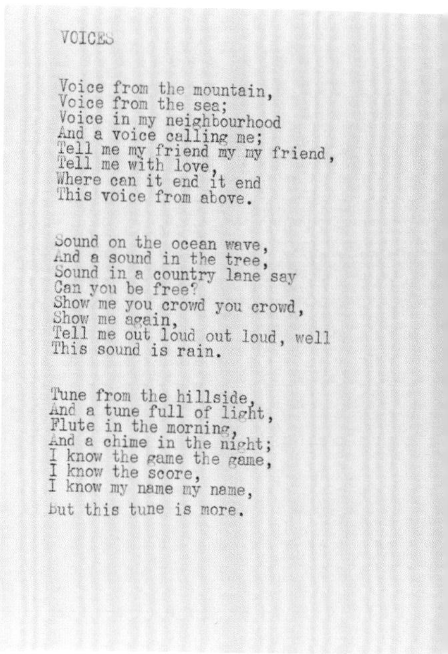
VOICES

Voice from the mountain,
Voice from the sea;
Voice in my neighbourhood
And a voice calling me;
Tell me my friend my my friend,
Tell me with love,
Where can it end it end
This voice from above.

Sound on the ocean wave,
And a sound in the tree,
Sound in a country lane say
Can you be free?
Show me you crowd you crowd,
Show me again,
Tell me out loud out loud, well
This sound is rain.

Tune from the hillside,
And a tune full of light,
Flute in the morning,
And a chime in the night;
I know the game the game,
I know the score,
I know my name my name,
but this tune is more.

Chris Healey: Dropping the G string down to E gives Nick new voicings of some straightforward chords, and adds an unexpected extra E note to others. Having that E in the 'home' A major chord instead of a high A also gives the same effect as in 'Northern Sky' – the top C# (the 'happy note') has no top A supporting it, lending the whole song a more fragile and uncertain tone than it would have in standard tuning. It's a great example of how being unwilling to just use the chords we're used to hearing can help to elevate a song – something Nick managed to do, even to the end.

Black Eyed Dog

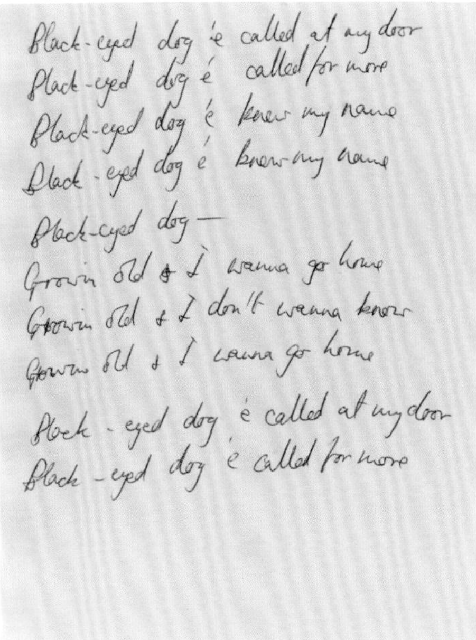
Black-eyed dog 'e called at my door
Black-eyed dog 'e called for more
Black-eyed dog 'e knew my name
Black-eyed dog 'e knew my name

Black-eyed dog —
Growin old & I wanna go home
Growin old & I don't wanna know
Growin old & I wanna go home

Black-eyed dog 'e called at my door
Black-eyed dog 'e called for more

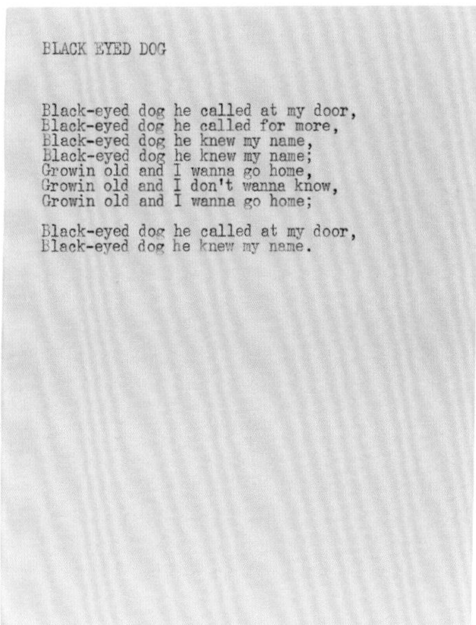
BLACK EYED DOG

Black-eyed dog he called at my door,
Black-eyed dog he called for more,
Black-eyed dog he knew my name,
Black-eyed dog he knew my name;
Growin old and I wanna go home,
Growin old and I don't wanna know,
Growin old and I wanna go home;

Black-eyed dog he called at my door,
Black-eyed dog he knew my name.

A black-eyed dog 'e called at my door
A black-eyed dog 'e called for more
A black-eyed dog 'e new my name
A black-eyed dog 'e knew my name

A black-eyed dog
A black-eyed dog

Growin' old and I wanna go home
Growin' old and I don't wanna know
Growin' old and I wanna go home

A black-eyed dog 'e called at my door
A black-eyed dog 'e called for more

Nick almost never used harmonics – notes generated by gently touching a plucked string without fretting it. 'Black Eyed Dog', however, has them as a fundamental feature, though not for ornament or for a bit of showing off, the way many acoustic guitarists use them. He uses the eerie sound of combined low-string harmonics, with sympathetic resonance from other open strings in his GGDGBD tuning, and even vibrato (also very unusual for him), to create something otherworldly, sounding nothing like an everyday acoustic guitar tune.

The feel is modal (compare 'Three Hours') – even one chord change, you feel, would break the extraordinary spell of this three-minute evocation of Nick's terrified mental state. The song is in a heightened condition of mortal fear: the two lines of guitar before the verse are almost shivering, as Nick worries away desperately at the D string with the edge of his fingernail.

Rider On The Wheel

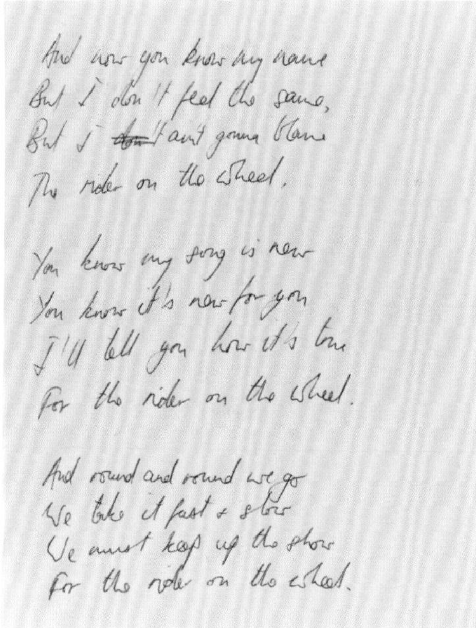

And now you know my name
But I don't feel the same,
But I ~~don't~~ ain't gonna blame
The rider on the wheel.

You know my song is new
You know it's new for you
I'll tell you how it's true
For the rider on the wheel.

And round and round we go
We take it fast + slow
We must keep up the show
For the rider on the wheel.

And now you know my name
But I don't feel the same
But I ain't gonna blame
The rider on the wheel

You know my song is new
You know it's new for you
I'll tell you how it's true
For the rider on the wheel

And round and round we go
We take it fast and slow
We must keep up the show
For the rider on the wheel

For the rider on the wheel

. . . know my name
I don't feel the same
But I ain't gonna blame
The rider on the wheel
Rider on the wheel

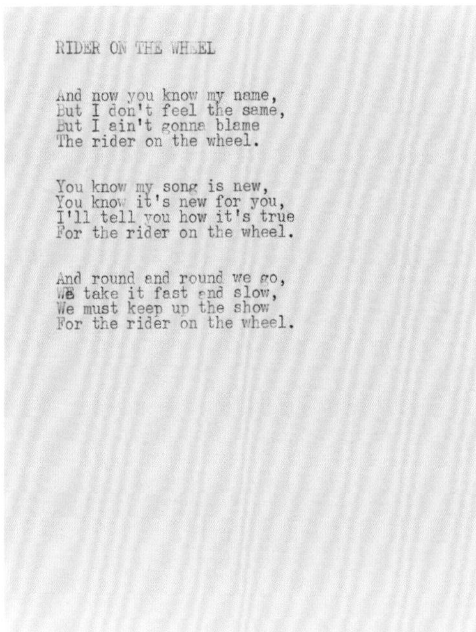

RIDER ON THE WHEEL

And now you know my name,
But I don't feel the same,
But I ain't gonna blame
The rider on the wheel.

You know my song is new,
You know it's new for you,
I'll tell you how it's true
For the rider on the wheel.

And round and round we go,
WE take it fast and slow,
We must keep up the show
For the rider on the wheel.

Pretty and intricate, if harmonically conventional, the instrumental section feels almost like a setting out of some internal debate. Its last line signs off with a conclusion that leads us into the here-and-now of the verses, which (like 'One Of These Things First') hint at Buddhist concepts.

There's a lovely thing going on in the verse guitar part. While the first three lines feature monosyllabic rhymes over (essentially) the same chords and melody, setting up the feel of going round and round, the first chord of each line is subtly different each time. It's not enough to destroy the circular feel. But try playing it with exactly the same chord each time and the repetitive effect overwhelms everything – the song feels dull and uninspired. A single-note difference at the start of each line makes the song work.

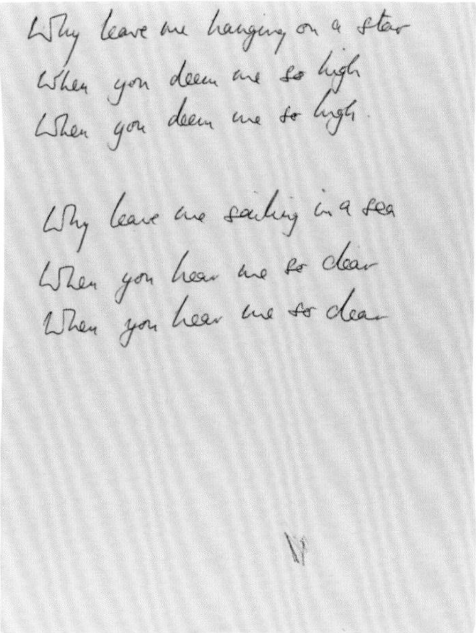
Why leave me hanging on a star
When you deem me so high
When you deem me so high

Why leave me sailing in a sea
When you hear me so clear
When you hear me so clear

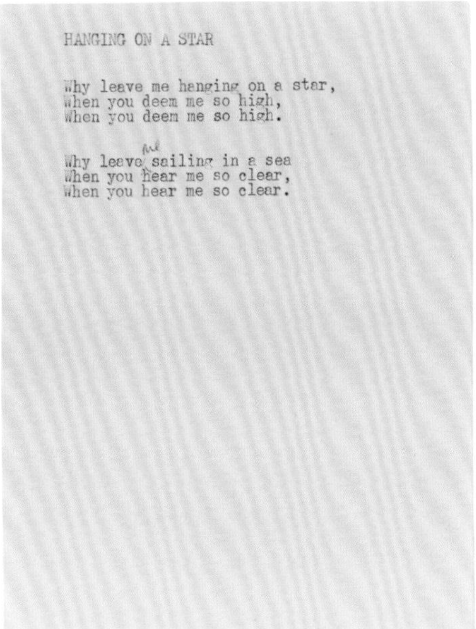
HANGING ON A STAR

Why leave me hanging on a star,
When you deem me so high,
When you deem me so high.

Why leave me sailing in a sea
When you hear me so clear,
When you hear me so clear.

Hanging On A Star

Why leave me hanging on a star?
When you deem me so high
When you deem me so high
When you deem me so high

Why leave me sailing in a sea?
When you hear me so clear
When you hear me so clear
When you hear me so clear
Why leave me hanging on a star?
When you deem me so high
When you deem me so high
When you deem me so high

The two versions of this song on *Time Of No Reply* and *Made To Love Magic* differ considerably in right-hand picking. Despite being more intricate, the latter version features orthodox picking patterns and is possibly easier to play. In both, the left-hand shapes in CGCFCE – which with the exception of the odd high note can be played with one finger – are very familiar from such songs as 'Which Will', among others.

The descending riff in the intro is also practically note-for-note the same fingering and picking as the original version of 'Magic' – just played on a differently tuned guitar. Nick may have been starting to run out of ideas – he didn't rate what came out of the last session very highly himself.

Tow The Line

This day is the day that we rise or we fall
This night is the night that we win or lose all
This time is the time that we wait for a while
This year is the year that we wait with a smile
If you call we will follow
If you show us, we can tow the line

Now that you're here you can show me the way
And now that you're here we can try to make it pay
While you were gone it was hard, it was cold
While you were gone, we were time, we were old
If you call we will follow
If you show us, we can tow the line
If you call we will follow
If you show us, we can tow the line

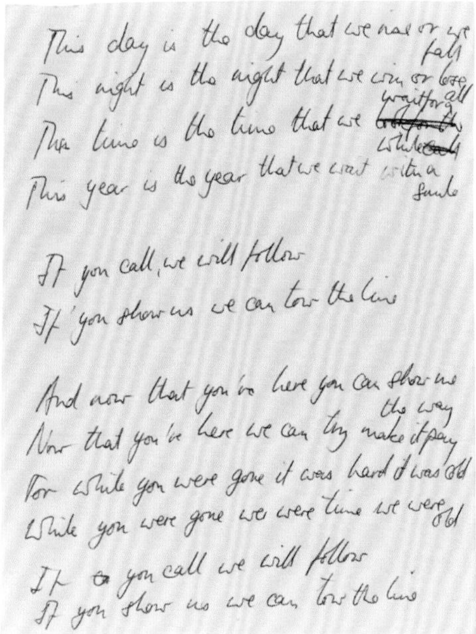

This day is the day that we rise or we fall
This night is the night that we win or lose all
This time is the time that we wait for a while
This year is the year that we wait with a smile

If you call, we will follow
If you show us we can tow the line

And now that you're here you can show us the way
Now that you're here we can try make it pay
For while you were gone it was hard it was cold
While you were gone we were time we were old
If you call we will follow
If you show us we can tow the line

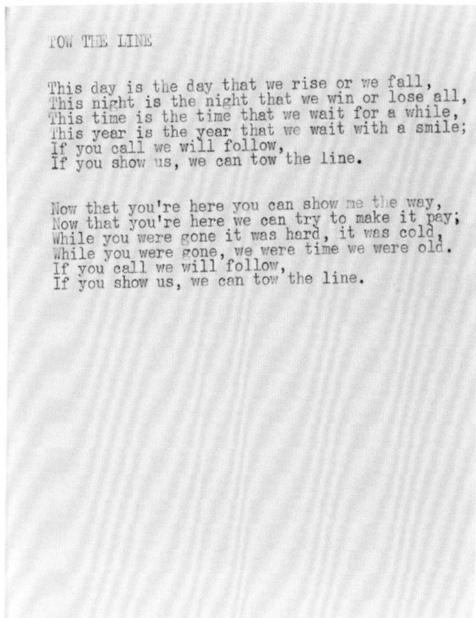

TOW THE LINE

This day is the day that we rise or we fall,
This night is the night that we win or lose all,
This time is the time that we wait for a while,
This year is the year that we wait with a smile;
If you call we will follow,
If you show us, we can tow the line.

Now that you're here you can show me the way,
Now that you're here we can try to make it pay;
While you were gone it was hard, it was cold,
While you were gone, we were time we were old.
If you call we will follow,
If you show us, we can tow the line.

The verses here have a familiar descending pattern. In essence they're a minor-key version of 'Parasite', played over a root note repeated on two strings tuned to the same pitch (their slight detuning giving the verses a nervy, uncertain texture). Unlike 'Parasite', though, the last note of the pattern does not continue down but goes back up to the home note of the minor chord, producing a curiously neutral feeling at the end of each line. Nick sings about coming to terms with the compromises the world demands, and musically the effect is of something dispiriting reluctantly accepted.

The 'If you call . . .' section, however, contains the song's key moment; although Nick is giving in and going along to try and 'make it pay', his submission is not an easy one. The discordant flat fifth note on the word 'tow' lets us know how conflicted giving in will make him.

Saw You On A Starship

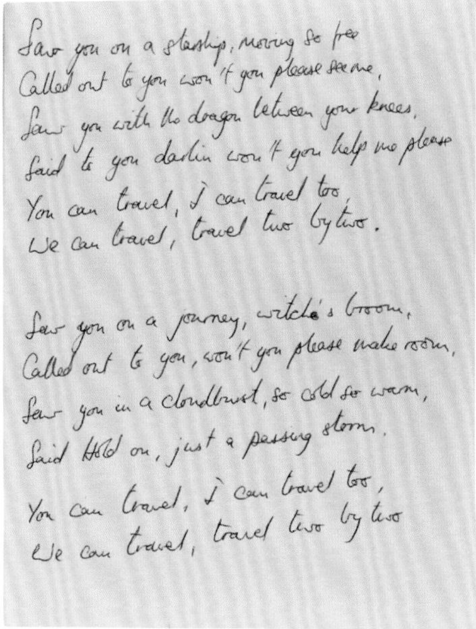

Saw you on a starship, moving so free
Called out to you won't you please see me,
Saw you with the dragon between your knees,
Said to you darlin won't you help me please
You can travel, I can travel too,
We can travel, travel two by two.

Saw you on a journey, witch's broom,
Called out to you, won't you please make room,
Saw you in a cloudburst, so cold so warm,
Said Hold on, just a passing storm.
You can travel, I can travel too,
We can travel, travel two by two

Sailing easy, flying high

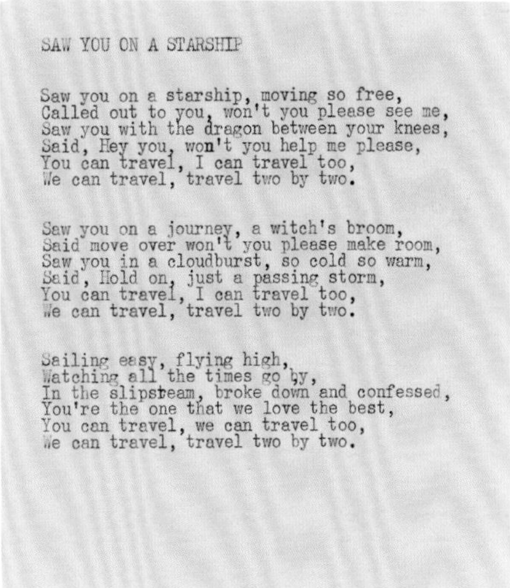

SAW YOU ON A STARSHIP

Saw you on a starship, moving so free,
Called out to you, won't you please see me,
Saw you with the dragon between your knees,
Said, Hey you, won't you help me please,
You can travel, I can travel too,
We can travel, travel two by two.

Saw you on a journey, a witch's broom,
Said move over won't you please make room,
Saw you in a cloudburst, so cold so warm,
Said, Hold on, just a passing storm,
You can travel, I can travel too,
We can travel, travel two by two.

Sailing easy, flying high,
Watching all the times go by,
In the slipstream, broke down and confessed,
You're the one that we love the best,
You can travel, we can travel too,
We can travel, travel two by two.

Old Fairytale

OLD FAIRYTALE

You open the door, don't you make a sound,
The light come in,you spread it all around,
And you cast your spell right across the ground,
It's an old fairytale.

The days go by, you're looking for a theme,
The night come down you go to bed to dream,
While the people there they change from blue to green,
It's an old fairytale.

So call the tune, don't you call for me,
What you see is a mystery,
You can say it has to be
An old fairytale.

You open the door don't you make a sound,
The light come in you spread it all around,
And you cast your spell right across the ground,
It's an old fairytale

Even Now

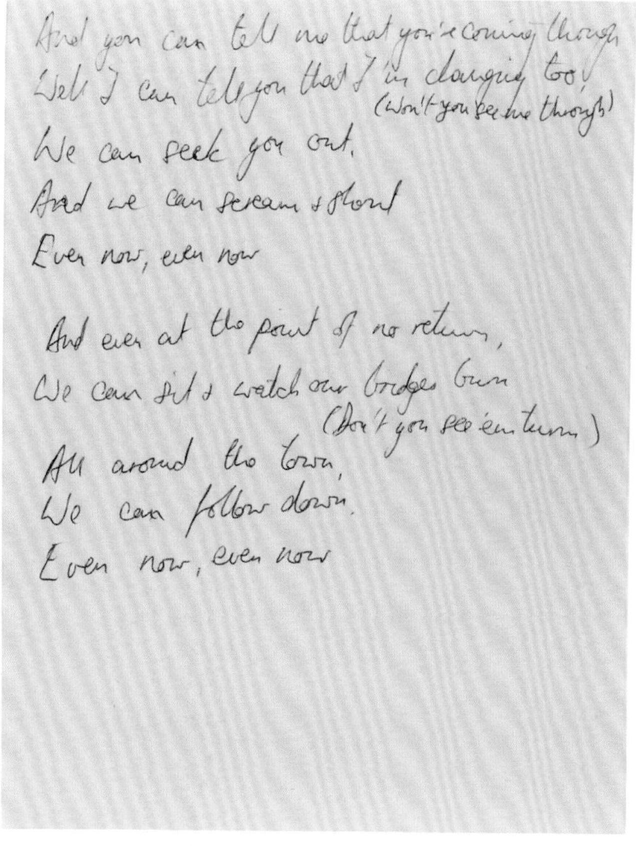

And you can tell me that you're coming through
Well I can tell you that I'm changing too,
(Won't you see me through)
We can seek you out.
And we can scream & shout
Even now, even now

And even at the point of no return,
We can sit & watch our bridges burn
(Don't you see 'em turn)
All around the town,
We can follow down.
Even now, even now

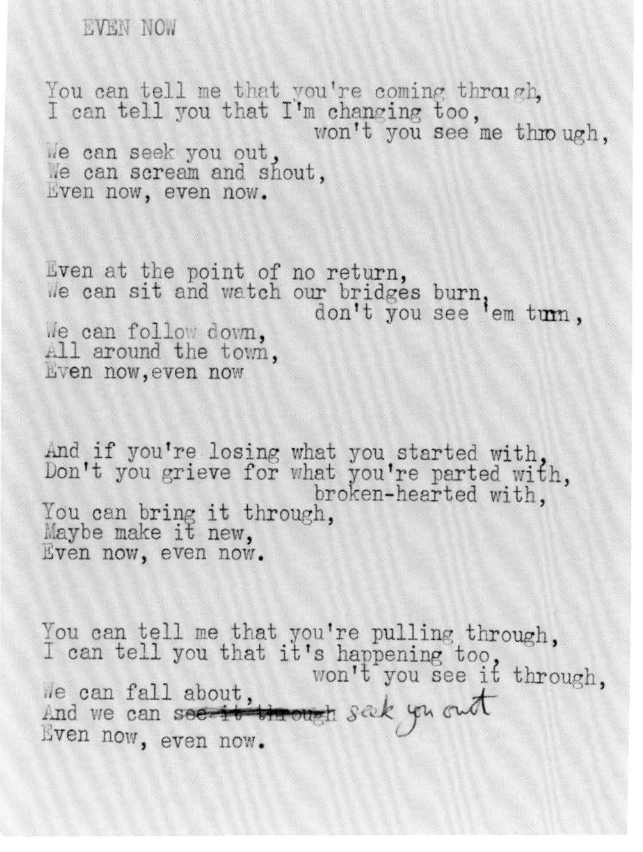

EVEN NOW

You can tell me that you're coming through,
I can tell you that I'm changing too,
won't you see me through,
We can seek you out,
We can scream and shout,
Even now, even now.

Even at the point of no return,
We can sit and watch our bridges burn,
don't you see 'em turn,
We can follow down,
All around the town,
Even now, even now

And if you're losing what you started with,
Don't you grieve for what you're parted with,
broken-hearted with,
You can bring it through,
Maybe make it new,
Even now, even now.

You can tell me that you're pulling through,
I can tell you that it's happening too,
won't you see it through,
We can fall about,
And we can ~~see it through~~ seek you out
Even now, even now.

On This Day

A train just won't run
Good time just won't come
On this day,
On this day.

New face just don't shine
New love just ain't mine
This old time
This old time

~~Seen you~~ New day just don't dawn
New love just ain't born
On this day
On this day.

ON THIS DAY

'A 'train just don't run,
Good time just won't come,
On this day, on this day.

New sun just don't shine,
New love just ain't mine,
This old time, this old time.

New day just won't dawn,
New love just ain't born,
On this day, on this day.

See you coming, Iknow the score
And I know that you know it too,
See you going, ask you for more
'Cos I know that you want it too,
See you coming, I can't be beat
And I tell you it's for real,
See you going, bring on the heat
Won't you tell me how you feel.

'A 'train just don't run,
Good time just won't come
On this day, on this day.

See you comin I know the score
An I know that you know it too
See you goin ask you for more
Cos I know that you wannit too
See you comin I can't be beat
An I tell you it's for real
See you goin bring on the heat
Won't you tell me how you feel

A train just won't run
Good time just won't come
On this day
On this day

Long Way To Town

LONG WAY TO TOWN

Well I don't wish to deceive you more,
And I don't wish to call you down;
And I don't wish to deny my name,
But it's a long long way to town.
A long long way to town,to town,
A long long way to town.

Sing A Song

SING A SONG

Sing a song, sing it low,
Sing a song, make it slow,
Sing a song, let it show,
I am yours from now on.
All new games we can play,
All new words we can say,
All new love won't betray,
I am yours from now on.
You are my treasure-trove,
You are my stars above,
Hold on tight, let me prove,
I am yours from now on.

Paid Brain

PAID BRAIN

Well they's paying him in gold,
And they's paying him in smiles,
And they's payin for his brain,
And they's payin for his wiles;
He's a paid brain,
Lord say he should be so,
Yes he's a paid brain
And the Lord say he should be so.

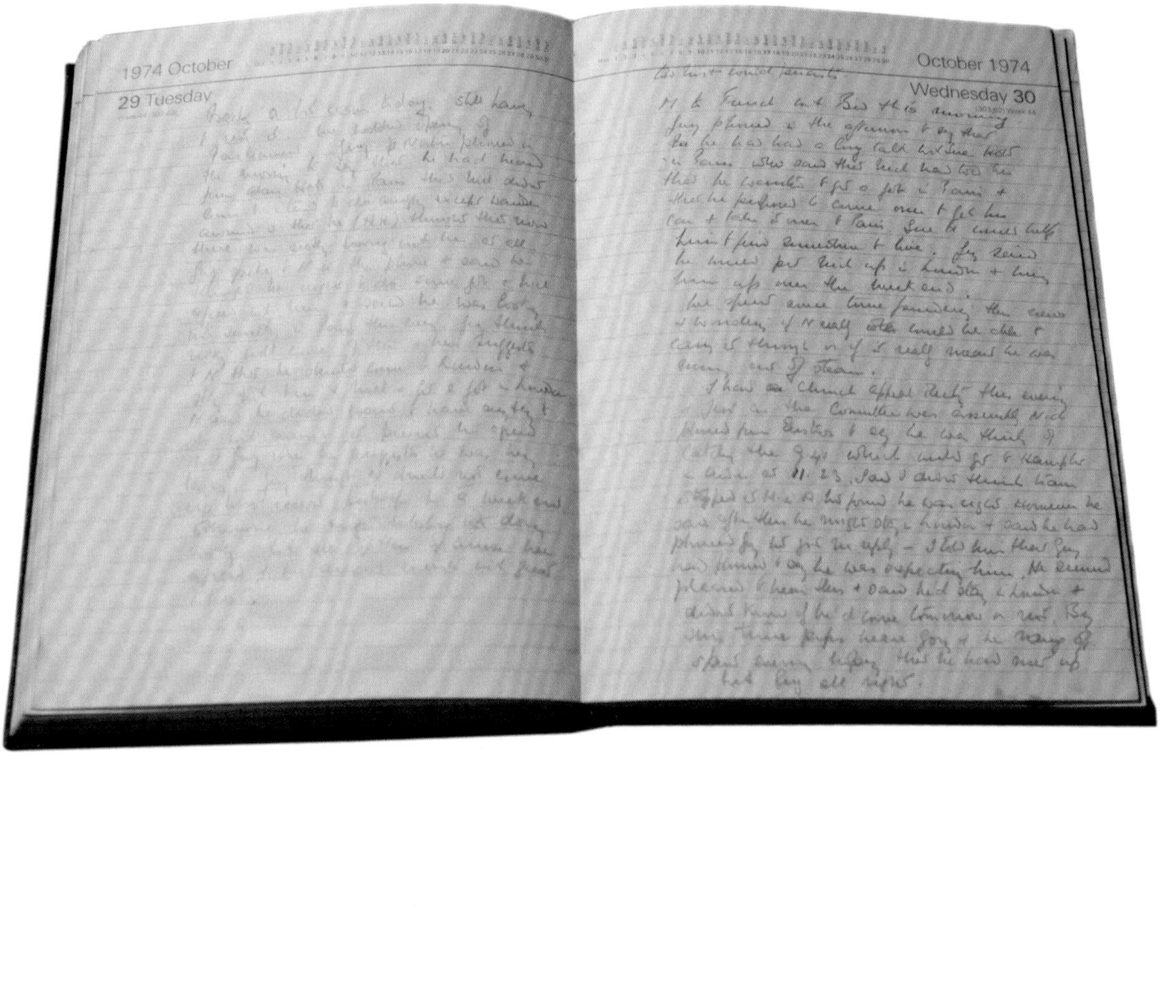

1974 October
29 Tuesday
October 1974
Wednesday 30

Remembered For A While

The Diaries of Rodney Drake

Annotated by Gabrielle Drake

What prompted Rodney Drake to start keeping a daily record of his son's mental difficulties? It has been suggested that it was a course of action encouraged by one of the doctors attending Nick. But, at the time the record starts – quite arbitrarily, on 21 March 1972 – Nick was receiving no medical attention, and denying that he needed any, so this suggestion seems unlikely.

A year earlier, in 1971, Nick had taken up random residence in his parents' home in Warwickshire. There had followed a year during which he seemed to slip further and further into an abyss of gloom. In August 1971, he was in acute pain, and diagnosed with a kidney stone. There was relief at the thought that Nick's mental depression might have a physical cause, a relief that almost seemed to be justified when, in September of that year, he returned to London to record his third, stark album, *Pink Moon*. But Keith Morris's *Pink Moon* photos all too bleakly attest to the fact that Nick's depression still sat heavily upon him.

Nick's specialist, Dr Weinstein, pursued tests, but eventually declared Nick to be physically fit. He did, however, acknowledge that his patient needed psychiatric help, and he introduced Rodney to a local psychiatrist.

But Nick refused to accept that there was anything wrong with him mentally, and certainly rejected the idea of any psychiatry. Nevertheless, he became increasingly withdrawn – increasingly wrapped in inertia, disliking where he was, but unable to leave. For Molly and Rodney, the frustration of being unable to help a beloved son in his hour of need was acute. But they were made of stern stuff, and came from a generation that knew how to take up the cudgels against an elusive enemy.

For in a sense, all three of them – Molly, Rodney and Nick – became involved in an epic struggle: a struggle against a wily protagonist that assumed many different guises, certainly to Nick, who spearheaded the battle. At times, his parents became the enemy for him, and at times, his closest cohorts. The difficulty for Molly and Rodney was that they could never predict which mantle had descended on them in their son's eyes. Molly's solution was to hold herself ever ready: she would later recount that, for many months, at the beginning of Nick's illness, she never left the house, preferring to be resented for her presence rather than for her absence. And if Nick appeared at the door – as he occasionally did – and said 'Are you busy?' she would drop everything and sit down with him, and he would talk: sometimes in despair, sometimes illogically, often incomprehensively, but at least he was talking.

Rodney's solution – his attempt to bring order into the chaos – was to keep a diary. The journal of Nick's last three years is, for the most part, a factual document, devoid of emotional baggage, which endeavours to give an objective view of a situation that fluctuated daily. It was written at the end of each day, as Rodney sat in bed waiting for his wife to join him, and as such, it is an accurate reflection of the day's events, though often, inevitably, humdrum and repetitious. For Rodney, with his engineer and inventor's mind, knew that the collection of data was of vital importance. Here was a problem, the like of which he had never before encountered and for which, in those days, there was precious little help or support offered to the *families* of those going through mental trauma. It was written in pencil, in a practically indecipherable hand. Rodney wrote fluidly and fluently, but his handwriting was notoriously difficult to decrypt.

What follows are extracts from his diaries, which attempt to give an idea of the progression of Nick's difficulties as witnessed and lived through by those closest to him, who were, apart from his parents:

Naw, the other member of the Far Leys household: she was the Drake's Karen servant, who had come over from Burma and was more a member of the family than a servant, referring to Molly and Rodney as Mummy and Daddy, and sharing all their joys and sorrows.

Nick's sister **Gabrielle**, who is variously referred to as 'Gay', 'Birdy' or 'B'.

Her husband (at that time partner), **Louis de Wet**, referred to as 'de Wet', and the house they lived in (which Nick would occasionally visit) as 'the Porte Grise' (its full name being *La Porte Grise Ouvrant . . .*).

Molly's sister **Nancy** ('Nan Non') and her husband **Chris**, who had been very close to Nick throughout his life: both were extremely musical. Chris in particular had an affinity with Nick, who would often seek him out even when avoiding the company of others.

Rodney's sister **Pam**, who came to stay at Far Leys from Canada after her diagnosis with Alzheimer's in late 1973.

Then there were Nick's friends from his university days: **Robert Kirby**, his orchestrator; **Paul Wheeler**, Cambridge friend and fellow singer-songwriter, who was also trying to make his way in the music business and was then living with his wife **Diana** in Tittenhurst Park, Ascot, the house of John Lennon and Yoko Ono whose personal assistant she was.

And friends and collaborators from his musical world: **Joe Boyd** his producer, **John Wood** his sound engineer, and **John and Beverley Martyn**, already by now established singer-songwriters.

For the sake of accuracy, and in homage to Rodney's thoroughness, the many cuts that have been made in the text of the diaries are marked by ellipses (. . .).

The first entries are brief, as though Rodney is finding his feet. But they attest to a situation that has been ongoing for some time:

Tuesday 21 March 1972

Went to London with Nick to get car. He went to bed after supper. V. silent but reasonably OK.

Thursday 23 March 1972

Nick off again early, then back for a few minutes and off once more and rang up to say that he would not be back for lunch. In fact did not return at all.

Rose pruning.

Friday 24 March 1972

. . . Found Nick asleep in his car. I woke him at about 9.30 a.m. and suggested he should go to bed. Not pleased and drove away. He returned for lunch and seemed better.

Chris & Nancy arrived . . . and Nick attended supper – not too bad but of course very silent – he wasn't bad after supper.

Sprayed roses for blackspot.

Saturday 25 March 1972

Bad day with Nick.

He came down in morning whilst C and N were playing croquet but after grapefruit returned to his room where he stayed for the remainder of the day lying on the floor and ignoring all attempts to rouse him.

Came down late in the evening and made a cup of coffee – berated Molly for not leaving him alone which was 'all he wanted'.

Said he was not ill (or rather shook his head when asked if he was).

Sunday 26 March 1972

Adopted policy of leaving Nick alone – as requested by him . . .

Monday 27 March 1972

Finished off pruning etc. in 'secret' garden a.m. . . .

Nick reappeared about midday without car, which apparently broke down shortly after his departure last night (10 p.m.). He got it towed to Branson's Cross garage and then spent the night 'somewhere' . . .

Tuesday 28 March 1972

. . . Nick stayed at home but seemed well and played his guitar most of the day. In the evening he walked to Beoley garage to collect his car . . .

Cold and windy – no gardening except for pruning of last few roses.

Wednesday 29 March 1972

Surprise – Nick rose early and washed his car! After good

breakfast set off in his car complete with guitar and new coat (& passport etc.). Said goodbye to Molly (I was gardening) but as usual no information about where he was going or how long he would be away.

However, he seemed in reasonable form and we feel happier about him than usual (which isn't saying very much).

Better day – planted onions and sowed cabbage and sprouts.

These first entries set the tone for what followed over the next two and a half years. The pattern of Nick's life – with a careful recording of the meals he ate, the music he played (or didn't), and the unexplained car journeys (and breakdowns!) – was set against the background of Molly and Rodney's quotidian lives, which they tried to maintain, and in which they endeavoured to include him whenever he would allow them to. Throughout the diaries there are entries concerning the garden – either at the beginning or at the end of the day's events: as though the round of the seasons, and the work nature demanded, were stabilising anchors in the turmoil that threatened to engulf them all.

Over the next few weeks, the situation with Nick deteriorated. He became increasingly withdrawn and depressed. Sometimes a flight from home would result in a phone call, but only to say he was stranded somewhere:

Monday 3 April 1972

. . . Nick rang at about 8.15pm to say that he had abandoned his bike and was at Shipston on Stour without money. Went to fetch him and also his bike which he had left in a ditch some 4 miles south of Shipston. No conversation!

Often his withdrawal would cause alarm:

Saturday 8 April 1972

. . . Found [Nick] locked in upstairs loo . . . After some time we became alarmed and I broke the lock and opened the door to find him seated with head down but refusing to talk and apparently unwilling (or unable) to move. Suddenly, however, proved himself perfectly well, swearing loudly at Molly, which angered me and caused us to leave him. Rang up later to find he was OK and it transpired he had a good supper, watched TV. Extraordinary chap!

But at least this provoked a rare moment of communication (Nick's way of apologising?):

Sunday 9 April 1972

. . . Had a short talk with [Nick] during which he said he was going through a difficult time – but didn't seem able to enlarge on this. Agreed that 'at times' he disliked being at home and the way of life here (and presumably us too) but it was at least a roof over his head (gratifying reflection for us). However, he at least talked a little – first time for weeks . . .

And then, a longer flight from home:

Wednesday 12 April 1972

. . . Nick . . . left in the morning about 10 a.m. after good breakfast and making two telephone calls. Reverted to his oldest coat and took a knapsack with him. Asked by Naw if he was going to London – he said 'No, further'. Car had to be pushed to start. Naw said he 'seemed happy'. Let's hope perhaps he has some project in view.

This time, Nick was away for six nights. But any hopes of improvement were dashed on his homecoming:

Friday 21 April 1972

. . . Returned home about 7.30 p.m. and found Nick here, seemingly very gloomy but not at his worst. He had supper with us and revealed that he had been to Paris where he had eaten 'pig's foot'. The only other item of news we extracted was that he had returned by hovercraft . . .

He seems to have even less use for us than ever, but has he for anyone else, being so totally withdrawn?

Paris only seemed to have aggravated a worsening situation. Nick retired to his room, and remained there for two days, seemingly comatose, and neither eating nor drinking. It was the crisis that provoked the next development in the saga:

Monday 24 April 1972

Went to see Nick at 7.30 a.m. and he seemed completely out and made no sign of hearing anything I said. Very pale.

Rang Weinstein who said he would come over at 12.30. He arrived late however, and whilst we were awaiting him Nick suddenly appeared downstairs fully dressed and announced that he was about to leave for London! It seemed essential that he should see Dr Weinstein and we managed to keep him until Weinstein arrived . . .

Weinstein had longish talk with him in the music room and emerged looking very serious and grim. Said Nick was obviously in grave need of psychiatric help (had talked amongst other things of suicidal thoughts) but would have none of it. Weinstein considered it his duty to see that Nick was examined in a hospital and that we must agree to the necessary action being taken. Horrible situation. Compulsory entry last resort which we hoped desperately to avoid. However, W saw Nick again and obviously brought great pressure to bear on him and Nick consented to go voluntarily. He took Nick (and we followed) to Louisa Raynes new wing at Warwick Central Hospital, Hatton. Had few words with Dr Dickens who after seeing Nick briefly, declared him to be 'very sick' . . . [Nick] sat in the car with us – very 'low' of course and very upset about being 'forced' to come. We explained that his entry was voluntary and he was not forced to stay. After saying 'You won't take me home then?' he seemed to make up his mind, took the suitcase and strode purposefully back to the hospital . . .

A really dreadful day. Not much sleep for either of us!

While we were talking to Dickens, Nick came out and said he wants six weeks to 'sort himself out'. Poor old Nick – he's been trying to sort himself out for the last two years and as Molly says, it is time someone else tried to help him.

And with that squaring of his shoulders, Nick seemed to bite the bullet, and accept that the auxiliary forces of medical help were needed in this battle to regain his mind. It was a resolve he questioned, rescinded, and then re-embraced many times over the next two years, but in this first instance, he remained – voluntarily – at the Louisa Raynes for some six weeks – with occasional trips home – forming a relationship with Dr Dickens, whom he respected, that he would try to maintain (sporadically) for the next two years.

To begin with, Molly and Rodney went daily to visit Nick:

Tuesday 25 April 1972

Miserable day.

Went over about 4 o'clock to see Nick . . . he wouldn't speak to us and was angry and resentful. But he did not seem distressed about being where he was . . . But we're obviously in the doghouse.

Until they were gently told that this was probably a bad idea:

Sunday 30 April 1972

. . . Had talk with Aniya, the coloured Duty Officer (or whatever he's called). Very nice man. Were delighted to hear from him that he thought Nick was settling down. Aniya seems to have talked quite a lot with him. Said he seems 'muddled' about his relations with his parents. (Aniya obviously thinks too frequent visits a bad thing.) Said Nick seems to have a guilt complex about leaving Cambridge and talked a lot about his music . . .

Friday 5 May 1972

. . . Aniya told us that Nick seemed to have settled down and to be co-operating well . . .

We also saw Dickens . . . His findings were that Nick had a deep anxiety complex which has made him turn completely in upon himself but the great thing was that he had accepted the hospital and was taking the drugs they were giving him.

Friday 19 May 1972

Dick Mills, Social Worker, came to see us. Very young, and enthusiastic about idea of transferring Nick to London and Leon Redler (Dr Ronnie Laing's right hand man) for psychiatric treatment. Misgivings after he left. What does Dickens think? Seems a pity to change horses . . .

Saturday 20 May 1972

I visited Nick and found him quite talkative . . . He says he 'has decided' that he does not want to go to London but wants to finish his course of treatment there. He asked me in to the sitting room for the first time. Thought he seemed better. Nick said . . . he was not unduly worried about electric shock treatment but did not want 'psychiatric' treatment.

Why was Nick so resolutely set against psychotherapy (he remained so for the rest of his life) – even preferring to contemplate the drastic interference of Electric Shock Treatment? Was it too humiliating – a final admission of defeat? Or did he fear that by revealing the inner recesses of his mind to another human being he risked the final destruction of his already ailing muse? Whatever the reason, even his Cambridge friend Brian Wells was unable to persuade him, though Brian was the only friend Nick allowed to come and see him at this time.

Monday 22 May 1972

. . . Very interesting and pleasant meeting with Brian Wells who came to see me after seeing Nick. Obviously very fond of Nick and greatly worried about him. Brian is becoming a Doctor and is almost qualified. Seems to favour the Laing/Redler set-up for Nick but agrees Nick won't accept it. Seemed an unhappy young man but charming in his own way and clearly very genuine.

Dr Brian Wells is today one of Britain's leading psychiatrists and an internationally recognised expert on drug abuse. His friendship for Nick continued up till, and beyond, Nick's death, and embraced, from the time he met them, the members of Nick's immediate family, to whom he became a necessary ally. By the time he came to see Nick again, the latter had discharged himself from the Louisa Raynes:

Tuesday 6 June 1972
Stydd House, Lyndhurst . . .

Nick rang up at about 7.30 p.m. to say he had walked out of Louisa Raynes and was at home! . . . Rang Dickens who . . . was disappointed Nick had left as he thought he had decided to stay at least until we came back. Seems he thought that Nick's trouble was emotional rather than cerebral (to do with the intellect), and thought therefore that prognosis was good. He said Nick should go on taking pills . . .

After considerable discussion at Stydd House, decided we must return tomorrow.

Wednesday 7 June 1972
. . . Eventually, got home at 1.45 to find poor old Nick very depressed, tears at lunch. In afternoon he asked Molly if he could speak to her and she had the first long conversation with Nick we have either of us had for years. He spoke of his great worries – his fear of London – anxiety about the future and much more . . .

He had said during the afternoon that he wanted to go to London and we persuaded him to wait until tomorrow and go with me.

Thursday 8 June 1972
Started off for London with Nick about 9.30 but as we were approaching Stratford he said, 'This won't work, I ought to go back to Louisa Raynes.'

He felt that he was doing what Dickens had said, 'running away' rather than leaving because he felt the place could do nothing for him. Had a long talk in Stratford and eventually returned home – rang up Louisa Raynes and arranged for Nick's return. Left him there at 11.30 a.m. He borrowed £5 off me and I feared in the end he might be going to walk out. However, his return was a good effort.

At about 2.30 he rang up to say he had tried but just could not stick it. So I went back for him . . . Nurse asked us to wait for Dickens, which was a good thing as he talked to Nick and changed the position. He agreed Nick should not stay if he was unhappy but extracted a promise from Nick that he must go on taking pills for time being . . . Nick got his car out and set off 'for London'! Returning however after a very short time as he couldn't make it.

It transpired that the reason – or one of the reasons – Nick was anxious to get to London was to visit Sound Techniques in Chelsea (the recording studio he knew so well), where Françoise Hardy was recording. History doesn't relate whether or not this was an arranged appointment – perhaps the subject of the letter he had received 'from my publisher' the previous weekend. Whatever the case, after another abortive attempt to set off on his own, Rodney offered to take him.

Friday 9 June 1972
Filthy weather.

. . . We set off for London after early lunch. Nick drove for first hour and then me – supposedly for 1 hour but actually for most of day as Nick did not feel up to it. He saw his publishers for a very short time and we then went to the recording studio where Françoise Hardy was recording, but this time Nick was reluctant. However he went in once and apparently said hello, came out again and said he would go back. Did so three more times without making further contact – obviously lost his nerve. Very depressed and unhappy. I could do nothing with him to make him try again. Changed his mind several times – once 10 miles out of London – but eventually asked to go home and seemed ill. Couldn't drive. Had good supper however and early bed. Some day!

It must have taken considerable courage for Nick to even attempt to go in to Sound Techniques that day: his last two albums made there – *Bryter Layter* and *Pink Moon* – had met with even less success than his debut album *Five Leaves Left*. All three had, it seemed, failed utterly; he had just come out of hospital, about which he felt ashamed; and he was visiting someone who was an established star in the music world from which he seemed to be excluded. Was this his attempt to obey Dr Dickens's instruction not to 'run away'? In any event, it was small wonder his nerve failed him. Small wonder he plunged back into depression. But at least he was more communicative:

Saturday 10 June 1972
. . . Nick up early but seemed very depressed. I had long talk with him in the morning – discussing his symptoms etc. and found him unexpectedly responsive but very difficult to convince about taking his pills . . . restless and

anxious to try someone else . . . He took his pills in the afternoon. Hates doing so he says – against his principles. It's going to be a difficult week.

Pontoprint
POSTCARD
Printed & Published by G. & G. Ponton Ltd., Glasgow
Thinking of you,
See you soon.
love
John + Bev
X
Mr. Nick Drake
Far Leys.
Tanworth in Arden
Warwickshire.
P8. WATERFOOT, CARRADALE
Colour Photograph by Gibson Ponton F.R.P.S

Nick's aversion to taking medication was always an obstacle for any doctor. However, by now, he seems to have accepted that he needed help from the medical profession. As he sank once more into depression and self-hate and the fear that he was a 'nutcase', he embraced the idea of Electric Shock Treatment. At his behest, an appointment was arranged:

Friday 23 June 1972
Nick appeared in our room at 3.10 a.m. this morning to say he was very worried about . . . the EST . . . From then on there wasn't much sleep for anyone. Molly went down and brewed tea – Nick wandered about and eventually settled down between us after Molly had give him a couple of sonneril. A little sleep after this . . .

We had promised Nick he need not have EST if he didn't want to but surprisingly after arrival at the hospital he told 'John', the nurse in charge, that he was prepared to go through with it. Left him there apparently ready to co-operate in day's programme.

During [lunch] Nick rang up to say that he had decided against having EST . . . Went in at 3.30 to fetch him back and saw [the specialist] who confirmed he could not take Nick unless he was prepared to start off with some EST. Thought him 'a very sick boy who was badly in need of treatment'. Only trouble is of course Dickens decidedly against EST . . .

A fact Dr Dickens vehemently endorsed the next time he saw Rodney.

Monday 26 June 1972
Dickens . . . said that if he had a son like Nick . . . he wouldn't consider EST for a moment since it would perhaps add unbearably to his anxiety, possibly to the point of suicide. It seems we must be guided by Dickens and consider once again the possibility of London and Ronnie Laing.

But this was an idea Nick still stubbornly resisted. It was as if he was unwilling to explore the havoc within, preferring instead to seek a discipline that could be imposed from without.

He talked about joining the army:

He told Molly he had twice tried to get into the Army but had been turned down by Colonel Whittaker as unsuitable.

getting a job:

Seems clear that he definitely wants to give up his music and get a job (bank?).

even joining the Church:

He spoke of Christianity and probably becoming a Catholic to control forces of evil. He is clearly in great distress.

Molly and Rodney were now on a rollercoaster, becoming alternately his confessors:

Before lunch he made quite an effort to tell us his problems and feelings and we began to think he really needs some pure psychiatric help. But London seems impractical and dangerous

or the enemy:

[Nick] extremely withdrawn, silent and seemingly hostile this morning . . . Told Molly he felt his treatment had done him no good and that he regretted everything he'd told us about himself . . .

For all three of them, this must have been a time of despair. But if Nick gave up, his parents didn't. They were given a contact with a leading psychiatrist in London, John Pollitt, whom, with Dr Dickens's blessing, they arranged for Nick to see.

Monday 3 July 1972
Dickens had no objection to our going to Pollitt but thought he would want to have him in to hospital. Said there was danger in changing medication without supervision . . .

Tuesday 4 July 1972
Nick seemed very slightly less depressed and played a little music in the morning . . .

Said he would 'make it one day' but didn't know if we would live to see it. Seemed worried that we might 'abandon' him if he went to London hospital – reassured him . . .

Wednesday 5 July 1972
Lovely weather at last.

[Nick] talked despondently to me about being insane and nothing could be done. Said he'd finished his life's work and had done more than many in a lifetime. One day people would realise. Seemed utterly despondent and sat with closed eyes or head in hands . . .

Nick was proved right. Rodney would not live to know how prophetic his son was being. But he had no intention of abandoning him now, instead arranging the appointment with John Pollitt. Nick, as usual, vacillated, disappearing to London, refusing his pills, taking to his bed for whole days, and eventually, in a rare moment, confiding in his sister:

Saturday 9 July 1972
After supper started talking to Gay about his problems and listening to her very well put questions. So Molly and I cleared out and left them to it. Nick talked for quite a long time (for him) and told Gay of his 'friends at Hastings' (presumably John and Beverley?) who he said he loved but who, it seemed, had great influence over him which he thought was working against his submitting to medical treatment. Useful conversation with Gay and she felt closer to him than she has for years.

So his sister swung into action:

Wednesday 12 July 1972
. . . Gay phoned to say that she had contacted both Joe Boyd, with whom she and de Wet had had a long talk on the transatlantic phone last night, and also John Martyn, both of whom were going to phone Nick . . .

John Martyn rang at lunch time and spoke to Nick, suggesting he should come up today. Nick agreed and asked him to spend the night. Nick seemed very pleased about this at first, then predictably was overcome with misgivings and worry about it all . . .

Joe Boyd rang about 7 p.m. and spoke to Nick – evidently told him he ought to see doctor. I went with Nick to fetch John, who proved to be a very charming and cheerful young man with a guitar.

Nick in good form and for him, very talkative and responsive. Continued to be so throughout supper (he took John round the garden earlier), but he ran out of steam soon after supper, leaving us to have a very pleasant chat with this very likeable young man.

Thursday 13 July 1972
[Nick] pretty silent and low all morning . . . Did say to Molly however that he thought going to Pollitt would be all right now that he knew his friends agreed that he ought to go. Said he recognised that he was 'very sick'.

Friday 14 July 1972
Quite a day . . . Arrived at Pollitt's consulting room at 6 p.m. Nick in a fearful state in waiting room . . . He pulled himself together the moment Pollitt appeared, who took him off and had over ¾ of an hour talk with him, whereafter Nick returned to waiting room and we went in.

Pollitt had found Nick to be in a very depressed state . . . We are therefore to set off on another course of pill taking . . . We must phone Pollitt next Friday to report progress and meantime Nick must stay very quiet and must not drive or cycle. Nick very silent and dour after this and refused to speak. Went to Boots all-night Piccadilly branch with prescription. N refused to come with us for a meal, and also refused to promise that he would not disappear if we had one. We were dead tired and could not help rebuking him for his selfishness . . . Nick sullen all of the way home and refused drink and sandwiches on M4.

Rather a scene when we got back. He seized parcel of pills and we had to remove them. He took two which Molly gave him but refused to take any water with them and seemed not to have swallowed them. He made a display of anger – fury really – to Molly, which caused us to lecture him in fairly strong terms on his attitude, ingratitude and so [on]. We feel we cannot take much more from him (but of course we shall!). A bad ending to a most exhausting day.

There followed days and weeks of unresponsive silence, which began to take their toll on Molly especially:

Sunday 23 July 1972

. . . Nick continuing to 'want to be alone' and to stay in bed. Molly gets greatly discouraged and distressed by his failure to respond to all efforts on her part to get through to him and she finds it difficult to reconcile herself to the only alternative which is just to leave him there and try not to worry about him. Afraid it is beginning to get her down . . .

Friday 4 August 1972

[Nick] said that . . . he 'ought to have his head examined' for agreeing to take the pills! However he is taking them and we must wait to see what happens. He seems to want to stay in a comatose state and not to come back into the world.

No one can know what was going on in the recesses of Nick's mind at this time, nor what effect the pills were really having, but Rodney notes that Nick would play his radio ceaselessly:

Told Molly he had 'got the horrors' and feared to turn off the radio

And he told his sister, during one of her visits home, that

Talking to people made him feel physically sick . . . Said he had nothing to build on and was in a muddle and didn't know how to communicate. Said he had found Pollitt sympathetic.

But now he stopped taking his pills; or at any rate, he stopped taking them regularly. This particular situation came to a head towards the end of the month:

Tuesday 22 August 1972

When Molly . . . was coming downstairs, there was an explosive sound and a crack which alarmed both Naw and Molly. Molly went back to the nursery and found Nick to her astonishment in a fuming rage having vented his spleen on a chair and broken it. A long tirade followed about hating everything – having to say thank you, his upper-class voice, our way of life, the oppression of the poor, Molly's 'failure to mix' and much more. Molly completely taken aback, but countered his arguments and emerged very upset by whole incident. I arrived late on the scene and added mild remonstration. An unusually gloomy lunch followed.

After tea Pam and Janie turned up (followed by John) and rather unexpectedly Nick joined the gathering and acquitted himself quite well – particularly with Pam, with whom he discussed Pollitt and ECT. Some signs during the evening that he was ashamed of his lunchtime outburst but he could not bring himself to make anything in the way of an apology for his behaviour. Molly very disenchanted with him.

But not for long:

Friday 1 September 1972

In the afternoon [Nick] came to see Molly who was having a rest and said he felt desperate and wasn't getting any better at all. Went down to drawing room and had long talk – at one point he cried and Molly felt desperately sorry for him. In the evening he was quieter and calmer.

For a while, Nick seemed to improve – small steps, which meant much: finding himself able to get to Birmingham on his own and returning with a box of chocolates for his parents; or asking his father to have a drink with him:

Thursday 7 September 1972

[After] some discussion we went . . . to Beoley Cross where he stood me a beer and talked quite a lot about his problems. Said his main problem was having no goal in life, which affects everything – also admits that before he went to L[ouisa] R[aynes] he had thought that he was finished and 'the sooner the better'. He no longer felt that now. Felt he ought to start tackling his communication problem soon and thought that after Pollitt's next examination he might go to Paul Wheeler for a while who lives at Ascot (his wife being John Lennon's secretary).

However, when Molly decided she must have a short break and made plans to go and see her sister Nancy in the New Forest:

Nick asked Molly this morning not to go to Lyndhurst and of course she acceded to his request. He seemed grateful and ready to try to be more helpful and responsive than he has been.

And then, another unexplained and worrying disappearance:

Tuesday 12 September 1972
. . . In the afternoon he disappeared and at 8.30 p.m. when we were really worried, de Wet phoned to say Nick was in London and on his way to them, wanting to borrow the fare home. Gay rang later to say Nick was there and was catching (with her help with car) the 11.10 from Euston . . .

Wednesday 13 September 1972
. . . I tackled him on yesterday's escapade which I suggested was both undignified and immature. Had quite a good discussion and tried to impress on him that this sort of thing must stop and also that we would not stop him from going to London if he wanted to. He admits he is irresponsible but doesn't seem to care or to be prepared to do anything about it. The inconveniences suffered by others seem to be matter of little moment to him.

But perhaps Rodney was wrong about this:

Friday 15 September 1972
[In] the evening before supper Nick joined me in the drawing room for a long talk . . . He felt that his pills were only going to carry him to the point where he could just resume his previous existence and he wanted more than that . . . As a result of this he thought be must reconsider ECT and he proposed to ask Pollitt on Friday to explain more about it. He felt that he was perhaps paranoiac amongst other things . . .

Looking through the diary entries for these months, it is remarkable that, whenever Nick's behaviour had been particularly antisocial, difficult, or even cruel, his mind turned to ECT. Was it remorse? Throughout Nick's life, remorse was an emotion that came easily to him. He hated cruelty. To find himself hurting those he undoubtedly loved – or had loved – perhaps made him feel invaded by an alien being. Did he think that with ECT he could jolt this being out of his body?

For the next two months, Nick swung between despair and optimism, inertia and enterprise:

Friday 6 October 1972
. . . Unexpected phone call from Joe Boyd before supper (from London). Put life into Nick who discussed his communication fairly fully with us afterwards and was obviously pleased that Joe had rung . . . .

Evidently Joe Boyd urged him not to give up his guitar and afterwards Nick talked about buying a 'good one' – seems to have sold his old 'good one' . . .

Sunday 22 October 1972
Nick in gloomy form this morning . . . Said he was desperate, was no better, had nothing to be thankful for and nothing worse could happen to anyone than what was happening to him. Later . . . Molly got him into a happier vein and he talked about Chris Blackwell and the future in general.

Monday 23 October 1972
. . . Chris Blackwell phoned later which obviously cheered Nick up considerably. He asked if Nick was making any progress with a new record. It seems that he has in fact some material and he talked to him about getting going again soon. All very surprising but very excellent that he should have something to think about.

Wednesday 25 October 1972
Uneventful day but not very good. Nick dead silent and spent day in nursery listening to his radio . . .

Thursday 9 November 1972
This morning Nick asked if I could possibly consider financing a trip to Paris as he has decided he wanted very much to go there to see Françoise Hardy. Long but constructive discussion on this between the three of us followed and attempts by Nick, after at last finding FH's number, to contact the girl. This he failed to do but he still felt so much that he wanted to go that we decided to allow the episode and let him have a go as we feel that any venture of this sort is a step forward – something that Nick himself feels too. It is of course a great boost for us to have Nick in discursive, friendly and adventurous mood.

But alas, Mlle Hardy was out. Nick returned home the same day.

Monday 13 November 1972
[Nick] told Molly he found he had no spark of music in him at the moment . . .

The front-line troops

Tuesday 14 November 1972
[Nick] has put both his guitars away in their cases, which is presumably a gesture of some sort. After lunch . . . he bewailed the fact that he had no friends and no one he could talk to . . . he told Molly he was giving up taking his pills as he felt he'd been on them long enough.

However, a few days later, after an abortive trip to London:

Friday 17 November 1972
. . . In the afternoon he phoned to say that he had rung up Pollitt but got on to Mrs Repp and told her that he wanted to have ECT! . . . It seems he never left Euston and it was anger and frustration at finding himself unable to carry out his mission that had prompted him to phone Mrs Repp.

Saturday 18 November 1972
Important feature of the morning was a good talk between Birdy and Nick in the music room . . . Told her of his difficulties – home conflict and so on, also about Paris and ECT idea . . .

But this time, it was John Pollitt himself who rang and dissuaded Nick from such a course of action.

Tuesday 21 November 1972.
[Nick] talked of 'settling for' a life of isolation but also of establishing himself in London again to do music. I suggested we might help him do so. Also talked a little about ECT. He seems less nervous about it now (since talking to Brian Wells).

And then:

Wednesday 22 November 1972
Nick swore at Molly when she went in to the music room this morning to say good morning to him but immediately said he was sorry and seemed genuinely so when he saw that he had upset her. A certain amount of guitar playing followed.

All quiet after lunch but at about 4 p.m. suddenly emerged from music room and asked me for Pollitt's number – rang up and fixed ECT appointment for 1 p.m. next Monday. This must have cost him quite an effort and afterwards he played classical music until suppertime.

So, one week later, Nick had his one and only session of Electric Shock Treatment. He was supposed to have his second session three days later. But he cancelled it.

Thursday 30 November 1972
. . . Nick taken through to ward to lie down but told Sister he was not wanting to have treatment. Pollitt went to see him and then came and told me that he couldn't persuade Nick and that in view of this he thought it best not to bring pressure to bear and to give way. Recommends carry on with pills. Nick obviously impressed by Pollitt and also by kindness of Sister and said as we went out that he felt bad about not having treatment, that in fact

it had done him good but 'in wrong sort of way'??

Home by 5.45 and Nick in quite talkative vein. Said he wished now he had had ECT today! Thought Pollitt a most reasonable man.

Two days later, Brian Wells, with whom Nick had been in regular communication about his treatment, rang:

Saturday 2 December 1972

... Brian Wells rang at about 4, which cheered Nick up ... Said Brian Wells had told him he ought to have gone on with ECT ...

But Nick had no more ECT.

And so the last month of the year passed with Nick once more fluctuating between good days and bad. But gradually, he became more sociable, unexpectedly attending two weddings – one locally, at which he re-established contact with friends from his early youth – David and Kirstie Lodder – and one further afield, where he met, almost for the last time, his friends from the Jeunesse Dorée, at the wedding of Julian Lloyd and Victoria Ormsby-Gore. To them, he seemed cured – the old Nick back again. But all too often, once back home, Nick plunged into gloom:

Saturday 23 December 1972

... After supper Nick had short talk with Birdy and told her he thought he was 'damned' and would never get better.

Nevertheless, the New Year started well:

Monday 1 January 1973

... Nick in much better form and announced to Molly that he wanted to go to Ascot tomorrow to go with Paul W to buy a new guitar, and also that he wants to ask Dave and Kirstie to supper. This he did and they duly came after Molly had taken Nick to Stratford in p.m. to visit Austin Reed.

Evening a success, finishing up in music room and Nick still in good form. Said he was glad to have said goodbye to the worst year of his life.

David Lodder was Nick's childhood friend. Together they had tobogganed, biked, splashed about in streams and got happily mucky.

'They were the best times, at Far Leys,' recalls David:

'Nick and I got into many a scrape. And then there was Rodney with his machines, which we'd try out in the garden. He would come home with a prototype invention, which would never quite work – vital bits would still be tied on with string. There was the go-cart, and a ride-on mowing machine (rare in those days), which turned over whenever you went round a corner ... but best of all was staying the night, and in the evening, Rodney would bring out this vast contraption which was a recording machine, and we'd record our voices – a complete novelty.'

Later, much later, after their schooling, both Nick and David had to go to a crammer to pass their university entrance exams: 'We'd go off to Bantock's together,' David remembers, 'with Nick driving Molly's Morris Minor – much too fast, always. Good days – we had a lot of laughs. But then we went our separate ways as he became more involved in his music.'

David's wife Kirstie was once Nick's girlfriend – probably his first. Blonde, petite, gentle, but more daring and adventurous than Nick, she led him into adulthood. By her own confession, she knew little about music, but would listen to Nick for hours, sitting on his knee whilst he played his guitar around her. Then, as Nick's music became more important to him, they grew apart. She met David: he was a better lifetime choice. They married, had their first child, and moved to Sheffield.

It was a happy chance that, at the time Nick was emerging from one of his caverns of despairing inertia, Kirstie and David moved back to Warwickshire. Now, it was probably the very fact that music was not primary to their lives that made them so accessible to Nick. Their home became his bolt-hole, and their visits to Far Leys became rays of light – particularly when they brought their small son Joe. Kirstie felt Nick and Joe had a special bond: Nick always responded well to tiny children. And Joe's first spoken word was 'Nick'.

But Nick's New Year euphoria, mild as it was, did not last. He now vacillated about his music. After his proposed visit to his friend Paul Wheeler:

Wednesday 3 January 1972

... He appeared without guitar but with some records. Said he had decided against paying out so much money (£125) on guitar – although it was a very good one – until he was sure he was going to be playing again ...

Nick then seemed to briefly flirt with the idea of becoming involved with the Church. He was introduced to Canon Peter Spink of Coventry Cathedral:

Thursday 4 January 1973

... Reminded him before lunch of his visit to Jill Bennett at 2.30 p.m. to meet Spink. Strongly against going at first

. . . However, he eventually decided he would go . . . He and Spink and Jill arrived up for tea soon after 4 p.m. Spink keen to fix another meeting which he did for the 12th at Coventry. Seemed a reasonable sort of chap. After they left could get no information at all out of Nick about his talk with Spink or his opinion of him. Sat gloomily in drawing room with head bowed and eyes shut until supper.

Saturday 6 January 1973
Nick continuing in gloomy form . . . Just before I went to bed I tackled him about Spink and suggested that if he doesn't want to go on with seeing him it would be best for us to say so now. He shook his head in surly manner but when I pressed him to speak he said that it was his affair now and he happened to want to go on with it, so of course I said that this was fine.

Sunday 7 January 1973
Nick again in silent, inactive gloom . . .

He sat through long TV programme without glasses or lenses but seemed to be able to see. This refusal to wear glasses is ominous, we feel, and indicates something or other but God knows what. There seems to be evidence that he has cut down on his pills.

Monday 8 January 1973
[Nick has] started wearing his glasses again and playing some music and reading. Seems that he has started taking his pills again.

Tuesday 9 January 1973
Nick again very uncommunicative . . . He really seems quite all right but just determined not to talk to us!

Then another visit to Pollitt:

Wednesday 10 January 1973
We got away at 10.30, Nick looking very smart in suit and black T-shirt. Picnic lunch. Nick still upholding oath of silence or whatever it is . . . Pollitt said he had told Nick he can drive but must regulate this so that he does not do so less than 4 hours after taking valium. . . . He wants him to . . . take a simple job . . . Seemed a little dubious about Spink but thought it worth trying . . .

Drove straight back (still total silence) . . . Birdy arrived at 10 o'clock and Nick brightened up straight away and became quite chatty. Molly and I took the opportunity to slip off to bed fairly early and left Nick and B talking downstairs. Subsequently heard that he had quite a talk with B. Told her he had been impressed by Spink and could tell him anything – evidently looking forward to his trip to Coventry.

Thursday 11 January 1973
. . . Spink rang early to speak to Nick . . . Nick reverted to silence with us, which is beginning to irritate us more than somewhat . . .

Friday 12 January 1973
. . . Spink took him round the cathedral and they lunched in cathedral staff canteen. Spink had suggested possibility of job in music shop so Nick must have raised subject. Spink has proposed another trip soon to a social function. Altogether the trip seemed to have been successful and Nick was in good form when he returned . . . Spink phoned after supper and it seemed that after this Nick, who was playing his guitar quite a lot, deteriorated . . .

And then the dam of silence broke:

Saturday 13 January 1973
. . . After ultra silent tea Nick suddenly returned to drawing room from which he had withdrawn and started talking . . . We talked of his big problem of whether to go on with his music or not and if Far Leys has become the 'seat of indecision' as I suggested. He thought he might get a room somewhere near (Birmingham or Coventry e.g.) and I encouraged this idea . . .

Monday 15 January 1973
. . . Found Nick awaiting me downstairs this morning to say that he wanted to get a job but didn't know how to go about it. Discussed possibility of bank and army and suddenly he suggested computer programming. Phoned [Roger Slater] who suggested Nick should come and spend the day on Monday next to see if he thought he could do the job . . . Told Nick all this on return and he seemed still interested . . .

Wednesday 17 January 1973
[Nick] seemed restless in the evening [and] left us abruptly about 10.45, as we thought to go to bed. Evidently however he had gone out without our hearing for at 1.15 a.m. after we had gone to sleep the telephone rang and Dave Lodder was on to say that Nick was with them and spending the night! Bit of a shock and more than somewhat disturbing.

Nick had in fact arrived on the doorstep of the Lodders at 11 p.m., and had spent the whole night talking to Kirstie:

clearly he was worried about his impending job interview. She and David had become concerned that Molly and Rodney would be worried, so David had slipped out of their cottage (in which there was no phone) and driven to a phone box several miles away, to reassure the Drakes. He had not expected Rodney on the doorstep the following morning: it was perhaps one of the few wrong moves Rodney made.

Thursday 18 January 1973

Me due to go to Swindon today but first went down to Dave and Kirstie's at 8.30 a.m. There I found Nick having a boiled egg breakfast with Dave – Kirstie appeared later. Couldn't talk much as Nick there and felt I'd done the wrong thing by referring to Dave's phone message last night . . .

Indeed he had: for Nick set off immediately for London. However, he returned that evening:

. . . Got home (through fog) at about 4.30 p.m. to find Nick just arrived back from London in contrite mood for having taken car (and so he might well be!) Apologised to Molly and seemed altogether in much better form. Said he had seen 'friends' in London.

And then the day of the interview arrived:

Monday 22 January 1973

A notable day. Nick duly paraded for a 10.20 departure for Droitwich – a little late after one or two changes of dress . . . Very silent on the way down and obviously 'uptight'. Took him up and introduced him to Roger Slater and left him. Returned home with Molly.

Nick eventually arrived back at 4.30 p.m. . . . It transpired that he had had a pretty full day . . . finishing up by doing 5 intelligence tests . . . He seems keen to get the job and says he will work hard at it if he succeeds in doing so . . .

A good day – let us hope a turning point.

Wednesday 24 January 1973

Letter from Droitwich arrived and came in from garden about 11 to find Nick pacing around with it in kitchen having opened it and found that he had been offered a job as computer programmer trainee at £700 p.a. for six months. Obviously pleased and excited, though at some pains to conceal the fact. He wrote a reply accepting straight away . . . Talked freely about it all at his early lunch – (I heard later from Roger Slater that he had done 'as well or better' than other trainees in his tests) . . .

We both felt tremendously relieved to think that Nick had got this job.

Their relief was to be short-lived.

Thursday 1 February 1973

Nick's first day at work.

[He] returned about 6.15 and was at first quite communicative. It seems he is to start a course in London on Monday and hotel accommodation has been booked for him for Mon/Thurs nights next week. We had not expected this to happen so soon and were rather perturbed that he should have no time to settle in. We feel he is a bit overwhelmed by the prospect himself but will not admit it, of course. He very soon relapsed into silence . . . Anyway, he has started this job and that was something which we never expected to happen in the foreseeable future.

Monday 5 February 1973

. . . Phoned Birdy at 9.15 p.m. to find that Nick was there at La Porte Grise for supper but evidently didn't want to talk to us. B phoned later to say that Nick had been in low form when he arrived but had cheered up at the end. Said he found the day's work pretty incomprehensible but that so had others. Said he was going to stick with the course. B took him back to his hotel.

Wednesday 7 February 1973

. . . Rather frustrated about Nick. B phoned hotel and found that Nick had left that morning . . .

Thursday 8 February 1973

[Nick's cousin] Gogs rang to say that she had been through to Honeywells where the course was being held and found that Nick had left at midday on Tuesday without any explanation . . . All very depressing. The job in Droitwich is obviously scuppered.

Friday 9 February 1973

. . . Increasing worry about Nick as he failed to ring up . . . we feel he has probably moved in with friends, but who?

Saturday 10 February 1973

Spent most of day wondering how Nick was faring . . .

In the evening phoned Paul Wheeler who said that Nick had been out to see him last Tuesday afternoon and had told him of the course he was supposed to be doing. He didn't seem unduly worried about it, Paul said, and got up early on Wed. morning . . . in order, as he said, to be back in time for it . . .

Nick did not, apparently, have difficulty in admitting to his friend and fellow songwriter that he had turned his back on his music in favour of an 'ordinary job'. On the contrary, his difficulty apparently came in admitting that he had walked out of this job. Was he ashamed? Or did he at that point intend to return to the course? Nevertheless, his next port of call was to his great musical collaborator, Robert Kirby:

. . . Phoned Kirby and found that Nick was there – it seems they were playing a tape of a recording session they had had the previous night. Spoke very briefly to Nick . . . Said he was all right and when I asked if he was going to stay up for next week's course said 'yes', but not very convincingly.

So, at least we know that he is all right and our worry about his well being has been replaced by our annoyance that he should have walked out of his course without any word of consideration for anyone.

So Nick returned home:

Sunday 11 February 1973

. . . Found Nick at Coventry station without any luggage and pretty subdued . . . Said at first he had left the course 'because he wanted to do something else', but modified this later to include his inability to make anything of the course. Lectured him at some length and urged on him the vital importance of going to Droitwich tomorrow to explain the position to R. Slater . . . He appeared contrite when he arrived home and went straight to bed.

But Nick's nerve failed him.

Monday 12 February 1973

Nick put on a tie this morning and set off to Droitwich to see Roger Slater and explain his failure to complete the London course. In ¾ hour he was back to confess that having arrived at Nuways he couldn't find the courage to go in. I spent most of the morning trying to persuade him that he must go. In the afternoon . . . I phoned Roger Slater myself, who was most sympathetic, very concerned, and offered to come up tonight or tomorrow morning if Nick would like to talk to him. This unexpected and undeserved kind gesture threw Nick into utter confusion and he didn't know what to say . . . I took him for a drive (to collect bits and pieces for his car stereo) but still he was very stuck . . . [Roger] arrived at 9 p.m. and . . . had a long private talk with Nick and it was agreed amicably between them that Nick should give up the idea of computer trainee work. All very sad really, but much better to end it like this than just to run away as Nick had planned to do.

Another triumph for the subtle enemy, who had cunningly led all three protagonists down a false avenue.

With hindsight, the idea of Nick becoming a computer programmer could be seen as risible. But at the time, all three collaborated in wishing and hoping that this mirage might just be the light at the end of the tunnel. Let there be no doubt, however, that Nick, who set the whole machine in motion, wanted it to succeed. But just as he was the one to start the procedure, perhaps he was also the first to come to his senses and see what a hopeless venture it was. Nevertheless, he must have felt its failure keenly:

Tuesday 13 February 1973

. . . Nick doesn't look very well and we think yesterday's proceedings were probably a pretty good strain on him.

Quite possibly this was an understatement. Nick now seems to have been frantic to try and prove that music was what he was meant to be doing. He left home for several, unexplained days, which in the circumstances caused inevitable worry at home. In fact, he contacted John Wood, and started travelling back and forth between London and Suffolk. His parents understood him well enough to realise where he might have gone:

Tuesday 20 February 1973

. . . Phoned John Wood at 6 p.m. to learn from him that Nick had left 'for Muswell Hill' (presumably Kirby) after lunch and moreover that a recording session had been booked for him tomorrow evening. John Wood had found Nick 'much better' and thought that he had enjoyed his visit.

We found all this rather encouraging and decided that we must keep quiet for the present and see how things work out with Nick.

This is how John Wood remembers that time:

'Much to my surprise Nick phoned out of the blue and said he wanted to go into the studio . . . So Nick and I went into Sound Techniques for a couple of sessions, which I do recall were afternoon and early evening. At this stage Joe was not involved in any way and was still working at Warner Pictures in Hollywood . . . What was unusual about these short couple of sessions was that Nick wanted to record the guitar parts only, something he had never done before, always previously having put down the vocal and guitar parts together. He told me the reason for this approach was that he was struggling to arrive at finished lyrics. I have always thought that Nick just wanted to get back into the studio and unusually for him was willing to arrive in this haphazard way . . .'

John was surely right. Nick must have been desperate to prove that the job debacle was for a reason: that if he could get back to his music, if he could just go into a studio – even if unprepared – he would once more find himself able, assured, and in command. What a devastation it must have been to find that this was not so. Three days later, he returned home:

Friday 23 February 1973
. . . After supper . . . Nick walked in (about 10.30 p.m.). Seemed OK, though unshaven and unkempt . . . Told us he had done 'some work' on Wednesday and had slept in the car in London (which we did not like, as this smacked of the old days) . . . A great relief to have him back.

Another short-lived relief. Two nights later, Nick took an overdose of valium.

Mercifully, here too he failed.

Monday 26 February 1973
. . . Molly went to him and had a long talk. He revealed that he had taken the whole untouched bottle of valium containing 36 pills and he said moreover that he had done so with the object of finishing himself off. He said everything was in a mess, that his music wasn't coming properly, that he couldn't get on with people, that he didn't like being at home but couldn't stand being anywhere else. Molly tried to persuade him to start his pills again but without avail and spoke to him for a long time. He came down for lunch but was very shaky and eventually agreed that he should put off the recording session due to start at midnight tonight in London with John Wood, which he had told Molly this morning he was going to go through with . . .

We are left wondering what will happen when he recovers and what the next move will be.

In fact, Nick soldiered on:

Wednesday 28 February 1973
He is obviously struggling to get some material ready on his guitar and obviously finding it difficult . . .

Nick rang John Wood and seemed to be making a provisional arrangement to do some more recording. He continued to zigzag across the country, travelling between Warwickshire, Suffolk and London.

Tuesday 5 March 1973
Woke up to find Nick's car back in its place in the drive and it transpired that he had returned at 4 a.m. . . . Nick did not as usual tell us much of his activities but said he had been up to London after Suffolk. He has with him a tape recording of some new songs of his . . .

Was this tape the fruits of those seemingly abortive studio sessions? A provisional work tape of Nick Drake's last songs?

John Wood remembers that 'after a couple of days we put everything on hold, allowing Nick some time to come up with final songs'.

Wednesday 6 March 1973
. . . Nick told Molly after tea that he is stuck for words and Molly suggested Paul Wheeler as a lyricist. Biddy phoned and suggested lunch with her and Cyril . . . [Nick] seemed depressed about this . . . It transpired that he resented us going out and evidently feels that we must remain with him all the time and go nowhere when he sees fit to be here. All alarmingly unreasonable . . .

Thursday 7 March 1973
. . . I had a bit of a talk with Nick and he said he was in great difficulty over words for his songs . . .

Nick told Naw at lunch that he was looking forward to May, when Joe Boyd would be back and (presumably) might be able to help him with his music.

Wednesday 14 March 1973
No change in Nick – he had a bath in the evening which sometimes means preparation for an expedition. Played guitar quite a lot. He postponed last Friday's recording session for a week, so maybe he will be off on Friday – we will wait and see. Meanwhile he is taking no pills.

This lack of pill-taking must have been anguishing for Rodney and Molly, although, as always in the diary, he merely states it as a fact. But Pollitt had warned them that such a move could be dangerous. And they had been made all too aware of how volatile Nick's situation was.

Friday 16 March 1973
. . . Before tea he had a bath and after tea set off for London with his two good ordinary guitars and also his electric guitar. He said he thought he'd be back tomorrow and took no luggage with him. We are left wondering if

he is going to a recording session as planned or what. And why does he need three guitars?

Tuesday 20 March 1973
[Nick] turned up (about 10.30 a.m.) looking pretty dishevelled and unshaven. Molly had a few words with him and remarked that Chris was coming this evening, shortly after which, after telling Molly that he hates being at home and couldn't think why he'd come, he stormed off in the car, leaving her very upset. However, as often happens on these occasions, he returned quite soon . . . in time to meet Chris. Talked a little to Chris and told him he was doing some recording but only found it possible to compose in studio.

And so the pattern continued: unexplained absences –

Nick up earlyish this morning and set off in his car at about 9 a.m. for an unknown destination. However he returned again about 10.45 but did not reveal where he had been or why he had gone there . . .

and silent returns –

Oath of silence or whatever it is still much in evidence . . .

punctuated by days when Nick emerged briefly from his black hole – often apparently following a rare moment of exasperation from his parents:

Saturday 14 April 1973
Molly told Nick a few home truths this morning about his personal cleanliness, the signs of his retreating to where he was this time last year, and the necessity for him to do a bit around the house – at least to help Naw with the coal. No noticeable effect – beyond expression of annoyance at the time – but no doubt a good thing.

. . . after tea agreed to play me a game of croquet – big breakthrough! He defeated me after a good game.

And the next day:

Nick filled up Aga hods this morning!

Most days, he played his guitar – often it would be the same phrase played over and over again:

A lot of electric guitar playing – simple theme repeated ad nauseam.

And always there were the car trips:

. . . Molly thinks perhaps he acquires musical inspiration from driving.

Mostly, however, Nick left his parents perplexed, and desperate to understand what was going on:

Monday 16 April 1973
. . . I phoned Brian and we had a long and helpful talk. Brian reckoned that Nick's present behaviour was a typical phase of his mental trouble and the only thing to do was to let him soldier through it in the hope that he would eventually come to terms with life. He said he thought Nick would back soon and sure enough he reappeared about 10.45.

And again, in an effort to understand, they turned to John Wood:

Wednesday 18 April 1973
. . . Tried to phone John Wood to try to get some information about his music as we thought difficulty with this might be at the root of the trouble. John Wood out but had long and helpful conversation with his wife – clearly knows [Nick] well and is fond of him. Seems that Joe Boyd has said he wants to make a record with Nick when he comes over in May. Nick had been trying to persuade John Wood that he has enough material to record now and wants to do so. John disagrees and recently (Monday) Nick phoned to say he now agreed that he should wait till May. Joe Boyd's visit is clearly a big thing to him and maybe that is what's worrying him.

Spent most of day wondering where he was.

Nick spent several days away from home, causing Molly and Rodney to fret as they prepared to take their first holiday for some years, and wonder whether in fact they would have to cancel it.

Saturday 21 April 1973
. . . Just going to bed at midnight when Nick appeared in bedroom much to our relief. Molly re-dressed and got him some supper. He was quite talkative and told her that he was planning to go to Spain on Tuesday! Said that he was 'on a razor's edge', that it could go right or it could go terribly wrong, and he could be 'in real trouble' . . . We don't know what on earth to make of all this and must hope that we shall hear more tomorrow.

Sunday 22 April 1973
. . . As we were finishing breakfast, Naw came in to say that Nick's car had gone, and sure enough he had slipped quietly out and away whilst we were in the drawing room. Left no clue of course as to where he'd gone – probably Spain.

So we remain as mystified as ever – is this all a gesture against our proposed week in France or is he running away from the coming next month of Joe Boyd? We shall perhaps never discover the real reason.

So Molly and Rodney left – not knowing whether Nick would go to Spain, or join them in France, as he had been invited to do. In fact he did neither. Instead, when they returned, they discovered that he had re-signed himself into the Louisa Raynes.

Wednesday 2 May 1973
. . . We were just reflecting that this rather surprising Louisa Raynes development was a good thing when the sister on duty phoned (about 10.30 p.m.) to know if we had any news of Nick as he had left during afternoon and not returned. So we returned upstairs to unpack and go to bed in the state of uneasiness that Nick seems to have perfected the method of inducing.

Thursday 3 May 1973
Telephone rang at 7.15 a.m. Nick on the line to say that he was walking along the Pershore Road from Birmingham and that he had left Molly's car at the beginning of M4 near Maidenhead. Somewhat stunned and mystified by these seemingly irreconcilable developments, and set off to meet Nick and picked him up just off the Pershore Road in Birmingham outskirts. Very uncommunicative and completely unapologetic but managed to gather that he had set off for London yesterday in Molly's car but finding he was running out of petrol and having already run out of money he abandoned car, hitchhiked into London for some unspecified reason, hitchhiked to Birmingham via M1, and then started walking home. Wouldn't talk to me (I found it difficult to be sympathetic) but did talk quite a lot to Molly, told her he couldn't stick Louisa Raynes, couldn't talk to any of the people and so on. He wouldn't phone Louisa Raynes as we wanted him to.

Why had Nick left the Louisa Raynes so soon after signing himself in? Having taken the decision to go there, it seems that disillusion set in rather quickly, even for Nick.

Had he perhaps gone up to London to see Joe Boyd who he knew was due back in England at the beginning of May? If he had, he probably failed in this too, since Joe has no recollection of a meeting at this time. But if this was another abortive venture by Nick, it would have surely reinforced every ounce of self-worthlessness he felt, and it may explain his surly behaviour.

But then, following a familiar pattern, remorse apparently set in:

. . . He was obviously pretty whacked and sat despondently in the drawing room until Molly and I decided we had better go with him to get the car, whereupon he went and had a bath, and then insisted on driving us all the way to where Molly's car was and did it very well despite the lack of sleep and food . . . On our return Naw told us she had had anxious calls about Nick from Louisa Raynes, from doctor (?) and from police. Nick said he would do the phoning and to our surprise rang up to tell them he was going to go back. After he had done this he was suddenly relaxed and talkative and although full of misgivings about his ability to stick it there, seemed in quite good form. Took him over at 5.30 and he went in by himself at his own request.

Whereupon he stayed at the Louisa Raynes for nearly three weeks. And after this he drove to London to see his friend Brian Wells, who now, for a while, takes centre stage:

Saturday 19 May 1973
. . . Brian Wells phoned to say that Nick had been with him for several hours and that he, BW, was concerned about him and thought he ought to be in hospital . . .

Sunday 20 May 1973
. . . Brian Wells phoned after dinner to ask if Nick had come home. Brian felt something positive should be done . . . Said he thought possibly Leon Redler might be worth considering if Nick prepared to see him.

Monday 21 May 1973
. . . After lunch Brian phoned to say Nick had called in and seemed considerably better . . . He had talked to Nick about the Philadelphia Association, which is Leon Redler's place, and Nick had seemed quite enthusiastic . . . Later Brian rang again to say that he had been on to Leon Redler's assistant . . . Way was open, Brian thought, for Nick to go in to Philadelphia Association as an inpatient . . . N.B. Brian, it seems, has spoken to Leon Redler himself who seems interested in the case.

Tuesday 22 May 1973
. . . Phoned Brian about 7 p.m., who told us he had already

spoken to Nick who seemed quite bright and also quite enthusiastic about Leon Redler still. Brian had told him that he must write in and Nick had undertaken to try and do this.

Wednesday 23 May 1973

Chelsea show today in not very nice weather . . .

Phoned Brian in the evening to learn that he had heard from Nick who said he has written a letter to Leon Redler and was going to tell us about it on our return. (He returned to Far Leys in the afternoon). This all sounds encouraging

Thursday 24 May 1973

. . . Arrived home about 4pm . . . Found Nick completely sealed up and unresponsive in the music room and apparently sleeping. Sure enough his letter to Redler was on the hall table left open, and Naw told us he had said he was leaving it for us to see. Nick came in for supper but of course wouldn't speak. After he had left to return to the music room we read his letter and were most impressed with it – a very clear résumé of his present state and what had led up to it . . . Told him we had read his letter and were most impressed with it – he seemed pleased. He watched TV for a while but wouldn't talk about his letter. Left him standing aimlessly in the drawing room. Molly went down later and found him in a chair – seems pretty bad.

This was the letter Nick wrote to Leon Redler, copied by Rodney before it was put into the post:

Dear Dr Redler,

It was recently suggested to me by a friend, Brian Wells, that I should try to get in touch with you, and he told me that the best thing was to write. It's a long time since I wrote a letter so I hope it won't seem strange.

I'll try and briefly outline what's been happening to me and I suppose that's what this letter is meant to be about. At 18, I got into Fitzwilliam College, Cambridge, and a year later went up there to read English. While there, I did read English but spent much time playing music and writing songs. After two years, I left to go to London, where I made three albums, two produced by an American, Joe Boyd, and the third produced by me. (If they would be of any interest, I would be happy to send them.) There was a lot of pressure around, and I suppose I sort of cracked up. After completing them, I went to Spain for a while and then came home here to my parents' place, where I have been for about the last year and a half. Fairly soon after arriving, I was placed by a local doctor in the 'Louisa Raynes' ward of the Warwick Central Hospital, pretty much against my own will. I spent six weeks there under a Dr Dickens, during which time I met Dick Mills, who I think is now working with Ron Laing, and he suggested that I should come and see you. However, what with one thing and another I didn't, and ended up seeing a Dr John Pollitt, of St Thomas' Hospital. He treated me for depression, and to tell the truth he was pretty helpful, although I never really understood the word, and felt that 'confusion' was more apt. Just lately I went back to Louisa Raynes as a voluntary patient, but didn't stay there very long. I could probably go into detail about what's going on now but I don't think this is the place.

I still write songs, but they have become a little too 'far out' for comfort and don't stand up very well in the studio.

My parents seem anxious to help but when I try to communicate with them I get completely tongue tied, which is a problem. Come to think of it, it's getting harder to talk to everyone now. I don't know too much about your work, so I've just said what springs to mind about me. I'm sorry if it all sounds trite or presumptuous or anything, but I would really like to hear from you.

Yours,
Nick Drake

So, for the first and only time in his life, Nick considered psychotherapy: human rather than chemical help. But it obviously cost him dear:

Friday 25 May 1973

Nick down at a reasonable hour and went out for a short time during the morning arriving back in time for lunch. Having heard from Naw that he had broken a guitar, went to inspect and found that he had broken both. Obviously in a fit of frustration and despair. He now only has his electric guitar. This is bad . . .

Thursday 31 May 1973

Letter from Leon Redler in reply to Nick's arrived this morning. Nick took it off to the music room and left it on the piano where we read it after he had set off in his car for an unknown destination (as usual). The letter proposed an interview with Redler on Sat. June 2nd and asked Nick to say a) if he would come and b) if he would mind if a student or trainee was present with Redler at the interview. We think all of this probably defeated Nick and he went off in his car . . .

And that was that. Perhaps it was the request for another person to be present at the interview that defeated Nick. Perhaps it was the reality of an actual session. But Nick never attempted psychotherapy again.

Meanwhile, the staff at Louisa Raynes, including Dr Dickens, were wondering where Nick was. Rodney phoned them, and managed to speak to Dickens himself:

Friday 1 June 1973

[Dickens] said that he had told Nick that he could come to LR whenever he liked and could stay as long as he wanted but he could do nothing for him until Nick was prepared to take treatment. Said Nick . . . seemed to be 'shopping round' trying to decide what to do. D said that until he was prepared to put himself in someone else's hands and do as he was told he would not get better and might get worse. But he thought that if Nick would do as he was told the prospects were very good. Asked him if it was Schizophrenia and he said that nowadays in psychiatry that was a meaningless word covering a whole host of psychic maladies. Said he thought Nick was suffering from an intellectual insufficiency which he (Nick) found unacceptable and which could be cured. D said all we could do was to soldier on as we were and hope that Nick would soon come round to accepting treatment – he thought him intelligent. All very interesting stuff.

Just before supper Nick walked in. He and I settled down in drawing room with drinks and I told him about the happenings of the day, including most of what D had said and although he was silent and made not a single comment he was clearly interested and perhaps pleased.

Saturday 2 June 1973

. . . I spoke to Brian again today on the phone – he thinks Nick will eventually come round to going to Redler and agrees with Dickens' thoughts. Agrees there is nothing we can do but await further developments.

Which was what Rodney and Molly did: indeed, they had little choice, faced with Nick's deepening retreat into his silent world, punctuated by apparently meaningless comings and goings in his car. Occasionally these would be explained:

. . . Molly met Kirstie in Henley in the morning, who told her that Nick had been to see them a fortnight ago, had gone to a pub with Dave and had been 'fine', playing darts.

But mostly they were in the dark. Nevertheless, they were always relieved when he came home:

. . . His bedroom light was on when we returned so Molly went to say goodnight but he hid his head under his wing, poor thing. Seems very low – but at least he came back.

For Nick's twenty-fifth birthday on 19 June, Rodney, understanding his son's phobia of wearing glasses, offered him a pair of contact lenses:

Tuesday 5 June 1973

. . . I phoned Brookes opticians to get particulars of new contact lenses, which sound a tremendous improvement on previous type. Went down to tell Nick to cheer him up, I thought, but he had gone again . . .

Tuesday 12 June 1973

Expressed hope that he would keep his appointment [at opticians] tomorrow that is if he wanted to take advantage of my offer. Did he? No answer. What is one to do?

But Nick did, at least, keep the appointment:

Wednesday 13 June 1973

Nick up early but did not go off as we had feared and when I went down early to ask him if he would be coming into Brooke with me he nodded. Sure enough we set off together at 10.25 (Nick making no sartorial concession to the occasion and remaining in the sweater and trousers he now lives and sleeps in). After a silent wait we were ushered into the presence of the great Brooke who put up his usual impressive performance . . . He was asking Nick about the difficulties and discomfort he had experienced with his contacts when Nick rose to his feet and stalked from the room. The great man never turned a hair and went on talking to me as though nothing had happened. I explained Nick's troubles and he remarked that of course he had been in difficulties if he couldn't see properly.

The solution in a nutshell! If only life could be that easy . . .

The situation regarding his new lenses is worrying. Must assume he is still wearing them as they are not back in the containers in his bedroom . . . I am faced with the dilemma of having to pay for them without being able to find out if they are all right . . .

But then, Nick posed many a dilemma – to himself, no doubt, as well as to his parents.

Asked him . . . if he could go up to village at 6.30 p.m. to meet Naw. He left just after 6.30 as we thought to fetch Naw but she arrived on foot to say that she had seen him driving off in opposite direction. What a strange chap he has become!

. . . He looks very pale and not very well but it is impossible to find out how he is feeling . . .

Seems to be eating well which is something but still looks very thin . . . All attempts to talk to Nick seem to be hopeless now.

I told him that we were very sorry that he seemed so down but until he could bring himself to tell us, there was nothing we could do but offer him shelter and food and be ready to help him in any way we could. No response of course.

Still, Rodney ploughed on – and, maybe, made progress.

On his twenty-fifth birthday Nick had inherited a small lump sum from a family trust.

Saturday 28 July 1973
. . . I had a go at talking to [Nick] today and amongst other things suggested he should consider getting going in his music again with a new guitar which he could now pay for himself (Pam's trust). He sat throughout my dissertation with eyes closed and face completely expressionless and I eventually left him and returned discouraged to the garden. However shortly after he sought me out in the workshop (most unusual) and stood there for a short while obviously wanting to say something but unable to.

Monday 30 July 1973
Nick . . . made the tea this afternoon and got the coffee after supper – small enough incidents but straws in the wind perhaps – anyway, we clutch at them.

Monday 13 August 1973
. . . Molly talked to him and I tackled him in the kitchen. Felt that he had some project in view but couldn't tell us . . .

We didn't expect to see him again today but he returned at about 7.15 with a brand new guitar! No doubt this was the project. We tried to express the right amount of interest without overdoing it.

As ever, Molly and Rodney were walking on eggshells. As ever, they moved from being central to peripheral and back again to whatever force was driving Nick.

He tried now to move away from home, and seems, briefly, to have rented a room in London:

Friday 24 August 1973
. . . I opened a letter addressed to Mr Drake to find it was for Nick from 21 Cranley Gardens, SW7, the writer saying that he assumed Nick did not want the room he had booked and that he had let it and wanted the keys posted. Tackled Nick about this in his room and talked for some time but he wouldn't say anything.

At the beginning of September, Nick apparently spent two weeks in London, staying in a hotel somewhere. For what purpose, history does not relate – and nor did Nick.

Thursday 6 September 1973
. . . No sign of Nick still – rather a long time away . . . in the evening I rang Robert Kirby who said that Nick had been round yesterday and he'd had about four hours with him. He had got the impression that Nick thought no one wanted to see him now . . .

Thursday 13 September 1973
Letter from Nick today! From 'Belsize Park BO', presumably 'PO'. He asked for his trust money to be credited to his deposit account, said he was going to spend it all but that was what he wanted. Sent him a form to sign and meanwhile credited his current account with £150. Spent day wondering what this new development portended – good or bad. Molly upset and worried but maybe it's all right.

But a few days later, Nick was home:

Thursday 20 September 1973
. . . Noticed that his suitcase was in the car and as the hotel key was no longer in his pocket we must assume he has given up the hotel room. Car boot locked which is unusual so one hopes new guitar is there . . .

Nick once again became a furnace sealed, with only an occasional eruption:

Saturday 29 September 1973
. . . I went to try to get him to come and sit down but he turned on me and shouted at me to leave him alone. Tried to reason with him but he said something was burning him up and he couldn't stand it. Denied that he hated everything as I suggested and flounced off upstairs to bed. Have recorded the incident in some detail as it is extremely rare these days for him to display any emotion.

Only an occasional raising of the portcullis:

Monday 8 October 1973
A day with an unusual event . . . He told me (with long

gaps of silence in between) that he expected that the time had come when he would suddenly be better and then he would leave home. That he had no wish now to go back to London. That he has tried some religious meditation in London recently but it hadn't appealed to him . . .

. . . After tea he went to stand in the dining room where Molly was arranging flowers . . . and then came and sat with me in the drawing room. Stranger still he came into our bedroom where Molly was changing to go out to dinner . . . and told her that he wanted to speak in a way that he hadn't spoken before. Molly did all she could to encourage him but to no avail . . .

It was as though Nick had been imprisoned by an invisible captor, who allowed him an occasional appearance at a barred window, but snatched him back and muffled him before he could cry out in communication.

Tuesday 16 October 1973

Paul Wheeler phoned this morning to say he and friend were coming up to Stratford on Saturday – asked him to lunch and handed phone over and Nick explained the way up here and talked quite a bit.

Had a bit of a talk with Nick this morning and managed to get a little out of him. Said he wouldn't now consider a routine job under any circumstances whatsoever. Didn't want to be a down-and-out – had tried it once and found it very frightening . . . Said he couldn't write because he couldn't observe or be impersonal. Self-expression seemed to boil down to music, I said. No answer.

No answer. Time Of No Reply . . . Because here, perhaps, was the nub of the problem: Nick the observer could no longer find himself in the turmoil of the force that drove him onwards and inwards. It even denied him the succour of friends:

Saturday 20 October 1973

A sad day really. Nick went off in his car after an early breakfast and we thought he had decided to miss the lunch party (Paul Wheeler and friend). However he returned quite soon having filled up with petrol. Paul phoned to say the party would now be 4 instead of two and he wouldn't be here until late (about 12.45). However by 2 p.m. they still hadn't come and after his third beer Nick slipped out of the music room door and left in his car. The party arrived about a quarter of an hour later. A very jolly lunch, Paul and wife (Diana) with friends Charles and Sandy. All very sad however that Nick wasn't there. They told us that Nick was still a real name in the pop or folk world and that plenty of people would be delighted to get him on their books for a record. They seemed to think he didn't want to do anything at all now but I doubt this.

Rodney knew his son, and was undoubtedly right in his doubt. Evidence of recognition could not have cured Nick: but it would surely have comforted him. The force however was implacable; despite Nick's avowal that he had no wish to return to London, the motorway became his treadmill, as he travelled incessantly to and from the capital.

Sunday 21 October 1973

. . . He said he had no alternative at present to going back and forth to London regularly because he had things to do there which I wouldn't understand and moreover he couldn't stay in London before he had got something going because London ate one up in such circumstances. He said little likelihood at present of the situation changing. He was off again in his car at 2.30 and got back at about 8.15 (just time to have done London and back).

Occasionally it was further afield – but for just as brief a time:

Monday 29 October 1973

. . . Molly found from ticket stubs that Nick must have set off for Malaga on October 24th having bought a return ticket there for £54 and then decided to return when he got as far as Paris as he took another ticket from there for 100 francs. It was after that expedition that he brought back his new guitar. All very mysterious!

Now a further complication entered their lives: Rodney's sister Pam, who lived in Canada, had developed Alzheimer's disease and become incapable of looking after herself. Rodney flew her back to England and she became a temporary member of the Far Leys household.

Wednesday 31 October 1973

A better day on the whole. Tackled Nick in the music room in the morning and told him that Pam was arriving next Wednesday instead of us going over there [originally, Rodney had thought that he and Molly would have to go over to Canada] . . . Before tea he came and talked with me for a bit – first time for a long time – said something was lifting now and that he had been worrying about something so much he'd forgotten what it was. Found driving about was a sort of therapy. We are wondering if he had been worrying about us going to Canada.

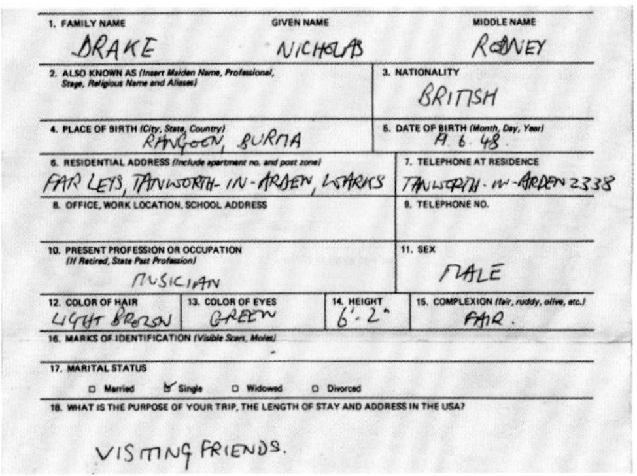

1. FAMILY NAME DRAKE GIVEN NAME NICHOLAS MIDDLE NAME RODNEY
2. ALSO KNOWN AS (Insert Maiden Name, Professional, Stage, Religious Name and Aliases)
3. NATIONALITY BRITISH
4. PLACE OF BIRTH (City, State, Country) RANGOON, BURMA
5. DATE OF BIRTH (Month, Day, Year) 19.6.48.
6. RESIDENTIAL ADDRESS (Include apartment no. and post zone) FAR LEYS, TANWORTH-IN-ARDEN, WARKS
7. TELEPHONE AT RESIDENCE TANWORTH-IN-ARDEN 2338
8. OFFICE, WORK LOCATION, SCHOOL ADDRESS
9. TELEPHONE NO.
10. PRESENT PROFESSION OR OCCUPATION (If Retired, State Past Profession) MUSICIAN
11. SEX MALE
12. COLOR OF HAIR LIGHT BROWN
13. COLOR OF EYES GREEN
14. HEIGHT 6'.2"
15. COMPLEXION (fair, ruddy, olive, etc.) FAIR.
16. MARKS OF IDENTIFICATION (Visible Scars, Moles)
17. MARITAL STATUS ☐ Married ☑ Single ☐ Widowed ☐ Divorced
18. WHAT IS THE PURPOSE OF YOUR TRIP, THE LENGTH OF STAY AND ADDRESS IN THE USA?
VISITING FRIENDS.

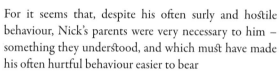

Nick applies for a visa to visit the USA.
It remained unposted

Christmas at Far Leys

For it seems that, despite his often surly and hostile behaviour, Nick's parents were very necessary to him – something they understood, and which must have made his often hurtful behaviour easier to bear

But the arrival of Pam Harwood was a complication:

Saturday 10 November 1973
Nick was up and prowling about during the night . . . Seemed in ultra bad form and told Molly he was 'in a terrible mess' but of course wouldn't expand on this despite the questioning

Friday 16 November 1973
. . . Nick appeared and . . . unburdened himself to Molly in strong but as usual rather incomprehensible terms about not being understood, very 'pissed about', denied human rights – clear something very wrong. Molly replied pointing out that we were doing all we could and expanding on this, at the end of which Nick left saying that that was what he had wanted to hear – Molly thought this was said in relief and not sarcastically. We feel that the presence of Pam and her claim on our attention is probably niggling him . . .

Sunday 18 November 1973
. . . We returned to find [Nick] sitting in the drawing room watching TV with Pam who seemed pleased that he had sat with her but unable to recall if any words had passed between them (what a strange household we have become to be sure!).

Nick see-sawed between irrational behaviour –

Monday 19 November 1973
Nick appears to be in a permanent suppressed rage these days and we can only assume that it is the presence of Pam that is accountable for this.

and sanity –

Thursday 22 November 1973
. . . Had a brief conversation about Pam with Nick, which was notable for the fact that he started it. Thought Pam was probably lonely and that we should go over to Canada to see the circumstances in which she lived . . .

with Rodney as wry bystander:

Saturday 8 December 1973
Nick . . . seemed to be playing quite a lot during the day and had a good lunch. Seemed very depressed at tea – a strange meal with Nick gazing in utter gloom at the floor and Pam standing about not really knowing what to do next but seemingly unable to relax and sit down. Would all make a good Chekhov play no doubt but not a very happy one in which to find oneself participating.

And so the year wound rather dismally to its end, with little change in Nick's pattern of behaviour. Very occasionally a chink can be glimpsed in the armour of Rodney's endurance – particularly when he felt the burden great on Molly:

Friday 21 December 1973
. . . At lunch time it became clear he was in one of his ultra unsociable moods. Refused at first to come in and then

when later he did he found our company unendurable and moved into the kitchen . . . What a bore it all is to be sure. There is no understanding his moods and in the midst of the great pressure of Christmas, which is upon Molly – it all becomes pretty hard to take – particularly with the added complication of Pam.

Then, a tiny glimmer of sun:

Saturday 22 December 1973
. . . notable event of the day – he reappeared whilst we were watching 'Upstairs Downstairs', removed the trolley and proceeded to wash up and put away the supper. A very long time since he has done anything of this sort!

Sunday 23 December 1973
Nick seemed in reasonable form today . . . asked Molly if he could help with decorations and put up mistletoe.

And just after Christmas:

Thursday 27 December 1973
. . . after tea Chris and Nan Non and Nick played Mozart and a modern trio in music room. Nick seemed to do well and to enjoy this.

Friday 28 December 1973
. . . Chris went in to music room and got Nick to play him some music. Nick forthcoming and volunteered to play a particular record (Nico) which impressed C rather. Told Chris that he thought he had 'rounded a corner'.

Rodney obviously had his doubts about this:

Monday 31 December 1973
. . . The end of a pretty ropey year for Nick (and us too of course) – let us hope for better things for him in '74 but we can't see much at present to justify such a hope.

The year 1973 could perhaps be summed up in Nick's own words from 'Bird Flew By':

> The list of false starts and crumbled broken hearts
> Comes from the need to play so many parts . . .

So many parts attempted; such a long list of false starts and dead ends: from his dalliance with the Church, embodied in an undoubtedly charismatic priest, Peter Spink – a relationship that seems to have fizzled out very quickly – to his bid to train for an entirely unsuitable job in computers, via the medical intervention of pills, ECT, and even – though fleetingly – the contemplation of psychotherapy, and finally, meditation. All these were tried and found wanting as Nick wrestled to overwhelm an adversary that threatened to destroy not only his personality, but also the very core of his being – his music. Even his time in the studio with John Wood must have seemed to both of them to be a dead end. And yet . . . this work tape that Nick had come home with, the result of those hours at Sound Techniques with his friend and sound engineer – did it not contain the germs at least of his last five songs: of 'Voice From The Mountain', 'Rider On The Wheel', 'Hanging On A Star', 'Tow The Line', and perhaps most importantly 'Black Eyed Dog'? The muse might have changed direction – but it wasn't dead.

But the New Year did not start well:

Tuesday 1 January 1974
. . . We feel we are both in the dog house in a big way and that [Nick] is in a very paranoiac state at the moment. Rather disturbing as there seems to be nothing we can do.

Nick was taking no medication of any sort. As far as Rodney was aware, the familiar pattern of apathy and hostility, with the only activity being endless unexplained car journeys, continued throughout January and February. If Nick saw Joe Boyd during this time, he did not mention it to his parents.

Then the situation began to improve:

Friday 1 March 1974
. . . Brian Wells phoned – said Nick had been to see them on Wednesday and had announced that he intended to get in touch with Joe Boyd to try to get to the States. Phoned there and then, but JB away for a fortnight. Nick spoke to Brian on phone and seemed in better form afterwards.

Nick started medication again –

Wednesday 6 March 1974
. . . Before supper he came into the drawing room to try the new piano and spoke a little with me afterwards. Said he was still taking pills in response to my asking but that he didn't like to get in touch with Pollitt as he thought he would put him back on everything . . .

– and started to be more civil:

Thursday 7 March 1974
. . . Soon after 10 p.m. Nick phoned from Wootton Wawen to say he had run out of petrol . . . V. apologetic –

said he had intended to go further but large filling station just outside Stratford closed so he knew he'd had it and turned back. Felt fully repaid for inconvenience of having to turn out at night by his responsiveness!

Rodney's gratitude for a drop of humanity from his son is telling:

Saturday 9 March 1974

. . . Came back after 4 and at tea Nick came in, asked how the lunch had gone and then proceeded to talk quite a bit – much to our delight . . . Said he'd been on the hook so long and couldn't get off. His plans were always being exploded – his own fault. Walked about while talking. All fairly incomprehensible but the great thing is that he is talking. We pray it may last.

Monday 11 March 1974

. . . Before lunch I was in my dressing room writing when Nick knocked on the door and came in. Said his girl friend had said she was coming this weekend and then proceeded to talk as he hasn't done for about a year. Thought he was coming through his difficulties – 2 years up in 3 months – pressures of his recording life – trying to get his two lives together – now was the 'crunch' – wanted to go on with music – thought his contacts still intact, and much more. After lunch he talked to Molly in the dining room about his emotional troubles – importance now of making relationships and more . . . Afterwards again talked to me in drawing room – about anxieties and worries. All slightly incomprehensible but wonderful for us both to have him talking again, of course.

Tuesday 12 March 1974

. . . Came back and found Nick in an apparent state of gloom in drawing room. However, he did speak and told us he had had a good morning and lunch and a bad afternoon. Quite a lively discussion after this. Tried to talk him out of a delusion he seemed to have built up that we were trying to get him back to being a 'straight up and downer'. Feel that talk did him a lot of good. He asked me to help him over getting his contact lenses put right – they still mean a great deal to him. Said he was all set to enjoy himself and various other as usual non sequiturs and rather incomprehensible remarks – but the GREAT thing was that he talked.

And then Nick decided to buy a 'new' (very second hand) car. Rodney was not entirely enthusiastic:

Wednesday 20 March 1974

Nick told me he had paid a deposit on a 1969 Sunbeam Rapier . . . All sounds a pretty rackety sort of deal with petrol prices as they are and no proper insurance but seems important not to step in as he is at least doing it himself. Moreover he is sensitive about this and accused me of being possessive when he thought I used the term 'we' instead of 'you' regarding the deal!

Two days later:

Friday 22 March 1974

. . . When we got back Molly told us that Nick had done the deed and traded in the Austen 1300 for a quite immaculate-looking and very classy Sunbeam Rapier . . . We all enthused genuinely enough about his new acquisition and he seemed pleased and agreed to drive Birdy and me over to see Pam in the afternoon . . . We had a very good drive over and the car seemed in very good trim considering its age (1969) and mileage (64,000) . . . After our return, Nick and Birdy had quite a long talk in the drawing room. He has been talking quite a lot all day really . . . Nick told me that he and Birdy had hatched a plot for getting us to and from London airport (he would take us on Monday).

For Rodney had decided somewhat reluctantly that it was necessary for him and Molly to go to Canada to wind up his sister's affairs there.

Monday 25 March 1974

A longish day! Up very early, 6.45 call, to be ready for a 9.15 a.m. start for London. Some apprehension as to whether Nick would fulfil his undertaking to drive us to Heathrow. But sure enough he was ready in time and drove us up in the Maxi very well. Drove straight away after wishing us good luck. Subsequently learned that he returned later to see that all was well with us . . .

Alas, when they returned from Canada, Nick was back in the dumps:

Friday 5 April 1974

Lovely day and 'grand to be back'. Nick appeared later – pretty silent – clam-like in fact initially but opened up later . . . Nan Non phoned in evening which seemed to put Nick in thoroughly bad form and after having his supper in the music room, whither Molly carried it, he went off to bed without a word to either of us. So we are back in our accustomed positions in the dog house.

And there they stayed for some time:

Sunday 7 April 1974
... It is clear that he has to make a considerable effort to stay in our company these days.

Monday 8 April 1974
Nick in profound gloom (for all appearances) all day ... Communication seems to be at the lowest level.

Tuesday 16 April 1974
I had a bonfire day today and found to my surprise that yesterday evening Nick had taken his two old broken guitars and thrown them on the heap ready for burning. Duly cremated them.

Then, a gradual thawing, and a partial explanation:

Friday 19 April 1974
... After six, Birdy persuaded Nick to come with her for a drink and they were out for over an hour and had a good discussion. Seems he is not feeling well but thinks this is due to his mental state.

Wednesday 24 April 1974
... Day made notable by a long talk between Molly and Nick during the morning in which he ranged over quite a number of subjects ... He has a project to go to New York in June or thereabouts by which time he reckons 'he will be better' ...

Monday 29 April 1974
... After tea I suggested croquet but he didn't seem keen so I started gardening. However, shortly after, he appeared with the mallets and we had a very good game lasting until 7.30 with Nick seemingly in relaxed form – quite a treat ...

The see-saw continued:

Monday 6 May 1974
... Nick said he had meant to go to London – indicated I had left him with nowhere to go to, having rung up all his friends and interfered with his life and much more. Tried to reason with him but it seems clear that in his present mood I am held responsible for most of his difficulties.

However, a few days later:

Saturday 18 May 1974
... we had a happy time fitting up his cassette into his car. All very relaxed and natural. Afterwards he went out and bought a 'Melody Maker' and we discussed possibility of his going to London to start up again ...

But later that same day he 'relapsed into non-communicativeness'.

Tuesday 28 May 1974
... we had a long talk for about 1½ hours in which he unburdened himself of much – his feeling that he could not adapt himself to anything but his music which he was really scared to return to and a general review of his life since he left Cambridge – a sensible and I think and hope from his point of view useful talk ...

Let us hope this is a sign of an improvement in him. He is taking his pills again.

And herein would seem to lie the clue. Whenever Nick took his pills, life became easier.

But:

Wednesday 5 June 1974
... A bit annoyed with himself for being dependent on pills, which he was 'taking religiously'.

Which inevitably meant, some weeks later:

Thursday 11 July 1974
Nick seemingly pretty low today. Practically no music. We have a feeling he may have stopped taking his pills.

But before that, a rare entry from Rodney about himself:

Friday 7 June 1974
... Self out of action with back trouble.

For all his dispassionate recording of Nick's troubles, finally these seem to have taken their toll. Rodney's back trouble would now persist, on and off, for many months, though it is only minimally referred to in the diary. Nick continues to take centre stage.

Wednesday 26 June 1974
... Nick failed to finish his lunch – very uncommunicative. He went out again in the afternoon and on his return came up and gave me a copy of a pop music magazine called 'ZigZag' which had a long and interesting article about himself. He left me with it and I read it to Molly. Most interesting and impressive. Later before supper Nick

came in and we had quite an animated talk. It seemed clear that the article had given him a boost and we talked about how he could get over his difficulty in talking to people. Managed to get quite a lot of things said to him and he took them well and argued intelligently.

Dr HOOK NICK DRAKE MOBY GRAPE LOVIN SPOONFUL
FREE ● JOHN STEWART ALBERT HAMMOND AND MORE
zigzag 42
VOL5 No2
15PENCE
ANDY FRASER & PAUL RODGERS

Then Nick disappeared to London – apparently with positive results:

Saturday 6 July 1974
. . . Nick said he was starting on another record – that he thought he was going to be able to work for Island again and that there was a chance of staying in the flat of Joe Boyd (who was shortly going away) with the people who were moving in, who were 'old friends'.

Tuesday 9 July 1974
. . . As Molly and I were coming to bed Chris went into the music room and had a talk with Nick who told him that he had made a start on a new record and had already recorded 4 things in the studio.

Monday 15 July 1974
. . . Nick and Birdy had a talk in the drawing room and he told her he was hoping to form a 'super group' possibly with John and Beverley Martyn. Also told her about his 4 tracks towards his new record.

So Nick talked freely about the last four tracks, which he presumably had recorded at the beginning of the month in London with John Wood and Joe Boyd, as documented by them both. But, as we also know from both Joe and John, Nick had been in a fearful state in the studio, unable to perform with his customary faultless confidence. The pain expressed in those recordings is evident. However uncommunicative Nick was in life, however hidden, he could not be in his music. And it is that pain that should be borne in mind as one considers Nick's trajectory through the last months of his life, erratically swinging between stony silence, vocal aggression, occasional normality, and numbing, incapacitating despair. It was a pain that his parents shared, and understood on a profound emotional level, if not always on an intellectual one.

Saturday 20 July 1974
. . . During the morning I suggested to Nick that he might take the empty petrol tins up to get them filled and at the same time fill up his car (this seeming to me to be a good way of getting him over the difficulty he experiences in getting petrol for his car). He agreed and we got in the car but it was only after two false starts, during which we got only as far as the gate, that we got away, only to find Tanworth garage out of petrol. So we came back, took the Maxi to get the tins filled at Hockley Heath and then returned and took his car (having put a little petrol in) to Beoley. Then we filled up and delivered some church appeal circular letters on the way back. Nick relaxed (seemingly) and quite talkative so that I felt rather pleased with myself for having arranged this activity. Was greatly taken aback therefore when soon after our return Nick launched an attack on me for pressurising him, all I was interested in was getting authority over people and much more in the strongest terms. Not long after this he returned to the music room to which he had retired and made a sort of apology and said everything was in an awful mess. He survived lunch and also supper but was perpetually restless after – to-ing and fro-ing and sighing. Eventually Molly went up to him and had a long talk with

Guy Norton, 1974

him – starting with accusation against us which we have heard before and eventually quieting down and becoming more rational as Molly talked to him . . .

Tuesday 23 July 1974
. . . Later in the morning he came out onto the terrace where I was installed in chaise longue and started talking as a result of which we had well over an hour's conversation. A good deal of old ground but a lot of sensible exchanges. He tried to explain how important it was to him not to be disturbed when he was working on some composition. He seemed in much more relaxed form for the rest of the day.

And occasionally, there was light relief for them all:

Thursday 25 July 1974
. . . Jeremy Harmer phoned asking for Nick and asking if he could come up at 2.30. I went to find Nick but . . . couldn't . . . So I told Jeremy he would ring back (thinking in fact that he probably wouldn't). However on hearing it was Jeremy, he did phone and agreed to his coming up . . . Jeremy arrived . . . They had a good long talk together and played some music . . . At 4.30 Molly produced tea and Nick and Jeremy joined us on the terrace. V. interesting account from Jeremy of his life in Mexico. He left about 5 o'clock taking Nick's 'Pink Moon' with him. Nick seemed in quite good form afterwards . . .

But the pendulum swung back –

Saturday 27 July 1974
. . . This is obviously a 'no pill taking' stage we are going through now and we must just hope that it won't last too long. No good at all trying to say anything of course . . .

Wednesday 31 July 1974
. . . Don't know what's up with him but just at present he seems to want to shut himself away from everyone even more than ever.

– and forth:

Thursday 1 August 1974
A day with a good ending.

. . . Later in the afternoon he went out again, stayed out for some time and returned shortly before five clearly in much better form which obviously arose from his having at last succeeded in getting a fill-up from the Tanworth garage – a great achievement as this has been a stumbling block for a long time. He got the tea for us and afterwards said he would come for a drink to the Lodders . . .

Wednesday 7 August 1974
. . . To our surprise and much to our delight, Nick decided to accompany us to our lunch appointment with Jackie, Gad God and Gingey [Nick's aunt, uncle and cousin] at the Trout Inn, Lechlade . . .

Nick's aunt, Lady Gwladys Harman ('Gad God') wrote to her sister the very next day:

Bathurst Cottage
8 August 1974

. . . Yesterday was so lovely, my darling ones, and we did so much love it, and especially seeing my poor Rodney so much better, thank God . . .

Barge shown on left (Photo: Susan Holt)

But what I really want to tell you about was the really fantastic improvement I found in our poor old Nick's condition. I do really feel he has broken through AT LAST. He tore my heart (a condition to which yours have been subjected all these last years, I know well, my darlings) all the time he was talking to me, as he was trembling and I could see the enormous effort he was making, and it's obvious there's still a long way to go BUT all he said was strong and thoughtful and responsible, and made a deep impression on me, for I felt that for the first time for I simply forget how long I was through to him. I started by asking him about the songs he's already done, and about the remaining six or so that are needed to make up a new long-playing record. I asked him if working on these brought him satisfaction or even pleasure; his answer was no, not at present, he found it the most terrible effort, but that he thought the satisfaction or pleasure would return, and that he was absolutely determined to press on and get himself back. He then said (heart-rendingly) 'It's the only thing I know I can do well' – I rejoined 'And How' or words to that effect, and went on to rub in how, in spite of him having been out of things for so long he hadn't been forgotten, as proved by the 'ZigZag' article 'Where Is Nick Drake?' – I got the impression . . . that this article had really been the starting-point of his beginning to surface from the slough of despond. He then spoke of having 'so much to fill in' . . .

I didn't really understand what he meant, but I took it to mean that he'd felt he hadn't been mature enough to cope with his success so I pointed out that things were very different now, that anyone who had been through, and come out of, the ghastly unhappiness that he'd endured these last years had no need to ever worry again about lack of maturity and this he appeared to entirely agree with. He finished up by saying that he worried about not making any money, to which I replied . . . that I was pretty sure that this was the very last thing that either of you cared about, and that all you wanted, and ever had wanted, was his happiness, first and foremost. And so our talk finished. I do so HOPE I haven't bogged it but he did seem to be so sensible, and able to take a detached view, and truly, at times, just like the old Nick, which I, at the too-few times I've seen him, simply haven't even glimpsed all these last years. Please God I'm right . . .

So take heart, my darling ones – it may still be a very long dark tunnel but there really does seem to be a light at the end, doesn't there? I was afraid Boyd might be pressing him for the next batch of songs but he assured me strongly that this wasn't so, that he's very understanding and is ready to wait . . .

What made it possible for Nick to unburden himself to this aunt whom he saw comparatively rarely? Was it the fact that, whilst family, she was not so involved with his struggle? Was it her sympathetic ear? Gwladys Harman was a woman of renowned beauty, whose innate charm masked a steely authority that fitted her admirably for her role as a general's wife. With Nick's tacit co-operation, she was quite capable of unshackling him, for a brief while, from the interior turmoil that bound and gagged him. But even she observed that it cost him dear.

And afterwards, inevitably, the old silent enemy exacted a penalty:

Nick's bedroom (Photo: Rodney Drake)

Friday 9 August 1974
. . . Birdy said she had watched TV for a bit with Nick in the music room after her return from Pebble Mill and that he had shown her that he had broken his electric guitar. We found him sitting in the music room and said goodnight to him and he went up soon after. Returning for further investigation we found he had had a real smash-up – electric guitar apparently smashed down onto piano, breaking music holder, vase and Perspex cover of tape recorder. This is the first smash-up we have had since the window of the Austin 1300.

Tuesday 20 August 1974
Nick seems to be cutting himself off entirely from us. He spent a large part of the day sitting on the step of the outside door of the music room, gazing gloomily out into the drive.

Wednesday 21 August 1974
. . . Much to our surprise and gratification, Nick appeared amicable and talkative to Birdy when she arrived and she had quite a long talk with him in the music room. He told her that at the beginning of this week he thought that he could not do any music and then suddenly it came right . . . and he seemed suddenly quite relaxed and jolly. A very strange and unpredictable chap.

Saturday 7 September 1974
. . . He stayed upstairs most of the morning but came down to lunch seemingly in great distress. 'Had no idea what was the matter'. After lunch I took up my position in drawing room and after much restless passing to and fro he settled down and started to talk – clutching his head and exclaiming loud and long about the condition he was in. Back to where he was, he said, after Louisa Raynes. Couldn't go on living like this. All very distressing . . . told me he would go to hospital if he could go now! Said he had taken 4 Stelazine and 2 Mogadol [Rodney probably meant Mogadon] – perhaps not a good combination. stayed in bed for a while but appeared for supper and later in the evening sank into another trough of depression. We tried to help him get on to Brian Wells but couldn't locate him . . . He really seems in a very bad way but we don't know what to do.

Sunday 8 September 1974
. . . Nick down at fairly normal hour and seemed in much better trim . . . later I went in and found him in the drawing room wanting to talk. He said he had thought things over this morning at 6 a.m. and decided he must either go ahead with his musical career or chuck it all. I suggested he might try something else for a bit but he said no. Talked about his pills. The trouble was he thought he would have to do it the 'mad' way and he was trying to pluck up courage to put a phone call through to an ex-directory number. We talked for quite a long time – all very natural – and I eventually left him to his phone call which he never put through. Brian Wells phoned just before lunch and Nick had a long talk . . .

Just at this low ebb, when the situation seemed to be without solution, a friend appeared:

Friday 20 September 1974
. . . Guy Norton phoned and asked for a game of croquet and came for it at 4 p.m. . . . I asked [Nick] to play and I think he would have liked to but couldn't make himself – nor did he appear afterwards whilst we were having drinks. Guy disappointed not to see him.

Guy Norton and his parents had been friends of the Drakes since his childhood. In Guy's own words:

'In 1952, when I was twelve, Rodney and Molly Drake, with their two children, Nick and Gay, moved to Far Leys in Tanworth-in-Arden, about four miles from where we lived, and we soon met the family.

'They were a sort of perfect family. Molly and Rodney were two of the most wonderful people that I have ever met and I knew them very well right up to their deaths; they were very special in my life. I did a terrible thing when I was fourteen: I told my parents that I wished that Rodney and Molly were my parents. They seemed to be so upstanding and yet so very warm. I used to go to their house very often, most often to play croquet with Rodney. They seemed so impeccable and faultless, and yet so amusing and such fun.

'Gay was a perfect English rose, very attractive and, again, very warm; I took her out when I was about seventeen and she was thirteen and I remember that we went to see the film *Gigi* two or three times!

'Nick was sort of perfect too, and the first time that I got to know him was when Rodney said that Nick was having trouble with his Maths O-levels and I offered to give him some tuition. (I remember that one time I had trouble explaining to Nick what a rhomboid is, and I thought of cutting up a bit of cheese to explain it to him, so I went into the kitchen and asked Molly if she had some cheese and Molly replied, "Oh! Guy, are you hungry?"). He was, of course, delightful and easy to teach and most appreciative (and he passed O-level Maths!).'

Guy was an explosive force of energy, and by 1974, he was already well on the way to being a successful entrepreneur. He had just returned from South Africa.

'Of course, when I saw Rodney and Molly I always asked after Gay and Nick and when I asked on 20 September 1974, when I had just come back from living in South Africa, Rodney told me that Nick was not great – he had gone into a depression and had not come out of his bedroom for a few months. I asked if I could do anything and he said that, of course, anything would be a great help. So I rang Nick next morning and asked him if he would come and have a drink with me at a pub that evening, and he agreed.'

Saturday 21 September 1974
. . . At tea time Guy Norton phoned, asked for Nick and asked him out for a drink. Guy came and collected Nick at 6.45 and he dropped him off at 9.45.

'I picked him up next day and, not only did we have a drink, but he stayed on to have dinner with me too. I remember that one of the things that was bothering him was that he suddenly left Cambridge before he was due to take his degree in his last year and he didn't know why he had left and couldn't explain it. I said to him that people often do things for no apparent reason; they cannot explain even to themselves why they did it, but other people will not accept this, so they make up reasons for having done things which are not true, but, at least it satisfies people.'

Guy now felt sure he could help Nick; on 26 September, Rodney received a letter from him:

. . . I think I can help him. This sounds terribly arrogant but I do think I have a tremendous advantage; I am not a psychiatrist and therefore do not start with his resentment as a psychiatrist would . . .

The reason for my writing this letter is that if you think I am doing him any harm you must please let me know and I will of course stop seeing him . . .

Rodney replied immediately:

. . . Far from thinking that there is any possibility of any harm, we are, on the contrary, absolutely certain that this will do Nick an enormous amount of good. The fact that he can talk to you is in itself a tremendous thing because we're quite sure that at the moment the one thing he wants more than anything else is someone he can unburden himself to. He can't talk to us at all, and I don't think there is now really anybody before whom he is prepared to open up – certainly no psychiatrist . . .

So Guy, never one to let the grass grow under his feet, steamed into action:

Tuesday 1 October 1974
. . . Nick announced today that Guy had asked him to go out to supper at 7.30 this evening. . . . Nick pretty restless before he arrived and had a drink or two but all was well and he went off looking very smart . . . Nick returned from his outing with Guy about midnight we think, tho' we didn't hear him.

And the next day:

Wednesday 2 October 1974
. . . Guy phoned and asked for Nick who, after a fairly brief conversation came in and announced that he was going to Paris with Guy and his wife, Noel – staying the night in London with them on Friday and flying out with them on Saturday. What a surprise!

Perhaps even more of a surprise was the fact that Nick made it to Paris – after a shaky start:

Friday 4 October 1974
Anxious morning for Molly and me wondering if Nick was going to make his getaway for London this afternoon . . . As the time approached for his departure he was obviously nervous . . . but we got away, he and I, at 3.10 to catch the 3.40 from H-in-A . . . When I got back to Far Leys I found Molly very worried because Nick had phoned from Coventry to say he didn't think he could make it. Molly tried very hard to persuade him to go and get to Guy if he possibly could, but he seemed dubious and said he might get a taxi home. However by 7.30 he had not come and Guy had not phoned so we assume he must have made it to Guy's after all . . .

Which he had, as Molly and Rodney heard a few days later:

Wednesday 9 October 1974
At about 7 p.m. Guy Norton phoned from London with the glad news that Nick was still in Paris. The trip had been a success and at his request Nick was staying till Monday with the couple on whose boat on the Seine he and Guy had been staying with. Thus were our worries

The book Nick brought back from Paris for his mother

over the past few days happily disposed of and we treated ourselves to ½ bottle of wine.

Thursday 24 October 1974
Guy Norton phoned from London during the morning to tell us that he had heard from Alan Holt in Paris that all was well with Nick ('talking volubly') and that he was staying in Paris (excellent news).

Friday 25 October 1974
. . . Guy and Noel came to lunch and we had most interesting time hearing about Nick in Paris. Seems he talks in French – the children all talk French all the time – and that he walks around Paris a lot . . . Felt very encouraged by all they said.

Guy, it has to be said, might have been painting a rather rosier picture than the reality of what was actually happening in Paris. 'Talking volubly' seems to have been something of an exaggeration – whether in French or English. Some forty years later, Susan Holt remembers that, after a couple of days' wandering around Paris, Nick did not leave the barge, but sat silently watching the world go by. Without the dynamo of Guy's presence, Nick's battery was running out of charge. Nevertheless, he stayed in Paris until the end of the month. When he returned to England, it was with the intention of preparing his affairs for a more permanent move to Paris.

Thursday 31 October 1974
A notable day. Nick phoned in the morning and told Molly that he was coming up by train . . . [Guy] confirmed that Nick was on his way and moreover said that he was just going to pick up his car and a few things and return this evening to Guy's in London with the intention of driving to Paris tomorrow. Molly duly met Nick and found him much more communicative than we have known him for a very long time. He told her he was going straight back, answered her questions about his doings and listened to our news. He was glad his car was ready. As soon as he arrived he phoned Royal Insurance to make ready a green insurance card for him to pick up later, after which we had lunch and then he packed up some clothes and set off for Henley (bank) and on to Birmingham (insurance). He couldn't get his car registration but left it with me to post. He came back to Far Leys for tea, still seeming quite responsive and we discussed his plans cautiously. He said he would try to get something to do in Paris and gave us the address of Alan and Susan Holt on the Seine. He eventually set off at 4.45, leaving us happy to think of him so much better but worried by the thought of all that lay before him. (Getting the car over, perhaps living alone and so on.) But he is anyway taking an initiative and trying to and indeed achieving something. Had a few words with Guy on phone after Nick left. He seems very confident that Nick will make it now in some way or another. We must pray he is right.

Friday 1 November 1974
Spent most of day wondering how Nick was getting on . . . In evening about 6 p.m., Guy phoned . . . said Nick arrived in London about 7.15 last night and was in good form – laughed a tremendous amount . . . Nick went off in good form this morning . . . and presumably, as we have heard nothing, he must have driven down to Dover and

crossed to France for Paris. Guy seemed full of confidence that this was the right thing for Nick and it seems to be what Nick has decided for himself, so we must hope and pray for the best. He certainly seemed yesterday more 'together' than we have seen him for years.

But . . .

Wednesday 6 November 1974
. . . We returned to hear from Naw that Nick had phoned, sounding she said cheerful and asked her to tell us that he was in England and on his way up to Suffolk (presumably to see John Wood). This left us speculating on what this can signify – is he going to do more music? Has he brought his car back? Has he finished with Paris? . . .

The next day Nick was back at Far Leys:

Thursday 7 November 1974
. . . [Nick] told us he was planning to go back to Suffolk tomorrow for weekend but was going first to London. Planned to take his tape recorder and guitar. He told us quite a bit about Paris – had evidently enjoyed his time on the boat very much. Said he tried to get a job but failed – though probably because he didn't really want one. Felt he was 'nearly there' now and that he must keep going . . . He does seem uncertain about his next move, though apparently he is veering towards going back to music. But he could easily be diverted from this. Anyway he is a very different and vastly improved person.

Friday 8 November 1974
. . . He was more silent than yesterday and perhaps finding home atmosphere difficult but he was quite all right otherwise. Immediately after lunch he made final arrangements to go (putting in place his guitar and tape recorder), came and said goodbye to us all (was kissed by Molly and Naw) and set off – presumably to Suffolk via London.

Monday 11 November 1974
. . . Nick arrived home at about 3.30 – greeted by Molly and came up to see me in dressing room at her suggestion. At tea told us he had been to London on Friday and again today (as well as to Suffolk) and that he was going again tomorrow. He was not communicative but seemed quite OK and reasonably responsive. Said he was going to play some music when I asked him what next. Seemed to be playing very attractive stuff which we didn't remember hearing before . . .

A tantalizing piece of information . . . what swan song might this have been?

Wednesday 13 November 1974
A discouraging day as far as Nick is concerned. He was down late and seemed to be back in his old 'closed up' condition . . . We are most worried that he may be slipping back into his old misery.

Thursday 14 November 1974
Nick came in to the bathroom this morning whilst I was shaving . . . to say that he had decided to return to Paris and try to get a job. He proposed to leave immediately. Not much time to think of what to say but I encouraged him . . . Said he would send his address when postal strike was over . . .

At about 6.30 heard music-room door open and Nick was back . . . Later he told me he had got halfway to Dover and then decided he didn't want to go to Paris after all. Thought now he would try his music again. Said his difficulty was he was halfway to getting back to his music and halfway to getting a job. And kept switching from one to the other. Of course the truth is he can't find the resolution or inspiration to do either and unless he does we are back to square one of miserable silence. Pointed out to him that home didn't suit him, that he must do something if only from the practical point of view of earning his living – but no good. He enjoyed his supper and then withdrew to music room. All very disappointing.

Friday 15 November 1974
. . . After tea, Nick and I had a good discussion . . . We talked of Paris and he agreed that he had 'sorted out' several things there. He often felt he wanted to drop out and that there was nothing for him but that, though he didn't really understand that feeling. He's been thinking more about his music and about performing which he didn't like though he does get a thrill out of it . . .

Saturday 16 November 1974
Nick did not emerge until lunch time today – looking very rough – said on being asked by Molly, that he'd had a bad night but had taken some Tryptizol . . .

Monday 18 November 1974
To our distress, Nick seems to be pretty well back to where he was before his trip to Paris. He seemed to spend the whole day more or less just sitting in the music room – very little music going on . . .

Why had Nick returned to Far Leys? What malefic force compelled him to return – a force greater than the combined wills of his parents and himself? What black-eyed dog lurked in his bedroom, in the music room? Certainly it was now calling for more . . . For retribution in the face of the one vibrant power that had threatened to overwhelm it – and continued to do so:

Saturday 23 November 1974

A good day for Nick. Guy phoned in the morning and asked him to lunch at Carpenters Hill – he accepted. We had fears when it came to the point that he wasn't going to make it. But after a couple of false starts, Molly suggested he might like to borrow her car. This sparked him off a bit and he strode off to his car and off he went. At 4.45 Guy phoned to say Nick and 'the girls' were walking over for tea and sure enough they all arrived at 5 . . . Guy said on the phone that Nick had been fine and talking a lot but he was very silent with us. Guy came with car at about 6 p.m. and took them all back – with Nick, who he had asked for supper.

Sunday 24 November 1974

Nick apparently only just got back before us last night so he was fairly late. However, he was completely silent this morning and wouldn't answer when we asked him how he had got on. But just before lunch he did open up a little, pacing the drawing-room floor and saying what an extraordinary chap Guy was for getting people to do things . . .

In the evening he would not stay with us at all but went up to bed early having been out and back through the music-room outside door once or twice.

Nick's restless last night: did he spend it in a blackness of isolation? Or was he set upon by voices – from the mountain, from the sea, in his neighbourhood: all calling, all clamouring, until the cacophony became unbearable? Did he know he was taking a fatal overdose? Or did he just up the amount of tablets in a desperate attempt to find some temporary respite? From the uproar? Or from a spiritual desert, a musical silence which he found unbearable? We will never know. Does it matter? The result was implacable and unalterable.

Rodney's and Molly's despair was clothed in few words. The facts were recounted faithfully, as ever in this diary:

Monday 25 November 1974

. . . Naw had looked in on Nick at 11.45, found him lying across bed and called to Molly who went in and found him dead. After desperate phone calls we got Ackroyd and shortly after, an ambulance which of course was too late as Ackroyd had declared Nick to be dead and to have been so for some hours . . . The contents of a Tryptizol bottle were missing . . .

Only the first and last sentences of the day point to a lifetime of grieving that was to follow:

The worst day of our lives . . .

. . . So ends in tragedy our 3-year struggle.

NOW WE RISE
AND WE ARE EVERYWHERE

Grief takes many guises. Rodney and Molly would strive for the rest of their days to make something positive of this, the worst of tragedies to befall any parent. Like so many of their generation, routine and order had always helped them cope with the crises of life: war, displacement, death. And it was to routine they now turned. Rodney continued to write his diary, and did so for the rest of his life. Molly insisted they stay on in Far Leys 'until,' she said, 'we have made it a happy house again.' And they did. Happiness, as Molly knew from within herself, is fragile but tenacious. It can be coaxed into being despite all the despairing odds against it. The tools they used to accomplish this were varied. Rodney sought more information, joining the Schizophrenia Society, and eventually, after a year, finding it possible to write to Dr Dickens, the one doctor who had any consistent effect on Nick.

27 September 1975

Dear Dr Dickens,

I expect you will remember the case of my son, Nicholas, who was at Louisa Raynes in May and June 1972 . . .

The reason I am troubling you with this letter is to ask you a favour. My wife and I are finding some comfort in gathering together as much information as we can about Nick, mostly about his music, for which he had carried a considerable reputation both here and in America. And this survived, notably enough, the last three years when he was too ill to produce anything.

But though we struggled our hardest to try and understand him and to help him with his problems from the time he came home to live here during 1971, we remained as mystified as we were distressed by his illness.

It would be a great help to us if we could learn more about this now. Of those few that tried to help him – despite his lack of co-operation – you were the one, we both feel, who understood him best – and certainly were the only one to whom Nick seemed to be prepared to listen at all.

Could you tell us what in your view the nature of his illness was? We would be so grateful to you if you could tell us – and I would ask you please not to temper your comments in any way to spare our feelings . . .

The letter they received in reply is remarkable for its sincerity and compassion:

29 September 1975

Dear Mr and Mrs Drake,

Thank you very much for your letter. If you do not find this letter gives you the information you require then please do not hesitate to ring my secretary . . .

I had, indeed, learned of the death of Nick and I was very saddened by that news – many people assume that doctors become hardened in their responses to such tragedies but I can assure you that this is not so. I did not write to you as I was not sure how you would feel about receiving a letter of sympathy from someone who had failed, albeit tried, to help your son – this is why I was so pleased to receive your letter.

I believe that Nick was suffering from an illness which is called in the text books simple schizophrenia, but I must add that I think such labels are meaningless and to a large extent, cover our lack of understanding of such illnesses. However, this illness as described over the years, tends to occur in late adolescence and can occur in people of all types including intelligent young people coming from stable family backgrounds. I think many in psychiatry believe that in time to come there will be found an underlying physiological or biochemical disturbance in those who manifest the symptoms of this illness. The symptoms are usually those of progressive deterioration in intellectual ability with the loss of abilities to comprehend new information and think abstractly. There is also a loss of initiative, loss of the ability to concentrate the attention and a tendency to withdraw from the world of reality into the world of fantasy. The outcome of treatment is variable. With the drugs available to us and other methods of treatment there can be no doubt that some patients can be helped considerably; others, however, cannot. I think the problem in treating Nick was what would be called his lack of motivation to treatment – his inability to see himself as being a sick man. In circumstances like this I feel one has the unenviable choice of enforcing treatment, which anyway cannot be guaranteed successful, or waiting with patience and some anxiety for the patient to accept treatment. I have but little doubt in my own mind that you, as his parents, did all that you possibly could to encourage Nick to seek the help he required and I believe also that the doctors concerned with him did their best in the circumstances. I am afraid that we all must accept that Nick posed an insoluble problem . . .

It would be quite impossible for anyone to understand what was in or on Nick's mind when he took the overdose of tablets. I think it would be absurd, knowing Nick, to believe that he killed himself in order to avenge himself on others or upon society at large.

All I can tell you is, first, that I believe that in no way at all did you or your wife in your handling of Nick over the years contribute to or exacerbate his illness and secondly, your lack of understanding in no way reflects upon you as parents. People who have studied this illness all their lives have no better understanding of patients than you had of Nick. I must emphasise (and I am not, as you asked me not to, in any way simply reassuring you) that neither you nor your wife have anything at all to reproach yourselves about. I think you did everything possible in the circumstances to try and see your son through an illness which, even now, is very little understood and which, alas in so many cases, simply cannot be treated adequately.

I hope that this letter will help to answer some of the questions that are obviously in your minds. The final point that I would make is that whatever behaviour Nick indulged in after the onset of his illness should be seen as being the outcome of that illness and not in any way should moral judgement be passed upon what he did. I think his flirtation with drugs was simply a manifestation of the need he had to try and understand the changes that were taking place within him.

I do hope that you and your wife will in due course of time be able to come to terms with this tragedy and, of course, it goes without saying that if I can help in anyway at all you only have to make contact with me.

Yours sincerely,
Gerald Dickens
Consultant Psychotherapist

Gerald Dickens's letter must have been one of the foundation stones on which Molly and Rodney were able to start rebuilding their lives: lives forever altered, but in which Nick never ceased to be present. In the time that remained to them they co-operated with every opportunity that arose to promote their son's work, despite the indifference of the majority of the musical press.

They met Nick's friends and musical colleagues – Joe Boyd in particular, who showed them great kindness – and offered a temporary refuge to the tiny, but steady trickle of fans who, despite all odds, had discovered Nick's music, and who would suddenly appear on the doorstep of Far Leys. These fans would have been, for Molly and Rodney, the small, precious harvest from their son's endeavours. They would never know how the yield would multiply as the years rolled by – flourishing long after they themselves had become part of the 'stock in the ground'.

The Harvest

Our memories are card indexes consulted,
and then put back in disorder by authorities
whom we do not control

Cyril Connolly

You Look To Find A Friend

Brian Wells interviewed by Cally

Occasionally and sporadically Rodney and Molly Drake would see Brian Wells. They knew that Brian was a doctor, and must have been aware that he was thinking of becoming a psychiatrist, but Rodney never told him about the diaries he had kept. Probably because he set no particular store by them.

However, by 2014, Dr Brian Wells had become a Fellow of the Royal College of Psychiatrists, and was an international Addiction Psychiatrist based in central London. Recently he read the entire journal, being in a unique position to interpret the entries from three points of view: as a current medical expert; as a friend and contemporary of Nick Drake; and as one of Rodney Drake's key allies at that time.

After he had read the diaries, I conducted an interview with Brian which took the form of a series of poignant, sometimes funny, often technical, and at times retrospectively emotional conversations. All that was missing was the patient himself.

The following is an edited account of Brian's thoughts and recollections:

Rodney Drake's three diaries provide a rare insight into the progression of a cluster of emotionally based symptoms with some physical components: what some would refer to as a mental or 'formal' psychiatric illness.

The thing that really struck me in the diaries was the length of time the whole process took, and, because Nick was a friend, how unaware I was of what was going on in his head until it became obvious. I actually had no idea about the duration of Nick's (let's call it) 'illness'. But having read the diaries, I can now see elements of what became palpable in Rodney's 1970s accounts as far back as 1967, when I first met Nick.

On the one hand, Nick had a quick and dry sense of humour, and was fun to be with in the early days, with a lot of laughs, often directed towards the expense of someone or something else; on the other, he wasn't always an easy guy to be around. He had a great sense of the ridiculous and when we were friends at Cambridge we had good times, sometimes falling about with laughter. He could also be quite superior in some ways. He clearly thought at times that I was a bit of an 'un-cool twit', and a fairly hopeless musician (true), compared to the likes of Paul Wheeler; and that was kind of obvious. I hung out with people whom he also quite liked, but he would dip in and dip out. He would never really engage unless we were sitting in a room listening, for instance, to the Arthur Lee *Love* album or some such. We'd listen to the whole album. We'd play certain tracks three times. We'd get a bit stoned and would listen to Vaughan Williams's *Tallis Fantasia*, or endlessly to Dylan (*Blonde on Blonde*), or Donovan, who was a big influence. You know that album with 'Hampstead Incident' – I think it was called *Sunshine Superman*? – We would sit and listen to that for bloody hours and smoke dope, and then at three o'clock in the morning, he'd quietly disappear. He didn't drink very much, Nick, and he didn't actually smoke a lot of dope. You sometimes got the feeling that you couldn't really get close to him, and that he was always in a slightly different 'zone', often picking up on things that I hadn't even noticed (like the violin on Frank Zappa's *Hot Rats*: most of us thought it was a guitar).

What I find interesting is that Nick's choice of music, not only the music that he wrote and played, but the music he liked – Van Morrison (*Astral Weeks*), *The Notorious Byrd Brothers*, obscure soul music I'd brought from America, Leonard Cohen, Randy Newman, Nina Simone – as sometimes incongruous for the period. If one talks about 1967, you are minded to talk about Pink Floyd and *Sgt Pepper*, but with Nick it was often more unpredictable and at times esoteric. He was the 'cool' guy. He knew Joe Boyd and Joe Boyd was seen as very cool. He would show up in Cambridge with The Incredible String Band, who were not exactly pop music. Joe had a reputation: the guy who started the UFO club; the guy who was connected in America and looked after people that one respected, like Fairport, John and Beverley Martyn and the String Band. Joe presented a famous performance at the Festival Hall, with Tim Buckley supported by the String Band; people still talk about it. And Nick knew Joe pretty well. He would disappear to London, then mysteriously return (usually with an ounce or two of excellent hash) and sort of imply that he was writing songs and making a record with the (almost) legendary Joe Boyd, whom Nick would refer to as 'his friend'. No one seemed to know what was really going on!

At the same time Nick would compartmentalise people . . . He was quite *defended* (which would be the technical term). Compartmentalising is to do with being defended. It's to do with not letting others in and controlling the boundaries; it's to do with being self-conscious, mysterious, or even a bit narcissistic. Until I read the diaries, for instance, I didn't know that Nick had bad eyesight. I don't think I ever saw him wearing glasses. I had no idea he was wearing contact lenses, which is written about in the diary. And there's another little note somewhere where it says he had a 'phobia about getting fat'. I think Nick was very aware of his image and his looks – these narcissistic quirks that we all have. I think he was quite vain, yet no more vain than the rest of us.

The way that Nick always appeared to me, until he became unwell, was the way he looks on the cover of *Five Leaves Left*. He would shave, and always look clean, but he would wear that same stuff all the time. I never saw him buying or wearing new clothes. He was tall. He was elegant, and he was aware of it. He wasn't bedraggled. He wasn't scruffy. There was usually an air of 'mysterious cool' about him that wasn't manufactured. I never saw him look in a mirror, and doubt that he often did. A lot of women, including my first wife Marion, were drawn to him. Probably they could recognise a vulnerability there. I doubt that it was about sexual attraction or wanting to have his babies! More about wanting to knit him a sweater or something. He was clearly very intelligent, and could be quite haughty and arrogant at times, but this was low key. He was not at all theatrical.

And he could sometimes be annoying – you couldn't really rely on him to keep to an arrangement – say to go and see a movie. He would arrive, but sometimes halfway through the film. Everything was done rather spontaneously in a pleasant but somewhat muddled manner. You never knew when he was going to get up and leave, even back then. Later on, when he was clearly becoming unwell, there was a lot of getting up and leaving the room, and just driving off. It was like, 'Is Nick still here? Was he offended by something? Was he bored? Did he eat anything? Where's he gone? . . . Oh well. He'll show up again sometime. He'll be fine.'

Nick was not good at openly sharing his vulnerabilities. In his songs he is mostly a perceptively sensitive observer: 'What will happen in the morning when the world it gets so crowded that you can't look out the window in the morning?' It's somebody standing back and saying, 'These are little films or vignettes that are playing in front of me.' And they are beautifully portrayed.

I never really sensed that when Nick sang 'Fruit Tree', he was singing about himself. He was just saying, 'Of the significant people I've observed, they eventually seem to wither and die, and then people celebrate their lives afterwards.' There was a controlled and observational distance between Nick and the subjects in the songs, until *Pink Moon* and songs like 'Parasite' came along. I once commented to him that 'Man In A Shed' sounded to me like a 'Nick Drake love song' ('But the man is me, yes, and the girl is you'). He just muttered something like 'Oh yeah?', gave a quick and diffident laugh, and then the conversation moved on without any further comment. He certainly wasn't about to discuss any deep lyrical interpretations.

There are exceptions, of course. I mean, I can feel Nick being himself in something like 'From The Morning'. I can feel 'A day once dawned, and it was beautiful / A day once dawned from the ground'. There's something really moving about that. It's not just an impersonal observation. There's a sense of appreciative emotion . . . but then he goes on to say, 'And go play the game(s) that you learnt / From the morning', which I guess could be interpreted as somewhat disparaging – although maybe that's just me. I'm sure he wasn't talking about skipping light-heartedly through the fields and admiring the blossom and so on, or maybe these were simply lyrics that just 'came out'.

I guess if a man is used to defending himself, compartmentalising, being self-contained, when his life collapses, for whatever reason, the tendency may be, not to give up, collapse or surrender, but to put up even stronger defences. Which is what I think Nick did.

I completely understood why he dropped out of Cambridge. I think he was suddenly in a situation where he felt that he could deliver something he was passionate about, which was *Five Leaves Left*. He dropped out before his final year, soon after the album had been released.[1] For him it was a big deal, getting together with Joe Boyd, and Nick probably felt: 'If I don't take this chance now, I might not get another one.' Quite a brave and rebellious move, actually. Not many of us would have done that. We'd have been sensible, and got our degrees first.

After Nick left Cambridge, I went on seeing him in London. *Five Leaves Left* did not go mega, but he was OK about that. He got into making *Bryter Layter*. I think he started writing that in Haverstock Hill, cos I remember going around there with Robert Kirby once, and Robert and I were a little stoned and 'chatty', and Nick got a bit irritated with us, and snapped, 'Can we do some music now?' Robert and I were yacking about whatever, and Nick was irritated that I was there, so that he didn't have Robert's full attention. I felt a bit awkward that I'd sort of intruded on what was meant to be a 'professional' situation. Nick was clearly proud of what he was producing, and wanted it to be taken seriously.

Certainly by Haverstock Hill, you could see him starting to withdraw.

I was doing a lot of drugs then, and I would go around with some hash, and it would get sort of 'edgy' and then would all become uncomfortable relatively quickly . . . Mind you, a lot of this was probably in *my* head. I would give him a lift somewhere, we'd go and pick up John Martyn, and take him to Regent's College, say, where he'd be doing a gig, after which Nick and I would have a curry and then Nick would get up and leave to be on his own. Because I was often stoned and probably a little paranoid, our contact wasn't always warm and fuzzy, there was often a bit of an edge to it . . .

But it wasn't just me – there were other signs too. Richard Charkin, who went to Morocco with Nick, remembers going to Haverstock Hill at a time when things should have been good. But Nick wouldn't answer the door. Rick went around the back and looked through the window. He didn't tap on the window cos he felt it would be intrusive. Nick was sitting there, just staring at the wall. That was well before he packed up and went home to Tanworth.

It wasn't an overt drugs problem: Nick wasn't ever a drug addict. I don't think he was especially damaged by drugs, and certainly not by alcohol. He wasn't smoking a lot of dope. I mean, he really wasn't. Nick wasn't into instant gratification in the way someone like I was, or someone who becomes an addict is. He was the guy who would have a puff on a joint and pass it on . . . Quite often he'd say 'No thanks'. Whereas I was the guy who'd get red-eyed and paranoid. I think 'A Skin Too Few' is a very good description of Nick Drake. He was highly intelligent, he was sensitive and perceptive, and became uncomfortable easily. But he wasn't an addict. I'm really clear about that. That's what I do: I sense it fairly quickly, and then perform an in-depth professional assessment to determine the presence (or otherwise) of dependence or addiction. Of course, I'm not always right! It's an art based upon as much evidence as possible, and this requires the trust and honesty of the patient/client and any 'significant others'. It's never a good idea to do professional work with friends or close colleagues with whom one has a personal or emotional relationship.

And so he made *Bryter Layter* – listening to Joe afterwards, they were very proud of it. They really expected this to be a big thing. Nick was kind of waiting for it to happen. And I think he found it all very tough. Anyone I've ever met who's famous has *wanted* to be famous – but in order to get there, and then sustain it, they've got to be pretty ruthless and thick-skinned. No way was Nick Drake ruthless. He was certainly ambitious. But I think the reality of appearing on stage, and the fact that he was playing something that people sometimes had to struggle to listen to – that he was not playing loud guitar chords, that he was playing a beautifully structured, subtle guitar with a very fragile vocal – meant that any 'live concert great reputation' was, in those days just not going to happen. The reality of Nick playing his stuff live in the sort of venues where John Martyn would play . . . no way could he do it. He was too sensitive, he was too uncomfortable, and people weren't going to listen. John had a rapport with his audience, and was a charismatic showman.

Nowadays, in some clubs, people respectfully shut up and listen, but even today, in venues like The Troubadour, there's a lot of drinking and noise coming from the audience by the bar (who are there for Happy Hour or whatever). Nick couldn't have coped with that.

Do I think making three albums which were ignored by the public could be traumatic? Absolutely.

I don't think Nick was expecting any of them to be *Top of the Pops*-type chart hits or anything. I think he was hoping that he would get recognition from the kind of people who thought that Joe Boyd was cool: 'Wow, that's Nick Drake! He wrote *Five Leaves Left*!' Interestingly, I once asked Nick if he would ever consider appearing on *Top of the Pops* (some band or other was recording a rock version of 'Free Ride') and he surprised me by saying that 'A few years ago he wouldn't have dreamt of it but now . . . why the hell not?'

Subsequently (in 1974, just before Nick died) I became friends with Mike Appleton, who produced *The Old Grey Whistle Test*, and I asked him if Nick would ever be likely to appear on that show. Mike responded along the lines of, well, maybe, but it had been felt that the material they'd heard – probably *Pink Moon* – was a bit on the melancholic or bleak side. Recently, I reminded Mike of this old conversation. He suddenly looked a bit sad and said, 'You know, one of the very few regrets I have is that we never had Nick Drake on the *Whistle Test*. It's such a shame that there's no live footage of him playing anything.' I also know that Bob Harris, who presented the show at that time, thought that Nick was 'wonderful'.

The main thing that leapt out at me from reading the diaries was that for Nick, it wasn't at all about 'I'm gonna be a big star'. You never got the sense that Nick wanted to be a Jim Morrison, for instance, but you did get the impression that his 'drive' had been knocked for six after the failure of *Bryter Layter*, and Joe Boyd having to go off to America.

It wasn't about stardom; it was more about recognition and feeling fulfilled and appreciated and admired in some way.

I remember talking with Nick in the music room at Far Leys, when he showed me the tuning for 'From The Morning', and then we went and played some tracks off *Bryter Layter* on the Dansette record player. I remember saying to him, 'My God! If I'd made an album like that and it hadn't been successful, I don't know what I would have done.'

And he replied, 'Well, now you know where I'm at.'

And in another conversation, I remember him visibly trembling, and saying, 'All the nerves are exposed. All the defences are down,' or something like that. But that's partly because I was the kind of friend who would be trying to get that out of him. Nick would drop in from time to time. And it was on one of those occasions – when I'd said, 'Nick, how are you *really* feeling?' (you know, 'Don't give me all this crap, you look dreadful. What is going on with you?') – that he just said, 'I can't cope.'

One can use somewhat meaningless terms like 'nervous breakdown' or 'highly strung'. To actually say 'I can't cope' was quite a statement from someone so *defended* as Nick Drake.

I am of the view today that Nick did not have an illness that was going to be cured, or even improved, by chemicals, by drugs alone. I think even modern-day antidepressants and/or antipsychotics (in small doses) wouldn't have 'fixed' Nick Drake.

But . . . back then, if you were a psychiatrist confronted with someone like Nick, what would you do? You would diagnose a 'depressive illness', and you would try to treat that. But in the face of Nick's personality, and resistance, it was difficult.

I think that Dr Dickens, who was a caring and good doctor, didn't know what the hell to do for him – I mean, what *would* you do? In retrospect, a diary of data, with particular emphasis on Nick's mood, appetite, sleep patterns, and any unusual or alarming behaviour – any possible precursor to, or signs of, potential self-harm – might have been useful. But it's doubtful whether Dr Dickens ever knew of the existence of Rodney's diary. Or if he did, there's no mention of him asking to see it.

Any psychiatrist would have tried giving Nick antidepressant medications, which in those days would most likely have been Tryptizol,[2] probably with a low dose of Stelazine[3] to take the edge off things. A lot of these drug actions are 'dose-related', so their effectiveness will often depend on the dosage taken.

Also, they wouldn't have worked unless Nick had taken them regularly. I think the sort of thing that would have boosted Nick in the short term would have been something like a good slug of amphetamine, or some other stimulant that would have made his mood go up for a short while, but would have worn off. It would also have been a pretty irresponsible thing to have prescribed . . .

Rodney's second opinion came from a Doctor Pollitt, in London. He was an eminent psychiatrist in those days, at St Thomas's (the London teaching hospital), who also had a private practice in Harley Street. The 'doyen' at that time was a psychiatrist called William

Sergeant. Pollitt was his ally. It was Pollitt and Sergeant who were then the 'top psychiatrists', and Rodney found them. Sergeant's big thing was depression. At that time they had MAOIs,[4] Tricyclics,[5] and ECT.[6] They were basically the only treatments that they had.

Rodney mentions in the diary that Pollitt thought that Nick might be schizophrenic. Nick's doctor back in Warwickshire, Dr Dickens, said (and I would agree) that in those days 'schizophrenia' was just a word, or a label, that was fairly meaningless. At that time, 'schizophrenia' was a term that was often applied to anybody who was just a bit odd, and has since been used by non-professionals as a term to describe a split personality ('I'm feeling a bit schizophrenic today').

Since the late 1960s, though, psychiatry has got its operational definitions a lot more organised in order to be more precise about what we mean by such terms as 'bipolar' and 'schizophrenic'. But in Nick's day, people like R.D. Laing were lone voices in being critical of the state of psychiatry that would give electric shock treatment to people who were 'just a bit strange'.

R. D. Laing was a former military (Air Force) psychiatrist, who wrote a book called *The Divided Self*, which is a seminal work; everybody still regards it as a masterpiece. But then Laing became something of a 'Star': a bit of a hippie-guru, who was very critical of 'traditional' psychiatry – often with good reason. Laing himself had a very unhealthy relationship with alcohol, and probably died a premature death as a result. Leon Redler, whom Rodney mentions in the diaries, was his American protégé, who came over to work with him.

They founded an organisation called the Philadelphia Association, which was a commendable attempt to provide patients 'asylum', in the true sense of the word, without locking them up or giving them electric shocks, and 'chemical coshes', which they were very critical of. They suggested that if you just allow the patient to 'be' – and don't criticise them – simply allowing them to hear their 'voices' (auditory hallucinations) or whatever, rather than treating them with these 'dangerous drugs' that produce horrible side effects, then that's probably a healthier way to try to help them. These attitudes remain very influential to this day, and are highly regarded by many modern mental health professionals.

As I say, I don't think that Nick's problems were ever likely to have been solved by medication alone, whether antipsychotics or antidepressants. I would instead compare Nick's deterioration in personality to somebody who's been taken hostage or kept in prison, something like that. An analogy would be with someone who's been kidnapped and tortured for several years: you do see disintegration in personality, and even hallucinations and flashbacks, and so on, as one sees in cases of post-traumatic stress disorder. So I would view it more along those lines. Nick was a hostage to the system that was driving him for a while. The music industry – the commercial making, marketing and selling of records – in reality just didn't work for him.

He was 'unwell' – I'm not disputing that. What I do challenge is that whether it was treatable with chemicals alone. I think his problems were more 'cognitive'; so I ask myself: If *Bryter Layter* had been a hit, do I think that Nick would have deteriorated in the way that he did? And the answer is: I don't think so. I think that if *Bryter Layter* had received acclaim, it would have given Nick a new buoyancy and a confidence. That's my take on it, both as a friend and as a psychiatrist.

When you are depressed, your cognitions present something like: 'I am miserable. The world is a horrible place. Nobody loves me. No one will ever love me.' And then what the cognitive therapist says is: 'Whoa! Hang on a second. *No one will ever love me?* Why are you saying that?' And it's actually an erroneous cognition. It's a lie. But your brain gets into that way of thinking when you get depressed. So cognitive therapy starts with what is called a 'cognitive analysis'. It then helps the patient to understand that there are a number of cognitions, which make up a thought process, that are erroneous: you're lying to yourself. *No one will ever love me* is the type of cognition that leads to a style of thinking that someone who's depressed can get into. But things can be restructured – which is essentially what cognitive therapy is all about.

CBT (Cognitive Behavioural Therapy) is an extension of cognitive therapy. In my view, it's the difference between, on the one hand, internalising and changing, as opposed to, on the other, simply gaining insight and understanding. Insight on its own does not necessarily facilitate change. You're more likely to change if you experience the solution for yourself. You learn what the problems are, and then solve them by experiencing a different cognitive response, accompanied by actions that reinforce the progress you have made.

This is what a CBT therapist tries to facilitate: insights as well as actions (or behaviours) that can lead to improved confidence and mood, and when performed well, this can be very powerful. (Often the use of some compatible medication can enhance the process.)

Motivational work can also be very powerful. So, for instance, I don't say to my patient: 'The reason you fell down the stairs is because you were drunk. And the reason why you were drunk is because you are an alcoholic and you need to go into recovery or rehab.'

What the motivational interviewer does instead is to ask open-ended questions: 'Help me understand a bit more about you falling down the stairs.'

So the response may be: 'I'd had a few drinks.'

'Ah, OK, could you tell me a bit more about that?'

'Well, you know, I'd been arguing with my wife.'

'Why might you and your wife have been arguing?'

'Well, she was saying I drink too much. And so, angrily, I went upstairs and I was staggering about and slipped, and . . . Well, I probably was a bit drunk.'

So instead of saying: 'You were drunk. You were drunk every night that week. You're an alcoholic, go to rehab!', you may say something like: 'So try to tell me a bit more about your relationship with alcohol.'

'Well, I was drinking on Tuesday, and I think Wednesday as well. So, maybe I think I am probably becoming an alcoholic.'

'OK, so how can we move forward together, constructively in a direction that is going to help to resolve this issue?'

'Maybe I should get some help?'

'Ah, OK. Any thoughts about what is likely to be of help?'

'Well . . . er . . . maybe I should try a spell of "rehab", like my sister did.'

So you see that the insights and suggested actions have, as it were, come from the patient, even though the therapist was covertly trying to direct the patient into this way of thinking.

I think that these types of approaches, or treatments, could possibly have had more of an impact, which Nick Drake may (or may not) have responded to.

If Nick had had a serious, chronic, enduring mental illness that required strong anti-psychotic medications, then it's unlikely that he would have driven 700 miles in two days as described in the diary.

As far as the driving is concerned, there was indeed something 'pathological' about it, I think. I mean, the mileage that Nick was racking up wasn't typical of any psychotic condition (other than possibly a bipolar disorder), but was more likely to be due to the mindset of someone who felt lost, miserable, and didn't know what else to do. It could, I suppose, have simply been pure escapism resulting from boredom.

The term 'psychosis' means different things to different people. What it means to a psychiatrist like me is that you're 'not in touch with the real world'. You're lacking in insight. I think that Nick became indecisive, and that he couldn't make decisions; couldn't make clear choices. I think that he was definitely ill, but that it had more to do with deteriorating confidence and a desperate form of thinking – having lost his sense of purpose and meaning – rather than suffering, say, from any auditory hallucinations or delusions.

He wasn't hallucinating. If Dr Pollitt thought he was schizophrenic, he can't have been referring to florid symptoms such as hallucinations or delusions, because Nick simply didn't have them. And the problem would have then been that the available treatments for schizophrenia would not have been effective. A simple form of the 'deteriorating personality' type of schizophrenia is rarely improved by the use of antipsychotic medications alone.

This is why I stand by my belief that Nick's condition was more of a cognitively induced deterioration, rather than a florid biological condition. He did not have a major psychiatric illness that would have responded well to psycho-pharmacological treatments. I'm just as convinced of that as I am that Nick was not dependent on addictive drugs, and I am *totally* convinced of that.

Tryptizol was not a bad drug to try out. He just didn't take it properly. He was storing medication, he was self-medicating throughout the entire period. Rodney would hand out tablets for him to take to London, but Nick wasn't taking them as prescribed by Dr Dickens. He was storing them up for when he felt low, and they don't work if you do it like that: you've got to get an adequate and consistent blood-level of antidepressants in order for them to be effective. Not that I think the medications, even if taken properly, would have been very effective in the long term. But it's evident that Nick wanted to be in control – of when he took the pills and when he didn't. He was self-medicating, also, with small amounts of alcohol at times. But he wasn't really misusing alcohol. That's maybe why he was so difficult to treat effectively: because it would have meant losing control – surrendering to the suggestions and prescriptions of someone else. He was a classic non-compliant patient (which of course, is not at all uncommon).

I don't think Nick committed suicide. I don't think that Nick (or Molly or Rodney) had any idea that Tryptizol could cause the heart arrhythmias that probably caused his death. Molly and Rodney would have locked the pills away, as they did with aspirin, say. There's a big difference between 'I don't care if I don't wake up' and 'I want to, and am determined to, kill myself'. The latter demonstrates suicidal intent, for which there needs to be evidence when recording a verdict of suicide. Men who commit suicide shoot themselves, jump in front of trains, hang themselves, or take an overdose of aspirin. If you have suicidal intent, you do something that you believe will kill you, and you may well leave a note for someone. With Nick, I'm inclined to think it was more a case of 'Oh God, I'm so depressed and fed up, I just want to go to sleep and I don't care if I don't wake up!'

Having said that, the coroner was presented with a privileged young man, who had been treated for depression over a number of years, who had ingested over thirty tablets of Tryptizol. It was difficult for him to record a verdict of 'misadventure' under those circumstances.

Would Nick have been better off with the sort of treatments that he might have been offered today? I don't know. These days, we think we are becoming more sophisticated, but for much of the time we still don't know in great detail what we are doing in the world of emotional health.

As with many other areas of medicine, psychiatry remains an art, based as far as is possible upon the scientific evidence available at any given time; so really: who knows?

Nick Drake was a much-loved friend who, when I knew him, was an increasingly complicated young man. Memories of him are variable. Joyous, fun and ridiculous. At times I felt breathtaking admiration; then intense worry as things deteriorated; and finally, profound grief and enduring sadness.

He left a beautiful, at times disturbing, and always fascinating legacy.

I often think about him.

'It is closing time in the gardens of the West and from now on an artist will be judged only by the resonance of his solitude or the quality of his despair.'

Cyril Connolly

Brian Wells, 1967

Notes

1. *Five Leaves Left* was released on 3 July 1969, and Nick left Cambridge in October 1969.

2. Tryptizol (Amitriptyline, in those days combined with Nortriptyline, I think) remains the most widely used Tricyclic Antidepressant (TCA), and is an efficacious treatment for major depressive disorder (clinical depression).

3. Stelazine (Trifluoperazine) is a typical or 'conventional' antipsychotic. The primary application of Trifluoperazine is for schizophrenia and 'psychotic conditions', but in low doses it can enhance the effects of antidepressant medications. Other official indications may vary from country to country, but generally it is also prescribed for use for patients with agitation and behavioural problems, severe nausea and vomiting, as well as severe anxiety. Trials have shown a moderate benefit of this drug in patients with borderline personality disorder.

4. MOAIs (Monoamine Oxidase Inhibitors) are chemicals which inhibit the activity of the Monoamine Oxidase enzyme family. They have a long history of use as medications prescribed for the treatment of depression. They are also used in the treatment of Parkinson's disease and several other disorders.

5. Tricyclic Antidepressants (TCAs) are chemical compounds used primarily as antidepressants. TCAs were first discovered in the early 1950s and were subsequently introduced into treatment later in the decade.

6. ECT (Electroconvulsive Therapy), formerly known as 'electroshock', is a standard psychiatric treatment in which seizures are electrically induced in patients to provide relief from psychiatric illnesses. ECT is usually used as a last line of intervention for major depressive disorder, schizophrenia, mania and catatonia. A usual course of ECT involves multiple administrations, typically given two or three times per week, under general anaesthetic, or 'sedation', until the patient improves sufficiently. It has recently moved back into vogue as an effective treatment for 'resistant depression', despite its controversial reputation by those who remain cynical or critical of psychiatry as a whole. Advocates of ECT will often view it as a 'life-saving treatment' that can produce dramatic and rapid results.

Nick and Jeremy in the Marlborough quad (Photo supplied by Jeremy Harmer, taken by his mother)

Memory
Whether you knock it, split it,
Eat it, can't bear to eat it
There it sits on your table
Thump-ripe
Already spoiling.

Cate Kennedy, 'Welcome'

Migajas

by Jeremy Harmer

Nick and Jeremy Harmer met aged thirteen at Marlborough College. But it was only once there that they discovered their families lived quite close to each other, so their meetings were not restricted to school only. Since both boys shared an interest in music, it was inevitable that they should become friends.

Here is an extract from a letter Nick wrote to his parents in February 1962, describing their first meeting.

Barton Hill
Marlborough
Sunday 18th
. . . Last Wednesday I asked the Harmer boy if he lived near Stratford. He does, and he said he recognised the name Drake, and also that he new [sic] Tanworth-in-Arden. Since then he's become terribly friendly and now actually calls me Nick! He's a very amusing type . . . He says he's going to call me over to his house in the holidays . . .

And a week later:

. . . Yes, J. Harmer is very keen on jazz, and also on Shakespeare, which seems rather funny as there's so much difference between the two . . .

There was a time, back then, when I knew someone exceptional, someone with an extraordinary talent for putting into words and music a gentle doubting, and a plangent search for beauty.

We were, what? Friends, or perhaps almost-friends, or probably just acquaintances; or, more reliably, sons of friendly parents; or, incontrovertibly, boys who went to the same school; or just people who loved playing the guitar.

And we would have – had almost – drifted away from each other. Different paths, different lives. I was no big part of his reality, even when we knew each other best. And so what would have happened in different circumstances, I have often thought, is that the music would have stayed on (of course it would). But it would almost certainly have faded into all the other musics of that time, one blissful sound amongst the deliriously hectic accompaniment to growing through our twenties. And we might have met again from time to time. But how can I tell? There's such a jumble of people and sights and sounds and places from an accumulated life that it's often difficult to see what has actually happened. Trying to guess what might have been is even less easy to understand.

Because he died, poor boy, and the legend started and the stories got told and re-told, and every time those particular events of the past started to slide away, again, there was another article, another new song, another memory, apparently thump-ripe all over again, pushing his short life back into the present of our thirties, and then our forties, and now our fifties, so that meetings and conversations which were, by themselves, unimportant, have become weighted down with history and myth;

and a relationship of what was most likely only minor importance keeps getting nagged back into prime position, refusing to go away.

Do all the other major and minor characters in the story of his life have the same experience? Do the musicians and singers from that period, the virtuosic instrumentalists, the fellow travellers, friends, do they find themselves obliged to live the same old memories, time after time when the phone rings from Holland because someone heard that they knew him, or when the newspapers are again full of the story of a short-lived poet whose music just refuses to go away as it is rediscovered yet again? Who are the people on the end of the phone? Who are the unknown e-mailers?

These are the new discoverers: they write on websites about how the songs saved them when they 'had lost their way a bit'. They key in words like 'timeless' and 'beautiful', and 'melancholic' and 'uplifting', and talk about becoming completely entangled in the music the moment they first heard ''Cello Song' or 'Northern Sky'. But it isn't quite like that for us, the survivors. Listening to 'River Man' isn't a new discovery. Perhaps, instead, it's a memory. But of what? An event? A person? No, I think it's a feeling, like the yearning for something better, a second grace, something he knew, and we, despite his absence, keep re-learning.

The real memories – unlike recollections of that twenty-something ambience – aren't in the music; the real memories are crumbs, *migajas*, little tableaux of when we were younger and, it seemed there was more future than past.

Jeremy Harmer photo album

August 1974: Tanworth-in-Arden

Now, when I think back, I remember the kind of mid-England summer afternoon that makes you nostalgic when you are living far away from home. We sat on the terrace, looking out onto a luxurious garden, with two tall hedges like aristocratic pinball flappers. My hosts, friends of my parents who had once known me moderately well, encouraged me to talk about myself with every appearance of loving interest. It was, I seem to think, a talent of theirs, a bone china elegance, and as I picture them now I can hear their smooth voices, his all molasses, hers jewelled and poised. And so I talked of my life in Mexico, showing off about my ease with foreign living, and joked about what it was like to be back in the hot-leafed greenery of Warwickshire. I told them of my girlfriend and about teaching and pyramids and the glittering Caribbean. I drank my tea and crunched the offered biscuits. And felt, as before, and ever since, the dull ache of guilt, making the words brittle and hollow, as if I had no right to be active and – as I was then – almost as happy as a person could be with a present and a future of such ease.

He was there too, you see, sucking the summer out of the day, making my words callous with his uneasy blankness. We talked around and through him, his parents and me, keeping a hospital jollity in the blue as if we were all just fine. And then I went off with him, back to the music room of old, followed by their blessing, another hope, perhaps, that someone, anyone, could make it better. Listen, that's how I see it now, but I could be wrong. But I visualise me sitting opposite him trying the old talk-listen-empathy trick of easy contact that can sometimes pass for intimacy. But it didn't work with him. He didn't seem to be interested in other lives, for one thing, and there was too much distance, for another. In those days I didn't know how to close that kind of gap because I had not met enough people living in his kind of despair. It's less surprising now. When he told me about putting his foot through a Martin guitar because it felt like the right thing to do and, he said, I think, that he was just angry, I thought it was weird, not tragic. And so, as he sat there, arms across his chest, his beautiful head slumped, uglied by trouble, I talked my way out of it because I could not listen properly in to it.

I would have gone to see him anyway. We had been almost-friends. Before, we had been to each other's houses, played tennis, winter-sported in Switzerland, attended the same school, played songs together, but he suddenly became so extraordinary that, as with his presence, you would not want to touch his music with your own ordinariness. I loved his parents' house too, the gentle welcome of it, the kindness that seemed to seep through it. But of course I would have gone too because of that music, the constant threnody of nostalgia and beauty that flooded my time then, and echoes hauntingly down the years, discovered again and again, by everyone who comes across it, a universal beauty that is timeless and exquisite.

I didn't hear of his death until a month or so after it happened. I had gone back to Mexico. No e-mails or internet then, and no mention in the airmail *Guardian*, delivered irregularly through the post, like buses. My mother's letters didn't come through that often either, or perhaps she just didn't tell me until she wrote it with the greetings my girlfriend brought back with her. And so the sheer joy and happiness of seeing my lover after an eternity of autumn was interrupted by the uncomfortable fact of too many pills in the night; and now, all at once, his music, those three extraordinary records, assumed a mythological invincibility, and though I play no real part in his story, so often told and re-told, he still, inescapably, plays a part in mine.

January 1971: London

Down the Fulham Road, a dark night, wet and unapproachable, and we were in search of something to eat. Spaghetti, probably. In those days there wasn't much choice. Not like now when you can find whatever you want just by thinking about it.

I remember the place, steamy against the damp gloom. But we were happy, I think, my companion and me, as we barrelled down the pavement in search of something to enjoy. We turned into the doorway in between the curving glass of the tabled bays. Hunger and the anticipation of warmth and cheerfulness. A heady feeling of possibility.

He was coming out, head down, the way we would have to get used to seeing him. I remember a battered old green anorak, some ill-fitting outdoor garment pulled tight around him, defensively, like armour.

I greeted him. I can hear myself now. 'Hello, hello.' I do a good hello, all loud and insistent. You really ought to listen. And respond.

He did. A mumbled greeting. So I went on. (You have to, really.) 'How are you? Haven't seen you for a bit.' Well, we were friends. Sort of. He was a bit of a hero, I suppose. I would tell people I knew him. Especially the right kind of people. They'd have listened to his first two records by then.

There weren't many of us, the listeners, but it was as if we knew each other, those of us who had recognised instantly that he was something special. That was his problem, in a way. There weren't enough of us, and the knowing of that fact ripped him to pieces – or so we understood later.

Was he angry with the world around him, already down and depressed, his sophistication blunted? Was that why he wouldn't stay to chat? It's true that he looked even worse than I did, but we were all unkempt and scarecrowed in those days. It was important. But his was a shambolic uncouthness, and even then it had almost buried his ethereal beauty.

So he didn't stop to talk. He said he was fine, but (this is what you can tell from dropped heads and flattened intonation) he either wasn't or he really didn't want to say one way or the other. He wasn't alone (the fading picture in my memory smudges back at me), so me and my companion were probably awkwardly met. Whatever. He walked away down the Fulham Road, a man with a purpose, but, apparently, with nowhere to go.

That's the thing with memory, though. He might have been alone, but it doesn't feel, now that I am thinking about it, as if he was. And if he was, would that have made him unhappier? Or is memory always fatally compromised by what we know now, what we've read? Did I imagine his solitariness? I'm sure of the shapeless green coat, though, and the lank hair, and the un-tempered muttering. But the rest is weighed down with the books and articles; perhaps what I know now is no longer really what I knew then at all, but is rather absorbed through the limpid guitar, that precious, gentle, angry voice, and – how to describe this? – the legend.

Later all of us – friends, acquaintances, colleagues – learned, separately, about the compartments he had us in, little syntactic clauses, never joined up. One of us – one world only – at a time. It was the way he was. I think now of his life surrounded by little specks of matter, never a whole vessel of friends and acquaintances, just crumbs flaking out around him. But that is fanciful.

There was a day, sometime around then, when we drove back to Warwickshire together, through the night, the Oxford bypass, Woodstock under a shiny yellow moon, and we stopped, as you would, the bright stars glittering, and he was beautiful again, and, I thought, so was I, and sweet and vulnerable. The days when the future hangs bloated before you, rich, mysterious and entrancing. Always just out of reach. Days of wonder. When we knew we could be anything, and what a lot of time for us to *be* in. Why, I now reproach myself, can I not remember what we talked about? But I feel a sense of relaxed optimism, thinking about it, and jokes. So that if I let the light of the Woodstock moon still shine down upon that stopped car, off the road, a gate interrupting a farm wall by a copse, why, then the future – not the one we all imagined but the future that came to pass – can be postponed indefinitely.

Autumn 1969: London

He must have rung up, I suppose. There was a coin-operated telephone somewhere in my basement in Randolph Terrace, just near the Warwick Road tube. My flat was owned and occupied by Clem, an actor of the old school, tall, thin and nobly bearded. And I rented a little room from him, a bedsit, containing my guitar, some books, and a Hacker gramophone with its rich deep resonance, so unlike the tinny portables then on offer. It sat on the floor. I had to be sure not to play it too loud because otherwise the violinist in the next cubicle – a nervous kind of man playing for one of the London orchestras – might not like it, and Clem might descend from the curtained stage where his bed sat at one side of the vast sitting room and express his exasperation. It didn't bother the other guy. He thought he was a songwriter too and had even less right to that fantasy than I did.

Anyway, he rang, and I agreed to be in. It was an afternoon. True, my room was a bit like a prison, but I had nowhere really to escape to. It was that after-university what-do-I-do-now strangeness that I do not look back on with nostalgia except for the books I read to cover my lack of direction. And so he turned up. He wore a proper jacket as if we were still at public school. He was cheerful and open, pleased to be there in my not very des-res. Then he asked whether I would like to hear it.

Well, I knew he was making a record. We all knew. Word gets out about that kind of thing. And I supposed it would be folk music, guitar-based songs, because that's what we had played before he *really* started playing and left us behind, and anyway that's what I had heard, but what kind of songs I did not know. Jealous? Of course. I'd had to pay for the LP I'd made, and then I'd had to sell it to people around the campus until I got my money back. And the thing is, I still entertained hopes of success in that direction, though I hadn't yet started the club-singing, and the endless round of fruitless record-company visits with my dodgy demos, that would occupy the next eighteen months of my life. Or the busking in echoing underpasses.

But not that jealous. And anyway, why not listen? A record with a plain white label because this was a first test pressing. I eased it over the kink in the turntable spike. Well, you don't let your friend's new album fall from a height. It's not seemly. The needle slithered across the outside rim, directed itself until it found the groove, and settled. And then it started.

Memory plays tricks. I've said that. But I think I knew, straight away, how good, how especially good it was, from those first plucked chords, the extraordinarily present acoustic-ness of the guitar, 'Time Has Told Me', to the accompanying piano and guitar, and the stringy edginess of the double bass. And then the voice came. That's when jealousy, I suppose, gave way to awe.

We didn't say much. We just listened, and occasionally I tried to offer a compliment, one of those hollow ones, so unlike what I was hearing: that's fantastic! And he'd say, that's – and reel off the name of one of my musical heroes, and the thing is we were sitting in my basement cell where I was not much of anything and this music *was* something, and he was sitting there with a rapt smile on his face as he listened to what he had done, and he saw that it was good. And, well, so did I. I have read since of people who were instantly captivated by different tracks: the entry, lolloping down the stairs, of Danny Thompson's bass in 'Man In A Shed', the haunting strings behind that delayed chording of 'River Man', the contrast between the acerbic finger-picking and the cello's long melodic line. But me, I heard it all there, with him, and could not believe my ears.

Of the three albums it is still my favourite. The first amazing statement. But more than that. There's a freshness about it, a young man's optimism. I mean in the introspective world of a young twenty-something. Before the frown and the knowingness sets in. Don't misunderstand me. I love 'Poor Boy', and the viola, and 'Please give me a second grace'. Those are heart-wrenching in their way, just as some of the *Pink Moon* tracks, in hindsight, are almost unbearable, and perhaps the best of all (not to mention those last later recordings). But *Five Leaves Left* still and always convinces because it is a young man's celebration of his prodigious talent, a talent he knows and recognises and glories in. Which, despite the piercing discomfort of inferiority I experienced, is what I recognised that afternoon as the music sang out of my Hacker and I looked at the man-boy in front of me as if I had never known him before.

Sometime in 1968: Cambridge

It wasn't as bad as the time on Park Lane. Then the policeman had looked into the car, hood down, me driving an impossible love of mine (impossible because I did not know, have never known, perhaps, the art of love), and said – see: the words are engraved on my heart – 'I don't know who you're trying to impress, sir, but you don't impress me.' And I had the grace to feel embarrassed and a bit angry because in those days it didn't seem too bad to roar up Park Lane at a speed far beyond the limit.

Ah well, we know better now.

But this time, with the girl from Essex University (and from just near me at home), I was pleased to be driving out of East Anglia proper to the city of Cambridge, a magic seat of art and learning that I could only dream of. We were (rightly, it turned out) unsure of each other, my Warwickshire friend and I, but I said we should visit my friend, the Cambridge student, companion from earlier times, co-musician, someone special.

I pass the place where he used to live quite frequently now as I drive through Cambridge, no longer mysterious since, some twenty years ago, it became my home town. The building still looks imposing, and the river still bubbles away in front of it, though I have never seen signs of the river man of the song, as the tourists gather round the weir of Jesus Green. 'River Man' is a different bigger place.

Still, that day, having been stopped by the police for going too fast, which is a bit of a downer when you are speeding through the countryside in your Triumph Vitesse convertible, twenty-first-birthday present for an upper-middle-class boy, we finally found the building and, greeted, I am sure, by a landlady, we came into the room where he lived, all long dark overcoats and gloomy romanticism. And look, we were pleased to see each other and Dinah (that was her name) was, I believe, impressed by his sheer presence, the statement of the way he carried himself, so sure, so urbane, so (I know I've used this word before) sophisticated. So distant.

I have a strong memory of that day (how strange that I can never remember the endings, the goodbyes, difficult or hasty exits, only an incident, a moment pinned like wings). We smoked some pot (now come on: that was what it was, that was how it was named) which was probably his, or hers, but not mine, I think. And he had some headphones, great big cans which enveloped your ears, the first I had ever come across. So he told me to put them on and I did. It felt as if I disappeared into them. Selfishly, I can't remember what she was doing, only what he did, and what I experienced.

What he did was put on a record from his collection which I had not, until then, come across. What he said was 'Listen to this', and with these great big cans on my ears and, I suspect, slightly stoned, I was suddenly assaulted by the blast of a ship's hooter, the first obbligato profundo in a building wall of sound, water, guitars and drums, 'Song for our Ancestors' by the Steve Miller Band. So good, so damn good – man – that you wanted to shout it out. Yes I know, it's just a track, another band trying to change the world and hardly making an impression, but it has always seemed more than that to me. A gift. Something I was given. And if, sometimes, I come across it, of all the music I know, it has the power to transport me back to that sombre room, and the long black-overcoated figure who, even before I knew, really, what he could do, seemed suffused with a strange and slightly awe-inspiring luminescence.

1965, perhaps: Verbier and Marlborough

That was the year when, charging down a mountain in a white fog I smashed a ski, but not, thankfully my leg, on a cheeky rock lurking beneath the featureless snow. That was the year my father broke a rib and my mother got hit on the head as she skied the path underneath the chair lift. It was a time when you could only take £50 per person out of the country, and no credit cards.

I don't know why my sister wasn't there. But I remember he came with us, and the mystery is why there are no photographs. I should explain: my mother, an inveterate photographic chronicler would never rest until she had recorded family groups, friends, posed harmony. All the years have their photographic images thanks to her, so that you can check age and fashion over the decades by studying the Christmas photos and the holiday cine films. But for the Verbier holiday there is nothing, just flickering images in the decaying spools of memory.

We took our guitars, gut-stringed and Spanish I think, and played to the other guests in the hotel bar. Awkward chords, unoriginal fingerings, E-A-D-G-B-E, none of the fancy tuning of later years, nor any of the lilting 5/4 rhythms or the flickering finger-pickings that we now know so well. Peter, Paul and Mary, probably. And I reckon we sounded what we were at the time: two young boys with great enthusiasm but no great understanding or talent. Listen to that! But I am sure it hadn't happened yet, whatever process it was that transformed base metal into gold. It can't have done.

There is a photo from around then, back in the UK, taken at Marlborough College, school for the sons of the clergy (originally), set in the heart of the Wiltshire Downs. There were around 800 of us boys back then (no girls in those days!), and there was music (for both of us) and acting (for me) and sport (for him – he was an outstanding sprinter), a Combined Cadet Force, and, I seem to remember, some learning.

The photograph must have been taken on some form of open day, or Parents' Day perhaps, where the heroes played matches, and we declaimed speeches or blew trumpets to make our mothers and fathers glad with admiring love. What strange places schools are. But in the photo no one seems over-impressed as we stand with our guitars in front of C-House, the old coaching building on the route of the old Bath Road. And as so often, his enigma remains gentled and hidden, his back to the camera, whilst I sing out unsubtly to my mother's pointing lens. One day, perhaps, when memories shift and buried shards are squeezed back up to the surface, I will remember what song it might have been, what songs we sang.

Always Summer: Tanworth-in-Arden and Stratford-upon-Avon

When I think of his parents' house it is always summer, and the brown shade into the kitchen welcomes you in from the heat. And the music room. We seemed to have spent hours in the music room, guitars and pianos, and a tape recorder. The easy companionship of music making.

Or a tennis court a mile outside Stratford which my parents had caused to be constructed, next to the old farmyard, restored, and with that raised round swimming pool. Everyone played tennis well and with enthusiasm. My sister was determined. The brothers from Preston-on-Stour had talent. The girl from Clifford Chambers seemed austere to me. The others. Everyone wore tennis whites and there was lemonade and orange juice. I mostly watched.

They called him Nicky, boy-child name, almost effeminate, well-chosen perhaps because that's a quality that never left him. I have a fragment of a photo in which he stands at the net, slightly stooped and eager, and 'Nicky' is what I wrote underneath it in my teenage hand. He was tall and thin, white and pressed, alert and sporting.

Think of it. All of us there, potentials hovering around my parents' garden in the summer air. The future actress, the future lawyer, the teacher, the professional clown, a psychologist (semi-retired), a teacher-writer, a folk-music legend, the future living, the future dead. The idyllic face of a comfortable Englishness. You could invoke it with elegant nostalgia, tinge it with regret for what was to come, for all the things that have happened since. But of course it wasn't perfect then, just as it isn't perfect now. The young carry doubts and fears with them just as older people try to balance regrets with their satisfactions, and write their triumphs in the furrows of their disasters. But still, the sun shone down and the smell of cut wheat hovered in the air, and as I sit here now temporarily isolated in a Buenos Aires hotel room on a cold grey morning, I can almost call it back to mind and feel the summer breeze upon my cheek. But then it fades again and I am left with nothing more than a crumb of recollection. I would need to find the music for it, or bring it alive with that one piercing scent if I really wanted to be back there. Just like I need the Woodstock moon or the London rain; just as I long for the hazy intoxication of a Cambridge student room or the expanse of a school court, a bar in a Swiss hotel, or a basement bedsit, Far Leys in the summer with those particular living people in it. But memory doesn't work like that. Thump-ripe spoils and rots away, changes and dissolves, however hard we try to cling to it. We are, in the end, what we leave behind, but we too spoil in the memories of others, augmented or diminished as they try to trap and pin us. Just as I have tried, unsuccessfully, to preserve a few memories, the ones I can bring to mind, that is, of someone I knew all those years ago: memories which are never allowed to dissolve because each time they start to do just that, some new resurrection rolls the stone away, again, from the cave mouth.

But what if we leave behind something which comforts and enthrals people long long after we have gone? What kind of gift is that? For however memory fades, the music, in the end, does not. You read the web postings of people who have just come across the songs of the young boy in his tennis whites, all optimism and enthusiasm for the future, and though you can't help comparing him with the huddled unhappiness that came later, still there is hope in the way a teenager from Bath or a middle-aged woman from California have found comfort, so many years later, in the present-ness of his past magic.

Nick Drake: Orpheus Visible

by Robin Frederick

When I listen to the songs of Nick Drake – to Nick Drake singing his songs – something shifts. The world slips just a little bit sideways. An ancient, unfamiliar door opens and I can see something beyond my everyday life. Beyond that door is a world that has more depth, more truth. It's a feeling that only exists in the present moment, when I'm listening to Nick singing, then it slips away again below the surface.

What is it about this voice and these songs that transport me, and so many others, far away from this world and into another? Is it the storyteller who, with hushed tones, draws his listeners closer around the hearth? Is it the hypnotic, grounding rhythm of the guitar, the melodies that drift above as if unhinged from the earth, chords rich in warm harmony and dark dissonance? Or is it the words that describe, in sometimes awkward phrases, a young man facing desire, shyness, ambition, need, and the fears we all share?

There are certainly other popular singer-songwriters whose work touches us, but few whose songs and voice resonate on such a deep level of the psyche and so long after they're gone. So many listeners describe Nick Drake's music as 'timeless', yet he was certainly the child of a particular time and place.

Over the years since I first knew him, when we were both teenagers busking around the south of France, taking a few university classes and playing in tiny clubs, I've spent many hours listening to and learning from Nick's music. As a songwriter myself, I can see the tremendous bursts of brilliance, as well as the painstaking effort and hard-won breakthroughs that went into the writing of those songs.

I love sharing these discoveries with others. I've had the privilege of writing about Nick's innovations in album liner notes and magazines. But I've always shied away from talking about how his songs affect me personally. Maybe it feels too revealing. Nick gives all of us plenty of room to project ourselves into his work. Or maybe it's because I need to know why I feel before I can explain what I feel.

The music journalist Ian MacDonald once told me that when he listened to Nick Drake 'the glamour came over him'. He used 'glamour' in its rich, archaic meaning – being under a magical spell or trance. The music has that effect on me, too. And, like all curious songwriters, I want to know why. What could be more important, and perhaps more dangerous, than seeking to understand the source of a magical spell?

Orpheus

There has always been more than a hint of magic around songs and singers. There's the irresistible song of the Sirens, the hypnotic chant of the shaman, the angels we have heard on high. But perhaps the most memorable and magical of all is Orpheus, the mythical youth with the golden lyre whose songs were so entrancing that trees uprooted themselves to follow him. Legend says he caused the sun to rise with the sheer beauty of his music. His songs brought peace to the hearts of all who heard them and lived on long after he was gone. In him, life, love, and art were interwoven, inseparable.

I sometimes catch the shimmer of that ancient wraith

peering through Nick's music, as if he embodied, for a short time, the ghost of Orpheus himself. In his songs, Nick steps easily into the mythic role of the Seeker, the Poet, and the Wounded Healer. He expresses the truth of the psyche, conveying insights into life that go deeper than any biography. In this sense, Nick's songs mythologise his own life – as many good songwriters do. As Sean Ono Lennon once put it: 'Songs are myths about things that happened to you.'

The Musician-Magician

By what art did Orpheus create music so alluring, so moving, and so magical? And what do those songs have in common with the songs of Nick Drake? Why do they, too, move listeners deeply and live on long after their maker is gone?

In the ancient world, Poetry – the most revered of all the arts – was synonymous with Song. It never lay still on the written page; it was always sung. The ancients knew that words alone are not as potent as words sung to music. In a song, the emotional message of melody, voice and chords combine with the images and associations in the words to create a perfect storm – lyrics and music building, one on the other, increasing the power of both, until they're able to deeply touch and move the listener.

Creating that magical effect takes knowledge and skill. I wonder if anyone ever asked Orpheus how many long nights he spent rewriting a song to make sure his audience felt it. Inspiration comes in a moment, but the making of a powerful song is an intoxicating brew of creativity, skill and craft. Out of this brew comes magic. We can no longer hear the songs of the mythical Orpheus, but if we look closely at the songs of Nick Drake, we may catch a glimpse of how it was done.

The Spell of Rhythm

The regular, rhythmic beat of a drum, the steady throb of a bass string, the whispery pulse of chanting voices – all cast a kind of hypnotic spell over us. These things tug on the body, pulling it toward a rhythmic centre, entraining it, capturing it. When you listen to a fast-paced, steady rhythm, it will cause your breathing and heart rate to gradually increase. An even, unhurried beat will slow down your heart and breathing rate. This is the magic of musical rhythm – it communicates with the physical body in ways that are outside of your awareness and beyond your control. That's one reason why so many cultural and religious rituals involve the steady rhythm of drums or voices. When the body becomes entrained, the mind follows, falling into a kind of rocking motion; thoughts becoming steady, repetitive, trance-like and open to suggestion.

Listening to the incantatory drone of Nick Drake's guitar on tracks like 'Three Hours' or ''Cello Song' is to let your mind and body be drawn into that hypnotic place. You might not notice it at first. In fact, if there are too many distractions, you might not feel its influence very much at all. But if you listen late at night, when life is willing to leave you alone for a while, and you focus on the rhythm of a Nick Drake track, you'll slowly begin to experience a sense of vertigo, of being pulled out of your own internal sense of time and into his.

The magical qualities of rhythm obviously held a fascination for Nick. From the very earliest songs, he can't resist playing with time and beats. 'They're Leaving Me Behind' is one of the first songs he ever wrote. In it, he plays guitar twice as fast – or sings the melody twice as slow – as anyone else would dream of doing. (You can hear this song on the *Family Tree* album.) This is an early attempt to produce an effect that Nick will come back to over and over again – making the melody float, seemingly disconnected, over an underlying, steady beat. It creates in the listener a feeling of disorientation: of floating, yet still being anchored in the rhythm.

Singing the melody for this early song requires an enormous amount of breath control. It almost sounds like a breathy tenor saxophone line. Just the sort of thing a sax player like Nick would sing. The melody lines sustain in long, smooth curves while the guitar creates a continual, steady patter underneath. The singer and guitar player almost seem like two people, not one. This would be the case in many of Nick's songs.

Within eighteen months of writing his first songs, Nick Drake created an acknowledged masterpiece of pop music in a time signature – 5/4 – that is challenging even when used in jazz and contemporary classical works, let alone the pop genre of the 1960s! Once again, rhythm played a pivotal role, and in ways that few other songwriters have attempted since.

The River Man

Nick's song 'River Man' is all about those two inescapable, elusive things: time and motion. It's really just another way of saying 'rhythm' because rhythm is the pattern of musical motion over time. And here is where the musician-magician begins to work his spell. By using rhythm to evoke the flowing motion of a river, Nick draws you into his song – or rather puts the song literally into you in an immediate, physical way.

The vast majority of popular songs are based on groups of four beats – it's what we're used to hearing. By writing a song about a river that is based on groups of five beats (5/4), Nick subtly conveys the feeling that there's an extra beat, one that spills over into the next group of beats, pulling you forward, like the momentum of a river current. Over the top of that, he lays a round of chords that tip back and forth from light to dark, from major to minor, in a slow, repetitive motion like the gentle rocking of a boat. And then, to complete the effect, he lays down a vocal melody with phrases that overlap the chord changes. Everything is in wave-like motion, everything is flowing with a rhythmical, swaying feel that literally picks you up and carries you down the river.

He did all this to underscore the lyric – to deliver it in a physical way straight to the body, making you physically feel his message rather than think about it. The lyric is all about motion – about the freedom to move, or the lack of it. What could feel freer than floating down a river? And that's what the music is meant to do, remind you of how good it feels to be free. Only Nick is immobile, imprisoned by 'the ban on feeling free'. He consults the River Man, the embodiment of eternal motion, but the River Man's words do not help, and Nick watches, powerless, as others come and go. 'Oh, how they come and go.'

Who hasn't felt the terrible sensation of being caught in a stifling backwater where nothing moves or changes, while all around you others, like the character Betty in the song, are getting on with their lives? It's a bittersweet experience for listeners since the music draws us into the free-flowing river while the words tell of the loss of that freedom.

Now, let's go back and revisit that very early song, 'They're Leaving Me Behind'. There's that same fear of being trapped – it's right there in the title. Meanwhile, a free-floating melody line is carried along on the momentum of the guitar. There's freedom in music, Nick seems to be saying, but very little of it in life. If you want an insight into the emotional life of Nick Drake, here it is – as plain as he could possibly say it. Themes of abandonment and loneliness are at the heart of most of Nick's songs – 'Time Of No Reply', 'They're Leaving Me Behind', 'River Man', 'Day Is Done', 'Saturday Sun', 'One Of These Things First', 'Poor Boy', 'Parasite', 'Hanging On A Star'. The name Orpheus, some say, sprang from the same dark root as 'orphan'.

Casting the Spell

Throughout Nick's songs, he seems to be reaching for a kind of salvation – as if, through music, he will find all he needs – love, happiness, fulfilment, and even a temporary escape from the ban on being free. He lets music take him to exotic places where the restraints of life are loosened. A friend, Colin Betts, recalls jamming with him 'in the Arabic style' after a trip to Morocco. These modal tunings have a mystical, exotic sound that springs from the ancient culture of the eastern Mediterranean. Nick poured it all into one song – 'Three Hours' – a trip to the East, a master in search of a slave, a floating melody sung over a rolling train-like drone of a guitar track, perfectly played even on bootlegged out-takes and home demos.

The very flawlessness of Nick's performances suggest that he invested something close to ritual significance in getting his guitar part exactly right. Like a shaman, he needed to perform the ceremony perfectly in order to get the result he was looking for. And if the result he sought was to draw people to him, to banish the fear of abandonment, to never again be left in the time of no reply, then he needed to connect, as Orpheus had done, compelling listeners to come to him.

Chords

Harmony, like rhythm, has a seemingly magical effect on listeners. It works its spell on the emotions, echoing and deepening feelings, pulling people into a world of sorrow or joy or a bittersweet combination of both. We experience the fatalism of 'Day Is Done' in the downward drift of the chords, a prayer-like pleading in the 'amen' chords of 'Way To Blue', and the yearning for rest in the constant return to the simple home chord (the tonic chord) in 'Place To Be.' Nick's ambivalent feelings for 'Hazey Jane I' are conveyed by rich clusters of notes that include both dissonance and warmth. We feel what he feels. This is the mysterious power of chords. But, as a guitar player, Nick had a problem – what if the chords you hear in your head are complex piano chords, ones that are nearly impossible to play on guitar? Nick had to come up with new tunings for the guitar that would allow him to easily play through those chords. It was a deliberate and difficult process that he began alone in a small, bare, antiseptic-white room in the south of France shortly after I met him. Within a very short time, it resulted in remarkable songs like 'Fruit Tree', 'Place To Be', and 'Hazey Jane I', songs whose chord progressions have more in common with the sophisticated cabaret tunes written on piano by his mother, Molly Drake, than the folk-inspired style of his contemporaries. (A comparison of the chords in Molly Drake's 'How Wild the Wind Blows' with the bridge in Nick's 'Fruit Tree' makes that clear.)

Only a handful of singer-songwriters used these complex chords in the pop and folk styles of the day. Even among them, Nick Drake stood out for the fluidity and emotionally expressive quality that he brought to this technique.

The Descent into Darkness

In the myth of Orpheus, the poet was driven to despair by the loss of his beloved Eurydice, his muse. On this level, the tale is a passionate story of a love so strong it challenges Death itself. But if we look beyond this mythic love story, we can read another tale, an allegory of the artist's desperate struggle to hold on to his creative spirit.

No one knows why some people are driven to create songs, paint pictures, make sculptures, write poetry, plays, novels. It's a profound need at the core of an artist's life. During the process of creation, there are great highs and lows, moments of joy, pride and intense excitement, and other moments of gnawing self-doubt and despair. The making of art requires energy, will, focus, time, determination and drive; it exacts a high price. Even when the artist isn't actually engaged in making art, it is giving shape and meaning to life.

What happens, then, when something severs the connection to this spiritually necessary and compelling activity? Orpheus was willing to go to hell and back, literally. He nearly succeeded in reuniting with his beloved but, at the last moment, failed. With hope and inspiration lost to him for ever, nothing could console him. I imagine him sitting in a darkened room, much as Nick did towards the end, in an overstuffed chair, endlessly, softly, fingering the strings of his lyre. Mute.

'Darkness', 'lamentation', 'separation' – these words are at the heart of the name Orpheus. This is the aspect that allies him with the Underworld and ultimately squares him with his tormented fate. It made him a favourite with poets like Baudelaire, Rimbaud, and Novalis. Orpheus is the patron saint of all night-loving, black-wearing artists who sing the praises of the dark, of rebellion and chaos. But being a true rebel means more than just wearing a T-shirt with a picture of James Dean or Kurt Cobain on it and, for the real poet-outsider, what starts as a pose may descend into something much more serious.

In his autobiographical study of depression, *Darkness Visible*, author William Styron singles out loss as the real engine of despair. Whether it's the early loss of a parent, or loss of creativity and inspiration, given the right combination of genetics, need and external triggers, it can lead to a vicious downward spiral – a true descent into the Underworld. Styron describes with careful detachment the sense of dread and alienation, anxiety and numbness that sapped his energy and wiped out any chance of writing.

For Nick Drake, depression's shadow appears early on. At first, it's a temporary chill. In the early lyric/poem 'Blue Season', he describes it as a 'mist at my window' and a 'heart full of shadow'. Still, it's something he expects will fade with time. Later on, it becomes a black-eyed dog – a single-minded beast that never grows tired and cannot be shaken off.

So much of Nick's music is cradled in darkness, he sometimes makes it feel like a second home: 'Safe in the womb / Of an everlasting night / You find the darkness can / Give the brightest light' ('Fruit Tree'). Or simply a natural conclusion: 'When the day is done / Down to earth then sinks the sun / Along with everything that was lost and won' ('Day Is Done'). It's a place for the worship of moons and the road that leads to the stars. Embracing darkness, though, is not the same as finding yourself shrouded in it, surrounded by it, cut off from light, life, and love. In Hades.

The songs on the *Pink Moon* album, and the five final, posthumously released songs, are the ones that trace Nick's own journey into the Underworld. The magic here is in the absolute intimacy of singer and listener – as if Nick Drake has finally succeeded in drawing the listener – no, compelling the listener to come to him. But it is just as he himself is turning away. 'Know I'm not there.'

He included some songs on *Pink Moon* that were written previously but he seems to have saved up for the final blow-out. The awful self-image of 'Parasite' and the paranoia of 'Things Behind The Sun' belong here and not on earlier albums. The regret in 'Place To Be' is palpable. And then there are the songs written on the downward spiral leading up to the album. 'Road' is a settling of accounts. It seems to say, 'I know we've had our disagreements but I finally accept you for who you are, and myself for who I am.' But in acceptance lies resignation, a sense that he will never achieve what he really set out to do. 'I can take a road that will see me through', not the road that leads to the stars as he had meant to. He sounds tired, ready to stop fighting. In 'Know', the artist finally disappears altogether.

For me, the most haunting (and haunted) song on

the album is 'Harvest Breed'. The title itself refers to birds that are bred to be hunted and killed, animals whose unavoidable fate is an early death. The rest of the imagery consists of flowers bending in a soft breeze and a kind of gentle freefall that suggests a dreamlike state. The Afro-Cuban rhythm of the guitar evokes a sensuous world that envelops and protects even as the dreamer falls to his death. There is a very real sense of mortality and the possibility that Nick envisions death as a welcome release rather than a frightening end – the only escape from the depths of unrelenting anguish.

'And now we rise . . .'

How to deal, then, with 'From The Morning' – that magical, mystical final song that clears the clouds away and lights up life like a beacon of gold? Here the poet-magician dissolves into nature, becoming one with it, expanding into something without boundaries, larger than himself. Like the tribal shamans of old, he has reached through the darkness and emerged on the other side where all things are One.

Who knows what triggered this release from the grip of depression. In *Darkness Visible*, Styron describes the moment that turned him away from the depths as occurring when he heard 'a sudden soaring passage from the Brahms Alto Rhapsody'. Nick's repeated listening to Bach's Brandenburg Concertos may have been his own form of self-medication. Whether it transported him back to happier times or raised his spirits with its chiselled beauty and arcing builds, we can't know. Something broke through the gloom long enough to allow him to write this exquisite, simple love song to life.

The Legacy of Orpheus

In the 1959 French/Brazilian film *Black Orpheus* (*Orfeu Noir*), a handsome guitar player convinces the local children that his songs make the sun rise. Shortly afterwards, he meets his Eurydice and their fate follows the familiar pattern of the myth. After his death, one of the children takes Orfeu's guitar up to a hilltop and plays as the sun rises. It's a moment that captures the genesis of a musical legacy.

In the original myth, Orpheus's lyre continues to play long after he is dead. So, too, the songs of Nick Drake continue to be played. And they live on in other ways; his distinctive melody and chord style laid a solid foundation on which today's singer-songwriters build new works. His musical legacy grows as his songs find their way to new generations, into new ears and hearts year after year, long after the youth with the golden lyre is gone.

All singer-songwriters share in the nature of Orpheus. Every songwriter and musician who has longed to create a magical effect – a change in mood or deepening of understanding within the listener – is stretching towards that mythical being whose music was so sweet, so powerful, so irresistible it could command nature itself. As the poet Rainer Maria Rilke wrote in *The Sonnets to Orpheus*: 'It's Orpheus whenever there's a song.'

Of course, Nick Drake never refers to himself as Orpheus. He doesn't need to. He slips easily into the mythic persona – the musician and poet whose gentle nature and compelling songs tame the wilderness, whose quest for hope and salvation through art takes him into the darkness of the Underworld. Over and over in Nick's songs, we hear him describe the world in terms even the ancient Greeks would have recognised as the voice of the Musician-Magician. He is the poet who speaks to the River Man, who seeks to understand the light among the trees, the one who holds emotion in the palm of his hand and knows we are all made to love magic. He is the singer who lives through his songs and speaks to his listeners whether he is present in this world or not.

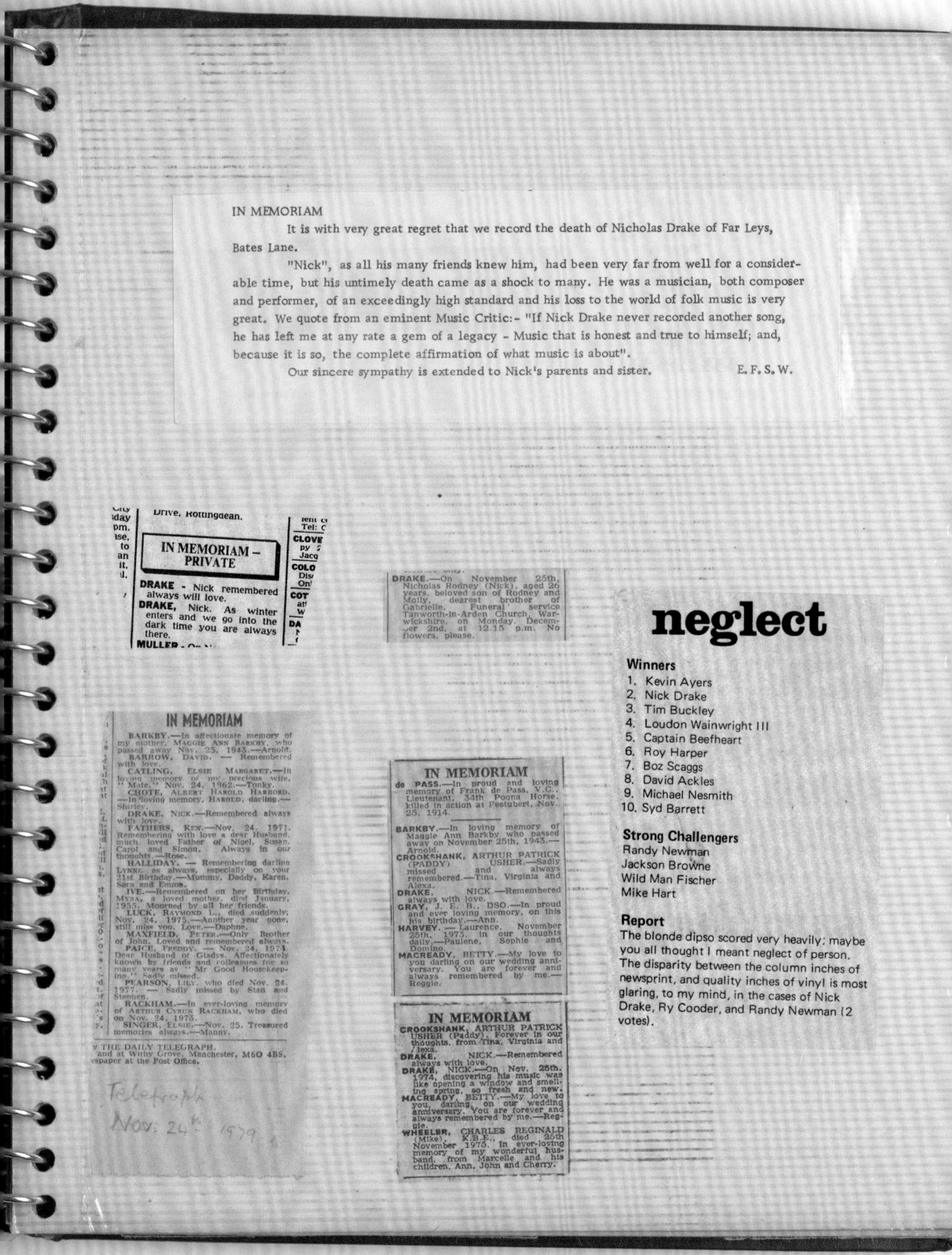

IN MEMORIAM

It is with very great regret that we record the death of Nicholas Drake of Far Leys, Bates Lane.

"Nick", as all his many friends knew him, had been very far from well for a considerable time, but his untimely death came as a shock to many. He was a musician, both composer and performer, of an exceedingly high standard and his loss to the world of folk music is very great. We quote from an eminent Music Critic:- "If Nick Drake never recorded another song, he has left me at any rate a gem of a legacy - Music that is honest and true to himself; and, because it is so, the complete affirmation of what music is about".

Our sincere sympathy is extended to Nick's parents and sister. E. F. S. W.

Drive, Rottingdean.

IN MEMORIAM – PRIVATE

DRAKE - Nick remembered always will love.

DRAKE, Nick. As winter enters and we go into the dark time you are always there.

MULLER - On N...

DRAKE.—On November 25th, Nicholas Rodney (Nick), aged 26 years, beloved son of Rodney and Molly, dearest brother of Gabrielle. Funeral service Tanworth-in-Arden Church, Warwickshire, on Monday, December 2nd, at 12.15 p.m. No flowers, please.

neglect

Winners

1. Kevin Ayers
2. Nick Drake
3. Tim Buckley
4. Loudon Wainwright III
5. Captain Beefheart
6. Roy Harper
7. Boz Scaggs
8. David Ackles
9. Michael Nesmith
10. Syd Barrett

Strong Challengers

Randy Newman
Jackson Browne
Wild Man Fischer
Mike Hart

Report

The blonde dipso scored very heavily; maybe you all thought I meant neglect of person. The disparity between the column inches of newsprint, and quality inches of vinyl is most glaring, to my mind, in the cases of Nick Drake, Ry Cooder, and Randy Newman (2 votes).

IN MEMORIAM

BARKBY.—In affectionate memory of my mother, MAGGIE ANN BARKBY, who passed away Nov. 25, 1943.—Arnold.

BARROW, DAVID. — Remembered with love.

CATLING, ELSIE MARGARET.—In loving memory of my precious wife, "Mate," Nov. 24, 1962.—Tonky.

CHOTE, ALBERT HAROLD HARBORD.—In loving memory, HAROLD, darling.—Shirley.

DRAKE, NICK.—Remembered always with love.

FATHERS, KEN.—Nov. 24, 1971. Remembering with love a dear Husband, much loved Father of Nigel, Susan, Carol and Simon. Always in our thoughts.—Rose.

HALLIDAY. — Remembering darling LYNNE as always, especially on your 21st Birthday.—Mummy, Daddy, Karen, Sara and Emma.

IVE.—Remembered on her Birthday, MYRA, a loved mother, died January, 1955. Mourned by all her friends.

LUCK, RAYMOND L., died suddenly, Nov. 24, 1975.—Another year gone, still miss you. Love.—Daphne.

MAXFIELD, PETER.—Only Brother of John. Loved and remembered always.

PAICE, FREDDY. — Nov. 24, 1973. Dear Husband of Gladys. Affectionately known by friends and colleagues for so many years as "Mr Good Housekeeping." Sadly missed.

PEARSON, LILY, who died Nov. 24, 1977. — Sadly missed by Stan and Stephen.

RACKHAM.—In ever-loving memory of ARTHUR CYRUS RACKHAM, who died on Nov. 24, 1975.

SINGER, ELSIE.—Nov. 25. Treasured memories always.—Manny.

...y THE DAILY TELEGRAPH, ...and at Withy Grove, Manchester, M60 4BS, ...wspaper at the Post Office.

Telegraph Nov: 24th 1979

IN MEMORIAM

de PASS.—In proud and loving memory of Frank de Pass, V.C., Lieutenant, 34th Poona Horse, killed in action at Festubert, Nov. 25, 1914.

BARKBY.—In loving memory of Maggie Ann Barkby who passed away on November 25th, 1943.—Arnold.

CROOKSHANK, ARTHUR PATRICK (PADDY) USHER.—Sadly missed and always remembered.—Tina, Virginia and Alexa.

DRAKE, NICK.—Remembered always with love.

GRAY, J. E. B., DSO.—In proud and ever loving memory, on this his birthday.—Ann.

HARVEY. — Laurence, November 25th, 1973. In our thoughts daily.—Paulene, Sophie and Domino.

MACREADY, BETTY.—My love to you darling on our wedding anniversary. You are forever and always remembered by me.—Reggie.

IN MEMORIAM

CROOKSHANK, ARTHUR PATRICK USHER (Paddy). Forever in our thoughts, from Tina, Virginia and Alexa.

DRAKE, NICK.—Remembered always with love.

DRAKE, NICK.—On Nov. 25th, 1974, discovering his music was like opening a window and smelling spring, so fresh and new.

MACREADY, BETTY.—My love to you, darling, on our wedding anniversary. You are forever and always remembered by me.—Reggie.

WHEELER, CHARLES REGINALD (Mike), K.B.E., died 25th November 1975. In ever-loving memory of my wonderful husband, from Marcelle and his children, Ann, John and Cherry.

Below right: *ZigZag*, September 1974

Time goes by from year to year,
And no one asks why I am standing here,
But I have my answer as I look to the sky
This is the time of no reply

Exiled from Heaven

by Ian MacDonald

Originally published in the millennium edition of Mojo

During the academic year of 1968–9, Cambridge University felt an alien influence from beyond its sober curtain walls. Solemn flagstones frowned up at kaftans, wooden beads and waist-length hair. Staid courtyards winced to the strains of *Beggars Banquet*, *The White Album*, *Big Pink* and Dr John the Night-tripper drifting through leaded windows. The stately air was fragrant with marijuana and no one seemed to be doing a stroke of work.

It was counterculture time, heady aftermath of the Year of the Barricades. In every half-hip college room, hirsute youths lolled in drug-liberated converse while fey girls curled worshipfully at their feet or came and went with mugs of scented tea. When the holy relics of the moment weren't revolving on the turntable, out came the acoustic guitars. It was all very cool and tasteful in a faintly post-Beat, elliptically knowing way. Dylan was God. A word out of sync and one's cred could be toast.

One spring afternoon in 1969, my room in King's happened to be where it was at. The door was open; people entered and left as they pleased. A dozen or so loafers were listening to the folk/jazz musicians among us when my friend Paul Wheeler put aside his guitar and introduced a fellow singer-songwriter sitting beside him: 'Nick.' After a few moments to check his tuning (or to let the intervening hubbub hush), this tall, elegant person – at whom all the women were now intently gazing – began to play, craned over his small-bodied Guild guitar and staring at the carpet, his long fingers moving unerringly across the fretboard while he sang low in a breathy beige voice: 'Time has told me . . . you're a rare find . . . a troubled cure . . . for a troubled mind . . . ' My eyes met those of another friend, a pianist with a jazz penchant. He silent-whistled: *What have we here?* 'Wow,' chorused the gathering at the end of the song, 'that was great, really nice', etc. Protocol was that those playing did a couple of numbers before giving way to someone else. Nick whoever-he-was finished another bout of tuning and began to play again. In 5/4. Not many folk guitarists play in 5/4. And he sang: 'Betty came by on her way . . . said she had a word to say . . . 'bout things today. . . and fallen leaves . . .'

Few present are likely to have forgotten that afternoon. When, six months later, *Five Leaves Left* appeared in its Lincoln green sleeve on the prestigious Island label, we were impressed, but not surprised. Nick Drake was 'class'. We all knew that.

And that's enough of the legend, the personal recollections. In the brief period I was at Cambridge at the same time as him, I exchanged barely twenty words with Nick Drake. Three or four years later, I seem to recall him visiting my flat in London with Paul Wheeler. In my memory, I told Nick, earnestly, that his latest album, *Pink Moon*, was a masterpiece; but while I certainly held that opinion, perhaps I imagine this scene. The chronology doesn't pan out. And the sad fact is we were all fairly constantly smashed in those days – into ourselves and our own things more than the outside world (or other people, especially 'difficult' ones). The Me Decade had succeeded the We Decade.

A year or so later, I heard that Nick Drake had died.

During the Eighties, I drifted away from the music scene. When I returned, I was surprised to find that Nick was becoming famous. Like most of those (make that *all* of those) who'd known him in whatever way, I'd got used to thinking of him as a private thing, an artist relegated to the exclusive periphery, one for the connoisseur. As time went by, I watched his fame grow. The ardour of those discovering him – young people, often born since his death in 1974 – was, I found, intense. When, in conversations, I mentioned that I'd known him, reactions were wide-eyed. 'You *knew* him? No shit! Did you see him walk on water?' Well, not that intense, but genuinely galvanised, urgently fascinated.

What are they transfixed by? Patrick Humphries, in his biography *Nick Drake* (1997), ponders this question at length in the company of a dozen or so people who knew the man far better than I, to the extent that anyone really knew that elusive soul at all. The myth, Patrick concludes, is powerful: the golden youth with the silver spoon who drifted into the dark, beyond the reach of the many who loved him, passing out of this life at the far end of a silent corridor he'd moved through during the last three years of his time among us. And more, of course: the small, death-limited body of often perfect work he left; the promise unfulfilled; the wan conjectures on what might have been. The mantle of romance shrouding Drake's story in retrospect is alluring, but its attraction wouldn't survive if the work didn't hold up: if fellow songwriters weren't so intrigued by the forms and changes, if fellow guitarists didn't puzzle admiringly over the unusual tunings and finger-picking techniques, if singers weren't drawn to the sighing melodies and cryptic lyrics. More crucially, new listeners, hearing this understated voice a quarter of a century later, love it for itself rather than for the aura of romantic doom which accompanies it like some unwanted orchestra dubbed on by sentimental hindsight. Nick Drake means something today. But what?

Nowadays we live in a loud, shiny, mechanised musical ethos of shallow excitement: glamour and clamour. On the one hand, titanic drum-sounds shudder the ground with the massive Metropolis robo-fours of club culture; on the other hand, post-Punk Indie-rockers scrub their guitars like crazed archaeologists grubbing for expression beneath the coarse signal distortion they're generating. It's not a subtle time. To listen to Nick Drake is to step out of this world of pose and noise, and enter a quiet oak-panelled room, dappled with sunlight – a room opening, through French windows, into a lush garden, quiet because we're in the country, far from the sound of the city. It's summer, bees and birds are abroad in the shade, and, beyond the nearby trees, a soft tangle of voices and convivial laughter can be felt, along with the dipping of languid oars in the rushy river winding through cool woods and teeming meadows hereabouts: an English landscape with Gallic ghosts from Le Grand Meaulnes and La maison de Claudine. And an acoustic guitar playing gently beyond the hedgerow in jazzy 5/4: 'River Man'.

Postmodern urban cynics will already be deconstructing this. A bourgeois fantasy of rural life that never existed; a dream, an evasion. Well, yes – up to a point. I've lived in the countryside for fifteen years and I can see what it 'really' is as I speed through it in my car. Certainly, it's as much a social construction as anything else is, or isn't. But after writing the previous paragraph, I went downstairs to make a cup of tea and, when I paused to look out of the window, the utilitarian landscape of interlocking lanes and fields and neatly pruned woodland which I normally see was suddenly deep, suddenly enveloping. I'm living in the country, I realised, as if briefly coming awake. And it's magical. Minutes after the kettle boiled, my ecstasy lapsed and the view had returned to normal. So was the experience real? It arose through contemplation summoned by writing 'poetically' about the outer world as inner experience. And the fact is that if we could live in that state all the time, that enveloping, magical view would be reality.

> I was made to love magic,
> All its wonder to know,
> But you all lost that magic,
> Many many years ago.

That's from 1968: an otherworldly Drake *chanson* called 'I Was Made To Love Magic'. And how very late Sixties. Magic! No room for that now, in the twenty-first century. Another religion-deriding article by Richard Dawkins, another dull reduction of love by an evolutionist: day by day, reality thins further into mere physical matter as that seemingly obsolete spirit-stuff evaporates. At the turn of the millennium, 'spirit' is being squeezed out of our materialist society. To say that 'it's not what you do, it's the way that you do it' is still acceptable, but to put it another way – to suggest that what matters is the spirit in which we live – would strike most of us as antiquatedly idealistic. The 'spirit'? A fantasy, a dream, an evasion. Yet the difference between the view seen normally and the view seen 'magically' is the spirit in which the seeing is done.

Penetrating the meaning of Nick Drake's work, beyond the instinctive attraction which so many continue to feel upon encountering it, starts from this apparently innocent proposition about magic and spirit. Beyond that, things soon get starker – and ultimately dark, as dark as it gets – but the corridor to the heart of Drake's vision is always lit by a mysterious light; and the pure luminosity of his work, the ultimate source of its attraction, emanates from its final redeeming revelation. If there's an artist of the last thirty years whose work speaks to us both directly and profoundly at this millennial transition, it's got to be Nick Drake. So, then: do you want to go deeper?

Drake's small opus – three albums (four, counting the posthumous collection *Time Of No Reply*) – is a slim claim to fame. But it's quality that counts, and this is obvious and timeless. The repeated refrain of those coming late to this music is that 'it could have been recorded yesterday'. More curious is that these songs speak to such diverse people. New Age idealists, dark-side nihilists, neo-Romantics, bedsit shoegazers, straights, gays, feminists, even the 'nothing matters, get loaded, enjoy the trip' faction – all tip their hats to an artist whose work touches them. Hailing Drake in 1992, The Swans' Michael Gira declared: 'I know people as diverse as metal/industrial merchants to classical/art-music collectors who speak his name with a respect reserved for only a handful of songwriters or composers.' Yet Drake's biographer Patrick Humphries is not alone in describing his output as 'frozen in immaturity'. How do such disparate views converge on the same work?

As presented by Humphries, Drake's friends are oddly uncertain of who he really was. Some, debunking the usual image of fragile translucence, stress his determination in advancing his career during 1968–9. They point to an image-conscious acuity in casting himself as the Sensitive Outsider, stress his featherlight irony and his ability, in his earlier days, to laugh his amusement out loud. Others allege a willingness to play up the mental dishevelment of his later years – to make winsome vagueness an excuse for unreliability, lack of commitment and living by his own private sense of time.

Through this demystification runs a persistent motif: judge the artist, not the art; defuse expression by treating it as a symptom. Of course, sometimes what seems like deep meaning is actually just flailing obscurity. Indeed, Drake's allusiveness is such a magnet for misinterpretation that some have asked whether any real significance exists beneath its beguiling surface. Investigating Drake after his death in 1974, Nick Kent conceded the evocative power of the songs, but thought their author 'confused'. Reviewing the 1994 anthology *Way To Blue*, Stuart Maconie put the same opinion more forcefully: 'Eulogies about Nick Drake often make romantic noises about his being "not of this world" and the like while ignoring the fact that he was mentally ill. To treat him as some super cultural sage rather than a gifted, sick, unhappy young man is both to cheapen his tragedy and undervalue his music.'

How 'ill' Drake was is anyone's guess. His father Rodney thought the shrinks who examined him were shooting in the dark. Brian Wells, a psychiatrist who knew Drake, doesn't believe he was 'biologically depressed' at all; rather that he was rationally, if hypersensitively, responding to outer events. Yet to stop washing and let one's finger nails grow like Howard Hughes is abnormal behaviour by any standard, especially for a guitarist. The fact that, by then (1972–3), Drake had done his best work shouldn't distract us from the evidence that, in the months after he recorded *Pink Moon*, he descended into a truly parlous state, whatever that state actually was. Distinguishing between deep introspection, sorrow, indifference and the spiralling serotonin-depletion of clinical depression remains, twenty-five years later, difficult even for experts. When, for example, Drake recorded his 'four last songs' in February 1974, some of his friends thought him much recovered; others thought not. To further complicate matters, there's an unconfirmed suggestion that, during his final years, he became a heroin user – which, if true, might account for facets of his behaviour till now taken to be diagnostic criteria for depression.

There's no reliable link between Drake's work and anything we know, or think we know, about his states of mind. What an observer sees as blank passivity may, to the person experiencing it, be a logical sequence of sane, if sombre, thoughts obscure to those not much given to reflection. Psychology textbooks admit that 'depressed' people are often more realistic than the well-adjusted. Many of the world's wisest minds have been retrospectively classed as unipolar (non-manic) depressives, including a striking number of poets. (See Kay Redfield Jamison's *Touched with Fire*, 1993.) All of which is to say that Drake's 'illness' and his creativity are not necessarily connected. Certainly, he'd become monosyllabically withdrawn long before serious unhappiness set in after *Pink Moon* in 1972, but we must recall that he was shy and introspective by nature. We should also bear in mind that he who curbs his tongue may see much that others miss.

Contrary to legend, Drake did laugh, and more than occasionally. School friends found him warm and amusing, yet understated enough for them to concede that they never knew the real Nick. Innate reticence kept him on the edge of any social event, as if always on the verge of leaving. 'You felt there was a very reflective, pensive mode to his psyche,' says one friend from Drake's days at Marlborough. 'While he joined in the fun and the laughter, he was always a little apart from the crowd.' At Cambridge, where peer-shock obliges newcomers to straighten up and study their cool, Drake's laughter was shared only with close friends; otherwise, his humour graduated to gentle irony. In 'Poor Boy' (from *Bryter Layter*) he mocks the idea of himself held by some who claimed to know him, deriding those who thought a wife would shake the 'self-indulgence' out of him ('He's a mess but he'll say yes / If you just dress in white'). A similar irony shades the line 'Pink, pink, pink, pink, pink ... pink moon', where Drake, always careful with tunings and their relationship to his vocal range, sings a descending line that takes him below his viable bottom note. If he hadn't meant this to be subtly wry, he'd have used a capo; the effect is intentionally graphic ('down we go ...') and, again, faintly mocking.

If one good reason not to get carried away with the 'romantic otherworldly sage' interpretation of Nick Drake is his understated irony, that's also a reason for giving him credit for knowing what he meant and saying it with intelligent consistency. As his friend and fellow singer-songwriter Robin Frederick observes (*Mojo* 63), Drake's lyrico-musical unity of expression was precise: words move organically with melody, harmony, rhythm and metre. Yet if he was dry enough to control his art so adroitly, he was more of an observer, and less of a victim, than many take him for. Despite the prejudices of our noisy society, to be solitary and contemplative is not in itself to be maladjusted. Far from immature, Drake's taste for solitude represents a deep scepticism about aspects of life which many take for granted. In truth, he's been more psychoanalysed than addressed on his own terms, his message obscured by misconceptions based on his image and outward behaviour.

The idea that a man as reserved and frightened of audiences as Nick Drake had such a thing as a 'message' to convey in his work verges on the counter-intuitive. This being so, it's important to see his later silence in perspective. Asked about him in 1979, Nick's mother Molly painted a picture of him at odds with the neurotic introvert of legend: 'I think he had this feeling that he'd got something to say to the people of his own generation. He desperately wanted to communicate with them, he had a feeling that he could make them happier, that he could make things better for them, and he didn't feel that he did that. He said to me once: "I have failed in everything I have tried to do." I said, oh Nick, how can you! And then I elaborated all the things that he had so patently done. It didn't make a difference. He *felt* this – that he'd failed to get through to the people that he wanted to talk to.'

Molly Drake's use of the word 'generation' may have been a misunderstanding. The 'generation gap' was never wider than in 1967–9. Parents then were challenged by their offspring, whose attitudes struck them as revolutionary rather than merely playfully rebellious. Mothers and fathers – particularly mothers – were disturbed by this and some tried earnestly to bridge the chasm before it was too late. No doubt Molly Drake was one such and, in her anxiety to maintain contact with Nick, she may have superimposed a 'generational' focus on what he himself saw in more universal terms. Whether she correctly understood him is, for now, less important than the fact that he confided such a concern *at all*. How are we to square the silent solitary of 1970–4 with the Nick Drake who impressed his parents with his wish to make the world a better, happier place? Was this wish unserious – a passing pretension put on to bolster his musical ambitions? The second question may be answered tersely: Drake, though mild, was not trivial. The rest depends on deducing what his message might have been.

While correcting the romantic myth of Nick Drake as a man of constant sorrows, Patrick Humphries' research, partly because incomplete, creates its own imbalance. That Drake could be genial company comes as no surprise to those who knew him, but it so undermines the stereotype that critics too easily conclude that he was either a happy man overtaken by depressive illness or a gifted adolescent whose cultivated sensitivity turned pathological. Neither idea is just. The unfashionable probability is that Drake was *different*, seeing things in a way normal people don't: an incarnation of the poetic temperament – a reflective mind endowed with unusual perceptions.

Having said that, it's crucial to recognise that Drake was not a poet and that it's misleading to treat his lyrics as verse, rather than as the verbal aspect of a creativity manifested through his music, his voice and his guitar. Because of this, we shouldn't expect, and be disappointed not to find, self-sufficient poetry abstractable from musical context. Some of Drake's lyrics are vague, awkward, even gauche, as if dreamed up and cast into a waiting musical form with little effort to refine them. Yet *the whole* is what matters in his work: the mood and movement of which the words are part. Often the aura of his songs is incantatory. A song like 'Way To Blue', with its plagal cadences, verges on plain-chant. At times it's as if Drake is half-asleep, daydreaming of something on the spiritual threshold of the material world. This being so, it's hardly surprising that he should cleave to the more mystical poets – Blake and Yeats, alike drawn to automatic writing – or that people new to his work often speak of its soothing, healing, timeless quality.

If Drake's lyrics can't be removed from this whole without risk to their meaning, they nevertheless work in a consistent way. Using one-syllable rhymes, his songs employ metaphors and images so rarely that when such things turn up, they seem incongruously artful (e.g., 'Autumn reached for her golden crown' in 'Time Of No Reply'). A dreamy boy, he switched to English in his last year at school, when he was allowed to spend a lot of time reading by himself. This late-awakened interest – together with the fact that his first love was music – would account for the lack of conventional word-play in his lyrics. Instead, he invokes a range of symbols and codes, almost all of which are drawn from nature: the seasons, the days of the week, and natural phenomena: sun, moon, stars, sea, rain, flowers, trees, leaves, sky, mist and fog. Allied to these are a set of recurring actions (falling, flying, showing, leaving) and some symbolic non-natural objects (clock, fence, floor).

Drake may have derived this haiku-like simplicity from books on the shelves of every hopeful young writer in the mid-Sixties: *The Penguin Book of Japanese Verse* and Basho's *The Narrow Road to the Deep North*. On the other hand, his symbols and codes form a harmonious system reminiscent of those of Blake and the seventeenth-century mystic Henry Vaughan. Temperamentally, Drake had more in common with Vaughan (e.g., the latter's 'They are all gone into the world of light!'); in practice, his affinity was with Blake, whom he studied at Cambridge. Larry Ayres, an American who came on a pilgrimage to Drake's home village of Tanworth-in-Arden in July 1980, mentioned his own love of Blake to Molly Drake, whereupon she produced her son's copy of the complete works (Erdman's edition) and told him that Nick had believed Blake to have been 'the only good British poet'. A number of parallels exist between Blake and Drake, not least that both worked in more than one medium. Doubtless the main fascination for Drake, though, was Blake's concern with awareness and its relationship with reality seen in the normal way and potentially seen in other ways according to one's quality of consciousness.

Quality of consciousness was the key motif of the counterculture's revolt against consumer materialism in the Sixties, running, for instance, through The Beatles' work from *Revolver* onwards and reaching a zenith with 'A Day In The Life'. The nub of the countercultural critique was that the 'plastic people' of 'straight' society were spiritually dead. New Leftists spoke of 'consciousness-raising' while hippies offered a programme of 'enlightenment' through oriental mysticism supplemented by mind-expanding drugs. In today's pleasure-seeking world, introspection holds no appeal and the Sixties' focus on innerness is ignored or derided as a cover for Nineties-style chemical hedonism. The truth was otherwise in 1965–9.

Nick Drake was no hippie, but one didn't need to wear flowers to concur with the counterculture, which any sensitive youngster of that time would have endorsed. Drake's 'generation gap' conversations show that he was one such, as does the fact that he often sang Dino Valenti's hippie anthem 'Get Together'. Paul Wheeler, whom he met at Cambridge in 1968, recalls that when *Easy Rider* was screened there in 1969, Nick left the cinema in mild shock, seemingly stunned by the film's conclusion. Wheeler didn't pursue this – it wasn't done to be explicit in those days – but he remembers other occasions on which his friend was shaken by things which clearly held significance for him. Drake's reaction to *Easy Rider*'s death-of-hippie message, with its pessimistic estimate of the chances of achieving inner freedom in a conformist world, confirms that he took the clash between 'straight' society and counterculture seriously. More significantly – though no causal link is necessarily to be inferred – it coincides with the first signs of his social withdrawal.

Sharing interests and values, Drake and Wheeler conversed in oblique exchanges, on principle never voicing the literal or the obvious. This allusive 'hip' style began in Forties bebop culture, whence it was picked up by figures like Jack Kerouac, Lord Buckley and Lenny Bruce, and later transmitted to Britain through Soho's jazz and R&B clubs, and the writings of the Beats. As a teenage habitué of the Marquee and the Flamingo, Drake had an early grounding in such *de rigueur* understatement, finding it congenial to his own reserve. The Beats, too, would have lured him, perhaps via their link with French existentialism, but more likely by their creed of self-realisation and advocacy of natural psychedelics. Indeed, he may have come to Blake partly through Ginsberg (who set Blake's 'songs' to music) and partly through a key book of the sixties, Penguin's 1963 dual edition of Aldous Huxley's *The Doors of Perception* and *Heaven and Hell* – accounts of the author's pioneering experiments with mescalin and LSD which alike borrow their titles from Blake.

Drake's interest in drugs is well documented but less well understood. Nowadays associated with pure pleasure, drugs meant something different in the Sixties, being often linked with the mysterious Eastern quest for 'enlightenment'. Taking a mind-expanding drug then bore little comparison with taking Ecstasy during the Second

Summer of Love of 1988. The goal of the counterculture's use of psychedelics was peaceful inner exploration, the very opposite of the 'shooming' communal body rush of Dance Culture. (According to the US Drug Enforcement Administration, the average Sixties LSD dose was five to ten times purer and more powerful than today's acid.) Drake, of course, smoked dope for fun like everyone else, but we'd be getting him very wrong if we supposed that, even at its most casual, his drug use did not involve a fascination with perception and reality – the countercultural focus on quality of consciousness.

Paul Wheeler recalls Nick describing a party at which someone showed him a blackberry, saying: 'Look, a bunch of grapes.' 'The amazing thing,' Drake laughed, 'was that there was *no question*: it *was* a bunch of grapes.' Told by and to anyone else, this might be shrugged off as a typical drug anecdote. Confided to a close friend in the late Sixties, it carries a different weight: an allusion to the contemporary interest in drugs and perception. To infer this would be less reliable if Drake hadn't been demonstrably absorbed in the way we perceive things and what they mean to us. As often as not, guitarists together will talk about guitars; Wheeler recalls that Drake never conversed in those terms. 'We used to talk about . . . well, phenomena. Nick would point at a tree, and it'd be like: "What d'you think of that?" It was very oblique, we never explicitly discussed it.' While naturally reluctant to be pinned down on events so long past, Wheeler confirms that Nick was intrigued by perception in relation to the intrinsic reality (the 'is-ness') of what we see. He's also sure that Drake 'had a thing' about trees.

References to trees recur throughout Drake's lyrics (except those for *Pink Moon*). He enjoyed the garden at his family home of Far Leys and there is reason to believe that the trees there may have assumed a special meaning for him. Similar meanings seem woven into the symbolism of his lyrics, especially early (unpublished) ones like 'Rain': 'Rain's the way you move now / Sun the way you seem / Leaves the way you wonder / Flowers the way you dream.' This suggestion of a personal system of 'correspondences' – reminiscent of French Symbolists like Rimbaud, Verlaine and Mallarmé, whose work Drake encountered on his visits to France during 1965–7 – seems at first too personal to be dependably decoded. Such lines clearly flow from a contemplative mind immersed in nature, but their almost deliberate imprecision might as easily be dismissed as teenage romantic indulgence as taken for anything more considered. Sensitive young people often have a horror of being understood for fear of losing their sense of uniqueness and, in the process, finding that they're not as 'deep' as they'd like to think. There's a suggestion of this in these lines, as well as a feyness Drake later rejected. (His father Rodney recalled him as scornfully self-critical, repudiating his early songs as 'childish and foolish'.) Yet there's also a sense, even in Drake's juvenilia, of an outlook too individual and developed to be set aside as mere adolescent musing. More crucially, the same outlook appears, in more austere and experienced form, in his later work.

Rain, in fact, is an abiding Drakeian symbol (probably the most obsessive of all), occurring in his work from his earliest pieces to the last song in his published canon, 'Voice From The Mountain' (recorded in 1974, but possibly written as early as 1969). What, then, did rain, trees and the rest of his range of symbols mean to Nick Drake? Answering these questions depends on deducing his outlook from his life and work.

According to his sister Gabrielle, Nick had an idyllic childhood. The son of wealthy parents, he grew up quietly in the heart of England's countryside during the peaceful Fifties. Like his parents, he was musical, and, as a child, he would have heard his mother play her elegant, bittersweet songs, couched in the West End styles of Noël Coward, Sandy Wilson and Julian Slade. Nick soon found his way on to the piano stool and began making up his own infant ditties. Later, we may picture him in the garden, listening to the sounds from the family gramophone: the lucid counterpoint of Bach (reflected in Molly Drake's compositions and bequeathed in the patterns of his own music); the pastoralism of Delius and Vaughan Williams; the Gallic magic, perhaps, of Ravel's diaphanous collaboration with Colette, *L'Enfant et les sortilèges*, with its exquisite transition from house to garden ('Ah! Quelle joie de te retrouver, Jardin!'); and, for contrast, the gloomy north-facing realm of Sibelius's saga music.

Living in the country confers heightened sensitivity to the procession of the seasons, and all four feature, schematically, in Drake's lyrics. Summer, in particular, figures centrally in the early work of his late teens – the heart of the youthful idyll, as it is in the memory of most people fortunate enough to have had happy childhoods. In Drake's case, though, awareness of autumn, when the leaves die, was rarely far behind, together with a fateful anticipation of loss and sorrow unusually poignant for a youth of seventeen. The contrast between the diffidently smiling, drily chuckling young man of Cambridge in 1968–9 and the deep-seated sadness of *Five Leaves Left* presents the enigma of Nick Drake at its most acute. Again the question arises: who *was* he?

His father Rodney confirmed that his son 'thought deeply about things' and was 'depressed about the world'. As such, some of his sadness may have stemmed from a little-remembered yet formative aspect of the Sixties: the shadow of The Bomb. Behind the fun, colour and seemingly endless sunshine of that era lay an awareness that we were always four minutes from nuclear annihilation. Since Drake is known to have been impressed by Dylan's macabre monument to the Cuban Missile Crisis, 'A Hard Rain's A-Gonna Fall', fear of global catastrophe may have been one source of his angst; indeed, Rodney Drake recalled that 'Nick always thought 1980 was going to be the time'. (David Bowie and Marvin Gaye each harboured nearly identical presentiments.) It would be false, though, to deduce that this was the sole extent of Drake's sadness. For one thing, his work makes no reference to such a fear (although some claim to detect it in the song 'Pink Moon').

The sadness of *Five Leaves Left* points to something more intense and existential than simple anxiety about The Bomb. Apart from its permeating melancholy, the album's preoccupations are with time and natural phenomena. Superficially, these may seem to be standard themes of adolescence, but taken as a whole with the music (and with Drake's extraordinary vocal and instrumental performances), something more profound is apparent: something mesmerising and almost subliminal. People now discovering Drake speak of approaching what they take to be yet another Sixties singer-songwriter, only to meet something much deeper than they'd expected. Indeed, the strongest rebuttal to the claim that Drake's appeal resides solely in the morbid aura which death-romantics project on him is that his work displays a power beyond our preconceptions; if anything, it projects into us, rather than the other way around.

Part of the mesmerising quality of *Five Leaves Left* derives from Drake's vocal technique: a low, close, sustained sound, rich in chest vibration yet entirely without glamorous vibrato. It's the sound of incantation: slow, deep, OM-like. His phrasing is riverine, flowing across metre and through bar lines as though detached from normal time. It's as if he's seeking to impress upon us the sense of another way of being. Meanwhile, the guitar part proceeds with eerie perfection, every passing note picked out in precise place by a technique at times entailing the entire right hand. So striking is the independence of voice and instrument in Nick Drake's performances that expert American guitarists coming late to his records have often found it hard to believe that he didn't record the two separately: guitar first, voice afterwards. The mutual detachment of these elements is arresting – especially in the context of his later strange behaviour – but the *timeless* aspect of Drake's vocal delivery is the key.

Almost every photograph of Nick Drake (appropriately, there's no action footage of him) presents him as observing or ruminative. Most portraits on singer-songwriter albums are similar, yet the stills of Drake are especially rapt and thoughtful. He posed himself in these ways, so conscious decision played a part; however, suggestions that this was all mere image-manufacture miss the fact that he genuinely was unusually introspective. Other young bards cultivated the contemplative image; Drake was the real thing – so much so that he worried about it. An early song, 'Blue Season', reflects on his sense of being just a little too different: 'Everything's wrong and you know you're to blame / Nothing will change while you're still the same.' A similar disquiet is heard in 'At The Chime Of A City Clock' from *Bryter Layter*: 'A city star / Won't shine too far / On account of the way you are.' In another early song, 'Leaving Me Behind', the world 'hums on at its breakneck pace' as 'people fly in their lifelong race', rushing into a future he fears he'll never catch up with. That his peculiar sensitivity was at times a burden is ruefully implied by another *Bryter Layter* song, 'One Of These Things First'.

Rodney Drake spoke of his son's early bent for solitude, acknowledging that Nick often seemed to slip off into a world of his own. It's hard to avoid concluding that a personality still and quiet enough to sit for hours, gazing into the distance or poring over his guitar, was not only fundamentally detached from life from the outset, but also in some way absorbed in his own senses, as if perceiving the world in a different way from the rest of us. If this was so, it raises the further possibility that he wasn't fully aware of how far his way of seeing things was from the norm, and of how much his view consequently required 'translation' – that when he spoke of trees or flowers, the meaning they had for him was not necessarily akin to the meaning (if any) they held for other people. This would explain his very plain use of such symbols, unassisted by explanatory similes or metaphorical cues. It also suggests he may have imagined he was more commercial and communicative in his work than he actually was; hence his bewilderment at his failure to sell records.

The impressionistic tinge in Drake's early unpublished lyrics conveys an almost inert immersion in experience: 'Drifting in lights of the fairground / Floating away on the breeze / Dazzled by scenes of a merry-go-round' ('Mickey's Tune'); 'When Joey first came, the light seemed to rise / Though it came in the night and left with her eyes . . . / As I sit in her city in fog and in steam / Everything's blurred, for blurred is my dream' ('Joey In Mind'). The effect is of a vaporous, time-forgetting absorption in the appearance of things – as if, in gazing at leaves rustling in a tree, Drake might have seen them in slow motion, a shade uncanny and perhaps preternaturally beautiful. Such sensitive 'slow vision' would account for much about his work, in particular the songs on *Five Leaves Left*; yet, while it may always have been there for him to explore, the youthful vagueness of his early work was gone by 1968. For we must remember that Nick Drake was not a passive receptor in thrall to sensory and emotional input but, on the contrary, careful and considerate as a human being and an artist. What he saw and experienced, and what he concluded about this, he strove to shape into forms of expression which, by touching people, would 'make them happier, make things better for them'. At the same time, his peculiar sensitivity may have misled him as to the extent of the communication gap he had to bridge in order to accomplish this. It certainly cost him dear in other ways.

Contemplative solitude breeds reflections on existence; the more so if accompanied by an unusual sense of detachment from the world. The mood and meaning of Nick Drake's songs from *c.* 1966 to 1969 suggest that he was able, perhaps at will, to drift into a mild form of heightened perception – a 'sensitive' quality of sight in which, under conducive circumstances (rural scenes), things took on a depth or translucence which he found evocative of transcendence. This would account for his partiality for silent withdrawal even as a child, as well as his later attraction to the writings of Blake and Yeats. Of course, compared to Blake's visions of angels, Drake's 'sensitivity' would have been small beer. Yet it's a short step from contemplating the 'is-ness' of phenomena to pondering their *meaning*: to wondering why they're there. The ultimate philosophical question – Why is there anything at all? – had clearly stolen up on Drake by the time he came to write his early unpublished songs, which turn obsessively on the slow cycle of the year, with its springtime 'gain' of leaves and flowers, the convivial warmth of the summer, the loss and sorrow of autumn and the dark, deathly emptiness of winter. While 'well-adjusted' people accept all this as the given elements of life, Drake was plainly uneasy about the way the seasons symbolise the recurrent suffering intrinsic to being alive – what the Christian writer C. S. Lewis called 'the problem of pain'.

'One would like to wonder the reason / What's the point of a year or a season?' This, the chorus of an early song called 'Bird Flew By', would strike most boys of Drake's age (then seventeen to eighteen) as mawkish – understandably so, for few people ever have such thoughts. Without feeling the turmoil induced by wondering why things exist, let alone empathising with the suffering which existence involves, it's nigh on impossible to comprehend what Drake is saying. Even so, such issues have dogged history's greatest minds; indeed, 'depression' and the ultimate questions of existence are often interwoven. That the teenage Drake not only thought about such things but felt deeply about them is painfully clear from other lines in 'Bird Flew By': 'Your life flies away / As the night turns to day / If you start once to think / Your hair will soon turn grey . . . / The wind and the rain / Shook hands again / Untouched by the world / They managed to stay sane . . .' Here is a sensibility already racked by anxiety, long before the descent into darkness which began at the appallingly early age of twenty-two.

Viewing the world as a beautiful but painful enigma, Drake had a choice: seal himself off and numb his feelings by artificial means (or deliberate self-centredness) – or find solace with others, empathising with their woes and trials, and seeking love. Idealistic, he had no hesitation. Rodney Drake recalled that his son's detachment didn't preclude intense sympathy with what he saw: 'His heart often carried him away. He carried other people's troubles and worries on his shoulders, and was always terribly depressed when something happened to somebody he knew. He was always the one that friends would come to with their worries. He rarely spoke of himself . . .' Paul Wheeler concurs: 'If there's one word for Nick that everyone who knew him would pick, it'd be "kind". I'd say kindness was his outstanding quality as a person.'

Sensitive to falsity, Drake was careful whom he trusted and adapted himself to the expectations of those he felt obliged to assist. This took its toll, as another verse of 'Bird Flew By' ruefully testifies: 'The list of false starts and crumbled, broken hearts / Comes from a need to play so many parts.' Yet he was not a perpetually tragic figure. His presence was warm enough to have left him with no known enemies – on the contrary, with a long roster of men and women who loved him and agonised over their inability to penetrate his growing sadness. More than this, he set out on his creative path in good heart and with paradoxically self-effacing resolve, working at his craft and even discreetly networking in London to advance himself. (No one knows how he got on to the bill at the Roundhouse in February 1968 where Ashley Hutchings saw him, afterwards alerting Witchseason producer Joe Boyd.) Nor was he precious in his tastes, which embraced everything from jazz, folk, classical and pure pop to some of the raunchiest stuff on the club circuit. (I can personally confirm that it was possible, like Drake, to mix a yen for bookish solitude with a hankering for the filthy R&B of Graham Bond's *The Sound of '65*. I'd also like to take this opportunity to point out the similarity of the verse chords of 'At The Chime Of A City Clock', on *Bryter Layter*, to those of Cream's arrangement of Skip James's 'I'm So Glad', not to mention 'Deserted Cities of the Heart' on *Wheels of Fire*.)

Drake did live in the same world as everyone else and, to a fair extent, enjoyed it. On the other hand, most of his social engagement was through music which, being his only certain pleasure, became first a form of escapism and finally the only thing that made life tolerable for him. (He's known to have had a long-term girlfriend and other partners are rumoured; the most compromising blank in Patrick Humphries' biography is its lack of testimony from the women its hero was close to.) Yet, behind his smile, Drake was far from confident in the world. To his sister Gabrielle, he seemed to have had one less layer of emotional insulation than other people. Observing him around 1970, Witchseason's PR Anthea Joseph saw something more acute: 'I felt he was really terrified of the human race. Everything was a nightmare. He really was frightened.' If this outright fear was a late development, its roots can be traced back to Drake's early unpublished songs when his worldview was to a large extent already formed. Among fans, one of the most discussed parts of Drake's legacy is 'the monologue' – a muffled soliloquy taped at home in Far Leys in a tipsy state after a party sometime in 1966–7. Apparently addressing someone else (possibly a girlfriend to whom he meant to send the tape), Drake wavers between self-deprecating irony and genuine self-disclosure, speaking in soft and rapid upper-middle-class tones of how easy it is to forget 'the lies, the truth, and the pain'. It's a young man's voice and a faintly stagey one, like a confessional character in a scene by Terence Rattigan. (This accent had modulated into something less class-defined by the time he reached Cambridge.) Amid some consciously absurd murmuring about 'the essence of the romantic', there's much dry humour, as well as a curiously detached attitude to happiness, which he clearly sees as essentially transient and as such to be distrusted.

The same ambivalent attitude to happiness appears in a letter which Drake, at nineteen, wrote to his sister Gabrielle from Cambridge: 'It may surprise you to hear that during the last few weeks I've been extraordinarily happy with life and I haven't a clue why . . . I think I've thrown off one or two rather useless and restrictive complexes that I picked up before coming here.' This brief insight into his inner progress (for which, characteristically, he immediately apologises) confirms the impression of someone looking at human behaviour, including his own, with an almost alien detachment.

Not to beat about the bush, these traits – scepticism about the phenomenal world, compassion for others, awareness of falsity and of the ephemerality of happiness – are the hallmarks of Buddhism. (In fact, they're also the hallmarks of most of the world's mystical systems, but of none more classically than Buddhism.) After 1967–8, Western spirituality turned decisively eastwards, especially towards India, bringing with it the New Age fascination with gurus and systems of personal development which flowered in the Seventies. The solitary Sixties precursor of this was Buddhism, as embraced by the American Beats and introduced to Westerners by two Englishmen, Alan Watts and Christmas Humphreys. In the early sixties, anyone in the gathering counterculture with a spiritual interest that ran deeper than a flip through the *Bhagavad Gita* would have turned to Buddhism or its 'hip' Chinese–Japanese variant, Zen. David Bowie, for instance, became so serious about Buddhism in the mid-Sixties that he nearly went to Tibet to become a monk.

The sparse shelf of books in Drake's room at Far Leys included one on Buddhism. The title is unknown – if he was like Bowie, it would have been Humphreys' *Buddhism* (1951, 1963); if not, then probably Watts's *The Way of Zen* (1958). All that matters is that Drake, who retained very few possessions, kept such a book. Bowie's interest in Buddhism probably sprang from his sharp sense of personal unreality – from the 'masks' which, as early as the mid-Sixties, he was toying with in an attempt to discover his true self. By contrast, Drake's interest in Buddhism almost certainly stemmed from his special way of seeing things: from his contemplative detachment and the profound philosophical unease this induced. Another of Alan Watts's books is *The Wisdom of Insecurity*. It's not hard to picture Drake identifying with this concept.

Buddhism contends that life is suffering. The cause of this suffering is beguiling transience (Bowie: 'the stream of warm impermanence'). Happiness, says Buddha, is an illusion; not that it doesn't exist but that, like everything else, it doesn't last and thus, being fugitive, is itself a source of suffering. The key to Buddhism is reincarnation: no matter how happy we are, if we fail to grasp the ephemeral quality of things, we'll be reborn into further lives in which happiness is rarer. Nothing lasts but the Self, yet this is the key to redemption – for while, as heedless creatures, we're bound to the Wheel of Becoming and doomed to rebirth and more suffering, if we can 'realise' the Self our outlook will transform, freeing us from the Wheel and letting us merge ecstatically with the Whole: the ground and source of love behind the scheme of appearances.

The pantheistic aspect of Buddhism – the idea that everything is both illusory and holy – parallels Blake's sense of a way of seeing in which all things become divine: 'If the doors of perception were cleansed, everything would appear as it is, infinite.' This is the focus of his poem *Auguries of Innocence*, from which comes the title of the 1985 Drake anthology *Heaven in a Wild Flower*. Here Blake proclaims that everything is sacred and hence profoundly consequential, urging a universal compassion shared by Buddhism. 'Innocence', in Blake's sense, is a state as yet unclouded by experience of the material world. It's the outlook of the child's soul, fresh from heaven and still on the threshold of life. Buddhism, like other mystical paths, seeks to recover this innocent way of perceiving by stilling 'the mind', a tool or faculty we acquire through experience but which comes to dominate our perceptions, among other things subtly creating our sense of time. Time, say the mystics, mysteriously, is the illusion of all illusions.

Nick Drake wasn't a literal disciple of Blake or Buddha. There are no clear Blake references in his lyrics, nor is he likely to have treated Buddhism as more than a confirmation of concepts he'd arrived at through his own experience. Nevertheless Blake's mystical vision and the tenets of Buddhism illuminate a great deal of his work. Drake's outlook seems to have boiled down to the linked recognitions that life is a predicament and that the world is ultimately an irreducible mystery. Why it exists, why we exist in it, *why there is anything at all*, we haven't the slightest idea. From this sense of predicament and mystery flows all his work, and also his message to us. More than that, the same influences shaped the growth and decline of his life.

The centrepiece of Drake's early period, both artistically and in terms of his personal outlook, is one of the sky-high classics of post-war English popular music: 'River Man'. A fatalistic cameo of calm perfection, 'River Man' presents itself in jazz-swung 5/4 (presumably developed from Brubeck's 'Take 5', which shares its late melodic entry on the fourth beat of the bar). Beginning with a deceptively simple C major pattern (Paul Wheeler: 'get a guitarist to explain to you what's happening, and he won't be able to'), the music shifts into chilly C minor for the first line before circling through two unclassifiable flat chords – made provisional by suspensions and anticipations, and turned into momentary clusters by the motion of the melody – thence returning to C major . . . only to shiver again into the shadows of C minor for the next verse. There's no harmonic resolution and, while the central lines for strings descend over the basic sway between C minor and C major, the cycle is implicitly endless, the track fading in discreet dissonance. Contemplatively still at the heart of this, Drake's cool breathy voice rolls and flows like whispered honey around the perfect steadiness of the rhythm – a passionless detachment natural to him, but so fluidly elusive that some wonder if he recorded the guitar first and added his voice afterwards. He didn't. He did it exactly the same way in my room at King's in 1969. (The version of 'River Man' on *Five Leaves Left* is a live take with strings arranged and conducted by Harry Robinson – though not, as often stated, in the style of Ravel, but instead in the manner of Drake/Robinson.)

The perpetual cycle of 'River Man' is echoed, in other forms, throughout Drake's work. Where his songs have harmonic releases, they almost always return to some cyclical pattern, even if this is merely a finger-picking figure. The sense of things, as Yeats wrote, 'turning and turning', is ubiquitous in Drake's songs, deriving chiefly from his country-bred sensitivity to the circle of the seasons (cf. his early song 'Blue Season' and Yeats's 'The Wheel'), but also reflecting the Buddhist Wheel of Becoming and the associated concept of the Law of Karma (cause and effect) which keeps the Wheel revolving. As such, the lyric holds three of Drake's key words: time, rain, summer.

Summer is Drake's symbol of Blakeian innocence – an idyll of heaven on earth prior to meeting the world of experience. Melancholic with autumnal anticipations of loss, *Five Leaves Left* is nonetheless a summer album, that season's languor ensouling the lyrics and the bee-buzzing hum of Drake's vocal phrasing. Summer for him meant a slumberous miscellany of 'summer sea-dream haze' ('Strange Meeting II'), 'people laughing, smiling with the sun' ('Blossom'), 'midsummer nightsongs' ('Mickey's Tune'), and 'endless summer nights' ('From The Morning'). Almost predictably, he included Gershwin's 'Summertime' in his teenage repertoire, and for similar deep-set reasons, as we'll see. However, the classic Drakeian homage to summer, as both life-memory and poetic metaphor for heaven on earth, is 'River Man'.

Once its karmically wheeling chord sequence is perceived, the lyric of 'River Man' becomes clear. The River Man is the Demiurge, the lesser god who is the mysterious proprietor of this mysterious world. The river is the realm of material life wherein the senses wander and the mind gets lost in the flow of time and thought. Time, say the mystics, is the mind's self-created prison. In reality, there is only *now* . . . forever. If we can just *be here now* – mindlessly present, which is very difficult and the goal of all methods of meditation – our Blakeian 'mind forg'd manacles' will drop off, leaving us free of attachment and beholding reality as it truly is: infinite, holy and illuminated. Some sensitive people – poets and such – are said by Buddhist mystics to experience occasional spontaneous glimpses of this state of 'enlightenment' (called, in Zen, *satori*). To judge from the outlook conveyed in 'River Man', Drake was one of them.

Few enjoy glimpses of *satori*. Some, though, deduce, through contemplation or suffering, that the cause of all sorrow is the unenlightened mind. They're then faced with the question of what to do with that intuition. Will they gamble on it – leave temporal life, as the Buddha did, and search for the Self without any guarantee that they'll find it? Or will they cash in their gains and go back to the life they're familiar with – the life of time, the mind and the material world – even though they know that it creates suffering? Betty, the heroine of 'River Man', is that sort of person. Her name signifies the wager. Will she (to put the spiritual spin on Leary's psychedelic exhortation) turn on, tune in, and drop out? Or will the uncertainty frighten her?

The river of material existence rolls on; only detachment shows us the process in motion. Naturally detached, Drake lived on the river bank, observing ('If he tells me all he knows / About the way his river flows / I don't suppose / It's meant for me'). Betty is on the verge of leaving the everyday river life for the life of detachment, but this is a rather stark – not to say lonely – proposition. She's aware of transience and suffering ('Said she had a word to say / About things today / And falling leaves'), but she doesn't know how to live beyond the incessant current of habit, with its clock-driven rat-race fight to win security ('Hadn't had the time to choose / A way to lose') – although she suspects there must be something better ('But she believes'). To leave the river, Betty must transcend her mind, with its enslaved attachment to time; yet the discomfort of her immediate dilemma is too much for her and she returns to the river's lulling flow: 'Calling for her mind again / She lost the pain / And stayed for more.' Here, string dissonances fret in cross-rhythm before relapsing back into sustained chords: Betty torn between lives, crying, running back to the world. 'Oh, how they come and go,' sighs Drake, watching her recede. 'Oh, how they come and go,' he repeats, cadencing fatalistically from his wider perspective – lives appearing like bubbles in the flowing river of time, travelling for a while and then vanishing.

The final lines of 'River Man' – recalling the refrain of 'Eleanor Rigby' ('Ah, look at all the lonely people') – suggest that Drake believed in reincarnation, and bolster the case for an underlying Buddhistic outlook. The same belief seems to be indicated in 'Saturday Sun' ('People in their season and time / Returning again and again / And again / And again') and in a variant of the last chorus of 'Magic', preserved on a handwritten sheet: 'You all lost that magic / Many many deaths ago.'

In 'River Man', the gap which Drake sees between his outlook and that of others offers an unsuspected insight into his later 'illness'. It also shows the clarity of his vision, which verges on the Gnostic. It's possible he'd read David Lindsay's awesome 1920 fantasy *A Voyage to Arcturus*, reissued to intrigued reviews in 1963. (The novel features a generative river which materialises the phenomenal world. The River Man and Lindsay's Demiurge, Crystalman, are aspects of the same idea, while E. H. Visiak's preface to the 1963 edition of *Arcturus* points out the book's 'Blakeian nomenclature' and 'Buddhistic teleology'.) It goes without saying that the counterculture was based on opposition to 'straight' society, seeking, ever so ironically, to steal its children by showing them the free, self-directed way one could live outside the mainstream. Yet Drake's rejection of the 'river' of everyday material life runs deeper: no easy hippie hedonism for him. He liked his music and was probably fonder of sex than has been suggested so far, but otherwise he held aloof from worldly attachment even as a boy.

Recalling that conventional social attainments meant nothing to Nick, his father Rodney admitted that 'there was something else going on in his mind all the time'. Molly Drake detected in her son no desire for stardom and no interest in money or clothes: 'He wanted to be totally without material possessions at all, I think.' Larry Ayres's impression of Drake's study room at Far Leys was of 'monk-like' bareness.

So, is 'River Man' a Buddhist song? No. It's a late Sixties song which reflects the countercultural concern with perception and enlightenment, but through a personal lens, compounded of elements of Drake's literary interests and his own contemplative gift. The almost militant joy of the counterculture is as absent from 'River Man' as it is from The Beatles' 'A Day In The Life' – nor is the comparison invidious. Both are tragic-transcendent songs of exceptional quality and startling originality, bridging the personal and the universal as only the best art can. But whereas 'A Day In The Life' rises above sorrow with its massive final chord, 'River Man' is ultimately a sad song.

The summer rain that draws Betty back to the river is Drake's most subtle (and Buddhistic) symbol. 'Rain's the way you move now,' he sings in his eponymous song. Rain, then, is transformation: the power that produces growth and change, setting things in motion. But by creating the impermanence which is the source of all suffering, rain is essentially tragic. Without a sense of permanent value in life, we're adrift: 'Countries and people caught in the rain / When will they learn to feel fine again / Wandering lost now for nothing is clear / Waiting for signs of the turn of the year' ('Blue Season'). Buddhism seeks permanence in the realised Self: the state of enlightenment. Christianity seeks permanence in God, representing it to the eye with the church steeple and to the ear by the chime of bells. Pre-Christians found symbols of divine permanence in rocks and mountains, but also in trees, which live so slowly that they seem almost immune to time, living emblems of contemplation. Nearly all of these symbols of permanence, stillness and peace appear in Drake's songs.

Trees seem especially to have fascinated him. He may have identified with – at times even imaginatively merged with – their dreaming, unworldly detachment. (In 'Northern Sky', on *Bryter Layter*, he sings of 'feel[ing] sweet breezes in the top of a tree', which suggests empathic projection into the object of his gaze; in 'Poor Boy', from the same album, he chides the mundane world for lacking such imagination: 'Nobody's eyes / Make the skies / Nobody spreads / Their aching heads.' What kinds of being spread their 'heads'? Again: trees.) Unfortunately, his own natural mysticism wasn't enough to sustain him. It must have been easier, and in the short term more rewarding, to explore drugs. If one wants magical realities, LSD will do the trick; if one wishes to feel like a rock or a mountain, immune to time and pain, heroin will oblige. But the costs to mind and body are heavy. Perhaps bankrupting.

Drake started smoking dope in 1966, around the time he stayed in London with his sister Gabrielle. A sensibility as impressionable as his would have been enthralled by the altered states which drugs create. No doubt he expected an imminent revelation, and he may have experienced just such a thing at Aix-en-Provence near Marseilles in January–March 1967. Friends say he suddenly became markedly more absorbed in his music, practising intently and spending hours tuning his guitar to unorthodox open chords. The scene in Aix was stimulating in itself – a hippieish array of like-minded souls, including nineteen-year-old American singer-songwriter Robin Frederick, with whom Drake played songs and whose 'Been Smokin' Too Long' he immediately took into his repertoire. But drugs were the secret of Drake's new intensity. Frederick recalls that the local hash was cheap and very strong; what's more, there was enough of it around to allow for casual indulgence: 'We used to eat it, which really knocked you down. I remember seeing *Jules et Jim* that way – eating hash at the start of the movie, then trying to stand up at the end and leave. Didn't get very far before I had to sit down. Watched the whole movie again and it was completely different.'

Looking back on the dope days and doomy folk-blues of her youth, Robin Frederick sees the Aix period as formative for Drake. She believes, and I agree with her, that 'Saturday', as used in his lyrics, is his code for Aix and for his experiences there. Closing *Five Leaves Left*, 'Saturday Sun' reflects wistfully on a time that combined the idyllic with the revelatory: 'Saturday sun came early one morning / In a sky so clear and blue / Saturday sun came without warning / So no one knew what to do.' Drake's early song 'Joey In Mind' refers to 'Saturday's gain', suggesting a significant advance of some kind, and concludes with the cryptic couplet 'Together we'll sit in the Saturday rain / And dream of Joey or Mary Jane'. Mary Jane (Sixties slang for marijuana) was probably the young Robin Frederick; Joey is one of two women: either a local girlfriend, mentioned in private by Molly Drake (in which case, the city of 'fog and steam' may have been Birmingham), or Jo D'A***, who was also present in Aix.

For Drake, 'blue' (as in the sky 'so clear and blue' in 'Saturday Sun') was a quite specific state of mind, possibly with Buddhistic resonances. Christmas Humphreys describes the dawning of Karuna, or compassion (called, in Buddhism, 'the law of laws'), in these words: 'Some there are whose lives are sufficiently unhappy, or who have sufficiently withdrawn themselves from the appearance of happiness in their own or in their neighbours' lives to be able to hear, in the stillness of the night or above the turmoil of the day, the ceaseless cry of anguish which rises from a blindly groping, sorrow-laden world.' In his early song 'Blue Season', Drake sees winter as a period in which the tragic aspect of existence is laid bare: 'Blue season / Won't you turn your wheel / Hide your heart of steel / Blue season, turn away.' In the hymnic 'Way To Blue', written after the Aix interlude (perhaps during the winter of 1967–8), 'blue' becomes a religious symbol for this state of lamentation and compassion.

Though couched in calm baroque cadences, the sad loneliness of 'Way To Blue' is intense. Yet, despite its sorrow, there's a sense of assurance in this song – assurance that its melancholy perceptions are correct. Probably this derived from a direct apprehension of truth on Drake's part, based on his own mysticism assisted by drugs: 'Have you seen the land living by the breeze / Can you understand a light among the trees?' The key to these enigmatic questions may be another recurring Drakeian cypher: the sun. Source of light and warmth (and presiding power of summer), the sun is a universal symbol of God or, more precisely, of celestial influence on earth – and hence of heaven itself.

There's little doubt that what happened in Aix unlocked a new level of creativity for Drake. All of the *Five Leaves Left* songs appeared over the next year or so, plus several hours of taped fragments and patterns, and perhaps a dozen other finished songs, including two important ones, 'Time Of No Reply' and 'I Was Made To Love Magic' (diverted from the album in favour of the lighter 'Thoughts Of Mary Jane' and 'Man In A Shed' so as to provide variety). More fundamentally, the Aix revelation seems to have changed Drake's attitude to other people. His innate kindness mirrored the focus on compassion found in Buddhism and Blake, and the trippy Aix hash may have reinforced his sense of cosmic meaning; however, such powerful drugs always instil estrangement from everyday life. During 1967–8, the word 'strange' is everywhere in his songs. For example, 'Princess Of The Sand' (musically, a variation on Jackson C. Frank's 'Milk and Honey'), was retitled 'Strange Meeting II', seemingly to reflect the 'strange' motif, but perhaps also to stress the idea of lamentation ('the heavy toll of a thousand sighs') associated with the theme of compassion. (The Great War poet Wilfred Owen wrote the original 'Strange Meeting', which is a meditation on pity.)

Along with deeper estrangement came a more acute sense of transience. 'Who has dressed you in strange clothes of sand?' Drake asks in a song on *Time Of No Reply*, sand being a symbol of impermanence, possibly suggested by Shelley's 'Ozymandias'. (The subject of the song has been carried away by the delusory river of material life, taking her 'far from my land'.) The fatalism of Drake's view of the wheel of the seasons now becomes personal and premonitory. Learning Robin Frederick's 'Been Smokin' Too Long', he made a pregnant change: 'Got the marijuana blues' became 'Got no other life to choose'. 'Day Is Done', a very Gallic *chanson*, is weighed down by fateful pessimism, again of a personal kind; 'Leaving Me Behind' laments that 'the chances they come, but the chances have been lost / Success can be gained, but at too great a cost'; the eerie 'Fruit Tree' predicts that fame won't be his until after his death. Whether it was the Aix dope or the consequences of a seance he attended there (Humphries, p. 51), something fundamental changed for Drake in 1967.

Artists worth their salt are bound to be somewhat apart from everyday life. As long as this detachment remains benign, they're safe – but when it declines into alienation, trouble beckons. Notwithstanding his instinctive compassion, Drake's drug-enhanced perceptions of people seem to have acquired an edge of disappointment, if not of sorrowful cynicism. The 'Saturday rain', which moved him on from Aix-en-Provence and the midsummer night's dream of his early work, logically carried him through to 'Sunday', the bittersweet finale from *Bryter Layter*, for which album it might fairly be considered the subtitle. In Drake's scheme of things, Sunday was not a happy day.

It's been said that *Five Leaves Left* is to *Bryter Layter* as Blake's *Songs of Innocence* are to his *Songs of Experience.* In Drake's scheme, the 'Sunday' of *Bryter Layter* is a time of disenchantment, an album of metropolitan motion after the rural stillness of its predecessor. Not that he didn't positively embrace the challenge of writing a new record in three or four months (the last of 1969). He believed he'd succeeded with *Five Leaves Left*, which had not yet failed to sell, and got down to work in his Hampstead bedsit in good spirits; but by mid-1970, things were different. Exacerbated by his drug intake, his introversion had become isolation and he'd lost his nerve for performing live. Never loquacious, he was becoming silent and withdrawn, saying scarcely a word to Richard Thompson or John Cale at the sessions for *Bryter Layter*.

Drake had long been detached from normal human intercourse, as much out of idealism as of reserve. His disappointment with people is detectable in 'Blue Season' ('Lovers and losers who fail in the night') and in the secretive third verse of 'Three Hours'. The latter song also reveals a distanced cynicism about even a special friend like Jeremy Mason, who generously ran errands for him in Aix. But, by 1969–70, he'd taken a good look at the denizens of wheeler-dealing London, compared to whom even the least of his friends from Marlborough, Aix and Cambridge were preferable. Now he was writing – and mysteriously holding back – quietly apocalyptic reports of the soul-degradation of city life, empathising with the losers ('the people who live on the floor') and drawing a line between himself and those others, predatory or merely indifferent, who lived without conscience on the proceeds of exploitation.

The alienation of songs like 'Things Behind The Sun' and 'Parasite', held back for *Pink Moon*, is anticipated on *Bryter Layter* in the 'speed' songs 'Hazey Jane I' and 'II', and in the chary sarcasm of 'Poor Boy'. The crowded lines of the first verse of 'Hazey Jane II' – the last pitched so as to give the impression of faint hysteria – testify to his city-jangled sensibility and partially explain his increasing need for quiet, solitude and cool darkness. For the rest, we need only consider the brusque impersonality of urban life. An essentialist, drawn to spirit more than matter, Drake needed contact with other people's inner beings, an infrequent experience in the best of places, and especially on the Northern Line. Another lyric motif is 'the fence' (in 'Hazey Jane I', 'Fly' and an unsung verse of 'Three Hours'), which represents every sort of barrier or division. Evidently, Drake believed the fence was there to be crossed, yet he found few, if any, takers: 'Nobody smiles / If I cross their stiles' ('Poor Boy'). 'At The Chime Of A City Clock' is obsessively shielded in circumlocution, as if to illustrate its theme of the withholding of self. In the city, it's vital to 'put up your road block', to have a 'face' (social mask) to hide in, and not to show your hand. 'Fly', a song in two vocal octaves (one high, one low), finds Drake in anguished dialogue with the earthbound outlook of the 'well-adjusted' – a lonely soul begging to be let into another's inner being ('Please tell me your second name / Please play me your second game'), only to be fobbed off with the complacent invitation to sit on the fence in the sun and agree, as between men of the world, that 'it's really too hard / For to fly'. Hardly surprising that he saw the world as a 'theatre full of sadness' ('Fruit Tree'). His wail, in 'Way To Blue', of 'Don't you have a word to show what may be done?' was clearly heartfelt.

Drake's growing disappointment in people must have been agonising for one so committed to direct soul contact. Apart from music, reaching other hearts was all he cared for; the rest of life was, for him, mostly distraction. Yet few, even in that era, are likely to have understood him. The counterculture was carnivalesque, its optimism compulsory. Drake saw deeper. For him, with one foot in the spiritual profundity of the past, the counterculture's let-it-all-hang-out hedonism must have seemed like another snare of attachment – as much of a riverish delusion as the soullessness it sought to replace. To Drake, the world's suffering must have seemed inbuilt. It *was* the world. Only the individual spirit, the Self, could be relied on. Like Blake, he was as rooted in tradition as he was sympathetic to reform.

There are, then, many rational reasons why Drake might have begun to withdraw around 1970. There's also the possibility that this was accompanied, and worsened, by some form of clinical depression, probably intensified by the drugs he used to raise his consciousness above the mundane. Physical illness can precipitate depression; he had kidney stones around this time. Occultists might indicate the Aix séance as a door through which something dark might have come, drawn by his presumably unusually luminous aura. Everyone will have their own theory, but the fact remains that Drake had several causes to withdraw from life at that time, not the least being that his records, contrary to prediction, weren't selling.

By 1971, the solitude into which he'd begun to retreat in 1970 had become a source of such worry to his family that doctors were called in and he was prescribed the anti-depressants which eventually did for him. Such drugs can set the mind in concrete. Drake, though, refused to take the pills regularly and, with amazing inner resolve, somehow managed to go on writing songs – among the best of his short life. His stay at Chris Blackwell's villa in Portugal in late 1971 gave him space to work on a new album, and the sun probably helped too. Judging by his positive reactions to southern climates, he may have suffered from Seasonal Affective Disorder, otherwise known as winter sadness. This could explain his superstitious aversion to winter and his association of his 'blue' outlook with the northern sky.

Having 'failed' with the relatively outgoing *Bryter Layter*, Drake seems to have decided to return to his first theme of Blakeian 'innocence', although this time the innocence in question was of an adult kind. Apparently he wished to finish a trilogy: the Saturday of *Five Leaves Left*, the Sunday of *Bryter Layter* . . . and finally: Monday. Moon Day.

In the major arcana of the tarot, the card known as the Wheel of Fortune is said to be equivalent to the Buddhist Wheel of Becoming or the Law of Karma. If one were to assign tarot cards to Nick Drake's last album, *Pink Moon*, they would probably be the Moon, the Fool and the Hanged Man.

Pink Moon has an eerie reputation, in part derived from the circumstances of its creation. Drake appeared at John Wood's Sound Techniques Studio towards the end of 1971, recorded the album (which lasts twenty-eight minutes) in two midnight sessions with one overdub on his eleven voice/guitar live takes, took the master, and left it wordlessly at Island Records. Apart from approving the cover art (painted by Michael Trevithick), he had no more to do with the record and, a few months later, suffered a form of breakdown, subsequently going home to Warwickshire to live with his parents (where, they later told writer T. J. McGrath, he 'spent hours looking up at the sky').

Pink Moon draws the gothically inclined and repels the fearful. It's spoken of as bleak, skeletal, nihilistic, ghoulish, a suicidal plea for help. This grim view is unfair, the crowning misconception created by viewing Nick Drake as a troubadour of tragedy. He certainly went through his Dark Night of the Soul; indeed, he never emerged from it, and it killed him. Nevertheless he was a soul of light, a Romantic idealist – and this uncanny, magical record, far from bleak and ghoulish, is a stark, sparingly beautiful meditation on redemption through spiritual trial. *Pink Moon* isn't about death, but about resurrection. A grave blessing on the solitary soul sundered from the world by his or her sensitivity, it's religious music for our time.

The pathetic unmasked clown of 'At The Chime Of A City Clock' (*Bryter Layter*) reappears in *Pink Moon*'s 'Parasite', as one aspect of a concept album about a rite of passage into adult independence. ('And I was green, greener than the hill.') Yet the psychological process Drake uses as a focus draws an unusually deep response from him. Evidently he identified with his subject. His own journey – the Schubertian *Wintereisse* he'd been on, with its rural solitude, its search for humble meaning and its quest for the last bare shard of authentic identity at the heart of the maze of false selves – is entwined with a more universal journey towards release. He stands aside from this, singing of what's real and what is not, of who to trust and of whom to beware. He offers counsel in 'Things Behind The Sun', reassurance in 'Harvest Breed' and unveils a happy ending to the night of loneliness in 'From The Morning': the Self restored, new and healed, in a pantheistic vision of glory ('And now we rise / And we are everywhere'). *Pink Moon* is a sombre record, but it's also a redemptive and uplifting one, and to miss that is grievously to misunderstand it.

'Things I say / May seem stranger than Sunday / Changing to Monday.' These lines are from 'Poor Boy' on *Bryter Layter*, a song which confides several insights into how Drake saw himself. But these insights are veiled, as if in ironic recognition that what he had to say, though simple, could not be said in so many words and still be understood. In the light of what's suggested here, such lines are clearer: the change from Sunday to Monday is both a metaphor for the essentially enigmatic cycles of earthly life and an allusion to the day symbolism of Drake's trilogy of albums. More significant, though, is his acknowledgement that things he says may seem 'strange'. In 'Things Behind The Sun', on *Pink Moon*, the addressee of the song is advised to 'Open wide the hymns you hide / You find renown while people frown / At things that you say / But say what you'll say'. Drake's message is an uncommon one – not because it is wilfully obscure, but because it emanates from a place our society is fast forgetting: the seer-domain of poetic apprehension of reality. The realm of 'magic'.

By 'magic', Drake meant an experience evocative of transcendence, which, in personal terms, signified something genuine, direct and heartfelt. In 'Northern Sky', from *Bryter Layter*, he tells his lover that he 'never felt magic as crazy as this'. This sort of magic is spiritual and timeless – the opposite of the busy, materialistic world of 'the river', which has its own lower form of magic: the lunar magic of delusion.

The moon, in Drake's scheme, symbolises the magnetic pull of attachment to materiality: the moon's tug on the world is the world's tug on the soul. To 'fly to the moon' ('Mickey's Tune') is to lapse into beguiling delusion. In his early song 'Come Into The Garden', another Betty-like heroine is said to have 'lost her grip / At the tip of life's finger / Went home and worshipped the moon'. In 'Clothes Of Sand', Drake asks his estranged addressee 'Can you now return to from where you came / Try to burn your changing name / Or with silver spoons and coloured light / Will you worship moons in winter's night?' Here moon worship is linked with winter, the season of death. In other songs, the moon's delusory glamour is associated with the effects of drugs.

The moon moves the sea, but in Drake's symbolism the sea is a place where rain, having flown to it in many rivers, merges into Oneness (e.g., 'Leaving Me Behind', 'Clothes Of Sand'). The sea symbolises the dissolution of the false self (mind or Ego) into the Whole. Thus: 'I never saw moons knew the meaning of the sea.' (The moon, mistress of false magic, rules the false self.) Of course, the cycle goes on: water vapour rises from the sea and falls again as rain, keeping the river flowing – a metaphor for reincarnation. The sea itself is a *process*, a recurring experience of Oneness which doesn't last. Karma will send us back to the world. The only salvation is to escape time and transcend the false self (find the way to the sun). Hence the vow in 'Time Has Told Me': 'Someday our ocean / Will find its shore.'

Drake may have developed his symbolism from his own contemplations. On the other hand, the same symbols are universal in transcendental thought, in particular cabbala, tarot and 'magick'. He may also have studied myth and folklore, perhaps after reading another very 'Sixties' book, Robert Graves's *The White Goddess* (1948, reissued 1961). One apparent folklore motif is his allusion to the magic of names. In traditions around the world, to name someone is to gain power over them; thus, people have secret names, or assume other names to protect themselves. In several Drake songs, the name is contrasted with the true Self: 'Can you now return to from where you came / Try to burn your changing name?' ('Clothes Of Sand'); 'Please tell me your second name' ('Fly'). Three of the four songs he recorded in 1974 feature 'name' references, while the fourth, 'Hanging On A Star', is a cry of bewilderment at being recognised yet neglected. Each of the other songs puts a different spin on the proposition that to know his work is to know his 'name'. 'Black Eyed Dog' involves both the 'name' concept and another folklore motif: an uncannily gazing dog (not itself always black, but having eyes which blackly fixate the beholder) – this creature being universally regarded as an emissary of death. The 'name' further suggests an outward label for an unnamable inner essence: the stripping away of 'faces' to find the true Self – 'To keep on trying / 'Til there's no more to hide' ('Time Has Told Me').

If Drake's symbology seems complex, it's only because such traditional seer-poetry is becoming lost to modern society. Lacking belief in transcendence, we're unused to this frame of thought, and see complexity where in fact only simplicity exists. Some will recoil from all this, not wishing to be confronted by anything which asks for a special kind of attention. To be disabused of this prejudice, they need only allow the magic of the music – Drake's presence – to work on them. That and to recognise how vulnerable he was. For while his inner strength and irony kept him going in a world where no one understood him, his loneliness must have been increasingly unbearable. His despairing anxiety humanises him for us, letting us hear his message without being put off by it.

Just how difficult it was for Drake to cope with the project of living is evident in an early unpublished song, 'Outside'. Locating itself on the cusp between the worlds of innocence and of experience, this lyric entwines three ways of leaving home: the physical act of quitting the cradle of the family, the mental act of shifting from the personal to the interpersonal, and the spiritual act of moving from the magical timeless prelude of childhood into the disenchanting adult world of temporal-material life. The most striking thing about 'Outside' is its revelation of how acutely sensitive Drake was. His post-1970 preference for solitude in shade or darkness – usually assumed to be an effect of his 'illness' – is here prefigured in fears that the outside world (also the world of outsides, of appearances) will be too blatant and noisy for him. Even more eye-opening is that he anticipates having to come home 'to hide' as a result. It's disturbing to consider this in the light of the alienation of 'Black Eyed Dog', recorded seven years later: 'I'm growing old and I wanna go home / I'm growing old and I don't wanna know.'

Outside

Seems the time is near
For finding a place outside.
Seems the time is here
For holding the window wide.
So I'm going to try
To open up one eye,
But if the world is too wide
I'll be home to hide.
Keep it warm inside
If it's strange, outside.

Seems the time has flown
When we lived inside a cloud.
Seems the time has gone
When nothing we said was out loud.
Going to find a word
Make myself be heard,
But if the world is too loud
I'll be home from the crowd.
Keep it soft inside
If it's strange, outside.

Seems the time has come
For banging our feet to the ground.
Seems the time has come
To see if the world is round.
Sweep the smoke away
Reach the earth today,
But if the world is all wrong
I won't be staying long.
Keep it cool inside
If it's strange, outside.

Here is someone so absorbed in the heaven-world of Blakeian innocence that leaving home is equivalent to 'reaching the earth', to landing on the planet. Drake invokes a world of cloud and smoke in which nothing's said out loud, as against the realm of matter in which feet are banged to the ground and words must be found in order to make oneself heard. Clearly, 'home', in his symbolism, was only one step from heaven itself – the threshold to another dimension in which communication is pictured as taking place directly: not in words but in thought feelings. Like other visionaries, Drake seems to have had so intense an apprehension of transcendence that it gave him an abiding sense, in this earthly life, of being exiled from heaven. No wonder, despite his longing for freedom, that he ended his life back at 'home' in Far Leys (with, as in the lyric of Gershwin's 'Summertime', 'daddy and mammy standing by'). For him, freedom was an inner thing – the ability to detach from phenomenal reality and see heaven in a wild flower. In a sense, it didn't matter where he lived; in another sense, returning 'home' completed a profound psychological cycle for him.

With his transcendental streak, Drake must have found almost everything about earthly life provisional and hence nearly impossible to commit to. His attempt, with *Bryter Layter*, to step out into the everyday world was admirable, but contrary to his deepest instincts. He'd seen the nature of life on earth at an early age and saw no reason to keep repeating the lesson, year after year ('What's the point of a year / Or a season?'). He was, in effect, waiting – waiting to be released from life and returned 'home' to heaven. Yet, while here, he felt obliged to make things 'better, happier' through his work, and that entailed engaging with the world. His predicament is encoded in the title of his first album, *Five Leaves Left*, which, to any dope smoker running out of rolling papers, means: 'Soon you'll have to go out (to buy more)' – i.e., engage with life. *Bryter Layter* can likewise be read as a code for Drake's 'waiting' disposition, though more likely, in view of the album's outgoing tenor, is that it's an ironic comment on the facile optimism of those in the 'river life' who never ask why (Y) they exist and are so enslaved to time that they live by chasing tomorrow, rarely if ever 'being' here now.

Such questioning of the 'river life' is recurrent in Drake's output: 'Seems so easy / Just to let [life] go on by / Till you stop and wonder / Why you never wondered why' ('Fruit Tree'); 'Do you like what you're doing / Would you do it some more / Or will you stop once and wonder / What you're doing it for?' ('Hazey Jane I'). Similarly, the false existence of 'the river' is associated with the loud life of the crowd, against which Drake naturally juxtaposed himself (e.g., 'Outside', 'Time Of No Reply', 'Voice From The Mountain', ''Cello Song'). His world is that of fleeting magical perceptions ('the mist where the melody flies'). The river-world, by contrast, is an earthbound, mind-heavy, materialistic place of clocks and analysing and counting, often symbolised by the ground or the floor ('Counting the cattle as they go by the door / Keeping a carpet that's so thick on the floor'). As Drake's lyrics repeatedly stress, time rules the river-world. An unused extra verse of 'River Man' makes this clear (perhaps too clear): 'Betty fell behind awhile / Said she hadn't time to smile / Or die in style / But still she tries / Said her time was growing short / Hadn't done the things she ought / Where teacher taught / And Father flies.' (Saturday, of course, is Saturn's day; and Saturn is Chronos, alias Old Father Time.) 'Three Hours' – which takes its title from Jeremy Mason's phrase for anything that'll take a tiresomely long time (Humphries, p. 51) – is a less forthright statement of the same ideas. Jeremy flies on his temporal mission, purposely avoiding the sun; meanwhile no one wants to stand out from the crowd by speaking of timeless, transcendent things. Further unused lines ascribe this evasion to the divisive mind: 'We had all the time, but failed to make sense / From one side to the other we fell to the fence.'

Drake's stance *vis-à-vis* the river-world is almost precisely analogous with the general Sixties counter-cultural view of 'straight' society. The Buddhistic *be here now* formula for enlightenment was familiar to those in the counterculture who'd moved from psychedelic drugs to Eastern mystical systems. In this sense, Drake is very much a child of his time – the essence of the late Sixties spiritual revolt in its purest form – and he can't be fully understood without seeing his work in historical context. In a more essential, timeless way, he transcends his era by virtue of the very purity which made his work too allusive – and not mundanely optimistic enough – to appeal to his contemporaries. For where Drake differed from the counterculture was in the world-fleeing intensity of his quasi-Gnostic vision. ''Cello Song', one of a set of what might be called 'Princess songs' written to female muses during 1967–8, calls to some heaven-touched soul to 'lend a hand and lift me / To your place in the cloud'. (Cloud and mist symbolise the adjacency of the realm of transcendence.) Drake's ideal woman, like him, is a wandering, waiting exile from heaven ('A troubled cure / For a troubled mind') – someone barely touching the materiality of earthly life ('A sole with no footprint / A rose with no thorn') who will join him in leaving 'the ways that are making you be / What you really don't want to be', and who knows that the escape is through the strait gate and narrow way of the extreme present, of which experience the mind cannot conceive and words cannot ultimately speak ('There's really no way / Of ending your troubles / With things you can say').

Such is the message of Nick Drake's work – and, if it can seem forbiddingly priestly, we must remember the smiling, gentle man beloved of almost everyone who knew him. Remember, too, that Drake wasn't a sage in the sense of mastering his own salvation, but an intuitively transcendental lyrical troubadour who saw in the seer-style of the traditional poet, but failed to realise the Self in the mystical way ('I could be / Here and now / I would be, I should be / But how?') – and, misunderstood, perished of isolation. Living always on the threshold of normal life – hanging near the door at parties, as if he might need to leave at any moment – he must sometimes have been uncertain of his own reality. Letting others talk, or shielding himself by discussing 'things' (guitars, techniques, arrangements), he peripheralised himself even in conversation: he wanted not to exist. The world was too gross for him, too much for his too-open senses. There again, he was paradoxically drawn to the down-to-earth: the strong, the straightforward, the dry and funny.

Such people, with their sharp, wide-awake ability to orientate and operate in this world, would have been very interesting to him; but they could no more grasp what was in his mind than those temperamentally more akin to him.

Too finely tuned for the rough and tumble of this world, Nick Drake found a way of getting through by focusing on his music – a focus so keen that he turned himself from a beginner to one of England's most original finger-style guitarists inside two years. His melodic/harmonic inspiration was of a high order bestowed by the same sensitivity that left him so vulnerable in other situations. Elsewhere, outside the circles of friends which he kept apart from each other like islands in a personal archipelago, the gale of the world blew hard on him. A Marlborough friend describes him as 'stooped forward, holding his head quite low in his shoulders, as if there was always a cold wind blowing'. For Drake, there was such a wind: the coldness of life beyond friendship, 'the ceaseless cry of anguish which rises from a blindly groping, sorrow-laden world'. Expecting him to behave with the usual amount of human resilience would have been about as silly as counselling a Mahler or a Dostoevsky not to get so upset about things.

The tragic aspect in his work is notoriously compelling. More of it is discernible in the light of this account, in particular the burden of his artistic mission, as expressed in the heart-rending prayer for relief of 'Voice From The Mountain': 'Tell me my friend, my friend / Tell me with love / Where will it end, it end / This voice from above?' Clearly, Drake felt inspired by something beyond him ('I know my name, my name / But this tune is more'). That this was a religious intuition of some kind is clear enough from the 'Christian' references to chimes in 'Parasite' and 'Voice From The Mountain', and the hymnic forms and references in other songs. Equally obviously, this transcendental link couldn't sustain him, even though it was still with him in 1974. He seems never to have entirely given up on reaching 'the crowd' with the spirit of his message, even if his attitude to the 'well-adjusted' of the river-world remained dry. (Those smug bystanders who judge the innocent fool in 'Pink Moon' are themselves altered by the trials he undergoes: 'And none of you stand so tall / Pink Moon gonna get ye all.')

But the end was darkness. 'Black Eyed Dog', with its Carnatic raga scale (probably derived, like 'Horn', from veena music), wails its longing for death with an intensity matched only by the hellhound blues of Robert Johnson or Dylan's debut album. It would be less unbearable to listen to if it hadn't been predicted by many fate-harried songs from seven years earlier. Suicide had been on Drake's mind for a long time. In this connection, Paul Wheeler recalls his friend's agitated reaction to Stephen Stills's '4+20', on Crosby, Stills, Nash and Young's *Déjà Vu* (1970). Yet Drake could not justify the act to himself: 'To leave there is no way' ('Time Of No Reply'). Like Wheeler, he may have read Doris Lessing's *Briefing for a Descent into Hell* (1971) in search of some map by which to orientate; this, perhaps, would account for the archetypal aspects of some of his later songs. For the rest, he was effectively on his own, despite the drugs which his doctors prescribed, and the anxious ministrations of those closest to him.

Without ill will, Nick Drake has been described as a depressed young man whose art never matured. Yet depression can be rational, while sorrow and unease are legitimate responses to life. As Buddha pointed out, sorrow, not happiness, cultivates compassion. (An example of the way a 'depressive' worldview can fall short of clinical depression is given by Randy Newman's 'I Think It's Going to Rain Today', Drake's favourite song from one of his favourite albums.) To ascribe a song like 'Time Has Told Me' to maudlin adolescence is absurd; there's simply too much suffering in it. Indeed, this is classic Romanticism of a kind that must have broken female hearts wherever Drake went. (Though a love song, 'Time Has Told Me' shares the worldview of 'River Man'.)

Everything ostensibly uncommitted or self-withholding in Drake's make-up is comprehensible, and forgivable, once his basic outlook is understood. In truth, far from immature, he grew up, philosophically, very quickly, almost as if he'd seen it all before and was simply going through it again. Yet this left him perpetually on the threshold of life, looking 'inwards' at the world of transcendent reality as much as outwards into the world of material fact. While Nick liked the garden at Far Leys, his father told Larry Ayres that he never helped maintain it. Drake's work is liminal in this sense, but no less legitimate and conceivably more inspired because of it. What remain contentious, in this materialist age, are his subjects: magic, the spirit, transcendence. Drake wished to address his contemporaries, but found that, on these issues, this was 'the time of no reply' (a concept with echoes of C. S. Lewis's *Out of the Silent Planet*). Of course, the followers of Richard Dawkins and company will find only delusion in Drake's work – yet materialism is bound to reject any claim that the world of spirit is real; Darwin and Mendel are our new gods. Even so, materialism has no answer to the mystical proposal that our minds are the very things which prevent us perceiving transcendent reality.

Human tastes and preoccupations are mostly time-bound and trivial. Drake's work opens a door on the eternal. In his songs, we find in action the Romantic ideal that beauty can elevate consciousness. The proof? The fact that so many are drawn to his work by its contemplative refinement without any awareness of its transcendental inspiration. Even if his lyrics weren't so considered, his music would still transfix us with its timeless harmony. Nick Drake is far more than merely a rather special singer-songwriter of the late Sixties. More significantly, he speaks to us from a tradition almost lost today, though nonetheless vital. His pantheism, his sense of the holy in nature, may be anomalous in our modern world, but it seems we need it.

The World Health Organisation predicts a vast upsurge in clinical depression in the first quarter of the coming century. Already, doctors report that half of their patients display signs of this illness. Can it be that the materialist worldview, in which there is no intrinsic meaning, is slowly murdering our souls? Nick Drake's work reminds us that life is a predicament and that the world is an insoluble mystery. It tells us that a 'magical', contemplative way of seeing can keep us aware of this, preventing us from destroying the world through the arrogant assumption that we know what it is. We do not. We're all exiled from heaven, though some of us don't realise it. But when magic reveals heaven to us in a wild flower, we remember. And then we hear the chime.

Nick Drake: death of a 'genius'

Sounds Dec. 14. 74

Jerry Gilbert

NICK DRAKE died in his sleep two Sundays ago, leaving a legacy of three superb, stylised albums on the Island label. He had been ill — perhaps weary is a better expression — for some time, but at the time of his death his enthusiasm had never been as high for he was totally immersed in the prospect of completing his fourth album.

"He was a genius," proclaimed arranger Robert Kirby when I spoke to him last week. "There was absolutely no one to touch him in England." Kirby worked on Nick's first two albums.

Nick Drake was a complete enigma. He seldom spoke and few knew what was going on inside his head. John Martyn tells of trips Drake would make down to his home in Hastings, stay the weekend and then leave as mysteriously as he had arrived, having uttered scarcely a word.

He hated performing, and although in the heyday of Joe Boyd's Witchseason Management he would be found opening shows for bands like Fairport Convention at the Festival and Queen Elizabeth Halls, personal appearances had petered out almost entirely by the end of 1970.

There was an ominous portent in a lot of his work and for Nick Drake the outside world was something he found difficult to look squarely in the face. He seldom raised his eyes from the ground and would walk around with a curious enigmatic half-smile most of the time.

My one attempt to interview Nick back in 1970 was a total disaster — no words, just the smile.

Nick's first album "Five Leaves Left" was widely acclaimed, as was the quite remarkable "Bryter Layter". The final album was "Pink Moon": Drake arrived at Island's Basing Street offices one day, introduced himself, handed over the finished master and disappeared. No-one even knew he'd made the album except engineer-producer John Wood, who probably knew Nick better than anyone.

That album was, for the most part, a grim acceptance of death, intensely personal — as with all his music. Robert Kirby is right when he says that Nick Drake should not be built into a legend or some kind of posthumous superhero in the way that Jim Croce was. He would never have wished for that.

Yet whilst respecting Nick Drake's life in obscurity it is important to at least hint at the influence he had upon musicians like John Martyn and mention the extrovert brilliance as recalled by Robert Kirby when Nick was out of the public eye, sitting back relaxing and playing blues and ragtime pieces like you wouldn't believe.

"People don't realise but he had remarkably broad tastes," says Kirby. "One of the biggest shames is that no-one will ever hear him play blues.

"He was the happiest I'd ever seen him just before his death, but he was usually despondent simply because he had nothing to do and couldn't see a direction for himself. I think London upset him, he didn't like it here at all, in fact he was upset by a lot of things that he saw and heard, he was just too sensitive.

"He was ready for death alright, I just think he'd had enough, there was no fight left in him. All his songs were epigrams — little extracts of philosophy and you could either take them optimistically or pessimistically.

"Yet I get the feeling that if he was going to commit suicide he would have done so a long time ago."

Newsweek, November 8, 1976

Pop Gems

NICK DRAKE: *"Five Leaves Left" (Antilles).* This is the first American release of a 1969 landmark album by a brilliant, sinuous British singer-songwriter who died two years ago, an apparent suicide. Drake is accompanied by bass, percussion and his own acoustic guitar, but the real instrument here is the dreamily sensual, jazz-inflected voice he brings to his songs' eerie, disjointed imagery. Drake's hints of quiet panic become all the more chilling in retrospect.

OS 3

Last month brought two pieces of very sad news. First we heard of the death of Mike Leadbitter, eminent authority on the Blues, and advertising manager for Let It Rock. Mike was undoubtedly one of the most popular personalities in the business and I know that all the many people who considered him a friend will miss him greatly. Then a week or so ago we heard the tragic news that Nick Drake had died. I know a lot of you are very fond of Nick Drakes' music, after the many letters we received as a result of Connor's article in issue 42, so I'm sure you'll feel as sad and brought down as we do.
Apparently he was working on a new one and had been in his happiest frame of mind for a long time so the question of him taking his own life seems very unlikely. In fact he died peacefully in his sleep.

Above: *Sounds*, 14 December 1974 Below right: *ZigZag*, December 1974

The Land Without Music

by Stuart Maconie

Every nationality has its way of identifying, outfoxing and humiliating outsiders. With the French and the Chinese it's the food: things that sweat and smell, putting things on the menu that you find on the bottom of old plant pots and eating the bits of the animal that even the animal thinks are its worst features. With the Americans it's stupidly complicated sports rules, and with the Germans, traditionally, it's been completely unjustified military invasion.

With us, it's language. The only good reason to pronounce Worcester 'Wuster' is that it gives bar staff a chance to snigger at American tourists when they ask for the sauce in their tomato juice. We can be so insular and protective that we have even invented linguistic mantraps and trapdoors for lesser members of our own tribe. All those Featherstonehaughs (Fanshaws), Belvoirs (Beavers) and Cholmondleys (Chumleys) are really there to act as a kind of password into rarified social strata. If you know the pronunciation, you're in. It works the same way as saying 'I'm a friend of Big Dave's' in certain after-hours Bermondsey drinking clubs. The shutter slides shut, the bolt slides off and you're in.

Hergest Ridge is pronounced 'Hargest' with the 'g' hard as in garden. You'll find this out as soon as you ask for directions. The lady in the newsagent's will snigger, the paper boy will join in and you'll finger the cookies in your pocket that the nice lady in Ludlow gave you. You're lost, as she predicted, and in a foreign country.

Well, nearly. Hergest Ridge is a big, shapely, friendly hill that sprawls on the English–Welsh border. Certain long ways up begin in Wales, but whichever way you come, climb high enough and you'll end up in England as the summit lies there. From the top – a large green sward made for kiting or striding or lying on your back chewing grass and listening to the drone of light aircraft on summer afternoons – the view is sweeping and grand. East and south lies Wales, land of song, of trilling harps, of valleys ringing with the sweet upraised voices of sooty-faced coal miners singing of love and chapel and community and keeping a welcome in these hillsides. West and north, though, lies England. And silence.

That's what our old friends the Germans used to think anyway. In 1904 Oskar Adolf Hermann Schmitz published a book about England entitled *Das Land ohne Musik*, or 'The Land Without Music'. Admittedly the years leading up to the First World War were not the most cordial for Anglo-German relations and the book was intended to pander to chauvinistic feelings in his homeland, but the central premise – that England cares about music less and produces less music than all its European neighbours – had currency in general and specialist circles for centuries. The quote 'Das Land ohne Musik' had first been used half a century earlier by the German music scholar Carl Engel, and Schmitz, in his book, goes on to try to diagnose our national tin-ear.

'I have asked myself what is missing from this nation. Kindness, love of people, humour or aesthetic sense? No, one can find all these attributes in England, some of them more noticeably than among ourselves. Finally I have found something which distinguishes English people from all other cultures to quite an astonishing degree, a lack which everybody acknowledges therefore nothing new, but has not been emphasised enough. The English are the only cultured nation without its own music (except street music). This does not mean that they have less sensitive ears but that their life overall is much poorer for it. To be immersed in music, even ever so little, means being able to lose yourself.' Ralph Waldo Emerson also said in his *English Traits* of 1856: 'England has no music. It has never produced a first-rate composer and accepts only such music as has already decided to be good in Germany and Italy.'

The poet Heinrich Heine – guess what, another German! – even dissed our moves on the floor, alleging that: 'The sons of Albion are themselves the most awful of all dancers, and Strauss assures me there is not a single one among them who could keep time. He too fell sick unto death in the county of Middlesex when he saw Olde England dance. These people have no ear, neither for the beat nor indeed for music in any form, and their unnatural passion for piano-playing and singing is all the more disgusting.'

Which is a bit rum when you take into account The Beatles, The Rolling Stones, Vaughan Williams, Elgar, Bax, Nick Drake, The Clash, Kate Bush, Harrison Birtwistle, Delius, The Smiths, Paddy McAloon, The Human League and a thousand other rock and rollers, jazzers, rappers, composers, choirs and folk singers.

However, and however galling it might be, up until roughly the turn of the twentieth century these slurs and canards may have contained a goodly portion of truth. While Bach, Mozart, Beethoven, Verdi, Wagner et al were churning out masterpieces by the yard in Vienna, Leipzig, Salzburg, Bayreuth and Rome, we were quiet as church mice when we weren't hammering and welding and forging our way to industrial supremacy. We didn't have much in the way of opera or string quartets, true. What we did have, though, was a fabulously rich folk music tradition: drinking songs and working songs, songs from farms and mills and latterly factories, murder ballads and bawdy tales, songs about generals, rascals, cutpurses, children, lusty wenches and peevish masters and the whole panoply of life as it was lived in the raw by the ordinary people of England, not the gods in Valhalla.

As has so often been the case, because this canon was the preserve of ordinary working people rather than the privileged classes, it was dismissed. The parlours and drawing rooms of middle-class England, tinkled to the sound of prim gavottes and mazurkas written in Paris and Prague whilst outside the window, a gardener whistled 'Barbara Allen' or 'Dives and Lazarus' or 'Lovely Joan'; beautiful old melodies worth in a few bars the whole tedious cabbagey length of *The Ring*, ja.

Then around the start of the twentieth century, a handful of enlightened individuals began to see the worth in our indigenous music. First came Cecil Sharp, a light composer who chanced upon some Morris dancers in an Oxfordshire quarry and fell in love with English traditional music. Sharp was something of a prude – he bowdlerised many of the songs to remove their erotic allusions – and he was rather prescriptive about what counted as folk music, dismissing much Lancastrian music because it originated in factory and mills and wasn't 'rural' enough. But he was crucial in a sea-change in the way we saw and heard our own music. Inspired by Sharp, a young composer called Vaughan Williams began to travel across Middle England, collecting and transcribing the folk melodies he found in pubs and farmers' fields and village squares. Other like-minded individuals took up the cause and soon a kind of English music revival was under way, spearheaded by Vaughan Williams, Bax, Ireland, Moeran, Butterworth and more, who unashamedly took as their wellspring the deep traditions of English music. Later they would become misunderstood and mocked for this. Vaughan Williams in particular, the greatest English composer ever, I'd say, was unjustly looked down on for years. His work was dismissed as 'cowpat music' by Elizabeth Lutyens, a dry intellectual of the serial music school that dominated in the 1950s, and Constant Lambert, another vastly inferior composer, said sneeringly of his wonderful Pastoral Symphony that it was the musical equivalent of a cow looking over a gate. Recently his transcendently lovely and radiant 'The Lark Ascending' was voted the nation's favourite piece of classical music in one of the polls that appears every day in modern Britain. The music critic of *The Scotsman*, Ken Walton – not to be confused with the former all-in wrestling commentator Kent Walton – sniffed that it was 'a very safe choice . . . it's fair to say that he is loved by middle England'.

There is real snobbery here, not just about music but about Middle England itself. Lutyens's arid, forgettable music was written in the style of the Second Viennese School of Schoenberg, Webern and Berg. If Vaughan Williams's is the cowpat, it may be that hers is the squeaky gate at the corner of the field. Implicit in her comment is the notion that music rooted in the verdant, rich and passionate soul of England cannot be worth our serious attention, merely a pretty diversion, an amusement. She was wrong. Vaughan Williams was right. And in some ways, in their insistence that popular song, the songs of the people, the tunes whistled and danced to and loved to and wept to by the great mass of us were as worthy as grand opera, Vaughan Williams and Cecil Sharp were the forefathers of English pop and all its glories. That, as the title of the late music scholar Ian MacDonald's book reflects, truly is the People's Music.

The First World War haunts English music and culture for long passages of the twentieth century. This national wound may be at the core of the ineffable, indefinable sadness and loss beneath the loveliness of so much of Middle England's music and poetry. It is a cliché to talk of a lost pre-war idyll and such. But it is also true. A generation was lost, amongst it writers like Wilfred Owen and composers like George Butterworth. For those who saw the bloodshed of Ypres and the Somme, the tranquil beauty of the Shires would forever after contain that sense of deep melancholy that the end of a late summer evening has, ripe with the sweet ache of mortality. It's become a motif, a meme, of English art. And before we leave pop music, we should say that pop has not been immune to this Middle English melancholy, embodied in two lost talents whose stories echo those of Butterworth and Owen and the rest. These two young men didn't go to war. But they did go missing in action.

To reach the grave you take the curving path around the church and into the quiet wooded section to the rear. A very English vista opens up: mixed woodland and rich Warwickshire pasture land stretching towards the horizon where a line of comfortable houses stand. To the right of the path stands a fine oak tree and, below it, the family grave of the Drake family, who lived in nearby Far Leys House. It's a late spring Saturday evening, the sun is slanting through the branches and glinting on the stained glass of St Mary Magdalene. The evening is golden but a chill is creeping into the sunlit air. There is no one here but me. It is, in a melancholy and very English way, perfect.

The headstone tells you that here lies Rodney and Molly Drake and their son Nick. But more telling is the sign attached to the oak tree: 'Fans are requested to pay their respects by leaving only small tokens or flowers.' By and large, they have done that. There is no gruesome cairn of tat like the one at Jim Morrison's grave in Père Lachaise, Paris, just a few Rizla papers and a couple of plectrums. Nothing much to suggest that Tanworth-in-Arden is a place of pilgrimage.

Nick Drake could not have been a more different kind of pop star than Jim Morrison. Morrison of The Doors swaggered about in ludicrous leather trousers, was prone to getting his penis out on stage and partial to the odd armful of heroin or cocktail of narcotics. He sang about wanting to sleep with his mother, violent revolution and other very 1960s Californian notions, and fronted a full-on psychedelic assault that made him a very rich and famous man.

Nick Drake, on the other hand, was a quiet, bookish acoustic guitarist who sang plaintive, muted, lyrical songs about fruit trees, rivers, loneliness and lives quietly wasted. He studied at Cambridge but opted for a failed career as a musician. He sold few records, certainly far fewer than his talent deserved, and that fact only deepened his existing sense of depression and isolation. Nick Drake died when he was twenty-six, Morrison when he was twenty-seven, both deaths the result of drug use. Except Morrison died coughing up blood after a fix of heroin in a Paris bathroom and Nick Drake passed out in his parents' house in a sleepy Warwickshire village after what may have been an accidental overdose of Tryptizol, an antidepressant.

Drake died in the winter of 1974. At that time his music was at best a coterie enthusiasm, largely ignored. Part of Drake's problem was to have been an introspective balladeer at a time when rock music was at its loudest, most physical and most communal. In the intervening years, however, his cachet has grown to the extent that Brad Pitt, Jennifer Aniston and the late Heath Ledger have queued up to eulogise him. Documentaries and front covers abound now, a bitter irony given that one of Drake's saddest songs, 'Fruit Tree', concerns lack of recognition during life, concluding, 'Safe in your place deep in the earth / That's when they'll know what you were really worth.'

Phil, the husband of the churchwarden at St Mary Magdalene's, is standing in the sunlit doorway of the Bell Inn sipping his pint and looking contentedly at the sunset over his village church. He has much to be contented about. Tanworth feels like a delightful place to live, but it has seen the same changes that many of the villages of Middle England have. Once it would have been a self-contained community with its little shop, its blacksmith's, its cluster of surrounding farms, possibly even its paternalist squire. You'd have worked here, in field or forge or mill or workshop. Now you probably work in Birmingham, and Tanworth, smarter than it once was, is a dormer village, a commuter's dream, just half an hour from central Brum by performance car or 'ultimate driving machine'.

Inevitably, then, the older villagers, the farmers and such, drink elsewhere. Though not in the bar of the Crossroads Motel. For many years Tanworth played the village of Kings Oak in that long-running and much-mocked Midlands soap opera, and it's odd to think that while Noele Gordon et al were hamming it up criminally for a film crew on the village green, Nick Drake may have been hunkered in his room just some yards away, writing the beautiful, stately songs that no one would listen to till after he was dead. In the graveyard, coincidentally, there lies another son of Middle England: the nine-times motorcycle champion Mike Hailwood, who drove his car into the path of an oncoming lorry one dark winter's night taking his daughter to the chip shop. Phil tells me this as he sips his pint thoughtfully on the pub's threshold.

Inside the doorway is a sign proclaiming that this is one of the fifty best pubs in England and by it hangs a picture of Nick Drake. It is a typical picture, the handsome young man with his thatch of modish 1970s hair and his inscrutable, wry, slightly pained half-smile. Inside, the restaurant is bustling and the bar is full of tanned, smart, new locals in smart casuals from Boden and Next. Is this Middle England? I ask one. 'Oh yes, absolutely, and the best place on earth too. God's own country,' he says, draining half his pricey continental lager at a pull. He is wearing an aftershave full of woody top notes, wearing a Hugo Boss shirt and the keys to a top-marque German car are on the bar by him.

Not everyone agrees with him. Some locals feel that the gentrification of the village has gone too far. 'Overpriced food and beer obviously appeal to the wealthy villagers living behind their electronic gates' is one comment on a local Internet forum, whilst another reads, 'I got the feeling that proper local villagers would only be welcome if they had suitable cool and trendy clothes on that would blend in with the modern surroundings. It is interesting to wonder (had he lived) what Nick Drake would have made of his new-look local.'

I don't know if Nick Drake went in for pubs much actually. I somehow can't see him sinking a pint of Grolsch while watching Chelsea on the big-screen telly or engaging in ribaldry with the barmaid before putting money in the quiz machine. The church across the way is somehow more in his line. Phil is taking the choir to the Royal Albert Hall tomorrow for a competition. He shows me around. There's a brass organ stop in memory of Nick, paid for by Rodney and Molly, and the visitors' book is full of tributes to Nick from pilgrims from all around the world. They have come from Albuquerque and Athens, from Milan and Moscow. They leave sweet messages and quote his lyrics. Once a year what began as the organist playing a recital of his music has blossomed into a small, very Middle English festival. They come from far and wide, in BMWs and camper vans, pitching tents in the local farmers' fields. They don't, as a rule, stay at The Bell. When Rodney and Molly were alive, they'd let them in, make them copies of Nick's home recordings, let them be photographed in his room. The new owners are, understandably, a bit less welcoming of these zealous strangers camping on their doorstep and hammering at their door.

'We do get older people, the sort who might have bought Nick's music the first time round, but it's mainly younger ones. They're often . . .' Here Phil chooses his words delicately – 'they're often a bit lost, I think . . . a bit unsure of themselves. A bit like Nick really.'

This Saturday evening, a young girl who fits the above description rather well is sitting in the church porch on the bench below the parish notices. She is pale and thin, smoking furtively and reading from a battered paperback novel. When she sees me, she smiles and even gives a little wave but scuttles away before I can talk to her. I decide she's a local girl getting out of the house for a crafty fag rather than an acolyte come from afar. But even so, it seems an apt image: a lost young woman in a twilit English graveyard where one of Middle England's lost young men lies asleep.

Syd Barrett was asleep, lost, even dead you might say, for three decades before his actual death. Like Drake, he was a well-brought-up son of Middle England. Like Drake, he spent his formative years in Cambridge and, like Drake, he was a delicate, attractive youth whose promise was lost due to mental fragility. In Barrett's case, though, the former front man and initial genius of Pink Floyd was seemingly waylaid and devastated by a cataclysm brought on by hallucinogenic drug use in the late 1960s. Barrett's music, both his solo work and that with Pink Floyd, teems with images of childhood and innocence and, lurking behind it, menace: scarecrows, gnomes, wonky bicycles.

For me, Nick Drake and Pink Floyd are as much the sound of England, indeed the sound of Middle England, as 'Greensleeves' and the 'Enigma' Variations. Though they fall loosely under the auspices of rock music – very loosely in Drake's case – their sound and their mien are literal and metaphorical miles from The Clash or Oasis or even The Rolling Stones. Mick and Keith are good suburban Kent boys rather than the plantation-owning piratical pimp hustler drag-queen romantic poets they would have you believe, but nothing in their work echoes Middle England like Drake or Floyd, with Barrett or after.

With Nick Drake, it's in the actual sound. The finger-picked acoustic guitar with its hint of minstrelsy and the delicate pastoral arrangements provided by his Cambridge friend Robert Kirby. No synthesisers or searing electric guitar solos here, but the plaintiveness of oboes and cellos, the sweetness of celesta and chamber strings. Drake's voice too – deep, refined, thoughtful

– is more Keats than Keith Richard and more given to regretful reveries than sexual braggadocio.

Pink Floyd, especially after Barrett's departure, evolved into a rock behemoth, massively amplified, hugely successful. But at the heart of their work is a comparable melancholy. On their magnum opus *The Dark Side of the Moon* they actually sing of 'plans that either come to naught or half a page of scribbled lines' and 'hanging on in quiet desperation is the English way'. You don't come across 'naught' in many Bon Jovi or Guns N' Roses lyrics. And even though their music is self-evidently rock, it is full of evocations of otherness, a very Middle English otherness: the tolling of bells, the ticking of clocks, murmured conversations. It is an eerie world, reminiscent of Lear or Belloc, and dates back to Barrett's earliest work with the group.

Barrett was a fairly common sight around Cambridge, shopping, cycling, largely undisturbed by locals if occasionally hounded by door-stepping journalists and fans. Pictures of him from this time show a bald, overweight, middle-aged man in dowdy T-shirts and shorts. Whenever a new one of these saw the light of day, taken without his consent or approval by some tittle-tattler or hack, the ensuing commentary would revolve around how terrible he looked. In truth, he doesn't look that terrible. He looks depressingly like quite a lot of fifty-odd-year-old blokes in modern England. No, the problem is that he doesn't look like Syd Barrett, the dark-eyed lysergic romantic of the summer of love. 'He were a good-looking lad, alright, if you look at his old pictures,' says the chatty, amiable lady in the very Budgens where Syd bought his provisions (milk, potatoes, cheese, eggs, nothing fancy). 'Such a shame. That's drugs for you,' she says sadly, standing in front of her rows of Blue WKD, Smirnoff Ice and Marlboro Lites.

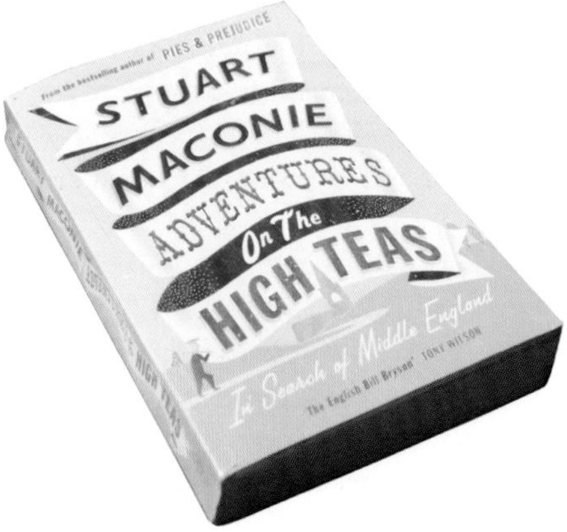

NEW MUSICAL EXPRESS
NEW MUSICAL EXPRESS

Pics: KEITH MORRIS

February 8, 1975

Requiem for a Solitary Man

ON October 25th, 1974, at approximately six in the morning Nick Drake, a 26-year-old singer/songwriter, died from an overdose of *Typtasol*, an anti-depressant, in the bedroom of his parents' house in Tamworth, Arden, not far from Stratford-upon-Avon.

The coroner's verdict was death by suicide, culminating from prolonged mental illness, which, in turn, was manifested through heavy introspective depressions. This verdict will be contested in the following article.

I GUESS I must have become, for want of a better expletive, an aficionado of Nick Drake's music when I found myself ensconsed for a time at University. In retrospect, it all seems pretty logical now: straddled at the tail-end of a self-indulgent bout of thoroughly-earnest teenage introspection, which had manifested itself through long solitary gambols over village greens, vague, confused affairs with willowy, callous girls, occasionally picking away tardily at cheap open-tuned guitars in an effort to "express myself," studious, worshipful dialectics over the hidden gem-like enunciations on "Blonde on Blonde" — above all, that arch-affectation of the world-weary Misunderstood Youth.

It was fun for a while, and Nick Drake with his fragile quasi-bossi-nova inflected voice and almost overwhelmingly gentle hypnotic music fitted into the landscape perfectly for that time. Drake, mind you, had probably risen from roughly similar circumstances. Born while his parents were stationed in Burma, he was brought to his homeland when aged six and, through a long illustrious sojourn within England's educational network, later landed himself a place in Fitzwilliam College, Cambridge.

Once in Cambridge Drake had become a part of both that whole cerebrally obsessive elitist capriciousness that the likes of Cambridge and Oxford seem fond of cultivating, and the activity on the outer periphery of the town itself. Cambridge was at that time (early '68) starting to simmer with a certain well-honed enthusiastic self-enveloping energy: the Pink Floyd had probably set the ball rolling the previous year, their appearance providing a spotlight for the area which carried on through to such cultural events as the staging of a "Cambridge Free Festival," John and Yoko doing one of their dynamic displays of "bag-ism" at the Lady Margaret Hall — a four-hour avant-garde extravaganza which also featured John Tchicai (a black saxophonist who had once worked with Archie Shepp), and the whole of the Cadentia Nova Danica.

Drake had won his scholarship to study English Literature but, according to friends and fellow-pupils, seldom attended lectures, preferring instead to get further into music — and his guitar playing and song-writing in particular. (A previous article about Nick Drake has claimed that he went through an almost permanent depression whilst at Cambridge, which couldn't be further from the truth, according to Brian Wells, one of Drake's best friends at Cambridge and one of the quite a few "frustrated" musicians resident there at that time.)

Cambridge, according to those who have resided there, has harboured a number of such figures in its time. Drake, however, easily shone forth from this company in most every respect: a prolific songwriter, a dauntingly-fine-to-the-point-of-innovative guitarist and — a moot point this — the possessor of a more than fair vocal style, a charming, almost-breathy sound that fitted in somewhere between the incredibly diverse likes of Kevin Ayers and a male Astrid Gilberto. According to Wells, Drake was also always the first on his block to pick up on a new sound.

Randy Newman and Tim Buckley albums were to be found among Nick's collection before other music devotees had got the message; "Astral Weeks" was another Drake Cambridge listening innovation; "Blonde on Blonde" was never far from the stereo, neither was Donovan or Jim Webb's work with the 5th Dimension.

Friends are, in fact only too eager to point out Drake's undying enthusiasm for most things, principally music, during his two years at Cambridge, his own musical progress being most spirited. It was later brought to the attention of, amongst others, one Robert Kirby, a music student from another college in the University complex who became most eager to work on arrangements for Drake's songs. One number for example, "Way to Blue" Kirby saw in terms of endowing with a quasi-Handel string ambience; another, "Riverman" with an hypnotic set of string charts to embellish the already all-pervasive dreamy quality. Thus was consummated a firm, totally-fruitful relationship that was to last (professionally) through two out of three albums and (personally) up to the closing months of Nick's life.

DRAKE, by this time had reach the stage where private performances in friends' lodgings (Wells mentions that certain facets of Nick Drake's talents have never been brought to public attention, not the least being, for example, an adeptness at 12-bar blues improvisations) were turning to public performances in Cambridge itself. It was at one of these that he was "discovered" — by Ashley "Tyger" Hutchings, then bassist for Fairport Convention (later founder member of Steeleye Span and all-round die-hard ethnic English folk music pioneer), at that particular time very much the apple of Witchseason's eye. Witchseason, was of course, the company that managed numerous high-quality-low profile "Underground" acts motivated — and more or less run single-handed — by the incomparable Joe Boyd.

Boyd's credentials were, and still are for that matter, quite peerless. Absolutely *the* vital organising body for London's whole Underground movement — the U.F.O. and Middle Earth

— production credits on the Floyd's first single "Arnold Layne", Incredible String Band Svengali, the Fairports of course . . . the list is endless and positively oozing with a kind of dead-eye sense of good taste and (a hackneyed word, sure, but most relevant here, I'd say) *integrity* easing up even to contemporary projects like that marvellous Hendrix movie and production credits for Maria (and currently ex-hubby Paul Butterfield's Better Days luminary, Geoff) Muldaur.

Boyd was informed of Drake's talents by Hutchings, went down to see for himself and at once became the third figure of the Drake-Kirby-Joe Boyd triumvirate which created . . . well first, of course, there was "Five Leaves Left". The title refers to the dilemma of roll-yer-own smokers when the cigarettte papers are running out, and was of no particular relevance to anything much really except that it sounded like it might be a good album title.

The cover said more: Drake the silent observer staring out of a window, dressed in an utterly nondescript functional style, the corners of his mouth curling ever so slightly on a face that screams with a kind of low-profile sensitivity. On the back a stranger is caught by the camera paralysed in mid-sprint, while Drake leans against a wall quite motionless, his face betraying no semblance of an expression. The gate-fold shot is unfortunate only in that it portrays Drake The Artist-head and shoulders cloaked in pitch-black darkness, prone like some earnest John Donne student of metaphysical introspection.

It's that word "introspection" that constantly springs to mind when Drake's name is mentioned, which is a large part of 'the image' sure, but really Robert Kirby says it when he views Nick Drake the artist as remarkable for "his ability to observe, mainly. I see his work above all as a series of extremely vivid, complete observations and not mere exercises in introspection as some might. They're almost like little epigrammatic proverbs. The music and the words are welded together in such a way as to make the atmosphere in all his songs the most important facet. I know that that was Nick's primary purpose — I don't think for example that he was hung up about his lyrics being 'great poetry' or anything. They're there to complement . . . to compound a mood that the melody dictates in the first place".

THE LATTER point seems to be one that meets with general agreement among acquaintances and admirers (only one person I spoke to made any statement about "Nick being primarily a poet"). Whatever, its omnipresence on all Drake's albums carves out a whole lustrous landscape that has seldom been touched and certainly never bettered by his singer-songwriter peers. "Five Leaves Left" is one of those albums that seem tied to exhorting and then playing on a particular mood in the listener — like "Astral Weeks" and "Forever Changes" certainly and arguably stationed on that particular echelon of creativity (though I wouldn't personally like to enter into that particular argument).

The album's qualities are variable, of course, even if smoothed over by a utterly seductive continuity of mood (a *Time Out* review of "Pink Moon", the third album, made mention of "Nick Drake's exquisite 3 a.m. introspections", which is one way of putting it, I suppose).

"Riverman" is easily the album's finest track: an utterly hypnotic guitar coda played with a kind of deceptively ambling sensuousness, almost throwaway lyrics edged with an oblique mysticism that acts in exactly the way that

Kirby states, and then Kirby's stunning string arrangement that suddenly swells up and levitates spiralling upwards and out, it is Drake at his most supremely spine-tingling effective.

The rest of the album is charming, fragile, observant . . . the adjectives roll off as easily as the melodies.

Island Records (the company Drake was signed with through Boyd's Witchseason connection) loved it, critics drooled, everybody who made it their business to know exactly what was happening in music nodded in their arch pseudo-sage-like pose and predicted great things and Drake immediately became the object of the "But, my dear, have you heard?" conversations. The public largely ignored the album of course, but it had sold "encouragingly" if nothing else and who could blame a highly elated Nick Drake, whose academic leanings had long become quite dormant anyway, for leaving Cambridge to pursue his musical bent?

The company he was keeping in that sphere was perfect anyway: Boyd produced and was a source of constant encouragement, illustrious, folk like Richard Thompson were helping out, Chris Blackwell was a modest but admiring benefactor. And then there was John Martyn and wife, Beverley, another pair of Witchseason hopefuls

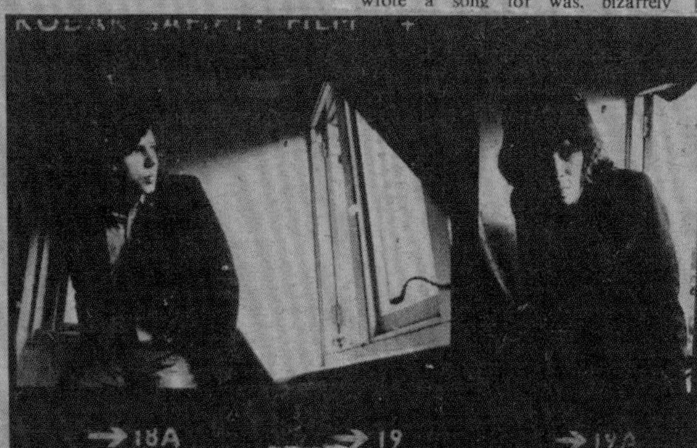

with whom Drake struck up a strong friendship and mutual appreciation society.

Drake was a great admirer of the Martyn accoustic guitar technique and this state of affairs was undeniably reversed to a point where John, according to friends, picked up much of the former's instrumental style.

Robert Kirby again: "Nick was an absolutely phenomenal guitarist . . . that's a fact which is all too often merely glossed over. He was very adept at highly complex double-pick rhythms with the thumb on the bass-string and the other fingers working on as many as four tunes at a time. He was a master of counter-point to that extent. I know for a fact that John Martyn was very influenced by Nick's work in that respect."

Drake's guitar-playing revolved around several complex open-tunings, principally certain mutations of the open-ended D and G chords. The instrumentals on "Bryter- Layter" give one potent example of the personal technique which was to reach full fruition on "Pink Moon". "Bryter Layter" is Nick Drake's most out-ward-going and consequently commercial album. It is also the biggest seller, notching up something in the region of a humble 15,000 sales.

The personal positurism inherent in Drake's psyche at the time cannot be overstated (if only to act as a contrast for the depressing bleak states that were to follow). Not that Nick was ever exactly one to be motivated by a sense of "drive" or ego — there is the story of the time Francoise Hardy, whose whole style and winsome breathy chantease must have obviously been drawn to Drake's similar, superiority-wrought style, phoned Island Records, more or less ordering Drake over to France to write songs for her.

After much goading, Drake, ticket in hand, doggedly set off to the Hardy chateau and after a long journey arrived at the door which was answered by the maid. When asked who he was, Drake muttered, "Um . . . I'm Nick . . . Nick" prompting the maid to become suspicious. Upon questioning the guests present (Ms. Hardy was unfortunately not there at that particular moment) as to whether they knew who "zis Ne-ek is", and getting blank looks for replies, she more or less shut the door in his face.

Drake wandered back to England straight afterwards, a touch bemused by the whole incident.

Drake and Francois Hardy did record together eventually, though nothing appeared from the sessions.

There is talk of some emotional attachment between the two, though little is known as to the exact nature of their relationship or even how long it lasted?

The only other person Drake ever wrote a song for was, bizarrely enough, Millie, of "My Boy Lollipop", who recorded a reggae song of his called "Mayfair" one of those "quaint" pieces of observation — a rich lady getting in a chauffeured limousine while a tramp ambles past at the exact same moment. That was released as a single (Robert King was arranging for Millie and got the song from Drake utilising it thus, on mere impulse). It did absolutely nothing.

BACK TO "Bryter Layter", though. The cover wasn't as good this time. The front, for example, is a twee, unnecessary Nigel Waymouth photo of Drake the Homely Folkie sitting moon-faced and dozy-eyed pouring over a Spanish guitar and fronted by a pair of "bumper"-styled brothel-creepers.

The music though . . . well for a start there was more variety. The melodies were more fluid and easy. "Hazy Jane II" was as close to rock as Drake was ever to get — with a free-wheeling swing-style that you could dance to, plus horns, no less, and great Richard Thompson guitarwork. The personnel were stronger and more varied than before, still using Fairport members plus Danny Thompson (with whom Drake talked about forming some sort of band, without anything ever coming of it) but excursions into a kind of atmospheric cool jazz like "Poor Boy" and "At The Chime Of The City Clock" usurped Ray Warleigh on alto sax and Chris McGregor of Brotherhood of Breath on piano — even spade chick back-up singers Pat Arnold and Doris Troy. And then there was John Cale — at that point somewhere between his A & R gigs, first for Elektra and then Warner Bros, who was living with Joe Boyd at the time and played keyboards and viola on "Fly" and "Northern Sky" — both, interestingly enough, very much precursors to Cale's own sound and style on "Paris 1919" and even some of the new songs from his superb forth-coming album.

The cover again — the back-shot gets closer to the truth of the time. It's a follow-up to the running/standing-still ambience number from the first album sleeve, except this time Drake's on a highway watching a car speed by.

He has his back to the camera.

Actually, Nick Drake never really felt comfortable in front of a camera, though strangely enough photographs of him (principally those of Keith Morris, who was the only photographer to ever get anywhere near him) are all too depressing statements of his personal decline through introspection, depression and, above all — and this is the word that friends choose with great care — confusion.

From 1970, which marked the release date of "Bryter Layter" Drake's final "up" period of any real length and consistency, up to and throughout 1973, Nick Drake's life reached a bleak unhappy state of affairs that it's perhaps unwise to dwell on in too much detail.

I earlier mentioned "Bryter Layter's" commercial potential. It was released at the same time as Cat Stevens' "Mona Bone Taken". Both were artistes striving for public acclaim: Stevens received just that but Drake was pitifully ignored.

Not that even that has much to do with the depressions. Drake was always the archetypal loner. He had his friends — Kirby, Wells, Keith Morris, John Wood, his engineer — but as often found himself in strange surroundings. He would occasionally consort with debutantes and the whole triple-barrel moniker brigade, even though he found their chosen life-styles utterly facile.

He didn't have many girlfriends, though many girls found him an incredibly romantic figure for fairly obvious reasons.

His confusion was something wrought via his destiny — though friends say there was no choice in the matter: no posing, no poetic gestures of the misunderstood troubadour. It was all a matter of course.

Drake slowly became more introspective, less easy to communicate with and everyone became concerned, worried and anxious for his well-being. He eked out a remarkably frugal existence living in Hamstead on £20 a week and became so poor at one point he couldn't even afford a new pair of shoes.

It never crossed his mind to ask a friend to give him a pair. It was just accepted as a fact of life.

Positive moments were few and far between and often conversations, when there were indeed conversations at all, might well dwell on topics like madness, schizophrenia. And occasionally suicide.

Island Records, by now, had given up even *thinking* in terms of Drake as some financial investment, though they still admired his talent and were only too willing to finance albums. It was Island Records indeed, that paid his way to Spain for a short stay there just prior to the making of "Pink Moon". This album was in fact recorded in two sessions over at Sound Techniques with just Drake and John Woods in attendance. Joe Boyd was busy in the States at the time — but, strangely, even he wasn't missed.

"Moon" is, I suppose, what you might call the Artist's Key Work. Brian Wells returned from abroad to find it already in the shops and marvelled at the fact that Nick, though quite lost in confusion and personal depression, could produce a work that captured him in the complete creative ascendant. His guitar playing for example, is quite remarkable here — easily the best he ever allowed onto a record.

"Pink Moon" though, is a strange, somewhat disturbing album. Wells likens it to a kind of Van Gogh statement (which, is one way of looking at it) some of the songs do have obliquely sinister overtones to them; "Know" is a kind of paean to schizophrenia, that Syd Barrett would've loved to have written.

"Know that I love you/know that I don't care/know that I see you/know I'm not there" — while even supposedly-placid songs like "Harvest Bread" bear painful, oblique images of death in them:

"Falling fast you kiss the flowers that bend/And you're ready now for the harvest bread".

Drake's lyrics occasionally ring with a certain pos'tivism, but mostly they are filled wit'i a kind of sad dark sadess, and bitter, resignedly cold observations. Photographs taken by Morris of Drake for the "Pink Moon" cover capture him staring into dull air, his face bearing that horribly doomed dough-like pallor of the terminal depressant — the one that ends up on the gate-fold sleeve is inverted into a kind of mysterioso, doomed negative; while a shot of Drake shuffling away from the camera with a dog running by his legs was used in advertisements for the album.

Media coverage was, not surprisingly, sparse — one interview for Melody Maker is vague to the point of rendering itself totally "nada", while an Island press release is something of a bad joke.

AFTER "PINK Moon" Drake spent some time in various mental hospitals. He'd left London in despair and returned to his parents' house in Tanworth, and it was there that he sought help.

Mostly, though, it wasn't followed up. Nick would check himself in and leave the same day. Everything from the taking of all manner of pills, to electric shock treatment was advised but seldom heeded. Friends became resigned to the imminent news that Nick Drake had taken his own life. It seemed all too inevitable.

And then something happened. The first thing anyone knew about it? The news came that Joe Boyd had driven to Island Record's Hammersmith offices and promptly entered to inform said company that Nick Drake was ready to record again. Drake stayed in the back of the car.

Sessions were laid on at Sound Techniques and in a couple of sessions during the Summer of 1974, Nick Drake, with Joe Boyd and John Woods, got to lay down four new tracks. To all intents and purposes Nick Drake was back on something approaching the right track.

That's only half the story, though.

What had occurred appears to have been something approaching a total psychic re-birth for Nick: he looked and sounded happier than in literally years. He was writing songs again and he even had a steady girl-friend.

He was also smiling again.

His parents, who had also lived with that daunting imminence of suddenly finding their son dead were, not unnaturally, elated. Everyone was.

Up until the night of October 25th the situation had been brightening even further. Drake, always something of a perfectionist where his music was concerned, had scrapped the four tracks (though Woods and Boyd considered them quite beautiful), and was determined to return to the studios again and record better songs.

While anticipating Boyd's return from the States, he'd gone over to Paris for some two weeks to live with a commune on a barge.

He returned more contented than ever.

On the night of October 24th, in his bedroom at Tanworth, where he was still living, Nick Drake had been playing some new riffs and songs over in his pyjamas and recording them on a cassette player. Obviously nobody knows exactly what happened during those hours up to his death at approximately 6 a.m. the following morning, but the subsequent suicide verdict seems ludicrous — if only because of the fact that were Drake to have actually wanted to kill himself, there were bottles full of asprins and barbiturates on hand for such a task.

Anti-depressants are the last thing to take in these circumstances, particularly someone like Drake who, like most of us probably, was fairly ignorant of the potency of such tablets. The tryptasol he was prescribed were so potent that, were even one to be taken over the prescribed limit, death could easily follow in purely accidental circumstances.

All of Drake's friends and acquaintances — including, as it happens, a student doctor I spoke to — are quite adamant: there was no suicide-note, no grand flourish which so often tends to typify the self-imposed taking of ones life.

All things being considered — and, particularly given the circumstances and nature of Nick Drake's death — the coroner's verdict deserves, at the very least, to be questioned.

OBITUARIES ARE probably the hardest of all pieces to write, particularly when you've never actually met the person whose death you're mourning. I always wondered what it would be like to write my first obituary, and decided ultimately that I'd never let myself be placed in a situation where I'd have to do just that.

All I can say when all is said and done that I liked Nick Drake. His music was the proverbial good companion at a time when I appreciate such a commodity. It was strange really after turning my back on that whole particular era of my life some two and a half years ago, I only recently rediscovered how fine his music was some few weeks before his death was reported (and it must have been the most pitifully under-publicized death in the whole ugly, depressing tradition of the whole "death" in rock thing.)

Island Records have not decided anything yet concerning any kind of recorded memorial (e.g. a "Best of" which could utilize the four recently-rrecorded tracks) and, sure, it might be cited as a tasteless gesture — *but* Nick Drake's music should be heard by more people. Its own tastefulness speaks for itself.

And finally, of course, one could make a lavish play on the incredible irony of Nick's death coming at a time when he had regained a certain personal balance, but that gesture would ultimately merely compound the grotesque tragedy of it all.

NICK KENT

FROM NEW MUSICAL EXPRESS DATED 15/2/75.

I FEEL I must clarify a point which I hope you will wish to correct as soon as possible.

In Nick Kent's article on Nick Drake he states at some length that I was responsible for the arrangement of the track "River Man" on the album "Five Leaves Left". In our discussion on the phone, I pointed out to Mr. Kent that at that time Nick and myself agreed that I was not able to arrange such a complex song. It was beautifully scored by Harry Robinson (as stated on the sleeve).

As the majority of people who know and love Nick's music agree that this is probably his finest orchestral song, I would hate to be thought in any way responsible for such a misrepresentation (though obviously accidental) against Mr. Robinson, who is probably Britain's most skilfully original string arranger. — **ROBERT KIRBY, Muswell Hill, London N10.**

WELL DONE, Kent! The article on Nick Drake was one of the best I have read in NME. I had never heard of Nick Drake before and the article still made a profound impact on me.

To people who knew Nick Drake or knew his music, this article must have impressed them tremendously. The article came over, to me at least, as a very well thought out and honest view of Nick Drake's life and his death.

Nick Kent wrought this article in a very moving way; he must have a great respect for Nick Drake. I think everybody who read the article must now know a lot more about the early years in the wilderness of a rising star.

It seems a great pity that this star never made it on a wide scale. Thank you again Nick Kent for a great article. — **IAIN WATKINSON, Leicester.**

WE'D LIKE to thank Nick Kent and NME very much for last week's sensitive, informative piece on Nick Drake.

There's just one point I'd like to clear up: we have no intention of repackaging Nick's recordings, either now or at any time in the forseeable future. His three albums have never been deleted, and they will remain available for those who wish to discover and enjoy them.

Furthermore, Nick himself expressed dissatisfaction with the four songs he recorded late last year; consequently John Wood has destroyed the 16-track master tapes — with our full approval. — **RICHARD WILLIAMS, Island Records, London W.6.**

● Sensitivity, 'twould seem, triumphs again. We (that's us) thank you (that's you) all. (That's that).

Of one thing he is adamant — the music world could not afford to lose the like of Nick Drake, who was a close friend of John's.

"It's the first time I've ever been exposed to anything at such close range. It's a great waste and a great shame but I would say it's the world's loss and not his." — JERRY GILBERT

JOHN MARTIN "SOUND" Feb 1st 1975

NICK DRAKE

The Final Retreat

The amount of coverage Nick Drake's death had in the weekly musical comics just about sums it all up, really. Jerry Gilbert did a beautiful piece for 'Sounds'—and they cut it down to half-a-dozen paragraphs. No-one else mentioned his departure with much more than a cursory nod of acknowledgement.

OK, so the guy did no more than a dozen gigs before more than 150 people, and they raised no ripple you'd notice. He released three albums in four years, and together they probably didn't sell enough to cover the cost of one. What the hell do you want?—front page in 'The Times'?

So you look at the facts and have to agree that when The Bay City Rollers have a new Number One and Gary Glitter's made his comeback after what we've been told is a crucial throat operation, there's precious little space left for the accidental death of some recluse folkie.

But.

The biggest three-letter word in the dictionary, that. But Nick Drake was a lovely cat. But he wrote songs that'd tear your soul out if you relaxed for a second. But in a world full of bullshit, hype, glittery horrors with the talents of dead oxen and the integrity of starving rats, Nick Drake was a man of sincerity, an artist of tremendous calibre and one of the few entitled to be called unique. But what the hell do they care?

Connor McKnight cared enough to research a superb piece on Nick Drake in ZZ42. Jerry Gilbert cared enough to pressure 'Sounds' into printing a shortened obituary. A lady who worked with me at Island Records when Nick's second album 'Bryter Layter' was released cared enough to cry when I told her he was dead. Joe Boyd and John Wood, his former producer and recording engineer, care like hell. And I do too.

I have no intention of making this short appreciation much more than that. This history, if you haven't read it and care to, is contained in Connor's story and is as complete as time allows. There is some to add.

Since ZZ42, when Connor's story ended, Joe Boyd, John Wood and Nick Drake did get together in the Sound Techniques Studios and put down some tracks.

Nick and Joe had got together in February 1974, while Joe was on a fleeting visit to London. At the time Nick told Joe that not only didn't he have any words left, he also didn't have any tunes anymore. What Joe didn't tell Connor is that he was shocked enough by this response to give Nick a good talking-to. Joe describes it as a pep-talk, but what he did was to tell Nick that he was wasting and abusing a real and valuable talent and that he ought to stop pissing about and knuckle down to work.

In July, Boyd was in London again and heard from Nick. He wanted to go into the studio to try out four new songs he'd pretty well got together. Nothing elaborate was done in that session—just guitar and voice tracks.

"Nick couldn't sing and play at the same time," Joe recalls. So they recorded the guitar and then the voice. It was shaky, but the melodies—the factor which elevates Drake's work above any of his rivals—were as beautiful as ever. Apart from a general dissatisfaction with the vocals, Nick, Joe and John were happy.

Boyd had to return to the States for more work and left Nick with every intention of returning in the autumn to continue what they decided was the beginning of a fourth album. Success with a number of projects, not the least being the Maria Muldaur albums, forced Joe to spend all his time in American studios, so the planned grand reunion never came off. By the end of November Nick Drake—described by everyone around him as being more happy than they'd known him for a long time—was dead from an

accidental overdose of sleeping pills.

Joe Boyd is clearly still upset about Nick's death and honest enough to express sorrow that he didn't make it back. His relationship with Nick was pretty special to him. "In a lot of ways it was a frustrating one, because although I felt I was able to get through to him and deal with him as a musician, I was never really able to handle him as a person. I don't think I ever gave him the feedback he needed."

It was a problem most people encountered, mainly because of Nick's own personality which changed discernibly through his last few years. John Martyn was someone originally close to Nick, someone with whom Nick communicated eagerly, both as a musician and as a person. But even John, and his wife Beverley, were eventually unable to handle Nick's moods. He'd turn up at their home in Hastings, unannounced but welcome, sit around for a couple of days without saying more than a few monosyllabic words, and leave as unexpectedly and abruptly as he'd arrived. It upset both of them; they tried to help and draw him out, but they got nowhere fast.

My few dealings with Nick at Island were at the time when he was withdrawing more and more away from all but a few people. He was non-communicative to the point of pain and spent a lot of time in a secret world of his own making. He'd vanish for long periods. Traced to a house full of flats in Hampstead, you'd discover that no-one even knew his name, or that he'd taken the flat in an assumed one.

But to contradict any generalisations made about his mental state, he would keep in touch with Joe Boyd and John Wood, still call Robert Kirby, the old friend from his days at Fitzwilliam College, Cambridge, who was brought in to arrange 'Bryter Layter'. And he still managed to come up with the songs which made his last album 'Pink Moon'.

The album was stark—just Nick's voice, his guitar and occasional piano. It reflected his mood at the time, and the dissatisfaction he felt about the way 'Five Leaves Left' and 'Bryter Layter' had sounded. At the time of 'Bryter Layter' I got the impression from Nick that he didn't like the strings, or the way the album was presented. Fine, if his studio relationship with Joe Boyd and Robert Kirby had been as bad as Tim Hardin's was with the people at Verve.

In Hardin's case, the rhythm and vocal tracks had been laid down, Hardin had split and strings shoved on when he was far away.

Nick Drake personally supervised every aspect of Kirby's arrangements, working with him and—as Joe Boyd tells it—mainly getting Kirby to chart out what Nick had, in the main, already planned. 'Bryter Layter' took a year to make because Nick Drake spent that long making damn sure it was precisely the way he wanted it.

So if Nick Drake had failed to realise the sounds he heard in his head, 'Pink Moon' trusted to the Drake audience to hear them for themselves. Maybe he did it that way so he could play it at home and hear the different arrangements himself.

But what Joe Boyd calls "the steady progress of retreat" was going on, and Nick spent more and more time at his parents' home in Stratford-upon-Avon, and latterly in Paris. His deal with Island had ended, and with it the regular 15 quid a week salary/pocket money Joe had arranged with Chris Blackwell before handing over the Witchseason stable to Island. Joe isn't sure how Nick made ends meet. There certainly weren't any royalties coming in.

Nick had enough friends to ensure that he had somewhere to stay and to watch out for him. Joe and he had talked about getting a new deal together so that he could get some kind of advance, but a hoped for meeting between Nick, Joe and a still-interested Chris Blackwell never came off because Nick just didn't want to commit himself to any kind of contract.

And that's pretty well the way it ended. Unfinished, inconclusive and typically up in the air.

If you haven't heard Nick Drake's work, dare I suggest you go out of your way and do so? It won't change the ending of the story, but it could change you. Don't take my word for it—Joe Boyd says it far heavier than I ever could:

"Of all the albums I've ever made, the two albums I produced by Nick are the ones I'm most proud of. I listen to them often because Nick Drake was extraordinarily good. Nothing he ever did was less than striking, and he had the gift of writing melodies of incredible beauty."

Joe Boyd, it may be worth reminding you, has been responsible during his career for some of the definitive British folk and rock albums, including Fairport's 'Unhalfbricking' and 'Leige And Lief', for John and Beverley Martyn's 'Stormbringer' and for the best Incredible String Band albums.

Two pictures of Nick Drake pretty well sum up what I think his relationship with us norms was. The first was on the cover of 'Five Leaves Left'. Nick stands, supporting and being supported by a wall, static and observing while a figure blurs past. Nick tended to let a lot of the world blur past—and was probably smart to do so.

The second was the back view of Nick—shoulders hunched, hand in scruffy jacket pocket, trouser turn-up torn—used to illustrate the ads for 'Pink Moon'.

We spent a day with Nick, taking innumerable excellent arty shots of him with a romping Gus the Labrador, or sat on park benches with a wistful, far-away (and bored?) look in his eyes. But that retreating back said it all.

And it still does.

☐ **DAVID SANDISON**

19
NOVEMBER 35p
AUSTRALIA $1 NEW ZEALAND $1·10
CANADA $1·40 MALAYSIA $3

NOVEMBER

1978

3

MUSIC

In Memory Of

This month sees the release of what is, without question, one of the most remarkable albums of the past 10 years. A tall claim, perhaps, but *Nick Drake* (Island) is a collection of the entire recorded works of an artist whom some regarded as one of the most talented singers and writers of his generation but whom providence cheated of his rightful recognition during his life. Nick Drake died four years ago at the age of 26. As a performer, all we have to remember him by are three albums of staggering beauty and a handful of tracks previously unreleased, now included in *Nick Drake*.

His performances were few. Crippled by shyness, he never was at home on stage. He never gave interviews. During his life, he somehow escaped the close scrutiny to which public figures are usually subjected. And it is only since his death that his records have sold in any quantity. His upbringing was archetypal English upper-middle class. He went to public school then Cambridge where, at a May Ball, he first performed the songs he had been writing. That performance led to a recording contract and, in 1969, his first album *Five Leaves Left*.

The first thing that strikes the listener about *Five Leaves Left* is its intense sense of privacy. Drake's performance makes one feel almost like an interloper who has stumbled inadvertently upon a diary to be at first abashed by the confidences disclosed then absorbed by the honesty and vulnerability of its author. His voice is never strident, rather it is a gentle, almost husky murmur, complemented by simple, acoustic guitar-picking and baroque string arrangements which enhance the songs' melancholic quality.

By any standards, it was an extraordinary performance—for the first album, even more so. But, mysteriously, the record was not a commercial success, neither was Drake's second album, *Bryter Later*, indisputably his finest hour. While *Five Leaves Left* was steeped in folk-music origins, with *Bryter Later* Drake wrought a style which was inimitable, bringing a jazz-accented shuffle to songs like 'Poor Boy' (where a girl chorus gently mocks the singer with the line "So sorry for hisself") and adding woodwinds to the evocative string arrangements to bring a dreamlike atmosphere to much of the album.

Seven years after its release, *Bryter Later* sounds as fresh as it ever did. But its pervasive mood of sadness and estrangement accurately reflects the trouble Nick Drake was having in making sense of his life at that time. In a profile in *New Times*, an American magazine, Arthur Lubow described how Drake was becoming increasingly insular and remote, his behaviour increasingly erratic. At the instigation of his parents, he underwent psychiatric treatment.

"He was very detached," a friend, Paul Wheeler, told Arthur Lubow. "He kept withdrawing until he just disappeared . . . "

Pink Moon, his third and final album, reflects that isolation. Drake recorded the album in two nights, alone, accompanying himself on piano and guitar. Stripped of the lush arrangements which had cushioned *Five Leaves Left* and *Bryter Later*, Drake sounds defenceless. But neither anguish nor pain are in evidence, the sadness is resigned, tranquil.

After *Pink Moon*, Drake's melancholia became more profound. He went to Paris to live, saying he no longer wished to record but to compose for other artists, instead. Paris seemed to do him good. His family thought he had rarely seemed happier, but it was short-lived.

He was back at home when, on 25 November 1974, tragedy struck. That morning Nick had appeared to have slept late. His mother went to wake him and found him lying in his bed, dead.

He had died from an overdose of anti-depressants. The coroner's verdict was suicide. MICK BROWN

The Listener 19 and 26 December 1974

Pop Music

The year in pop by John Peel

Our hearts were uplifted at the start of 1974 by loose talk of a vinyl shortage. Such a shortage, surely, would cut down marvellously on the flood of sub-standard records released by those companies that operate on the scatter-shot principle. This principle, long a record-biz staple, is based on the simultaneous issue of 15 or 20 records in the hope that one will somehow stick. However, with fiendish ingenuity, these companies have largely dodged the proclaimed shortage, and the deluge of nightmarish records has continued.

On the credit side, the most obvious LP successes, in musical terms, have come from two young and fiercely independent labels, Island and Virgin, which make certain that *every* release counts. Island have been with us since the early Sixties, starting as a label devoted to West Indian music, and developing throughout the progressive boom into a label that could be depended upon, by 1970, to produce work that was always interesting, usually excellent. Free, Fairport Convention, Traffic, Nick Drake, Spooky Tooth, the Incredible String Band, King Crimson, Mott the Hoople and Cat Stevens are just some of the names associated with the label during this period. Through 1972 and 1973, Island's output was generally less interesting, but in 1974 they have experienced a resurgence that has been most gratifying. In a later LISTENER, I hope to thrill you with a list of the ten LPs of 1974 that I consider to be the very best. Currently, my working list contains some 45 records, so the final ten are still in considerable doubt, but I suspect that Richard and Linda Thompson's *I Want To See The Bright Lights Tonight* will be my LP of the year. Richard and Linda record for Island, and during the year the label has also released dandy music from Eno (twice), Sparks, (twice), Bad Company, Nico, John Cale, Jess Roden, Robert Palmer, Traffic, Fairport Convention, Roxy Music, Bryan Ferry, Andy Mackay, Bryn Haworth, Sandy Denny, King Crimson (twice), Sharks and the Sutherland Brothers and Quiver (twice). Anything from this impressive list will bring pleasure into the homes of persons

NEW MUSICAL EXPRESS March 19th, 1977

Information CITY

EDITED BY FRED DELLAR

Nick Drake: the remaining albums

I HAVE just listened to "Pink Moon", an album by singer-songwriter Nick Drake, and thought it really excellent. I've never heard of him before — could you tell me if he has any other albums available? — **DAVID JONES, Mayford, Woking, Surrey.**

IS NICK Drake dead? If so, when and how? — **DAVE HOWARTH, Chipping, Preston, Lancs.**

● Drake, a brilliant singer-songwriter, died from an overdose of an anti-depressant at his parents' home at Tamworth, Arden, on October 25, 1974. The coroner's verdict was death by suicide caused by prolonged mental illness. But Nick Kent, in a superbly constructed investigation into the life and work of Drake (NME 8-2-75), contested these findings. Whatever the truth of the matter, all that remains to remind us of his talent is a trio of albums — "Five Leaves Left" (Island ILPS9105), "Bryter Later" (ILPS9134) and "Pink Moon" (ILPS9184).

The late NICK DRAKE

Rodney And Molly

by Gorm Henrik Rasmussen

It's 1979. And November again. Exactly one year after my first encounter with *Pink Moon* I find myself in London, looking for people who can help me in my quest for Nick Drake.

Island Records have provided me with the address of Nick's parents, but not with their phone number, so I get hold of a Warwickshire directory and find an R. Drake, Far Leys, Tanworth-in-Arden. The name 'Far Leys' mystifies me. Is it a street? Or a manor house, perhaps? A long time passes before the ringing phone is answered.

'Yes, hello?'

The tone is aristocratic, the voice is light and sonorous; no doubt it belongs to an elderly, distinguished gentleman.

'Hello, is this Rodney Drake?'

'Yes, it is. Whom am I speaking to?'

I introduce myself as a young Danish poet, and in my best classroom English I try to explain my plans of writing a book about Nick Drake. Would it be possible to get an interview?

A long pause follows.

'I really don't know if we have got anything interesting to tell you.'

It's been five years since the young songwriter swallowed a handful of antidepressants, which had dangerous side effects on the heart.

I tell his father that I am convinced his son is one of the greatest songwriters to come out of England in the Sixties, and that it's a bloody shame his music is not better known. I say that it will not be possible for me to return to England in the foreseeable future.

Rodney Drake hesitates and then disappears from the phone for a minute. As far as I can hear he has a muted exchange with a woman. The only sentence I catch is, 'It's a poet from Denmark.' A minute or two go by. Then he returns.

'All right, we would like to meet you.'

'Ask him if he will read some of his poems!' shouts the woman in the background.

'Did you hear what my wife said?'

I reply that I'll be sure to bring my poems, but that unfortunately they are all in Danish.

'Oh, that doesn't matter. Then you can just translate one or two for us. That'll be fine.'

A few days later Rodney and Molly Drake pick me up in Birmingham and we drive through the green landscape of Warwickshire, heading for Tanworth-in-Arden, the village where Nick spent his childhood. The sun is shining from a cloudless November sky. The pleasant atmosphere in the car has an edge of natural awkwardness as we sound each other out. Rodney and Molly are an elegant, extremely polite, elderly couple – she is in her early sixties, he is over seventy – but they appear youthful as they sit in their comfortable car, chatting with me about the culture and music that I perceive as part of *my* history. It is unusual to hear people over fifty referring to Fairport Convention, and the London underground scene of 1967, as if it were the most natural thing in the world. They tell me of the time Nick met the Rolling Stones on a trip to Morocco, and to my utter astonishment they have listened to *Revolver*. They know the individual songs. Molly praises the string arrangements, and Rodney singles out 'Eleanor Rigby' as one of the high points of *The Beatles Songbook*.

We roll through the idyllic village with the church on one side and the pub on the other, while eagerly discussing the influence of J. S. Bach on rock music. When Rodney stops the car in front of a large house at the end of a lane, I realise that we have arrived. This is Far Leys, not a street or a manor, but rather a house with many windows. The solid redbrick walls are covered in ivy. Nick's childhood home. And final abode.

Rodney and Molly lead me down a path to the back of the house and give me a tour of the garden. I'm here in a rural village being shown around a picture perfect English garden. Trees and bushes circle a well-tended lawn; here and there flower beds break the straight lines and angles created by the mower. Behind the bushes, more garden: a square lawn especially laid out for playing croquet, the English summer sport.

We take a moment to enjoy the view from the croquet lawn. The garden opens onto a hilly landscape, cut across with creeks; stubble fields, moss-grown stone fences, little copses and meadows as far as the eye can see. I try to imagine what it must have been like to grow up here. Boys need a lot of space to romp about in. If I were a songwriter and my point of origin was this spot, the likelihood would be that words such as 'sky', 'sun', 'rivers', 'leaves', 'wind' and 'grass' would slip into my vocabulary with the same ease as moving one's feet or drawing a breath.

'Nick would often roam around on his own,' Rodney tells me of the early years in Tanworth-in-Arden. 'One would find him in the garden or in the meadows behind it. Nick always knew how to amuse himself. I wouldn't go so far as to say that he kept himself to himself or had a hard time making friends . . . but he was a loner by nature.'

In contrast to his elder sister, Gabrielle, Nick was an introvert. He was an observer who enjoyed watching the world while keeping it at a safe distance.

'Of course, he couldn't really do that,' Rodney continues, smiling briefly, and then turning serious again. 'Nick was so sensitive. He took the grief and worries of others upon himself, and if anyone he knew were in trouble, he would feel terribly sorry for them.'

'On the other hand we mustn't forget that Nick had a terrific sense of humour,' Molly adds. 'It was as if from a very early age he could see through the absurdities of adult life – from the way in which people dress to the discrepancies between what people *say* and what they actually *do*. When I think back on his childhood, that is probably what I remember best. All those hours he and I spent together laughing.'

We have come inside the house and are now sitting between bookcases and mahogany cupboards in a spacious living room. The furnishings bear witness to the years that the family spent in the Far East. There is wicker furniture, Oriental jute mats, strange lamps and bric-a-brac, Chinese figurines, and sofas upholstered in floral patterns. There is a comfortable area with a fireplace; on the black piano in a corner facing the garden is a vase with freshly cut roses. The sun streams in through the many windows. The warm colours of the Orient meet a tasteful traditional interior; the styles of two separate worlds brought together in one grand house.

'Nick had a special sense of humour, it's true,' Rodney concurs. He is a tall, powerfully built man with an owl-like head. His movements are slow and dignified. He appears to be a rock of calm as he sits there in his brown cardigan and grey, recently ironed, trousers, his hands folded around his knee, leaning back in the comfortable sofa. At his side sits one who at first glance appears to be his complete opposite: Molly Drake, a vivacious and delightful lady, gesticulating, entertaining. She is being the hostess, and her husband enjoys that. She speaks passionately about music and tells me that she writes songs as well, as her husband nods and smiles. The couple have been married for forty-two years. They are respectful and attentive towards one another. They know each other like a well-travelled duo, and when Molly begins a sentence, Rodney will often finish it, and vice versa. They both speak in this old-fashioned English, which rings clear as a bell with open vowels and voiced *s*'s, a natural musical tone that leads easily into song. Nick Drake sang in this language. He never adopted any alien accent, even though almost all his musical heroes had their roots in African American rhythm and blues.

'How did he do in school?' I ask.

'Fine,' says Molly.

'Amazingly well,' Rodney chimes in. 'Nick had top grades in nearly all subjects. At his first school, Eagle House in Berkshire, where he spent five years, he was elected captain of the rugby team. Later, when he went to Marlborough College, he beat the school record in the hundred-yard dash.'

'He was a fast runner, very fast.' Molly nods. 'He had the perfect height and build. He was a born athlete.'

'The funny thing is that he wasn't really interested in sports,' Rodney says. 'Neither track events nor rugby were important to him. He was just amazingly fast on the track. Another paradox: our boy didn't like being in charge. He just wanted to potter about quietly and mind his own business. Yet he was made head boy. His classmates loved him. He was also well-liked among his teachers. But in the last report card he had at Eagle House

– an exceptionally good report card – his headmaster wrote "*None of us really knows him*".

Molly: 'When he changed schools at thirteen, he came home overjoyed and said: "You know what, Mum, the thing I like best about Marlborough is that I shall have no responsibilities there. Now I can finally relax." And what happened? His new classmates made him head boy *of his junior house*. It was no use protesting. They *wanted* him as head boy.'

Rodney hesitates a bit. 'Early on in his life there was a pattern emerging. He found himself at the centre of his friends' and teachers' attention, and at the same time he felt that he was an outsider. A strangely uncomfortable position to be in. If you listen to his lyrics, you'll see that *that* is the dilemma some of them deal with.'

'You couldn't put anything across Nick. You couldn't cheat him in any way. He would know quickly what you were really thinking. He had a very shrewd way of summing people up'.

Molly Drake

Rodney and Molly both play the piano. They come from families with musical traditions. After only a short time with them I have the distinct impression that Nick grew up in a household where music was much more than a diversion at teatime; it was quite simply an important part of family life. Molly wrote songs for her children from the time they were in their cradles. She taught Nick the piano when he was five. Later, when he went to Marlborough, he learned to play the clarinet and the saxophone. Although it has been five years since his death, I can feel how much he is still present at Far Leys. Nick is here, there and everywhere. Molly goes to the piano and strikes a series of chords. She looks at me inquisitively.

'"Way To Blue",' I say, feeling slightly disoriented.

'That's right! Nick wrote his songs on the guitar, but "Way to Blue" is actually a piano piece. When Robert Kirby did the arrangements for the piece, he had the idea of replacing the piano with a string quartet.'

There is something puzzling me. When Rodney and Molly discuss when and where Nick wrote something, a number of the songs they keep referring to are quite unknown to me. His parents are throwing about quotes from what appears to be a hidden treasure of songs.

Nick Drake recorded three albums. They are displayed on the table in front of us in their new packaging, next to a little pile of clippings from English and American music magazines. But there was a time before these records; a very creative period when Nick lived in the south of France. As far as I can gather, the songs from this period are simpler and more youthful than the ten that Nick selected for his debut album. The titles sound intriguing: 'Bird Flew By', 'Mayfair', 'Blossom Friend' and 'My Love Left With The Rain'.

'He met a girl in Aix-en-Provence and wrote a song for her,' Molly explains. 'The girl's name was Joey. He must have been quite in love with her. It is a song about unrequited love.'

'Just like "Princess Of The Sand",' Rodney interjects.

'A lovely one,' Molly nods.

'One of his best,' Rodney agrees.

'And he never recorded it?' I ask.

'No, not on any album. But we have it on a tape, together with the other songs. You can hear them if you like.'

'Rodney managed to smuggle the tape out of the music room and hide it in a drawer,' Molly says.

'We had to be very careful, or the songs would have been lost,' Rodney continues. 'Nick was so hard on himself. He would record a number twenty times and then erase it all. Later he would mock his early songs and call them childish and silly. We, however, thought they were wonderful. And we still do – even though the sound quality is very bad.'

The door to the music room is open. From where I sit in the living room I can see a music stand, a stool and a small shelf where some tape reels are lying about. On the wall there is a frame containing the original cover of *Pink Moon*. The room has been left more or less as it was on the night Nick left it five years ago, after he had been listening to Bach's Brandenburg Concertos. The turntable is still there, and Nick's record collection. While Rodney is kneeling in front of the shelf, looking for the tape of Nick's early songs, I quickly glance through Nick's records. The covers are well-worn. Nick Drake must have been an inveterate coffee drinker, for they all have dark stains and cup marks on them. He had been listening to *The Freewheelin' Bob Dylan* and *Rubber Soul*. Here are albums by Bert Jansch, Tim Buckley, Randy Newman, Miles Davis and Tim Hardin. Van Morrison's *Astral Weeks* has also seen some heavy use. A select, very refined collection of records, although it gives no clues as to how Nick Drake, aged nineteen, could present a song like 'River Man' to his friends in Cambridge . . .

'Are you ready?' Without waiting for my reply Rodney starts the tape. First comes the guitar. The basic riff is immediately catchy. It is simple. The fretwork is virtuoso. Then the words. Nick's voice, muted, darker than one is used to:

Deep down in the depth of forgotten dreams
So far away, so long ago it seems . . .

'One day he showed up with a guitar; he must have been fifteen or sixteen,' Rodney tells me as the tape plays on. 'Nick's instruments were the clarinet and the saxophone, so naturally we were curious . . . We knew some of the tunes. It seemed as if he found it easy to absorb other songwriters' stuff and he quickly finished with them. But his own songs he played over and over. Often he would practise till late at night, sometimes without switching on the lights when it got dark. He would just sit and strum for hours on end.'

Rodney must have sensed my fascination with these songs that Nick obviously considered unfinished, because when we have finished our tea and I have met the Karen housekeeper Naw, he returns to the music room. He comes back from there waving the cassette tape in his hand and gives it to me.

'You can keep this.'

I thank him, moved and amazed by this gesture, and ask him if he knows when the songs were recorded.

'1967 and '68,' he says without hesitation. 'Some are from Nick's time in Aix-en-Provence, but most of them are recorded here at Far Leys – under rather primitive conditions, as you can probably hear.'

On the way to the station we go by the cemetery at the Church of St Mary Magdalene in Tanworth-in-Arden, and the couple show me Nick's grave. His plain, grey, arched granite stone carries the inscription 'Now we rise and we are everywhere'. Rodney bends down and with quick movements of his hand brushes away some wet and golden brown leaves that surround the little plot.

'We were looking for a line from one of Nick's songs that wasn't too sad a memory of his much too early death,' Rodney says while rubbing some soil off his hands. 'We chose "From The Morning" because that song has hope in it. It says "nothing disappears".'

It is pitch black when we get to Wolverhampton and the two of them accompany me into the train station. We say goodbye. As I wave farewell from the compartment window, I have no way of knowing that in less than a year I would once again be sitting at the living-room table drinking tea with them, in an atmosphere so warm and hearty that I almost feel a part of the family.

'Come and see us in the merry month of May,' Molly wrote to me, 'then we will be able to have tea in the garden.'

That was in the winter of 1987. This letter turned out to be the last I would ever receive from Far Leys. Much later I discovered the reason for that: Rodney had died.

He left behind a little black book: 'For Molly'. Written in his tidy little hand, the book had a number of small chapters: 'How to pay the bills'. 'How to deal with the tax'. 'How to set the aerials' . . . Through their long marriage Rodney had learned that it was no use trying to burden Molly with practicalities; she wrote poetry and songs, was a good mother and a loving wife, and that was more than enough for him.

Rodney, the engineer, made sure that his family stayed safe and comfortable even after he himself had gone. On the surface he seemed rather reserved and awkward, a bit of a stereotypical, conservative, English patriarch. But one did not have to spend much time with him before he let his guard down and revealed his loving, gentle nature. What struck me about Rodney was how expansive he was. One always got an urge to discuss things with him, to egg him on and provoke him, because he showed you so much respect. In Rodney's universe, poets were at the top of the social ladder, on a par with kings and war heroes. This esteem for artists was probably old-fashioned. I confess I enjoyed his company very much.

Precipice Of Loneliness

by Will Stone

Truth is a power. But one can see that only in rare instances, because it is suffering and must be defeated as long as it is truth. When it has become victorious others will join it. Why? Because it is truth? No, if it had been for that reason they would have also joined it when it was suffering. Therefore they do not join it because it has power. They join it after it has become a power because others had joined it.

Søren Kierkegaard

I

'Who could he have been?' asked the great German-language poet Rainer Maria Rilke of his direct contemporary, the Austrian visionary Georg Trakl, following the latter's suicide by an overdose of drugs in November 1914, in a mental hospital, in Krakow, Poland. One might be tempted to ask the same of the poet who departed the earth in not dissimilar circumstances almost exactly sixty years later, in the barely comparable surroundings of the picturesque Warwickshire village of Tanworth-in-Arden in England.

The legend, for want of a better word, of poet singer-songwriter/guitarist Nick Drake is but a few decades old, and the global fame he now enjoys roughly counts for a third of that time. Many facts surrounding his life remain obscure and therefore his movements through creative ascension and mental decline have become hopelessly obscured by skeins of rhetoric and been awarded almost mythical and often misleading properties. However, one remains resolutely stark and clear. Drake died by his own hand from an overdose of prescribed drugs in November 1974, aged twenty-six, following a prolonged period of what is generally termed 'clinical depression'. My aim in this essay is to avoid as far as possible a conventional approach to Nick Drake's art, where the pecuniary-drawn plough never stops turning up another scrap of extinct ordnance or a dubious treasure. For this recycling of soundings and propositions always misses the overlooked essential, the touchstone of Drake's being, the visionary element.

For above all else, Nick Drake was a genuine poet with a heightened introspective faculty overwhelmed by an on-going and unfeigned existential interrogation. The injurious mental malaise Drake suffered and which invariably led to his life being cut short, was a by-product of this rare faculty, causing him to exist in a state of subliminal precariousness, in states intricately bound and in some sense interdependent on each other. Although the depressive ailment that bore down on Nick Drake was not unique to him, since many artists who engage in their own 'struggle with the demon' are held in the grip to some extent by Blake's 'mind-forg'd manacles', it was in his case all-encompassing and surely decisive. His relatively rapid ascent, the sector of the music world he was obliged to navigate, and his creative peak occurring at a certain cross-generational point in history, may also have had some bearing on the self-destructive propensity of his mental decline. Drugs of course also have their part to play and cannot be glossed over, however wearying the music that habitually plays from their malicious fairy pipes. But the extent to which they informed his lyrical gift remains ambiguous. Although no one is refuting Arthur Rimbaud's call for intoxication to render a complete upheaval of the senses in order to access visionary states, and despite the all-pervading LSD culture of the late Sixties, it is important in Drake's case to see drugs as no more and no less than indifferent servants standing patiently in the vestibule leading to the chamber of breakdown. They appeared, so to speak, both at the right and the wrong moment. For with or without drugs, an artist of Drake's calibre was already perfectly poised to circumnavigate the abyss.

To make matters worse, Drake was a highly erudite, sincere and intelligent young man who was ashamed of his own parlous state as depression took hold. Despite on the surface being able to employ a wry wit and delicately dry sense of humour, Drake was irrevocably drawn, via the dark romanticism he fostered, into something of a self-fulfilling prophecy. This sense of being one of the few who only receive their artistic laurels after death is articulated throughout his lyrics, but none more overtly it would seem than in the mournfully numinous song 'Fruit Tree', whose sumptuous melody seems to make the clearest of statements. And yet one must be careful not to jump to apparently inevitable conclusions, since, knowing Drake's eventual fate, such lyrics take on a greater significance than they may really have harboured. Having said this, since we only have the lyrics we cannot overlook them, nor pass them off as mere unsubstantiated symbols, for they are all we have. But whether the extraordinary lyrics of 'Fruit Tree' were strictly personal, or merely a melancholy tainted fanfare for the universal forgotten prodigy discovered by later generations, cannot be properly determined, nor should be. If one is tempted to settle somewhere between the two, this would not be, it seems to me, a wholly uncomfortable or presumptuous position. Particularly as the awareness and acceptance of alienation and the seed of posthumous resurrection is witnessed some time before the oft-cited lyrics of 'Fruit Tree', namely in Drake's earliest songs, penned at a time when, it has been suggested (largely by biographers eager to observe their own torch beam play in the gloom), Drake was as yet untainted by any pernicious existential disturbance. But the nimbus shadow that almost always passes across these early songs demonstrates a darker conclusion. These youthful lyrics are in fact tentative precursors to those from the more desolate latter stage. Through a quasi-symbolist mist, we make out the same concern for the deceptions of earthly existence. The reaction to this is an increased sense of apartness, of being a son of perennial nature rather than of modern humanity. 'I was made to love no one / No one to love me / Only the wind in the long green grass, / The frost on a broken tree,' laments Drake in his paean to the elusive magic of elsewhere.

The great German poet of the Romantic era Friedrich Hölderlin, two centuries before, passionately identified with unsullied nature, as he sought to fasten himself poetically to the eternal, to those regions of the spirit that convey a nobler, purer caste and where natural phenomena take on a persuasive personality. His fear and rightful foreboding before so-called 'madness' claimed him, was to be subsumed in a lonely vigil cut off from the literary activity of his time. His 'stock' too was in the ground but no one in his era had as yet noticed the freshly disturbed soil. The intellectual minds around Hölderlin during his lifetime were simply not yet in the right gear to properly detect or absorb his imaginative powers. Hölderlin's poetry had appeared too early to fuse meaningfully with the existing readership of his time, but by the very nature of its unique poetic apartness, it could germinate only in that time, and therefore Hölderlin's path would necessarily be a tragic one of isolation. Nick Drake's songs on the other hand were recognised as uniquely gifted works by a minority of discerning people. But any mass audience (while he lived) was unable to distinguish his proper contours against the glut of singer-songwriters thronging the airwaves at the time, and chose to worship other lesser or more commercial artists because the art and the recipient in these cases were in a more easily won synchronicity 'of the moment', whereas Drake's mass audience were moored out of sight, an armada only prepared to sail out of the future. Drake's personal tragedy, i.e. the sense of failure, is that he expected an audience to respond enthusiastically, he yearned to see his own generation take strength from his art, but an audience 'proportionate' to his generous creative donation could not manifest itself in his lifetime. The frustration engendered by this perverse constellation is then the impetus for the protracted fall.

As with Hölderlin, the yearning for a higher place shorn of the earthbound occurs throughout Drake's lyrics. Often it is the wind or the breeze which serves as chief symbol for escape from the oppressive weight of being. In 'Bird Flew By', one of the most affecting and enduring early songs, he suggests that the elements remain uninfected, sacrosanct, are left in a quasi-sacred state by their insulation from the contrasting pestilent chaos of the human world. 'The wind and the rain shook hands again, untouched by the world, they managed to stay sane.' And later in 'Northern Sky', one of Drake's flagships, he returns to the high foliage with the line 'Or felt sweet breezes in the top of a tree', following on from the nod to William Blake's 'infinity in the palm of your hand' in his 'never held emotion in the palm of my hand'. So always the wind, purified by the crown of leafage, and crucially high off the ground is where Drake would feel safer and more at home, where he too, if he could just jettison the skin of his earthbound existence might manage to 'stay sane'. Furthermore, it is perhaps pertinent to compare the revealing early song 'They're Leaving Me Behind', recorded in the summer of 1967, to the lyrics of 'Bird Flew By' of roughly the same period. Then compare these to later more accomplished works such as 'Day Is Done', 'Road', or ''Cello Song', or to the languorous downstream drift of 'At The Chime Of A City Clock' and the harrowing honesty of 'Parasite', Drake's urban Calvary. All these songs and more morph into one another with that now familiar essence of romantic wistfulness offset by refined bitterness, displaying a longing for transcendence and the peeping shoots of self-loathing. All are habitual concerns for the uncompromising poet who must respond artistically, *literally* in order to survive, for only through the creation of an alternative landscape in which to reside can he hope to support his insecure and increasingly burdened presence. It is, then, this fundamental struggle between the increasing weight of his own existence and the purging counterbalance of his songs that forms the ebb and flow of Drake's survival, the barometer that measures his suffering. In those telling lyrics of 'They're Leaving Me Behind', Drake laments thus: 'The chances they come and the chances have been lost, success can be gained but at too great a cost, for some there's a future to find, but I think they're leaving me behind.' And this written years before the fatal depression begins. Again such concerns are echoed in the equally lamenting yet stoically elegant lyric of 'Bird Flew By': 'The list of false starts and crumbled broken hearts, comes from a need to play so many parts.' For Drake even at this time, when he was enjoying the wild thyme and dope-scented air of Provence with his friends, a recurring set of concerns were ominously crouching, darkening the palette, moving him onto another level from the regular folk blues standards transposed onto a reel-to-reel tape recorder in the music room at Far Leys. Also in that South of France summer of 1967, the visible apartness of Drake begins to impose itself on his increasingly awestruck entourage, and during that bucolic pause before his course is set, one can assume his prolific gifts fatefully converge.

II

I think there are very few poets who do not suffer between their twentieth and thirtieth year, an essential crisis where the fate of their gift is played out. A crisis, that is to say, a judgment by the forces in attendance – an always tragic confrontation of ambitions, powers, ideals, memories and premonitions. In a word, a battle of all the elements of contradiction, of all the antagonistic themes that a life already long enough and enough experienced to have reunited all of them, offered to their torn soul, which in turn imposes conflict on the organism in distress.

Paul Valéry

Like many with a rare gift, the acutely sensitive and self-critical Drake found his work well respected by an immediate inner circle during his lifetime; loyal friends, other musicians and artists who urged him on and gave him the will to at least endure the completion of his albums. After the commercial failure of *Bryter Layter*, and adrift in London's overbearing metropolis, which seemed now to crowd its afflictions in on him, Drake's confidence in his audience, his record company, his advisors and most destructively himself dramatically began to fade, pitching him onto the downward slope of the breakdown which eventually compromised his social faculties as an effectively inter-relating human being. Drake was a perfectionist, inclined to see success and failure in purely black and white terms. His guitar technique, a method of picking using both nail and flesh seemed perfectly formed for him alone. This delicate yet powerful, clean and confident sound was, according to Joe Boyd, John Wood and others, almost always meticulously executed, something which cannot help but remind one of the iconic pianist Glenn Gould, who legend has it was always note perfect, whichever radical and controversial way he chose to play a work by Bach or Beethoven. But like Gould, this technical perfectionist was also a romantically attuned seeker fully aware of his responsibility as a creative renegade, who, though warmly personable, empathic and companionable within his artistic limits, fostered a lofty detachment that quickly communicated itself to listeners and commanded respect from his peers. At first this detachment worked in his favour, but when the dream of connection with a significant audience died, the sense of apartness became a burden, a disability so to speak, which seemed to the frustrated Drake to be the result of yet another deception.

As morbid depression edged its way in, feelings of personal failure and hopelessness seeded all too readily in a mind perilously poised between chronic states of despair and idealism. A romantic yearning for the world to be otherwise snagged relentlessly on the cultivated and hypersensitive Drake's consciousness. The onset of realisations of communicative impotence and the prospect of tepid reception and grubby compromises sapped his reserves of mental stoicism. Frustration with ill-starred concert appearances where he witnessed amorphous crowds talking through his songs, seemingly oblivious to his astringently created art, turned to apathy and despondency. Drake was struggling to find and lead the right audience from the raucous thicket of the music world to the more serene uplands of his rarefied vision.

Drake's dissatisfaction with the opulent arrangements on *Bryter Layter*, following the unexpectedly poor reception of the album, are often quoted in articles. But it is hard to ascertain the consistency of Drake's true feelings about the merits of these arrangements on his albums: although Kirby's sensitive grafting of cello and flute on *Five Leaves Left* are almost unanimously accepted as in keeping and inspired, in the wake of *Bryter Layter*'s commercial failure, it seems Drake may have viewed the more cluttered layering on that album as playing to commercial demands and having the effect of veiling his guitar, the engine of his art. Or perhaps this is merely a handed-down judgement, now set in stone, an even more tempting assumption since the unadorned *Pink Moon* was what followed. But was *Pink Moon* a reaction to *Bryter Layter*'s complexity, or was it simply an evolution that Drake envisaged even before or during the making of *Bryter Layter*? In any case, 'No more frills' was his firm declaration and the lonely vigil of the oncoming *Pink Moon* recording sessions the consequence of such a remark. John Wood, who appeared to be one of the few people Drake could tolerate and confide in by this time, testifies to his artist's absolute insistence on producing a stark album shorn of other players. Wood recalls how during those all-night sessions, a desolate Drake 'kind of stared blankly at the wall' and stated, 'Well, I really don't want to hear anything else, I really think people should be just aware of me and how I am, and the record shouldn't have any sort of "tinsel".' (This last word Wood acknowledges to be his own rendering, but something similar was used by Drake to refer to the orchestration.) What is significant here is that Drake is preparing to shed collaboration and seek artistic integrity on his own terms. His reliance on others and their advice for better or worse is waning. The much touted rawness and acoustic nakedness of *Pink Moon* is an overt expression of aloneness. 'I am here where it is growing darker and you are out there where the light still prevails . . .' is what Drake implicitly states. 'You can say the sun is shining if you really want to, / I can see the moon and it seems so clear . . .' The acute lack of instrumentation appears a clear statement of intent, but is that just the seductive pull of hindsight? The third album is not so much a turning point in terms of the songs, but in the thorny wilderness of silence that surrounds them. *Pink Moon* is a final raising of the drawbridge and a retreat to the keep.

The see-saw arguments concerning Drake's suicide – yes he did, no he didn't – are of course ultimately futile. The fact is that an artist of Drake's singular introspective propensity is always vulnerable to a premature exit in a desperate pre-dawn moment. Although there is evidence he was finding his feet again that autumn in 1974, with trips to Paris, a serious love interest and at last a renewed acquaintance with his guitar, this does not mean Drake was off the hook and less likely to commit suicide. On the contrary, such an act could have actually been provoked by the more optimistic climate that restored his family with hope. This brief period of positive energy may sadly have been Drake's swansong, a last surge before the final collapse. The unavoidable fact is that Drake, shambling about the borders of an obscured maturity was crushed beneath the insupportable weight of his own existence, unable to bear the load which had settled on his ironically so broad shoulders. As he himself confessed to a close friend, 'I can't cope, all the defences are gone. All the nerves are exposed.' Where others could shake off the nefarious realities that customarily assail humankind, he was unable to follow. Instead Drake wrote *Pink Moon*, taking the supreme symbol of solitariness, that indifferent glacial eye in the ether, and tainting it a maleficent pink. To call *Pink Moon* a suicide note is a rhetorical impulse unworthy of the repetition it enjoys, but when Drake says in the song 'Road', 'You can say the sun is shining if you really want to, / I can see the moon and it seems so clear, / You can take the road that takes you to the stars now, / I can take a road that will see me through . . .' what do you think he is saying? Typically, Drake tells the listener something, but not quite enough, of his intentions. There is always an ambiguity in his symbolism which permits a slightly less desolate interpretation. (In this context see also 'Harvest Breed'.) Is the road he is taking to a permanent plot in Tanworth churchyard, or is it a road leading to some as yet unspecified new horizon, or is it just a commitment to sit tight until the danger passes? I suspect Drake planted this ambiguity because he himself did not know and wanted to communicate his confusion, to leave a record of his deliberation.

At the same time as suggesting there may be deliverance, a rope ladder unfurling down into the abyss, he is always toying with the possibility of imminent departure. Towards the end he wrote a last clutch of famously coruscating songs. Of these the most harrowing, 'Black Eyed Dog', is self-evidently a response to Robert Johnson's 'Hellhound on my Trail', but for Drake the dog is nothing less than a canine reaper calling to collect, baying at his door. Drake tells us in no uncertain terms he is ready for death, or rather release. But with the accusing solemnity of 'Hanging On A Star' there is more, a question encompassing again the disbelief in his lack of achievement after so much promise and assurance from others. Here Drake issues a howl from the crater he is now occupying in no man's land, questioning with that characteristic sometimes-arcane erudition of language that seems to enhance his apartness. 'Why leave me hanging on a star when you deem me so high?' One can be in no doubt that these last recordings stand alone and will remain in their caskets of black ice for eternity. Not only had Drake's voice cracked through mental exhaustion into a kind of clattering of wintry twigs against a wall backlit by a crematorium fire, but the songs themselves seem unable to bear their own presence, like the mortally wounded trying to fight off sleep, they seem to drift in and out of wakening with an almost opiate heaviness, that is both their burden of dissolution and their vital artery. They sound like no one else and will never be repeated. It is my belief that death was never far from Drake's mind during the length of his brief adulthood. I imagine he lived daily with the idea of non-being, with the option always there as a counterweight to the powerlessness of being adrift in a life which never came up to his abstracted expectations. Probably even before he seriously broke down, he savoured the bittersweet taste of the concept, the precarious notion of the ability to control at least his own time, in a 'time of no reply'.

Nick Drake was a visionary artist who appeared at a certain specific moment in history, in England, and demonstrated his poetic vision through the music of his time, using the most appropriate medium available to him. But because of his fateful situation at a point when everything in the service of his art became perfectly aligned, Drake stands apart in the musical domain in which he expressed himself, the rare gift of his music immune to generational changes or limited to any one particular epoch. But looking at Nick Drake, what do we see? A well-educated, upper-middle-class young man with a sensitive disposition, sired from a colonial background, already by the mid Sixties something of an anachronism, a man suffused with classical music, song and poetry from an early age. A young man both clearly of his time and out of his time. One who sees himself as a remnant from a past endowed with more authenticity, but also one who, without sounding dated, can say, using the hippie parlance of the era, 'Hey, take a little while to grow your brother's hair.' Drake draws on the past and is worked on by the present, only to rise and be everywhere in the future. At the same time he develops a poetic capacity steeped within the English romantic imagination, underscored by the rural idyll in which he lives. He will leave a very English pastoral wash over his songs; but equally he is drawn abroad, especially to France. He draws on the root of European poetry, art and philosophy, directing this tributary into the broad delta of country blues and jazz, traditional song and classical music, so his overall visionary impact is a complex synthesis of melodic assurance, compositional originality, and lyrical intensity whose architecture is equably both English and European. All is carried within the vessel of song, a rowing pattern of multiple oars that serves to power the single craft.

Of course there are many great songwriters who are essentially poets, but with Drake, something else is going on in the mix, in terms of the nuances brought to bear and the intricate veins supplying his art. This ingredient is probably impossible to express and to discuss it may prove futile. But its location is presumably found somewhere in that unique fusion of landscapes, both physically real and deeply imagined, the subtle weaving in of dream imagery, and this indefinable coalescence emerging at a precise moment in the calendar of consciousness when all elements harmonise. Early lyrical attempts are not great poetry in themselves, but ciphers to trigger the embryonic forming of a mood, usually concerning youthful hope in an idealistic love, then disillusion when the dream dissipates. They are sufficient for their purpose. For example, the artistic power acting on the listener in a sub-courtly love dreamscape such as occurs in the song 'Princess Of The Sands' is borne by an almost hallucinated synthesis of guitar and vocal, a ghostly repeating melody like waves turning on the shore at night, and a delicious melancholia which is never shoe-horned in. 'She moved her mouth but there came no sound, the message she brought can never be found.' 'I looked at her and I saw in her eyes, the heavy toll of a thousand sighs.' Again and again Drake spins his reverie: that ultimately he is only a visitor to this world, who will stay for a while, observe the potential for transcendence in the solitude of nature, but then, realising that this will be stymied by the destructive energies released by material reality, resolves to depart before being tainted. And this suspicion of the present 'season' being continually threatened by a toxic unknown, that malevolently crouching future, or a 'sorrow waiting round the bend', proclaimed in the early songs, evolves into the fully fledged despair of the later period, when suspicion, unease and fear, the confounding of the romantic gene, transforms into the terrifying reality of morbid narcissism, listlessness and self-destruction.

And the photographic legacy is there, material

evidence of eternity. Here is the proof for all to see, for this Drake is not tainted by physical decay. Likewise in his meticulous song archive, there are no lacklustre albums, no embarrassing changes of direction, no shameful stunts, no fallow periods, all is pristine, crafted to the highest standards. For Drake the increasingly vulgar reality of spiritual poverty, loneliness and alienation becomes the rack on which he prostrates himself. Only the fast dwindling dream holds real security, where there is at least a possibility for the ideal to prosper. His path towards the frontiers of maturity is therefore one of decline, a descent, slow at first then suddenly gathering speed towards his breakdown and hospitalisation in early 1972. But even on the way down the last steep descent, Drake recognises the latent chance to awaken: 'Falling fast you stoop to touch and kiss the flowers that bend / And you're ready now / For the harvest breed.'

This mounting urge to divulge his intuitive anxiety at the human condition, overlaid with his personal trials, was the way Nick Drake sought to vocalise his brief stay on earth and to pass this message on to those who might profit from it. When he sings in 'Fruit Tree' of fame not coming 'till its stock is in the ground', the stock is his songs, though his body is what ended up in the ground, two-thirds of a full life. But the fallen fruit has gone back into the earth and been resurrected again with each new season. The songs have survived in their initial perfection, just like the fruit that returns year on year. Therefore they can never die.

III

Speak more softly to be better heard by a deaf public . . .

Joseph Joubert

So when Drake stepped out from the youthful enclosure of his early songs towards something more mature and far-reaching, how could he know then that it was the journey itself, the resulting pressures and trials down the path chosen for him by fate that would turn the dial up on the art, that his own evolving despair, in effect the light that ebbed away, would power the creative generator? As far as poetry goes, most journalistic articles on Drake reference the same names as influences: namely, that he admired Blake above all, 'to hold an ocean in the palm of your hand' ('Northern Sky'), had a penchant for Wilfred Owen ('Strange Meeting II') and explored the English Romantics and First World War poets during his studies at Cambridge. But of course this is not the whole story. For Drake was also, as already indicated, naturally drawn to European poetry of the late nineteenth century, most notably the symbolist period, or that known as the fin-de-siècle, mainly in the French language, but not necessarily only French poets, why not Franco-Belgian as well? This is not altogether unlikely for at the time there was a significant increase in translations of poetry and prose from the literary era which ushered in modernism. Drake's lyrics are awash with symbolism and though he was also exploring surrealism, illustrated by comments he made, books in his library, as well as by his dabbling in popular 'existentialist' texts like Camus's *The Myth of Sisyphus* for example, it is crucially the influence of symbolism, which is most dominant and consistent in his work.

Solitariness, melancholia, refined meditation and an elite distancing from the world, the whole languidly anguished tenor of the fin-de-siècle period seems to sit naturally alongside Nick Drake's vision. Ever since his fabled trip to Aix in the summer of 1967, Drake was increasingly drawn to France whose geographical space and continental cultural depth, not to mention recent revolutionary fervour, must have seemed like a necessary escape from the narrow confines of England in the early Seventies. Shortly before he died, Drake enjoyed a brief respite from his mental strife staying with friends on a canal boat moored on the Seine. One is tempted to conclude that had Drake lived he might have been drawn back to the French capital, or to provincial France, whose national tradition of providing sanctuary for the artist was at that time still relevant. For France was surely more attuned to Drake's intellectual and artistic tastes than England was, having retained and consistently celebrated those elements of its past culture which served to reinforce an intellectual aesthetic. France then as now offered a horizon which both metaphorically and literally seemed wider and less hemmed in than England. Paris too, was the scene of a student revolution in 1968. London was not. There, through a communal romantic impulse for change, the weight of being was momentarily lifted and an unknown outcome mischievously teased the naive hearts of radicals and mavericks. England was familiar, ponderous, inspirationally stodgy, and crucially held the burden of one's history, a place where class dictated, and one walked through clay, and knew one's place, where people grumbled behind their papers, but never revolted. France must have seemed a wider horizon, a lighter load, and crucially more exotic, a potential restorative exile for the jaded Drake.

It is also not impossible to imagine that Drake read some German literature in translation, not only the then fashionable hippie guru Hesse, but perhaps he may have delved into Novalis, Rilke and Hölderlin, or why not

Schopenhauer and Nietzsche alongside the oft quoted French stalwarts of Verlaine and Rimbaud? For here is a man whose wheel is not just following the tramline along the popular counterculture books of his age, but driving deeper into the European storehouse. This brings me back to the Austrian poet Georg Trakl with whom I began this essay; he whose melancholy autumnal-tinged poetry sits so comfortably alongside the tenor of Drake's lyrics. The whole mood of Trakl's eerily beautiful and morbidly afflicted imagery, his mysterious evocations of mankind's spiritual downfall has distinct echoes across Drake's albeit very English canvas. Did Drake read Trakl's poetry? This is entirely possible since a pioneering collection of his poems translated by the poet Michael Hamburger and others was published by Jonathan Cape in 1968, its covers suitably sporting the same Emerald green shades as *Five Leaves Left*. But even if Trakl remained invisible to Drake, both these seers in their different homelands and in different epochs had tapped into a seam where the creatively born dream image forms both a sanctuary and a consistently reinforced bulwark to an increasingly insupportable conventional reality. Time appears compressed and eschews linear rationality, when one reads a poem by Trakl or listens to a song by Drake. They synthesise through their intensity of feeling and the credible heroism of their artistic stance. Although their backgrounds, biographies, nationalities and periods are so utterly different, the music of Drake with its minor key cascades and strong currents of apartness and decline, seems to gesture unconsciously to the more linguistically complex poetic landscape of Trakl. Here music becomes confused with verse and imagery with music. Mediums dissolve instinctively as vision assumes mastery. It is pertinent to note that Trakl's explicitly tonal and almost painterly poetry, replete as it is with symbolic colours, has consistently attracted leading classical composers, from Webern to Knussen, drawn to such obliging musical qualities. But another uncanny crossover with Trakl occurs in an equable use of mysterious names for those half-real, half-spectral characters who move in and out of their respective works, unspeaking muses or personae whose story is itself veiled by insubstantiality, mere suggestion. Drake's indefinable 'Joey', 'Betty' and 'Jacomo', for example, seem somehow to inadvertently shadow Trakl's equally inscrutable and mysterious 'Elis', 'Helian' and 'Sebastian'. In each case it appears that these are personalities of the imagination, wraiths who follow their respective introverted duties across the stage of the subconscious, significant only within the hermetic enclosure of the song or poem. However, both these artists through their determination to offset reality with a sustaining beauty born from deep interior labours, manage to produce a poetry which though melancholy, is not nihilistic, but in contrast, strenuously spiritually affirming and bound for transcendence. Though both are eventually consumed and their final communication is ashen despair, they never lose the capacity to deliver a poetic utterance which is entirely authentic and without the slightest pretence. Moreover, it seems almost too poignant to add here that Trakl himself died a presumed suicide from a drugs overdose, whilst undergoing treatment for acute depression in the early months of 1914, during the conflict that would devour a generation. He was just twenty-seven.

Although it seems preposterous to employ such a hackneyed label, Drake really was the genuine tortured artist, not one who claimed to be, wished to be, or aspired to be. Today, in an era where mediocrity is regularly dressed up as greatness, and marketing-led 'profiles' are everything, one can only be struck yet again, as if for the first time, by the haunting apartness of Drake. But he confronted a society he had no functioning role in, a society mortally incompatible with his psyche and from which he could not escape alive, a society that was in too much of a hurry to entertain the advanced party of its own self-destruction, to properly flag up his life-changing music. An organic inability to bend to the contours of this hostile environment was the true essence of his malaise. And this society had no qualms in deleting Drake as soon as possible, in fact 'suiciding' *him*, since he was clearly at one with a higher consciousness, and was, as Antonin Artaud claimed of Van Gogh, perhaps even on the verge of divining something which might prove troublesome to that society.

Drake's songs rose out of his own existence to such a profound extent that eventually he could exist only from out of those songs. Once his art had achieved all it could, i.e. when the circle was complete, and there were no more songs left, he simply fell away, a husk after the abundant flowering. As a deeply subjective artist, Drake absorbed what he needed from the exterior world and transformed it poetically through his interior imagination. But ultimately this process reaches a point where nothing more can be absorbed. Religion, marriage, or some other diverting or nurturing crutch, can enable an angst-corroded artist to realign their trajectory, but Drake was unable to subscribe. Pinioned between despair and bittersweet resignation, Drake found himself rudderless soon after *Pink Moon*. 'I have songs running through my head all the time, but I just can't get them down,' he lamented. The rhetoric in such a tragedy is that Drake only experienced a third of an average man's full life. We will never know what he might have done with those lost years, sixty years perhaps, which he traded in unknowingly on the night of his death. But then one is of course tempted to ask, what are sixty years of conventional life compared to an eternity of unsoiled artistic integrity?

Drake's grave famously carries the following epitaph, a line from the song 'From The Morning': 'And now we rise and we are everywhere.' It is like so many aspects of the Nick Drake enigma, both fitting and fateful. For only now three decades on from his death has he risen with such unforeseen power and the full force of his vision been released, which seems somehow to have coincided with the appetite of a new, more quietly desperate generation born into the uninviting anchorage of late capitalism. Here they find a fraternal figure who seems romantically set against the age of commodity, an unlikely figurehead for authenticity and incorruptibility, one who spent everything of himself in his songs, then shambled off stage in silence to simply vanish. Those few dozen songs, supremely resistant to decay, travel now reassuringly alongside our own impermanence, a lifetime's subservience to tides and seasons that he, in soaring for a while, so resolutely overcame.

Suffolk, May 2014

BRIDGET ST JOHN

Musician

Dear Nick

Why is it so hard to put finger to key to write down thoughts and memories of days and stages shared?

I have never consistently documented my life – so there are few written references of those times, and we were not yet in the days of the perpetual shutter – so images of you stay soaked into various parts of my memory. And you – as with many others of my brothers and sisters in music – accompany me shadow-like down the days.

. . . One night in 1969 – sitting side by side, scrunched on the kerb outside the pub a little way up from Les Cousins on Greek Street – I still sense our silent communion as we both prepared to perform . . .

Les Cousins – big Andy Matteou on the door (later, in the early morning hours, his father, Loukas, would feed us all his glorious moussaka in the family restaurant above the club) . . . no dressing room . . . one flight of steps both entrance and exit . . . a crowded basement with one, somewhat noisy, fan for ventilation – strong coffee in industrial-thick mugs as I remember . . . a small raised platform, a stool, two mics, and the audience seemingly inches away . . .

John Martyn ran the evening – self-assured but protective and mindful of both of us – somewhat daunted, inexperienced and shy in our different ways. You were one kindred spirit near the beginning of this journey into live performance . . .

. . . An afternoon (one day when?) – Paul Wheeler's flat – listening to and watching you, Paul and John playing – in awe of all three of you – able to absorb some small portion of different tunings and fingerings that I would later imperfectly remember but be so excited to try . . . Without saying a word you were one of my teachers . . .

. . . One evening in 1970 – you and I opening for Fairport Convention at the Fairfield Halls in Croydon. A dressing room for each of us . . . a huge stage with enough room for choirs and orchestras, Fairport's audience masked by myriad stage lights . . . and you and I needing still, in this case, a chair, two mics, taking the stage one after the other . . .

My memory of watching you remains that you looked like your photo on the cover of *Bryter Layter* – (still one of my favourite albums, and one of the few vinyls I brought with me to New York in 1976) – hair mostly obscuring your face, your body curved over your guitar, eyes closed for the most part . . .

In a review of the gig, never mentioning us by name, the writer (who shall remain nameless!) cobbled us together: 'The only thing I do not understand is why the promoters bothered with the first half.' That hurt me for some time after – and I imagine you felt the same . . . But time has shown us you're a rare, rare find – your ocean found its shore . . .

I am thankful for your companionship in those early days, and for the endless river of your music that still threads through . . .

MICHAEL CHAPMAN

Musician

We went to see Nick at the Haworth Arms in Hull, playing to a crowd of baying, beer-swilling chorus singers who ignored him. Nick went into his shell and never said a word all night. Outside, after the gig, Andru noticed him standing alone under a streetlight and said, 'Never mind those arseholes, the people who know and care about music were enthralled. Are you waiting for a ride to your accommodation?' (They hadn't even bothered to provide anything.) 'Get in the car, come with us.'

At our apartment, guitars, wine and dope appeared. I thought I knew more than a few guitar tunings but Nick left me for dead. In the morning he was gone; I have no idea how he got there or how he left but I have heard stories since of Nick drifting into your life and then drifting out. And that's how it happened with us.

ROGER MICHELL

Film director

Early in 2013 I was finishing work on *Le Week-End*. In one scene in the film a man in his early sixties (played by Jim Broadbent) listens to a piece of music on his iPod that he witnesses a stoned teenager nodding along to much later in the story. I knew the music had to be reflective, beautiful, solitary, and something that crossed the generations. Mulling this over, I was driving my teenage son up the M11 back to Cambridge where he was an undergraduate. It was overcast and we'd hit the flatlands around Duxford and he stuck *Pink Moon* on the CD player: one of his and my own favourite albums. As we drove into town, past the Fen Causeway and the Catholic Church, and then up Regent Street, the light fading, I worked out that Jim's character and Nick Drake would have been contemporaries at Cambridge in the late Sixties. In my imagination they bumped into each other in a smoky back room of The Eagle, or at a late-night screening of a Godard movie at the Arts Cinema: and perhaps had a nodding acquaintance of each other.

The sad, level sweetness of the music fell into my lap, and the next day we fitted it to the picture.

MATT JOHNSON
Musician

I first heard Nick Drake in 1978 when my older brother Andrew brought home a copy of *Bryter Layter*. When the needle dropped onto the vinyl and began its slow spiral through the grooves I was transported instantly by the deep velvet softness of his voice and the intricate fingerpicking and mysterious chord-work chiming from his acoustic guitar – it all seemed to hang in the air long after the record had stopped playing.

But it's strange, really, the way time plays tricks upon our minds. When I was a teenager Nick Drake's voice and music seemed to hold within it such maturity, yet now, listening to his recordings as a very experienced man in my fifties, what I mainly hear is all the life torn off too soon, all the lovers he would never know, all the places he would never go, all the yearnings for things that would never show – a life over before it had even begun.

Having suffered a similar bereavement within my own family – my younger brother Eugene was also in his mid-twenties when he died – I empathise deeply with the devastation caused by such a tragic loss. We can only ever wonder what the future may have held – both for them and for us.

Yet a small consolation – due in no small part to their sensitive shepherding of his small but potent catalogue – is that the Nick Drake Estate have ensured his legacy not only survives but thrives, by accruing an ever-expanding audience who deeply appreciate the magic that lies inside his timeless songs. I think Nick Drake can finally rest in peace.

MARK ELLEN
Writer and broadcaster

I first ran into him when I was fifteen in 1969. Island Records put out a sampler called *Nice Enough To Eat* – a whole album for only 14 and 6! – and I remember staring at his name on the cover, alongside the label's big stars, like Jethro Tull and Mott the Hoople, all of them spelled out in letters made of pastry. We played his track 'Time Has Told Me' over and over again, trying to plumb its fathomless depths, marvelling at his guitar tunings and his stoned, lazy intonation – 'wayzzzzz of making me love' – and arguing about whether the second line was 'You're rare I find' or 'You're rare refined'. (It was neither.) And wondering where he'd bought his velvet jacket on the *Five Leaves Left* sleeve they'd printed on the back. Such were the captivating mysteries of adolescence.

DAVE MATTACKS
Musician

Bassist Dave Pegg and I heard about Nick through Joe Boyd; he and Nick asked us to play on some tracks for his next recording – that was to be *Bryter Later*.

At that time, Fairport were living together in Little Hadham, and Nick came up from London to the house to rehearse the songs with Dave and myself.

I recall sitting in Dave Pegg's room with Nick running through the songs, Pegg with a small bass amp 'on 1', and me with a pair of sticks and a practice pad. I recall Nick being very shy.

The sessions at John Woods's Chelsea Sound Techniques studio soon after were simply wonderful – as was the case then, everything was recorded 'live'.

Though my freelance work started off with people like Nick, Sandy Denny and John Martyn, it was illuminating over the next few years to realise how much those people were not 'the norm' with regard to quality of song-writing, singing and playing. It's a source of pleasure knowing Nick's work has endured.

PHIL SELWAY
Musician

Like many others at the time – the early Nineties – I came late to Nick Drake's music. His records went straight to the heart, where they have remained ever since. However, much as I love Joe Boyd's production and Robert Kirby's string arrangements, my favourite Nick Drake recording is a bedroom demo of 'The Fly'. The scene is set with the sound of birdsong in the background. As Nick accompanies himself with just an acoustic guitar, it's almost as if you have stumbled across a very intimate and unguarded moment. It feels so heartfelt, and is one of the most affecting pieces of music I know. Even though the version on *Bryter Layter* is beautifully arranged, and the lyric is more developed, this demo says it all: incomplete, yet somehow fully realised.

DAVE PEGG
Musician

I've played on hundreds of albums in my forty-eight years of playing music for a living, and one that I still love hearing is Nick's *Bryter Layter*: joyful sessions, helped enormously by John Woods' engineering and Joe [Boyd]'s 'laissez-faire' approach giving the artist lots of freedom. Nick played and sang most of the songs live in Sound Techniques studio in Chelsea. Dave Mattacks and I had rehearsed a few of the songs at The Angel (the Fairport hovel in Little Hadham, Hertfordshire). One could never be sure if Nick was happy with what we did or not, but we certainly were in terms of appreciating his wonderful performances. An iconic album for sure – with Robert Kirby's beautiful arrangements. I am often flattered when youngsters come up to me at Fairport gigs and thank me for playing on that album, and Nick has certainly been highly influential in developing great taste in up-and-coming singer-songwriters. Of course we all wish he was still with us, and it would be fascinating to see what he would be doing musically today. I look forward to reading the book and discovering more about a truly wonderful writer.

MARK RADCLIFFE

Broadcaster, musician and writer

Nick and the Running Man

Who was that man? Where was he going? Why was he running?

The essence of Nick lies here as he languorously lolls against the wall.
The anonymous brick wall.
The blankest of canvases.
And yet, and yet . . . the deepest of thoughts are behind those watchful eyes.
Eyes suspicious of the wider world.
The hurried world.
The world rushing by.
Haven't we all felt like that sometimes?
We are in the wider world but often at a remove.
In a reverie.
Behind a veil.
There is something that keeps us from throwing ourselves into the rushing torrent.
We loll against our own brick wall and try and make sense of those running by.
It's at those moments that Nick Drake sings to me.
Inside my head.

ULRICH SCHNAUSS

Composer and musician

I heard Nick Drake's voice the first time singing the words 'three hours from sundown' – poignantly describing the ambiguity of hopeful anticipation while already acknowledging that our dreams of a better life will most likely never materialise.

Soon after, the gorgeous string arrangements of 'River Man' made me cry – and I've been hooked ever since.

Some people manage to describe the cold harshness of our reality, a few even succeed in mapping out a framework for a utopian alternative – but it's a true art to accurately portray the ambiguity of our existence in between – and Nick Drake was a master.

JOHN PARISH

Musician

As a producer, I have a very select few albums that I use as benchmarks for particular styles – not to try and emulate, but to remind myself of what a great record can make me feel. For bare-boned acoustic guitar and voice I use Nick Drake's *Pink Moon*. It is beautifully recorded, but it's an invisible beauty – as though there was no recording, and you are simply listening to a compelling intimate performance taking place in front of you.

His delivery is unaffected and seems effortless. His guitar and voice are locked. Each song is perfectly weighted. It is a truly timeless album, and a source of inspiration.

BEN WATT

Musician

I was nineteen when I first heard Nick Drake. Someone on my course at university had stolen his brother's *Fruit Tree* box set. It was 1982. I was already fascinated by English outsider-folk singers like Robert Wyatt and Kevin Coyne. I was enthralled. I think it was in part because my natural singing voice seemed to come from a similar place. Un-Americanised. Clean and direct. And there was a melancholy grace to his work that spoke to me. I remember finding out some stuff was still in print and ordering a new vinyl copy of *Pink Moon* from the record shop in town, in Hull, where I was studying. It took two weeks to arrive. I mimicked some of his guitar rhythms. The title track to my debut album *North Marine Drive* (1983) owes much to 'Things Behind The Sun'. I recently returned to songwriting and guitar-playing after a ten-year break and realised how much I still owe him.

NICK DRAKE

Poet

The deserted second hand record exchange;
Just a bald guy and his ponytail
Guarding the memory palace of dead vinyl;
Multiple copies of *Rumours* and *Blue*
And the *Carpenters' Greatest Hits* in brown and gold;
Pink Moon's playing on the sound system,
Nick Drake's last LP; soon he would die
On the night Lord Lucan disappeared, Miss World
Lost her crown as an unmarried mother,
And the sun's November mercury slipped
Off the indigo horizon at 4.04 p.m. . . .
I browse the bins, and luckily I find
Fruit Tree, the deleted posthumous box set –
Five Leaves Left, *Bryter Layter*, *Pink Moon*;
Three big black discs, acetate ammonites
Coded for ancient technology.
I offer Bela Lugosi my credit card;
He contemplates the name, my face, then up
To the shivering strip light and the obscure ceiling
Where sound waves collide with dust to conjure
Nick's sad ghost in the live air, whispering:
Know that I love you, know that I care,
Know that I see you, know I'm not there . . .
Then the song fades to recorded silence –
The hushed acoustic of his after-life –
Before the static, the perpetual heart-beat trip
Round the record's inevitable zero . . .
Lugosi stares from the dark vacancy,
The tangled wires, the drifting golden motes
In the creaky auditorium of dust
Where the ghost had sung and disappeared; he grins;
'Oh man, oh man, I thought you were *dead . . .*'

JOHN ALTMAN

Musician

I first heard and met Nick Drake at an anti-Vietnam War gig at the Roundhouse in London in 1968 at which my jazz group also appeared. Nick was the only person on that day's list with whom I ever played. Painfully shy of public appearances, he was happy to play his new songs and jam with other musicians in the comfort of John and Beverley Martyn's front room in Hampstead. John and Beverley attracted a wide circle of talented songwriters including Bridget St John and Andy Fernbach – they themselves were immensely talented too, and some of the music made in front of five or six people would amaze people today in the age of YouTube and instant videos on people's phones. As it was, I wish someone had brought a camera or a tape machine, but who was to know that within a few years Nick would become a legend?

I remember playing flute on some of the songs that found their way on to *Bryter Later* where Ray Warleigh, later a member of my big band, was the saxophonist and flautist. I also recall playing flute at John Martyn's flat with Bridget St John, and then appearing with her in clubs and on John Peel's radio show – but Nick never showed any interest in playing gigs or clubs. His own gigs were usually disastrous: I attended one where the audience talked throughout and he sat and stared at the floor. When I would play with John or Bridget or Cat Stevens or Mimi Farina at the all-nighters at Les Cousins, Nick would never perform although he might show up in the audience.

JOHN MARTYN

Musician

You've been taking your time
And you've been living on solid air
You've been walking the line
And you've been living on solid air
Don't know what's going 'round inside
And I can tell you that it's hard to hide
When you're living on solid air

And you've been painting the blues
And you've been looking through solid air
You've been seeing it through
And you've been looking through solid air
Don't know what's going 'round in your mind
And I can tell you don't like what you find
When you're moving through solid air

I know you, I love you
And I can be your friend
I can follow you anywhere
Even through solid air

You've been stoning it cold
You've been living on solid air
You've been finding it cold
You've been living on solid air
I don't know what's going on inside
I can tell you that it's hard to hide
When you're living on solid air

You've been getting too deep
You've been living on solid air
You've been missing your sleep
And you've been moving through solid air
I don't know what's going on in your mind
But I know you don't like what you find
When you're moving through solid air

I know you, I love you
I will be your friend
I will follow you anywhere
Even through solid air

You've been walking your line
You've been walking on solid air
You've been taking your time
But you've been walking on solid air
Don't know what's going on inside
But I can tell you that it's hard to hide
When you're living on solid air

You've been painting the blues
You've been living on solid air
And you've been seeing it through
And you've been looking through solid air
I don't know what's going on in your mind
But I can tell you don't like what you find
When you're living through solid air

I know you, I love you
And I can be your friend
I can follow you anywhere
Even through solid air

Solid air

RICHARD & LINDA THOMPSON

Musicians

Called him poor boy
You took him for fun
He dressed for the tinkering trade
He dressed for the tinkering trade
Now the poor boy is taken away

No use waiting
Like a ghost in a dream
The world has no comfort to bring
The world has no comfort to bring
He left you, took everything

No use standing
Waving adieu
The penny won't drop in your mind
The penny won't drop in your mind
The old flame has left you behind

No use crying
In a room full of memories
You never will find yesterday
You never will find yesterday
And the poor boy is taken away

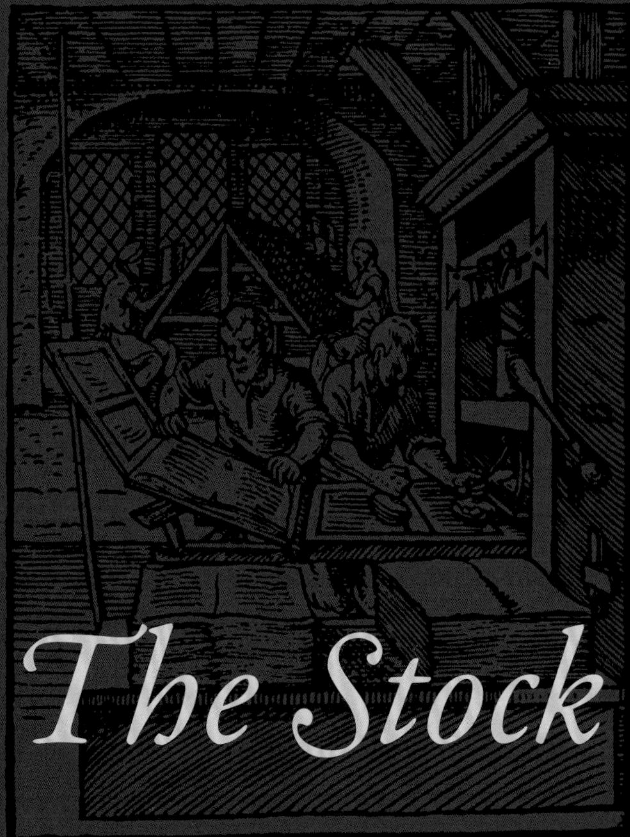

The Stock

STUDIO ALBUMS

FIVE LEAVES LEFT

LP July 1969 Island ILPS 9105
CD March 1987 Island CID 9195

Time Has Told Me
River Man
Three Hours
Way To Blue
Day Is Done
'Cello Song
The Thoughts Of Mary Jane
Man In A Shed
Fruit Tree
Saturday Sun

Released on both Musicassette and LP vinyl.
Later released in the USA in 1976 on Antilles (AN7010).

Original CD released as part of the Island 25 Years celebrations.

BRYTER LAYTER

LP March 1971* Island ILPS 9134
CD May 1987 Island CID 9134

Also released on 8 Track Cartridge

Introduction
Hazey Jane II
At The Chime Of A City Clock
One Of These Things First
Hazey Jane I
Bryter Layter
Fly
Poor Boy
Northern Sky
Sunday

* Original set release date 1/11/70.
Delayed until March 1971.
Released in Australia on the Island/Festival label, where the LP labels titled the album 'Bryter Bryter'.
Released in Holland with mis-spelled labels.
Also released on Musicassette.
First released in the USA in 1976 on the Antilles label (ANC 7028).
Original CD released as part of the Island 25 Years celebrations.

PINK MOON

LP February 1972 Island ILPS 9184
CD April 1990 Island IMCD 94

Pink Moon
Place To Be
Road
Which Will
Horn
Things Behind The Sun
Know
Free Ride
Parasite
Harvest Breed
From The Morning

Released in the USA on Capitol simultaneously.
Released on Musicassette.
Spanish pressings credited Nick as Nick Darke.
Also released in New Zealand (SIL-934506) in a single sleeve.
CD release came later than the previous two albums as it was Nick's poorest selling album.

COMPILATIONS

NICK DRAKE

Island/Capitol SMAS-9307 (July 1971)

Island Records did not exist as a stand-alone label in the USA: titles were licensed out to other labels, notably A&M and Capitol. Perhaps due to a recommendation from manager and record label mogul David Geffen, the Capitol label issued a composite of Nick's first two albums in the USA simply titled *Nick Drake.* The tracks were culled from his first two albums:

'Cello Song
Poor Boy
At The Chime Of A City Clock
Northern Sky
River Man
Three Hours
One Of These Things First
Fly

This album was re-released in 2013 to celebrate 'Record Store Day' both in the USA and the UK; pressings and sleeves differed slightly between the two.

FRUIT TREE

Island Records issued a boxed set of Nick's album as early as 1979. In 1979, boxed sets were virtually unheard of for even the most popular artists.

LP 09/3/79 Island NDSP 100
Original blue box with drawings by Paul Ellis on individual covers, designed by Bloomfield/Travis.
3 LP boxed set with last known 4 tracks from the unfinished fourth album added to the end of *Pink Moon.* John Wood is credited as being producer of *Pink Moon* for the first time. The set included a booklet with an essay by US journalist Arthur Lubow, which replaced the original rejected notes by UK journalist Nick Kent. This edition also had a one-sided promo vinyl album sampler issued to the media prior to release of the full box (Island RSS 7).
The boxed set also gained a full release in Italy on the Orizzonte label (ORL 1007).

LP 08/86 Hannibal HNBX 5302
Violet boxed set version with replica paper inner sleeves on each album, 4 LPs including *Time Of No Reply* LP of extra tracks and out-takes. Same essay as above. US release only.

CD 12/91 Hannibal HNCD 5402
Turquoise boxed set (4 CDs including *Time Of No Reply* CD variant of the above). US release only via Rykodisc.

Fruit Tree was later issued on Hannibal as a compact CD-only set in a smaller slip case.

Fruit Tree was then reinstated as a CD and vinyl edition in a replica of the original blue box on Island. Both CD and vinyl included a new booklet, 'A Much Updated Ruin From A Much Outdated Style', plus a DVD of the documentary 'A Skin Too Few' Island Records (2007).

HEAVEN IN A WILD FLOWER

Nick's first single LP compilation with sleeve notes by Ian Cranna and erroneous production credit to Joe Boyd for all tracks.
The album managed a release only in the UK, Italy and Germany.
It was also released as a Musicassette.

LP 28/5/85 Island ILPS 9826
CD 04/90 Island IMCD91

Fruit Tree
'Cello Song
The Thoughts Of Mary Jane
Northern Sky
River Man
At The Chime Of A City Clock
Introduction
Hazey Jane I
Pink Moon
Road
Which Will
Things Behind The Sun
Time Has Told Me

TIME OF NO REPLY

A later release for an album that was once included with the Fruit Tree boxed set as a 'bonus' title.
Licensed from Island Records by Joe Boyd's own Hannibal label for both the UK and US.

LP 03/87 Hannibal HNBL 1318
CD 03/87 Hannibal HNCD 1318

Time Of No Reply
I Was Made To Love Magic
Joey
Clothes Of Sand
Man In A Shed

Mayfair
Fly
The Thoughts Of Mary Jane
Been Smoking Too Long
Strange Meeting II
Rider On The Wheel
Black Eyed Dog
Hanging On A Star
Voice From The Mountain

TAMWORTH

French CD compilation given away with Les Inrockuptibles magazine (Hannibal/Rykodisc; RYKINRK 001, 1992)

Fruit Tree
'Cello Song
River Man
Things Behind The Sun
Northern Sky
The Thoughts Of Mary Jane
Time Of No Reply

WAY TO BLUE – AN INTRODUCTION TO NICK DRAKE

Though Chris Blackwell was not enthused by a single album composite of Nick's three albums (both Chris and Joe Boyd damned the 'Heaven In A Wild Flower' title), he warmed to the idea of a series of unsung Island artists getting an 'An Introduction To' treatment as a library set of five titles. These were selected as Nick Drake, John Martyn, Sandy Denny, John Cale and Julian Cope. The series started with Nick Drake and proved to be his biggest-selling title. Combined US and UK sales soon bettered 200,000 copies, aided by the Volkswagen Cabriolet TV advert that was shown in the USA and Germany and used the song 'Pink Moon' as its soundtrack.

Universal bought out the parent Island Records company PolyGram and soon took the series of 'An Introduction To' across to some 200 other artists. The track listing for *Way To Blue* was chosen by Joe Boyd, and John Wood oversaw the mastering process for CD. Simultaneously, John Wood re-mastered all three studio albums for CD and they were given new sleeves and slip cases.

CD 31/5/94 Island IMCD 196

'Cello Song
Hazey Jane I
Way To Blue
Things Behind The Sun
River Man
Poor Boy
Time Of No Reply
From The Morning
One Of These Things First
Northern Sky
Which Will
Hazey Jane II
Time Has Told Me
Pink Moon
Black Eyed Dog
Fruit Tree

MADE TO LOVE MAGIC

Time Of No Reply having been long deleted, the idea was revisited to release an album of out-takes, different mixes and the last four songs from the unfinished fourth album. During the remastering process, John Wood discovered the unmixed, previously undiscovered, song 'Tow The Line'. Robert Kirby discovered his orchestral manuscripts for the original string arrangements for 'Time Of No Reply' and 'Made To Love Magic' and technology did the rest. From this album two singles were released (the now correctly titled), 'Magic' and 'River Man' both of which entered the UK pop charts.

CD 24/05/04 Island CID8141
LP 07/06/04 Island ILPS8141

Rider On The Wheel
I Was Made To Love Magic
River Man
Joey
The Thoughts Of Mary Jane
Mayfair
Hanging On A Star
Three Hours
Clothes Of Sand
Voices
Time Of No Reply
Black Eyed Dog
Tow The Line

NICK DRAKE – A TREASURY

In 2004 it was deemed appropriate to re-jig Nick's long-selling *Way To Blue* single CD, taking it away from the now-overused and somewhat diluted 'An Introduction To' series as well as including some of Nick's instrumental pieces that Joe Boyd had been reluctant to include before.

CD 04/10/04 Island CID8149
LP 04/10/04 Island ILPS8149

Introduction
Hazey Jane II
River Man
'Cello Song
Hazey Jane I
Pink Moon
Poor Boy
Magic
Place To Be
Northern Sky
Road
Fruit Tree
Black Eyed Dog
Way To Blue
From The Morning
Plaisir D'Amour (added as a hidden track to the 5.1 mixed version of the CD)

FAMILY TREE

CD 04/07 Island CID8149
LP 01/08 Sunbeam SBR2LP5041

By the mid 2000s Nick's fame had generated a demand for bootleg pressings of his early home recordings, many of which were poorly mastered and pressed and sold at inflated prices. Some even contained tracks by an impersonator of Nick Drake. Adopting the idea set by The Everly Brothers, 'family' album *Roots*, Nick's own home recordings were remastered by John Wood, adding two songs by Molly Drake and some recently found Cambridge University recordings by Robert Kirby. The track listing configuration altered slightly for the US, for iTunes and for mainland Europe, however, a complete list of songs follows:

Come Into The Garden (Introduction)
They're Leaving Me Behind
Time Piece
Poor Mum (Molly Drake)
Winter Is Gone
All My Trials (with Gabrielle Drake)
Kegelstatt Trio
Betty And Dupree
Strolling Down The Highway
Paddling In Rushmere
Cocaine Blues
Blossom
Been Smoking Too Long
Black Mountain Blues
Tomorrow Is A Long Time
If You Leave Me
Here Come The Blues
Sketch 1
Blues Runs The Game
My Baby So Sweet
Milk And Honey
Kimbie
Bird Flew By
Rain
Strange Meeting II
Day Is Done
Come Into The Garden
Way To Blue
Do Your Ever Remember? (Molly Drake)

TUCK BOX

CD 11/13 Island 0602537538546

In November 2013, with the ever-confusing CD details posted on sites like Amazon, all five of Nick's CD titles were re-issued in cardboard sleeves as a uniform set, then also grouped together in a 7-inch square box portrayed as a replica of Nick's school tuck box. This package came at a competitive price with 5 original-design posters inside. The box (and posters) were available separately for those that had already bought some of the CDs, allowing them to house the complete works inside their own Tuck Box.

OTHER TITLES

INTERPLAY ONE

(Longman, 1971) Single album with booklet

Described by Robert Kirby to Gabrielle Drake on 10 April 2008:

Around 1970/'71, a lady-friend of mine was employed by the publishers Longman. They were producing an educational book on early Australian settlement, which was accompanied by an LP of readings and music. Through her contacts I was asked to produce performances of . . .

'Full Fathom Five'
On this I hired a female session singer named Kathy Fowler, with whom I had worked on other productions. She was the wife of the famous boy-actor, and later Fifties and Sixties character actor, Harry Fowler. Nick provided the solid accompaniment on guitar from my basic chord charts.

'The Swagman'
This one, *I* sang. I was asked to make sure of clear enunciation, so it is in my best Cantab choral-scholar baritone – somewhat bizarre, considering the lyrics! Nick was highly amused by the incongruity of the culture clash! Again, Nick provided the accompaniment, which I believe we practised during the thirty-minute train journey from Liverpool Street to Harlow Mill Station (where the Longman offices were located), to the amusement of fellow passengers. I'm so proud to have a track with Nick backing me for a change.

'I Wish I Was a Single Girl Again'
Kathy sang this. I wanted a banjo, so enlisted the services of 'Rockin' John' Wilkinson – an amigo of my older brother. When not rebuilding old Morgan vehicles (which had ash and elm frames – I digress – but I feel it is relevant, so there!), he would play his banjo. He lived near Harlow, in fact near Spellbrook Lock on the River Stort, in Pig Lane. He was a very quiet guy and got on well with Nick. My grandmother, Fanny, had been the pastry-and-cake cook at 'The Big House' in Pig Lane (owned by the Frère family) in the 1920s – but now I *really* digress . . . It badly lacked a bass part, so Nick played bass superbly on the bottom string of his guitar! Nick's guitar parts are the best thing here. Oh, and we were paid!

Oh, and oh! Last year, a copy of this was sold on eBay for nearly £2,500 – without the booklet! I had bid up to £1,000, as I lost mine years ago . . .

MICK AUDSLEY

(UK Sonet SON 641, 1972)

Nick Drake has been wrongly credited as a guitar player on the above album. Mick Audsley wrote the following:

I met Robert Kirby when I was a student at the Royal College of Art in 1969. We got along like a house on fire, and ended up living together in Cranley Gardens. He was Nick's great friend, of course, so I ended up seeing a lot of Nick too. He used to just show up, and I'd think, 'Wow! Where did he come from?!' Then we'd play for a while, and suddenly at about 2 in the morning you'd notice he'd gone. Nick was a beautiful man in every sense of the word, and very charismatic, but he was the most private person I'd ever met. He was profoundly shy, to the extent that he even played the guitar facing the wall. I remember feeling it would be inappropriate to take a photo of him. At one point Robert was working on a musical entitled *Man Of Destiny* that was being put together by John B. Howse, and he offered Nick and me some money to record demos of some of the material. We therefore spent a couple of afternoons rehearsing at Cranley Gardens, then went and recorded the songs at Marquee Studios. Two tracks I remember were 'Money Honey' and 'How Do You Keep On Moving?' Nick was a fabulous player, of course, and a far faster learner than me, so I did the rhythm and he did the fingerstyle parts. I think that's what Robert must have been thinking of when he said Nick had played on my first album – I don't recall him being there, and if he had played on it, we would certainly have featured him more prominently! After he went to live back with his parents, he used to post little quarter-inch tapes of his material off to Cranley Gardens. I remember hearing one of 'Black-Eyed Dog' three or four days before he died, and thinking, 'Now that's a song!' I remember being sure it couldn't have been suicide, because he'd been writing quite a lot of new songs at the time. I also felt frustrated that he wasn't regarded in the way he deserved. I mean, we all knew!

The Shell

Living grows round us like a skin
To shut away the outer desolation,
For if we clearly marked the furthest deep
We should be dead long years before the grave.
But turning about within the homely shell
Of worry, discontent and narrow joy
We grow and flourish, and seldom see
The outside dark that would confound our eyes.
Some break the shell.
I think that there are those
Who push their fingers through the brittle walls
And tear a hole: and from this cruel slit
Stare out across the cinders of the world
With naked eyes: they look both out and in,
Knowing themselves and too much else beside.

Molly Drake

There are so many people who have made this book possible, and to whom we – and Nick – owe great gratitude. Our thanks go out to them all, in particular, of course, to each of our named contributors, and to every person mentioned in this book. All gave generously of their time and, in many cases, of their hospitality. Without them there would have been no book.

There are many equally important, unnamed contributors, who worked behind the scenes, and they include: Stella Macpherson, Jane Cowburn, Sîan Murray and Courtney Sieberling who risked serious damage to their eyesight deciphering Rodney Drake's letters and diaries (not to mention Nick's postcards), and for transcribing the hours of interviews; Henry and Constance Kirby who filled in the facts about their father's life and spent time finding photos of Robert in their family archives; Richard Morton Jack of *Flashback Magazine* whose prodigious knowledge and extensive research has increased, beyond measure, our knowledge of Nick's press coverage; Martin Wilkinson who gathered together the 'Jeunesse Dorée' and helped with the editing of the pieces that concerned them; Dr Terry Rogers, Marlborough College archivist; Clare Morris and Caroline Edwards, custodians of their late husbands' portfolios who allowed us to use Keith's and Tony Evans' photos of Nick; Jeremy Mason and Simon Crocker whose snapshots of Nick in Aix are rare images of an important era in Nick's life; likewise, Jean-Louis Pujol who generously allowed us to use his photographs of Robin Frederick in Aix-en-Provence; Donna Ranieri who was, and still is, an invaluable ally for all things Nick in the USA; Gavin Bush, photographer, film-maker, designer and builder of our websites; Mike Schutzer Weissmann and Sarah Talmage who gave us information about The Loungers Club. Our thanks also to David Barber, Marijn Van Beck, Richard Charkin, Jason Creed, Bill Forsyth, Colin Harper, Paul Hillary, Susan Holt, Matt Hutchinson, Steve Kelly, Tod Lloyd, Beverley Martyn, Denise Offringa, Peter Rice, Michael Trevithick and Nathan Wiseman-Trowse.

The team at our publishers, John Murray, have been unendingly supportive, enthusiastic and helpful, most especially our editor, Mark Richards, backed by Nick Davies; our printmasters Amanda Jones and Joanna Seaton; marketeer Bea Long; copy-editors and proofreaders Nick de Somogyi and Caroline Westmore; typographer Janette Revill; and Lyndsey Ng, our media firewall.

Mention should also be made of our graphic engineer Nik Rose, who regularly went without sleep to achieve Cally's vision for the book during its six-year gestation.

Finally, we need to say a profound thank you to two people who had little to do with the actual book, but without whose constant support Cally and Gabrielle would have wilted: Jennie Callomon and Louis de Wet.

Book art direction and design by Cally (www.antar.cc).

www.brytermusic.com

First published in Great Britain in 2014 by John Murray (Publishers)
An Hachette UK Company

1

Extract from *Frozenlight: True Tales of the Sixties* by Colin Betts (Floating World, 2007), reprinted by permission of the author. 'Live Air' by Nick Drake, from *From the Word Go* (Bloodaxe Books, 2007), reprinted by permission of the publisher (www.bloodaxebooks.com). Lines from 'Welcome' by Cate Kennedy reprinted by permission of the author. 'Exiled from Heaven: The Unheard Message of Nick Drake' from *The People's Music* by Ian MacDonald (Pimlico, 2003), reprinted by permission of The Random House Group Limited. Extract from *Adventures on the High Teas: In Search of Middle England* by Stuart Maconie (Ebury, 2009), reprinted by permission of The Random House Group Limited. Lyrics from 'Solid Air' by John Martyn, from *Solid Air*, reproduced by kind permission of Warlock Music/BMG. Extract from *Pink Moon – A Story about Nick Drake* by Gorm Henrik Rasmussen, translated from the Danish by Bent Sørensen (Rocket88, 2012), reprinted by permission of the author. Lyrics from 'The Poor Boy Is Taken Away' by Richard Thompson, from *Pour Down Like Silver* by Richard and Linda Thompson, reproduced by kind permission of Richard Thompson and Island Music Ltd.

A CIP catalogue record for this title is available from the British Library

ISBN 978-1-444-79259-1
Special boxed edition ISBN 978-1-444-79260-7

Typeset in Garamond Premier Pro

Printed and bound in Italy by Graphicom S.r.l.

John Murray policy is to use papers that are natural, renewable and recyclable products and made from wood grown in sustainable forests. The logging and manufacturing processes are expected to conform to the environmental regulations of the country of origin.

John Murray (Publishers)
338 Euston Road
London NW1 3BH

www.johnmurray.co.uk